Global Politics

Engaging a Complex World

Global Politics

Engaging a Complex World

Mark A. Boyer
University of Connecticut

Natalie F. Hudson
University of Dayton

Michael J. Butler
Clark University

McGraw Hill

Connect
Learn
Succeed™

GLOBAL POLITICS: ENGAGING A COMPLEX WORLD

Published by McGraw-Hill, a business unit of The McGraw-Hill Companies, Inc., 1221 Avenue of the Americas, New York, NY 10020.

Some ancillaries, including electronic and print components, may not be available to customers outside the United States.

This book is printed on acid-free paper.

1 2 3 4 5 6 7 8 9 0 DOC/DOC 1 0 9 8 7 6 5 4 3 2

ISBN 978–0–07–802481–8
MHID 0–07–802481–1

Senior Vice President, Products & Markets: *Kurt L. Strand*
Vice President, General Manager, Products & Markets: *Michael Ryan*
Vice President, Content Production & Technology Services: *Kimberly Meriwether David*
Managing Director: *Gina Boedeker*
Director: *Matthew Busbridge*
Brand Manager: *Meredith Grant*
Director of Development: *Dawn Groundwater*
Content Development Editor: *Thomas Sigel*
Editorial Coordinator: *Ryan Vivaini*
Digital Development Editor: *Amy Flauaus*
Marketing Manager: *Josh Zlatkus*
Director, Content Production: *Terri Schiesl*
Content Production Manager: *Debra B. Hash*
Buyer: *Susan K. Culbertson*
Designer: *Margarite Reynolds*
Cover/Interior Designer: *Amanda Kavanagh / Ark Design*
Cover Image: *Stephen Strathdee*
Content Licensing Specialist: *John Leland*
Photo Research: *Emily Tietz / Editorial Image, LLC*
Compositor: *Aptara®, Inc.*
Typeface: *10.5/12.5 Garamond Premier Pro*
Printer: *R. R. Donnelley*

All credits appearing on page or at the end of the book are considered to be an extension of the copyright page.

Library of Congress Cataloging-in-Publication Data

Boyer, Mark A.
    Global politics / Mark A. Boyer, Natalie F. Hudson, Michael J. Butler. – 1st ed.
        p. cm.
    Includes index.
    ISBN 978-0-07-802481-8 — ISBN 0-07-802481-1 (hard copy : alk. paper)
    1. International relations. 2. World politics. I. Hudson, Natalie Florea. II. Butler, Michael J. III. Title.
    JZ1305.B69 2013
    327—dc23
                                    2012027257

www.mhhe.com

brief contents

contents

Mark A. Boyer is a Professor of political science and Scholar-in-Residence at the Center for Environmental Science and Engineering (CESE) at the University of Connecticut. He was Editor of *International Studies Perspectives* from 2000–2004 and Co-Editor of *International Studies Review* from 2008–2012. He is author or co-author of numerous books and articles, including *Defensive Internationalism* (with Davis B. Bobrow and published by University of Michigan Press, 2005) and *International Cooperation and Public Goods* (Johns Hopkins University Press, 1993). His articles have appeared in such journals as *International Studies Quarterly*, *Journal of Conflict Resolution*, *Journal of Peace Research*, and *International Journal*, among many others. Long an advocate of active learning approaches to international studies education, Dr. Boyer is a former Pew Faculty Fellow and recurrently writes on pedagogy issues. His current research focuses on climate change and the interplay of global and local politics in coping with the challenges of climate adaptation.

Natalie Florea Hudson is an Assistant Professor in the Department of Political Science at the University of Dayton, where she also serves as the Director of the Human Rights Studies Program. She specializes in gender and international relations, the politics of human rights, human security, and international law and organization. Her work has appeared in the following academic journals: *International Studies Quarterly*, *International Studies Review*, *Journal of Human Rights*, *International Journal*, *Simulation and Gaming*, and *Global Change, Peace and Security*. Her book, *Gender, Human Security and the UN: Security Language as a Political Framework for Women* (Routledge, 2009) examines the organizational dynamics of women's activism in the United Nations system and how women have come to embrace and been impacted by the security framework, locally, and globally. Dr. Hudson has also consulted in areas related to gender mainstreaming and UN Security Council Resolution 1325 for the European Union and the United Nations. With the support of a McGrath Human Rights Fellowship (2011–2013), her current research centers on the deployment and impact of female military and police personnel in UN peacekeeping missions.

Michael J. Butler is an Associate Professor in the Department of Political Science at Clark University. His research and teaching interests converge in the areas of conflict and cooperation, foreign policy, and global governance. He specializes in the study of military intervention and conflict management and resolution. Recent publications have appeared in journals including *International Studies Quarterly*, *Journal of Conflict Resolution*, *International Studies Review*, *International Studies Perspectives*, *International Negotiation*, *Canadian Journal of Political Science*, *Global Change, Peace, and Security*, and *International Journal*. He has also authored two books—*International Conflict Management* (Routledge, 2009) and *Selling a 'Just' War: Framing, Legitimacy, and U.S. Military Intervention* (Palgrave Macmillan, 2012). Dr. Butler serves on the editorial boards of the journals *International Studies Review* and *Simulation and Gaming*, as well as the Governing Council of the International Studies Association-Northeast. In 2010–2011, he was voted Outstanding Teacher as well as Adviser of the Year by the Clark student body. His current research focuses on the legal and political implications of the Responsibility to Protect (R2P) doctrine relative to sovereignty, human security, and third-party intervention.

preface

What are the crucial elements of a strong Global Politics program?

This is the question we posed to instructors around the country. The answer: **critical thinking** and **theory**. These constitute the foundation of *Global Politics: Engaging a Complex World*. This contemporary presentation stresses the importance of global events and offers students a number of lenses through which to view the world around them. *Global Politics* challenges students to actually **apply what they're learning** throughout an **integrated print and digital content program**.

Geared toward undergraduate students taking a first-time international relations course, this highly accessible, comprehensive, yet concise text will help students develop a deep appreciation of global politics—equipping them to encounter the threats and opportunities of their generation.

Critical thinking and theory

Connect Global Politics

McGraw-Hill's Connect® Global Politics offers a wealth of assignable and assessable interactive course materials. Features such as Analyze the Issue, Join the Debate, Challenge Your Assumptions, and simulations encourage students to apply what they're learning and hone critical thinking skills. Detailed reporting helps students and instructors gauge comprehension and retention—without adding administrative load. A fully searchable, web-optimized eBook provides instructors and students with a reliable source of course content.

CRITICAL THINKING QUESTIONS

1. Why do you think states choose to cooperate and form international organizations like NATO or NAFTA? What motivates that choice? In your answer, consider which theoretical perspective informs your belief system.

2. What do you see as the most critical function of IGOs and why?

3. Compare and contrast the membership and voting structure of the UN Security Council and the General Assembly. What are the advantages and disadvantages of each? Should the Security Council be reformed in ways that make it more democratically representative? Why or why not?

4. In what ways are regional IGOs different from global IGOs? Do you think that regional integration is more plausible than global integration? Using the case of the EU, what are the major challenges for further consolidating regional organizations?

Critical Thinking Questions

End-of-chapter Critical Thinking Questions reinforce the concepts from each chapter and promote problem solving. For example, Chapter 5 covers International Organizations. After reading this chapter, why do you think states choose to cooperate and form international organizations like NATO or NAFTA? What motivates choice? In your answer, consider which theoretical perspective informs your belief system.

Challenge Your Assumptions

Found in the print book and Connect, these real-world scenarios prompt students to critically evaluate the highlighted case and form their own opinions and ideas, thus enabling them to analyze, evaluate, and apply course content to their everyday lives. For example, the Challenge Your Assumptions feature in Chapter 10 compares and contrasts the global views of Economic Nationalists and Critical Radicals and then asks students to test their own world view by deciding on several policy issues such as whether the U.S. should repeal its long-standing embargo on Cuba, or whether a Chinese company should acquire a controlling interest in a major U.S. corporation.

Thinking Theoretically

Thinking Theoretically features highlight and apply significant international relations theories beyond the chapter content. Through the use of empirical, real-world cases, this feature enhances students' appreciation of the ways one can interpret and explain a political issue as well as an opportunity to formulate well-reasoned opinions. For example, the Chapter 8 Thinking Theoretically encourages students to think about the responsibilities, legitimacy, and jurisdiction of international courts. Should their role be to assuage transboundary conflicts and wrongs that are brought to them by arresting and punishing criminals, or should they serve a much wider, sociological purpose of holding perpetrators accountable for crimes in the eyes of their victims and communities?

History Matters

Unlike many other texts that relegate history to one stand-alone chapter, the History Matters feature provides a historical context to material in each chapter, which encourages students to think critically about important historical connections—and how they illuminate current political events—throughout the entire semester. For example, the Chapter 4 History Matters examines whether globalization is really new and provides a brief history of international trade beginning with records as early as ancient times and continuing to the present.

flexibility

The first step to academic success is having access to course materials. With a variety of delivery methods and pricing options, *Global Politics* gives your students the flexibility they desire in securing access to the content they need.

McGraw-Hill create Craft your teaching resources to match the way you teach! With McGraw-Hill Create™, you can personalize your book's appearance by selecting the cover and adding your name, school, and course information. Order a Create book and you'll receive a complimentary print review copy in three to five business days or a complimentary electronic review copy (eComp) via e-mail in about one hour. To get started, go to www.mcgrawhillcreate.com and register today.

Introducing McGraw-Hill Create ExpressBooks!

ExpressBooks contain a combination of preselected chapters, articles, cases, or readings that serve as a starting point to help you quickly and easily build your own text through McGraw-Hill's self-service custom publishing website, Create. These helpful templates are built using content available on Create and are organized in ways that match various course outlines across all disciplines. We understand that you have a unique perspective. Use McGraw-Hill Create Express-Books to build the book you've only imagined! www.mcgrawhillcreate.com.

CourseSmart The text is available as an eTextbook at www.
Learn Smart. Choose Smart. CourseSmart.com. At CourseSmart your students can take advantage of significant savings off the cost of a print textbook, reduce their impact on the environment, and gain access to powerful Web tools for learning. CourseSmart eTextbooks can be viewed online or downloaded to a computer. The eTextbooks allow students to do full text searches, add highlighting and notes, and share notes with classmates. CourseSmart has the largest selection of eTextbooks available anywhere. Visit www.CourseSmart.com to learn more and to examine a sample chapter.

McGraw-Hill Tegrity McGraw-Hill Tegrity Campus® is a service that makes class time available all the time by automatically capturing every lecture in a searchable format for students to review when they study and complete assignments. With a simple one-click start and stop process, you capture all computer screens and corresponding audio. Students replay any part of any class with easy-to-use browser-based viewing on a PC or Mac. Educators know that the more students can see, hear, and experience class resources, the better they learn. With Tegrity Campus, students quickly recall key moments by using Tegrity Campus's unique search feature. This search helps students efficiently find *what* they need *when* they need it across an entire semester of class recordings. Help turn all your students' study time into learning moments immediately supported by your lecture.

McGraw-Hill Higher Education and Blackboard® have teamed up. What does this mean for you?

The Best of Both Worlds

1. **Your life, simplified.** Now you and your students can access McGraw-Hill's Connect and Create from within your Blackboard course—all with one single sign-on. Say goodbye to the days of logging in to multiple applications.
2. **Deep integration of content and tools.** Not only do you get single sign-on with Connect and Create, you also get deep integration of McGraw-Hill content and content engines right in Blackboard. Whether you're choosing a book for your course or building Connect assignments, all the tools you need are right where you want them inside Blackboard.
3. **Seamless gradebooks.** Are you tired of keeping multiple gradebooks and manually synchronizing grades into Blackboard? We thought so. When a student completes an integrated Connect assignment, the grade for that assignment automatically (and instantly) feeds your Blackboard grade center.
4. **A solution for everyone.** Whether your institution is already using Blackboard or you just want to try Blackboard on your own, we have a solution for you. McGraw-Hill and Blackboard can now offer you easy access to industry-leading technology and content, whether your campus hosts it, or we do. Be sure to ask your local McGraw-Hill representative for details.

Online Learning Center

The password-protected instructor side of the Online Learning Center (www.mhhe.com/boyer1e) offers test banks, PowerPoints, and an instructor's manual to accompany *Global Politics*.

Ask your McGraw-Hill representative for password information.

acknowledgments

We would like to acknowledge a number of scholars who were instrumental in the development of this text. Their input and ideas as reviewers were invaluable in the process. They are:

Heather Smith Cannoy
Lewis & Clark College

Kathleen Collihan
American River College

Peter Davies
California State University—Sacramento

Jalele Defa
University of Nebraska—Lincoln

Steve Dobranksy
Kent State University

David Dreyer
Lenoir-Rhyne University

Colleen Driscoll
Quinnipiac University

Renee D. Edwards
Washington State University

Jeannie Grussendorf
Georgia State University

Michael M. Gunter Jr.
Rollins College

Nancy N. Haanstad
Weber State University

Maia Hallward
Kennesaw State University

Patrick J. Haney
Miami University

Jeneen Hobby
Cleveland State University

Julie Keil
Saginaw Valley State University

Marwan Kreidie
Villanova University

Bob Mandel
Lewis & Clark College

Julie Mazzei
Kent State University

Andrew D. Musila
Lock Haven University of Pennsylvania

Fernando Nunez
The Ohio State University

Lawrence Olson
George Washington University

Sunil V. Ram
American Military University

Maria Sampanis
California State University—Sacramento

William P. Schaefer
Suffolk County Community College

Kendall Stiles
Brigham Young University

contrast, we use *international relations* to signify the social science field that focuses on the study of global politics. Thus, when we are discussing global financial flows, we will use *global politics*. But when discussing theories applied in our field, we would use *international relations*. We have tried to maintain this distinction throughout the chapters in the book, even if we occasionally slip back and forth (though we hope we haven't done so).

Global Actors

Unlike those in most of the interactions in your daily life, most of the actors involved in global politics are organizations, not people. That is not to downplay the influence of individuals in global politics, but merely to recognize that organizations are comprised of groups of people with established practices of interaction that condition the impact of individuals. **States** (countries) are one type of organizational actor, and are primary actors in global politics. Simply put, a state is a territorial entity inhabited by a population with some form of organized government. Currently, there are almost 200 states in the global community, but as is obvious from reading any newspaper or watching the news, some states are more involved in global politics and some less so. A variety of factors including (but not limited to) power, history, and geographic location dictate this level of involvement. Regardless of a state's power and position relative to others, all states base their global authority on the concept of **sovereignty,** the legal claim that there is no higher global authority. It is this sovereign status that separates states from other players in world affairs.

State sovereignty also means that there is no world government to actively or passively control the action of states in a way similar to that of a federal government, which controls other lower governmental units within its borders. This lack of central authority can, and often does, leave states and other global actors in conflict with one another—a condition called **anarchy.** While all states are legally equal, the reality is that states participate in the global system in very different and asymmetrical ways. The United States is certainly among those few states that exist in a position of privilege, and therefore power, exercising significant influence over global interactions along with China, Russia, Japan, Germany, and some others. Conversely, countries like Andorra, Vanuatu, and Gambia have much less power and influence over global interactions, and even, in some cases, their own affairs.

Even though states hold the global legal status that sovereignty brings, **international organizations** are playing increasingly significant roles in contemporary global politics. The most prominent of these are the 300 or so **intergovernmental organizations (IGOs)** whose membership is made up of states. Some are global, like the United Nations; others are regional, like the European Union. Even more numerous are transnational organizations that reach across and even permeate states. One prominent example, **nongovernmental organizations (NGOs),** has individuals primarily as members. There are thousands of NGOs, and their concerns touch virtually every aspect of international politics ranging from the AIDS crisis (the International AIDS Society) to zero population growth (Population Connections) to human rights (Amnesty International). **Multinational corporations (MNCs)** are another prominent type of transnational actor. The annual earnings of some of these companies rival the economic output of midsize states and dwarf most of the smaller ones. In a largely unregulated world economy where money is the source of power, MNCs are important players to consider.

International relations
Used in this book to describe the *academic* study of global politics.

States
A political actor that has sovereignty and a number of characteristics, including territory, population, organization, and recognition.

Sovereignty
A central tenet of global politics first established in the Treaty of Westphalia, which holds that the administrative unit of the state has the sole right to govern its territory and people.

Anarchy
Contends that global politics is best understood as a self-help struggle for survival between and among states and other actors given the lack of any effective overarching central governing authority in the system.

International organizations
Organizations with an international membership, scope, and presence.

Intergovernmental organizations (IGOs)
International/transnational bodies that are composed of member-countries.

Nongovernmental organizations (NGOs)
International/transnational organizations with private memberships.

Multinational corporations (MNCs)
Private enterprises that have production subsidiaries or branches in more than one country.

Individuals, even those not holding official positions, can impact global politics. Celebrity diplomacy has helped raise the profile of a number of important issues globally in recent years, as did Angelina Jolie's humanitarian work with suffering populations in several developing regions.

Finally, people also are important actors on the world stage. Usually individuals exercise their influence on global politics as decision-makers, protesters, voters, or in some other role within the bounds of a state or IGO. Sometimes, however, individuals play roles that transcend national and other institutional boundaries. Former U.S. President Jimmy Carter's role over the last thirty years as a crisis mediator demonstrates how individuals can play separate roles from any official status they hold in the state system. Similarly, the Irish rock star Bono has made significant waves in crusading for various causes of importance to global affairs, including debt forgiveness and the HIV/AIDS crisis—a type of activism we sometimes call "celebrity diplomacy" (Cooper, 2008).

Ordinary people also make a difference in the way the world works every day. Take Edna Adan, a Somalian woman, who with great persistence obtained an education—a rarity for girls like her—and became her country's first qualified nurse-midwife. After working for the World Health Organization, Edna returned to Somalia to build the country's first maternity hospital. With the help of supportive donors, Edna completed her maternity *and teaching* hospital (Kristof & WuDunn, 2009). In a world where 500,000 women die in childbirth each year—over half of them in Africa—maternal mortality is a critical issue where change can happen and individuals make that change occur.

Interpreting Global Politics

This book begins from the assumption that how the world is organized and how global politics proceeds are undergoing considerable transformation. Long-dominant structures, ideas, and practices have all changed substantially and at an increasing rate during the past century or so. Traditionally, global politics has been tumultuous and often violent, centering on independent and self-interested countries using their power to compete against other countries in a largely **anarchical global system**, where there is no central authority to set and enforce rules and resolve disputes. While this remains a central characteristic of global politics, one can see new trends and forms of interaction emerging. Some of the differences that distinguish the traditional view of global politics from emergent trends are shown in Table 1.1.

You might argue that the emergent trends the table shows are idealistic and even unrealistic in our world, but to ignore the tangible evidence that those trends are in fact happening would limit our ability to understand the world around us. First, these emergent trends in global politics are really reflections of how we interact as individuals inside our own countries. Certainly, we pursue our own interests

Anarchical global system
The traditional structure of world politics in which there is no central authority to set and enforce rules and resolve disputes.

TABLE 1.1	Traditional vs. Emergent Trends in Global Politics	
Aspect of Global Politics	**Traditional Perspective**	**Emergent Trends**
Human organization	National societies	Global community; globalization, local ownership
Interests	National/self-interests	Global and regional interests; local identity-based interests
Interaction	Competition	Cooperation
Pursuit of Security	Self-protection	Collective action
Pursuit of prosperity	Self-help	Mutual effort; recognition of interdependence
Ultimate authority	Sovereign states	International organizations
Conflict resolution	Power prevails	Law prevails

in domestic systems, with considerable freedom to do so, and we partly rely on ourselves for our own safety and welfare. However, in domestic political systems, individuals also recognize rules, are accountable for obeying them, and have some sense of common identity, common good, and shared responsibility to achieve the common good and help struggling members of society.

Second, while the traditional view continues to prevail as the primary way we analyze global politics, it is not as dominant as it once was in academia or in the policy community. If a century ago a professor had written a global politics text predicting a world organization (the United Nations) with all countries as members, a legal community of 27 European countries (the European Union), the virtual disappearance of tariff restrictions under the World Trade Organization, tens of billions of dollars a year in economic aid flowing from rich to poor countries, an International Criminal Court established to try war crimes, or many of the other realities of today, that text, if printed at all, would have been consigned to the fiction section of the library. Such a historical perspective is critical in the study of global politics, and therefore each chapter will feature a historical narrative that contextualizes the examined global politics issues allowing for further critical analysis of contemporary challenges and opportunities. For the first of these "History Matters" boxes, see below.

Exploring and comparing the traditional and emergent approaches underlies almost everything in this book. To begin, the next section of this chapter will present two ways to think about global politics theoretically. The first approach is **realism,** which reflects the view that competitive self-interest drives world politics, and therefore, that the central dynamic of a global system is a struggle for power among countries as each tries to preserve or, preferably, improve its military security and economic welfare in competition with other states. This is the traditional and often dominant theory in international relations.

Realism/realist
The view that global politics is driven by competitive self-interest, and, therefore, that the central dynamic of the global system is a struggle for power among countries.

Liberalism/liberal
The view that people and the countries that represent them are capable of finding mutual interests and cooperating to achieve them.

The second mainstream theory in international relations is **liberalism,** the view that people and the countries that represent them are capable of finding mutual interests and cooperating to achieve them, by forming ties between countries and also by working together for the common good through international organizations and according to international law. Following this presentation, and throughout the remainder of the book, we will also introduce other theoretical approaches to the study of international relations, as their perspectives provide unique and valuable insights into the topics of discussion.

In continuing to draw on multiple theoretical lenses to understand global politics, chapters 2 through 5 examine processes, structures, and actors. In each chapter, we will use different perspectives to analyze the material at hand, in an effort to demonstrate how the theoretical lens you use colors your interpretation of global politics and its impact on your life. Indeed, those who espouse particular political views, whether conservative or liberal, capitalist or Marxist, view their philosophies as the "truth." However, we will see that the "truth" is much more subjective than most of us would like to admit. Your truth is built on the assumptions that you make about the way individuals, states, and international organizations interact in world affairs.

The remaining chapters of the book, 6 through 12, each tackle a substantive topic in global politics ranging from security through environmental issues. Again, we will use multiple theoretical lenses in our analysis and discussion, but we also will draw upon the discussion from earlier chapters about process, structure, and actors. Throughout these chapters, we will recurrently discuss the ways that the traditional and emergent trends are in tension both in terms of the ways that they manifest themselves in the global community and in terms of how we analyze what we observe as social scientists. In sum, there are few clear-cut, "truthful" answers to the big questions of international relations. Rather, by using multiple theoretical lenses to understand our world, we are able to gain insights into the complexity of the interactions that take place among individuals, states, and organizations in a changing world.

THINKING THEORETICALLY: TOOLS FOR STUDYING GLOBAL POLITICS

Organizing our thinking about world events is important because it allows each of us to make sense of what is going on in the world. Given the impact that seemingly random events have on our daily lives, organizing our thinking about them gives us a chance to act in ways that help us live productive and secure lives. As we wrote this book, the headlines in daily newspapers were dominated by the tsunami and subsequent nuclear explosions in Japan, the democratic revolutions in places ranging from Tunisia to Egypt to Libya, continued armed conflict in Afghanistan and Iraq, and the global economic recession and prospects for recovery. Each of these stories encompasses a unique issue we often present and debate discretely, yet each is also part of a larger context. If you are not familiar with these issues or others that dominate the news as you read this book, then we encourage you to begin reading the newspaper, hard copy or online, and consulting other reputable news sources in order to better understand what we discuss in daily, concrete ways.

To get a better perspective on these and other stories, we must also put them in both a historical and a theoretical context. As discussed above, we will draw on theory throughout this book to help analyze events from diverse perspectives. In addition, as you will see in more detail in the next chapter, we will also draw on the history of global politics to give you insights into why the events of today are partly the product of decades, and even centuries, of ongoing sociopolitical relationships in some cases. You will see that good reporting of world events in the news media will often include some historical background, however brief. For example, returning to our discussion of the recent global recession, it is critical to understand that financial crises have been a recurring feature of the global system. From the Great Depression of the 1930s to the Mexican debt crisis in 1982 and the Asian financial fallout in the late 1990s, market booms and busts are a part of the narrative. What aspect of the recent crisis that we choose to focus on, however, very much depends on our theoretical perspective. For some, the recession demonstrates the fatal flaws of capitalism and its eventual demise. Others see a system that has once again achieved equilibrium, even though it has been slower to come than previous economic downturns. Further, this broader context also helps us to understand what role governments can and should play in addressing financial crisis. While U.S. citizens largely relied on the government for help and solutions, people in Greece demonstrated in masses, challenging, and subsequently weakening, their government's role in the economy. Clearly, both history and theory help us to better understand and think critically about the world around us.

As we seek to explain and think systematically about global politics and all its complexities, the use of theories becomes an indispensible tool in our toolbox. A **theory** is a connected set of ideas and concepts that seeks to explain why things happen and how events and trends relate to one another. Theories allow us to explain and even predict phenomena. For instance, theories allow analysts to argue that the oil spill in the Gulf of Mexico is not just an environmental catastrophe, but also the product of lax environmental regulation and oversight of major corporations, as well as larger structural forces shaping the global economy. As you begin to think theoretically, consider this advice from James Rosenau (2004:330):

> [Thinking theoretically] is a technique that involves making a habit of asking a six-word question about anything we observe. . . . The six-word question seems quite simple at first glance. It is: "Of what is this an instance?" The "this" in the question is anything you observe (be it in world or personal affairs) and it is a powerful question because it forces you to find a larger category into which to locate that which you observe. That is, it compels you to move up the ladder and engage in the theoretical enterprise.

There are many advantages to thinking theoretically. One is that it helps us build knowledge. If we confine ourselves to treating every event as unique, then our past and present are little more than a complex jumble of seemingly random events. By thinking theoretically, we look for patterns that help us understand more clearly what has occurred and, perhaps, even predict what may occur. Another is that thinking theoretically gives us a better chance of evaluating policy. One example is assessing the debate over whether the United States and other democracies should work to

Theory

An interconnected set of concepts that seeks to explain why things happen and how events and trends relate to one another.

history matters

International Relations Theories in Context

"Those who cannot remember the past are condemned to repeat it."
   George Santayana, *Reason in Common Sense, The Life of Reason,* Vol.1

Santayana's quote provides ideas that we will engage throughout this book. Santayana tells us that leaders must know something about history in order to learn and evolve as individuals and for their communities. Understanding history is essential to effective governance, citizenship, and democratic participation and choice. Second, Santayana implies that for us to understand the world around us, we must understand how it got to be this way. How has our history shaped what exists today and how does it constrain what might emerge tomorrow in the political world? While we can learn many lessons from history, we must also avoid drawing simple conclusions from historical cases and be wary of using oversimplified political analogies to understand the complex dynamics of global politics.

Each chapter makes a point of identifying one aspect of the relevant historical context as it applies to that chapter's focus. Our historical understanding begins with the Peace of Westphalia in 1648, which marked the birth of the modern nation-state system when it ended the Thirty Years' War. The Treaties of Westphalia granted sovereignty to virtually all the small European states, effectively ending the rule of the Holy Roman Empire or any other higher authority. The monarchs governing these new states could now determine their own domestic policies, including the practiced sect of Christianity and the development of national militaries.

The emergence and eventual triumph of the state as the dominant mode of governance and organizing principle had profound consequences for the global system. One of these consequences was that states became the primary actors in the post-Westphalian global system and remain dominant, though challenged, today. Central to this state-centric system is sovereignty, which is one of the most basic factors impacting state behavior, albeit to a varying degree, today.

The sovereign state's dominant place in global politics is a central reason why realism has long been the dominant lens through which to analyze them. Realism's focus on the state as the primary actor in world affairs and the state's monopoly of power allow the theory to provide powerful and logical explanations for much of what we will discuss throughout this book and observe every day in the news.

However, realism's dominance began to break down with the emergence of new thinking about the future of diplomacy and global politics in the early 20th century. President Woodrow Wilson's Fourteen Points, the creation of the short-lived League of Nations after World War I, and the eventually more entrenched United Nations after World War II signaled that some state-level decision-makers perceived a need for global governance structures above the state, even if they were unwilling to cede power to those organizations at the moment.

With the rise of liberalism and its appeal over the past 50 years is the growing sentiment that states have increasingly confronted challenges to their sovereignty and, some would argue, even their power as independent players in global politics.

We have also seen the weakening of the Western orientation of the global system as a result of the expansion of the number and power of non-Western states. The colonial empires established by the imperial Western powers collapsed after World War II, and in the ensuing years over 100 new countries, mainly located in Africa, Asia, and other non-Western regions, gained independence. A few, especially China, have achieved enough power to command global attention and may even challenge the United States for global leadership in coming years.

Along with the changing polar configuration and the rise of non-Western states, the rise of non–state actors to the fore in many global political venues is also affecting the 21st-century system. This idea of **globalization** popularly captures a multifaceted concept that represents the increasing integration of economics, communications, and culture across national boundaries.

The historical evolution of global politics and the interactions that it entails impact what theoretical lenses are most valuable and accurate for analyzing world affairs. Other theoretical approaches throughout this book will help us organize and understand the current and evolving character of global politics.

promote democratization in the Middle East, Afghanistan, and elsewhere. Chapter 9 provides some insight into the exploration of the "democratic peace theory," which is the idea that democratic states seldom, if ever, go to war with one another (Chernoff, 2004). If this theory is correct, then the path to world peace may be through world democratization. This would make promoting democracy not simply an altruistic ideal, but also a significant contribution to national and global security. Thinking theoretically also pushes us to think more critically about our own biases and assumptions as we examine our world. In this way, "thinking about how we think" helps us to ask new questions and open our minds to alternative perspectives.

As you begin to think about events and to decide "of what is this an instance," do so expansively and do not worry for now whether your ideas seem controversial or even contradictory. Rosenau once ended up with 23 answers when he thought about one event and asked himself of what it was an instance. From such beginnings, you can test and refine your thinking to see what seems to hold up and what does not.

You will encounter discussions of various theories throughout this book, but a good place to begin is with a range of ideas that have been put forth to address the study of international relations in its most general terms. To that end, we will proceed somewhat chronologically in the development of modern international relations theory by first discussing two macro theories: realism and liberalism. After we discuss those two theories in some detail, we will briefly introduce a number of other important theories that we will revisit at later points in this book. This is not to imply that these theories are any less valuable than realism and liberalism in their explanatory power and accuracy. Rather, we decided to present theories this way for two primary reasons: 1) we don't want to overload the reader with too many theories too fast; and 2) we recognize that realism and liberalism are the two most widely applied theories in our field. As a result, we will work with other theories in detail later in the book, and introduce them where their application has been most significant from an explanatory perspective. We also recognize that some scholars, teachers, and students may disagree with our theoretical choices, but we will try our best to be evenhanded in our explanation and application of alternative approaches. That said, Table 1.2 outlines the main points of realism and liberalism.

Before taking up these schools of thought in detail, four intellectual caveats are in order. First, none of these theories is truly comprehensive. Some scholars argue that even realism and liberalism are "best described as paradigm[s]" rather than full-scale theories (Geller & Vasquez, 2004:1). Such controversies are not our focus here, so treat "theory," "paradigm," "approach," and other such words as synonymous. Second, each theory has numerous variations because, "If you put four IR theorists in a room you will easily get ten different ways of organizing theory, and there will also be disagreement about which theories are relevant in the first place" (Jackson & Sorenson, 2003:34). There are, for instance, classical realists, neorealists, offensive realists, defensive realists, and other kinds of realists (Schmidt, 2004). We will briefly note some of these subdivisions, but will mostly concentrate on the major premises of the basic theories.

Globalization
A multifaceted concept that represents the increasing integration of economics, communications, culture, and many other aspects of global life across national boundaries.

TABLE 1.2	Realism and Liberalism	
Views/Emphasis	**Realists/Neorealists**	**Liberals/Neoliberals**
Human nature	Pessimistic: Humans self-interested and competitive	Optimistic: Humans capable of enlightened cooperation
Core concepts	Power, conflict	Cooperation, interdependence
Reality	Largely objective	Largely objective
Political stakes	Zero-sum	Non-zero-sum
Conflict in system	Central and inevitable	Central but not inevitable
International system	Anarchical	Anarchical, but growing order
Main cause of conflict	States pursuing conflicting self-interests	Lack of central processes to regulate competition
Best path to peace	Achieve balance of power	Increase interdependence, cooperation, and adherence to international law
Key organizations	States	IGOs, states
Morality	National interest is a state's moral imperative	Define and follow common moral standards
Policy prescriptions	Pursue self-interest, expand/preserve power	Cooperate to achieve mutual interests

Third, do not be fooled by the connotations of realism and liberalism. Realists do not necessarily see things as they "really" are. Also, do not equate the use of "liberal" here with left-of-center political parties in American domestic politics. In this context, liberalism is more closely tied to the writings of 18th- and 19th-century political philosophers like Jean Jacques Rousseau, Adam Smith, and Immanuel Kant than it is to the connotations that American politics and policy implementation use. For example, someone might call President Barack Obama a liberal in American politics, but one might understand his approach to some foreign and security policy situations, like those in Iraq and Afghanistan, from a realist lens.

Fourth, focus on what each theory has to offer rather than its shortcomings. Each of these approaches helps us to better understand world politics. Each also has its weaknesses. There are also considerable overlaps among theories, not only in terms of what they try to explain, but even in the manner by which they try to explain it and some of their key assumptions about human behavior and social structures.

Realist Theory

Realists
The view that global politics is driven by competitive self-interest, and, therefore, that the central dynamic of the global system is a struggle for power among countries.

Realism, as stated above, is based on the view that competitive self-interest, given the preeminent goal of survival, drives global politics. **Realists** therefore believe that the decisive dynamic among countries is a struggle for power in an effort by each to preserve or, preferably, improve its military security and economic welfare in competition with other countries. Furthermore, realists see this struggle for power as a **zero-sum game**, one in which a gain for one country is inevitably a loss for others. Realists also are prone to seeing humanity as inherently divided by national loyalty to countries or some other source of political identity such as religion or culture. As a result, realists focus on states as the primary actors, and some would even say, the only legitimate actors, in international relations. In this way, states are the filters through which all international interactions pass.

Military power remains a potent tool of foreign policy. President Obama, as commander-in-chief, has overseen wars in Iraq and Afghanistan as well as other more limited interventions such as the raid that killed Osama bin Laden.

Classical Realism and Neorealism As realist theory evolved, it split into two schools of thought based primarily on different views of the root cause of conflict. We associate **classical realism** with Hans Morgenthau and other realists who are pessimistic about human nature. They believe that political struggle among humans is probably inevitable because people have an inherent dark side. Therefore, classical realists believe that it is foolhardy to trust other countries and their people (Brewer, Gross, Aday, & Willnat, 2004). As one realist puts it, "The sad fact is that international politics has always been a ruthless and dangerous business and it is likely to remain that way" (Mearsheimer, 2001:2). Many realists trace their intellectual heritage to the English political philosopher Thomas Hobbes (1588–1679), who argued in *Leviathan* (1651) that humans have an inherent urge to dominate, which often causes them to "become enemies and . . . [to] endeavor to destroy or subdue one another." Similarly, Morgenthau (1945:17) described "the lust for power" in humans as a "ubiquitous empirical fact."

Neorealism also portrays politics as a struggle for power, but **neorealists** believe that the cause of conflict in the global system is its anarchic (unregulated) structure (James, 2002). As one neorealist puts it, the international system based on sovereign actors (states), which answer to no higher authority, is "anarchic, with no overarching authority providing security and order." The result of such a self-help system is that "each state must rely on its own resources to survive and flourish." However, because "there is no authoritative, impartial method of settling these disputes—i.e., no world government—states are their own judges, juries, and hangmen, and often resort to force to achieve their security interests" (Zakaria, 1993:22).

The two schools of realism also disagree on how countries determine their foreign policies (Cozette, 2004). Classical realists believe a country should follow the dictates of power, but they do not believe that they always do so (Williams, 2005). Instead, classical realists believe that national leaders can and do err by allowing morality, ideology, or anything else other than power realities to govern foreign policy. In contrast, neorealists pay little attention to the internal policy making in countries.

Zero-sum game
A contest in which gains by one player can only be achieved by equal losses for other players. See *Non-zero-sum game*.

Classical realism
A subdivision of realist thought, that believes the root cause of conflict is the aggressive nature of humans.

Neorealism/neorealists
The view that the self-interested struggle for power among countries is rooted primarily in the system's most fundamental concept: anarchy.

This is because neorealists believe that countries are *rational actors* and therefore will react similarly and predictably to power realities in a given situation no matter who is in office. Because neorealists see states reacting predictably to power, these theorists are interested in ascertaining rules about how states will react in a given set of circumstances. Chapter 2 provides examples of how these rules work in the discussion of power and global system structure.

What unites both realists and neorealists is that they doubt whether there is any escape from conflict. Classical realists believe human nature is immutable, and neorealists are skeptical about the ability of interdependence or international organizations to promote cooperation (Sterling-Folker, 2002).

Realism: An Emphasis on Power   Realists contend that struggles between states to secure their frequently conflicting national interests are the main impetus for global politics. Given this view, realists maintain that countries should and usually do base their foreign policy on the existence of what they see as a Darwinian world in which power is the key to the national survival of the fittest. In the words of one scholar, "In an environment as dangerous as anarchy," those who ignore realist principles will "ultimately not survive" (Sterling-Folker, 1997:18). From this perspective, realists define national interest mainly in terms of whatever enhances or preserves a state's security, its influence, and its military and economic power. For realists, then, might makes right—or, at least, it makes success.

With respect to justice and morality, Morgenthau reasoned that it is unconscionable for a state to follow policy based on such principles. He argued that "while the individual has a moral right to sacrifice himself" in defense of an abstract principle, "the state has no right to let its moral [views] . . . get in the way of successful political action, itself inspired by the moral principle of national survival" (Morgenthau, in Vasquez, 1986:38). This does not mean that realists are amoral (Williams, 2004). A realist might argue that the highest moral duty of the state is to do good for its citizens. More moderate realists contend that surviving and prospering in a dangerous world requires that we weigh morality prudently against national interest. One scholar has summed up this realist rule of action with the maxim, "Do 'good' if the price is low" (Gray, 1994:8).

Realism and the Competitive Future   There are many implications to the realists' pessimistic view that there is little hope for substantially reforming the anarchic global system. Morgenthau, for instance, argued that only a global government could permanently secure international peace and justice, but he concluded gloomily, "A world state cannot be established" (Speer, 1968:214). With meaningful change out of reach, realists advocate a pragmatic approach to world politics which we often call *realpolitik*. As a term first coined by scholars to describe the machinations of 19th-century power politics in Europe, the practice of *realpolitik* has several basic but important propositions. First, secure your own country's interests and then worry about the welfare of other countries, if at all, on the assumption that other countries will not help you unless it is in their own interest. This makes realists wary of what they see as the self-sacrificing policies liberals advocate (Goldsmith & Krasner, 2003). Such policies are not just foolish, but dangerous, according to Morgenthau (1986:38), because countries that shun realpolitik will "fall victim to the power of others."

Second, realpolitik holds that countries should practice balance-of-power politics. This means to strive to achieve an equilibrium of power in the world in order to prevent any other country or coalition of countries from dominating the system. Methods for achieving this goal include building up your own strength, allying yourself with others, or dividing your opponents.

Third, realists argue that the best way to maintain the peace is to be powerful: "Peace through strength," as President Ronald Reagan was fond of saying. Showing his realist side, President George W. Bush took a similar line, arguing, "We will build our defenses beyond challenge, lest weakness invite challenge" (Washington Post, 2001). Thus, realists believe that countries must be armed because the world is dangerous and they reject the liberal counterargument that the world is dangerous because countries are so heavily armed. As Morgenthau once claimed about disarmament, "Take away their arms and they will either fight with their bare fists or get themselves new arms with which to fight" (Speer, 1968:214).

President Reagan is widely viewed as a realist decision-maker. But even as a realist, he saw the value of compromise and peaceful conflict resolution. He and Soviet President Mikhail Gorbachev together facilitated the end of the Cold War, even though both led powerful militaries poised for conflict.

Fourth, realists advise that a country should neither waste its power on peripheral goals nor pursue goals that it does not have the power to achieve. This frequently makes realists reluctant warriors, not warmongers, as they are sometimes (mistakenly) portrayed. Morgenthau, for instance, criticized U.S. involvement in the war in Vietnam as a waste of resources in a tangential area. Many realist scholars also opposed the invasion of Iraq in 2003, arguing accurately and publicly in advance of that invasion that Iraq was not an immediate threat and, therefore, "Even if such a war goes well and has positive long-range consequences, it will still have been unnecessary. If it goes badly—whether in the form of high U.S. casualties, significant civilian deaths, a heightened risk of terrorism, or increased hatred of the United States in the Arab and Islamic world—then its architects will have even more to answer for" (Mearsheimer & Walt, 2003:58). More generally, one realist scholar claims, "America's . . . realists [have] . . . warned of the dangers that a hegemonic United States would over-reach itself and, by asserting its power heavy-handedly, provoke opposition to it" (Layne, 2006:46).

Liberal Theory

The main theoretical counterpoint to realism in international relations theory is **liberalism.** Liberals reject the realists' contention that politics is inherently and exclusively a struggle for power. Liberals do not dismiss power as a factor, but they add morality, ideology, emotions (such as friendship and mutual identity), habits of

Liberalism

The view that people and the countries that represent them are capable of finding mutual interests and cooperating to achieve them.

cooperation, and even altruism as factors that may, and do, influence the behavior of national leaders and the course of world politics. Liberalism also holds that global politics can be a **non-zero-sum game.** In other words, it is possible to have win-win situations in international relations where the gains of one or more countries do not have to come at the expense of others. Liberals also are proponents of cosmopolitanism, and as such are prone to think that all humans have a common bond that they can draw on to identify themselves beyond the narrow boundaries of their country or group and to identify and forge ties with people around the world.

Classical Liberalism and Neoliberalism
Like realism, we can divide liberalism into two schools of thought. Similar to classical realism, **classical liberalism** is based on its adherents' view of human nature. In contrast to the pessimism of classical realists, however, classical liberals are optimistic about human nature. In this sense, they trace their intellectual lineage to political philosophers such as Jean-Jacques Rousseau (1712–1778). He argued in *The Social Contract* (1762) that humans had joined together in civil societies because they found it easier to improve their existence through cooperation than through competitive self-reliance. Contemporary liberals apply this notion to global society, and argue that people and their countries can better their existence by joining together to build a cooperative and peaceful global society.

Neoliberalism, sometimes called **neoliberal institutionalism (NLI),** emerged in the 1970s and 1980s in a manner somewhat parallel to the emergence of neorealism. **Neoliberals** also place a decided emphasis on the structure of the international system, and agree with neorealists that competition among sovereign states in an anarchical world system causes conflict. Neoliberals, however, contend that the structure of the system is not nearly as anarchical as neorealists claim. According to neoliberals, **complex interdependence** marks the international system. This means that countries are tied together through trade and many other economic and social exchanges that both increase cooperation and limit conflict. Complex interdependence also promotes the increased use of international law and the creation of more and stronger international organizations to deal with the expanding ties among countries. In turn, the spread of international law and the importance of international organizations progressively serve to reduce anarchy and, therefore, conflict in the system.

Liberalism: An Emphasis on Cooperation
Unlike realists, liberals do not believe that acquiring, preserving, and applying power must be or even always is the essence of global politics. Instead, liberals argue that we should formulate foreign policy according to the standards of cooperation and mutual gain. This does not mean that liberals are never willing to use military force or other forms of coercion. Almost all liberals are willing to do so in self-defense or in response to overt international aggression. Many liberals also would use force, especially if authorized by the United Nations, to prevent or halt genocide and other gross violations of human rights. Beyond such cases, though, liberals differ. Some favor assertive liberalism, an approach that led Woodrow Wilson to send American troops to Europe in an effort to make the world safe for democracy and arguably

---

Non-zero-sum game
A contest in which gains by one or more players can be achieved without losses by others. See *Zero-sum game.*

Classical liberalism
A subdivision of liberal thought that is optimistic about human nature and believes that people can achieve more collectively than individually.

Neoliberalism/ neoliberals
The view that conflict and other ills that result from the anarchical global system can be eased by building global and regional organizations and processes.

Neoliberal institutionalism
Builds on liberal thought that states can cooperate through international regimes and institutions; focus is on long-term benefits instead of short-term goals.

Complex interdependence
Complex interdependence refers to the broad and deep interdependence of issues and actors in the contemporary global political system.

led George W. Bush to invade Iraq to foster democracy there, although many disagree with that spin on Bush's motives. Proponents of more passive liberalism argue that using force is often counterproductive and that it often leads to imperial domination even if the initial intentions were lofty (Morefield, 2004).

Whatever the exact formulation, liberal thought has had a clear influence on the actions of some post–Cold war leaders. For example, President Bill Clinton asked Americans to support sending U.S. troops to Bosnia because "it is the right thing to do" to prevent the continued agony of "skeletal prisoners caged behind barbed wire fences, women and girls raped as a tool of war, [and] defenseless men and boys shot down in mass graves" (New York Times, 1995). Echoing Wilson's resolve to make the world safe for democracy, President Bush pledged that "America will . . . support democratic movements . . . with the ultimate goal of ending tyranny in our world."[1] The goal of helping others also provides, at least, the rhetorical foundation for President Obama's commitment in Afghanistan, as exemplified by his claim that "I've been very clear that we are going to move forward on a process of training Afghans so that they can provide for their own security"[2]

This picture of the "world's most exclusive club" does little to illustrate the power and the frustration experienced only by the men who have held the office. It is an interesting thought experiment to think about how each of the four men might have handled any given world crisis. Are decisions made by the person or the office?

Such views do not mean that Clinton, Bush, Obama, and others with liberal internationalist views do not also pursue realist policies. When, for example, Clinton sought the presidency in 1992, he condemned China as a tyrannical abuser of human rights and assailed President George H. W. Bush for his realpolitik approach to that country. As president, though, Clinton learned that he could not afford to overly antagonize a country as powerful as China, and he tempered his liberalism. Clinton had to admit near the end of his first term, "it would be fair to say that my policies with regard to China have been somewhat different from what I talked about in the [1992 presidential] campaign."[3]

Liberals also dismiss the realists' warning that pursuing ethical policy often works against the national interest. The wisest course, liberals contend, is for countries to recognize that their national interests and the common interests of the world are inextricably tied. For liberals, this means that improving global economic conditions, human rights, and democracy are very much in the national interest of the United States and other economically developed and democratic countries. This was President Bush's argument in 2005 when he told Americans, "In the long term, the peace we seek will only be achieved by eliminating the conditions that feed radicalism and ideologies of murder. If whole regions of the world remain in despair and grow in hatred, they will be the recruiting grounds for terror, and that terror will stalk America and other free nations for decades."[4]

Liberalism and the Cooperative Future   Liberals believe that humanity is struggling toward a more orderly and peaceful global system and can and must succeed in that goal. All theories recognize the importance of the state in world politics, but whereas realists focus almost exclusively on the state, liberals put a great deal of emphasis on the UN and other IGOs as both evidence and promoters of greater cooperation. Liberals are divided, however, over how far cooperation can and should go. Classical liberals believe that just as humans learned to form cooperative societies without giving up their individuality, so too can states learn to cooperate without surrendering their independence. These liberals believe that the growth of global economic interdependence and the spread of global culture will create a much greater spirit of cooperation among the world's countries. Neoliberals are more dubious about a world in which countries retain full sovereignty. These analysts believe that countries will have to surrender some of their sovereignty to international organizations in order to promote greater cooperation and, if necessary, to enforce good behavior.

As for the future, liberals are encouraged by some recent trends. One of these is the willingness of countries to surrender some of their sovereignty in order to pursue and secure tangible gains. The EU, for instance, now exercises considerable economic and even political authority over its 27 member-countries. These member-countries were not forced into the EU; they joined it freely. Later in the book, we will discuss at length this and other indications that sovereignty is weakening. Liberals are further buoyed by the spread of democracy and economic interdependence. They believe that both tend to lessen the chances of conflict among states, and research shows that there is substantial validity to this notion (Kinsella & Russett, 2002). Liberals also condemn the practice of realpolitik. They charge that power politics lead to an unending cycle of conflict and misery in which safety is temporary at best.

Because realism and liberalism are what we might term as the two classical theories of international relations and are still the ones most often used to characterize and debate policies and events, it might be enlightening for you to explore which more closely represents your approach to world politics and which you believe your country should follow. In the following box "Thinking Theoretically: The Afghan War," you can see how these two dominant theories help us to understand the ongoing war in Afghanistan.

Theoretical Perspectives: Alternatives to the Dominant Schools

It is worth noting at this point that discontent with realist theory was (and is) not confined to those who fall into the liberal school of thought. Over the past several decades, various scholars have used postmodern, feminist, and constructivist perspectives, among others, to criticize the state of international relations theory, and especially realism. Additionally, there is a range of economic theories, some long existent, others more contemporary, that help us to think theoretically about world politics. As you will see at various points throughout this book, these alternative theoretical perspectives have provided valuable insights into the sociopolitical context in which global politics is embedded. For instance, neo-Marxist theories of international relations are powerful tools for understanding the tensions

thinking **theoretically**

The Afghan War

In October 2001, when the Taliban refused to give up *al Qaeda* leader Osama bin Laden, the U.S. initiated aerial attacks, bringing an end to Taliban rule two months later. Despite this quick triumph and the eventual killing of Osama bin Laden in 2011, the war in Afghanistan rages on as supporters of the hard-line Islamic movement have regrouped. Although the administration adopted a new constitution in 2004, the infighting between local commanders and tribal leaders over power and territory has risen. Since 2001, the war has cost approximately 2,700 American lives, 800 lives from the coalition forces, and an unknown number of Afghan civilians. The UN Assistance Mission in Afghanistan (UNAMA), in 2010, reported dead 2,777 Afghans.

Applying international relations theory helps make sense of the causes of this conflict and the problems that the global community faces. Realist and liberal theory push us to look at different interactions, actors, and institutions, to ask different questions about who and what really matters, and even to search out different solutions to one of the defining conflicts of the 21st century.

From a realist perspective, the initial decision to invade Afghanistan in 2001 is unsurprising given the theory's focus on states' inherent interest in surviving in a self-help, anarchical system. The U.S.-led coalition had no choice but to focus on bringing down the Taliban government and rebuilding Afghanistan as the best means for combating global terrorism. Realists argue that terrorist groups are dependent upon states and governments, like the Taliban regime. Focusing on destroying and then rebuilding the Afghan state is the only means to combating terrorism.

While realists would not ignore the domestic politics and insurgent uprisings occurring within the Afghan state, they would highlight that other nearby states, from Pakistan to Iran, are interfering. Realists situate the Afghan war within the broader struggle for power and security among regional states. "Winning the war" in Afghanistan continues to be, for most realists, a critical component of U.S. national security interests. The solution for Afghanistan involves establishing a strong state that not only has control of domestic actors, but that can serve to balance other regional powers. From a U.S. perspective, this means a regional democratic ally to tip the balance of power in its favor and in direct response to a potentially nuclear Iran. Such a power comes from coercive techniques, as the U.S.-led coalition and the emerging Afghan security forces demonstrate.

Liberal theory emphasizes the role of non–state actors, interdependence, and the prospects of cooperation in Afghanistan. While liberals are not naively optimistic, they do take seriously the idea that the conduct and practice of global politics is not solely nation-state oriented. For example, non–state actors and less legitimate organizations (terrorists/drug traffickers) "matter," today more than ever. Afghanistan is a clear case for this worldview. The capacity of a transnational terrorist network, such as *al Qaeda,* to execute major terrorist attacks (9/11) from its remote mountainous border region of Afghanistan and Pakistan makes both it and that geographic space crucial.

The liberal emphasis on interdependence reveals the extent and importance of the multiple pathways and avenues for the movement of goods, services, money, people, and ideas that weave across our world. The "complex interdependence" between and among economies, nations, and states allows *al Qaeda* to plan, organize, and execute acts of terrorism from such an isolated region. Liberals contend that this interdependence provides the primary opportunities for freedom, peace, and prosperity. They feel that the most effective solution is one that not only seeks to unseat *al Qaeda,* but also fully integrates Afghanistan into the international community. For liberals, this is the best way to ensure more effective and transparent governance, economic growth, full protection of human rights, and establishment of peaceful relationships with its neighbors. Interdependence makes it possible for states and non–state actors to cooperate on economic, political, legal, and military issues—and to form and commit to international institutions to do so. In light of the liberal emphasis on "positive sum" outcomes, all nations and states share a common stake in uprooting and defeating *al Qaeda* and in the rebuilding and stabilization of Afghanistan and Pakistan—explaining why so many states have come together and contributed to those efforts.

that exist in the global system as a result of disparate levels of economic development and the crushing effects of poverty. Feminist theories provide unique perspectives on the status of women as political actors throughout the world and on the gendered dimension of many of the "problems" and "solutions" that dominate the study and practice of international relations. We will introduce these alternatives in a number of later chapters, where we think they will be most valuable to you for understanding why events and interactions develop in the ways they do in our contemporary world.

WHY GLOBAL POLITICS MATTERS

The terrorist attacks on September 11, 2001, increased Americans' interest in the world around them, but only a little. Prior to 9/11, 33% of Americans said they followed international news "most of the time." That share had improved only slightly to 39% in 2006 (Pew Research Center, 2006). Young adults, ages 18 to 24, have particularly low interest and knowledge about global affairs. One indication was a National Geographic survey finding that 63% of Americans in that age group could not find Iraq on a blank map, and 70% were unable to locate Afghanistan, despite the fact that U.S. troops were fighting conflicts in both countries at the time of the survey (National Geographic Society, 2006).

It is important to note that this dearth of concern and information among Americans contrasts with the attitudes and knowledge levels in most other economically advanced countries. The study that we mentioned earlier, which presented 18- to 24-year-olds in nine countries with 56 questions about world geography and 8 questions about world affairs, found that Americans finished last among the eight developed countries and did only marginally better than young adults in Mexico, where educational opportunities are much more limited. One illustrative multiple-choice question about the size of the U.S. population revealed that only a scant 25% of Americans selected the correct answer, but, even worse, their score was lower than that of the respondents in any of the other eight countries.[5]

Although the United States is the most powerful country in world affairs, policy makers in the U.S. have had to increasingly account for forces and events beyond its borders over the past few decades. Whether because of transboundary policy problems like climate change or because of the terrorist attacks of 9/11, the "outside" is becoming more immediate to policy makers and citizens alike. Thus, we argue that it is important for you to recognize, and understand, that global events impact on your daily life and that you begin to formulate your own views on those happenings.

To help you start, you will find a number of "Challenge Your Assumptions" boxes in this book. Each asks you to evaluate an important policy issue and to formulate a position on it. The one in this chapter asks that you consider how global you are in very concrete ways.

To further highlight the importance of the world to you, we now turn to a number of ways, some dramatic, some mundane, in which global politics affect your economic well-being, your living space, and your very life. For example, in revisiting this chapter's focus on the 2008 global recession, consider governments' responses to the banking

challenge your **assumptions**

How Global Are You?

The word "globalization" is ubiquitous. Globalization is all over the daily news. It permeates our evolving culture and it impacts each of us in many, often unseen, ways. The challenge we pose to you throughout this book is to begin to think more consciously about the ways that the world impacts you. At the simplest and perhaps most abstract level, we ask that you contemplate the following questions each day this semester:

- In what ways are you global?
- How does globalization impact you positively? Negatively?
- How does globalization impact your country's national policy decisions?
- What are the most pressing problems that globalization raises for you and your country's decisionmakers?
- More concretely, do you have a passport?

At a much more specific level, we ask that you undertake a *Personal Global Inventory*. To accomplish this task, identify one complete day when you can spend time thinking much more consciously about how global you really are. Then, keep track of everything that you do that day that has global links. Some starting points for your inventory are:

- Check the labels on the clothing that you wear. Where were the clothes made?
- Did you drink coffee or tea? Where were the beans or tea leaves grown?
- What fruits or vegetables did you eat? Where were they grown?
- Did you use any electronics? Where were they made? Are the companies based in your country? Do they use production facilities abroad?
- Where was the paper made that you used in your printer?
- Did you use the Internet? What sites did you visit? With whom did you communicate?

If possible, take the time to compare your inventory with others in your class. Then maybe you'll have some sense of how global you are relative to others. Throughout this book we will focus on how the world impacts you and how you impact the world. Keep that in mind as you read. Each chapter addresses that theme in a slightly different way.

crisis that catalyzed the 2008 global recession. Following the collapse of two of America's financial titans, Lehman Brothers and Washington Mutual, with combined losses totaling over $350 billion, governments around the world began injecting large sums into the economy, and in some cases bailing out banks.[6] The term "too big to fail" emerged as a defining and highly controversial approach to the recession. For many policy makers, certain **international financial institutions (IFIs)** are so large and interconnected that their failure would mean complete disaster for the entire global economy; therefore, such institutions should receive financial and other support from governments to keep them alive for the sake of the greater good. Critics maintain that the policy is counterproductive and in complete contradiction to capitalist ideals and free market interactions. Furthermore, there is no room for accountability and corporate social responsibility with such an approach. Economists and Nobel Laureate Paul Krugman support a more tempered approach that allows for bailouts of certain financial institutions as long as they are well regulated and in proportion to their economic clout. As a taxpayer, do you believe that your government should be bailing out billion dollar MNCs? What if the bailout means economic stability not only for the U.S., but for many developing nations as well?

International financial institutions (IFIs)
Global financial institutions established or chartered by multiple states. Many of the most prominent IFIs are multilateral banks, such as the World Bank and the International Monetary Fund.

Global Politics and Your Finances

World politics affects each of our personal economic conditions in many ways. Sometimes specific events are costly. In addition to the human toll of the 9/11 attacks, they cost the United States at least $81 billion in destroyed property, lost business earnings, lost wages, increased security expenditures, and other costs during just the four months immediately following. More routinely, the global economy affects individuals in ever-expanding ways as national economies become increasingly intertwined. We shall see that the ties between national and international affairs are so close that many social scientists now use the term **intermestic** to symbolize the merger of *inter*national and do*mestic* concerns. To illustrate the increasingly ubiquitous connections between your personal financial condition and world politics, we will briefly explore just three of the many links: how global trade, global investment, and defense spending affect your finances.

Intermestic
The merger of *interna*tional and do*mestic* concerns and decisions.

International Trade and Your Finances

The global flow of goods (tangible items) and services (intangible items such as revenues from tourism, insurance, and banking) is important to your financial circumstances. One example is U.S. dependence on foreign petroleum. That reality came sharply into focus as crude oil prices rose more than 500%, from about $19 a barrel in January 2002 to about $88 a barrel in late 2011, driving up the prices of gasoline, heating oil, and other petroleum products to record highs in the United States. Thus, every time you pumped gas, you paid more, thanks to the realities of the global system.

Trade also wins and loses jobs. There is a steadily increasing likelihood that global trade and your job are related. Exports create jobs. The United States is the world's largest exporter, providing other countries with $1.84 trillion worth of U.S. goods and services in 2008. Creating these exports employed some 18 million Americans, about 13% of the total U.S. workforce.

While exports create jobs, other jobs are lost to imports. Americans imported $2.52 trillion in goods and services in 2008. Many of the clothes, toys, electronics, and other items they bought were once produced in U.S. plants by American workers. Now most of these items are produced overseas by workers whose wages are substantially lower. Jobs are also lost to service imports through *outsourcing* or *offshoring*. Once, most of those who answered calls to the service help lines of U.S. computer companies were Americans. Now you will most likely get technical help for computer problems from a technician in Bangalore, India. In a different realm, Americans who have no or inadequate

Just as 2008 saw the rise of the Tea Party, 2011 saw the rise of Occupy movements across the United States. Emphasizing social and economic justice and equity, those attesting to represent 99% of the population foisted a new agenda into American politics in down economic times.

health insurance are increasingly outsourcing some of their medical care to internationally accredited foreign hospitals and physicians. A few procedures and their comparative costs are: heart valve replacement, U.S.: $185,000, Singapore: $13,000; hip replacement, U.S.: $55,000, India: $9,000; and gastric bypass, U.S.: $55,000, Thailand: $15,000. There are no official data about the shift of service jobs overseas, but one recent study concludes that Americans are losing 90,000 business, professional, and technical jobs a year to outsourcing (Schultze, 2004).

Lost jobs are a serious matter, but if you are a U.S. citizen, before you cry "Buy American!" and demand barriers to limit foreign goods, it is important to realize that inexpensive foreign products improve your standard of living. For example, the United States annually imports more than $85 billion worth of clothes and footwear. What Americans pay for shirts, sneakers, and other things that they wear would be much higher if the items were all made by American workers earning American wages.

The Flow of Global Capital and Your Finances   The global flow of global finance affects you in more ways than you probably imagine. Chapters 4, 9, and 11 cover these in greater detail, but to begin to see the impact of **global capital**, we can look at international investment capital, the flow of money in and out of a country to buy companies, stocks, bonds, real estate, and other assets. The amounts of money involved are immense. In 2010, for instance, Americans owned slightly more than $1 trillion in foreign assets and foreigners owned more than $1.2 trillion in U.S. assets.[7] One way that this may affect you is if you receive financial aid from your college. Schools generate part of their scholarship funds by investing their endowments in stocks and bonds, including foreign holdings. So, the investment in these foreign assets and the dividends and capital gains that your college earns from them may be helping to pay your tuition. Another possibility is that you or someone in your family may be working for a foreign-owned company. Sometimes foreign investors buy faltering U.S. companies and rejuvenate them, thus saving the jobs of their American workers. In other cases, foreign companies open new operations in the United States. For example, American workers make Nissan automobiles in Tennessee, Hondas in Ohio, Toyotas in Kentucky, and Mitsubishis in Illinois. Overall, foreign-owned firms in the United States employ over 60 million Americans.

Global capital
Global financial resources that fuel economic development around the world.

Defense Spending and Your Finances   Paying taxes to fund your country's military forces is yet another way that world politics affects you economically. U.S. defense spending, for example, is $664 billion for **fiscal year (FY)** 2010. This amount is 20% of the U.S. budget and equals almost $2,200 per person in the United States.

There is a lively debate over whether defense spending is too high, too low, or about right. Chapters 6 and 7 examine that topic and other aspects of military security. Whatever your position on the funding debate, it is clear that military forces are expensive and that to a considerable degree the military competes with domestic programs for funding. The proper level of defense spending and how it relates to

Fiscal year (FY)
A budget year, which may or may not be the same as the calendar year. The U.S. fiscal year, for instance, runs from October 1 through September 30.

other programs is just one area that you can influence as a voter and politically active citizen of your country.

As you can see in Figure 1.1, countries set their spending priorities in different ways. Although there is not a one-to-one relationship between reduced defense spending and increased spending in other categories, it is worth noting that such decisions are at the heart of some of the budgetary problems facing countries around the world, including the ones depicted in this figure. For instance, the United States exhibits the highest spending on all three categories among the countries shown. These spending choices might be one of the reasons that the United States runs such a persistent federal budget deficit. And given the political deadlock that characterizes Washington, especially during this election year, it is unlikely that agreement will be found about where to cut spending.

From a different perspective, one might argue that maintaining spending in all these important areas is crucial to American and even global economic recovery. Substantial budget cuts would cause ripple effects that would economically damage

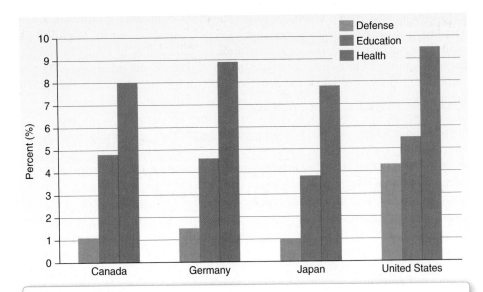

FIGURE 1.1

Comparative spending on defense, health, and education

In theory, defense spending involves a trade-off with other forms of government spending, such as education and health. This figure compares how much four wealthy countries spend in public funds on defense, health, and education as a percentage of their respective gross domestic products (GDPs). As is evident, the United States spent more on each category than each of the other countries in 2010. Even though each of the other three countries is also a wealthy, economically developed country, might the higher levels of spending in all three areas during 2010 be reflective of America's role as a global economic leader? A more telling story might be seen if we compared these figures over a much longer time frame to see how spending patterns have evolved. Remember: government spending priorities change and the world changes.

people in the United States and those in other countries. Thus, one can argue that deferring hard spending choices for now might be good economic policy. As one former defense official puts it, "both the administration and Congress . . . view defense as a federal jobs program."[8]

Global Politics and Your Living Space

Global politics affects more than your wallet. It also affects the quality of the air that you breathe, the water that you drink, and other aspects of the globe that you inhabit. For one, the growth of the world's population and its pressure on resources threaten to change the quality of life as we know it. It took 100,000 years of human existence for the world population to finally reach 1 billion. Now, only a little more than 200 years later, there are 7 billion people because, as Figure 1.2 depicts, each addi-

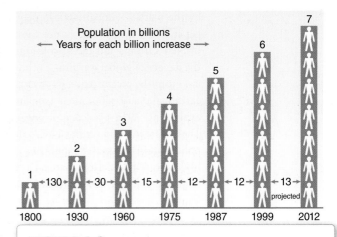

FIGURE 1.2

World population growth

From the time of the first humans, it took about 100,000 years for the world population to reach 1 billion in 1800. Another 130 years passed before there were 2 billion people. Now it takes only a little more than a decade for the population to expand by yet another 1 billion people.

Data Sources: U.S. Census Bureau, UN Population Fund.

tional billion people have been added in shorter and shorter periods of time. Although growth rates have been declining slightly, in October 2011, the UN Population Fund predicted that the world population had reached 7 billion. This represents a tidal wave of new humans. In 2007, for example, the world added 77 million people, a number somewhat larger than the population of Egypt.

Among other concerns, Earth's expanding population presents serious environmental dangers. Burning oil and other fossil fuels to warm, transport, and otherwise provide for this mass of people annually creates more than 6 billion tons of carbon dioxide and other gas emissions. These, most scientists believe, are causing global warming. The year 2005 was the warmest since scientists first kept records in 1856, and 9 of the 10 warmest years occurred between 1996 and 2005.

Warmer temperatures may be welcome to some, but the overall ramifications are worrisome. Among other things, many scientists claim that global warming is melting the polar ice caps, thereby raising sea levels and threatening to flood coastal areas of the world. Some Pacific island countries could even disappear under the rising seas. In addition, many scientists believe that global warming is increasing the number and severity of damaging weather events such as heat waves, droughts, hurricanes, and other forms of destructive weather. Highlighting the view that such cataclysmic climate events are a political issue, a group called Scientists and Engineers for Change and Environment sponsored billboards in Florida criticizing President George W. Bush's environmental policy during the 2004 presidential campaign. One such billboard showed a photograph of a hurricane swirling toward Florida accompanied by the words, "Global warming equals worse hurricanes. George Bush just doesn't get it."[9] The horrific hurricane season the following year, including the devastation of New Orleans and the surrounding Gulf Coast area in August 2005, underscored the danger of global warming to those who believe it will bring environmental calamity. From the recent string of devastating tornadoes in the American Midwest to the earthquake and subsequent tsunami that rocked Japan causing a series of nuclear explosions, 2011 proved quite deadly in terms of global environmental atrocities. These ongoing and serious environmental events not only impact our personal and political decision-making, but they highlight the interconnectedness of critical issues, like energy, population, natural resources, economic growth, and pollution. And when we consider the proliferation of nuclear power around the globe as shown in Figure 1.3, we begin to wonder whether the Fukashima disaster is a very rare, isolated occurrence or something that policy makers need to consider more seriously as our environmental demands grow. That question is at the heart of the debate about the world's energy future.

Numerous other by-products of human activity also threaten our living space. The United Nations Environment Program (UNEP) reports that 10% of Earth's land has been desertified or is in danger of desertification from over-farming and other harmful practices, nearly a billion people living in cities breathe dangerous levels of sulfur dioxide, and more than half the world's population could face critical water shortages by 2050. Certainly, world politics has not caused most environmental problems. However, we are unlikely to be able to stem, much less reverse, the degradation of the biosphere without global cooperation. As UNEP's director has put it, "We suffer from problems of planetary dimensions. They require global responses." You can find much more on this topic in chapter 12, which details global warming and other threats to the environment, but also discusses the views of those who believe that such concerns are overstated. It also explores the politics of environmental regulation and remediation.

Global Politics and Your Life

Global politics affects not only how we live, but in some cases, whether we live at all. Disease and political violence are just two threats to your life that are connected to global politics. So, although these threats are relatively unlikely to impact you personally, they represent what are often called **high-value, low-probability problems.** However, even problems like this can become much more urgent if policy makers do not deal with them. For instance, while it is unlikely that you would catch a serious infectious disease, left unchecked, the spread of disease globally could develop into a very difficult to control pandemic. Thus, high value, low probability problems are still worthy of thinking about in terms of your global interactions and the political decisions that others are making about your health.

High-value, low-probability problems
The nature of most problems or threats in which the likelihood of a given individual being impacted is very low, but the consequences if it occurs are very serious.

Transnational Diseases   Politics may not directly cause diseases, but we are increasingly in need of global responses to counter health threats that ignore national borders. Some diseases are the result of environmental damage. By spewing chlorofluorocarbons (CFCs) and other chemicals into the air, we have significantly depleted Earth's ozone layer, which helps shield us from the sun's deadly ultraviolet

Nuclear Electricity Production, 2009—TWh

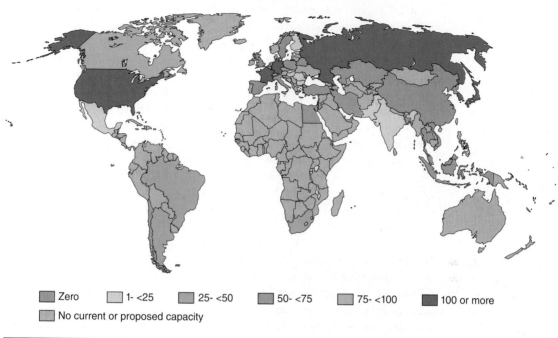

Zero   1- <25   25- <50   50- <75   75- <100   100 or more

No current or proposed capacity

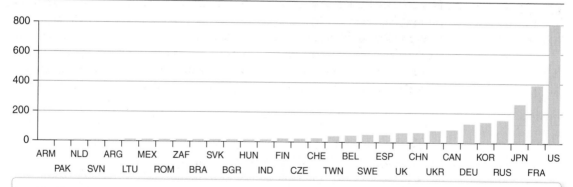

FIGURE 1.3

Nuclear power and its proliferation around the globe brings both positive and negative implications. Obviously, the energy generated is crucial to economic development globally, but some also find the risks (relating to waste, disaster, and failed technology) too great. Either way, as this map shows, nuclear power plays a large role globally.

rays. As a consequence, new cases of melanoma, the deadliest form of skin cancer, have skyrocketed. Among Americans, the chances of developing melanoma increased 20-fold between 1960 and 2000. Annually, doctors diagnose about 62,000 Americans with melanoma, and almost 8,000 die from it. Certainly, wearing sunscreen and taking other precautions will reduce your chances of developing skin cancer, but international agreements such as the UN-sponsored Montreal Protocol (1989) can greatly help achieve that goal. The Protocol mandates phasing out the use of CFCs and other ozone-attacking chemicals that manufacturers once used in such

To what lengths would you go to stay healthy? This mother and child wear masks to prevent infection, while the father goes uncovered. Disease and its prevention raises many personal choices that impact your health and ultimately the health of those around you.

common items as air conditioners and deodorant sprays. Now, because of international cooperation, CFC concentrations in the atmosphere are declining, and the ozone layer is gradually beginning to recover.

We also increasingly rely on global cooperation to prevent the spread of infectious diseases. Such diseases have always moved across borders, but modern transportation is now rapidly cutting the global travel time of many diseases as their human hosts jet from continent to continent. Since 1981, when the medical community identified the first cases of AIDS in Africa, the disease has rapidly spread worldwide, and more than 34 million people are now HIV-positive. AIDS is just one of several diseases that has emerged in recent years and rapidly claimed victims around the world. According to a top epidemiologist, the number of new infectious diseases and their ability to spread rapidly has made the period since "the 1970s, without precedent, the most rampant in the history of the annals of medicine" (Epstein, 2003). Of course, each country acts to contain transnational diseases and treat their victims. It is far more effective, however, to counter diseases where they first begin to appear than after they cross national borders, and it falls to the World Health Organization (WHO) to coordinate the global effort.

Transnational Political Violence War, terrorism, and other forms of transnational political violence are in many ways more threatening today than ever before (Horne, 2002). Until the 20th century, the vast majority of war deaths were soldiers. Civilian casualties began to rise drastically as military operations increasingly targeted noncombatants. Nearly as many civilians as soldiers were killed during World War II. Now more civilians than soldiers are killed. According to the UN, civilians accounted for more than 85% of everyone killed during wars in the 1980s and 1990s. In a nuclear war, military casualties would be a mere footnote to the overall death toll, and terrorists almost exclusively target civilians.

In addition to military forces, terrorists engage in international violence, as the attacks of September 11, 2001, underlined. Americans found that they were vulnerable to terrorism anywhere and at any moment in their daily lives. This unsettling reality has long been felt more acutely in other parts of the world that have been subjected to more frequent acts of international terrorism (Enders & Sandler, 2006; Laquer, 2004).

War is a special concern for college-age adults because they are of prime military age. Of the American troops killed during the Vietnam War, 84% were ages 18 to 22. The average age of U.S. soldiers killed in the Iraq War beginning in 2003 is higher than it was in Vietnam, in part because U.S. forces in Iraq are part of an all-volunteer military, whereas many U.S. soldiers in Vietnam were draftees. Still, young adults bear the brunt of American casualties in Iraq.

It is also the case that military combat is a matter that increasingly affects women directly as well as men. In the United States and elsewhere, the types of combat units in which women are allowed to serve are expanding. As a result, many more women may fight and die in future wars. More than 200,000 women are on active duty with U.S. forces, and as of late 2011, 141 American military women had lost their lives in Iraq.

INTERNATIONAL RELATIONS THEORY AND YOUR WORLD

As the previous sections illustrate, global politics is no longer a distant set of events and forces that have limited impact on you. Those personal impacts also suggest that finding ways to analyze global politics so that you can make better personal decisions is important for your prosperity and your impact on the world. We argue that using theory allows you to organize your thoughts and we ask that throughout your reading of this book you try to think explicitly about the theoretical application you are using to understand the content in this book and your course.

As you work to think theoretically, here are a few suggestions that may help. One that we made at the beginning of the theory section, but that bears repeating, is to avoid trying to referee the debate among the various schools of thought. Various well-educated, well-read scholars who have devoted their academic careers to studying theory profoundly disagree on which one is the best model of reality. You certainly may find that one theory or another appeals to you, but for the present, the best idea is to keep an open mind about all of them. Each has something important to say.

Also, observe that many of the theories have both empirical (factual) and normative (value-based) aspects. Empirically, any good theory should provide insightful *description*. That is, it should be able to describe past and current events in a way that tells you of what they are an instance, to recall Rosenau's standard from earlier. Harder yet, but still a valid test of the empirical worth of a theory, is how well it enables accurate *prediction*. Realists would probably predict diplomatic muscle flexing and perhaps even military action if, for example, two democracies are angrily disagreeing about each other's withdrawals from an oil field that lies under both their territories. Liberals would be more likely to predict that the democracies would not fight (democratic peace theory) and that, instead, they would negotiate a compromise or perhaps even submit the dispute to an intergovernmental organization such as the International Court of Justice. So, one thing that you can do to evaluate realism and liberalism is to watch developing events, think about how realists and liberals would predict their outcomes, and then see which proves more accurate.

Prescription is also an aspect of many theories. This involves policy advocacy, arguing what policy should be, rather than describing what it has been or is or predicting what it will be. Many realists, for instance, do not believe that countries always follow a self-interest course. Realists worry that their country may be persuaded by altruism, by ideological fervor, or by some other drive to pursue policies that are not in the national interest. Recall that realist Hans Morgenthau opposed the Vietnam War as a misuse of U.S. power and, more contemporarily, realist John Mearsheimer took essentially the same view of invading Iraq in 2003. Thus, you can use theory to organize your views about what your country's foreign policy should be and what the entire future course of world politics should be. If you do so from a solid grounding in theory, you will be far ahead of those who imagine that each event and situation is unique and not part of the ongoing drama on the world stage.

CRITICAL THINKING QUESTIONS

1. Who are the major actors in the global system? What is the relationship between these actors and how are they positioned in the global system?

2. What are theories and why do they matter in the study of global politics?

3. How would realism and liberalism differ in explaining the causes of the 2008 global recession? What would each theory predict in terms of the eventual outcome?

4. What contemporary global political issue is currently having the biggest impact on your daily life? In what ways is this global issue becoming personal and local for you?

chapter summary

- This book is organized to reflect that the global political system is evolving. Throughout, we will present theories where they apply to particular substantive contexts, but also will rely on realism and liberalism as the dominant theories of our field.

- We improve our understanding of world politics by putting events within the context of theory to see patterns and make generalizations about the conduct of international affairs.

- Realism focuses on the self-interested promotion of the state and nation. Realists believe that power politics is the driving force behind global politics. Thus, realists believe that both safety and wisdom lie in promoting the national interest through the preservation and, if necessary, the application of the state's power.

that the "soft power of the U.S.—its ability to attract others by the legitimacy of U.S. policies and the values that underlie them—is in decline as a result" (Nye, 2004a:16).

Absolute and Relative Power By one standard, power that indisputably exists and that one can potentially use is *absolute* power. An example is the approximately 5,000 nuclear warheads and bombs that the United States deploys on about 1,000 U.S. missiles and bombers. These weapons represent a material reality, and will have a specific impact if used. The destructive capability of these weapons has an absolute quality, affording the United States greater power and influence on the world stage than it would otherwise have, regardless of what other states or actors are concerned.

At the same time, power does not exist in a vacuum. Since power is about the ability of an actor to either persuade or compel another actor to act in the original actor's interest, assessing any actor's power requires one to also take into account the power of the adversary or competitor with which it is engaged. When attempting to accurately assess an actor's capabilities, then, we must consider *relative* power. The fact that China has the largest army in the world and the highest constant level of economic growth over the last two decades makes China powerful in absolute terms. However, it provides a more useful and practical appraisal if we talk about China's power in relation to other specific actors. Whatever the sources and extent of China's power, they afford China greater influence over a relatively small neighbor such as Vietnam than a regional power such as Japan, or certainly to a global power such as the United States. Similarly, the view of China's power by other powerful states may also differ, as shown in Figure 2.2.

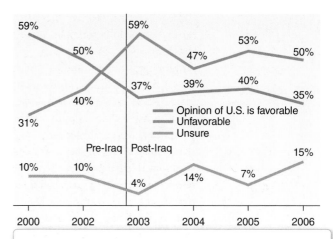

FIGURE 2.1
U.S. soft power and Iraq

Polls in six countries indicate that after the U.S. invasion of Iraq in March 2003 there was an increase in the share of people who viewed the United States unfavorably and a similar decline in the U.S. favorable rating. The shifts between 2000 and 2002 may be related to the fact that by the summer of 2002, when the poll was taken, there were already strong reports of a U.S. readiness to act against Iraq. This decline in U.S. prestige arguably undercut U.S. "soft power" and the willingness of other governments to cooperate with Washington.

Note: The question was, "Please tell me if you have a very favorable, somewhat favorable, somewhat unfavorable or very unfavorable opinion of the United States." The six countries were France, Germany, Great Britain, Pakistan, Turkey, and Russia. Pew reported the favorable data only for 2000; the two other data points for that year are estimated.

Data source: Pew Research Center for the People and the Press (2000, 2003, 2006).

Capabilities and Credibility Material factors substantially determine every actor's power. For states, important assets include military strength, economic assets, physical infrastructure, and a natural resource base. For non–state actors such as international or nongovernmental organizations, factors such as the capability of the organization's leaders, the size and source of its budget and staff, and its organizational efficiency and adaptability matter. Invariably, the material power assets that a state or non–state actor possesses have a major effect on that actor's potential for exercising power and influence in the international arena—in other words, on that actor's **capabilities**.

Capabilities
In global politics, the power and influence available to an actor as a function of its tangible power assets.

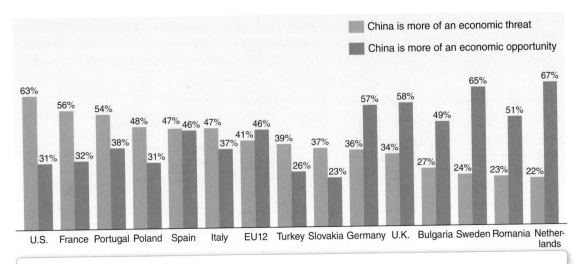

FIGURE 2.2
Divergent views of china: threat, or partner?

Source: "Transatlantic Trends: Key Findings 2011." The German Marshall Fund of the United States, 2011. Chart 11, "Does China Represent Economic Threat or Opportunity?" p.14.

Credibility
The power and influence available to an actor as a function of its ability and willingness to follow through on commitments and threats.

By themselves, though, substantial material assets may translate into capabilities, but not necessarily to a powerful global presence. That presence, and the power from which it is derived, is also contingent on **credibility**—meaning the actor's apparent willingness to carry through and utilize its material power assets in the pursuit of its interests, or to prevent another actor from using *its* material assets in the pursuit of competing interests. Together, it is the fusion of material capabilities with political will that equates to the effective use of power—a fact that highlights the political as well as material aspects of exerting power in global politics.

One example illustrating these two interrelated aspects of power is the decision taken by India in 1998 to publicly test nuclear weapons, thereby announcing to the world its status as a nuclear weapons state. Although India first tested a nuclear warhead in 1974, it did so covertly and maintained a climate of secrecy around its status, for both strategic and ideological reasons (Mistry, 2004). When domestic debate within India turned to the prospect of publicly testing in the mid-1990s, one surprising source of opposition was the more hard-line elements within the defense and security sector. This opposition stemmed not from an objection to India's possession or testing of nuclear weapons, but rather to revealing to the world India's possession of a nuclear weapons *capability* without a public articulation of a doctrine of first-use. The view of some of the more hawkish elements in India was that any enhanced power and influence associated with revealing the material capability of possessing "the bomb" would be offset by the reality that few other actors perceived that India would actually use it—thereby reducing the *credibility* of any threat to do so. What this scenario aptly illustrates is the degree to which power hinges on both capabilities and credibility.

Objective and Subjective Power   Just as an actor's power is influenced by a willingness to convert its assets in the pursuit of its interests, so too is power influenced by how other actors perceive those assets and the intent to use them. *Objective* power consists of assets that an actor possesses and is ready and willing to use. As such, objective power can be a major factor in determining whose interests prevail. Consider, for example, the run-up to the war in Iraq beginning in the summer of 2002. Much of the international community, including many traditional U.S. allies, opposed an invasion of Iraq. Yet diplomatic rebukes by countries such as France and Germany expressed through the vehicle of the UN Security Council were no match for the Bush administration's zeal for an invasion, particularly when a massive military arsenal and widespread domestic support backed it.

As with hard and soft power, while objective power may be simpler and easier to understand, it is not the only relevant translation here. It is crucial to remember the degree to which the pursuit, accumulation, and application of power in global politics takes place within a social context, where perception matters and where we can talk about power having a *subjective* dimension. For an actor to be truly powerful, to some extent, other actors must see it as powerful. Reputation matters. One recent study of the subjective or reputational aspect of power found that a state's power diminishes, and the possibility of future aggression against it increases, if other states perceive it as lacking the ability and willingness to follow through on commitments or to maintain a strong and consistent position in crisis settings (Foster and Palmer, 2006).

Because it is difficult to measure reputation, judging its impact is challenging. Some scholars conclude that concern over reputation is overdrawn, but that does not negate the case that an actor's power is to a degree based on others' perceptions of its current or potential power or its reputation for willingness (or not) to use it. We can argue, for example, that Saddam Hussein's willingness in 1991 and 2003 to risk war with the United States was based in part on his perception that Americans would not tolerate the cost and casualties necessary to invade Iraq and topple him. As Saddam put it prior to the first war, "The nature of American society makes it impossible for the United States to bear tens of thousands of casualties."[2]

Situational Power   The last characteristic of power in global politics we consider here points to the degree to which an actor's power varies according to the situational context. The situational power an actor has is often less than the total inventory of its capabilities. Military power provides a good example. During the last weeks of March and first weeks of April 2003, American and British forces faced those of Iraq in a classic conventional war situation. In that context, the conflict was one-sided with the U.S./U.K. forces quickly destroying and dispersing those of Iraq. During the postwar period, the conflict situation changed when forces opposed to the U.S./U.K. presence in the country turned to insurgent tactics. More U.S. soldiers died in the postwar period than during the war, and U.S. policy was in considerable disarray even though the American forces in Iraq were as numerous as the ones that had so easily toppled Saddam Hussein's regime. The difference was that in the very different situation after "victory," a great deal of the U.S. high-tech weapons inventory, its armored vehicles, and its air power were less effective in countering the insurgency in Iraq.

THE LEVELS-OF-ANALYSIS APPROACH

One way in which we can understand power in all of its manifestations is by taking into account where it resides. Who has power in global politics—and how do they use it? Of course, practically any major news story dealing with world events on a daily basis reflects the power and influence of individuals, states, and of the larger global political system in which they are embedded. These are things that we can evaluate more systematically by using the "levels-of-analysis" approach.

One reason for the utility of the levels-of-analysis approach is the way in which it helps reveal how people, states, and the international system all "matter" in global politics, both on their own and in relationship to one another. While the long-standing centrality of nation-states makes their power and influence—derived from military, economic, social, and natural resources—easy to grasp, we would be wrong to overlook either the increasing role of individual actors or the important constraints that the distribution of power in the global system places on states.

One particularly useful and recent illustration of the independent power and influence of individuals, states, and the global system as well as the interrelationship of the three on the conduct of global politics is, again, the "Wikileaks" saga, which came to the fore in late 2010 and early 2011. Advocates hailed this report as a breakthrough in investigative journalism, whereas its detractors viewed it as a dangerous and destabilizing challenge to political authority. The Wikileaks website burst into the public consciousness by revealing a steady flow of classified documents from governments and other official organizations.

The massive release of thousands of sensitive diplomatic cables in the winter of 2010–2011 garnering worldwide media attention (largely for the salacious descriptions of Sarkozy, Berlusconi, and others) was just one in a series of prominent Wikileaks revelations over the past few years. For instance, in October 2010, the site released almost 400,000 classified U.S. military logs detailing its operations in Iraq—a release that garnered worldwide media attention, as well as sharp rebukes from the Obama administration. This release came shortly after publication of nearly 90,000 top-secret military records pertaining to the U.S./NATO military strategy in Afghanistan, as well as the controversial April 2010 release of a video (contentiously titled "Collateral Murder") showing a U.S. Apache helicopter killing at least 12 people (including two Reuters journalists) during a 2007 attack in Baghdad (BBC, 2010). Other controversial documents hosted on the site include a copy of the Standard Operating Procedures for Camp Delta, detailing the treatment of prisoners at Guantanamo Bay.

Most observers think that the motivation behind these releases is a desire on the part of the Wikileaks site's owner (Julian Assange) and operators (collectively known as the "Sunshine Press") to challenge what they perceive as the unchecked power of the state, through a fully globalized form of media (the Internet). Whatever the motivation(s), as we will see throughout the rest of this chapter, the Wikileaks case clearly illustrates that in global politics, power can and does reside at the individual, state, and system levels.

U.S. Apache helicopter over Baghdad, spring 2010. Perhaps the singular event of the Wikileaks controversy was the April 2010 release of raw authentic video footage (dubbed "Collateral Murder") of airstrikes by an Apache helicopter in the streets of Baghdad, killing nine unarmed civilians.

Origins and Applicability

Introduced to the field of International Relations, with the emergence of **behavioralism** in the social sciences in the mid-twentieth century, early proponents argued that the "levels-of-analysis" approach offered a sophisticated set of "analytical models" for sorting through the complex problems that typify global politics (Singer, 1961). Some of the earliest translations of the approach considered it a blueprint for a more rigorous scientific analysis, providing a greater understanding of perennial problems such as the balance of power and the outbreak of war (Waltz, 1959). Although subsequent challenges to behavioralism have exposed some of its deficiencies, the levels-of-analysis approach continues to provide useful "lenses" through which we can interpret and analyze global politics in general, and the sources and use of power in particular. Among other things, this approach allows us to account for important unit-level (state and individual) as well as structural (system) conditions and phenomena. In that vein, we can use the levels-of-analysis approach to consider questions such as:

1. Which individuals have power in global politics? Which states? How do the players distribute power within the global system?

2. What are the sources of power at the individual, state, and system levels?

3. How do individuals and states use power within the global system?

In light of the varied array of actors and forces that shape the course and conduct of global politics, the levels-of-analysis approach provides us with a tool by which we can appraise power in one of three ways: (1) through **individual-level analysis**, in which we seek to identify and assess the power and impact of individuals or small groups on issues and problems in global politics; (2) through **state-level analysis**,

Behavioralism
The study of social and political phenomena using the scientific method—including, but not limited to, hypothesis testing and empirical analysis.

Individual-level analysis
An analytical approach that emphasizes the role of individuals as either distinct personalities or biological/psychological beings.

State-level analysis
An analytical approach that emphasizes the actions of states and the internal (domestic) causes of their policies.

history matters

Using Levels-of-Analysis: The Third Reich and the Outbreak of World War II

This chapter presents a useful tool for thinking about the accumulation and exercise of power by different categories of actors in the global system—the levels-of-analysis approach. Of course, while splitting off these three different levels is useful in the abstract, in the real world of global politics we probably best understand them as accounting for factors residing at all three levels of analysis.

One prominent historical example that suggests the merits of combining the three levels of analysis comes in explaining the role of Nazi Germany in the onset of World War II. From the standpoint of the "variables" or factors that we study at the individual level, few individuals provide a more fascinating (and frightening) case study than the murderous dictator Adolf Hitler. The well-known facts of Hitler's biography have generated numerous theories about the influence of his formative experiences (such as his failed attempt at becoming an artist, or the bitterness that he felt about the outcome of World War I) on his later development and emergence as a political leader. Similarly, there are numerous studies of Hitler's psyche, the cult of personality that he fashioned in interwar Germany, and the origins and impact of his racist and anti-Semitic views on his leadership and decision-making.

Given the singular influence exercised by Hitler after assuming the chancellorship in Germany in 1933, one would be well-advised in employing individual-level analysis when seeking to understand Germany's role in bringing about World War II. At the same time, there are numerous factors to consider relative to the German state and society during the interwar period that also help explain the outset of World War II. The weak Weimar Republic's incapacity to function, followed by the establishment of a one-party totalitarian regime, provide great insight into the consolidation of political power and the drive to remilitarization. In

societal terms, the legacy and perception of the terms of the Versailles Treaty in Germany and the crippling economic impact of the Great Depression are additional state-level factors that, both on their own and in conjunction with Hitler's skillful manipulation, contributed to Germany's movement down the path to war.

Likewise, a full understanding of the outbreak of World War II and Germany's contribution to it is not possible without also accounting for the nature and structure of the global system at the time. Many of the factors that reside at the system-level of analysis—such as the power vacuum caused by the United States' retreat to an isolationist position, the League of Nations' inability to have any impact, and the establishment of numerous vulnerable and weak states on Germany's doorstep in central and eastern Europe—are important in their own right, and to the extent that they interacted with individual- and state-level considerations.

In the end, this brief inventory of factors regarding Germany's role in triggering World War II demonstrates the merits of the levels-of-analysis approach. One can clearly see the necessity of studying individual leaders (here, Adolf Hitler), state and societal factors (here, pertaining to interwar Germany), and systemic considerations (such as the prevailing distribution of power in the world system at the time) in seeking to gain insight on that question. At the same time, a fuller and richer insight probably requires a broader, cumulative approach, in which we identify and consider the relevant factors at all three levels, not only independently, but in light of one another. Of course, conducting such an all-encompassing analysis would far exceed the time, resources, and capabilities of any one individual, which makes it fortunate that scholars of international relations and foreign policy readily and effectively employ all three levels for the benefit of our understanding of such complex questions.

System-level analysis
An analytical approach that emphasizes the importance of the impact of world conditions (economics, technology, power relationships, and so forth) on the actions of states and other international actors.

whereby we seek to identify and assess how the organization and functioning of the state and/or the society it governs influences those same issues and problems; and (3) through **system-level analysis**, in which the external forces and constraints which the global system exerts on states, individuals, and non–state actors alike are the central concern.

INDIVIDUAL-LEVEL ANALYSIS

Individual-level analysis begins with the view that at the root it is people who shape the conduct of global politics. This shaping can and often does come through the domain of foreign policy and the foreign policy process. As a result, the most common category of individuals who we study through individual-level analysis is political leaders, or those with influence on national or global political systems and processes. This focus on leadership tends to direct individual-level analysis toward the study of those individuals who exert significant independent influence due to their social status, rank, or position—and about whom we tend to have the most information. Examples include government officials such as heads-of-state, foreign ministers, or UN secretary-generals, or those outside the political realm, including highly prominent business leaders and philanthropists (George Soros or Bill Gates), religious clerics (Pope John Paul II), or leaders of transnational terrorist organizations (Osama bin Laden), to name just a few.

Individual-level analysis subsumes a focus on prominent leaders and leadership. This is especially true with the increasing ability of everyday individuals to influence the course of events on the global stage. The Wikileaks scenario is instructive here. We have also seen the power and influence of the use of "new media" or "Web 2.0" applications such as Facebook, Twitter, and YouTube, as in the "Arab Spring." Harnessing the technology we normally use on an individual-level basis, people have used these powerful social media platforms to affect global politics.

Of course, we must be careful to avoid overstating the influence and impact of Wikileaks or the impact of individuals on the conduct of global politics more generally. To be sure, neither the Wikileaks site nor Assange himself is going to usher in the demise of the state or the dismantling of the global system. At the same time, what the Wikileaks story (or that of the Arab Spring) tells us is that ordinary (if committed and savvy) individuals with access to information and technology—and in Assange's case, financial capital—can significantly impact and alter the conduct of global politics.

Individual-level analysis construed more broadly involves understanding how the ways in which humans function as a species and idiosyncratically helps to explain their thinking, decisions, behavior, and actions on matters of importance to global politics. Therefore, such analysis far surpasses just the study of major world leaders. So how does one go about analyzing the impact of individuals on global politics? In other words, when we want to take the influence of individual-level actors into account, what do we study?

Human Rationality and Its Limits

The central question for individual analysis is relatively straightforward. Do individual people influence the conduct and outcome of global politics—and if so, how? To answer that, a first step is acknowledging the important if often unstated assumption that humans are usually considered to be **rational actors** able to identify their interests and preferences and order their actions accordingly. To be sure, most humans possess the faculties to make "rational" (and self-serving) decisions when faced with

Rational actors
The assumption that individuals are prone to make informed and self-serving choices based on a careful accumulation and weighting of all relevant information.

important choices, and many attempt to do just that on a regular basis. Still, human beings are complex and notoriously difficult to predict, and often act in ways that hardly seem rational. Suicide bombers probably do not seem rational to many readers of this text, in that they appear to willingly give up perhaps the most precious resource of all (their lives) in service of some larger cause. On the other end of the spectrum, acts of selflessness or even altruism—such as members of the New York Fire Department rushing into the smoking hulk of the Twin Towers on 9/11—also seem to defy rational explanation. Of course, many of us do things every day that may be risky (such as driving a car) or self-defeating, and hence irrational, without thinking twice about it.

Bounded rationality
A concept that suggests the rational choices of individuals are bound or limited by time pressures, imperfect information, and biases that influence those choices.

Bounded Rationality   One way of reconciling our assumptions about individual rationality and the reality that human behavior may not match those assumptions is by recognizing that we often make rational decisions within limits. Factors such as how much information is available to the individual making the decision, time constraints, or cognitive biases establish these limits. The reality is that most individual decisions are a by-product of what the economist Herbert Simon (1957) referred to as "**bounded rationality.**" Individuals make choices within a contextual environment in which preference ordering and interests meet the "guesswork" reality imposes, so that none of us possesses all the available input we need to make optimum decisions that will maximize our power and influence over a particular situation.

These boundaries can be either external or internal. *External* boundaries include missing, erroneous, or unknowable information. To cite an example, President Bush and Prime Minister Blair had to decide whether to invade Iraq in March 2003, without knowing whether Saddam Hussein would respond with chemical or biological attacks on U.S. and British forces. *Internal* boundaries on rational decision-making are the result of human frailties—the limited physical stamina and intellectual capacity to study exceptionally complex issues. Whatever the "realities" were during the crisis leading up to the Iraq War in 2003, the universe of information available was far more than President Bush, Prime Minister Blair, or indeed anyone else could absorb.

Cognitive Factors

It may be comforting to think that individual actors , particularly those in a decision-making or leadership capacity with access to the levers of power, are fully rational. Yet it is important to remember that by virtue of their humanity (like all of us), cognitive, emotional, psychological, and even biological factors, as well as rational calculations, influence such individuals. Whether you are a foreign minister or a university student, you probably do not like to concede that you confront very real limits that impede your ability to "think through" a problem of consequence and come up with a rational solution. Human beings are prone to adopt one of a range of mental strategies for coping with our cognitive limits. Three examples of such coping mechanisms are cognitive consistency, optimistic bias, and heuristic devices.

Cognitive consistency
The tendency of individuals to hold fast to prevailing views of the world, and to discount contradictory ideas and information in the process.

Cognitive Consistency   Decision-makers tend to seek **cognitive consistency** by discounting ideas and information that contradict their existing views. The controversy over the snarl of information and misinformation about Iraq's abilities and intentions will continue for years, but it is informative to ask why top decision-makers in London and Washington were willing to accept intelligence reports that Baghdad was attempting to buy uranium from Africa. One reason is that this finding "fit" with the existing negative images of Saddam Hussein and his intentions, whereas believing information that there was no nuclear program would have created **cognitive dissonance** among decision-makers.

Optimistic Bias   Humans also justify our decisions by overestimating the likelihood that they will lead to a successful outcome (Johnson, 2004). Social psychologists refer to this phenomenon as "**optimistic bias**," which is particularly evident in the exercise of power by individual leaders. In the view of some scholars, this bias and the "illusion of control" it fosters explains why "hawkish" leaders often win out in policy debates concerning the use of force (Kahneman and Renshon, 2007).

Wishful thinking is common in human decision making. Saddam Hussein seemed to believe that he would politically survive a war with the United States in 2003 just as he had in 1991. This may have increased his willingness to risk war. Wishful thinking cannot change reality. Seven months after this photo was taken, Saddam was hanged for crimes committed against the Iraqi people.

For example, given the overwhelming forces that were mounted against him by the spring of 2003, it is hard to understand why Saddam Hussein chose to fight rather than retreat safely into exile. The reason, according to some of his former aides, is that he believed that he would survive in power despite all evidence to the contrary. In Saddam's mind, Iraq's military defeat in 1991 was only a tactical retreat. This wishful thinking was evident just before the 2003 war when a reporter pointed out that the forces facing him were even more powerful than those that had routed Iraq in the Persian Gulf War. The Iraqi leader replied, "In 1991, Iraq was not defeated. In fact, our army withdrew from Kuwait according to a decision taken by us. . . . We withdrew our forces inside Iraq in order that we may be able to continue fighting inside our country." Going further, Saddam assured the reporter, "If war is forced upon us, Iraq will continue to be here . . . [We] will not finish just like that, even though a huge power may want it to be like that."[3]

Heuristic Devices   A third way that humans deal with their cognitive limitations is by using **heuristic devices**. These are mental shortcuts that help us make decisions more easily by allowing us to skip the effort of information gathering and thorough analysis. *Stereotypes* are one type of heuristic device. For example, former U.S. Attorney General John Ashcroft voiced his biased and inaccurate view of Islam—in the process shedding light on some of the policies of the Justice Department he helmed toward suspected Muslim terrorists—with his egregiously offensive comment that "Islam is a religion in which God requires you to send your son to die for him. Christianity is a faith in which God sends His son to die for you."[4]

Cognitive dissonance
A discordant psychological state in which an individual attempts to process information contradicting his or her prevailing understanding of a subject.

Optimistic bias
The psychological tendency of individuals—particularly those in positions of power—to overrate their own potential for success, and underrate their own potential for failure.

Heuristic devices
A range of psychological strategies that allow individuals to simplify complex decisions.

		Total	Gender		Age				
		Adults	Men	Women	18–29	30–39	40–49	50–64	65+
Concerned that Afghanistan will become another Vietnam?	Very concerned	38%	37%	39%	51%	29%	31%	38%	42%
	Somewhat concerned	28%	26%	30%	19%	31%	27%	26%	36%
	Not very concerned	19%	23%	15%	16%	16%	29%	23%	12%
	Not at all concerned	6%	7%	5%	3%	10%	9%	5%	4%
	Not sure	9%	7%	11%	12%	13%	4%	7%	7%

FIGURE 2.3

The Vietnam Analogy and Afghanistan

National Survey of 1,000 Adults Conducted September 23–24, 2009 by Rasmussen Reports.

Source: Rasmussen Reports; http://www.rasmussenreports.com/public_content/business/econ_survey_questions/september_2009/toplines_afghanistan_september_23_24_2009

Analogies are another heuristic shortcut (Dyson & Preston, 2006; Breuning, 2003). We make comparisons between new situations or people and situations or people that we have earlier experienced or otherwise have learned about. One such connection that frequently figures in policy debates is the **Munich analogy**. This refers to the decision of France and the U.K. to appease Nazi Germany in 1938 when it threatened Czechoslovakia. World War II signified the failure of appeasement, and the "lesson" later leaders drew was that compromise with dictators encourages them. The Munich analogy was clearly in the mind of Secretary of Defense Rumsfeld when he urged action against Iraq despite the lack of definitive evidence of Iraqi WMDs, by arguing, "Think of the prelude to World War II . . . [and] all the countries that said, 'Well, we don't have enough evidence.' There were millions of people dead because of the miscalculations.[5] Analogous reasoning has also been used in comparing contemporary U.S. military operations to the Vietnam debacle (see Figure 2.3)."

Munich analogy
A prevailing belief among many post-World War II leaders that appeasement must be avoided at all costs—a "lesson" derived from the concessions made to Hitler by Britain and France at Munich in 1938.

Psychological Factors

Humans share a number of common psychological traits that also help explain why their decisions may be less than fully rational. One such approach is **frustration–aggression theory**, which argues that individuals or groups that are frustrated sometimes become aggressive. "Why do they hate us?" President Bush rhetorically asked Congress soon after the 9/11 attacks.[6] "They hate our freedoms," was the answer the President supplied to his own question. Perhaps, but others put the source of rage in a very different light. Based on polling in nine Arab and/or Muslim countries, one analyst suggests that rather than a hatred for freedom, the reason for the widespread negative opinions toward the United States is that ". . . the United States is 'ruthless, aggressive, conceited, arrogant, easily provoked, [and biased against Muslims]',"[7] as shown in Figure 2.4. One does not have to understand or agree with these views to comprehend the sense of frustration Arab societies feel over the lack of Palestinian statehood, the underdevelopment that characterizes much of the Arab world, or the sense of Western domination and subjugation (Zunes, 2005).

Frustration-aggression theory
A psychologically based theory that frustrated societies sometimes become collectively aggressive.

Perception and Misperception   The philosophical debate over whether there is an objective
reality "out there" or whether everything is only what
we perceive it to be is timeless. Either way, it is clear
that we all view the world through perceptual lenses
that distort reality to some degree. These distortions
have direct ramifications on how individuals pursue,
conceive of, and wield power. Whatever their source,
individual perceptions have a number of characteristics that influence global politics. The first, which
has two dimensions to it, is what social psychologists call **fundamental attribution error** (Ross,
1977) or **correspondence bias** (Gilbert & Malone,
1995). These two dimensions are an overvaluing of
dispositional factors and an undervaluing of situational factors when seeking to explain the behavior
or decisions of others, with these factors reversed in
our attempts at understanding our own behavior or
decisions. Following are some by-products of this
biased perception.

*There is a tendency to perceive opponents as
more threatening than they actually may be.* North
Korea's and Iran's nuclear programs have alarmed
many Americans. One survey found that 71% of
Americans considered Iran a threat to regional
stability and 77% saw North Korea in the same
way. By contrast, surveys in 20 other countries
revealed that only 40% believed Iran to be a force
for instability and just 47% perceived North Korea in that light.[8]

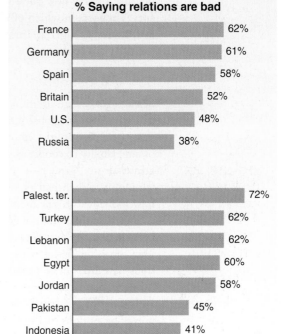

% **Saying relations are bad**

France — 62%
Germany — 61%
Spain — 58%
Britain — 52%
U.S. — 48%
Russia — 38%

Palest. ter. — 72%
Turkey — 62%
Lebanon — 62%
Egypt — 60%
Jordan — 58%
Pakistan — 45%
Indonesia — 41%

FIGURE 2.4
Most say relations between Muslims and Westerners
are poor

Source: Pew Global Attitudes Survey (July 2011)

*A tendency to perceive the behavior of others as more planned and coordinated than
our own.* During the Cold War, Americans and Soviets were mutually convinced
that the other side was orchestrating a coordinated global campaign to subvert
them. Perhaps more accurately, former Secretary of State Henry Kissinger
(1979:1202) has described the two superpowers as behaving like "two heavily armed
blind men feeling their way around a room, each believing himself in mortal peril
from the other whom he assumes to have perfect vision." Each, according to Kissinger,
"tends to ascribe to the other side a consistency, foresight, and coherence that its
own experience belies."

Difficulty in understanding others' perceptions. Misperceptions also produce a
"failure of empathy," in which we are unable to fully grasp or comprehend others'
perceptions of our own statements or actions, particularly when those perceptions are less than positive (Kahneman & Renshon, 2007). This failure was
evident in Former President George W. Bush's expressed amazement during a
press conference that ". . . there's such misunderstanding of what our country is
about that people would hate us. . . . Like most Americans, I just can't believe it

**Fundamental attribution
error (correspondence
bias)**
Overrating personality and
disposition and underrating
situational or contextual
factors when explaining
the observed behavior of
others—and doing the
exact opposite in seeking
to understand one's own
behavior.

because I know how good we are."[9] This perception stood in marked contrast to survey reports in which 60% or more of poll respondents in countries as diverse as Indonesia, Nigeria, Turkey, and Russia thought that the United States represented a direct threat.[10]

Sex and Gender

Sex and gender are additional factors to consider when thinking about the influence of individuals on global politics. Sex represents a biological variable, one that the study of global politics employs to explain how things like aggression, territoriality, or amenability to cooperation might differ in comparing men to women. To an even greater degree, gender—a social construct rooted in ideal types of masculinity and femininity, rather than a biological attribute—has become a crucial variable defining how individuals think about, define, pursue, and use power.

We base the notion of gender, as distinct from sex, on the belief that all or most behavioral differences between men and women derive from learned role definitions. Thus, sex is biological, whereas gender is behavioral. Crucial gender analysis applications have been most prominent in feminist IR scholarship, whether in looking at the gendered nature of military and defense issues (Cohn, 1987), hegemony (Weber, 1999), or the structural inequalities and discrimination that require us to rethink prevailing notions of the global order and how global politics "works"—including the marginalized roles and overlooked contributions of women in general (Tickner, 1992; Enloe, 1990).

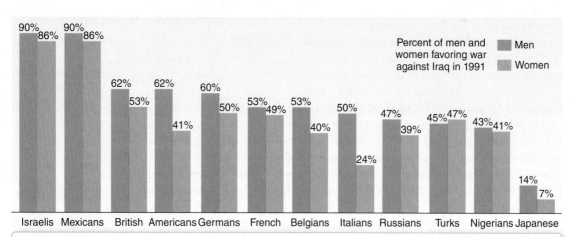

FIGURE 2.5

War and the gender gap

This figure shows the percentages of men and women in favor of using military force to expel Iraq from Kuwait in 1991. Notice that in all but one country, Turkey, more men than women favored using force. Also notice the variations among countries. Women cannot be described as antiwar, nor can men be characterized as pro-war because both men and women in some countries favored war and opposed it in others.

Note: The American response (Pew) was to a slightly different question than for all others (Wilcox et al.) and is used here as generally representative only. Except for Americans, the poll was taken in each country's capital city. Respondents in the Soviet Union were therefore mostly Russian.

Data source: Wilcox, Hewitt, & Allsop (1996); Pew Research Center poll, January 1991.

Social scientists are really just beginning to scratch the surface in empirically accounting for how gender explains behaviors and attitudes of importance in global politics, such as conflict behavior (Caprioli, 2000, 2004). In terms of attitudes, it is clear that a "**gender opinion gap**" exists between men and women on a range of issues, including the utility of war (see Figure 2.5). Public opinion surveys of Americans going back as far as World War II have almost always found women less ready than men to resort to or continue war. A study found this gender gap globally, with men in Australia, Canada, Great Britain, and Italy 10–15% more likely to hold a favorable attitude toward war than women.

Gender opinion gap
The difference between males and females along any one of a number of dimensions, including foreign policy preferences.

Problematizing Gender   Beyond introducing gender as a variable, taking up a gendered perspective when studying global politics also sheds light on critical and previously overlooked or ignored issues impacting women and girls, such as the systematic use of rape as a weapon of war or the transnational sex trade. One of the primary contributions of feminist IR scholarship is the extent to which it reveals the disproportionate, and disproportionately negative, impact that the "normal," everyday conduct of global politics has on women—and the degree to which not only this negative impact, but our limited understanding of it, is a by-product of patriarchal and exclusionary institutions, rules, and practices (Tickner, 2001). At the same time, the leading edge of contemporary feminist IR scholarship has attempted to advocate for the consideration of women as agents rather than victims, with an increased focus on analyzing the active role of women as warriors, human traffickers, and terrorists (Cunningham, 2003; Sjoberg and Gentry, 2007).

Leadership

As we noted earlier, while individual-level analysis is not and should not be solely concentrated on high-ranking leaders, the reality is that individual leaders and leadership do receive a much greater emphasis in individual-level analysis than do "ordinary folk." This is partly structural because, for a variety of reasons, the conduct of global politics and foreign policy is far more centered around a cadre of top leaders than is that of domestic politics. This is also partly pragmatic, in that IR scholars have more readily available information concerning individual leaders to obtain and analyze.

We sometimes refer to the branch of individual-level analysis focusing largely on particular individual leaders

Ellen Johnson Sirleaf was the first woman in Africa to be a democratically elected head of state. As the President of Liberia, Johnson has made special efforts to appoint women in her cabinet and has encouraged women to take a public leadership role.

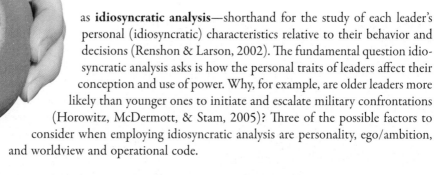

as **idiosyncratic analysis**—shorthand for the study of each leader's personal (idiosyncratic) characteristics relative to their behavior and decisions (Renshon & Larson, 2002). The fundamental question idiosyncratic analysis asks is how the personal traits of leaders affect their conception and use of power. Why, for example, are older leaders more likely than younger ones to initiate and escalate military confrontations (Horowitz, McDermott, & Stam, 2005)? Three of the possible factors to consider when employing idiosyncratic analysis are personality, ego/ambition, and worldview and operational code.

Personality   When studying personality types and their impact, scholars examine a leader's basic orientations toward self and toward others, behavioral patterns, and attitudes about such politically relevant concepts as power and authority (Dyson, 2006). There are numerous categorization schemes. One of the most well-known schemes places personality along an active–passive scale and a positive–negative scale (Barber, 1985). Active leaders are policy innovators; passive leaders are reactors. Positive personalities have egos strong enough to enjoy (or at least accept) the contentious political environment; negative personalities are apt to feel burdened, even abused, by political criticism.

Of recent U.S. presidents, Bill Clinton is a prime example of an active–positive personality. He reveled in the trappings of authority that came with his job and admitted that he was "almost compulsively overactive" in seeking to use that authority (Renshon, 1995:59). Scholars differ on President George W. Bush. One assessment is that he is an active–positive personality who "loves his job and is very energetic and focused" (DiIulio, 2003:3). Others have characterized Bush as positive–passive, in part due to perceptions of his "hands-off" delegation of authority to other top-ranking officials in his administration (Etheredge, 2001).

The more active a leader is in seeking and using power, the more criticism he or she is likely to encounter. Positive personalities take such criticism in stride, but negative personalities are prone to assume that opponents are enemies. Lyndon Johnson and Richard Nixon were both active–negative personalities who showed symptoms of delusion, struck out at their enemies, and generally developed bunker mentalities as their administrations faced mounting difficulties such as Vietnam and Watergate.

Ego and Ambition   Obviously, a leader's ego and personal ambitions can also influence his or her conception, pursuit, and use of power. One thing that arguably drove former Iraqi dictator Saddam Hussein was his grandiose vision of himself. According to one intelligence report, the Iraqi leader saw himself in "larger than life terms comparable to Nebuchadnezzar [the great Babylonian king, 605–563 BCE] and Saladin [the Sultan of Egypt who in 1189 defeated the Christians during the Third Crusade]."

The ego of President George H. W. Bush also may have influenced policy. He came to office in 1989, with a reputation for being wishy-washy, and *Newsweek* even ran a picture of him with a banner, "The Wimp Factor," on its cover. Seeking to counter this popular perception, a wounded Bush arguably overcompensated

Idiosyncratic analysis
An individual-level analysis approach to decision-making that assumes individuals make foreign policy decisions and that different individuals are likely to make different decisions.

with a hard-line foreign policy oriented around military power. Early in his first and only term, he ordered a military intervention in Panama, and his opposition to a diplomatic response to the crisis in the Persian Gulf after Iraq's invasion of Kuwait in August 1990 made war an eventual inevitability. Certainly, it would be outrageous to claim that Bush decided on war only to assuage his ego. At the same time, after the successful conclusion of the military interventions in Panama and Iraq, the president told reporters, "You're talking to the wimp . . . to the guy that had a cover of a national magazine . . . put that label on me. And now some that saw that we can react when the going gets tough maybe have withdrawn that allegation."[11]

Worldview and Operational Code Apart from a more general consideration of perceptions, an additional related factor that helps us understand the power and influence of individuals in world politics is the worldview and "operational code" of influential leaders. Whatever their source, the sum of a leader's perceptions creates his or her worldview (Hermann & Keller, 2004). Perceptions play a key role in policy because they contribute to a decision-making context that often shapes (if not determines) whether, when, and how to use power. In other words, individual leaders tend to act based on their perceptions of other actors or of situations, accurate or otherwise. For example, research shows that supposedly "**rogue states**" are no more likely than any other country to start a war (Caprioli & Trumbore, 2005). Yet most ranking officials in the Bush administration repeatedly asserted that Iraq, part of President George W. Bush's imagined construct of the "axis of evil" (along with Iran and North Korea), had WMD capabilities and intended to develop them more fully—a key factor driving the U.S.-led military intervention.

A related perceptual phenomenon is known as one's "**operational code**" (Schafer & Walker, 2006; George, 1969). This idea describes how any given leader's philosophical beliefs (assumptions regarding the fundamental nature of politics, conflict, power, and the individual) and instrumental beliefs (specific beliefs concerning the appropriate method for attaining the ends one desires) come together to influence that individual's conception of whether, when, and how to use power. Operational code analysis allows us to assess how a leader's propensities for choosing rewards, threats, force, or other methods of diplomacy help explain decisions and actions (Walker, Schafer, & Young, 1998).

For example, the roots of President Bill Clinton's operational code in a philosophical belief set in which the United States operates in a complex, technology-driven, interconnected world led him to favor a multilateral, diplomatic approach. Conversely, George W. Bush's operational code—derived from the fact that he was,

Kim Jong-il, who died in December 2011, was the long-time leader of the Democratic People's Republic of Korea (North Korea). He was at the center of an elaborate cult of personality that extended far into North Korean politics and society. Publicly referred to as "The Dear Leader," Kim Jong-il ensured that North Korea remained almost completely isolated from the outside world.

Rogue state
States which are perceived to be in noncompliance with the majority of prevailing rules, norms, and laws in the global system and therefore constitute a threat to order. This may mean, among other things, a state governed by authoritarian rule that severely restricts human rights, sponsors or condones terrorism, or seeks to obtain or promote the spread of weapons of mass destruction.

Operational code
How an individual acts in a given situation, based on a combination of one's understanding of the nature of politics and fundamental worldview.

in his own words, more a "gut" player than an intellectual (Daalder & Lindsay, 2003:7), as well as the influence of his religious convictions—led him to see the world in more dichotomous, "black and white" terms.[12] This belief set left Bush disposed to see the world as a dangerous place, prompting an instrumental belief set in which he viewed unilateralism and military force more favorably.

STATE-LEVEL ANALYSIS

For all of the importance of the various individual-level variables outlined previously (and others, such as physical and mental health or personal experiences), in global politics we most often associate power and its use with nation-states. For this reason, the sovereign state remains the central actor in contemporary global politics, making the study of state-level factors vital. By allowing us to identify and analyze the impact of the processes and institutions of the state on the use of power in global politics, state-level analysis provides another useful "lens" through which we can interpret events, decisions, and behavior in the global arena.

State-level analysis emphasizes the characteristics of states and how they make foreign policy choices and implement them (Hudson, 2005; Bueno de Mesquita, 2002). What is important from the perspective of state-level analysis is how a sovereign state's political structure and dynamics, as well as subnational actors, shape that state's decisions, behaviors, and overall use of power (of all types) on the world stage (Chittick & Pingel, 2002). Examining these factors allows us to better understand the sources of a state's power and how it exercises power, by peering inside the state's "black box."

We can return to the Wikileaks case to illustrate the degree to which states can and do use the power at their disposal to advance and defend their interests, even in a changing global political environment. For obvious reasons, states oppose the widespread public divulgence of sensitive information concerning the inner workings of their foreign policy process and the decisions it produces. Yet, as we discussed previously, the Internet is an extremely useful tool that allows for the rapid flow of vital information across borders and boundaries (physical and otherwise), making it something that is difficult for states to regulate. Impeding the flow of undesirable and possibly harmful information raises the related risk of impeding beneficial information. Consider the dependence of states and societies on the Internet for commerce, for instance. Either way, we can undermine even the attempt to restrict Internet activity by the simple relocation of a website to another server in another political jurisdiction, as Wikileaks has done repeatedly (BBC, 2010).

Yet while it might be the case that no single state can directly regulate the Internet or other transnational forces, keep in mind that power has many different facets and translations. The response of the United States and other states to Wikileaks is telling here. States have used indirect means to alter the behavior of private actors. The United States has been particularly effective in this regard. Following up on Secretary of State Hillary Clinton's promise to respond "aggressively" in November 2010, Amazon stopped hosting Wikileaks, Every DNS sought to rescind Wikileaks.org's domain name, eBay/Paypal promised to cut off financial transactions to Wikileaks associates, and Mastercard and Visa severed all relations with it. While none of these actions were able to "put the genie back in the bottle" and limit the availability of the information

Despite spelling confusion, (the "H" in Cyrillic is pronounced like the "N" in English), Julian Assange and Wikileaks captured the imagination of many protesters and critics of unchecked state power. Here, Russians express their support for Assange.

that Wikileaks has already leaked, they clearly did have an adverse impact on the long-run viability of Wikileaks as an organization. Thus, we can see not only the ability of the state to respond effectively to "new" transnational threats and problems, but also the degree to which the state remains a viable force that exerts influence on private actors such as multinational financial firms.

Beyond thinking about the ability of the state to control information flow or to influence private firms, state-level analysis affords us the ability to look specifically at where a state's power originates. Although it is common to think of national power as derived from military might and wealth, those elements of power depend on more basic factors including the type and efficacy of the government, natural resource endowments, technological infrastructure, and demographic characteristics. In the following sections, we provide an accessible (if simplified) grouping of these factors under the headings of governmental and societal sources of state power.

Governmental Sources

Traditionally, the state has been the central actor in the global system. Accordingly, each state's pursuit of its national interests through whatever implements of power are available to it has traditionally been the central force shaping global politics. When assessing a state's governmental pursuit and use of power, we are really concerned with its **statecraft.** Statecraft is the term that we use to encapsulate how a country applies its national capabilities through its foreign policy institutions and processes to achieve its foreign policy goals. Scholar Michael Mastanduno has defined statecraft as:

> the use of policy instruments to satisfy the core objectives of nation-states in the international system. . . . Statecraft is most usefully thought of in broad and multidimensional terms. It involves the application and interplay of multiple instruments—military, economic, diplomatic, and informational—to achieve the multiple objectives of states, including national security, economic prosperity, and political prestige and influence. (Mastanduno, 1988:826)

Statecraft
The use of military, economic, diplomatic, and ideational tools in the pursuit of clearly defined foreign policy interests and objectives.

Therefore, when conducting state-level analysis, it is essential to isolate and study those governmental factors or variables that explain the power that states have available at their disposal to effectively engage in statecraft. We now discuss four such factors—state sovereignty, governmental authority, military capability, and economic capacity.

State Sovereignty   The first and in many ways the most important factor to take into account when looking at governmental sources of power is **state sovereignty**. In an anarchical global political system organized around sovereign states, it is this condition that determines first and foremost whether or not a national group or political unit will have the status and "clout" necessary to engage in the conduct of global politics. The centrality of the sovereign state has been more or less the defining feature of the global system since the **Treaty of Westphalia** (1648), which ended the Thirty Years' and Eighty Years' Wars and helped institutionalize international law and diplomatic practice around the emergent state. In contemporary global politics, state sovereignty effectively rests on the satisfaction of four conditions:

1. The existence of a clearly defined and identifiable national group, oriented around some common characteristic(s), seeking self-determination

2. The recognized dominion of that group over a clearly demarcated territorial space

3. The formation and successful implementation of an effective governing mechanism by that group

4. The political and legal recognition of all of the aforementioned conditions by other states and the international community

In some ways it is the last, and most subjective, condition that is the most important of the four. The importance of the *recognition* of a state's sovereignty by other states underscores the degree to which state sovereignty has a social and reputational dimension. Following from this, it is not hard to see that sovereignty confers significant power on a national group that attains statehood, and significantly limits one that does not. Sovereign states have representation at the United Nations and all international conferences, signatory status on international treaties, and the legal right to noninterference in their domestic affairs (according to the UN Charter). These factors and more mean that state sovereignty serves as an important platform for the exercise of power in global politics—and help explain why stateless nations (such as the Palestinians) seek statehood, or why multinational nation-states (such as the former Yugoslavia) sometimes fragment along national or ethnic lines into multiple states.

Governmental Authority   Those who study statecraft are well aware that there is no such thing as a single foreign policy process. Instead, the way that states formulate and conduct foreign policy varies considerably. One fundamental variable of importance here is the country's government type. In the field of IR, we call this **regime type**. These types range along a scale that has absolute **authoritarian** governments on one end and unfettered **democratic** governments on the other. The more authoritarian a government is, the more likely it is that foreign policy will center itself in a narrow segment of the government, even in the hands of the chief executive. It is important to realize, though, that no government is absolutely under the

State sovereignty
A central tenet of global politics that holds that the state has the sole right to govern its territory and people, free from outside interference.

Treaty of Westphalia
The treaty ending the Thirty Years' War (1618–1648), giving rise to the modern state-based system.

Regime type
The type of government prevailing in a given society.

Authoritarian
A government that centralizes and exercises power and administers society with little or no input from or participation by the governed.

Democratic
A form of government established on the premise that the consent of the governed is necessary to the exercise of power and administration of society—and that the governed have obligations to participate in the political system.

thumb of any individual. States are too big and too complex for that to happen, and thus secondary leaders (such as foreign ministers), bureaucrats, interest groups, and other domestic elements play a role in even very authoritarian political systems.

At the other end of the scale, the conduct of statecraft by democracies is subject to a much more open process, with inputs from legislators, the media, public opinion, and opposition parties, as well as those foreign policy–making actors that influence authoritarian government policy. For one, the power of the executive may be practically fragmented or constitutionally limited. For example, in the United States, the Senate is given the authority to ratify (approve) all foreign treaties—which proved particularly unsettling to President Bill Clinton and many other world leaders in 1999 when the U.S. Senate refused to ratify the Comprehensive Test Ban Treaty that he had signed, thereby preventing the United States from becoming a party to the agreement.

Of course, the conduct of war and diplomacy long predates the emergence of democracy, with the authority to carry out such activities transferred to the sovereign state over a gradual process beginning with the Treaty of Westphalia. As such, a country's top leadership tends to dominate the practice of statecraft somewhat by design, regardless of regime type. In most countries, the executive branch is predominantly responsible for diplomacy and statecraft, particularly in matters deemed vital to national security. The degree to which the head of government and/or political executive dominates a state's foreign policy varies, of course—by not only regime type, but also by how the state allocates powers formally and informally, the situational context, and the effectiveness, motivation, and operational code of particular decision-makers.

The Nehru-Gandhi family is widely recognized as a political dynasty with a strong grip on Indian politics. Jawaharlal Nehru, the first prime minister of India, took office in 1947 and his descendants have been involved in politics since then. Among those pictured in this photo are Nehru's daughter, the former Prime Minister Indira Gandhi (center), her son Rajeev Gandhi (another former Prime Minister, to her left), her daughter-in-law, Sonia Gandhi, who is currently the President of the National Congress Party (to her right) and Rajeev and Sonia's son Rajeev Gandhi, (the young child sitting at Indira's feet) who is now a member of parliament.

There are multiple reasons for, and examples of, the centralization of state-level power at the "top" of the political system. For one thing, as public opinion and attitude surveys consistently report, in the vast majority of countries, foreign policy issues are generally less **salient** than domestic issues (Holsti, 2004). Issues about which the public knows or cares little are, naturally, issues over which political leaders tend to exert more, and more unfettered, authority. For instance, President Bush consented to expanding the North Atlantic Treaty Organization (NATO) by adding seven new members (Bulgaria, Romania, Estonia, Latvia, Lithuania, Slovakia, and Slovenia) in 2004. Even though this substantially added to U.S. defense commitments by including countries that border Russia, the move was nearly invisible within the

Salience/salient
In public opinion research, the issues or questions that are more meaningful and significant (or "matter" more) to a greater proportion of people.

United States. The media made little mention of it, pollsters did not even bother to ask the public what it thought, and the U.S. Senate unanimously ratified the amendment with little debate.

Another, related dynamic (often evident in crisis situations) is the "**rally effect**"—the propensity of the public and other domestic actors to offer broad and unquestioning support to political leaders during times of crisis, thereby enhancing the leaders' power base. Dynamics such as these have occurred in all states across the global system, regardless of regime type. In a similar vein, **bureaucracy** heavily influences every state, whatever its strength or type of government. Although political leaders legally command the bureaucracy, they find it difficult to control the vast understructures of their governments. During their leadership, President Vladimir Putin of Russia and President George W. Bush candidly conceded that gap during a joint press conference. The two presidents were expounding on a new spirit of cooperation between their two countries when a reporter asked them if they could "say with certainty that your teams will act in the same spirit?" Amid knowing laughter, Bush replied, "It's a very good question you ask, because sometimes the intended [policy] doesn't necessarily get translated throughout the levels of government [because of] bureaucratic intransigence." President Putin agreed. "Of course, there is always a bureaucratic threat," he conceded.[13]

Rally effect
The tendency during a crisis of political and other leaders, legislators, and the public to give strong support to a chief executive and the policy that leader has adopted in response to the crisis.

Bureaucracy
The bulk of the state's administrative structure that continues even when political leaders change.

Military Capabilities   In an anarchical global system in which there is no universal world government and states are locked in a self-help relationship, military power is obviously a huge consideration when assessing the state's power. The ability and willingness of states to amass and use military power in the face of few effective restraints has continued more or less without interruption since the 18th century. The importance of military power notwithstanding, assessing a particular state's military power objectively is trickier than you might imagine. Some aspects of military power, such as defense spending or uniformed personnel, are easy to count. Others, including training, preparedness, and morale, are harder to quantify.

Defense spending is one of the largest categories in most countries' budgets, and there can be little doubt that the level of spending has some impact on military capabilities. U.S. military expenditures ($698 billion in 2010, not including supplemental allocations for military operations in Iraq and Afghanistan; SIPRI, 2011) far exceed those of any other country. As such, there are probably few scenarios in which the armed forces of any other country could defeat U.S. forces in a conventional war. Yet none of the ways that governments commonly report defense spending is wholly satisfactory when attempting a state-level analysis of a state's military power, especially in a comparative sense. Looking at defense spending in the aggregate or on a per capita basis (controlling for population) can be misleading because it does not account for significant and potentially major differences in overall size and performance of a country's economy or the landscape of security threats and commitments.

Assessing and comparing the military arsenal of states is another approach. Here, the quantity of weapons overall, and by category, is certainly an important consideration. Knowing that the United States had 16,000 tanks and Iraq had 1,900 tanks prior to their war in 2003 is one indication of the relative power of the two countries' armored forces. Had the potential combatants been the United States and Russia or China, Moscow's 21,000 tanks or Beijing's 11,000 tanks would have made for a much different military situation. Yet aggregate numbers are only part of the military weapons equation—quality matters. Even if the U.S. and Iraqi tank forces had had equal numbers, Iraq's aging Soviet-export tanks would have been no match for U.S. battle tanks, which are capable of maneuvering at nearly highway speeds, using thermal sights and computerized targeting, firing shells coated with depleted uranium that can destroy almost any armored opponent, and clad in depleted uranium armor capable of repelling shells fired by Iraqi tanks.

Apart from defense spending or types of armaments, state-level analysis of military power can focus on a country's military personnel. Here too, we must account for a number of quantitative and qualitative factors. The aggregate number of troops, both total and compared to an opponent, is one factor. For example, China (2.3 million troops), India (1.7 million), the United States (1.5 million), and Russia (1.0 million) all have enough troops to play a major regional and even global role. By contrast, Belize, with about 1,000 troops, has very little military muscle to use as a diplomatic asset. Like spending, governments must measure sheer numbers of troops against the scope of their deployments and reasonable estimates of their potential use. For example, the large U.S. military force becomes less dominant when considering its numerous and extensive global commitments. Deployments in Afghanistan and Iraq have stretched U.S. forces thin, leading in the view of some analysts to **overstretch**.

Overstretch
A concept developed by historians that suggests a recurring tendency of powerful actors to overextend themselves by taking on costly foreign policy commitments that deplete their finances and generate domestic discord.

The quality of a state's military personnel is also important to consider. A military force comprised of intelligent, healthy, disciplined, and well-trained enlisted troops and officers is far more likely to be an effective instrument of state power than one that is undereducated, plagued by malnutrition and disease, undisciplined, or poorly trained in tactics, strategy, and weapons systems. Another related factor is whether a state's armed forces serve on an all-volunteer basis (as in the United States or France), or through conscription (as in Russia or Israel).

Conventional wisdom holds that an all-volunteer armed force is likely to attract better recruits and exhibit greater morale and professionalism than a force raised by the draft. Recent U.S. military involvements have called the efficacy of an all-volunteer force into question, with the wars in Afghanistan and Iraq requiring the call-up of reserves into combat and rolling (recurring) deployments due to recruiting shortfalls. For example, in 2005, the U.S. Army fell 17% below the target of 80,000 recruits. One response to these shortfalls has been lowering the standards for recruits. Between 2003 and 2006, for example, the number of waivers given for a criminal background jumped 65%, accounting for 11% of all Army recruits in 2006. Perhaps as a result, in 2010, all branches of the U.S. armed forces met or exceeded their recruitment targets.

Economic Capacity   While states utilize foreign policy to increase their economic strength, it is important to keep in mind that they also use economic power and resources to engage in statecraft (and vice versa). Some determinants of a state's economic power include financial position, natural resources, industrial output, and agricultural output. As a starting point, the center of any country's economic power is its basic financial position. The overall size of the economy is one factor, and here, bigger is better. Take the United States as an example. According to World Bank and IMF statistics, at $14.5 trillion, the U.S. GDP is immense: the world's largest, nearly three times that of the next largest country (China), and equal to 23% of the world's combined GDP. Other important measures of financial position include the scope of a country's exports of goods and services. Here again the U.S. position is good, with over $2 trillion in exports in 2011—slightly more than the next largest countries (Germany and China) and equal to approximately 11% of all exports. The extent of a state's foreign investment is also telling. Americans currently have more than $20 trillion tied up in assets abroad, far more than any other country.

With respect to financial solvency, the aggregate size of a state's economy or its flows of goods, services, and money does not give the full picture. The U.S. example, as well as that of Greece, Ireland, and Portugal (among others in Europe), illustrates the vulnerabilities and weaknesses that occur with large and expanding budget deficits and overall debt. The U.S. government has run a budget deficit for all but 4 of the 30 years between FY1980–FY2010. One result of chronic deficit spending is that the U.S. government has had to increasingly borrow money from foreign sources to finance the debt, as Figure 2.6 shows.

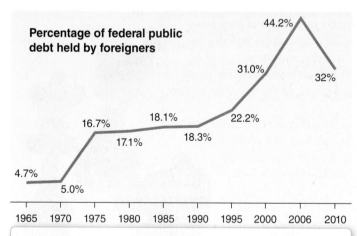

Percentage of federal public debt held by foreigners

44.2%
31.0%
32%
18.1%
22.2%
16.7%
17.1%
18.3%
4.7%
5.0%

1965   1970   1975   1980   1985   1990   1995   2000   2006   2010

FIGURE 2.6

U.S. foreign debt

To finance its budget deficits, the U.S. government borrows money, partly by selling bonds to foreign countries. Increasingly, as this figure shows, this creates vulnerabilities for the U.S. economy. In 2010, 32% of U.S. government debt was held by foreign governments.

Data source: U.S. Department of Treasury.

Deficit spending and debt financing leave states that engage in it vulnerable to external financial pressure, and increasingly subject to the twists and turns in the global financial market. Another measure of relevance here is a state's import-export ratio. Returning to the U.S. example, Americans import far more than they export, and have rung up a trade deficit during all but two years since 1971. The $500 billion trade deficit for 2010 was among the largest in American history, and far larger than that of any other country. Thus far, the immense size of the U.S. economy has been able to absorb these negative trends, but a prolonged recession has raised serious doubts about that prospect going forward.

A state's possession or lack of energy, mineral, and other natural resources has become an increasingly important power factor as industrialization and technology have advanced. Natural resources affect power in three related ways: (1) The greater a country's self-sufficiency in vital natural resources, the greater its power. (2) Conversely, the greater a country's dependency on foreign sources for vital natural resources, the less its power. (3) The greater a country's surplus (over domestic use) of vital resources that other countries require, the greater its power. The key here is not just how much of a given resource a country has and how much it extracts for use each year. It is production compared to consumption.

Oil is the most obvious example, as illustrated in Figure 2.7. For countries with large reserves, high production, and low consumption, this "black gold" has been a major source of revenue. Oil has also increased the global political power and significance of Saudi Arabia and other such oil-surplus countries. By contrast, the United States has limited reserves and uses far more petroleum than it produces. The resulting need for imported petroleum makes the country vulnerable to disruptions in the flow of oil and to fluctuations in energy prices that can have broadly harmful economic impacts.

Even if a country is bountifully supplied with natural resources, its power is limited unless it can convert those assets into industrial goods and, increasingly, services. On a global basis, industrial production is highly concentrated. For instance, just five countries (China, Japan, Russia, the United States, and South Korea) produce a majority of the world's steel. Vehicle production is another indication of industrial concentration. In 2011, the five biggest vehicle manufacturers (China, the United States, Japan, Germany, and South Korea) accounted for 58% of the global total. Conversely, about 85% of the world's countries (including all those in Africa) produce no, or only a negligible number of, vehicles.

A country's agricultural capacity adds or detracts from its economic power. Self-sufficiency varies widely in the world. The United States not only meets its own needs, it also earns money from agricultural exports. In 2010, the U.S. net trade surplus came to approximately $34 billion. Other countries are less fortunate. Some have to use their economic resources to import food. Sub-Saharan Africa and South Asia are in particularly bad shape. Senegal, for one, needs to import machinery, fuel, and other products necessary to diversify and industrialize its economy, yet it must spend 28% of its limited import funds to buy food.

Societal Factors

Assessing the power and capabilities of a state requires one to look beyond simply those factors related or subject to governmental control and authority. Undoubtedly, other variables associated with the society or territory over which a state has jurisdiction can and do contribute to a state's power or weakness—both directly and indirectly. We will discuss five examples: political culture, technological sophistication, geography, demographics, and human development.

Political Culture   Each country's foreign policy interests and orientation toward power usually reflect its **political culture**. This concept represents a society's widely held, traditional values and its fundamental practices that are slow to change, particularly concerning matters of governance and issues in the public arena (Paquette, 2003; Jung, 2002). We can describe political cultures as democratic, authoritarian, militaristic, procedural, or xenophobic, to name a few possibilities (Pye & Verba, 1965).

Political culture
A society's general and fundamental practices and attitudes toward governance and policy, based on historical experience and the values of citizens.

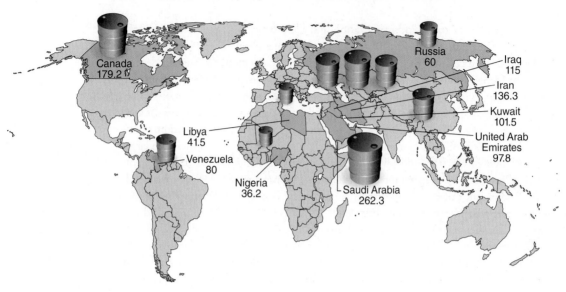

Proved Reserves 2007, Top 10 Countries in Billions of Barrels

Canada 179.2

Russia 60

Iraq 115

Iran 136.3

Kuwait 101.5

United Arab Emirates 97.8

Libya 41.5

Venezuela 80

Nigeria 36.2

Saudi Arabia 262.3

Fueling up

A look at key oil statistics, including proved reserves, the top 10 producers and consumers, and oil revenues of OPEC countries.

Producers	2007 estimates (millions of barrels per day)	Consumers	2007 estimates (millions of barrels per day)	Revenue	Estimated net oil export Jan.– Oct. 2008 (billions)
Saudi Arabia	10.2	United States	20.7	Saudi Arabia	$262
Russia	9.9	China	7.6	United Arab Emirates	$84
United States	8.5	Japan	5.0	Iran	$75
Iran	4.0	Russia	2.9	Kuwait	$74
China	3.9	India	2.7	Algeria	$64
Mexico	3.5	Germany	2.5	Nigeria	$63
Canada	3.4	Brazil	2.4	Angola	$62
United Arab Emirates	2.9	Canada	2.4	Venezuela	$56
Venezuela	2.7	Saudi Arabia	2.3	Iraq	$54
Kuwait	2.6	Korea, South	2.2	Libya	$51
				Qatar	$34
				Ecuador	$10
				Indonesia	-$5

FIGURE 2.7

As this graphic shows, oil production is not only a lucrative but also a highly concentrated endeavor. High energy prices ensure that many of the world's major oil producers and exporters have a source of tremendous financial revenue, which should correlate with a higher performing economy and a stronger state. Similarly, high levels of oil consumption indicate high levels of industrial activity—also a marker of a better performing economy and, by extension, enhanced state power. As with everything else, patterns of oil exports and imports are subject to an alternative interpretation, since a state's excessive reliance on a single export (such as oil) or excessive dependence on imports of a natural resource outside its control might also signal vulnerability and weakness.

Source: U.S. Energy Information Administration.

Despite great protests from the EU in the former case and the United States in the latter, the WTO rulings led to alterations in trade policies by the two actors—representing a limit to unchecked state sovereignty in both cases. The outcome here also represents an effective recognition by the two parties that some global governing authority was necessary to facilitate the extensive commercial interactions benefiting both sides. In the end, this example illustrates one of the primary arguments for expanding global governance and "vertical" authority in the global political system, as well as a reason for why it occurs when it does. We can say that international agreements such as the GATT, if all relevant parties agree to them and if they are enforceable, reduce what liberal international relations theorists claim to be one of the primary barriers to international cooperation: **transaction costs**.

Liberals argue that states are necessarily opposed to cooperation, but that they are reluctant to cooperate because of the risks involved—in other words, states need answers to important questions (Will both or all parties uphold the agreements that they reach? Can the law adjudicate when disputes arise?)

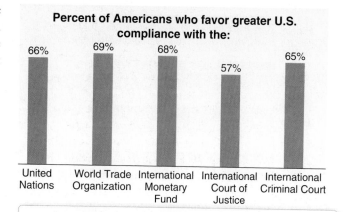

FIGURE 2.9

Attitudes about global governance

Most Americans say they support increased U.S. compliance with a wide range of international organizations even if their decisions differ from U.S. policy preferences. However, questions about specific issues that go against current U.S. policy often bring a less internationalist response by Americans. For example, 65% of them want the United States to join the International Criminal Court, but only 37% are willing to have the ICC try American soldiers accused of war crimes if the U.S. government refuses to do so.

Data sources: Chicago Council on Global Affairs, *Global Views 2004: American Public Opinion and Foreign Policy* (Chicago: Chicago Council on Global Affairs, 2005) and Pew Global Attitudes Project Poll, January, 2003; data provided by The Roper Center for Public Opinion Research, University of Connecticut.

that only governance can provide. In matters of international commerce in particular, we are able to see increasing evidence of reduced transaction costs and enhanced cooperation as a result of expanding global authority and support for it (see Figure 2.9).

Interdependence   A second structural characteristic of any system is the frequency, scope (range), and intensity (level) of interactions among the units. In the global political system, the frequency, scope, and level of interaction among actors (states, and increasingly, non–state actors) has grown extensively during the last half century. Economic interdependence provides the most obvious example, and is often the touchstone for liberal arguments about the rise of **complex interdependence** and the resulting decline in state sovereignty (Keohane & Nye, 2001). The volume and value of goods and services traded and foreign investment are continually expanding, and dwarf that of even a half-century ago. All but the most **autarkic** states (such as North Korea) are heavily dependent on other states for raw material inputs for goods that it produces, for finished goods and services that it needs, and/or as markets for products that it sells. Without foreign oil, to pick one obvious illustration, U.S. transportation and industry would literally come to a halt, explaining in part the degree of support for international engagement (see Figure 2.10). Without extensive exports, the U.S. economy would stagger because exported goods and services account for about 13% of the U.S. GDP (World Bank, 2011).

Transaction costs
Impediments to commercial or other cooperative ventures stemming from a lack of trust between and among involved parties rooted in concerns about the enforceability of agreements.

Complex interdependence
A term most associated with the liberal theorists Robert Keohane and Joseph Nye referring to the broad and deep interdependence of issues and actors in the contemporary global political system, and the ways in which this condition structures and conditions the conduct of global politics.

Autarky/autarkic state
A completely or nearly completely inwardly directed society with little or no connections to the outside world.

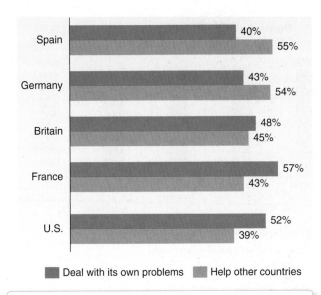

Spain — 40% / 55%
Germany — 43% / 54%
Britain — 48% / 45%
France — 57% / 43%
U.S. — 52% / 39%

■ Deal with its own problems   ■ Help other countries

FIGURE 2.10

Isolationism vs. engagement

As a survey conducted in Fall 2011 indicates, most Western countries accept, and even support, the realities of interdependence—though isolationist sentiment during turbulent economic periods remains significant.

Source: Pew Global Attitudes Center; The American-Western European Values Gap (Survey Report).

Transnational
Social, political, economic, and cultural activities and processes that transcend and permeate the borders and authority of states.

Data about expanding trade does not, however, fully capture the degree to which the widening scope and intensifying level of global interactions are increasing **transnational** contacts at every level. For individuals, the ease of travel and the expansion of modern telecommunications have made personal international interactions, once relatively rare, now commonplace. According to the U.S. Census Bureau, between 1990 and 2010, the number of Americans traveling overseas increased 38% from 44.6 million to 61.5 million. During the same period, the number of foreign visitors to the United States jumped 51% from 39.4 million to 59.7 million.

Information and communications technologies (ICT) such as the Internet, Web-based applications such as Facebook, Twitter, and YouTube, smartphones, and satellite technology are also expanding the scope, level, and intensity of information flow, both in terms of mainstream media, alternative or "new" media, and between and among individuals and social groups. Trillions of phone calls, letters, and e-mail messages add to the globalization of human interactions, and the Internet ignores borders as it connects people and organizations around the world as if they were in the next room. To cite just one example, satellite-transmitted television has revolutionized communications by providing more and different information to new and hungry audiences—as in the case of *al-Jazeera*, a Qatar-based global media conglomerate that first rose to prominence by offering an alternative to much of the state-controlled media in the Arab world.

The benefits of interdependence are many and often celebrated (Keohane & Nye, 2001; Friedman, 2007). Still, the reality of a persistent deficit in global governance means that the depth and expanse of networked interactions between and among societies and individuals can be hazardous. Most notable among these is the increased sensitivity and vulnerability of an ever-greater number of actors, including states, to an increasingly wide range of security threats (Baldwin, 1980). Put simply, just as we enjoy the benefits that a smaller globe brings in terms of enhanced information flows and access to a diverse array of consumer goods and services, the increasing intensity and penetration of global interdependence has also created a degree of densely networked and weakly governed connections in commerce, transport, energy and natural resources, migration, and information technology.

Power Relationships

The second grouping of systemic-level factors that we consider here are power relationships. System-level analysis reveals that in the "real world" the realities of power in the global political system restrain states and individuals much like the distribution of power in domestic society limits groups and individuals. At the systemic level, considerations such as the number of powerful actors predominant in the system, as well as the prevailing social context (e.g., dominant norms and ideas), heavily influence the practice of global politics at any point in time. Whereas the former consideration speaks to the importance of "hard" (coercive and material) power, as well as reminding us of the centrality of states, the latter suggests the impact that "soft" (persuasive and ideational) power can have on the wider global society of states.

Polarity   Historically, how many powerful actors exist during any given time period—a concept drawn from principles of magnetism, which we call **polarity** (Wilkinson, 2004), characterize the global political system. "Poles" are most typically states or imperial powers, although one can conceivably think of other, non–state actors (such as alliances or international organizations) in the same vein. Polarity is particularly important to the realist approach and its concern with the **balance of power**. Sometimes scholars use the term to describe the existing distribution of power, as in, "the current balance of power greatly favors the United States." More classically, though, the theory of balance-of-power politics the realists put forth holds that: (1) all states are power seeking; (2) ultimately, a state or bloc will attempt to become hegemonic, that is, dominate the system; and (3) other states will *either* attempt to balance that dominance by increasing their own power and/or cooperating with other states, *or* bandwagon with the hegemonic aspirant in order to capture the gains of allying with a dominant power (Walt, 1987).

System-level analysts concerned with polarity arrangements believe that the number of power poles in existence at any one time demonstrably shapes how states (and individual leaders) are likely to act. A **unipolar system**, in which one actor is dominant, is likely to approach a vertical hierarchy such as that which exists in most domestic societies, with less room for maneuver by weak states or adversaries to the dominant power. Unipolarity was arguably present in the immediate aftermath of the Cold War, with the United States the dominant actor. Conversely, a **bipolar system** exists when two superpowers roughly equally split power and authority in the system, leading to the formation of **blocs**. We can best exemplify bipolarity in the **Cold War** itself, with two superpowers, the U.S. and USSR, representing the two "poles" in the system. A third arrangement, a **multipolar system**, prevails when power is fragmented among several great powers that can shift from rivals to allies (and back). A classic example of multipolarity is the so-called **Concert of Europe**, prevailing from the end of the Napoleonic Wars in 1815 through the outbreak of World War I in 1914. Figure 2.11 depicts these power configurations (unipolarity, bipolarity, tripolarity, and multipolarity) and ways in which interaction patterns differ across them.

Polarity
The number of predominantly powerful actors in the global system at any given point in time.

Balance of power
A concept that describes the degree of equilibrium (balance) or disequilibrium (imbalance) of power in the global or regional system.

Unipolar system / unipolarity
A type of international system that describes a single country with complete global hegemony or preponderant power.

Bipolar system / bipolarity
A type of international system with two roughly equal actors or coalitions of actors that divide the international system into two "poles" of power centers.

Bloc
Grouping of materially interdependent and (often) ideologically aligned states.

Cold War
The confrontation that emerged following World War II between the bipolar superpowers, the Soviet Union and the United States. Although no direct conflict took place between these countries, it was an era of great tensions and global division.

Multipolar system / multipolarity
A world political system in which power is primarily held by four or more international actors.

Concert of Europe
A multipolar arrangement prevailing in Europe through much of the 19th century in which the major powers committed to a loose agreement to avoid war with one another while policing disorder and outbreaks of violence with and among smaller actors in the region.

Unipolar System

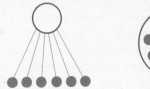

Traditional Hegemonic Dominance

World Federal System

One pole

Rules of the game are: (1) The central power establishes and enforces rules and dominates military and economic instruments. (2) The central power settles disputes between subordinate units. (3) The central power resists attempts by subordinate units to achieve independence or greater autonomy and may gradually attempt to lessen or eliminate the autonomy of subordinate units.

Bipolar System

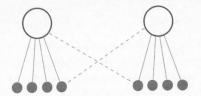

Two poles

Acute hostility between the two poles is the central feature of a bipolar system. Thus primary rules are: (1) Try to eliminate the other bloc by undermining it if possible and by fighting it if necessary and if the risks are acceptable. (2) Increase power relative to the other bloc by such techniques as attempting to bring new members onto your bloc and by attempting to prevent others from joining the rival bloc.

Tripolar System

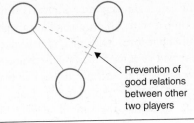

Prevention of good relations between other two players

Three poles

The rules of play in a triangular relationship are: (1) Optimally, try to have good relations with both other players or, minimally, try to avoid having hostile relations with both other players. (2) Try to prevent close cooperation between the other two players.

Multipolar System

Four or more poles

Rules of the game are: (1) Oppose any actor or alliance that threatens to become hegemonic. This is also the central principle of balance-of-power politics. (2) Optimally increase power and minimally preserve your power. Do so by negotiating if possible, by fighting if necessary. (3) Even if fighting, do not destabilize the system by destroying another major actor.

● Small Power   - - - - - - - - Short-Term or Potential Link

○ Large Power   ———————— Dominant and Lasting Link

FIGURE 2.11

The dynamics of international systems

The relationships that exist among the actors in a particular type of international system structure vary because of the number of powerful actors, the relative power of each, and the permitted interactions within the system. This figure displays potential international system structures and the basic rules that govern relationships within each system. After looking at these models, which one, if any, do you think best describes the contemporary international system?

challenge your assumptions

Toward an Era of Nonpolarity?

The concept of polarity, which we introduced in this chapter, assumes the existence of anywhere from one to several great powers. These actors possess significant military, economic, diplomatic, technological, and natural resource assets, so much so that they possess greater power and influence than the rest of the international community. Finally, the concept of polarity also assumes that the number of these great powers or "poles" has an important impact on the structure and functioning of the global political system—with the system ordered differently depending on whether there is one, two, or multiple poles.

But is it necessarily the case that the global political system will always have a small number of power centers to determine the scope and shape of the global order? Richard Haass, the President of the Council on Foreign Relations, the preeminent foreign policy think tank in the United States, has recently addressed this question. In grappling with a 21st century forecast for global politics, Haass—who previously served as the Director of Policy Planning at the U.S. Department of State (2001–2003)—contends that the system is moving toward an age of nonpolarity. Like many IR scholars and practitioners, Haass accepts the premise of a decline in U.S. power, which is the catalyst for nonpolarity. He sees no rising power sufficient enough to surpass the United States and assume the mantle of a unipolar hegemon, or even to balance the United States and create a new bipolarity (as in the Cold War). Haass also rejects the more common assertion that the decline in U.S. power is bringing the United States "back to the pack," and ushering in a new era of multipolarity (as was the case in the early 20th century).

Rather, Haass sees a world emerging in which nations diffuse power far beyond the narrow scope of a few great powers. While five states (China, India, Japan, Russia, and the United States) and one regional governmental organization (the EU) meet that distinction,

there are also multiple regional powers, for example, Brazil, South Africa, Mexico, and Nigeria (to name a few), with extensive internal power reserves. The real key to Haass's argument is the growing importance of new types of actors in global politics, drawing influence from a wider array of (nonmilitary) power assets. In a nonpolar system, we can reasonably consider international and regional organizations, nongovernmental organizations, corporations, terrorist organizations and paramilitaries, major media outlets, and even states and cities within nation-states all as centers of power.

The diffusion of power typifying a nonpolar system is also a product of globalization and transnational networks, and of the increased volume, velocity, and importance of cross-border flows of goods, services, money, and ideas moving along those networks. These flows are in a very real way the driving mechanism of nonpolarity. They particularly explain the rise to prominence of the range of the above-mentioned non–state actors. Yet, it is important to recognize, as Haass does, that an emerging nonpolar system is likely to be a world of great disorder. In a system where power is widely diffused, resulting in a void "at the top," the prospects for order and an effective response to important global issues such as energy, terrorism, and WMD proliferation may be limited as the necessary influence to bring about and enforce that order and those responses may also be lacking. In such a "flat," nonhierarchical system, it would seem that the importance of multilateralism, cooperation, and networked responses to networked problems would likely be magnified. What do you think?

- Are we entering a "nonpolar" era, or not?
- Does the concept of polarity still matter?
- If a nonpolar world does emerge, how would such a system change the ways states and individuals impact global politics?

Hegemony

Systemic arrangement in which one predominant actor possesses both the material capabilities and political will to introduce, follow, and enforce a given set of rules to lend order and structure to the global system. Also requires "buy-in" from at least some other actors who stand to benefit from those rules.

Hegemony   One illustration of how polarity actually influences global politics in practice is evident in the dynamics of a unipolar system and the related concept of **hegemony**. Unipolar systems frequently feature a hegemonic power that tries to introduce and maintain control of the entire global political system. For hegemony to prevail, there must be a dominant actor in the system that possesses three distinct attributes: commitment to a system governed by rules that players perceive as beneficial to most other major actors, the material capability to enforce those rules, and the political will to do so. From a system-level perspective, this impulse to power demonstrated by the hegemon dovetails with pressure in the system to maintain stability and order, providing "hegemonic stability" (Kindleberger, 1973).

The argument is that "a unipolar system will be peaceful," but only so long as the hegemonic power acts like one (Wohlforth, 1999:23). This leads some scholars to worry that if a hegemon is unwilling or unable to assume the responsibilities of maintaining order, the system could become unstable—triggering an onset of violence as well as extensive challenges to the "rules" underpinning that order which the hegemon is supposed to uphold (Ferguson, 2004; Lal, 2004).

Needless to say, there is considerable debate over such a rosy depiction of hegemony, with some critics contending that hegemony is a source of destabilization and disorder, and others dismissing it out of hand as a destructive imperialistic impulse (Gitlin, 2003; Lobell, 2004). From the standpoint of "offensive realists," the anarchical nature of the global political system means that states constantly strive for dominance—generating a "tragedy of great power politics" in which war and rivalry is endemic (Mearsheimer, 2001). From the standpoint of power transition theory, hegemony naturally produces challengers and aspirants to the power and rules of a hegemon, with similar consequences (Organski & Kugler, 1980). The urge to resist perceived hegemonic domination may help explain why France, Germany, Russia, and China were all opposed to U.S. action against Iraq in 2003. Certainly, those countries objected to the war as such, but it was also a chance to resist the attempts of the United States to exert hegemonic power (Carter, 2003).

Norms

Unwritten rules, principles, or standards of behavior that create expectations about how states and individuals ought to behave and interact in the global community.

Social Context   System-level analysts are concerned with the structure of the global political system, and the distribution and deployment of power within that system. As we have discussed earlier in this chapter, power is not only something that is coercive and material. Considering these factors, it is not hard to imagine how social context—and in particular the dominant values or **norms** in the global political system—provides a significant systemic constraint on the behavior of states and other actors. Power has persuasive and ideational dimensions that also help explain the system's structure, the most powerful actors in it, and the favored behaviors, practices, and arrangements.

The very premise of a global political system and structure implies that the actors in that system comprise a society of sorts. Like domestic society, to the extent that a global society exists, we can say that it can turn both on coercion and persuasion. Also like domestic society, a global society exhibits certain ideas, values, and behaviors that we favor or accept (what sociologists would call "normative"), and others that we do not favor or find unacceptable (which sociologists consider "deviant"). The commonplace label "rogue state," applied to regimes in places like North Korea

```
       UW-W TEXTBOOK RENTAL
      HOURS MON-FRI   8AM -4:15PM
   CHECK WEBSITE FOR  EXTENDED HOURS
  AT BEGINNING & END  OF EACH SEMESTER

            Account Sale
Receipt: R-0480702
Cashier: MIKE           01/18/17 12:40
StudentID:
Student Name:   Alexis Young
Email: YoungAC08@uww.edu


 1 BOYER / GLOBAL POLITICS
   10380222
   0-07-802481-1        N      $115.24
   XREF: 41020048900001790236
   Rental#: GENED 140 00456
   Cost: $86.41
   Fee: $0.00
   Due Date: 05/19/17

              Subtotal:      $115.24
Tax:

              Total:        $115.24
Tender:

UNDERGRAD RENTAL            $115.24

Change Due:                    $0.00

  PRICES ON RECEIPT FYI ONLY; NO CHG
 UNLESS BOOKS DAMAGED OR NOT RETURNED

  SPRING BOOKS ARE DUE BACK 5/19/17
    FINES BEGIN THE NEXT MORNING
  YOU HAVE 30 DAYS AFTER DUE DATE TO
  RETURN; AFTER THAT NO RETURNS; ALL
  BOOKS CHARGED TO STUDENT'S ACCOUNT
 WITH NO OPTION FOR RETURN OR CREDIT
```

```
    R - 0 4 8 0 7 0 2
```

...ile the ability of powerful members of a ...ive and what is deviant—and to promote ...ere near what it is in most domestic soci-...ies and practices, while others do not.

...democracies and international institu-...t democracy as a system of government ...sely, those same states and institutions ...plement punitive measures such as dip-...ary invasion threats. Similarly, marginal-...ate" actors carry out certain forms of ...hat states and institutions widely, if not ..."; whereas, powerful "legitimate" actors ...ts (military intervention or trade wars) ...t states and institutions accept, and even

...ociety, those social actors with the most ...nation of what is normative and what is ...n a global society, those actors are nation-...rominent proponents of this sociological ...states" (Bull, 1977). Further to that point, ...those with the greatest military and eco-...greatest influence on that determination, ...ility to promote what they deem "norma-..." should they choose.

...s exist in a world in which atrocities and ...basis. Moreover, it would be far too strong ...accepted standard of behavior—and cer-...eld. Yet whatever their limits or subjectiv-...lobal politics in both obvious and subtle ...o too have the prospects for greater con-...(and unacceptable) behavior and practices. ...ons of mass destruction (nuclear, chemi-...e widespread availability and destructive ...them an attractive tool for states seeking ...heir interests in an anarchical setting in ...rtainly, all forms of WMD have prolifer-..., and states and non-state actors have ...recently (such as by the United States ...d Nagasaki in 1945, by Iraq in the Iran-...al terrorist group Aum Shinryko in the ...te their pervasiveness, governments infre-...t the use of WMDs, translated through ...ide a partial answer. The revulsion and ...s of such weapons in the "court of world ...iety that does exist—has had some inhib-

CRITICAL THINKING QUESTIONS

1. What is power in global politics? How does it differ in the global context, compared to other situations and settings?

2. What is the purpose of the levels-of-analysis approach used in the field of IR? Are the levels more useful to your understanding of the "stuff" of global politics individually, or collectively?

3. Which do YOU think has the greatest role in shaping global politics—individuals, states, or the global system itself? Why?

4. To what extent do transnational forces and phenomena—such as the globalized media, information, and financial networks utilized by Julian Assange and "Wikileaks"—matter? Does globalization invalidate the "levels-of-analysis" framework, or can it be incorporated by it?

chapter summary

- Power dictates the *conduct* of global politics—requiring those engaged in the *study* of it to pay attention to considerations such as what power is, where it comes from, where it resides, and in what circumstances one can or cannot effectively use it.

- Power is mercurial, waxing and waning with time and by actor (or category of actor). For example, the Wikileaks saga shows us the degree to which power and influence resided with Wikileaks founder Julian Assange, the U.S. government, and the interdependent global political system.

- An appraisal of power requires us to focus on the motivations, perceptions, and other idiosyncratic characteristics of individual leaders, and the impact of these on decision-making.

- An appraisal of power also requires us to take into account states and the societies that they govern—whether factors such as the government, military, or economy, or the social forces that grant a state power or, conversely, limit it.

- Lastly, students and scholars of International Relations (IR) are wise to remember that both individuals and states operate within a system, one that is anarchical in nature and thus subject to definition and redefinition by its members. Power relationships between and among actors influence global politics, as do the norms, values, and ideas that help define the social structure of the global political system.

FIGURE 3.1
Map of Holy Roman Empire overlain on Europe
Attempts to sustain central and universal authority in Europe under Christendom were typified by the establishment of the Holy Roman Empire—which proved incapable of preventing the momentous political and social changes that led to its steady decline and eventual demise in the early 19th century.

Some of the earliest evidence of broad-based nationalism occurred in England during the reign of King Henry VIII (1491–1547). His break with the centralizing authority of the Roman Catholic Church and his establishment of a national Anglican Church headed by the king were pivotal events establishing the English nation. The conversion of English commoners to Anglicanism helped spread nationalism to the masses, as did the nationalist sentiments in popular literature. In an age when most people could not read, plays were an important vehicle of culture, and one scholar has characterized the works of William Shakespeare (1564–1616) as "propagandist plays about English history" (Hobsbawm, 1990:75). "This blessed plot, this earth, this realm, this England," Shakespeare has his King Richard II exult. In another play, *Henry VI,* Shakespeare notes the end of the authority of the pope in Rome over the king in London by having Queen Margaret proclaim, "God and King Henry govern England." This sounds commonplace today, but omitting mention of the papacy's authority was a radical step at the time (Maley, 2003).

Ascendant Nationalism   Nationalism in its modern form began to emerge in the 1700s. Until that time, the link between "the state" and its inhabitants was very different than it is today. Most people did not identify with, and were not emotionally

Popular sovereignty
A political doctrine that holds that sovereign political authority ultimately resides with the citizens of a state, to whom a state's rulers are accountable.

Social contract
A concept associated with liberal political philosophy referring to an implicit understanding between citizens and government detailing their mutual obligations.

attached to, the political authority in the territorial space in which they lived. Instead, the vast majority were merely subjects who a monarch anointed by God to govern (the notion of "divine right") ruled from afar. This changed with the doctrine of **popular sovereignty**, a by-product of political liberalism. Popular sovereignty and the idea of a **social contract** (as advanced by Hobbes, Locke, Kant, Paine, and others) holds that people are not subjects, but citizens who have a stake in the affairs of the state—and whom the state must therefore serve. Moreover, rulers are to be governed by the consent of the people, which subjects them to removal, at least in theory, if often not in fact (Heater, 2004).

Until the late 1700s, popular sovereignty was a nascent phenomenon confined largely to Switzerland, England, and the Low Countries. This changed dramatically with the outbreak of the American Revolution (1776) and the French Revolution (1789). These violent revolutions greatly advanced popular sovereignty and the concept of nationhood by abolishing kings altogether and in their place proclaiming, in the words of the American Declaration of Independence, that governments derive their "just powers from the consent of the governed." From these beginnings, the idea of popular sovereignty and nationalist sentiment began to spread around the globe—first throughout Europe in the Revolutions of 1848 and 1849, and subsequently beyond. Within 200 years after the American and French Revolutions, absolute monarchism—previously the most common form of governance—had virtually disappeared. Transnational ties among the elites also waned. When Great Britain's royal house of Stuart died out in 1714, it was still possible for the British to import a German nobleman to become King George I. Such a transplanted monarch or president would be virtually unthinkable today.

The spread of popular sovereignty and nationalism also radically recast the global political landscape. An important factor was the associated concept of self-determination. This is the idea that every nation should be able to govern itself as it chooses. Following this notion, some nations that were divided among two or more political entities coalesced to create a single state. The formation of Germany and Italy in the 1860s and 1870s are examples. In other cases, national states were established on the ashes of empire.

A major outgrowth of the emergence and spread of nationalism has been the decline and death of vast multiethnic empires. First, American colonists revolted against British colonial rule. Then the urge for self-determination contributed to the decline and fall of the Spanish empire in the 1800s, followed by the Austro-Hungarian and Ottoman empires in the late 19th century and early 20th century. In each case, many of the nations that had existed within these empires established states. By the mid-twentieth century, nearly all of Europe

Among other things, former U.S. President Woodrow Wilson was known as a staunch liberal internationalist and proponent of self-determination. His "Fourteen Points" proved instrumental for the fashioning of the League of Nations after World War I, as well as promoting national self-determination. As a result, a number of new (and relatively weak) states were established in central and eastern Europe in the aftermath of that war—states that became the target of Adolf Hitler's quest for *lebensraum* after his rise to power in 1933.

and the Western Hemisphere had been divided into nation-states, and the colonies of Africa and Asia were beginning to demand independence. The British and French empires were similarly doomed by nationalist pressures within them and fell apart in the three decades after World War II. Finally, the last of the huge multiethnic empires, Russia/the Soviet Union, collapsed in 1991, with 15 nation-states emerging. In the 20th century in particular, nationalism reigned virtually supreme around the world.

Patterns of Nation-State Formation

As the history of nationalism suggests, nations, nationalism, and nation-states can come together in various patterns. Sometimes nations and nationalism precede states, sometimes states precede nations and nationalism, and at other times nations and nationalism evolve along with states.

Nations Precede Nation-States

The easiest form of **state building** occurs when a strong sense of cultural and political identity exists among a people, and the formation of the nation precedes that of the state. This process is called "unification nationalism" (Hechter, 2000:15). Europe was one place where nations generally came together first and only later coalesced into states. For example, Germans existed as a cultural people long before they established Germany in the 1860s and 1870s. In much the same way, the Italian peninsula was fragmented after the fall of the Roman Empire and remained that way until a resurgent sense of Italian cultural unity and its accompanying political movement unified most of the peninsula in a new country, Italy, in 1861. Similarly, on the other side of the world in Japan, increased nationalism helped end the political division of the Japanese islands among the *daimyo* (feudal nobles) during the Tokugawa Shogunate (1603–1867), and restored real power to what had been a figurehead emperor.

> **State building**
> The process of creating both a government and other legal structures of a country and fostering the political identification of the inhabitants of the country with the state.

Nation-States Precede Nations

Another scenario is when the state is created first and then has to try to forge a sense of common national identity among the people and between them and the state. This approach to state-building is often fraught with problems. The decolonization process that began in the mid-twentieth century accounts for the existence of many states lacking in national unity. The forced coupling of populations with different tribal and ethnic backgrounds within the borders of their African colonies by European powers remains an enduring and problematic legacy of colonialism (Larémont, 2005). When those colonies later became states, most lacked a single, cohesive nation in which to forge unity once they had achieved independence. For example, Rwanda and Burundi are neighboring states defined by colonial boundaries that indiscriminately comingled Hutu and Tutsi people. With independence, these became national boundaries, as the map of Africa in Figure 3.2 depicts. The difficulty is that the primary political identifications of these people have not become Rwandan or Burundian. They have remained Hutu or Tutsi, and that has led to repeated, sometimes horrific, violence.

The difficulties of building national identities and a stabilizing state have also beset the United States, and to a degree other states, the UN, and regional organizations involved in the post-conflict reconstruction and statebuilding efforts required in places such as Somalia and the Balkans in the 1990s, and more recently in Afghanistan and Iraq. Outside powers can find themselves "stuck" because they

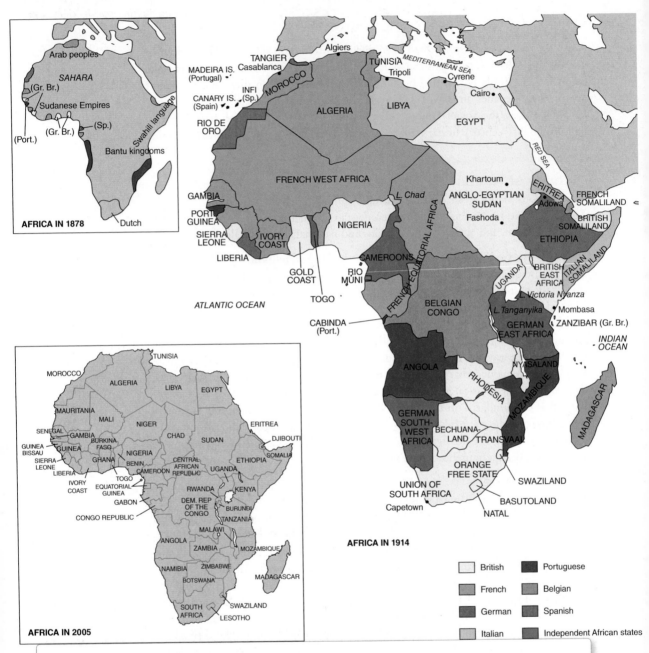

AFRICA IN 1878

Arab peoples
SAHARA
(Gr. Br.)
Sudanese Empires
(Gr. Br.)
(Port.)
(Sp.)
Bantu kingdoms
Swahili language
Dutch

AFRICA IN 1914

TANGIER
MADEIRA IS. (Portugal)
Casablanca
Algiers
TUNISIA
Tripoli
MEDITERRANEAN SEA
Cyrene
MOROCCO
CANARY IS. (Spain)
INFI (Sp.)
Cairo
RIO DE ORO
ALGERIA
LIBYA
EGYPT
RED SEA
FRENCH WEST AFRICA
Khartoum
ANGLO-EGYPTIAN SUDAN
ERITREA
FRENCH SOMALILAND
GAMBIA
L. Chad
Fashoda
Adowa
BRITISH SOMALILAND
PORT. GUINEA
ETHIOPIA
SIERRA LEONE
NIGERIA
FRENCH EQUATORIAL AFRICA
IVORY COAST
LIBERIA
CAMEROONS
BRITISH EAST AFRICA
ITALIAN SOMALILAND
ATLANTIC OCEAN
GOLD COAST
RIO MUNI
UGANDA
TOGO
L. Victoria Nyanza
CABINDA (Port.)
BELGIAN CONGO
L. Tanganyika
Mombasa
GERMAN EAST AFRICA
ZANZIBAR (Gr. Br.)
INDIAN OCEAN
ANGOLA
RHODESIA
NYASALAND
MOZAMBIQUE
MADAGASCAR
GERMAN SOUTH-WEST AFRICA
BECHUANA-LAND
TRANSVAAL
ORANGE FREE STATE
SWAZILAND
UNION OF SOUTH AFRICA
Capetown
BASUTOLAND
NATAL

AFRICA IN 2005

TUNISIA
MOROCCO
ALGERIA
LIBYA
EGYPT
MAURITANIA
MALI
NIGER
CHAD
SUDAN
ERITREA
SENEGAL
GAMBIA
GUINEA BISSAU
GUINEA
BURKINA FASO
NIGERIA
DJIBOUTI
SIERRA LEONE
GHANA
BENIN
CENTRAL AFRICAN REPUBLIC
ETHIOPIA
SOMALIA
LIBERIA
TOGO
CAMEROON
UGANDA
IVORY COAST
EQUATORIAL GUINEA
GABON
RWANDA
KENYA
DEM. REP. OF THE CONGO
BURUNDI
CONGO REPUBLIC
TANZANIA
ANGOLA
MALAWI
ZAMBIA
MOZAMBIQUE
NAMIBIA
ZIMBABWE
MADAGASCAR
BOTSWANA
SWAZILAND
SOUTH AFRICA
LESOTHO

British
French
German
Italian
Portuguese
Belgian
Spanish
Independent African states

FIGURE 3.2

The colonization and decolonization of Africa, 1878, 1914, 2005

The industrialization of the West was one factor that caused the colonization of Asia and Africa in the late 1800s and early 1900s. This map and its insets show that Africa was largely controlled by its indigenous peoples in 1878 (inset) but had by 1914 (larger map) become almost totally subjugated and divided into colonies by the European powers. Then, after World War II, the momentum shifted. Independence movements led to decolonization. Now there are no colonies left in Africa. Thus the West's domination of the world has weakened.

Source: Perry Marvin, Myra Chase, James R. Jacob, Margaret C. Jacob, and Theodore H. Von Laue. *Western Civilization: Ideas, Politics and Society,* Fourth Edition. Copyright 1992 by Houghton Mifflin Company. Adapted with permission.

are neither able to create stable political situations allowing them to withdraw, nor are they willing to withdraw and permit a violent struggle for power to ensue (Etzioni, 2004; Fukuyama, 2004; Migdal, 2004).

Nations and Nation-States Evolve Together   Frequently, nation-building and state-building are not locked in a strict sequential interaction, when one fully precedes the other—instead, they can and sometimes do evolve together. This approximates what occurred in the United States, where the idea of being American and the unity of the state began in the 1700s and grew, despite a civil war, immigration inflows, racial and ethnic diversity, and other potentially divisive factors. Still, as late as 1861, the country could see the limitations of nationalism when Colonel Robert E. Lee declined President Abraham Lincoln's offer of the command of the United States Army and accepted command of the militia of his seceding home state, Virginia. The point is that American nationalism was not fully developed in 1776. As has happened elsewhere, living within a state over time allowed a diverse people to come together as a nation through a process of *e pluribus unum* (out of many, one), as the U.S. motto says.

NATIONALISM RECONSIDERED

From the outset, the aim of those seeking to establish South Sudanese autonomy (and eventual statehood) was a unified and secular "New Sudan" in the south. The SPLM/A's accompanying manifesto dating to the 1980s rejected the interference of Khartoum in the region, while prevailing upon the South Sudanese to unify together and consider themselves a separate and distinct nation (Simmons and Dixon, 2006). Southern Sudan contains many more ethnic groups (with major groups including the Dinka, Nuer, Bari, Azande, Shilluk, and others) than the north, with corresponding linguistic differences. The divisions between these groups remain problematic, and the Sudanese government in Khartoum sometimes exploits them in an effort to undermine the new South Sudanese state. For example, the South Sudan government is currently confronting armed uprisings in at least 7 of its 10 states, with these uprisings largely playing out along tribal lines, triggered by disputes over political participation, civil rights, and the distribution of economic resources and opportunity. Fostering a sense of common South Sudanese national identity was (and remains) easier said than done.

Positive and Negative Aspects of Nationalism

Nationalism has clearly been a positive force in the development of the global political system, lending cohesion and order to many societies while also promoting the idea (and sometimes the reality) that well-defined and cohesive **political communities** have the right to seek and secure self-government. At the same time, as a catalyst for war and instability, nationalism has also brought great despair and destruction to the world. During an address to the Fiftieth UN General Assembly in 1995, the former Pope John Paul II spoke of these two strains of nationalism. One was *positive nationalism,* which the pontiff defined as the "proper love of one's country . . . [and] the respect which is due to every [other] culture and every nation."[1] The other was *negative nationalism,* "an unhealthy form of nationalism which teaches contempt for other nations or cultures . . . [and] seeks to advance the well-being of one's own nation at the expense of others."[2]

Political communities
As defined by the political scientist Karl W. Deutsch (1957), social groups with a process of political communication, some machinery for establishing and enforcing collective agreements, and some popular habits of compliance with those agreements.

thinking **theoretically**

Contending Views on Nationhood

The central role of the nation-state and national interests in realist theory points realists toward a general conclusion that the nation and national identity are powerful, persistent, and important phenomena. If, as realists contend, competing states engaged in the pursuit of interests (statecraft) define the conduct of global politics, it stands to reason that those states best positioned to compete are those with clearly defined interests and responsive and effective political systems. While not the only means to that end, a state in which a common national identity exists and in which the state and nation are mutually reinforcing entities (e.g., a "nation-state") is more likely to identify and pursue the "national interest" and provide for its own security than a state lacking such coherence. At least indirectly, realist theory treats nationhood as a crucial determinant of power in the global political system, in no small part because the nexus of nation and state tends to correlate with and prop up most of the more powerful actors in the global system—such as the U.S., China, Russia, France, and the U.K.

The other "grand theory" in IR—liberalism—places a more direct onus on nationhood. In its original (classical) form, liberalism treated nationhood as a natural aspiration for groups of people oriented around one or more common defining traits (such as ethnicity, language, religion, or ideology). Late 19th- and early 20th-century classical liberals such as Woodrow Wilson dubbed this aspiration "self-determination," and lobbied widely for it in conjunction with democratic governance (as Wilson did in his famous "Fourteen Points" proposal after WWI). Whereas realism considers the cohesion nationhood provides as a crucial underpinning of state power, classical liberalism treats the state as the end reward for a national group successfully attaining its "rightful" place among the community of nation-states.

However, the evolution of liberal thought and the expanding globalist focus of "neoliberalism" in the late 20th century brought with it a less optimistic view of nationhood and nationalism. Classical liberals felt that national self-determination would result in a pacific order of nation-states along the lines of what German philosopher Immanuel Kant (1795) dubbed a "league of nations" (his second definitive article of peace). However, the persistence of interstate and intrastate wars and rivalries propelled by self-determination throughout the 20th century has led neoliberals to place a greater premium on global identity and citizenship, as a by-product of Kant's *third* definitive article of peace, cosmopolitanism. Neoliberal thinkers tend to view nationalism and nationhood as somewhat outdated if not dangerous impediments to global and transnational interaction and cooperation.

More recent introductions to the theoretical conversation in IR have challenged both realist and liberal views on nationhood. In particular, constructivist thought points to the subjective, contextual, and relational dimension of social identity, which raises the possibility that "the nation" itself is, at base, a socially constructed entity. In this vein, in his seminal work on nationalism, Cornell University scholar Benedict Anderson (1991:5) introduces a definition of the nation as an "imagined political community" that is also "inherently limited." In Anderson's view, the nation is imagined in that while even the members of the smallest nations will never actually know or meet most of their fellow members, they all adhere to an "image of their communion" or a collective "we-feeling" that breeds a deep horizontal comradeship across the national group. Part of that image stems from the related consideration that nations are, by definition, also limited constructs—in other words, to exist in a group's collective consciousness, we must differentiate the nation from other nations or groups of people by real "boundaries"— territorial, linguistic, ethnic, religious, or otherwise. Anderson's view, and indeed the view of many other leading scholars of nationalism such as Gellner (1983) and Smith (1994), suggests that the treatment of the nation and nationhood as empirical "facts" or realities by realists and liberals alike requires reconsideration.

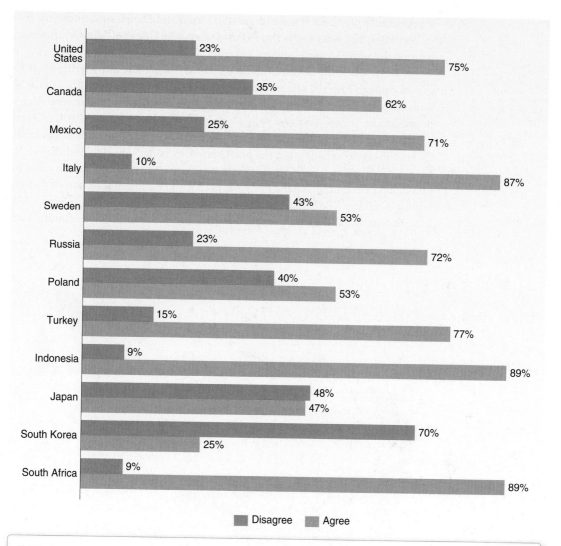

FIGURE 3.5
We should further restrict and control immigration
Attitudes toward immigration vary, but the vast majority of states and societies exhibit some significant anti-immigrant sentiment. With the movement of people around the world cheaper and easier than at any previous point in human history, the rising tide of immigration and of calls for greater restrictions and controls on immigration bear watching.

Source: Pew Global Attitudes Project, 2007.

myths and high degrees of nationalist ideology and rhetoric can and sometimes do exhibit imperial tendencies of their own. Rampant nationalism can lead to external aggression based on the belief that it is acceptable to conquer or otherwise incorporate other nations. Russian history provides an example. As is shown in the map in Figure 3.6, the country has long been a classic multiethnic empire built on territories that centuries of czarist Russian expansion seized and Soviet arms furthered. From its beginning 500 years ago as the 15,000-square-mile Duchy of Moscovy, Russia has become the world's largest country in terms of land area.

In 1991, when the Soviet Union fragmented, Russia lost many territories it had gained through imperial and nationalist exploits. In the current century—under the leadership of Vladimir Putin and Dimitri Medvedev—Russian nationalism is again on the ascent. It may serve one well to remember revolutionary socialist Karl Marx's warning (1818–1883) that "the policy of Russia is changeless. Its methods, its tactics, its maneuvers may change, but the polar star of its policy—world domination—is a fixed star."[10] Russian neo-imperial ambitions were evident in 2004, when in Ukraine's presidential election, President Putin supported the fraudulent election of Russian-leaning candidate Viktor Yanukovych over Western-leaning Viktor Yushchenko. Massive protests by Yushchenko supporters (the so-called "Orange Revolution") and

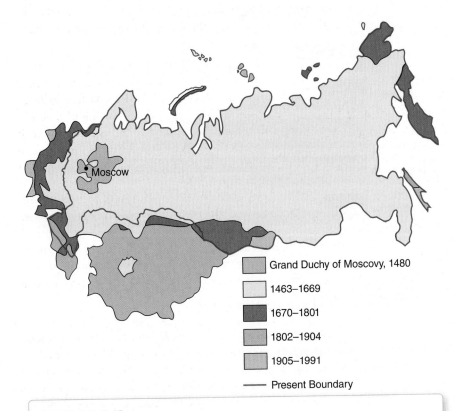

Grand Duchy of Moscovy, 1480

1463–1669

1670–1801

1802–1904

1905–1991

—— Present Boundary

FIGURE 3.6

500 years of Russian expansion

Nationalism has positive and negative effects, and both are illustrated in the history of Russia. Among the negative effects, nationalism often prompts expansionism. The Grand Duchy of Moscovy was about half the size of Maine when it was founded in about 1480. It expanded under Russian czars and then Soviet commissars to become what was the world's largest country.

pressure from the West forced Putin to stand aside as Ukraine called for new, internationally monitored elections, and Yushchenko won a resounding victory. Russia has also been deeply entrenched in the internal affairs of several other former Soviet republics (part of what it terms the "near abroad") over the past decade, by supporting Russian nationals in the breakaway region of Transdniester in Moldova and also assisting separatist movements in the regions of South Ossetia and Abkhazia in Georgia—the latter prompting a direct military conflict between Russia and Georgia in 2008.

Self-Determination as a Goal

An additional gap between the ideal and reality of nationalism is related to the wisdom of self-determination as a goal (Danspeckgruber, 2002). As with nationalism more generally, there are positive and negative aspects of self-determination. Consider the recent civil war in Libya and the widespread support for self-determination—including military support from NATO—the rebel forces centered in Benghazi received from much of the international community. While ousting long-time dictator Moammar Gaddafi would seem to have its clear merits, we do not know whether the forces of self-determination among the various factions of the opposition will lead to a fragmented or unified polity in Libya.

Positive Aspects of Self-Determination   Many observers have lauded the principle of self-determination. For one, President Woodrow Wilson believed that "self-determinism is not a mere phrase. It is an imperative principle of action."[11] Moreover, the origins of many nation-states are rooted in the demand for their nation's self-determination. For example, the Declaration of Independence begins with the proclaimed determination of Americans to "assume among the powers of the earth, the separate and equal station to which the laws of nature and of nature's God entitle them." Certainly, there are numerous reasons to support self-determination. In addition to the benefits of nationalism, which we noted earlier, self-determination ends many of the abuses that stem from ethnic oppression. If all ethnic groups were allowed to peacefully found their own sovereign units or join those of their ethnic brethren, then the tragedies of Bosnia, Chechnya, East Timor, Kosovo, Rwanda, Sudan, and many other strife-torn peoples and countries would not have occurred.

Concerns about Self-Determination   The principle of self-determination becomes more problematic when put into practice. The core problem is that there are literally thousands of ethnic groups worldwide, many with the potential to develop a national consciousness and to seek independence or autonomy. If the principle of self-determination is valid, how could the global political system possibly accommodate all of these groups and their desire to establish their own sovereign states? Before dismissing such an idea as absurd, keep in mind what the political scientist Benjamin Barber (1996) referred to as a "tribalist" impulse—the urge to break away from current political arrangements and, often, to form into smaller units. This impulse is particularly strong as a backlash to globalization's homogenizing tendencies.

Disentangling Groups Untangling groups is one challenge self-determination presents. In reality, many nations are intermingled within common territorial spaces or states. Bosnia-Herzegovina was a classic example of such ethnic heterogeneity and comingling. Prior to the ethnic conflagration in the 1990s, Bosnian Muslims, Croats, and Serbs often lived in the same cities, on the same streets, and even in the same apartment buildings. How does one disentangle these groups and assign them territory when each wants to declare its independence or to join with its ethnic kin in an existing country?

Dissolving Multinational and Multiethnic States   A second problem that the principle of self-determination in practice raises is the prospect of dissolving existing states in order to provide statehood to the various national and/or ethnic groups in their midst. Examples stemming from the existence of multinational states and multistate nations include Canada (Quebec), through Great Britain (Scotland and Wales), to Spain (Basque region and Catalonia). Americans also need to ponder this problem. They have long advocated the theory of a right of self-determination. One has to wonder, however, how Wilson would have applied this principle to national minorities in the United States, such as native Hawaiians who wish to reestablish an independent Hawaii?

Microstates   A third problem of self-determination relates to the rapidly growing number of independent countries, many of which have a marginal ability to survive on their own. Is it wise to allow the formation of **microstates**, countries with tiny populations, territories, and/or economies? Such countries have long existed, with Andorra, Monaco, and San Marino serving as examples. However, in recent years, as colonialism has become discredited, many more of these microstates have emerged. In the view of some observers, two of the world's newest states, Timor-Leste and South Sudan, face similar challenges (Cotton, 2007; Jok, 2011). Roughly one-third of the world's countries have populations smaller than that of Los Angeles, California, and about 10% occupy less land than that city. Such countries often cannot defend themselves, cannot economically sustain themselves, or both. This incapacity to perform one or both of two basic obligations of a state—to provide for its citizens' security, and to allocate public goods—undermines such states' reason for existing, increases economic burdens on the rest of the world, and creates potentially unstable power vacuums (Klabbers, 2006).

Microstates
Countries with small populations that cannot survive economically without outside aid or that are inherently so militarily weak that they are inviting targets for foreign intervention.

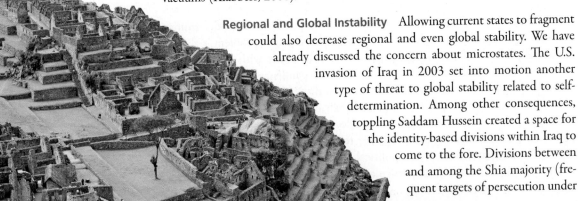

Regional and Global Instability   Allowing current states to fragment could also decrease regional and even global stability. We have already discussed the concern about microstates. The U.S. invasion of Iraq in 2003 set into motion another type of threat to global stability related to self-determination. Among other consequences, toppling Saddam Hussein created a space for the identity-based divisions within Iraq to come to the fore. Divisions between and among the Shia majority (frequent targets of persecution under

Saddam Hussein's rule), the influential Sunni minority (who dominated Saddam's Ba'athist regime), and the stateless Kurds residing in the north (also frequent victims of Saddam) have proven a source of ongoing violence and instability within Iraq and beyond. As we noted earlier, most Kurds' ultimate goal is an independent Kurdistan, with northern Iraq representing the most viable option. Trying to achieve that goal, however, would almost certainly meet with violent resistance from the Iraqi state.

Moreover, the Iraqi regime might find a ready ally in Turkey, which fears the implications of an independent Kurdistan for its own long-contested Kurdish areas. Yet another manifestation of this fragmentation is that Iraq's Shiite-dominated south and eastern region might fall under the sway of Iran—a Shiite-majority country governed by Shia clerics. Additionally, a weakened Iraq no longer serves as an effective buffer separating Iran from Saudi Arabia and the other oil-rich Arab states that lie to the south of Iraq along the western shore of the Persian Gulf. As such, the long-term consequences of the U.S.-led invasion are clearly regional instability and a power vacuum in the Persian Gulf region.

One problem to be addressed in attempting to create a unified Iraq is building Iraqi nationalism. Among other obstacles are the nationalist sentiments of the Kurds, symbolized by this young Kurdish boy wearing a jacket bearing the proposed flag of an independent Kurdistan.

The Persistence of Nationalism

While some scholars find traces of nationalism extending back to ancient times, most generally accept that nationalism has only been an important political idea for about the past 500 years—and that it did not reach its current ascendancy as a source of primary political identification until the 19th and 20th centuries. As such, nationalism has been and remains a contested concept.

World War II served as a watershed moment changing the views of many people about nationalism. They blamed fascism and other forms of virulently aggressive nationalism for the war itself, and for the other horrors of the period. Moreover, critics argued that the second global war in 30 years demonstrated that the state system based on national antagonism was not only outdated, but dangerous. The advent of weapons of mass destruction added urgency to the case, making "the nation and the nation-state . . . anachronisms in the atomic age."[12] As a counterpoint, the establishment of the United Nations in 1945 symbolized the desire to progress from competitive, often conflictive nationalism toward cooperative globalism.

The thrust of this thinking led numerous scholars to predict the imminent demise of the national state or, at least, its gradual withering away. As it turned out, such retirement announcements and obituaries proved reminiscent of the day in 1897 when an astonished Mark Twain read in the paper that he had died. Reasonably sure that he was still alive, Twain hastened to assure the world: "The reports of my death are greatly exaggerated." Similarly, one scholar notes that contrary to predictions of

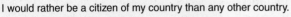

I would rather be a citizen of my country than any other country.

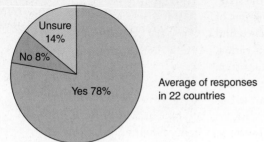

FIGURE 3.7
Nationalist sentiment

Nationalism makes most people feel attached to their country. One survey found that a large majority of the people polled in 22 countries worldwide felt that way. Only a small percentage was ambivalent; even fewer people were emotionally unattached to their country.

Data source: International Social Survey Program, National Identity Study, 2003/2004; Mayda & Rodrick (2005), Table 12, p. 1425.

nationalism's impending extinction, "this infuriatingly persistent anomaly . . . refused to go away" (Wiebe, 2001:2).

The continued strength of nationalism is unquestionable. Insistence on national self-determination has almost tripled the number of states in existence since World War II. For most of this time, the primary force behind the surge of nationalism was the anti-imperialist independence movements in Africa, Asia, and elsewhere. More recently, nationalism has reasserted itself in Europe. Germany reemerged when West Germany and East Germany reunited in 1990. More commonly, existing states disintegrated. Czechoslovakia became two states in 1993, and Yugoslavia eventually dissolved into six countries during the 1990s. Even more momentously, another 15 came into existence when the last great multiethnic empire, the USSR, dissolved in December 1991. Except for Eritrea, Namibia, Palau, South Sudan, and Timor-Leste, all of the states that have achieved independence since 1989 are in eastern Europe or are former Soviet republics. There are also nationalist stirrings—in some cases demands—among the Scots, Irish, and Welsh in Great Britain, the Basques and Catalans in Spain, and among other ethnonational groups elsewhere in Europe.

Another sign of persistent nationalism is the continuing attachment of people to their countries (Gijsberts, Hagendoorn, & Scheepers, 2004). As Figure 3.7 details, one cross-national survey found that a strong majority of all people said that they would rather be a citizen of their own country than any other. Somewhat unexpectedly, the strength of nationalist sentiment was not closely connected to a country's economic circumstances. For example, among those in relatively poor countries, 88% of both Bulgarians and Filipinos felt that way. By contrast, only 50% of the relatively wealthy Dutch shared that view (Mayda & Rodrik, 2005). Asking people if they would move to another country yields similar results. One such poll found that only 18% of those in relatively poor India would do so, while 38% of those in comparatively well-off Great Britain would.[13]

THE SOVEREIGN STATE

Nationalism continues to thrive and dominate our political consciousness in most ways. Yet, doubts about nationalism have increased in some circles. It has weakened somewhat, and there are those who predict and/or advocate its further diminution or even its extinction as the primary focus of political identification. Similar views prevail with respect to what remains the central unit of authority in the global political system—the sovereign state.

States, like nations, also have not always existed (Opello & Rosow, 2004). Humans have organized themselves in cities, leagues, empires, and other political structures at various times in history. In fact, the state is actually a relatively recent innovation, emerging late in the Middle Ages (ca. 500–1350). One part of that evolution occurred when European rulers expanded their political authority by breaking away from the Holy Roman Empire's secular domination and the pope's theological authority. The second phase occurred as kings subjugated feudal estates and other small entities within their realms. The facts that the state as a form of governance has a beginning and that most states are relatively young are important because they underscore the possibility for other forms and structures of political authority—a possibility that we take up in greater detail in subsequent chapters.

As we discuss more extensively below, sovereign statehood has certain requirements— among them a functioning and recognized government with unchallenged authority over a territorial space and population. South Sudan clearly possesses all of these attributes. The (now defunct) Southern Sudan Legislative Assembly ratified the Transitional Constitution two days before independence. The president signed it on Independence Day, establishing a mixed presidential system of government headed by a president, as well as a bicameral legislature and an independent judiciary. A number of major world powers, including the U.S., U.K., China, Russia, India, and perhaps most notably, Sudan itself, have extended diplomatic recognition to South Sudan. A landlocked country, South Sudan is located in the Sahel and borders Ethiopia, Kenya, Uganda, the Democratic Republic of the Congo, the Central African Republic, and of course, Sudan (see Figure 3.8). The country's estimated population of 8 million constitutes one of the most impoverished in the world, with a predominantly rural, subsistence economy.

Despite satisfying many of the requisites for statehood, the capacity and future prospects of the South Sudanese state remain in question. War has ravaged South Sudan's territory and population for decades, resulting in a lack of infrastructure and major destruction and displacement. Estimates of the dead from the two civil wars and continuing violence exceed 2 million, with figures for refugees and internally displaced persons in the range of 4 to 5 million.[14] The economy is one of the weakest and most underdeveloped in the world, with South Sudan having the highest maternal mortality and female illiteracy rates in the world as of 2011. With about 80% of the untapped oil in all of Sudan located in the south, the region's oil

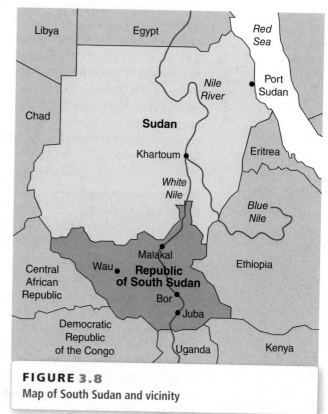

FIGURE 3.8
Map of South Sudan and vicinity

fields have been its chief source of revenue for decades.[15] At the same time, oil has proven a source of contention among the various ethnic groups within South Sudan and between South Sudan and Sudan over the allocation of that revenue. With South Sudan completely dependent on oil revenues (which make up approximately 98% of the new country's federal budget intake) and on Sudan for transport pipelines and refineries, the difference between sovereignty and independence, which we introduce below, is clearly on display in the case of South Sudan.

Requisites of Statehood

States are units of governance that exercise legal authority over specific territory and the people in it and that recognize no legitimate external higher authority. To the extent that they overlap with nations, states often take on great significance in the formation of people's political identity. Furthermore, states are the most powerful of all political actors. Some huge companies approach or even exceed the wealth of some poorer countries, but no individual, company, group, or international organization has anywhere near the coercive power that most states wield. Whatever their other individual differences, states share all or most of six characteristics: sovereignty, territory, population, diplomatic recognition, internal organization, and domestic support.

State sovereignty
A central tenet of global politics first established in the Treaty of Westphalia, which holds that the administrative unit of the state has the sole right to govern its territory and people, free from outside interference.

State Sovereignty   The most important requisite for statehood is **state sovereignty**, a condition that confers supreme legal authority on the state. State sovereignty means that states have the exclusive legal right to govern the territory and people within their borders and do not recognize the legal legitimacy of any outside authority. Sovereignty also denotes formal legal equality among states. One important application of this principle is evident in the UN General Assembly and many other international organizations, where each member-state has one vote. Of course, there are great disparities between and among states, which calls into question this formal equality in practical terms. For example, see Table 3.2, which compares the tiny republic of San Marino to the People's Republic of China. San Marino lies entirely within

The legal concept of sovereign equality is evident in the equal votes of San Marino and China in the UN General Assembly. Very different are the more tangible measures of equality, such as the two countries' territories, populations, economic production, and military personnel.

TABLE 3.2	San Marino and China: Sovereign Equals		
	San Marino	**China**	**Ratio**
Territory (sq. mi.)	24	3,705,400	1:154,392
Population	29,251	1,313,973,713	1:44,921
Gross domestic product (US$ millions)	880	2,455,900	1:2,790
Military personnel	0	2,225,000	1:∞
Vote in UN General Assembly	1	1	1:1

Note: ∞ = infinity
Data sources: World Bank (2007), CIA (2007).

Italy and is the world's oldest republic, dating back to the fourth century CE After years of self-imposed nonparticipation, in 1992, the UN granted membership to San Marino with the same representation in the General Assembly as China and every other sovereign state. "The fact of sitting around the table with the most important states in the world is a reaffirmation of sovereignty," explained the country's foreign minister.[16]

It is important to note that *sovereignty,* a legal and theoretical term, differs from *independence,* a political and applied term. Independence means freedom from outside control, and in an ideal, law-abiding world, sovereignty and independence would be synonymous. In the real world, however, where power is important, independence is not absolute. Sometimes a powerful neighbor so dominates a small country that its independence is dubious at best. Especially in terms of their foreign and defense policies, legally sovereign countries such as Bhutan (dominated by India), the Marshall Islands (dominated by the United States), and Monaco (dominated by France) possess little true independence.

Territory   A second requisite for statehood is territory. It would seem obvious that a state must have physical boundaries, and most states do. On closer examination, the question of territory becomes more complex. There are numerous international disputes over borders. Territorial boundaries can expand, contract, or shift dramatically, and it is even possible to have a state without territory. Pakistan provides an example of the limits to the idea of a state's territorial authority. The Pashtuns, an ethnonational group that is also the largest group in neighboring Afghanistan, control Northwest Pakistan. Pakistan's Punjabi-dominated government exercises only limited authority over these so-called "tribal areas" and their well-armed Pashtuns, a reality that explains in part why the region has proven a springboard for the resurgence of the Taliban (Islamic fundamentalists of largely Pashtun descent) in both Pakistan and Afghanistan in recent years.

Population   People are an obvious requirement for any state, but populations vary greatly from the 932 inhabitants of the Holy See (the Vatican) to China's approximately 1.5 billion people. Increasingly less clear in the shifting loyalties of the evolving global system is exactly where the population of a country begins and ends. Citizenship has become a bit more fluid than it was not long ago. For example, a citizen of one European Union (EU) country who resides in another EU country can now vote in local elections and even hold local office in the country in which he or she resides. Also a growing number of countries, now more than 90, recognize dual citizenship, being a citizen of two countries. For example, Mexico recently amended its laws to allow Mexicans who have emigrated to the United States and become U.S. citizens to retain their Mexican citizenship, vote in that country's presidential election, and even have their children who are born in the United States claim dual citizenship.

Western Sahara, a vast and sparsely populated territory in North Africa formally administered by Morocco, is just one of many regions in the world in which sovereignty over a particular territorial space is in dispute. These protestors from the Polisario Front are seeking independence and statehood.

Internal Organization   Statehood also normally requires some level of political and economic structure. Most states have a government, but statehood continues during periods of severe turmoil and unrest. Afghanistan, Liberia, Sierra Leone, Somalia, and some other existing states have dissolved into chaos during the last decade or so. Yet none of these chaotic states has ceased to exist legally. Each, for instance, continued to sit as a sovereign voting member in the UN General Assembly. Some of these disordered states have restored themselves to a modicum of order, but not all of them. For example, Somalia has not had a functioning government since 1991. For most of the time, Somalia's Transitional Federal Government (TFG) was located in Kenya because its lack of capacity and popularity made it impossible to meet in safety in Mogadishu, the Somali capital. Meanwhile, real control of Somalia was divided among various warring clans. In turn, the fundamentalist Islamic Courts Union (ICU), which sought to consolidate political authority through implementing *shari'ah* rule, defeated many of the clan factions by 2006. Subsequently, an Ethiopian-led (and U.S.-backed) military assault in 2007 almost immediately unseated the ICU, driving it from power, and returned Somalia to its previous anarchical state, where it remains at the time of this writing.

Diplomatic Recognition   Beyond these other material considerations, another important requisite for statehood is subjective or perceptual in nature. In the end, state sovereignty rests on both a claim to that status and existing states' extension of **diplomatic recognition**. How many countries must grant recognition before a country can achieve statehood is a more difficult matter. When Israel declared its independence in 1948, the United States and the Soviet Union quickly recognized the country. Its Arab neighbors did not extend recognition and instead attacked what they considered to be Zionist invaders. Was Israel a state at that point? It certainly seems so because both of the superpowers of the era recognized it as such. Such is the subjective nature of sovereignty, which hinges both on the sheer number of countries that extend recognition to a state, as well as *which ones*.

> **Diplomatic recognition** The formal recognition of one state's sovereignty by another, extended through the establishment of an embassy and/or consular relations. Diplomatic recognition is a key defining condition of state sovereignty, suggesting the relational and subjective aspect of sovereignty.

As a perceptual aspect of statehood, it is important to point out that a lack of recognition, even by a majority of other states, does not necessarily doom a state to nonexistence. For example, diplomatic recognition of the communist government of Mao Zedong in China came slowly after the Communists prevailed in the Chinese civil war and consolidated power in 1949. The U.S. withheld diplomatic recognition until 1979. Did that mean that the People's Republic of China did not exist? Clearly, the answer is no, because the U.S.'s stand that China's legitimate government was the defeated nationalists who had fled to Taiwan was obviously not credible. The issue of diplomatic recognition remains a matter of serious concern. Taiwan is for all practical purposes an independent country, with more than two dozen countries recognizing it as such. Yet Taiwan itself does not claim independence from China, and thus is a *de facto* (in fact) but not *de jure* (in law) state. Similarly, since the Iran Hostage Crisis of 1979–1981, the U.S. and the Islamic Republic of Iran have no diplomatic relations, although, of course, no one would claim either lacks statehood as a result.

Another contemporary issue involves the Palestinians. Almost 100 countries, including China and India, recognize the Palestinian National Authority (PNA) as the Palestinian nation's government. The PNA is also a member or an observer in several international organizations, including the United Nations. The UN Security Council

history **matters**

Max Weber and the Modern State

The gradual breakdown of the feudal system and universalistic (especially religious) authority in the West beginning in the 14th century (CE) created the conditions for a new form of governing entity. While alternative forms such as the mercantilist city-states of the Hanseatic League in the 13th through 17th centuries appeared, and older forms such as the imperial and monarchical systems of the Hapsburg, Russian, and Ottoman Empires persisted, ultimately it was the state that emerged as the primary actor in the global political system. Indeed, the triumph of the state as the dominant unit in the global system was both embodied in and advanced by the Treaty of Westphalia (1648), which settled the century-long struggle over political authority in Europe, catalyzed by the Protestant Reformation (1517) and the Renaissance (ca. 1350–1650).

Of course, there is more to the preeminent position of the state than its recognition as a sovereign reference point for diplomacy and international law in a 350-plus-year-old international treaty. Among other factors, the "economies of scale" associated with the state proved a boon to the emerging system of capitalism in the 17th and 18th centuries, and to the market system and commercial order that evolved from it. Second, the rise of popular sovereignty in conjunction with the Enlightenment, as embodied in the American (1776) and French (1789) Revolutions, furthered the emergence of nations and nationalism. Like capitalism, the forces of nationhood and nationalism found their natural outlet in the form of self-determination and the quest for governance via the nation-state.

These important considerations notwithstanding, the synergy between the state and economic and political liberalism also had much to do with the ability of the "modern" state to maintain social order and stability amidst the tumultuous social changes of the 18th and 19th century in Europe and beyond (Mann, 1993). To that end, the prominent 19th-century German sociologist and political economist Max Weber posited that the defining feature of the modern state, and a major wellspring of its power and authority, was the perception by a majority of the governed that only the state held a monopoly on the use of coercion. With the legitimacy of "the state" contingent on a widely held notion among the citizenry that it is the state and only the state that possesses the right to employ violence both domestically and on the world stage, one can see (as Weber did) an important (if perceptual) source of the sovereign state's power, coherence, and authority.

The Weberian monopoly, once asserted and (at least mostly) achieved at the domestic level, helps consolidate state power and eliminate potential challenges both to actual states and to the abstract concept of the state itself. Violence can be used to crush dissent or avert potential challenges to the government. At the same time, such a monopoly also contains an important external dimension. Possessing sole and unchallenged (or mostly unchallenged) authority to utilize organized violence similarly permits the state to employ violence to defend national interests and advance national objectives relative to other states, or even to divert attention from domestic problems by initiating armed conflict with "enemies." By virtue of possessing this "monopoly," individual states are able to secure their interests and protect their sovereignty while also advancing the central position of the state as the central and most legitimate actor in the global political system.

passed a resolution in 2002, calling for a separate Palestinian state, and the United States and many other countries claim to support the eventual creation of a Palestinian state as part of an overall Israeli-Palestinian agreement. Yet amid all the diplomatic maneuvering, it is clear that an independent, sovereign Palestinian state does not exist and that any of the diplomatic recognition that countries extend to the PNA is more a matter of legal nuance than practical reality. This point was driven home by opposition from the U.S. (and to a lesser extent the EU) to Palestinian leader Mahmoud Abbas' bid for Palestinian statehood in a speech at the UN General Assembly in late September 2011.

While the connection between statehood and diplomatic recognition is imprecise, it is an important factor for several reasons. One is that only states can fully participate in the global political system. For example, the PNA holds a seat in the UN General Assembly, but cannot vote. This is roughly analogous to Puerto Rico having only a nonvoting member of the U.S. House of Representatives. External recognition is also important because states are generally the only entities that can legally do such things as sell government bonds and engage in major and licit arms transactions. Israel's chances of survival in 1948 were enhanced when recognition allowed the Israelis to raise money and purchase armaments in Europe, the United States, and elsewhere. Similarly, the quick recognition of Kosovo by the U.S., U.K., France, Germany, Turkey, and others following its declaration of independence in February 2008 went a long way toward ensuring its survival as a sovereign state—while also continuing to be a point of tension and controversy in the region and the global system. Taiwan's prosperity shows that survival while in diplomatic limbo is not impossible, but it is such an oddity that it does not disprove the general rule.

Domestic Support   Another requisite of statehood, also of a perceptual nature, is domestic support. In its most positive form, a state's population is loyal to it and grants it legitimacy: the willing acceptance of the authority to govern. At its most passive, the population grudgingly accepts the reality of a government's power to govern. For all the coercive power that states usually possess, it is difficult for any state to survive without at least the passive acquiescence of its people. The dissolution of Czechoslovakia, the Soviet Union, and Yugoslavia are illustrations of multinational states collapsing in the face of the separatist impulses of disaffected nationalities. One of the continuing challenges confronting the Iraqi government, for example, is whether it will be possible to create sufficient domestic support for any government among the badly divided Shiites, Sunnis, and Kurds, all of whom, in turn, have their own internal divisions.

Embryonic and Failed States   As is evident from the foregoing discussion of the requisites of statehood, what does or does not constitute a state is far from an absolute. Because a state's existence is more a political than a legal matter, there is a significant gray area. Thus, there are political entities that well meet all the criteria and are indisputably states. Brazil, Canada, China, France, Egypt, and most of the existing 193 countries serve as examples. It is also clear that in that "gray area" there are a number of political entities that possess many, but not all, of the requisites of a state. It is possible to situate these types of entities in two groups: embryonic states and failed states.

  Embryonic states constitute the first group. Such political entities have many or even most of the characteristics of a state, yet they are not generally accorded the status of a full-fledged state. No country truly imagines that the Palestinians control a sovereign state, yet many countries recognize it as such for political reasons. By the same political token, Taiwan functions in most ways like a state, but China's power keeps it in a legal limbo. Regarding Tibet, no matter what the Tibetans and their Dalai Lama say and regardless of anyone's sympathies, no government has ever recognized it, nor is Tibet a sovereign state.

Failed states comprise the second group. These are existing states, but they have lost one or more of the characteristics that define a state. They remain legally sovereign entities by default because nothing else can be easily done with them and because other states are reluctant to acknowledge that a state can die due to such causes as lack of internal support, absent or incompetent internal organization, or the lack of real independence, as distinct from legal sovereignty.

One gauge of the number of failed states and states under stress is available in "The Failed States Index," a dataset compiled by the nonprofit organization The Fund for Peace. The Index's latest (2011) edition draws on over 130,000 publicly available sources to analyze 177 countries and rate them on 12 indicators of pressure on the state—from refugee flows to poverty and from public services to security threats. A country's performance on this battery of indicators, taken together, tells us how stable or unstable it is (see map depicting 2011 rankings in Figure 3.9).

Failed/failing state(s)
Countries in which political and economic upheaval are compounded by the fact that all or most of the citizens give their primary political loyalty to an ethnic group, a religious group, or some other source of political identity rather than the state itself. Such states are so fragmented that no one political group can govern effectively.

Purposes of the State

Although political philosophers have long disagreed over why humans create societies and establish governments, individual betterment is a common theme among them (Baradat, 2003). For example, this theme is evident in the writing of such classical theorists as Thomas Hobbes (1588–1679) and John Locke (1632–1704). Each

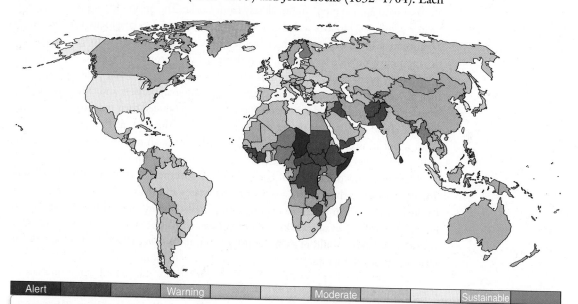

Alert | Warning | Moderate | Sustainable

FIGURE 3.9

Strong and Weak States: Relative Comparison

One gauge of the number of failed states and states under stress is available in "The Failed States Index," a dataset compiled by the nonprofit organization The Fund for Peace. With a possible range from 12 (absolutely stable) to 120 (absolutely chaotic), 13 countries led by Somalia (113.4) scored 100 or above and might reasonably constitute the failed state category. Another 22 scored in the exceptionally stressed 90s. Scoring 19.7, the Index characterized Finland as the most stable country, with the United States at a fairly stable 34.8. The map here presents categories of the states' rankings throughout the world.

Source: Foreign Policy / Fund For Peace Failed States Index Map, 2011

State of nature
A theoretical time in human history when people lived independently or in family groups and there were no societies of nonrelated individuals or governments.

contended that people had once lived as individuals or in family groups in a **state of nature**. Communities of unrelated individuals did not exist, and people possessed individual sovereignty; that is, they did not grant authority (legitimate power) to anyone or anything (a government) beyond their families to regulate their behavior. They also argued that people eventually found this highly decentralized existence unsatisfactory. Therefore, the theory continues, it was the desire to improve their lives that prompted individuals and families to join together in societies, to surrender much of their sovereignty, and to create governments to conduct the society's affairs. All this was based on an implicit understanding called a social contract (which we discussed previously) that specified the governments' purposes and the limitations on them.

Hobbes and Locke disagreed about what persuaded people to abandon the state of nature and merge into societies. Hobbes said it was fear, arguing that life without government was so dangerous that people created strong governments to provide protection. Taking a more positive view, Locke contended that people joined together in societies because they realized that they could improve their lives more easily through cooperation than by individual effort alone. Among other places, the ideas of Hobbes and Locke are clearly evident in the fundamental documents of the American Revolution and the United States. The idea in the Declaration of Independence that people had a right to "life, liberty, and the pursuit of happiness," and "that to secure these rights, governments are instituted among men," draws closely from Locke. The preamble to the U.S. Constitution combines Hobbes' emphasis on protection and Locke's focus on individual advancement in its words that the purpose of the new government is to "insure domestic tranquility, provide for the common defense, [and] promote the general welfare."

The key point about Hobbes and Locke is that they agreed that political units and their governments were instruments created for a utilitarian purpose and that governments were legitimate and should survive only as long as they fulfilled their practical mission and did not abuse their power under the social contract. The idea, as President Woodrow Wilson put it, is that "government should not be made an end in itself; it is a means only. . . . The state exists for the sake of society, not society for the sake of the state."[17]

How does this discussion of the purpose of government relate to global politics? The connection is that having a sense of what states and their governments are meant to do is necessary in order to evaluate how well they are operating. The ability to judge how well states are working will help you think about and determine whether and why the state should remain the principal unit of governance in the global political system going forward.

Regime Types and Governance

How states are governed has a number of ramifications for global politics. These implications relate to such questions as whether some types of government are more warlike than others, whether some are more successful in their foreign policies than others, and whether it is wise to promote a specific form of governance—as the United States has been doing in relying on democracy promotion as a centerpiece of its foreign policy.

We can begin to address these questions by dividing theories of governance into two broad categories. One includes *authoritarian governments,* those that allow little or no participation in decision-making by individuals and groups outside the upper reaches of the government. The second category includes *democratic governments,* those that allow citizens to broadly and meaningfully participate in the political process. As with many things that we discuss, the line between authoritarian and democratic is not precise. Instead, using broad and meaningful participation as the standard, there is a scale that runs from one-person rule to full, direct democracy (or even, according to some, to anarchism (having no government). The map in Figure 3.10 provides one way to order types of government, with the countries in shades of green generally democratic and the countries in other colors generally authoritarian. Recent events, particularly in the Middle East and North Africa, are likely to shift more countries into the "disordered" category, pending resolution of the domestic political upheaval they are currently experiencing.

Authoritarian Government   Throughout history, the most common form of governance was for an individual or group to exercise control over people with little or no concern about whether the people consented to it or agreed with the ruler's policies. This approach has included many garden-variety dictatorships that sprang from an individual's or group's urge to power rather than from any overarching theory of how to best govern societies. Yet there are a number of rationales supporting **authoritarianism**, rule from above.

One of the oldest forms of nondemocratic governance is **theocracy**, rule by spiritual leaders. Today, it has virtually disappeared, and the Holy See (the Vatican) is the world's

Authoritarianism
A type of restrictive governmental system in which people are under the rule of an individual, such as a dictator or king, or a group, such as a party or military junta.

Theocracy
A political system that is organized, governed, and defined by spiritual leaders and their religious beliefs.

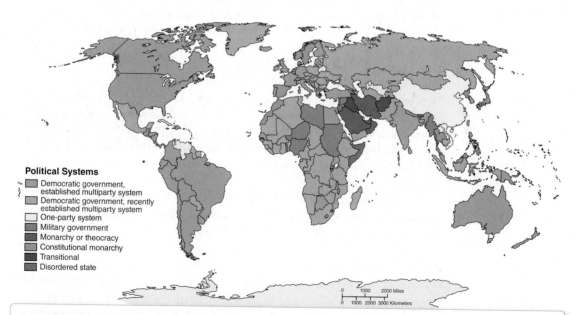

Political Systems
- Democratic government, established multiparty system
- Democratic government, recently established multiparty system
- One-party system
- Military government
- Monarchy or theocracy
- Constitutional monarchy
- Transitional
- Disordered state

FIGURE 3.10

Political systems

The democratization of the world's countries, which began symbolically with the American (1776) and French (1789) Revolutions, progressed slowly for 150 years, then accelerated after World War II. Now, as this map indicates, the majority of countries are full-fledged or quasi-democracies. Because of different criteria, this map takes a narrower view of what a "failed" or "disordered" state is than does the previous figure depicting state stability.

Perhaps the best example of a theocracy today is the Vatican, which serves not only as the seat of authority in the Roman Catholic Church but also enjoys the status of a sovereign state. As such, the Pope—here, Pope Benedict—technically serves both as chief cleric and head-of-state, and the religious and diplomatic activity of the Holy See are more or less indistinguishable.

only pure theocracy. Additionally, theocratic elements remain in the popular, if not the legal, status of Japan's emperor, Thailand's king, and (most strongly) Tibet's exiled Dalai Lama. Iran's government is also partly theocratic. Moreover, Islamic religious law (the *shari'ah*) plays a strong role, along with secular law, in a number of Muslim countries. Furthermore, the increased strength of religious fundamentalism in many places means that it is not unthinkable that a rejuvenation of theocracy might occur.

Arguments for secular authoritarianism are also ancient. For example, the Greek philosopher Plato (ca. 428–347 BCE), in his famous work, *Republic,* dismissed democracy as "full of . . . disorder and dispensing a sort of quality of equals and unequals alike." He contended that the common citizenry trying to direct the state would be analogous to sailors on a ship "quarrelling over the control of the helm; each thinks he ought to be steering the vessel, although he has never learned navigation . . . ; what is more, they assert that navigation is a thing that cannot be taught at all, and are ready to tear in pieces anyone who says it can." Plato's conclusion was that ships needed strong captains and crews that took orders and that "all those who need to be governed should seek out the man who can govern them."

Monarchism
A political system that is organized, governed, and defined by the idea of the divine right of kings, or the notion that because a person is born into royalty, he or she is meant to rule.

Communism
An economic ideology based in the works of Engels and Marx that holds the oppressed class of proletarian workers will eventually revolt against the bourgeois owners of the means of production, creating a new social order.

Totalitarianism
A political system in which the ruling regime recognizes no limit to its authority and seeks to regulate and control every and all aspects of public and private life.

Monarchism is one form of secular authoritarianism, although the theory that God had granted kings the divine right to govern contained a touch of theocracy. This system of governance through hereditary rulers has declined considerably. There are only a few strong monarchical regimes (such as the House of Saud in Saudi Arabia) scattered among a larger number of constitutional monarchies that severely restrict the monarch's power (as in the United Kingdom).

Communism as applied by Vladimir Lenin and his successors in the USSR, by Mao Zedong in the People's Republic of China, and by other communist leaders elsewhere, also falls within the spectrum of authoritarian governance. Karl Marx expected a "dictatorship of the proletariat" over the bourgeoisie as a necessary intermediary step during a transitional socialist period between capitalism and communism. Lenin institutionalized this view by centralizing power in the hands of the Communist Party, which in turn the Politburo and its head dominated. Party control over all aspects of society became so strong that its critics labeled it **totalitarianism**—an extreme form of authoritarian rule in which a single dominant party or leader seeks to control all aspects of social life, often through extreme repression, propaganda, and the fostering of a "cult of personality" around the leadership (as in the present-day North Korean regime).

Although strictly speaking it refers to a system of economic organization, in political terms, scholars often use communism to refer to regimes that Communist parties dominate regardless of the economic system structure they promote. Over the past two

Ethnic conflict between ethnic Chechens and the Russian government has dragged on for decades in the Caucuses. Here, Chechens mourn the dead and wounded in the aftermath of a harsh Russian military response to a three-day siege of School Number One, a primary school in the town of Beslan, by Chechen insurgents in September 2004.

During World War II, Moscow deported the entire Chechen population to Siberia in the east because Soviet dictator Josef Stalin suspected that the Chechens might assist the invading Germans in return for independence. More than one-third of all Chechens died during their time in Siberia, but they were unbowed. Once the USSR dissolved, the Chechen quest for self-rule redoubled. Amid ferocious fighting that left 100,000 dead, the Chechens achieved autonomy in 1996, then lost it in 2000 when Russian arms again overran them. The struggle continues, however, with sporadic, often brutal fighting in Chechnya and occasional Chechen terrorist attacks in Russia. The most ghastly of these occurred in the Russian town of Beslan, where Chechen terrorists seized an elementary school in 2004. During the ensuing siege, 330 people, mostly Russian schoolchildren, were killed. For now, Russia maintains a tenuous hold on Chechnya, but current Russian leaders, like czars and commissars before them, are finding it daunting to subdue a people whose national anthem asserts in part:

> Never will we appear submissive before anyone,
> Death or Freedom—we can choose only one way. . . .
> We were born at night, when the she-wolf whelped.
> God, Nation, and the Native land.

Many of the other FSRs also have complicated ethnonational compositions. As we noted above, Uzbeks and Tajiks not only live in Uzbekistan and Tajikistan, respectively, they also live in Afghanistan. To further complicate matters, numerous Tajiks live in Uzbekistan, and many Uzbeks live in Tajikistan. Numerous separatist movements also exist in the European FSRs, including those in the South Ossetia and Abkhazia regions of Georgia, the so-called Transdniester Republic within Moldova, and the Nagorno-Karabakh enclave in Azerbaijan. Each has seen fighting that could spread and bring neighboring countries into conflict. This possibility led nearby Romania's President Traian Basescu to describe the tensions as "transnational threats" to European stability. "We cannot leave the countries of this region as victims of European history, as unstable borderlands outside Eastern Europe," Basescu warned.[27]

CRITICAL THINKING QUESTIONS

1. What are the most important defining features of nationhood? Is it necessary to meet them all in order to consider an identity group a "nation"? Why or why not?

2. Are the concepts of popular and state sovereignty that we respectively associate with the nation and the state competing or complementary?

3. What does the reality that state sovereignty is, at least in part, a relational concept suggest about the nature and conduct of global politics?

4. What role does identity play in explaining disputes and conflicts between and within nation-states in global politics? In a global system predicated on state sovereignty—and by extension, self-determination—is there any way around this problem?

chapter **summary**

- Nations, states, and identity are all central to the organization and conduct of international relations, but also abstract and highly contestable notions.

- The success or failure of a state depends in large part on "buy in" from citizens and identity groups within a state's borders—and acceptance and recognition from outside actors.

- While nationalism and the state can and do provide coherence and order to both domestic and global society, they also can and do serve as wellsprings for conflict and contention.

- It is the overlap or lack of overlap of identity politics with the nation-state that serves as the "wildcard" helping determine whether a state, nation, or society is headed down a road of consolidation and stability or contestation and disorder.

- The world's newest state, South Sudan, reflects all of these claims. If South Sudan can settle internal divisions between its various ethnic groups and establish a national consciousness and identity, the prospects for the South Sudanese state are likely favorable. Conversely, if the triangular relationship between nation, state, and identity remains fractured, it is almost certain that the world's newest sovereign state and its citizenry will face adversities too great to overcome.

key terms

authoritarian

Communism

democracy

diplomatic recognition

Enlightenment

ethnonational group /
  ethnonationalism

exceptionalism

Failed/failing state(s)

fascism

Holy Roman Empire (HRE) / Holy
  Roman Emperor

identity politics

irredentism

microstates

monarchism

multinational states

multistate nation

nation

nation-state

nationalism

nativism

political communities

popular sovereignty

Protestant Reformation

secessionism

self-determination

social contract

state building

state of nature

state sovereignty

stateless nation

theocracy

Thirty and Eighty Years' Wars

totalitarianism

xenophobia

Zionism

Globalization: Politics from Above and Below

chapter 4

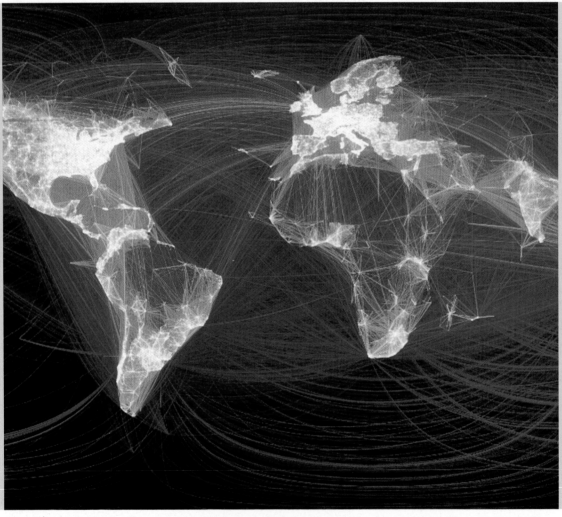

This photo attempts to visualize where people live relative to their Facebook friendships. Each line represents the cities of connected friends. The brighter the line, the more friends between those cities. Interestingly, the visualization produces a fairly detailed map of the world where certain continents and country borders are visible. It is also important to note the large areas of the world that don't appear—those vast areas and corresponding populations are not part of Facebook, and in many cases, not digitally connected at all.

LEARNING OBJECTIVES

This chapter introduces the concepts of globalization and transnationalism as complex, multidimensional forces of change operating in and impacting global politics. While these processes are certainly not new, they are shifting the nature of human interaction and political identification well beyond the traditional borders of the nation-state in important ways. Upon completion of this chapter, you will be able to:

■ Identify and explain the factors that are accelerating globalization and their relationship with the various forms of economic and cultural interchange

■ Grasp certain theoretical explanations of the causes and consequences of globalization, particularly along economic and cultural lines

■ Recognize and understand the various actors that constitute global civil society, how they organize themselves, and the range of transnational strategies that they employ in affecting change from below

■ Compare, contrast, and assess several different transnational movements in terms of their purpose, the nature of their advocacy, and their complex—and at times contradictory—relationship with the state

Many would agree with the idea that we live in an era of globalization. From the food we eat, to the clothes we wear, and to the issues with which we most identify, we are constantly engaging in global processes from our local positions while global events impact our local realities. People, as individuals and groups, are increasingly in contact with one another and these interactions are transformative at all levels. In this way, the world is more than just the sum of its parts. It is also a complex system, one which has many commonalities and connections that cut across political borders, national identities, and cultural differences.

Globalization is often the generic term that we use to describe this increasing integration of economies, polities, communications, and cultures. At a very basic level, economist Joseph Stiglitz (2002:9) defines globalization as "the closer integration of the countries and peoples of the world which has been brought about by the enormous reduction of costs of transportation and communication, and the breaking down of artificial barriers to the flows of goods, services, capital, knowledge and people across borders." These multidimensional processes "compress the time and space aspects of social relations," shifting organizational structure of human society and the power relations and reach within them (Mittelman, 1997:3). From the movement of people to the change in markets, globalization refers to the disruptive global forces, both positive and negative, that operate in our daily lives.

Globalization
A multifaceted concept that represents the increasing integration of economics, communications, and cultures across national boundaries.

Transnational/ transnationalism
Social, political, economic, and cultural activities and processes that transcend and permeate the borders and authority of states.

Global civil society (GCS)
The vast and voluntary assemblage of groups operating across borders and separate from governments with the aim of influencing the world.

Simultaneously, forces from below are bombarding our social spaces, whether from local organizations of which we are members, from the 24-hour news cycles, or from various social media networks. Increasingly, **transnational** actors, ideas, and movements that operate in a private or nongovernmental capacity shape our identity. **Transnationalism** refers to the range of cross-border political identities and signifies the social, economic, and political links—and related activism—among people and private organizations that transcend the sovereign state. We often call this open-ended civic sphere **global civil society (GCS)** as it seems to transcend international borders. Many of these regional or global links serve to promote or intensify a common sense of identity among people, and these ties can form the basis of political self-identification that in some cases can rival or supplant nationalism. Religious identity or gender roles, for example, often transcend political borders and identities. As with nationalism, transnationalism has both positive and negative consequences, at times simultaneously. While it can promote cooperation among some groups, it can also drive further divisions among others.

These complex and, at times, contradictory processes of harmonization and fragmentation were central to Benjamin Barber's (1992, 1995) theorizing about international relations, which he referred to as the intense struggle of "'Jihad vs. McWorld." For Barber, the political future that we face comes down to two forces of equal strength pulling us in opposite directions, neither of which moves us closer to a democratic society. The force he called "Jihad" is "a retribalization of large swaths of humankind by war and bloodshed: a threatened Lebanonization of national states in which culture is pitted against culture, people against people, tribe against tribe—a

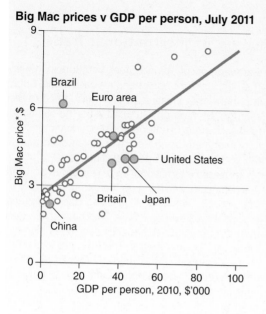

Big Mac prices v GDP per person, July 2011

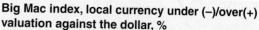
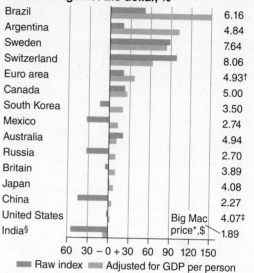

Big Mac index, local currency under (–)/over(+) valuation against the dollar, %

	Big Mac price*,$
Brazil	6.16
Argentina	4.84
Sweden	7.64
Switzerland	8.06
Euro area	4.93†
Canada	5.00
South Korea	3.50
Mexico	2.74
Australia	4.94
Russia	2.70
Britain	3.89
Japan	4.08
China	2.27
United States	4.07‡
India§	1.89

Raw index   Adjusted for GDP per person

*At market exchange rate (July 25th)   § Maharaja Mac
† Average of member countries ‡ Average of four cities

FIGURE 4.1

What the Big Mac says about overvalued currency

Published by *The Economist* since 1986, the Big Mac Index is an informal but creative way of measuring and comparing the purchasing power parity (PPP) between countries. The Big Mac PPP exchange rate between two countries is obtained by dividing the price of a Big Mac in one country (in its currency) by the price of a Big Mac in another country (in its currency). This value is then compared with the actual exchange rate; if it is lower, then the first currency is undervalued (according to PPP theory) compared with the second, and conversely, if it is higher, then the first currency is overvalued. For more, see http://www.economist.com/blogs/dailychart/2011/07/big-mac-index.

Jihad in the name of a hundred narrowly conceived faiths against every kind of interdependence, every kind of artificial social cooperation and civic mutuality." The second one reflects the "economic and ecological forces that demand integration and uniformity and that mesmerize the world with fast music, fast computers, and fast food— with MTV, Macintosh, and McDonald's, pressing nations into one commercially homogenous global network: one McWorld tied together by technology, ecology, communications, and commerce." One is driven by "parochial hatreds" from below and the other by "universalizing markets" from above. As Figure 4.1 demonstrates, we can even use a cultural phenomenon like the Big Mac to evaluate which currencies are at their "correct" levels. While global politics is clearly not this simple, Barber's theory helps us to think about the multiple, complex, and even oppositional forces that challenge the centrality of the state, and more important, the future of democracy in our world.[1]

While theories of globalization and strategies of transnationalism reflect so much more than Barber's notions of "McWorld" and "Jihad," a better understanding of these conceptualizations and their theoretical significance and historical context will help you in evaluating the explanatory value of Barber's theory on the forces

history **matters**

Is Globalization Really New? A Brief History of International Trade

International trade has existed between distant nations for centuries. Records as early as the 19th century BC indicate the existence of merchant-trading colonies in Mesopotamia (Laursen, 2011:42). Camels facilitated trade in spices and silk between the Middle and Far East. Arabian nomads facilitated the exchanges and reaped profits. These early traders initiated simple, makeshift trade routes that existed hundreds of years before planned routes between East and West.

The easiest ancient trade routes were waterways like the Nile, Tigris, Euphrates, and Indus Rivers, as well as the Mediterranean Sea, which allowed merchants to transport large amounts of goods, increasing their profits. Port cities developed around the Mediterranean between 3000 and 1000 B.C. as trade between empires increased. The Phoenician cities of Tyre (modern day Lebanon) and Sidon became important trading hubs, exporting luxury goods like cedar and purple dye to neighboring nations (Sommer, 2007:98). Trading vessels, however, were still unable to survive the long trips.

Land routes flourished as they reached inland metropolises. Empires in both the East and West strengthened, grew, and created an increased demand for international trade. The Greek and Roman empires in the West expanded into Persia (modern day Iran) and Syria, bringing with them their distinct culture and advances in technology. The Chinese Emperor Zhang Qian of the Han Dynasty continued to expand his empire westward, encountering Greek and Roman influences. The Hans brought horses and art back home, but more important, they created the Silk Road in first to second century BCE (Waugh, 2010:10–11). The Silk Road led to the creation of international economic policies, as Roman emperors and Han rulers established trade limitations depending on political climates.

Increased international trade resulted as populations grew and European living standards improved during the 12th and 13th centuries. Flourishing cities supported an emerging, wealthy upper class. They desired new luxuries from distant lands. Monasteries demanded high-quality fabrics, spices, and metals. The Crusades increased the contact between the average European and luxuries of the Middle East and Holy Land (Day, 1981:160–162). Venetian traders dominated the Middle Eastern market, utilizing their Mediterranean location to bring exotic goods to Europe. However, this trading boom did not last. The Black Death pandemic, which spread through these developing trade routes, affected every aspect of European society. Plague survivors now needed to focus on survival during the 14th century. It took 150 years for Europe to recover.

The 15th century brought the rise of the Ottoman Empire, which cut access to many land and water routes for European traders, forcing them to look for new paths for economic exchange. Advances in technology, particularly in ship-building and navigation,

from above and below and their impact on the future of global politics. Thus, throughout the chapter we will return to Barber's worldview and how it relates to the concepts that we discuss. We will ask you at the end of the chapter to consider how we can improve Barber's theory to better reflect the world in which we live.

GLOBALIZATION

Although globalization may seem like an abstract concept, it is a phenomenon that we can see and experience in almost everything we do and even touch on a daily basis. The computer keyboard that we used to type this book was made in Thailand, the mouse came from China, the monitor was produced in South Korea, and the flash drive to back up files was manufactured in Taiwan. During the day today we have all likely connected with websites in more than a half-dozen countries, and classes at our university this afternoon have students from a variety of countries beyond the United States. In short, globalization brings people and places closer together more rapidly

The movement of people and goods depends on the movement of information. Technological advances permit us to transmit images, data, written words, and sound easily and quickly all over the world. This is what drives globalization. Thus, it is almost impossible to overstate the impact that modern communications have had on global politics. In only a century and a half, communications have made spectacular advances, beginning with the telegraph, followed by photography, radio, the ability to film events, telephones, photocopying, television, satellite communications, faxes, and now computer-based Internet contacts and information through e-mail and the World Wide Web.

Many parts of Africa have experienced an incredible boom in mobile phone use over the last decade. Mobile phones are more affordable and reliable than computers in Africa, where its billion people use less than 5% of the world's electricity. From texting to banking, mobile phone use is on the rise throughout Africa and carries tremendous economic potential for many developing countries across the globe.

The Growth of Communication Capabilities   The flow of these communications is too massive to calculate precisely, but if the growth of international telephone calls is any indication, we are increasingly able to "reach out and touch someone" internationally, as the AT&T advertising slogan went. What is more, with the growth of mobile technology we are not confined to making calls in our homes or offices, but just about anywhere we can imagine. Approximately 68% of the world's population now have a cell phone, representing a dramatic jump from 11 million users in 1990 to an estimated 5.6 billion in 2011 worldwide.[3]

The technological revolution in communications has also meant that more and more people around the globe are obtaining their news from the select few media giants. The most obvious example is CNN, which now reaches virtually every country in the world and broadcasts in nine languages. And while CNN carries an American perspective to the rest of the world, non-U.S. news networks are bringing foreign news perspectives to Americans. *Al Jazeera*, which translates as "The (Arabian) Peninsula," is based in Qatar and began operations in 1996 as the first Arabic language television news network. Since then it has become well-known around the world for its broadcasts of, among other things, video and audio tapes of Osama bin Laden from his hiding place. In 2006, *Al Jazeera* added broadcasts in English originating in the United States, and the news agency also has Internet news sites in both Arabic and English, which, it claims, receive more than 160 million hits a year, making it the most visited Arabic language website and among the top 200 most visited sites worldwide.

Through the Internet, many people throughout the world are bombarded with instantaneous news and eyewitness coverage of all types of political events. Further, the number of people using the Internet is growing exponentially. Between 1990 and 2011, the share of the world population using the Internet soared from only 0.5% to 30.2% and the number of total users is exceeding 2 billion, as Figure 4.2 indicates.

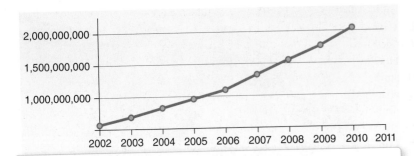

FIGURE 4.2
Internet Users Worldwide

This graph illustrates the Internet Users Worldwide ongoing increase of individuals around the world who are gaining access to the Internet. While this increase is occurring both in developed and developing countries, it is happening at a much faster rate in the former. Despite this progress, two-thirds of the global population does not have regular and reliable Internet access.

Source: The World Bank Development Indicators.

Social media
Internet-based programs that allow for the creation and exchange of user-generated content and interactive dialogue between individuals and groups.

Democratic internationalism
The theoretical perspective that the basic political and moral concerns of people will conflict with imperial domination and violence, and thus, people can place a (democratic) check on abuses of power.

Still, the Internet is more readily available in the economically developed countries, where regions like Europe and North America have approximately 58% and 78%, respectively, of their population connected compared to 11% in Africa, 24% in Asia, and 32% in the Middle East (http://www.internetworldstats.com/stats.htm). Furthermore, today's Internet users are not only able to access the Web, they can use it to communicate with one another via e-mail or through **social media** sites such as Facebook and Twitter, instantaneously sharing information or promoting their causes globally.

The Impact of Globalized Communications The communications revolution with its ongoing spread of global access to information and interactive communications in real time is of immense importance. One impact is **democratic internationalism**. Transnational communications have provided citizens from different countries with the ability to espouse causes of nearly every imaginable type, to exchange views, to organize across national borders, and to undertake political actions (Schmitz, 2004). Nowhere was this more evident than the series of democratic revolutions that constituted the Arab Spring, as chapter 6 discusses in greater detail. In the context of social media and other globalizing processes, transnational groups are flourishing and having an important impact on policy at the global level through the UN and other international organizations, and on the national level through the pressure brought on governments by the groups' national chapters.

Along these lines, global communications can also undermine authoritarian governments. Authoritarian governments still suspiciously greet the rapid mass communications that industrialized democracies take for granted. China tries to control the Web by using technology to monitor and block dissident communications and by imposing fines and imprisonment on those who the government claims endanger national security by transmitting dissident information and opinions. In the end, Beijing's efforts are probably doomed to failure. "The more they [Chinese authorities] do to block it, the more people want to get online," says Chinese dissident Liu Xiaobo. "People in China now understand a lot more about what's going on than . . . in the '70s and '80s. Then, the only contact we had with the outside world was through meeting the very occasional foreigner or somehow getting hold of a foreign paper or magazine."[4] From 2006 to 2010, Chinese citizens had access to Google, although the government restricted search results and prohibited YouTube. In 2010, Google partially pulled out of the world's largest Internet market (by users) over censorship concerns and a computer hacking attempt that Google claimed they could trace back to the Chinese government. This move to shut down mainland Chinese service is a major blow to the Chinese government and its international image as it signals a major corporation's unwillingness to continue to accept such censorship.

Government Policy   Just as government policy can resist globalization, it can also serve as a major catalyst in promoting it, especially on the economic front. After World War I, countries increasingly tried to protect their economies from foreign competition by instituting trade restrictions in the form of high tariffs and by impeding the free exchange of currencies. In hindsight, policy makers concluded this approach had been disastrous. Much of Europe struggled economically during the 1920s, and then experienced collapse at the end of the decade. Between 1929 and 1932, industrial production in Europe fell 50% and unemployment shot up to 22%. The U.S. stock market crashed in 1929, and the American economy soon imploded, as did the economies of Japan and other countries. Global trade plummeted and the world sank into the Great Depression. During the 1920s, fascist dictator Benito Mussolini had seized power in downtrodden Italy, and during the Great Depression, Adolf Hitler and other fascist dictators rose to power in Germany, Japan, Spain, and elsewhere. World War II soon followed, exacting a horrific price. Many observers argued that the restrictive economic policies after World War I had created the economic desperation that allowed fascism to take hold, which, in turn, led to World War II.

Based on their analysis of the causes of World War II, policy makers planning for the postwar period focused in part on preventing a reoccurrence of global conflict. On the economic front, the United States led the effort to create the **General Agreement on Tariffs and Trade (GATT)**, a treaty and an organization of the same name (later renamed the **World Trade Organization [WTO]**) meant to eventually eliminate the **trade barriers**. Policy makers also established the **International Monetary Fund (IMF)** and the World Bank, as we will discuss in chapter 9. Our belief in, and government support for, globalization remain powerful assumptions that help guide policy choices today. The government's role in promoting globalization tends to undercut former President Bill Clinton's argument that "Globalization is not something we can hold off or turn off . . . it is the economic equivalent of a force of nature—like wind or water."[5] Thus, globalization is not natural or inherent, but we must evaluate it as a product of policy choices that focus on internationalizing trade, investment, and capital, as well as liberalizing domestic economic systems through the dismantling of trade barriers, the deregulation of industry, and the privatization of state enterprises. These processes involve new rules and institutions, both formal and informal, increasing human interdependence and the reach of the global market. On the other hand, countries, especially acting collectively, can shape, restrain, or even reverse many aspects of globalization by increasing economic barriers, by restricting travel and interfering with transnational communications, and by other policies designed to make national borders less permeable.

Conceptions of Globalization

For some, globalization is about integration and harmonization. For others, globalization is about systems of domination and new forms of imperialism. Globalization

General Agreement on Tariffs and Trade (GATT)
A series of multilateral trade negotiations that reduced tariffs after World War II and continued into the early 1990s. Became the WTO in 1993.

World Trade Organization (WTO)
The organization, founded in 1995, that implements and enforces the General Agreement on Tariffs and Trade (GATT) and mediates trade-related disputes between and among states-parties to the GATT.

Trade barriers
Government-induced restrictions on international free trade, including tariffs, import quotas, licensing, subsidies, embargos, and currency devaluations.

International Monetary Fund (IMF)
The world's primary organization devoted to maintaining monetary stability by helping countries to fund balance-of-payment deficits.

can simultaneously support democratic reform and lead to environmental degradation. In order to understand this complex and multidimensional process, it is critical to distinguish between the economic and cultural processes of globalization. By doing so, we can see the important ways these processes are interdependent, mutually reinforcing, and at times, contradictory.

Economic Globalization

Economic interchange across borders is bringing the world together and creating economic interdependence in both positive and negative ways. Manufacturers produce goods more cheaply and distribution channels make them more widely available, but that also means that we send jobs to the places where we can pay the lowest (and not necessarily livable) wages. Chapters 9 and 10 detail the growth in free trade policies and agreements, the impact of international investment in developing economies, and the shifts in global monetary exchange practices—all of which have empowered international banks and multinational corporations as powerful actors in the international system. Thus, we will save that discussion. It is important to note here, however, two other critical aspects of economic globalization—the centrality of the informal sector and the impact of identity politics on economic exchanges.

When we look at formal sectors, economic globalization has often translated into growth and prosperity. However, it is also important to consider the impact of economic globalization on the market's informal sectors. These include both the legal and illegal profit-based exchanges that occur outside formal, market-based production. Political scientists and economists rarely count these areas, which are by definition unregulated, in economic studies or even in national assessments, such as **gross domestic product (GDP)**. From child care to housework, to street vending to petty trade, to drug dealing and the arms trade, these activities have dramatically increased in recent years and constitute more than half of all economic output. While measuring and assessing these often invisible work forms is controversial, the *Journal of International Affairs* documented this remarkable growth in an article entitled "The Shadow Economy" (2005). The article stated that the global economy, as we understand it, could simply not function without the informal sector and all the work, paid and not paid, legal and illegal, that it constitutes.

The formal sector also has personal implications. Global economic interchange is bringing people together transnationally through familiarity with one another and one another's products. For example, some of these contacts are interpersonal. More have to do with the role of international economics in narrowing cultural differences and creating a sense of identification with trading partners. About half of Japan's annual foreign trade is with the Western industrialized countries. The impact of this trade flow is evident in Japan's sense of affinity with others. One study asked whether Japanese people more closely associated with Asian or Western countries. Of those willing to respond, 54% replied, "Western countries." When asked why they identified with Western countries, 89% said it was because of "economic interaction" (Namkung, 1998:46).

Cultural Globalization

Much of the early development of different languages, customs, and other diverse aspects of world cultures resulted from the isolation of groups from one another. It is

Gross domestic product (GDP)
A measure of income within a country that excludes foreign earnings.

not surprising, then, that a degree of cultural amalgamation has occurred as improved transportation and communication have brought people of various societies into more frequent contact. Analyzing the blurring of cultural differences inevitably includes a great deal about fast food, basketball, rock music, and other such aspects of pop culture, but such analysis does not trivialize the subject. Instead, a long-standing bottom-up line of political theory argues that the world's people can build on commonplace interactions and increasing cultural commonalities that engender familiarity with and confidence in one another to create a global civil society where people begin to define themselves as global citizens. Some nations emerged from civil societies and, as chapter 3 discusses, carved out their own nation-states. By the same process, if transnational civil societies develop, then regional and even global schemes of governance could conceivably form and supplement or supplant the territorial state. Scholars who examine the bottom-up process of transnational integration look for evidence in such factors as the flow of communications and commerce between countries and the spread across borders of what people wear, eat, and do for recreation.

While it is premature to talk of a world culture, and that may never come, there is significant evidence of cultural amalgamation in the world. Chinese leaders once wore "Mao suits." Now they wear Western-style business suits. When dressing informally, people in Shanghai, Lagos, and Mexico City are more apt to wear jeans, T-shirts, and sneakers than their country's traditional dress. Young people everywhere listen to the same

music, with, for example, Rihanna's "Disturbia" on the Top-10 charts in many countries, including the United States, in 2008. One of the most alarming trends along these lines has been the spread of poor eating habits, particularly the increasing consumption of Big Macs, fries, and milk shakes around the world. The World Health Organization predicts that in 2015 there will be 2.3 billion overweight adults in the world and more than 700 million of them will be obese. This is up from the 1.6 million and 400 million in 2005. Despite the severe interpersonal, health, and economic costs of people getting fatter worldwide, more than 1 billion people in the world are suffering from hunger, according to the UN Food and Agriculture Organization.

Before looking further at the evidence of cultural amalgamation, one caution is in order. You will see that a great deal of what is becoming world culture is Western, especially

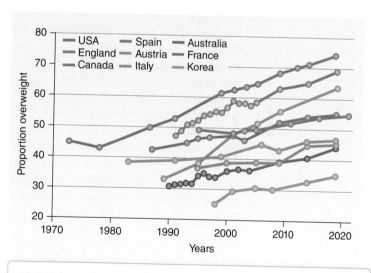

FIGURE 4.3
Obesity rates in OECD countries

Recent statistics from the advanced industrialized world clearly demonstrate a global obesity epidemic. As countries develop, obesity tends to increase as unhealthy eating habits spread and physical activity decreases—a dark side of globalizing ideas, culture, and technology. This concerning trend is problematic for a variety of reasons, including serious implications for individual health, community stability and prosperity, national economic systems, and public health care systems.

Source: Organization for Economic Cooperation and Development.

American, in its origins. That does not imply that Western culture is superior. Its impact is a function of the economic and political strength of Western Europe and the United States. Nor does the preponderance of Western culture in the integration process mean that the flow is one way. Many foreign imports, such as fajitas and sushi, soccer, and acupuncture influence American culture. The United States today prides itself on its melting pot status—a nation comprised of many cultures, ethnic and racial backgrounds, and religions that offer a multitude of diversity, but whose individuals, ideally, share the privilege of being citizens of a free and democratic society.

Language One of the most important aspects of converging culture is English, which is becoming the world's common language of business, diplomacy, communications, and even culture. Afghan President Hamid Karzai and many other leaders of countries or international organizations converse in English. A number of them, including UN Secretary-General Ban Ki-moon of South Korea, learned or improved their English while enrolled at U.S. universities. A bit more slowly, English is spreading among common citizens around the world. This is evident in differences among various age groups. In Europe, for example, 9 out of 10 students, in countries ranging from Italy to Spain to Austria to Norway to Greece and Croatia, now receive English instruction during their primary education.[6]

Modern communications are one factor driving the spread of English. There have been notable advances, such as the ability to search in nearly 100 languages through Google, in making the Web more accessible to non-English speakers. However, the vast majority of what is available on the Internet has been and remains in English. As the webmaster at one site in Russia comments, "It is far easier for a Russian . . . to download the works of Dostoyevsky translated in English to read than it is for him to get [it] in his own language." Business needs also promote the global growth of English. The U.S. status as the world's economic powerhouse makes it far more common for foreign businesspeople to learn the language of Americans than it is for Americans to learn other languages. The Japanese government issued a report declaring that "achieving world-class excellence demands that all Japanese acquire a working knowledge of English."[7] The use of English will probably continue to expand throughout the world because a majority of people in every region in the world believe that their children are more likely to prosper if they learn English.

Consumer Products The interchange of popular consumer goods is another major factor in narrowing cultural gaps. American movies are popular throughout much of the world. In 2010, for example, the two top drawing films globally were both Disney productions—*Toy Story III* and *Alice in Wonderland*. Moreover, foreign distribution is vital to the U.S. film industry, which earns approximately 67% of its revenue from international sales. In contrast, foreign films account for just 3% of the U.S. market.[8] Still, consumerism more generally is spreading rapidly. Consider the implications that China, the most populous country in the world, has surpassed the United States as the largest market for new cars, as well as the largest emitter of greenhouse gasses.

In short, there is a distinct and important intermingling and amalgamation of cultures under way. For good or ill, Western, particularly American, culture is at the forefront of this trend. The observation of the director-general of UNESCO, that "America's main role in the new world order is not as a military superpower, but as a multicultural superpower," is an overstatement, but it captures some of what is occurring.[9] While the sources of this common culture are certainly important, it is the actual and potential consequences of this cultural amalgamation that will be defining features of the 21st century. From local interactions reshaping a person's identity, to global environmental systems reworking how we understand "natural disasters," cultural globalization is real and intense. As noted, some analysts welcome it as a positive force that will bring people and, eventually, political units together. Others see transnational culture as a danger to desirable diversity and sustainability.

Evaluating Globalization

Very few would refute that globalization as a multidimensional process exists. At a factual level, there can be little doubt that the exchange of peoples, goods, services, and ideas across borders has sped up considerably. Evidence of the extraordinarily rapid globalization of communications and transportation is beyond dispute. The economic data are also clear. Measured by trade, investment, monetary flow, and every other standard, economic globalization has advanced quickly and far. Cultural globalization is harder to measure, but anyone who has traveled internationally over the past several decades will attest to how much more frequent the use of English, Western-style dress, fast-food restaurants, and many other aspects of a spreading common culture have become. From these cursory observations, many people seem to view globalization positively. It enjoys considerable popular support around the world. Yet critics of the process are legion and more vehement than its supporters. For others, the assumed benefits of globalization are for the few at the top, and more problematically, these benefits rely upon the exploitation of those at the bottom, even exacerbating their disadvantaged and often dependent state.

No matter where you come down, it is difficult to evaluate globalization as a positive or negative trend for the world. As the following discussion will demonstrate, in many ways, it is both.

Arguments for Economic Globalization   As we noted earlier, economic globalization gained momentum after World War II because it was promoted by American and other policy makers who believed in the causal sequence: reducing international economic restrictions would → increase prosperity, thereby → decreasing a source of potential conflict among countries. Many policy makers, scholars, and others continue to believe in the validity of this causal sequence and to promote globalization based on it. They also see additional links between globalization and peace. One thought is that globalization increases prosperity and that democracy is more likely in prosperous countries. Because democratic peace theory contends that democracies seldom, if ever, fight with one another, then a positive sequence is: globalization → greater prosperity → more democracies → fewer wars. Yet another argument is that globalization creates interdependent economies, which make it difficult and economically self-destructive to fight wars. Thus, another positive sequence is: globalization → increased interdependence → fewer wars. These sorts of rationales were certainly part of the justification behind the creation of the **European Union (EU)**, which began as the European Coal and Steel Community following the social and economic devastation of WWII.

Just as some policy makers and scholars see positive links between economic globalization and peace, some analysts believe that as globalization creates more

European Union (EU)
The European regional organization established in 1993 when the Maastricht Treaty went into effect. The EU encompasses the still legally existing European Communities (EC). When the EC was formed in 1967, it in turn encompassed three still legally existing regional organizations formed in the 1950s: the European Coal and Steel Community (ECSC), the European Economic Community (EEC), and the European Atomic Energy Community (EURATOM)".

This photo shows but a small piece of the protests against the WTO that rocked Seattle, Washington, in 1999. This massive demonstration in a major U.S. city was an incredibly significant moment in the history of popular protests. Not only did the protestors succeed in disrupting the meetings of the world's most influential trade-governing body, but the event drew together incredibly diverse constituencies representing a wide range of interests, many of which would seem incompatible on the surface. All, however, reflected a grassroot backlash to globalization.

personal interaction, cultural interchange, and amalgamation among people, it makes others seem less alien and threatening, and the resulting familiarity enhances peace. In this positive sequence we see: globalization → increased cross-cultural contacts and amalgamation → a decreased sense of difference among nations → less conflict. Whatever the precise sequence of the links, President Bill Clinton, when in office, expressed his belief in the general globalization → peace concept when he told Congress, "These are the challenges we have to meet so that we can lead the world toward peace and freedom in an era of globalization."[10] Numerous scholars also link globalization to peace, arguing in one case, "The United States and other major powers can best discourage conflict by promoting greater global economic ties" (Gartzke & Li, 2003:285). It is important to note, however, that not everyone agrees that globalization promotes peace, and even if it does, some believe that the process to get to peace and prosperity is often violent, repressive, and unstable. Thus, there are serious concerns about the impact of globalizing processes in the short- and long-term.

Concerns about Economic Globalization   We will analyze the complex impact of economic globalization in chapter 10. However, in this chapter we include an overview of the arguments. One concern relates to the causal arguments that link prosperity directly to peace or indirectly through democratization to peace. Although there is substantial evidence supporting these arguments, there are analysts who doubt them, either entirely or in part. Take Russia, for example. While Russia is certainly part of the global market in terms of oil, it is only quasi-democratic and semi-cooperative at best. According to one analyst, "The oil sector has effectively merged with the state, making Russia's deepening ties to the global economy a would-be weapon rather than an avenue of restraint. Russian economic liberalization without political liberalization is unlikely to pay the strong cooperative dividends many expect" (Goldstone, 2007).

Another broader concern about economic globalization relates to how governments and societies more widely distribute benefits. The basic argument critics make is that we do not distribute benefits equally, with the wealthy benefiting and the poor gaining little or nothing and sometimes even becoming worse off, at least relatively. The answer depends to a degree on which numbers we stress. Since 1945, world prosperity has grown overall. The economically developed countries (EDCs), which the United States has led, have done exceptionally well, and conditions in the less developed countries (LDCs) have improved overall. Many of them have made great strides, and while not truly prosperous, are not generally poor either. Yet there are still a billion people worldwide living in extreme poverty on the equivalent of a dollar or

TABLE 4.1	Top Global Companies: Which are the most profitable?		
Rank	**Company**	**2010 Profits ($ millions)**	**Profits % change from 2009**
1	Nestlé	32,843.0	242.0
2	Gazprom	31,894.5	29.9
3	Exxon Mobil	30,460.0	58.0
4	Industrial & Commercial Bank of China	24,398.2	29.6
5	Royal Dutch Shell	20,127.0	60.8
6	China Construction Bank	19,920.3	27.5
7	AT&T	19,864.0	58.5
8	Petrobras	19,184.0	23.7
9	Chevron	19,024.0	81.5
10	Microsoft	18,760.0	28.8

Source: http://money.cnn.com/magazines/fortune/global500/2011/performers/companies/profits/

two a day, and many countries remain desperately poor. Moreover, the gap between the per capita wealth of the EDCs and LDCs has expanded. In 1980, for every $1 of per capita wealth LDCs generated, the EDCs generated $14 per capita. In 2010, that 1:14 gap had grown to 1:26 (UN Human Development Report, 2011).

At the extreme, some contend that poverty persists and the wealth gap has grown because EDCs have utilized globalizing processes in ways that exploit the LDCs by pressuring them to open their economies to EDC penetration and domination. A related contention is that even within the EDCs, the elites are using globalization to increase their wealth and financial power through the **multinational corporations (MNCs)** that they control to escape regulations protecting the environment, workers, and consumers by either moving operations to a permissive country or pressuring governments to ease or end regulations. Those who see globalization as a process that is making the rich richer by exploiting both poor countries and the poor within wealthy countries advocate radical change in global economic trends and policy. A less dire interpretation of the causes of the expanding wealth gap and other unsatisfactory trends and conditions is that many LDCs do not have an adequate economic base to compete openly in the global market. From this perspective, the solution is to reform the globalization process with EDCs giving more economic assistance to LDCs by incentivizing improved local working conditions, by creating global environmental codes, and by instituting a wide variety of other reforms that will create a more equitable globalization process internationally and within countries.

Multinational corporations (MNCs) Private enterprises that have production subsidiaries or branches in more than one country.

Concerns about Cultural Globalization

Those who object to cultural globalization condemn it for undermining the world's rich tapestry of cultural diversity and potentially producing a less vibrant monoculture that one scholar has described as the "eternal yawn of McWorld" (Barber, 1996:vi). The alternative perspective is, "We should not fear that globalism will lead to homogenization. Instead, it will expose us to the differences that surround us" (Nye, 2002:1).

What do people around the world think of cultural amalgamation? The answer has several parts (Edwards, 2006). Most people welcome the availability of foreign culture. A worldwide survey in 45 countries found that 77% thought that having foreign products available was good, and 61% felt that way about foreign movies and other entertainment media. However, few people are unreservedly positive about importing foreign culture. When asked about foreign entertainment media, for instance, only 30% thought it was "very good," and another 31% said it was merely "somewhat good." Further, many people have conflicting views with a strong majority of people around the world arguing simultaneously that cultural imports are good and that their way of life is threatened and needs protection from outside influences. Part of public reaction to cultural imports relates to demographic patterns. Age makes a difference, with older people usually more averse to cultural imports than younger people. In the West African country of Senegal, for example, 76% of young adults (ages 18 to 29) favor cultural imports. Only 47% of adults age 50 and over favor them. In contrast, geography and the relative wealth of countries generally do not make a great deal of difference in the responses to various questions about cultural imports, although Muslim countries, especially those in the Middle East, are somewhat more resistant than other types of countries.

A final note about cultural imports is that countries sometimes try to restrict them either because governments want to drum up nationalist feeling or need to respond to the demands of nationalist groups. France and China provide two examples. At least 90% of the French favor popular culture imports and believe that their children should learn English. Yet the French government has strongly resisted the encroachment of foreign culture. Former President Jacques Chirac warned that the spread of English poses a "major risk for humanity." The government requires the exclusive use of French in teaching, business, and government, and pressures the entertainment industry to feature French-language movies and music. Such measures have not worked well. For example, *Harry Potter and the Deathly Hallows Part 1* was the highest grossing film in France for 2010, and Part 2 is set to be the highest grossing film of 2011.

Like their French counterparts, 90% of the Chinese also view cultural imports favorably. Yet dissenters worry about the loss of Chinese traditional culture. The end of 2006, for instance, saw a campaign on the government-controlled China Daily website that warned, "Western culture has been changing from a breeze and a drizzle into a wild wind and a heavy storm. This is vividly embodied in the rising popularity of Christmas," the site lamented, and it urged "our countrymen to be cautious about Christmas, to wake from their collective cultural coma and give Chinese culture the dominant role." Not everyone agreed. "It might not be a bad thing for traditional Chinese culture to make some changes under Western influence. There should be competition among different cultures," one posting on a blog objected. "It is not necessary to boycott Western culture. You just can't," was another post.[11]

TRANSNATIONALISM

Transnationalism generally springs from two sources. Globalization is one. Economic interdependence, mass communications, rapid travel, and other modern factors are fostering transnationalism by intertwining people's lives around the world and promoting a much higher level of transnational contacts. Human thought is the other source of transnationalism. "I think, therefore I am," philosopher René Descartes argued in *Discourse on Method* (1637). The ability to think abstractly allows humans to imagine—to see themselves beyond what they have experienced and to define how they wish to connect to people, ideas, and institutions. Transnationalism is based on this abstract self-awareness that brings people together.

Transnationalism has both action and identification elements. Regarding action, transnationalism is the process of people working together as individuals and collectively in private groups across borders with other individuals and groups to accomplish a common purpose. Regarding identification, transnationalism provides alternatives to nationalism as a source of political identity. This concept refers to how we see ourselves connected as individuals to ideologies (such as communism), religion (such as Islam), demographic characteristics (such as ethnicity or gender), region (such as Europe), or virtually any other perceived common bond. We will speculate on the future of transnationalism later in the chapter, but it is important to say here that most people will not abandon **nationalism** in the foreseeable future. It is also important to see, however, that things are changing, and that at least some people are shifting some or all of their political identification away from their nationalist identity and toward one or more other identities.

Nationalism
The belief that the nation is the ultimate basis of political loyalty and that one's nation is entitled to self-government.

As our discussion of transnationalism proceeds, you will see that it has the potential to significantly restructure the global system and its conduct. Some aspects of transnationalism tend to undermine nationalism and, by extension, the state. For example, some European Union citizens identify as Europeans, instead of simply as French, German, or some other nationality. In other cases, transnational identification and organization help change attitudes and policies around the world related to a specific area of concern. Issues, from climate change to gender equality often transcend national borders. This chapter will explore this dynamic by more closely examining the global women's movement.

You will also see that transnationalism is neither an inherent force for peace nor for discord. Some aspects of transnationalism promote greater global interdependence and harmony and, as such, are very much in accord with the liberal school's political thought vision, which we discussed in chapter 1. Yet globalization has also spurred illegal and violent transnational movements, particularly in terms of transnational crime. These forces from below, as Barber discusses them, can create an image of transnationalism in which the world is divided along cultural lines. Those who see transnationalism in this light tend to be realists, many of whom would strengthen the national state as a bulwark against the dangers of hostile transnational alignments. To explore transnationalism, we will first survey transnational organizations, then turn our attention to regional transnationalism, cultural transnationalism, religious transnationalism, and transnational movements before looking at the future of transnationalism.

Britain's Sarah Ferguson (L), Duchess of York, after giving a speech as United Nations Secretary General Ban Ki-Moon (C) and Hamidon Ali (R), president of the United Nations Economic and Social Council (ECOSOC), listen during the meeting "Engaging Philanthropy to Promote Gender Equality and Women's Empowerment" February 22, 2010, organized by ECOSOC at UN headquarters in New York. ECOSOC is the UN agency that assists nonstate actors and nongovernmental organizations in observing and participating in negotiations among UN officials and member-states.

Global Civil Society

For some, the term *transnational* is a bit too narrow, or understated so much that a single border crossing would constitute a transnational interaction. Under this definition, the world has been connected in this way for centuries. Many scholars and practitioners prefer the term *global* civil society to better capture the range of common identities that emerge from various localities across the world. Similar to Barber's "Jihad," these forces from below work to counter the globalizing forces from above. Global civil society goes beyond transnational linkages to include an expression of consciousness with a global reach, even if some participants do not have access to the Internet or even a telephone (Anheiner et al., 2001). According to the *Global Civil Society Yearbook,* "global civil society is the sphere of ideas, values, institutions, organizations, networks, and individuals located between the family, the state, and the market and operating beyond the confines of national societies, polities, and economies" (2001). Global civil society consists of value-driven actors aiming to influence the world. While some seek global citizenship, others may seek something closer to global domination. Global civil society can have desirable as well as harmful ambitions. This section will explore the nature and scope of GCS in terms of its membership and the ways such people often organize themselves.

NGOs: Driving Global Civil Society One indication of the increased strength and presence of global civil society is the phenomenal growth in number and activities of transnational organizations that we call **nongovernmental organizations (NGOs)**. These are organizations that operate across national boundaries, that have membership comprised of private individuals and groups, and that do not answer directly to any government. While government agencies may fund these groups in whole or in part, their members do not include state actors (Reimann, 2006). In many ways, NGOs are legally constituted not-for-profit organizations. From a purely technical viewpoint, terrorist groups and multinational corporations (MNCs) fit NGOs' definitional boundaries, but most IR scholars treat them separately, as we do in chapters 7 and 9, respectively.

Nongovernmental organizations (NGOs) International (transnational) organizations with private memberships.

The Growth of NGOs Between 1900 and 2005, the number of NGOs grew from 69 to over 11,400. Note that, by far, the greatest growth spurt has occurred since 1975, in parallel to rapidly advancing globalization. Of these NGOs, in 2010, close to 3,500 hold consultative status with the United Nations, up from 928 such groups in 1992 and 222 such groups in 1952.[12] These groups have a highly diverse range of interests that include peace, human rights, disarmament, the environment, and virtually every other public concern. Notably, the causes and consequences of many (if not all) of these areas of advocacy constitute transnational global challenges.

The increasing number of NGOs and their diverse range of interests and activities reflect globalization in several ways. First, as we noted previously, there is a growing awareness that many issues are partly or wholly transnational. For instance, one country's discharge of atmospheric gases that attack Earth's vital ozone layer increases the rate of skin cancer globally, not just in the country where the gases are emitted. Similarly, many women believe that the status of women in any one country is linked to the treatment of women everywhere. Second, NGOs have flourished because advances in transportation and communication have made transnational contacts easy, rapid, and inexpensive. Third, the growth of NGOs reflects disenchantment with existing political organizations based in or dominated by states in an age of globalization and transnational problems. As a result, people are seeking new ways to work with one another beyond traditional government-to-government diplomacy.

The Activities of NGOs   In essence, NGOs are organized interest groups that operate singly or in combination with one another to promote their causes. In the realm of environmental politics, for example, there are such groups as Friends of the Earth International, headquartered in the Netherlands. It coordinates a transnational effort to protect the environment and also serves as a link among 5,000 Friends of the Earth member-groups in 70 countries. Just like more domestically oriented interest groups, NGOs promote their goals by such techniques as attempting to raise public awareness and support for their causes and by providing information, argumentation, and electoral backing to policy makers in national governments and **intergovernmental organizations (IGOs),** international organizations in which the members are states.

On the domestic front, for example, government agencies often work with NGOs to accomplish goals and sometimes even seek their help to obtain funds and other types of support. Speaking before the U.S. Conference of Catholic Bishops in 2006, the head of the U.S. Agency for International Development (USAID) stressed that "the U.S. government and NGO community together must use their comparative advantages . . . in combating poverty." This not only means lobbying Congress, but utilizing the specific expertise and street credibility that some NGOs have about specific circumstances on the ground.[13]

NGOs also play a role in the UN's international policy making processes and those of other IGOs, who have long sought out relationships with NGOs. These ties have expanded greatly over time. Some scholars have found the relationship between IGOs and NGOs to be symbiotic (Reimann, 2006). For example, NGOs are active through their participation in multinational conferences that the United Nations and other IGOs convene to address global problems. Since the early 1990s, all such conferences have two components. One is the official conference that includes delegates from governments. The other is the parallel NGO conference, which exists to bring non–state actors together in an organized way to share information, mobilize, strategize, and ultimately work to influence state actors. The largest such dual conference was the 2002 World Conference on Sustainable Development in Johannesburg, South Africa, drawing some 41,000 delegates from more than 6,600 NGOs to its parallel meeting. In this way, NGOs provide a way for individuals to become involved in and have an impact

Intergovernmental organizations (IGOs), International/transnational bodies that are composed of member-countries.

on global events. Certain NGOs, such as Amnesty International and Doctors Without Borders, have received the Nobel Peace Prize for their contributions to humanity.

International conferences are both the result of NGOs' work and a vehicle that promotes their role by enhancing their visibility and by serving as a place where they can create **transnational advocacy networks (TANs)**. These networks, or coalitions, include NGOs, IGOs, foundations, professional groups, religious organizations, and even state-based agencies that are united by a common principled interest (Betsill & Bulkeley, 2004; Park, 2005; Rodrigues, 2004). For example, the effort to protect the environment combines the efforts of a TAN comprising national government agencies such as the U.S. Environmental Protection Agency, NGOs such as Greenpeace, IGOs such as the United Nations Environment Program, and communities of environmental scientists, such as those at the Earth Institute at Columbia University.

Transnational advocacy networks (TANs) IGOs, NGOs, and national organizations that are based on shared values or common interests and that exchange information and services.

The Impact of NGOs It is hard to measure the impact of NGOs or any other single factor on policy making, but there is evidence that NGOs are gaining recognition as legitimate actors and are playing an increased role in the policy process. One measure is funding. The amount of aid flowing through NGOs to economically less developed countries increased from $1 billion in 1970, to approaching $10 billion today. Historically, NGOs have received most of their funds from their members. More recently, some governments and IGOs have begun to channel some of their aid funds through NGOs. For example, USAID directs some of its funding through a number of NGOs and also gives funds to strengthen the NGOs in order to allow them to bring about economic development, democratization, and other desired changes.

NGOs have also helped move some of their causes to the center of the political stage by increasing public information and demanding action. According to a former British diplomat, "You used to have a nice, cozy relationship [between states]. Now you have more figures on the stage. . . . This adds to the pace and complexity of diplomacy."[14] For example, 50 years ago, the environment received little political attention. Now it is an important issue that generates world conferences (such as those in Rio in 1992 and Johannesburg in 2002). It is a frequent topic of conversation among heads of government and is the subject of numerous international agreements. This power to set the agenda and frame issues in politically expedient ways has proved to be a key function for many NGOs.

International NGOs and their national chapters also individually and collectively bring pressure on governments. In the United States, for example, the League of Conservation Voters lobbies legislators and agency officials and takes such public relations steps as maintaining a scorecard that rates the voting record of members of Congress on the environment. Also note that some forms of NGO activity can be destructive and, therefore, illegitimate in the view of most. Extreme examples include the violent acts by terrorist organizations, ranging from groups with a global scope like al Qaeda to those more locally focused like *Euskadi Ta Askatasuna* (ETA), the armed Basque separatist movement in Spain.

TANs: Organizing Global Civil Society As we noted above, NGOs often organize themselves into transnational advocacy networks (TANs). International relations scholars Margaret Keck and Kathryn Sikkink (1998) were among the first to theorize and then empirically observe the nature and impact of TANs. From their initial research on the human rights movement and the violence against women network, Keck and Sikkink defined TANs as a group of relevant actors bound together by shared values, a common discourse, and a dense exchange of information. TANs organized around "principled ideas" with the goal of changing the behavior and policy of states and IGOs. While NGOs often comprise the TANs' majority, these networks also rely upon and involve media groups, foundations, churches, trade unions, consumer organizations, intellectuals, and even parts of governments. These various actors come together in voluntary ways to campaign on a particular issue, and they serve to multiply the channels of access for non–state actors in a state-based political system. Similar to NGOs, TANs build new links among civil society actors, IGOs, and states.

TANs have been particularly influential in their ability to bring new ideas and **norms** into policy debates. According to Keck and Sikkink, this activism emerges in related but distinct forms:

Norms
Unwritten rules, principles, or standards of behavior that create expectations about how states and individuals ought to behave.

- Information Politics—the ability to quickly and credibly generate politically usable information

- Symbolic Politics—the ability to call upon symbols, action, or stories that make sense of a situation for an audience that is frequently far away

- Leverage Politics—the ability to call upon powerful actors to affect a situation where weaker members of a network are unlikely to have influence

- Accountability Politics—the effort to hold powerful actors to their previously stated policies or principles

Take, for example, the "Madres de la Plaza de Mayo," a group of mothers that began to meet and protest every Thursday in the late 1970s in the large Plaza de Mayo in Buenos Aires, the site of Argentina's government. They walked in nonviolent demonstrations

These two photos (1982 and 2005, respectively) depict the weekly protests led by the "Madres de Plaza de Mayo" in Argentina. This human rights organization, led by Argentine mothers, is demanding that the mothers be reunited with their children who were disappeared during the Dirty War of the military dictatorship from 1976 to 1983. They wear white head scarves with their children's names on them to symbolize the blankets of their abducted children. The name of the organization comes from the Plaza de Mayo in central Buenos Aires, where the bereaved mothers and grandmothers first gathered and continue to do so every Thursday since the repressive regime was in power.

demanding the return of their children who had disappeared during the "Dirty War" from 1976 to 1983. During the war, the military government abducted, tortured, and killed left-wing militants and anyone who they claimed were political opponents of the ruling regime. Many of those who disappeared were young people, college students like yourself, who expressed dissatisfaction with the regime. The women served as a powerful moral symbol of the country as mothers. They documented and disseminated the names of those missing, and leveraged human rights organizations outside of their country, as well as governments like the U.S. to put pressure on the military regime. The Madres served as the TAN's central element, which brought down the brutal ruling party and restored democracy in Argentina.

Regional and Cultural Influences

Regional and cultural influences have largely determined transnationalism. Although chapter 5 discusses regional organizations in greater detail, it is worth noting here that organizations like the European Union (EU) are an important example of regional transnationalism. Since its genesis after World War II, the EU has evolved to the point now where there is advanced economic and social integration among European states. Although at a slower rate, political integration has also proceeded. These changes are beginning to affect how Europeans define their political identity (Caporaso, 2005). Even if there is no doubt that nationalism continues to dominate, there is also a sense of other identifications taking hold. Among Europeans, 40% define themselves only as citizens of their country. Another 44% define themselves as citizens of their country first and as Europeans second. Even more transnationally identified, 8% feel more European than national, and 4% perceive themselves as exclusively European (with 3% unsure).[15] Thus, while nationalism reigns supreme, it is notable that about 12% of people in the EU have transferred a traditional national identification to a primary or exclusive sense of being European and that 60% of EU citizens have some sense of political identification with it, even if it is secondary. Also, there is a stronger European identification (15%) among younger Europeans (ages 15 to 24), with support dropping off to only 8% among older Europeans (age 55 or more).

There is no other area of the globe with a regional organization that even approaches the economic, much less the political integration of the EU. Thus, to date, any sense of regional political identity is almost exclusively confined to Europe. But in the 1950s, Europe's Common Market was just beginning, and it was limited to trade, much like several regional organizations such as the North American Free Trade Agreement (NAFTA, which links Canada, Mexico, and the United States) are today. What has evolved in Europe could occur elsewhere.

Regionalism drives and often coincides with cultural transnationalism, but it has distinct characteristics that can be as divisive as they are unifying. Considerable scholarship demonstrates how greater intercultural familiarity reduces stereotyping, suspicion, fear, and other divisive factors that promote domestic and global conflict. Therefore, the familiarity with different cultures that globalization brings, and even the blending of cultures, holds the prospect of reducing world conflict.

A darker view is that cultural transnationalism will lead to a clash of civilizations. The best-known proponent of this theory is Samuel P. Huntington (1993, 1996). Like many analysts, Huntington (1993:22–26) believes that nationalism will "weaken . . . as a source of identity." What will happen next is the key to his controversial thesis. He proposes that new cultural identifications will emerge that will "fill this gap," and countries will align themselves in "seven or eight cultural blocs," including "Western, Confucian, Japanese, Islamic, Hindu, Slavic-Orthodox, Latin American, and possibly African." These blocs, Huntington further predicts, will become "the fundamental source of conflict" as "different civilizations" engage in "prolonged and . . . violent conflicts."

Most Western scholars reject Huntington's theory (Henderson, 2004). However, it seems more plausible in other parts of the world. Additionally, some research has found evidence of increasing clashes between "civilizations" since World War II, although it has mostly involved the West and Islam (Tusicisny, 2004; Huntington, 1993). As a result, whatever the perspective may be from the United States or other Western, largely Christian-heritage countries, there is considerable suspicion among Muslims that a concerted campaign is under way to undermine their religion and its cultural traits. Note that the view of such actions as anti-Islam or, at least, reflecting cultural insensitivity, is not confined to Muslims. Just before his death, Richard Nixon wrote of the long delay before the West intervened to stop the slaughter of Muslims in Bosnia, "It is an awkward, but unavoidable truth that had the [mostly Muslim] citizens of Sarajevo [the capital of Bosnia] been predominantly Christian or Jewish, the civilized world would not have permitted [the atrocities that occurred]."[16]

As we will discuss later in the chapter, there is a history of conflict between Christendom and Islam that goes back more than a millennium, and to some Muslims current policy by the U.S.-led West is an extension of that conflict. Muslims making that case might point, among other things, to their perceptions of the following U.S. and/or European policies:

- Inaction while Christian Serbs slaughtered Bosnian Muslims (1992–1995)
- Exclusion of Muslim Turkey from the mostly Christian EU
- Opposition to Iraq or Iran obtaining nuclear weapons, while ignoring Israeli nuclear weapons
- Two invasions of Iraq and one of Afghanistan and the long-term presence of Western troops in both countries
- Sanctions on Iraq after 1991 that lasted longer than those on Germany after 1945
- Lack of sanctions on largely Christian Russia for its often brutal campaign against the Muslim Chechens
- Support of Israel

Whether or not such actions reflect a bias against Islam or at least cultural insensitivity, it is important to see that many Muslims perceive them as true. A survey of Muslims in 14 countries in Africa, Asia, and the Middle East found that nearly half felt that their religion was in danger. This perception has arguably fostered the greater sense of solidarity that a strong majority of Muslims also expressed in the survey.[17]

Transnational Movements

Transnational movements, both religiously and ideologically based, have emerged in the context of globalization and are challenging the state in new and critical ways.

These forces from below increasingly operate in a complex political space that both utilizes and critiques globalization. While these movements vary in terms of strength, influence, and goals, they tend to influence people's identity and focus on some aspect of the human condition. The following sections explore various types of transnational movements and their impact on the global system.

Transnational Religious Movements   Most of the world's major religions have a strong transnational element. It is particularly apt to exist when a religion, which is a basis of spiritual identity, becomes a source of political identity among its members. When religion and political identities become intertwined, members of a religion may take a number of political actions (Fox & Sandler, 2004; Shah & Toft, 2006). One is to try to align their country's laws and foreign policy to their religious values. Another is to provide political support for the causes of coreligionists in other countries. This sense of support is why, for example, Jews from around the world are likely to defend Israel and Muslims everywhere are apt to defend the Palestinians. Religion also helps explain why Osama bin Laden, a Saudi, was able to recruit Muslims from Egypt, Pakistan, Chechnya, and elsewhere, including the United States and Europe, to the ranks of al Qaeda and to find a base for the organization in Afghanistan.

As one international relations scholar reminds us, "You're constantly blindsided if you consider religion neutral or outside world politics."[18] Often, it is a force for peace, justice, and humanitarian concern (Johnston, 2003). It is also true that religion has been and continues to be a factor in many bloody wars, conflicts, and other forms of political violence (Fox, 2004). For example, religious identity tied to politics is an element of the conflict between the mostly Jewish Israelis and the mostly Muslim Arabs. Religion is also part of what divides Pakistan and India, each of which has nuclear weapons, giving rise to what some people believe is the world's most dangerous situation.

Religion also causes or exacerbates conflict within countries. In the 1990s, Yugoslavia disintegrated partly along religious lines into Catholic Croats, Muslim Bosnians, and Eastern Orthodox Serbs. More recently, religion played a role in the deadly cultural divide between Serbs and Muslim Albanians in Kosovo. Conflict can also occur within a religion, as the horrific violence in Iraq between Sunni and Shiite Muslims, and even between Shiite factions following the U.S. invasion in 2003 demonstrated.

Organized religion also plays a range of positive roles as a transnational actor. Among Christians, the World Evangelical Alliance, founded in 1846, is an early example of a Protestant NGO. Even older, the Roman Catholic Church is by far the largest and most influential religion-based NGO. The Vatican itself is a state, and the pope is a secular, as well as a spiritual, leader. Roman Catholicism's political influence, however, extends far beyond the Vatican. During the Cold War, for instance, the Church worked successfully to weaken communism's hold on Poland and other mostly Roman Catholic countries in Eastern Europe. Soon after the Soviet Union collapsed in 1991, its last president, Mikhail S. Gorbachev, wrote, "Everything that happened in Eastern Europe in these last few years would have been impossible without the presence of the pope and without the important role—including the political role—that he played on the world stage."[19]

The Strength of Religious Fundamentalism   One aspect of religion that has gained strength in many areas of the world is fundamentalism (religious traditionalism). One

CHALLENGING THE STATE FROM ABOVE AND BELOW

Throughout this chapter we have encouraged you to think about multiple actors in various spaces working to influence the way the world works. Sometimes those forces for change come from global systems and international structures imposing certain ideologies and discourses from above. For example, the logic of capitalism guiding international investment and development loans from the World Bank and the IMF demonstrates that Barber's globalizing notion of "McWorld" is alive and well, as we will discuss more in chapter 9. When we look at religious fundamentalist movements, particularly extremist groups, we see local forces coming together in transnational ways in search of change, for better or for worse. This is the sort of fragmentation and backlash from below that give credence to Barber's notion of "*jihad*."

The case of the global women's movement, however, raises some interesting questions for Barber's theory. While the women's movement has certainly emerged from local contexts and grassroots activism, hatred does not drive it and it does not seek to erase difference, but rather, it seeks to engage and embrace difference. Women within the movement have come to embrace women's different experiences and different forms of feminist activism that have emerged. While women have found commonalities and solidarity in their personal experiences, it is clear that not all women are oppressed and not all men enjoy privilege. The movement has recognized that gender is just one social cleavage that marginalizes certain sects of society—so too, does race, class, and age—all of which have implications for local identity and politics. The women's movement has also engaged with the globalizing forces from above in a way that respects cultural difference and encourages a diversity of perspectives in global institutions, such as in the newly formed UN Women. As you learned in this chapter and will read about in chapter 11, the global women's movement has been very active in organizations like the United Nations, in unified but context-specific ways. "The transnational nature of the feminist solidarity," is, as Niamh Reilly argues, driven by a "commitment to the bottom-up, critical (re)interpretations of universal norms, especially human rights" (2009:10). In short, the global women's movement challenges Barber's binary construction and encourages us to think about the way forces from below interact, reshape, and redefine forces from below and vice versa. It is an ongoing process, sometimes filled with conflict, but sometimes engaging in constructive ways.

Given what you have learned in this chapter about the power of globalizing processes and transnational activism, do you find Barber's theory on "Jihad vs. McWorld" to be a useful way to understand the world around you? What are the strengths and weaknesses of his theoretical paradigm? Consider how you might be able to improve his theory to better explain the world around you.

CRITICAL THINKING QUESTIONS

1. How does globalization operate as a force from above? What are some examples of globalization? Where do these top-down globalizing processes come from, and what is their impact at the local level?

2. Besides transnational religious movements and the transnational women's movement, what other examples of transnationalism are currently at work in global politics? In what ways are these transnational movements reactions to globalizing processes? Do these transnational movements serve to resist or reinforce globalization?

3. What are the strengths and weaknesses of NGOs in global politics today? Using a real-world NGO, discuss the achievements and limitations of this non–state actor.

4. How do globalization *and* transnationalism interact with the sovereign state? Do these forces from above and below challenge the primacy of the state? Do they depend on the power of state? Given what you have learned in this chapter, what is the future of the sovereign state in the global system?

chapter **summary**

- Globalization refers to the multidimensional processes that have increased interactions between political, social, and economic systems. While this integration and exchange is not new, the speed and intensity of global communications, transportation, and information technology is unprecedented. Globalization has made the world more interconnected and interdependent as barriers to the flow of goods, services, people, and ideas have decreased dramatically.

- Globalization is having both positive and negative effects on the global community. From raising cultural awareness to spreading democratic ideals to growing certain economic sectors, globalization has to an extent been a positive development. At the same time, globalization has also led to a greater awareness about cultural differences, nationalistic backlash, and a widening gap between the rich and the poor. Thus, this chapter pushes us to consider the ways in which we must monitor globalizing forces and understand their implications fully at all levels for all people.

- Transnationalism refers to another set of processes in part driven by globalization and in part a reaction to or a form of resisting globalizing forces. Transnationalism refers to the range of cross-border political identities and signifies the social, economic, and political links—and related activism—among people and private organizations that transcend the sovereign state.

- The recent growth in number and range of activities and of nongovernmental organizations is evidence of recent transnational growth. Further, nongovernmental organizations are increasingly allying themselves with a range of other state and non–state actors in the context of transnational advocacy networks. Transnational advocacy networks organize global civil society in ways that allow them to share information, raise awareness, set the global policy agenda, and influence the decisions and actions of world leaders.

- As the case study of Islam demonstrates, religious groups often have a strong transnational element that tends to unite all members of that religion despite national differences. However, given the political heritage of certain religious groups, it can be difficult to separate religious identity from political identity, and the link between these two identities varies significantly among those of the Islamic faith.

Like Christianity and Judaism, Islam is a very diverse religious tradition ranging from moderates to conservatives to fundamentalists to extremists and everything in between.

■ The case study of the global women's movement highlights activism coming from local experiences (from below) as well as from global institutions (from above). This renders Barber's binary construct of Jihad vs. McWorld problematic. While women's experiences and priorities certainly vary, the movement has identified common goals in terms of gender equality and women's empowerment. How we achieve those goals depends on cultural context and that difference has become an asset for the global women's movement to engage in society and embrace their beliefs.

key terms

democratic internationalism
European Union (EU)
fundamentalist/traditionalist
General Agreement on Tariffs and
   Trade (GATT)
global civil society (GCS)
globalization
gross domestic product (GDP)
industrial capitalism

International Monetary
   Fund (IMF)
Intergovernmental organizations
   (IGOs)
multinational corporations
   (MNCs)
nationalism
nongovernmental organizations
   (NGOs)

norms
social media
trade barriers
transnational/transnationalism
transnational advocacy
   networks (TANs)
transnational crime
World Trade Organization (WTO)

International Organizations: Global and Regional Governance

chapter 5

International organizations, such as the United Nations, the European Union, the North Atlantic Treaty Organization, and the Africa Union, deploy peace-keepers in conflict and disaster zones around the world. These peacekeepers serve a range of functions from military intervention to humanitarian assistance in hostile and often very poor environments. While the peacekeeping model, and peacekeepers themselves, demonstrate significant shortcomings, they often confront tremendous challenges in admirable ways. Pictured here are Brazilian peacekeepers deployed as part of the UN mission to Haiti in 2007.

LEARNING OBJECTIVES

This chapter chronicles both the nature and scope of global and regional international organizations, including why states choose to organize themselves collectively, how these organizations operate, and what impacts these global governing bodies can have on global politics, national behavior, and individual lives. In particular, the chapter will explore in-depth the United Nations and the European Union to illustrate the structures, policies, and controversies surrounding the world's leading international organizations. Upon completion of the chapter, you will be able to:

- Understand various theoretical perspectives on why intergovernmental organizations form and how these organizations function in the global system

- Identify the United Nations as a global international organization and comprehend the key debates related to the United Nations' structure, leadership, operations/activities, and founding principles in the current era

- Grasp the evolution of the European Union as a regional supranational organization and assess the current challenges to its governing structure and authority in the region

- Evaluate the relative success of international organizations as systems of global and regional governance in political environments that are constantly changing

From the United Nations (UN) to the European Union (EU), the World Trade Organization (WTO) to the North American Free Trade Agreement (NAFTA), or the World Bank to the Economic Community of West African States (ECOWAS), **intergovernmental organizations (IGOs)** are increasingly important actors in global politics today. While there is considerable diversity among IGOs, these organizations are distinct in that their membership is state-based. National governments rather than private groups or individuals constitute an IGO. In this way, IGOs often operate as alternatives to the traditional authority of sovereign states. This alternative can work to trump state sovereignty, reinforce state sovereignty, or sometimes do both simultaneously. In this way, the relationship between IGOs is complex and constantly shifting. The sheer number of IGOs has grown dramatically in the last 60 years, as has their reach, in terms of geography, issues, and actors involved.

Nowhere is this growth in numbers and expansion in activities more evident than in the case of international peacekeeping operations as a central approach to global and regional security governance. Peacekeeping missions have increased dramatically since the end of the Cold War and have expanded to address different types of conflict and take on different responsibilities. Further, no longer is peacekeeping under the sole purview of the UN. The UN, the EU, the North Atlantic Treaty Organization (NATO), and the African Union (AU), among others, now deploy peacekeepers as missions. Often these deployments overlap in certain areas. In Kosovo, for example, you could find peacekeepers from the UN mission, the (UN authorized) NATO mission, and from the EU under the European Security and Defense Policy. Another example would be the joint UN-AU peacekeeping mission in Darfur. With a force of approximately 26,000, which began deployment in 2007, it is the largest peacekeeping mission to date. While the various IGOs often "partner" in these peace missions, many times there is a considerable amount of overlap. Still, peacekeepers come from national armies representing their sovereign states. There is no standing army or peacekeeping unit, for example, at the UN ready for deployment. In most IGOs, peacekeepers are not vetted by the organization, but rather by the unique national military and government standards. In this way, peacekeeping as a case represents the simultaneous gains and challenges that IGOs face in coordinating collective action while also preserving and respecting the sovereign rights of states—both those that are contributing troops and police units to peace missions as well as those living and fighting in the target states. Thus, throughout this chapter, we will return to the case of peacekeeping to illustrate some key trends, achievements, and challenges of IGOs in the 21st century.

OVERVIEW OF IGOs

Intergovernmental organizations (IGOs)
International/transnational bodies that are composed of member-countries.

There is a great deal of variance among IGOs. Some of them, such as the UN, have many members. As of 2011, UN membership reached 193 with the addition of South Sudan. Other IGOs, like Africa's Economic Community of the Great Lakes Countries or NAFTA, each with only three members, are quite small. Relatedly, IGOs are different in terms of global and regional membership, the latter referring

Facilitator of Cooperation   Another IGO role is to promote and facilitate cooperation among states and other global actors. Secretary-General Kofi Annan observed correctly that the UN's "member-states face a wide range of new and unprecedented threats and challenges. Many of these transcend borders and are beyond the power of any single nation to address on its own."[7] Therefore, countries have found it increasingly necessary to cooperate to address physical security, the environment, the economy, and a range of other concerns. The Council of the Baltic Sea States, the International Civil Aviation Organization, and a host of other IGOs all came about to address specific needs and, through their operations, to promote further cooperation.

When cooperation develops in a number of related areas, then **regime theory** argues that the specific points of cooperation become connected with one another in more complex forms of interdependence called an *international regime*. This term does not refer to a single organization. Instead, *regime* is a collective noun that designates a complex of norms, rules, processes, and organizations that, in sum, have evolved to help govern the behavior of states and other global actors in an area of international concern. Central to international regimes are their association with a specific issue, such as nuclear weapons proliferation or food aid.

One such area is the use and protection of international bodies of water and the corresponding regime that has evolved for oceans and seas (Heasley, 2003). Figure 5.1 depicts this regime's array of organizations, rules, and norms that promote international

Regime theory
Derived from liberal tradition, regime theory argues that international institutions or regimes affect the behavior of states, assuming that cooperation is possible in the anarchic system of states.

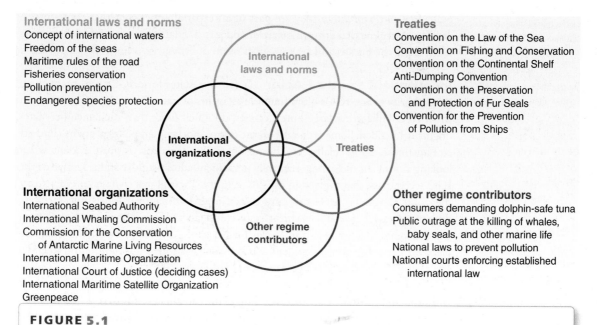

International laws and norms
Concept of international waters
Freedom of the seas
Maritime rules of the road
Fisheries conservation
Pollution prevention
Endangered species protection

Treaties
Convention on the Law of the Sea
Convention on Fishing and Conservation
Convention on the Continental Shelf
Anti-Dumping Convention
Convention on the Preservation
    and Protection of Fur Seals
Convention for the Prevention
    of Pollution from Ships

International organizations
International Seabed Authority
International Whaling Commission
Commission for the Conservation
    of Antarctic Marine Living Resources
International Maritime Organization
International Court of Justice (deciding cases)
International Maritime Satellite Organization
Greenpeace

Other regime contributors
Consumers demanding dolphin-safe tuna
Public outrage at the killing of whales,
    baby seals, and other marine life
National laws to prevent pollution
National courts enforcing established
    international law

FIGURE 5.1

Regimes for oceans and seas

The concept of an international regime represents the nexus of a range of rules, actors, and other contributors that regulate a particular area of concern. This figure shows some of the elements of the expanding regime for oceans and seas.

Note: Entries are only a sample of all possibilities.

cooperation in a broad area of maritime regulation, including navigation, pollution, seabed mining, and fisheries. The UN Convention on the Law of the Sea (1994) proclaims that the oceans and seabed are a "common heritage of mankind," to be shared according to "a just and equitable economic order." To that end, the treaty provides increased international regulation of mining and other uses of the oceans' floors and empowers the International Seabed Authority to help advance the treaty's goals. On a related front, the International Maritime Organization has helped create safeguards against oil spills in the seas, which have declined dramatically since the early 1970s. The International Whaling Commission, the Convention on the Preservation and Protection of Fur Seals, and other efforts have begun the process of protecting marine life and conserving resources. The Montreal Guidelines on Land-Based Pollution suggest ways to prevent fertilizer and other land-based pollutants from running off into rivers and bays and then into the oceans. Countries have expanded their conservation zones to regulate fishing. The South Pacific Forum has limited the use of drift nets that indiscriminately catch and kill marine life. NGOs such as Greenpeace have pressed to protect the world's seas. Dolphins are killed less frequently because many consumers buy only those cans of tuna that display the dolphin-safe logo. It is not necessary to extend this list of multilateral law-making treaties, IGOs, NGOs, national efforts, and other programs that regulate the use of the seas to make the point that *in combination* they are part of an expanding network that constitutes a developing regime that governs behavior and sets standards for states and other actors when using the oceans and seas.

Independent Political Actor   Given that states form IGOs and grant them the authority to act, IGOs often function as agents of states. There are times, however, when IGOs, like other large bureaucracies, do much more than their member-states originally intended. Some even take on the role of independent political actors (Barnett & Finnemore, 2004; Haftel & Thompson, 2006). This role is most evident when looking at some of the strong, relatively permanent administrative staffs, known as the IGO secretariats, that evolved in the 20th century. These global civil servants act to set the political agenda, persuade states to act, draft international legislation, facilitate diplomatic exchanges, and monitor state compliance. From inspectors determining whether uranium enrichment in Iran is for peaceful purposes to maintaining surveillance on a possible bird flu epidemic, IGO secretariats are important and influential actors in global and regional governance (Mathiason, 2007).

These individuals often identify with the organization and try to increase its authority and role. As a result, one scholar contends that IGOs have a "strong measure of autonomy from their member-states" and are "especially likely to act on their own initiative if states are indifferent to a situation." IGOs "may act, at least obliquely, against the perceived interests of member-states, even against the interests of important states" (Ferguson, 2005:332). Thus, an IGO may be a force unto itself, more than the sum of its (member-country) parts. Sometimes this independence is controversial, as we shall see in the discussions of the UN and EU that follow. In other cases, a degree of organizational independence is intended and established in the charters of various IGOs, such as in the International Criminal Court, particularly in the role of the chief prosecutor (Schiff, 2008).

Supranational Authority Some people believe that the world is moving and should continue to move toward a more established form of global government (Tabb, 2004). "The very complexity of the current international scene," one scholar writes, "makes a fair and effective system of world governance more necessary than ever" (Hoffmann, 2003:27). This model envisions a role for IGOs as **supranational organizations** in which legal authority transfers from the sovereign members to the IGO to the point that the IGO can override decision-making at the national level.

> **Supranational organizations**
> An organization that is founded and operates, at least in part, on the idea that international organizations can or should have authority higher than individual states.

Some IGOs already possess a degree of limited supranationalism in specialized areas because many states in practice accept some IGO authority in the realm of "everyday global governance" (Slaughter, 2003). For example, countries now regularly give way when the World Trade Organization (WTO) rules that one of their laws or policies contravenes the WTO's underlying treaty, the General Agreement on Tariffs and Trade (GATT). The Dispute Settlement Unit has become a very busy international adjudicatory body. In just 15 years of its existence, it has had over 400 disputes on its docket. While it resolved close to half of these cases before proceeding to the adversarial panel process, "with a few exceptions, the remaining disputes that did go to full-fledged panel proceedings were resolved by Members who brought themselves into compliance with the rulings and recommendations of the Dispute Settlement Body" (Agah, 2010:1).

The European Union exercises even greater supranational authority on a regional level, as we will discuss in greater detail in the next section. It not only has most of the structure of a full-scale government, but it makes policy, has courts, receives taxes, holds international popular elections, and in many other, if still limited, ways functions like a government of Europe. A major question for the future is whether and how far to extend the supranational authority of IGOs and how to structure such powerful new actors.

Ultimately, limited supranationalism might evolve into regional governments or a world government. The powers of any such global or regional governments also range along a scale based on the degree of power sharing between the central government and the subordinate units, as Figure 5.2 depicts. Unitary government is at the end of the scale where the central government has all or most of the power and the subordinate units have little or none. In such a system, countries would be nonsovereign subordinate units that serve only administrative purposes. A less centralized alternative would be a federation, or federal government, one in which the central authority and the member-units each have substantial authority. The United States and Canada are both federal structures, with the 10 Canadian provinces having greater authority than the 50 U.S. states. A confederation is the least centralized of the three main arrangements. In a confederal government, the central government has quite limited powers, while the members retain all or most of their sovereign authority. The least centralized model of all, though, and one that borders on not being a government at all, is a league, an arrangement in which the centralized government is mostly symbolic and has little, if any, functional authority.

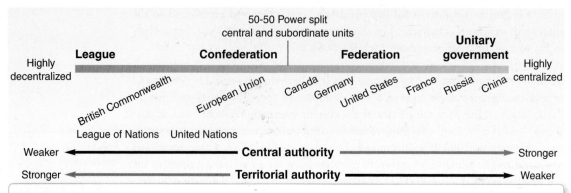

FIGURE 5.2

Power sharing in models of governance

Whether at the national, regional, or global level, governments share power between the central government and territorial governments in a variety of ways. In countries, territorial units are commonly termed states or provinces. In a global or regional government, countries would be the territorial unit. This figure shows the scale of possible power-sharing relationships. At one end of the scale, a league, the central government has little more than symbolic authority, and most power remains with the territorial units. At the other end of the scale, a unitary government, the central government monopolizes power and the territorial units perform only administrative functions. The most centralized international government organization today, the European Union, is a confederation.

Arguments for Expanding Supranational Authority   The arguments for greater global government begin with the criticism of the current state-based system, which chapter 6 details (Volgy & Bailin, 2002; Wendt, 2004). The World Federalist Movement (WFM), for one, argues, "Ours is a planet in crisis, suffering grave problems unable to be managed by nations acting separately in an ungoverned world." Given this perspective, the WFM calls for founding "world institutions . . . [with] actual and sufficient authority to make and enforce law in their given jurisdictions."[8] Note that the WFM and most others who favor greater global governance do not advocate the abolition of state sovereignty and the creation of an all-powerful world government. More common are calls for a federal structure, with countries retaining sovereignty over their internal affairs.

Arguments against Expanding Supranational Authority   Critics of greater global governance raise numerous objections (Coates, 2005). First, they argue that there are practical barriers. Their assumption is that nationalism has too strong a hold and that neither political leaders nor masses would be willing to surrender substantial sovereignty to a universal body. Second, critics of the world government movement pose political objections. They worry about the concentration of power that would be necessary to enforce international law and to address the world's monumental economic and social problems. Third, there is doubt whether any such government, even given unprecedented power, could succeed in solving world problems any better than states can. Fourth, some skeptics further argue that centralization would inevitably diminish desirable cultural diversity and political experimentation in the world. Fifth, some critics of the world government worry about preserving democracy. With power concentrated in a central global government and little countervailing power left to countries, the seizure of the world government by authoritative forces might, in a stroke, roll back hundreds of years of democratic evolution.

The idea of regional government does respond to some of these concerns. Regions would still have to bring heterogeneous peoples together and overcome nationalism, but that would be an easier task than addressing even greater global heterogeneity. Moreover, regional governments would allow for greater cultural diversity and political experimentation than would a global government. To this, skeptics reply that, at best, regional government is the lesser of two evils compared to global government. Opponents also contend that creating regional governments would simply shift the axis of conflict from among states to among regions. Indeed, in the novel *1984,* George Orwell predicted in 1949 that the future would find world political control exercised by three regional governments (Oceania, Eurasia, and Eastasia) all perpetually at war with one another. Making matters worse, democracy was a memory. The totalitarian iron hand of "Big Brother" ruled Oceania, and the other two megaregions were presumably also subject to authoritarian discipline. It is not hard to project the EU as the core of Eurasia, a U.S.-centered Oceania, and an Eastasia built around China. So, while Orwell's vision did not come to pass by 1984, opponents of regional or global government might contend that perhaps he should have entitled the book *2084.*

GLOBAL IGOs: FOCUS ON THE UNITED NATIONS

Of the growing range and importance of activities of IGOs at the global level, the United Nations' activities are by far the most notable. As Mingst and Karns argue, "more than sixty-five years after its creation, the UN continues to be the only . . . IGO of global scope and nearly universal membership that has an agenda encompassing the broadest range of governance issues . . . serv[ing] as the central cite for multilateral diplomacy" (2012:1). Therefore, this section focuses on the UN as a generalized study of the operation of IGOs and as a specific study of that key institution. We look at issues related to UN membership, voting procedures, executive leadership, administration and finance, and importantly, core functions and activities. Figure 5.3 provides an overview of the UN's structure, beginning with the six major bodies established by the UN Charter, the organization's principal constituent agreement. The figure also includes some of the specialized agencies and global conferences that have come to define the UN system's work and international capacity. Given the case study on peacekeeping in this chapter, it is worth pointing out the UN Department of Peacekeeping Operations is not one of the six founding bodies in the UN. The term "peacekeeping'" did not even appear in the Charter. Nonetheless, it has become a defining department within the organization operating under a separate budget and having deployed some 66 operations since 1948 when the United Nations Truce Supervision Organization (UNTSO) was authorized in the Middle East.

IGO Membership: Procedures and Challenges

Fundamentally, every IGO is an international organization whose membership comprises two or more states. Therefore, one key element of how an IGO operates is how it structures its membership, who it includes and excludes, and why. Membership matters in terms of the overall organization, as well as in terms of the

General Assembly
All 193 UN members, one vote per member
The main policy making and representative organ
Meets in regular sessions

UNITED NATIONS

Security Council
15 members
5 permanent, 10 serve 2-year terms
Veto power for permanent members
Responsible for maintenance of
   international peace and security
Establishes peacekeeping operations
   and international sanctions
Able to authorize military action under
   Chapter VII

International Court of Justice
15 judges, serving 9-year terms
Seated in The Hague
Settles legal disputes submitted by
   individual states according to
   noncompulsory jurisdiction
Gives advisory opinions on questions
   referred by other UN bodies

Secretariat
Headed by the Secretary-General, who serves in
   5-year terms
Carries out day-to-day operations of UN, ranging
   from dispute mediation to writing reports
   documenting and monitoring global problems

Trusteeship Council
Tasked to govern United Nations
   trust territories during decolonization
Task completed
Suspended operation in 1994

Economic and Social Council (ECOSOC)
54 members, serving 3-year terms
One vote per member
Coordinates activities of 14 specialized agencies,
   functional commissions, and regional commissions
Examines and recommends economic and social policies
   for member-states and the General Assembly

Specialized Agencies
Functional agencies affiliated with the UN but
   with separate governing structures
Under the Charter, they are incorporated under
   ECOSOC
Include IGOs such as the International Labor
   Organization, World Health Organization, and
   World Bank

Topic-Specific Conferences
Ad hoc events authorized by the UNGA or
   ECOSOC
Seek to raise awareness, develop new norms,
   and mobilize action on issues ranging from
   climate to LDCs to racism to women's rights

FIGURE 5.3
Structure of the UN system

various substructures within the organizations. For example, it is impossible to grasp the politics of the UN without awareness that the Security Council only has seats for 15 out of a body of 193 member-states, and 5 of the 15 are permanent seats reserved for China, France, Russia, the United Kingdom, and the United

States (also known as the **P5**). That means that the other 188 UN member-states must rotate on the Security Council, and therefore have a very limited say on Council matters like the deployment of peacekeepers around the world.

General Membership Issues Theoretically, membership in the UN and most other IGOs is open to any state that is both within the geographic and functional scope of that organization and also subscribes to its principles and practices. In reality, politics is sometimes an additional standard. Today, with the exception of the Holy See (the Vatican), the UN has universal membership, but that was not always the case.

Standards for admitting new members are a point of occasional political controversy. One instance occurred in 1998 when the General Assembly voted overwhelmingly to give Palestinians what amounts to an informal associate membership. They cannot vote, but they can take part in debates in the UN and perform other functions that states undertake. In late 2011, Palestinian President Mahmoud Abbas formally submitted a request to join the UN as a full member. The Security Council's Standing Committee on the Admission of New Members, at the time of this writing, is reviewing the application for admission. In order for the Palestinians to receive full admittance, they would need the UN Security Council's approval—9 votes out of 15 and no veto from any of its permanent members. Any Council recommendation for membership would then require a two-thirds majority vote in the General Assembly. However, the U.S. has made clear that it will wield its veto power in the Security Council before it ever reaches the General Assembly.

Sometimes successor state status can be a political issue. When the UN recognized Russia as the successor state to the Soviet Union, it meant, among other things, that Russia inherited the USSR's permanent seat and veto on the Security Council. Taking the opposite approach, the UN, in 1992, refused to recognize the Serbian-dominated government in Belgrade as the successor to Yugoslavia once that country broke apart. Instead, the General Assembly required Yugoslavia to (re)apply for admission, which it finally (re)granted in 2000.

Withdrawal, suspension, or expulsion is another issue. Nationalist China (Taiwan) was, in effect, ejected from the UN when the "China seat" transferred to the mainland. In a move close to expulsion, the General Assembly refused between 1974 and 1991 to seat South Africa's delegate because that country's apartheid policies violated the UN Charter. The refusal to recognize Yugoslavia as a successor state in 1992 began what was, in effect, an expulsion that lasted eight years until a less oppressive government gained power.

Membership in IGOs' Substructure As we mentioned earlier, not every internal decision-making structure in an IGO necessarily has representatives from each member-country. At the core of the UN and other IGOs there is usually a plenary representative body that includes all members. The **UN General Assembly (UNGA)** is the UN's **plenary body**. Such assemblies normally have broad authority within their organizations and are supposedly the most powerful elements of their organizations. In practice, however, the assembly may be secondary to the administrative structure or some other part of the organization. Another type of representative body is a **limited membership council**. Based on the theory that smaller groups can operate more efficiently than large assemblies, many councils have representatives only

---

P5
Refers to the five permanent members of the UN Security Council who have the power to veto resolutions. These include China, France, Russia, the United Kingdom, and the United States.

UN General Assembly (UNGA)
The main representative body of the United Nations, composed of all 192 member states where each state has one vote.

Plenary body
A session that is fully attended by all qualified members.

Limited membership council
A representative organization body of the UN that grants special status to members who have a greater stake, responsibility, or capacity in a particular area of concern. The UN Security Council is an example.

from some parent organization's membership. For example, the UN's Economic and Social Council (ECOSOC) has representatives from 54 members, elected by the General Assembly for 3-year terms based on a plan of geographical representation. Sometimes membership is limited on the theory that some members have a greater concern or capacity in a particular area. The UN Security Council (UNSC) has five permanent members who were the leading victorious powers at the end of World War II and, thus, founders thought had a special role to play in matters of security. Additionally, with the idea of keeping membership limited to improve efficiency, the UNSC set total membership at 15, with the UNGA choosing 10 nonpermanent members for 2-year terms. Do not interpret the emphasis on the P5's powerful role on the Security Council as meaning that the other 10 seats have little consequence. While secondary to the P5, the rotating seats are important and much sought after by members. Not only do these nonpermanent members share the limelight in a key decision-making body, but some of them receive increased foreign aid and other incentives from the United States and perhaps other big powers in order to win their cooperation (Kuziemko & Werker, 2006).

Controversy over Membership on the UN Security Council   The P5's permanent status and veto power reflect the distribution of military power in 1945, and have always been very controversial, particularly among small and middle power states. Given the many changes in the global system since the end of WW II and the fact that other states actually contribute more to the UN than some of the P5 members, individuals have raised many legitimate and serious criticisms against the UNSC. Lack of democracy is one line of criticism. Expressing this view, Zambia's president argued that the council "can no longer be maintained like the sanctuary of the Holy of Holies with only the original members acting as high priests, deciding on issues for the rest of the world who cannot be admitted."[9] Geographic and demographic imbalance is another source of criticism. Geographically, Europe and North America have four of five permanent seats, and those four permanent members are also countries of predominantly Eurowhite and Christian heritage. Yet other criticism charges that the permanent members are an inaccurate reflection of power realities. As the German mission to the UN puts it, "The Security Council as it stands does not reflect today's world which has changed dramatically since 1945."[10] From this perspective, Germany, India, Japan, and some other powerful countries have begun to press for permanent seats for themselves.

In recent years there have been a number of proposals to expand the UNSC's membership and, in some cases, to increase the number of permanent members, although to date no consensus has emerged of what direction such reform might take. Some reform proposals have sought to give the new permanent members a veto. Even more proposals have called for the elimination of the veto power of permanent members. Most countries in the UN favor reform, yet none has been possible because of the two nearly insurmountable hurdles to amending the UN Charter and altering the UNSC's composition. First, Charter amendments require the approval of two-thirds of the Security Council, and the P5 are not especially open to diluting their influence by adding more permanent members, by giving new permanent members a veto, or, least of all, by eliminating the veto altogether. Specific rivalries also influence the P5. China, for instance, would be reluctant to see either of its two great Asian power rivals, Japan or India, get a permanent seat. Beijing also complains that Japan has not apologized adequately for its aggression and

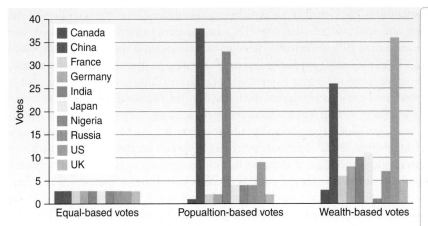

FIGURE 5.4

IGO voting formulas

To see the impact of various voting formulas, imagine that the UN allocated the 193 votes in the GA based on one-state-one-vote, population, or wealth. Voting power would vary widely depending on which formula was used. Which formula is the most fair? Which is the most equitable? Should other factors be taken into consideration such as a country's geographic territory or level of democracy domestically?

atrocities during World War II. Second, another hurdle for a Charter revision is to get a two-thirds vote of the UNGA. There, agreement on any new voting formula would be difficult, given the sensitivities of the 193 countries. For example, the proposal that India have a permanent seat alarms Pakistan, whose UN representative has characterized the idea as "an undisguised grab for power and privilege."[11]

Voting Formulas and Debates

One of the difficult issues that any IGO faces is its formula for allocating votes. At least one of the major IGOs uses three formulas—majority voting, weighted voting, and unanimity voting. The implications of various voting formulas are evident in Figure 5.4.

Majority voting is the most common formula IGOs use. This system has two main components: (1) Each member casts one equal vote based on the concept of sovereign equality, and (2) the issue is carried by a simple majority (50% plus one vote), reflecting the democratic notion that the will of the majority should prevail. The UNGA and most other UN bodies operate on this principle. A variation is supermajority voting. This requires more than a simple majority to pass measures. A two-thirds vote is most common, and some of the supermajority formulas, like the one the Council of the European Union uses, can be quite complex.

The objection to equal voting power is that it does not reflect some standards of reality. Should Costa Rica, with no army, cast an equal vote with the powerful United States? Should San Marino, with a population of thousands, cast the same vote as China, with its more than 1.3 billion people? Note, for example, that in the UNGA, two-thirds of the votes may be wielded by 128 states whose combined populations are less than 15% of the world's population. In contrast, the 11 countries with populations over 100 million combine for 61% of the world's population, yet they have just 6% of the available votes in the General Assembly.

Weighted voting allocates unequal voting power on the basis of a formula. Two possible criteria are *population* and *wealth*. As detailed later, the European Parliament provides an example of an international representative body based in part on population. The World Bank and the International Monetary Fund are based on member

Majority voting
A system that counts votes based on the concept of sovereign equality and the democratic notion that majority should prevail.

Weighted voting
A voting formula that counts votes depending on what criterion is deemed to be the most significant, such as population or wealth.

contributions. The United States alone commands about 17% of the votes in the IMF, and it and a handful of other top EDCs have majority control, yet combined have little more than 10% of the world's population. In contrast, China and India combined have 37% of the world's population, yet combined have less than 6% of the IMF votes.[12] This wealth-weighted voting is especially offensive to LDCs, which contend that it perpetuates the system of imperial domination by the industrialized countries.

Unanimity voting

A system used to determine how votes should count. In this system, in order for a vote to be valid, all members must agree to the proposed measure. Abstention from a vote may or may not block an agreement.

Unanimity voting requires unanimous consent, although sometimes an abstention does not block agreement. The Organization for Economic Cooperation and Development (OECD) and some other IGOs operate on that formula. Unanimity preserves the concept of sovereignty but can easily lead to stalemate. In a related formula, as noted, the rules of the UNSC allow any of the five permanent members to veto proposals. Taking exception to this arrangement, a Venezuelan diplomat described the veto as "an antidemocratic practice . . . not in accordance with the principle of the sovereign equality of states."[13] During the Cold War, for example, mostly the Soviet Union frequently cast vetoes. More recently, the number of vetoes has dropped sharply. During the Cold War the UNSC employed the veto power over 200 times, and since the end of the Cold War it has used the veto power in about 50 instances. Notably, the U.S. cast 69% of the vetoes between 2001 and 2011, 10 of 11 of which were cast under the Bush administration.

Although the use of the veto has declined dramatically, the power remains important. First, vetoes are still sometimes cast in critical cases. In 2006, for example, the United States vetoed a resolution calling on Israeli forces to withdraw from Gaza on the grounds that the resolution ignored the provocation—the kidnapping of two Israeli soldiers. Second, and more commonly, a veto threat can persuade countries not to press an initiative. For example, the United States and Great Britain did not push for Security Council authorization to take military action against Iraq in 2003 because it was clear that even if it could garner majority support, France and Russia would exercise their veto power. In 2006, the Security Council decided the race for Secretary-General in an informal vote. Voting was anonymous, but the P5's votes were coded distinctly, and every candidate but Ban Ki-moon received at least one "discourage" vote from a member with a veto. Recognizing reality, the other candidates all withdrew, and the Council soon nominated Ban. The veto can also serve as a diplomatic tool. The United States, for instance, has successfully pressured the UN to exempt U.S. troops serving as UN peacekeepers from the jurisdiction of the International Criminal Court by threatening to veto all UN peacekeeping operations.

Leadership

International organizations rely on member-states, executive heads, and even non–state actors to exercise initiative and leadership. Administrative structures, or secretariats, are critical to guiding and directing these large, multilateral organizations and often wield a significant amount of power in the process. The UN's **Secretariat** employs approximately 55,000 professional and support staff based in UN offices all over the world. The **Secretary-General (SG)** is the "chief executive officer" (CEO) of this complex UN system, serving as both the managing administrator of the Secretariat as well as the diplomatic figurehead of the entire global institution. Virtually all IGOs have some type of chief administrative officer with varying degrees of authority, legitimacy, and power.

Secretariat

The administrative organ of the United Nations, headed by the Secretary-General.

Secretary-General (SG)

The Secretary-General is the head of the Secretariat of the United Nations and serves as the UN spokesperson.

United Nations Secretary-General The SG, a complex and often highly political position, primarily answers to two constituencies: the Secretariat and member-states. In this balancing act, the SG is responsible for managing the Secretariat, preparing the UN's budget, submitting an annual report to the UNGA, overseeing studies conducted at the request of other major organizations, and bringing any issues to the UNSC that may threaten international peace and security. This is a tall order that at times grants the SG the authority to act independently and even progressively as a political actor. Such leadership has become largely dependent on the individual SG's personality. As the Thinking Theoretically box demonstrates, leaders like Dag Hammarskjöld have been particularly instrumental in putting forth a neoliberal institutionalist agenda and pushing the UN forward as a driver of ideas and new norms.

One indication that IGOs are important players on the world stage is the often intense struggle among member-countries over who will head various IGOs. Clearly, the selection process would not engender so much sound and fury if it were not important. Formally, the process of selecting the Secretary-General involves the Security Council nominating one or more candidates for the post and the General Assembly then electing one candidate for a 5-year term. Reality is less democratic than theory. In practice, the Security Council controls the choice by submitting only one name to the General Assembly. Moreover, each of the permanent members, the P5, can and does veto candidates, and still other possible contenders do not even bother to seek the office because of known opposition from one or more of the P5. The selection of Secretary-General Ban Ki-moon from the Republic of Korea (South Korea) in 2006 seemed somewhat less contentious than that of his immediate predecessors, but there was still considerable maneuvering, most of it behind tightly shut diplomatic doors. Not surprisingly, Ban Ki-moon, like those elected before him, comes from a relatively small and noncontroversial state.

Succeeding Kofi Annan in 2007, Ban Ki-moon became the eighth man to serve as SG and was just reelected to a second term in 2011. Like his two immediate predecessors, the Security Council selected Ban, in part, because of his reputation as a quiet diplomat and one who does not assert-

U.N. Secretary-General Ban Ki-moon talks to media during a press conference after the Istanbul Conference of Somalia, on May 22, 2010. He is appealing for global support to assist Somalia as it attempts to establish a stable and authoritative government. The Secretary-General has historically been a substantial advocate in the global arena for impoverished societies and failed states.

ively promote the role of the UN as an autonomous force in world politics. However, neither Boutros Boutros-Ghali nor Kofi Annan had complied with that expectation. What Ban's record will be in the long run remains unclear. He says of himself, "I may look soft from the outside, but I have inner strength when it's really necessary."[14] While this low profile seemed to work for Ban in persuading the Myanmar government to accept humanitarian assistance after the Cyclone Nargis in 2008, it has produced dismal

thinking theoretically

The Neoliberal Legacy of Dag Hammarskjöld

International organizations are often the products of collaboration among diverse people and groups. Their development is a result of the individuals who shape them during both their creation and their implementation. The United Nations is a product of many individuals, each with their own theoretical ideologies. Dag Hammarskjöld, the second Secretary-General of the United Nations, perhaps best exemplifies this. His actions as Secretary-General reinforced his neoliberal institutionalist identity and expanded the role of the Secretary-General into a more active agent and leader in the global community. He is one individual among many who demonstrated not only how theoretical worldviews matter, but also how individuals can play a critical role in the development and future impact of IGOs.

Prior to his April 1953 unanimous appointment by the General Assembly as the second UN Secretary-General, the relatively unknown Hammarskjöld served as a Swedish delegate to the UN as well as Secretary-General of the Swedish Foreign Office, and held numerous financial positions with the National Bank of Sweden. His 1953 to 1961 term was a time threatened by Cold War tensions and the sovereign control of nuclear weapons. During his tenure, Hammarskjöld redefined the role of the UN and Secretary-General in international relations,

often defying the egos and desires of powerful member-states in pursuit of common peace.

Hammarskjöld embodied the ideals and principles of neoliberal institutionalism. He believed that despite the system's anarchic nature and states pursuing their narrow self-interest, collectively members could identify common goals and cooperation could emerge. He pursued these common goals because he believed that such collaboration would mutually benefit the global community over the long run (Boehmer, 2006).

In this way, Hammarskjöld applied neoliberal institutional theory in practice through his actions as Secretary-General. One year after taking office, in an unprecedented move, the General Assembly asked Hammarskjöld to intervene on behalf of 11 American airmen imprisoned by the People's Republic of China, which had no UN representation (Dag Hammarskjöld Library, 2012). His success in negotiating their release demonstrated his strong diplomatic skills, and perhaps more importantly, the role that the UN can take in interstate relations, even with nonmember-states. Both the U.S. and China benefited from these negotiations. China released the airmen, and the negotiations established the groundwork for the admission of the People's Republic to the UN. Hammarskjöld's mediation enabled both sides to save face, and ultimately

results for Ban motivating states to meaningfully address climate change, one of his top priorities since his election.

As Ban's leadership at the UN develops, the debate over the proper role of top officials in other IGOs will continue. Traditionally, national states have sought to control IGOs and their leaders. As IGOs and their leaders have grown stronger, however, they have more often struck out independently and even in opposition to certain powerful states. As former SG Kofi Annan commented, all the Secretaries-General have carried out their traditional role as chief administrative officer, but they have also to one degree or another assumed an alternative role, one that Kofi Annan described as "an instrument of the larger interest, beyond national rivalries and regional concerns."[15]

Administration and Finance

Related to challenges of leadership, no organization can be successful unless it is well organized and efficient and also receives the staffing and budget resources it needs to accomplish its missions. Matters such as staff and finances are critical to the UN, like other IGOs, even though they do not often capture headlines.

cooperate for mutual gain. Many credit him with "inventing the idea of preventive diplomacy" (Mingst & Karns, 2012:85)

Hammarskjöld also initiated UN peacekeeping operations with the creation of the United Nations Emergency Force (UNEF). This force was meant to peacefully settle the dispute and quell the violence that erupted over the Suez Canal crisis in 1956. Importantly, the UN established UNEF to report to the General Assembly and it was not responsible to any singular nation. This was the first solely international military force and the predecessor to modern peacekeeping operations. UNEF met with great success, thus proving Hammarskjöld's diplomatic skills innovative and effective.

An extremely active Secretary-General, traveling the world, Hammarskjöld visited 21 African nations as part of the UN efforts to foster more inclusion and cooperation with African states. Hammarskjöld spent the last year and a half of his time as Secretary-General working to resolve violence in the Congo, including establishing the United Nations Force in the Congo (ONUC). The Soviet Union was extremely displeased with his actions, and called for his resignation. Hammarskjöld, however, stood firm in his beliefs and publicly dismissed this. Even if leaders and individual nations were not entirely in agreement, the goal was the greatest good for the most people. Hammarskjöld stayed loyal to this belief until his death in 1961.

A famous Hammarskjöld quote is, "The United Nations was not created to bring us to heaven, but to save us from hell" (Urquhart, 2011). Essentially, structures like the UN cannot bring about a perfect world where everyone gets exactly what he or she wants. What it can do, however, is save the world from another devastating world war. Hammarskjöld's actions and legacy at the UN paved the way for the negotiations and collaborations between many diverse nations. His neoliberal institutionalist ideals in the United Nations helped create the system that exists today.

Sources:

Boehmer C. 2006. Neoliberal Institutionalism. University of Texas El Paso, El Paso, TX. Available at http://utminers.utep.edu/crboehmer/Neo-Liberal%20Institutionalism.pdf

Dag Hammarskjöld Library. January 9, 2012. Dag Hammarskjöld: The UN Years. United Nations, New York. Available at http://www.un.org/depts/dhl/dag/index.html

Urquhart B. September 16, 2011. Learning from Hammarskjöld. *The New York Times*, New York. Available at http://www.nytimes.com/2011/09/17/opinion/learning-from-hammarskjold.html?_r=1

Administrative Challenges   The SG appoints the other principal officials of the Secretariat. However, in doing so, he or she must be sensitive to the desires of the dominant powers and also must pay attention to the geographic and, increasingly, to the gender composition of the Secretariat staff. For example, the UN has a relatively good record compared to most countries for increasing the percentage of management positions held by women. They now occupy more than 40% of the professional posts, up 11% since 1991, and, among the most senior UN positions, women fill about 28% of the jobs.[16] Still, this is far from 50% and no women have been among the top candidates for SG.

Controversies have occasionally arisen over these distributions, but in recent years the focus of criticism has been the size and effectiveness of the UN headquarters' staff in New York and its regional offices in Geneva, Nairobi, and Vienna. "Studies conducted both under the UN itself and by members such as the United States came to similar conclusions about the lack of coordination, the expansion of programs with little consideration of financial commitments, and weak to nonexistent program evaluation" (Mingst & Karns, 2012:58). In this way, the UN is like many other IGOs and, indeed, national governments, with allegedly bloated, inefficient, and unresponsive bureaucracies that have made them a lightning rod for discontent with member-governments.

Over the existence of the United Nations, its critics, especially those in the United States, have regularly charged that it costs too much, employs too many people, and manages its affairs poorly. Defenders reply that many of these charges reflect animus toward the UN rather than a balanced evaluation. As a commentary in the *Asia Times* put it, "unrelenting conservative attacks on the UN were never about 'mismanagement, waste and corruption' . . . [They were] always about policies and the temerity of the organization and its officials in defiantly holding onto policies that differed from Washington's."[17] There is an element of truth to this accusation, but even UN defenders have agreed that the organization's operation needs improvement. Soon after he became Secretary-General, Annan reported to the General Assembly that, to a degree, "over the course of the past half century certain . . . [UN] organizational features have . . . become fragmented, duplicative, and rigid."[18] To address these issues, the UN instituted many administrative changes. Budget increases have been modest, and the UN's staff member numbers have remained static despite significantly increased peacekeeping operations.

Bureaucracy
The bulk of the state's administrative structure that continues even when political leaders change.

As with almost any government **bureaucracy**, it is possible to find horror stories about the size and activities of IGO staffs. The oil-for-food program scandal and the evidence of sexual abuse of supposedly protected persons by UN peacekeeping troops and personnel that swept over the UN like a tsunami in 2004 are recent and particularly disturbing examples (Pilch, 2005). However, we need to put into perspective the charges that the UN and its associated agencies are corrupt and a bureaucratic swamp. It is important to recognize that all these problems also occur in national governments, including the U.S. government. The basic point is that the standards that one applies to the leaders of countries and those of IGOs should not differ, nor should reactions to bureaucratic blundering. Within countries, problems may lead to the abolition of a particular agency, but the thrust is reform, not destruction of the entire government. From this perspective, it is more reasonable to address problems at the UN through reform rather than by disbanding it.

Another way to gain insight about the size of the UN staff is to compare it to government employment in the United States. Between 1997 and 2007, there was nearly identical growth in the number of UN employees (11.3%) and U.S. federal, state, and local government employees (10.8%). The Secretariat's staff (44,134), which deals with a world population of 7 billion people, is about the same as the staff of San Antonio, Texas, which has 1.9 million people.[19]

Addressing these administrative challenges is especially difficult and complex in the UN where the Secretary-General has 192 bosses, each with self-interested views of bureaucratic arrangements and all squabbling among themselves as to what is superfluous and what is vital. In 2006, for instance, the Secretary-General proposed a plan to create several panels of countries to oversee UN finances, rather than leaving that task to the large, often unwieldy General Assembly. Many poor countries suspected, with some reason, that the proposal was meant to give additional financial control to the wealthier countries that contribute most of the UN's budget. "We should always remember that we are all equal partners in this organization, regardless of . . . how much we contribute to the budget of the organization," Egypt's ambassador asserted. With poor countries forming an overwhelming majority in the General Assembly, the proposal never moved forward, a fate that the British ambassador termed "destructive, a setback for the reform effort."[20] Reflecting such roadblocks, the U.S. General Accountability Office found that 70% of the reforms that the Secretary-General had initiated and could implement on his own authority had proceeded, but only 44% of 32 reforms needing member-country approval had made significant progress.[21] The implication of these data is that when members complain about the UN's operation, they might look to themselves as barriers to change.

Financial Realities in Context   All IGOs face the problem of obtaining sufficient funds to conduct their operations because most do not have independent sources of money and depend almost entirely on member-states for financial support. National contributions, while often assessed, are still voluntary, and IGOs have very little authority to compel member-countries to support them.

The United Nations budget system is complex. For the UN in its narrowest organizational sense, there are two budgets: the regular budget for operating the UN's headquarters, its organs, and major administrative units, and the peacekeeping budget to meet the expenses of operations conducted by the Security Council. Looking at the UN system in a broader sense also includes the specialized agencies budgets and the voluntary contributions budgets of the agencies and various other UN associated programs. The agencies raise some funds based on assessments on members, but they and some other UN programs rely for most of their funding on voluntary contributions of countries and private groups and individuals. UN spending through these budgets has increased considerably, but the lion's share of that increase has been caused by a sharp increase in funds for peacekeeping operations and money going to various UN socioeconomic programs, rather than to the central administration, as critics sometimes charge. These four budgets and some special budget categories, such as funding international tribunals, brought the total UN budget to about $18 billion in 2011.[22]

To pay for its regular and peacekeeping operations, the UN depends almost entirely on the assessments that it levies on member-countries. By ratifying the UN Charter and joining the UN, members accept a legal obligation to pay these assessments and may have their voting privilege in the General Assembly suspended if they fall behind by more than a year. A complicated equation that the General Assembly formulates based on national wealth determines the amount each country is supposed to pay. As a result, nine countries each have assessments of 2% or more of the budget. They and their percentages of the regular budget are the United States (22%), Japan (19.5%), Germany (8.7%), Great Britain (6.1%), France (6%), Italy (4.9%), Canada (2.8%), Spain (2.5%), and China (2.1%). At the other end of the financial scale, the UN assesses 48 countries at the minimum level, 0.001%. The assessment level for the specialized agencies is the same as for the regular budget. Because of their special responsibility (and their special privilege, the veto), permanent UNSC members pay a somewhat higher assessment for peacekeeping, with the U.S. share at 25%. Some criticize the assessment scheme on the grounds that while the nine countries with assessments of 2% or higher collectively pay almost 75% of the UN budget, they cast just 5% of the votes in the UNGA.[23]

Such numbers are something of a fiction, however, because some countries do not pay their assessment. In 2009, **arrearages** (unpaid assessments or debts) to the UN's regular budget exceeded $800 million, with the U.S. alone owing close to 90% of that total (Karns & Mingst, 2012:57). As a result, the UN's financial situation is always precarious because of the increasing demands to provide protection and help meet other humanitarian and social needs. "It is," a frustrated Boutros-Ghali observed, "as though the town fire department were being dispatched to put out fires raging in several places at once while a collection was being taken to raise money for the firefighting equipment."[24] The analogy between the UN's budget and firefighting is hardly hyperbole. During 2006, the public safety (police and fire departments) budget of New York City was larger than the UN peacekeeping budget.

Activities and Behaviors

The most important aspects of any intergovernmental organization are what it does, how well this corresponds to the functions that we wish it to perform, and how well it is performing its functions. The following pages will begin to explore these aspects by examining the scope of IGO activity, with emphasis on the UN. Much of this discussion will only briefly touch on these activities, which receive more attention in other chapters.

Peace and Security Goals

The opening words of the UN Charter dedicate the organization to saving "succeeding generations from the scourge of war, which . . . has brought untold sorrow to mankind." The UN attempts to fulfill this goal in numerous ways.

Creating norms against violence is one way. Countries that sign the Charter pledge to accept the principle "that armed force shall not be used, save in the common interest" and further agree to "refrain in their international relations from the threat or the use of force except in self-defense." Reaffirming the Charter's ideas, the UN (and other IGOs) condemned Iraq's invasion of Kuwait in 1990, Serbian aggression against its neighbors (the Croatian War of Independence from 1991–1995), and other such actions. These denunciations and the slowly developing norm against aggression have not halted violence, but they have created an increasing onus on countries that strike the first blow. When, for example, the United States acted unilaterally in 1989 to depose the regime of Panama's strongman General Manuel Noriega, the UN and the OAS condemned Washington's action. Five years later, when the United States toppled the regime in Haiti, Washington took care to win UN support for its action. Of course, norms do not always restrain countries, as the U.S.-led invasion of Iraq in 2003 demonstrates. Yet the efforts of U.S. and British diplomats to obtain a supportive UN resolution underlined the existence of the norm. Moreover, the angry reaction in many parts of the globe to the Anglo-American preemptive action and the postwar difficulties during the occupation may, in the long run, actually serve to reinforce the norm.

Providing a debate alternative is a peace-enhancing role for the UN and some other IGOs. Research shows that membership in IGOs tends to lessen

interstate military conflict (Chan, 2004). One reason is that IGOs serve as a forum in which members publicly air their points of view and privately negotiate their differences. Thus, the UN acts like a safety valve or perhaps a soundstage where players can carry out the world drama without the dire consequences that could occur if they would choose another method or locale. This grand-debate approach to peace involves denouncing your opponents, defending your actions, trying to influence world opinion, and winning symbolic victories.

Intervening diplomatically to assist and encourage countries to settle their disputes peacefully is another role that IGOs play. IGOs engage in such steps as providing a neutral setting for opposing parties to negotiate, mediating to broker a settlement between opposing parties, and even deciding issues between disputants in such forums as the International Court of Justice.

Promoting arms control and disarmament is another IGO function. The **International Atomic Energy Agency**, a specialized agency, focuses on the nonproliferation of nuclear weapons. The UN also sponsors numerous conferences on weapons and conflict and also has played an important role in the genesis of the Chemical Weapons Convention and other arms control agreements.

Imposing **sanctions** is a more forceful way to pressure countries that have attacked their neighbors or otherwise violated international law. As we will see in chapter 10, sanctions are controversial and often do not work, but sometimes they are effective and can serve as an important symbol of the views of the international community.

Peacekeeping is the best-known way that the UN and some other IGOs promote peace and security. chapter 7 extensively covers peacekeeping, but a few preliminary facts are appropriate here. Through 2011, the United Nations had mounted 68 peacekeeping operations, and they have utilized military and police personnel from most of the world's countries. These operations ranged from very lightly armed observer missions, through police forces, to full-fledged military forces. Never have international forces been as active as they are now. The number of UN peacekeeping operations has risen markedly in the post–Cold War era. As of November 2011, there were 16 UN peacekeeping forces of varying sizes in the field throughout the world, with about 98,000 troops and police from 115 countries deployed.[25] Fortunately, UN peacekeeping forces have suffered relatively few casualties, but almost 2,960 have died in world service. For these sacrifices and contributions to world order, the UN peacekeeping forces were awarded the 1988 Nobel Peace Prize. Peacekeeping has had successes, such as the Namibia mission from 1989–1990, as well as many failures including the UN's failure to act in Rwanda in 1994. Many individuals have criticized even the most successful cases. For example, Canadian political science scholar Sandra Whitworth (2004) raises critical questions about the deployment of soldiers who are trained to kill in traditional military organizations as *peacekeepers* tasked with maintaining law and order, rebuilding infrastructure, monitoring democratic elections, documenting gross human rights abuses, and providing humanitarian aid, among other tasks that we associate with **complex peacekeeping**.

Social, Economic, and Other Areas of Interest
In addition to maintaining and restoring the peace, IGOs engage in a wide variety of other activities. During its early years, the UN's emphasis was on security, a concern that has not abated, but

International Atomic Energy Agency (IAEA)
A critical organization in the nuclear nonproliferation regime, especially in its role in conducting international inspections of national nuclear facilities to promote safe, secure, and peaceful nuclear technologies according to the NPT.

Sanctions
Economic, diplomatic, or military actions put in place to punish a state in an attempt to coercively force states to comply with legal obligations.

Complex peacekeeping
International, multidimensional operations comprising a mix of military, police, and civilian components working together to lay the foundations of a sustainable peace.

has been joined by social, economic, environmental, and other nonmilitary security issues. This shift has been a result of the ebb and eventual end of the Cold War, the growing number of LDCs since the 1960s, realization that the environment is in danger, and changing global values that have brought an increased focus on human and political rights. "Peacekeeping operations claim the headlines," Secretary-General Annan observed astutely, "but by far the lion's share of our budget and personnel are devoted to the lower-profile work of . . . helping countries to create jobs and raise standards of living; delivering relief aid to victims of famine, war, and natural disasters; protecting refugees; promoting literacy; and fighting disease. To most people around the world, this is the face of the United Nations."[26] Recent examples of this effort include the UN program to supply emergency relief to people in the embattled region of Darfur in Sudan and the refugees from there who have fled to neighboring countries.

It would be impossible to list here, much less fully describe, the broad range of endeavors in which the UN and other IGOs are involved. Suffice it to say that they cover most of the issues that humans address at all levels of government. We will highlight many of these endeavors in subsequent chapters, so this discussion is limited to a few of the programs and successes of the UN and other IGOs.

Promoting economic development is an important role of the UN, with the United Nations Development Programme (UNDP), the World Bank, and a significant number of other global and regional IGOs working to improve the economic well-being of those who are deprived because of their location in an LDC, because of their gender, or for some other cause. The UNDP alone has a biennium income of about $10 billion and is the conduit of about another $1 billion in foreign aid from individual countries in support of thousands of projects globally.[27]

Advocating human rights is a closely related IGO role. Beginning with the **Universal Declaration of Human Rights** in 1948, the UN has actively promoted dozens of agreements on political, civil, economic, social, and cultural rights. The UN Commission on Human Rights has used its power of investigation and its ability to issue reports to expose abuses of human rights and to create pressure on the abusers by highlighting and condemning their transgressions. In an associated area, the International Labour Organization (ILO) leads the global effort to free the estimated 250 million children who are forced to work instead of attending school, to end the sexual predation of children that is big business in some parts of the world, and to eliminate other abuses that debase the meaning of childhood.

Advancing **international law** and norms is another important UN and IGO role (Coate & Fomerand, 2004). For example, international courts associated with IGOs help establish legal precedent. IGOs also sponsor multinational treaties, which may establish the assumption of law. Under UN auspices over 300 such treaties have been negotiated. As one scholar sees the norm-building function of IGOs, "The procedures and rules of international institutions create information structures. They determine what principles are acceptable as a basis for reducing conflicts and whether governmental actions are legitimate or illegitimate. Consequently, they help shape actors' expectations" (Keohane, 1998:91).

Improving the quality of human existence is a role that has many aspects. The UN High Commissioner for Refugees has provided shelter, fed, and assisted more than 34.4 million refugees from war, famine, and other dangers.[28] A wide variety of

Universal Declaration of Human Rights
Adopted by the UN General Assembly in 1948, it is the most fundamental internationally proclaimed statement of human rights in existence.

International law
The body of principles, customs, and rules regulating interactions among and between states, international organizations, individuals, and in more limited cases, multinational organizations.

on which they can later build. Still, others argue that international organizations are vehicles that states should manipulate to gain national political goals.

■ The United Nations provides an example of the development, structure, and roles of a global IGO, including peacekeeping, intervening diplomatically, imposing sanctions, promoting arms control, and supporting international law.

■ Fundamentally, every IGO is an international organization whose membership comprises two or more states. Therefore, one key element of how an IGO operates is how it structures its membership, who it includes and excludes, and why. Membership matters in terms of the overall organization, as well as within the various substructures within the organizations.

■ Closely related to the political challenges of membership is that of voting power. IGOs use a range of voting formulas, from majority-based to weighted to unanimity voting to give voices to its member-states. No voting formula is more consequential and controversial than the veto power of the P5.

■ The EU provides an example of the development, structure, and roles of a regional IGO. The EU has evolved considerably along the path of economic integration and is by far the most integrated regional organization.

■ The movement toward political integration is more recent and is proving more difficult than economic integration. The French and Dutch rejections of the proposed EU constitution were a significant setback in the process of EU expansion. The financial crisis beginning in 2008 continues to challenge European integration and demonstrates how integration is not necessarily linear or permanent.

■ However one defines the best purpose of an international organization, it is important to have realistic standards of evaluation both in terms of the organization's goals as well as what is possible in given time frames.

key **terms**

arrearages
bureaucracy
complex peacekeeping
euro (€)
European Coal and Steel
 Community (ECSC)
European Commission
European Communities (EC)
European Council
European Court of Justice
European Parliament (EP)
European Union (EU)
functionalism
International Atomic Energy
 Agency (IAEA)
international institutions
international law

Intergovernmental organizations
 (IGOs)
League of Nations
less developed countries (LDCs)
Limited membership council
Lisbon Treaty
Maastricht Treaty
majority voting
Millennium Development
 Goals (MDGs)
Montreal Protocol
neofunctionalism
Neoliberal institutionalism (NLI)
P5
plenary body
public goods
Regime theory

realism
sanctions
Secretariat
Secretary-General (SG)
self-determination
Supranational organizations
The Hague system
Treaty of Amsterdam
Treaty of Nice
UN Charter
UN General Assembly (UNGA)
UN Security Council (UNSC)
UN Trusteeship Council
Unanimity voting
Universal Declaration of
 Human Rights
weighted voting

Pursuing Security

chapter 6

Popular unrest throughout the Middle East and North Africa captivated the world's attention during the so-called Arab Spring. Tahrir Square in Cairo, pictured here, was the epicenter of the movement that ousted longtime ruler Hosni Mubarak and provided an opportunity for the enhanced security and well-being of millions of Egyptians in the process.

LEARNING OBJECTIVES

This chapter chronicles the fundamental importance of security in global politics, as well as changes in the way International Relations (IR) scholars and policy makers think about security from a conceptual and theoretical standpoint. Upon completion of the chapter, you will be able to:

- Identify and explain the defining features of security in the traditional (realist) view, including the concept of anarchy

- Grasp the basis for and main examples of efforts to "broaden" and "deepen" the concept of security over the past quarter-century

- Compare, contrast, and assess the differences in the conceptualization and provision of security from the differing reference points of the national, international/global, and human security approaches

- Recognize how broader structural transformation in the global political system since the end of the Cold War has created, or perhaps revealed, a so-called new security environment, which different rules, actors, problems, and threats define

onflict happens. Each of us engages in conflict with family members, roommates, and coworkers. However, most of us try rather hard to find ways to manage and resolve those conflicts short of violence, in ways that leave us better off in the long run. Unfortunately, that is not always the case when observing global politics. The next two chapters analyze various perspectives on conflict, ways to manage, reduce, and resolve it, and our collective desire to feel secure personally, locally, and nationally. We will do that first here by examining the evolving nature of the concept of security in theory and application before turning more directly to patterns of conflict and its (possible) resolution in the chapter that follows.

Many of the dilemmas involving security in the global political arena are evident in the so-called Arab Spring. This revolutionary wave of demonstrations and protests across the Middle East and North Africa began most prominently with an uprising against two decades of corrupt rule by Zine El-Abidine Ben Ali in Tunisia in December 2010, culminating in the collapse of Ben Ali's regime in mid-January 2011. This was followed by a revolution in Egypt, civil war in Libya, and major uprisings in Bahrain, Syria, and Yemen, as well as major protests in most of the remainder of the Arab world. Triggered by years of repressive and corrupt rule across the region, the Arab Spring—ignited by scores of mobilized young people, abetted by their easy familiarity with the tools of social media, and captured in the slogan *Ash-sha'b yurid isqat an-nizam* ("the people want to bring down the regime")—represents the greatest single example of mass political unrest since the end of the Cold War. It also sheds a great deal of light on the nature of security, and how that concept and our understanding and pursuit of it have begun to change. As such, we will return to the Arab Spring repeatedly throughout this chapter to emphasize key points concerning the central if evolving role of security in contemporary global politics.

THE TRADITIONAL APPROACH

Security
In global politics, a condition associated with individual nation-states, the global system, and/or individual human beings in which the subject is insulated from harm.

It is impossible to make sense of global politics without understanding the concept of **security**. It is a term that saturates the speeches of politicians, pundits, activists, and journalists who attach it to a range of issues at various levels of analysis. From energy security to food security, from the individual level to the global level, security is one of the most important and most contested concepts of our time. Security is the epitome of what the prominent social theorist W. B. Gallie referred to as an "essentially contested concept" (Gallie, 1956). Accordingly, one must accept that security is a relative, ambiguous, fluid, and subjective condition. At its core, the concept of security begs four fundamental questions (Williams, 2008:5):

- What is security?
- Whose security are we talking about?
- What counts as a security issue?
- How can we achieve security?

These questions highlight the fundamentally political nature of this concept, as security often determines who gets what, when, and how in world politics (Lasswell, 1936).

The traditional approach to security, particularly since the establishment of the Westphalian system, has emphasized the primacy of the state and the need for material capabilities to defend and advance the state's interests. This typically translates into states cultivating military preparedness in order to preserve their sovereignty and territorial integrity at all costs. Accordingly, **national security** has become synonymous with national self-defense, with the resulting state-level defense posture resting on the amassing of military force (including arms and projection capabilities) to deter aggression.

However, this traditional approach to security also has its evident drawbacks. In revisiting our consideration of the Arab Spring, such an approach places primary if not sole emphasis on the security of each individual state. At least, in theory this extends each state "carte blanche" to preserve and protect itself by any and all means necessary. From this perspective, the Tunisian, Egyptian, Bahraini, Syrian, or Yemeni regime (to name just a few) would have been well within their rights to assemble and deploy any and all resources necessary to ensure regime survival—whether in response to internal challenges from opposition forces, or external interference from the international community. Taken to the extreme, such a perspective would mean that any of these regimes capable of crushing their respective rebellions would be fully justified to do so, and above any criticism for it. From this extreme position we would also expect them to arm themselves, or perhaps even strike, against any outside state supporting such insurgency. Clearly, the fact that not all regimes act in this fashion, or support such acts, indicates that this traditional view of security has some problems in application—thereby opening the door for other ways for us to think about security.

Still, the power and appeal of the traditional approach and the ideas on which it rests persist. To that end, we need look no further than how the world spends its money in the pursuit of security (Figure 6.1). According to the Stockholm International Peace Research Institute (SIPRI), in 2011 the world spent about $1,740 billion on military expenditures, an increase of 1.8% from 2010. This relatively small increase was undoubtedly a by-product of the global recession. Consider, for example, that global military expenditure grew by over 5% each year from 2000 to 2009. Of 2010 expenditures, the U.S. allocated just under $700 billion to its national defense budget (excluding special allocations for the military campaigns in Afghanistan and Iraq), accounting for over 43% of total global defense spending. With this enormous amount of spending in the name of national security, it is worth asking

> **National security**
> The requirement to maintain the survival of the state through all available means. Originally (and still largely) focused on amassing military strength to forestall the threat of military invasion by powerful adversaries, national security now also encompasses a broad range of factors impinging on a nation's nonmilitary or economic security, material interests, and values.

The brutal response of government forces to civil unrest in Syria since the fall of 2011 has elicited widespread condemnation of the Assad regime from the international community, as well as the deployment of observers from the Arab League and the appointment of a UN Special Envoy, former Secretary-General Kofi Annan. Nevertheless, the violence has continued unabated as of the time of this writing.

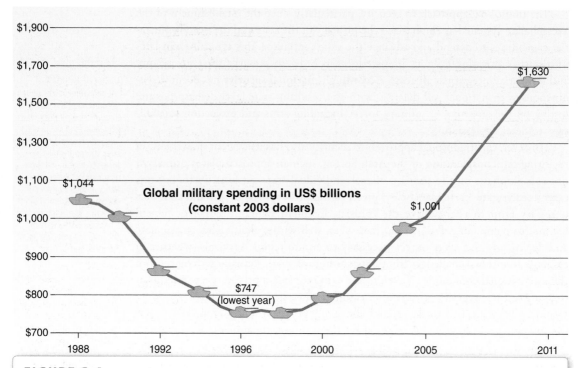

FIGURE 6.1

Global military spending

Global military spending peaked in the late 1980s at the end of the Cold War, then declined into the mid-1990s, reaching a low point in 1996 and being fairly steady for the rest of the decade. Beginning in 2000, arms spending began to accelerate more rapidly, increasing about 22% in constant 2003 dollars (adjusted for inflation) to just over $1 trillion in 2005, and crossing the $1.5 trillion mark in 2011.

Data Source: Stockholm International Peace Research Institute (SIPRI), 2004.

whether or not such policies actually make the world a more secure place. Perhaps the first Secretary-General of the United Nations, Trygve Lie, was onto something when he suggested that "wars occur because people prepare for conflict, rather than for peace."[1]

This chapter aims to think anew about security in light of humankind's failed effort to find it for extended periods of time. Because the emphasis on military defense has not brought us to a consistently secure place, it is only prudent to consider whether we can supplement, or even replace, traditional conceptions of security with alternative approaches to and ideas about security that are not similarly bound to the state. The origins of such alternatives require one to take seriously a range of diverse threats, "new" actors, and shifting global rules and norms. In examining these significant changes in the security landscape, this chapter seeks to understand better the dynamic of this **new security environment**, highlighting some of the most pressing security challenges of the 21st century.

New security environment
A catch-all term referring to the emergence of a multiplicity of "new" (or perhaps, newly recognized) threats to the security of states, individuals, and the global system in the contemporary (post–Cold War) world.

From the critics' vantage point, realism's unwavering emphasis on state sovereignty makes it unable to account for emerging security challenges that do not directly pertain to or impact the state, leading to potentially misleading or erroneous conclusions about the security status of a state and its citizens (Brown, 1998). For example, we might consider Haiti a relatively "secure" state in that it does not confront a major military challenge from any of its neighbors. Such a conclusion seems foolish in light of the crippling poverty and devastated infrastructure plaguing the country and leaving the vast majority of Haitians vulnerable and insecure. As a result, critics have called for the replacement of this "Westphalian" approach to security (so named for the Treaty of Westphalia, considered the basis for the creation of the modern state-based international system) with a "post-Westphalian" approach in which state sovereignty would no longer occupy a position of primacy, as Figure 6.3 depicts.

Security: The Westphalian View	Security: The Post-Westphalian View
Prevailing beliefs	*Prevailing beliefs*
• State sovereignty confers stability and order in world politics • Stability and order upheld by material power • Sovereign states have right to noninterference	• Political, economic, and social rights confer stability and human fulfillment in world politics • Stability and human fulfillment upheld by international institutions and law • State sovereignty entails responsibility on part of states to citizens
Trajectory	*Trajectory*
• Forceful preservation of interstate order begets . . . • interstate cooperation begets . . . • changing norms and values begets . . . • international peace and security.	• Changing norms and values begets . . . • interstate and transnational cooperation begets . . . • willing maintenance of global social order begets . . . • global peace and security.
Assumptions/implications	*Assumptions/implications*
• State sovereignty retains customary political and legal centrality • Security at state level, provided collectively via states • Security operations should be administered by states, and target interstate conflicts • Little role for international institutions, global civil society	• State sovereignty is in decline, requires reformation ("sovereignty as responsibility") • Security at global and individual level • Security operations should target intrastate as well as interstate conflicts • Major role for expanded international institutions, global civil society

FIGURE 6.3

Sovereignty and security at a crossroads

Much of the current debate over security turns on differing views of the importance of state sovereignty as a central organizing tenet of global politics.

Source: Adapted from: Bellamy, Williams, & Griffin (2010).

Broadening and Deepening the Security Agenda

The proliferation of ethnic conflict, humanitarian disaster, and general social disorder in Somalia, Bosnia, Rwanda, and beyond in the early to mid-1990s proved crucial to furthering the challenge to traditional definitions of security. While attempts to redefine security in the post–Cold War era proved controversial, consensus did emerge on two fronts.[2] First, it was impossible to ignore how globalization in all its speed, enormity, and complexity was impacting the security agenda at the local, national, and international level (Held & McGrew, 2001). Along these lines, one could not refute Rosenau's argument that "more than ever, security is elusive; more than ever, it is embedded in the interaction of localizing and globalizing forces" (1994:255). The increasing relevance and intensity of these local-global processes and interactions raised critical questions regarding the rationale for an exclusive focus on the state, and suggested that security might include concerns other than narrowly state-focused military ones and might point to responses beyond those associated with military capacity (Rothschild, 1995). In this way, it is becoming more and more difficult to draw clear lines between the pursuit of **global security** and national security.

On a second and related front, consensus began to emerge in both policy and academic circles on the need to focus on the individual as the subject of security rather than only on the state. We must understand this focus on the individual in the context of the 1990s when intrastate violence, civilian targets, and gross and systematic human rights violations that impinged upon the credibility of the state's claim to primacy in security increasingly defined armed conflict.[3] As a result, political scientists helped coin the term **human security**, intended to stand in contrast to the more traditional term "national security," thereby directing attention to a wider spectrum of security threats, both within and outside of the state. This new security conceptualization argued that, unlike under traditional approaches, people can be insecure inside a secure state and threats increasingly exist that lack identifiable enemies (Hamill, 1998).

This is where realist notions of security seemingly fall short. Kanti Bajpai (2000:51) observed that "realism's appropriation of the term security rests on the assumption that interstate war is the greatest threat to personal safety and freedom. This may or may not be the case at any given time." The conceptualization of human security, not merely the absence of military conflict between states, is a direct response to this critique. As Lloyd Axworthy (2001:19), a prominent Canadian politician, explains, human security "puts people first and recognizes that their safety is integral to the promotion and maintenance of international peace and security." At its core, human security has come to have meaning in terms of the individual, moving beyond purely state-based notions of military and territorial security.

One of the earliest statements concerning human security appeared in the UN's 1994 *Human Development Report*. The politics of security, the report made clear, must widen its focus and include not only "the security of borders [but] also . . . the security of people's lives" (UNDP, 1994:23). The final report from the UN Commission on Human Security further defined human security to mean "protecting fundamental freedoms . . . protecting people from critical (severe) and pervasive (widespread) threats and situations." (2003:4). The report further connects different

Global security
The efforts a community of states takes to protect against threats that are transnational in nature. The responses to these threats are usually multilateral, often involving regional and/or international organizations.

Human security
An emerging paradigm for understanding global vulnerabilities, proponents of which challenge the traditional notion of national security by arguing that the proper referent for security should be the individual rather than the state. Human security holds that a people-centered view of security is necessary for national, regional, and global stability.

types of freedoms—freedom from want, freedom from fear, and freedom to take action on one's own behalf—and offers two general strategies to address these fears: protection and empowerment. Expanding this notion, the report identified seven specific elements that comprise human security: economic security, food security, health security, environmental security, personal security, community security, and political security. The drafters of the report did not want to establish any definitional boundaries, but rather promote the "all-encompassing and integrative qualities of the human security concept, which they apparently viewed as among the concept's major strengths" (Paris 2003:255).

Many proponents of human security, however, do not see it as opposing or replacing traditional notions of security, but rather supplementing and complementing national security. According to the UN Human Commission on Human Security in its report, *Human Security Now* (2003:4), human security complements state security in four respects:

1. Its concern is the individual and the community rather than the state.

2. Menaces to people's security include threats to the state and conditions that have not always been classified as threats to state security.

3. The range of actors is expanded beyond the state alone.

4. Achieving human security includes not just protecting people, but empowering people to fend for themselves.

The report goes on to argue that human security and state security are "mutually reinforcing and dependent on each other." While many agree with these basic tenets, the report largely fails to address situations where human security and state security might be contradictory, and more important, how the international community ought to handle such contradictions and trade-offs when it comes to prioritizing resources.

Again, the Arab Spring provides an instructive tool for thinking about the redefinition of security and the notion of "human security." Whereas a narrow, state-centric conception of security might suggest that the security of the regional political order in the Middle East and North Africa take precedence, a broader reformulation of the concept points in a different direction. If we think beyond secure borders and stable regimes to consider the rights of actual human beings and the security of the social and natural environment they inhabit, then the plight of the majority of Arabs living under repressive and corrupt governments such as those administered by Zine Ben Ali, Hosni Mubarak, or Bashar al-Assad would point to massive insecurity

> Human security is predicated on a priority concern for the safety and well-being of individuals, especially civilians and noncombatants. Many contemporary peace operations are at least loosely predicated on this notion, and the need for peacekeepers to interact with the affected communities they seek to secure is vital to ensure the success of such operations.

under the veneer of a seemingly stable and secure state. From this alternative perspective, well-documented limitations on political freedom, educational and economic opportunity, and fair and impartial legislative and judicial procedures make Tunisians, Egyptians, and Syrians decidedly less secure than would the removal of such restrictions. Such has been the claim of many of the protesters and revolutionaries in these and other countries throughout the Arab Spring, as well as their supporters and sympathizers throughout the international community.

We can view the widely documented Arab Spring as, at least in part, triggered by the pervasive economic and political insecurity of people across the Arab world, as well as a response to the inability of their governments to advance policies to that end. Protesters in Tahrir Square in Cairo, Egypt (pictured here), sought to call attention to the lack of economic opportunity and affordable housing—both measures of insecurity from a human security vantage point.

Human security remains a highly contested and criticized concept, and "even some of the strongest proponents of human security recognize that it is, at best, poorly defined and unmeasured, and, at worst, a vague and logically inconsistent slogan" (King & Murray, 2001:591).[4] Critics often find the concept of human security inclusive to the point where it renders itself meaningless. Even for those who find validity in the concept, human security is still an "underdeveloped approach to understanding contemporary security politics" (Thomas & Tow, 2002:177). It still falls short of the efforts of critical scholars of security (sometimes referred to as the "Aberystwyth School," named for the Welsh university with which many proponents of such an approach have been associated) to advance a research program around what they consider the logical next step for security in the 21st century: namely, the recasting of security studies (and policies) to emphasize the security of the individual, defined as human emancipation (Booth, 1991, 2005; Krause & Williams, 1996, 1997; Wyn Jones, 1996, 2001; Sheehan, 2005).

While this approach encourages us to deepen our approach to security to individual and global levels of analysis, others, such as those from the Copenhagen Peace Research Institute (COPRI), have pushed for a broadening of security. Often referred to as the Copenhagen School, this group of scholars developed a theory of **securitization** that assumes a sectoral approach to security in which they introduced multiple realms of security concerns (military, political, social, economic, environmental, etc.) as a means of defining, analyzing, and responding to differing security threats. From this perspective, security does not refer to an objective reality corresponding with a distinct perception of threat, but rather to a speech act—that is, "the *word* 'security' is the act; the utterance is the primary reality" (Wæver, 1995:55). In other words, adherents to the Copenhagen School look at why some issues get securitized and receive priority treatment by states and international organizations, while others with crucial security implications for individuals, groups, and even nations do not.

One useful illustration here is what some have referred to as the securitization of climate change (Brown et al., 2007). Climatologists and security scholars alike have long warned that climate change threatens the security of food and water supplies, the allocation of important natural resources, and the very existence of coastal

Securitization
Assumes a sectoral approach to security in which multiple realms of security concerns (military, political, social, economic, environmental, etc.) are introduced as a means of defining, analyzing, and responding to differing security threats.

populations—all factors that could increase forced migration, raise tensions over scarce resources, and trigger armed conflicts. Such warnings went more or less unheeded in the United States until 2003, when the Defense Department commissioned a speculative analysis of the implications of climate change on international security.[5] In a textbook example of securitization, the 2003 Pentagon report sparked a flurry of media reports (including a *Fortune* magazine article famously labeling climate change the "mother of all security problems" [Stipp, 2004]), as well as further studies of the phenomenon by the American security and defense establishment. With respect to securitization, this example highlights the reality that securitization is a political act with real world implications, as you will read below with the case of energy security policy. As a result, not only can securitization legitimize the use of force and the ability of the state to take special measures, but it can also lead to the allocation of a substantial proportion of a state's resources to address a particular issue. Using security talk as a political framework for action elevates a particular issue or a vulnerable population, demanding that the state prioritize the issue or group.

Debating the Focus of Security

As we have discussed throughout this book, the theoretical lens through which one views global politics has direct implications for how you think about security. Theoretically inspired debates over the conceptualization of security illustrate the ways that theory matters in the real world. Decisions about who or on what to focus security concerns play an essential role in establishing who the most important actors are, what the chief threats to security are, and how states can manage and contain those threats.

A prime example of this is the debate over the appropriate security referent—the unit or actor that is the centerpiece of one's concern when thinking about security. Figure 6.4

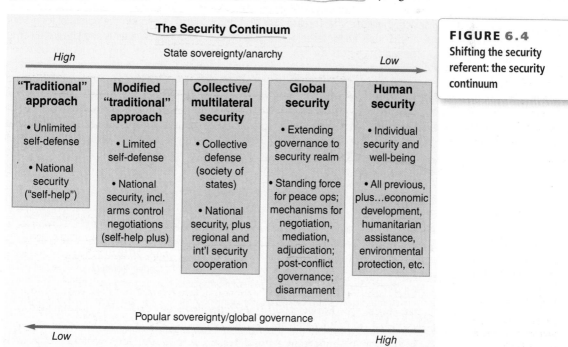

FIGURE 6.4
Shifting the security referent: the security continuum

thinking **theoretically**

The Drug War in Mexico

The debate over the appropriate reference point for security harkens back to the theoretical debates we introduced at the outset of this book. Consider, for example, drug-related turmoil in Mexico. According to a January 2011 estimate by Mexico's National Intelligence Service, more than 34,000 people have died in drug-related violence since the initiation of a major crackdown on Mexico's several powerful and competing drug cartels in December 2006. Although the violence appears to be spreading, the worst-hit areas have been the cities along Mexico's northern border with the United States (most notably Ciudad Juarez, just across from El Paso in Texas), as well as the states of Michoacan and Guerrero, major tourist centers along Mexico's Pacific coast.

From a traditional perspective, where the reference point for security thinking is the state, Mexico's security situation is hardly dire. Realists focus on the security of the state as something determined by the state's ability to identify and pursue its national interests, a function of the state's ability to guarantee its own survival. In other words, the state should seek to protect itself from attack by other states. Although the violent drug cartels are worthy of governmental attention, from a traditional security perspective they do not constitute a major security threat to Mexico, because the threat emanates from non–state actors operating largely within the domestic arena. The violent actors do not directly threaten Mexico's sovereignty and survival. The Mexican state is not likely to collapse, nor do any of its neighbors compromise Mexico's sovereignty. The world's preeminent military superpower, the United States, is working in close collaboration with and support of the Mexican government's crackdown. If anything, the deployment of more than 50,000 Mexican troops and federal police by the Calderon government demonstrates the Mexican state's viability and capacity.

Viewing the same situation through different security lenses, however, suggests that the security implications of Mexico's "war on drugs" are massive. If one considers the security of individual persons a prime concern (as some feminists and critical theorists advocate), the violent clashes between and among the cartels and the security forces clearly compromise the security of ordinary Mexicans. The discovery of mass graves has become commonplace, as have kidnappings, public beheadings, and other human rights atrocities. On the other hand, the security forces' broad leeway has led to intimidation, violence, and violations of the rights and liberties of Mexicans the government suspects of working with the cartels. The degree of corruption among the police further compromises the security of individuals as the police are woefully underpaid and therefore prone to bribery and infiltration by the well-funded cartels. This corruption makes threatened individuals reluctant to trust such unreliable sources of authority.

Another view of the drug war in Mexico comes from those concerned with the security of the regional and global system. The security implications of transnational activities involving non–state actors has become a hot button issue for liberal theorists, who emphasize the need for institutionalized cooperation in order to define and respond to security threats collectively. The Mexican cartels' domination of trafficking routes from South America to the United States suggests the regional, if not global, ramifications of these events. These are especially great for the U.S., which is the final destination for 90% of the cocaine trafficked through Mexico, a business enterprise estimated at $13 billion a year. The Mexican war on drugs is deeply intertwined with the United States, not only because of the insatiable demand from Americans for illicit drugs, but also through the potential for violent attacks on U.S. border patrol agents and citizens by drug traffickers. At the same time, the connection between drug trafficking and other transboundary phenomena such as migration, money laundering, gang violence, and arms transfers poses security problems not only for Mexico and the United States, but for all states in the region. This regional dimension is reflected in the Mérida Initiative, a multiyear commitment (currently totaling $1.6 billion) of equipment and training by the United States to law enforcement officials in Mexico as well as in Central America, Haiti, and the Dominican Republic.

Sources:

BBC, 2011. "Q&A: Mexico's Drug Related Violence."

BBC, 2010. "Mexico migrants victimized by drug cartels."

U.S. Department of State. 2010. *International Narcotics Control Strategy Report*. Under Secretary for Political Affairs, Bureau of International Narcotics and Law Enforcement Affairs.

U.S. Department of State. 2009. *Fact Sheet: The Merida Initiative*. Under Secretary for Political Affairs, Bureau of International Narcotics and Law Enforcement Affairs.

schematically depicts these different reference points and their corresponding approaches. Choosing the reference point for security is a crucial issue as policy makers and scholars attempt to make decisions about where to focus security policy attention in the real world and how to allocate resources to alleviate the identified security concerns.

THE "NEW" SECURITY ENVIRONMENT

Understanding the broadening and deepening of security as a concept, as well as the different "reference points," is crucial for comprehending the evolving security land-scape and the conflicts that characterize it. The remainder of this chapter highlights the real-world implications of this revised approach to thinking about security. The chapter synthesizes major contributions of contemporary security studies through discussion of the origins of the new security environment, the new and closely inter-related rules, actors, problems, and threats defining it, and the significance of these rules, actors, problems, and threats.

In revisiting the Arab Spring again, we can see how this new security environment affords us the ability to see the security implications of what a bygone era might have understood as "just" social protest or political unrest. In the realm of "rules," it is hard to dispute that an expanded and revised conception of sovereignty seeking to hold states to account with respect to how they treat their own people has risen to the fore both among the various opposition groups and in the international community at-large—so much so that NATO's military engagement cited this concept, dubbed the "**Responsibility to Protect**," or **R2P**, as a factor in intervening on behalf of the opposition forces in the Libyan civil war (Bellamy & Williams, 2011). So too has the diversity of actors capable of acting to advance their own security (and their own conception of it) shown itself within and across the various states experiencing unrest in the Arab world—whether in the form of NGOs, religious organizations, university students, or armed militia groups. In fact, the panoply of **non–state actors (NSAs)** has shown itself as more than a match for even the most tightly authoritarian and highly militarized states in the region. The efforts of these capable non–state actors to call attention to the insecurity of individuals and social groups under many prevail-ing Arab regimes—and the roots of that insecurity in such new security problems as insufficient economic opportunity, political corruption, inadequate housing supply, restrictions on political organization, and the like—offers copious evidence of the new security environment amid the Arab Spring. So too does the concern that some observers express about the range of possible new security threats that might result from such popular mobilization, particularly if the protestors' demands for change go unmet (Nasr, 2011). Such new threats could involve the expansion and intensifi-cation of transnational terrorist groups (such as al Qaeda and its affiliates), additional cases of intrastate fragmentation and conflict along ethnic, religious, or tribal lines (beyond Libya), or interruptions in the global energy supply and/or global commerce—to name just a few.

Post–Cold War Origins

A small cadre of residual Cold Warriors aside, the vast majority of scholars and prac-titioners concerned with security have come to accept, sometimes begrudgingly, the

Responsibility to Protect (R2P)
A global policy doctrine, endorsed by the UN in 2005, based on the idea that sovereignty confers responsibilities on states and their leaders—first and foremost, to ensure the well-being of their citizens. Among other things, R2P seeks to afford the international community the authority to address threats to human security in the event that a given state and its leaders are either unwilling to do so themselves, or are responsible for them.

Non–state actors (NSAs)
Entities participating or acting in the sphere of global politics; organizations with sufficient power to influence and cause change in politics that do not belong to or exist as a state structure or established institution of a state.

changing nature of security threats and responses. They also increasingly understand the often volatile and unpredictable nature of these changes. The notion that security, or at least how we think of security, has somehow changed has become mainstream. This characterization is difficult to dispute given the prominence of the "new security environment" as a point of reference in such disparate pockets of officialdom as UNESCO policy reports (UNESCO, 2001), position papers produced by the various U.S. war colleges (Yarger, 2010), and even keynote addresses by NATO military commanders (de Hoop Scheffer, 2005).

Those changes, and the recognition of them, are undoubtedly tied to the seismic geopolitical shift brought about by the collapse of the Soviet Union and the end of the Cold War. The end of a half century of **bipolarity** and the military, political, and ideological struggle that defined it cemented a transformation that began with Russian President Mikhail Gorbachev's reforms in the mid-1980s, continued with the fall of the Berlin Wall in 1989, and culminated in the collapse of the USSR in 1991. Differing interpretations of the significance of the end of the Cold War for global security ranged from proclamations of a utopian **"end of history"** (Fukuyama, 1989) to predictions of a multipolar balance of power arrayed across the United States, Europe, and Japan (Mearsheimer, 1990) to dire forecasts of an impending and all-encompassing **"clash of civilizations"** (Huntington, 1993).

The major, and perhaps only, common theme in attempts at forecasting the post–Cold War landscape was that dramatic changes were afoot. In a twist on President George H. W. Bush's much celebrated assertion of the emergence of a **New World Order** in conjunction with the international community's response to security challenges in the Persian Gulf and Somalia, one leading scholar referred to the post–Cold War period as one of "new world disorder" (Zartman, 2008). In this view of the contemporary security landscape, the end of the Cold War triggered or revealed a plethora of new or previously overlooked security threats and challenges. Included among these challenges were the increasing frequency of intrastate wars (many triggered by perceptions of non–state-based political identity rather than traditional national interests), the threat posed by the proliferation of weapons of mass destruction, the rampant spread of light weapons, the rise in both **failed/failing state(s)** and **predatory states**, the insecurity with competition over scarce natural resources, and forced migration.

Many observers have equated the transformation of contemporary security with the rise to the fore of transnational terrorism in the aftermath of the September 11, 2001, attacks on the World Trade Center and the Pentagon. Although continuous assertions that "9/11 changed everything" are rather trite, certainly 9/11 has had an appreciable effect on the ways that states define and pursue security. Perhaps most important from the standpoint of considerations of a new security environment, 9/11 illuminated for the first time for a mass audience, particularly in the United States, the importance of non–state actors and transnational forces and processes within the security realm. The importance of transnational terrorism notwithstanding, the concept of a new security environment, and the changing nature of security and conflict to which it refers, speaks to something much more fundamental and far-reaching than the perpetration of attacks by al Qaeda or its affiliates and subsidiaries. While we can certainly say that the changes at the heart of the aforementioned new security environment encompass transnational terrorism, they also include within their

Bipolarity
A type of international system with two roughly equal actors or coalitions of actors that divide the global political system into two "poles" or power centers.

"End of history"
Francis Fukuyama's thesis (1989, 1992) that the end of the Cold War marked the complete and total triumph of liberalism and therefore the end of "history" (defined by the 19th-century German philosopher Friedrich Hegel as the dialectical struggles produced by the existence of contending ideologies).

"Clash of civilizations"
Samuel P. Huntington's thesis (1993, 1996) that the source of future conflict will be along "civilizational" (e.g., cultural) lines, with conflicts emerging at the "fault lines" or interfaces of the most contentious of the world's major civilizational units.

New World Order
Refers to any period of history featuring a dramatic change in dominant norms and values and the associated balance of power.

Failed/failing state(s)
Countries in which political and economic upheaval are compounded by the fact that all or most of the citizens give their primary political loyalty to an ethnic group, a religious group, or some other source of political identity rather than the state itself. Such states are so fragmented that no one political group can govern effectively, undermining the capacity of the state and the security and well-being of those residing in the affected society.

purview ethnic conflict, state failure, ecological and natural resource wars, **genocide,** and numerous other security threats and challenges (C.A.S.E. Collective, 2006; Mathews, 1989). In that sense, we should understand events such as 9/11 or the end of the Cold War as reflections rather than causes of a deeper and more pronounced transformation in the global system that arguably began with the end of the Cold War.

Defining Features of the New Security Environment

The emergence of a new security environment occurred gradually, with origins stemming back decades. The extent to which its defining characteristics—shifting rules, newly emerging actors, intensifying threats—have reshaped and continue to reshape the contemporary security landscape renders them worth considering here.

Shifting Rules: State Sovereignty in Decline

State sovereignty has, of course, played a dominant role within the traditional approach to security. This characterization is borne out in the degree to which actionable security threats were almost exclusively those that compromised the political, legal, and/or territorial sovereignty of one or more states. Certainly, state sovereignty remains important today, and something that nations should not lose in a hurried embrace of a post-Westphalian conception of security. Yet in seeking to understand the complex dynamics of contemporary security, one must acknowledge that the preservation of state sovereignty is no longer the only important consideration. Empirical data suggest that states are increasingly unlikely to engage in even the definitive security concern of the traditional approach, armed conflicts. According to the estimates of the Uppsala Conflict Data Programme (Sweden), of the 30 active armed conflicts in 2010, none were interstate (UCDP, 2012).

Emerging Actors: The Impact of Non–State Actors

As we mentioned earlier, critics of realist theory often seek to rethink security beyond the singular emphasis on militarized interactions between competing states (Baldwin, 1997). The statist orientation of realism and its deliberate emphasis on power, order, and competing interests rendered realism highly useful for describing security threats and proscribing security responses in a Cold War world where states were dominant. Constructs like **deterrence, containment,** and **flexible response** undoubtedly provided the key intellectual grounds for the difficult balancing act nuclear bipolarity necessitated. However, given the central importance of social inequality, gender inequity, poverty and relative deprivation, resource scarcity and environmental degradation, organized crime, public health, external and internal migration, and the like to contemporary security threats and problems, the utility of such constructs is an open question. In a world in which the source, target, and delivery of a security threat may be only tangentially related to a state, its interests, or its military capabilities, a theoretical lens that emphasizes only those factors is inadequate. It is worth reading the "Challenge Your Assumptions" feature "Gender, Conflict, and UN Security Council Resolution 1325" to understand one situation in which this new security environment produced on-the-ground changes in the way the UN implements its peacekeeping operations in war-torn regions.

Predatory states
States governed by corrupt and repressive regimes that "prey" on the population and assets of the state and society they govern for the purpose of personal enrichment, and to the detriment of the collective well-being.

Genocide
The deliberate and systematic destruction of, or effort to destroy, in whole or in part, an ethnic, racial, religious, or national group.

Deterrence
Persuading an opponent not to carry out an undesirable action by combining both sufficient capabilities and credible threats so as to forestall that action.

Containment
A cornerstone of U.S. foreign policy during the Cold War, devised by George Kennan, which sought to prevent the spread of communism through a mix of coercive diplomacy, strong alliances, and military strength.

Flexible response
A defense strategy John F. Kennedy implemented in 1961 to address his administration's skepticism of Dwight Eisenhower's New Look and its policy of massive retaliation. Flexible response calls for mutual deterrence at strategic, tactical, and conventional levels, giving the United States the capability to respond to aggression across the spectrum of warfare.

challenge your assumptions

Gender, Conflict, and UN Security Council Resolution 1325

October 2010 marked the 10th anniversary of the passage of United Nations (UN) Security Council (SC) Resolution 1325. This landmark resolution was the first time the SC directly addressed the subject of women and armed conflict, not simply as vulnerable victims, but recognizing women as agents, with the right to participate in decision-making at all levels and during all phases of conflict and conflict resolution. Further, this unanimously adopted SC resolution calls for all participants in peace negotiations "to adopt a gender perspective" and "expresses its willingness to incorporate a gender perspective into peacekeeping operations" (S/1325/2000). In short, this resolution recognizes the importance of women in international peace and security policy, making women's needs and gender equality relevant to negotiating peace agreements, planning refugee camps and peacekeeping operations, designing disarmament, demobilization, and reintegration programs, generally reconstructing war-torn societies, and ultimately making gender equality relevant to every single Security Council action (Rehn & Sirleaf, 2002). In this way, Resolution 1325 represents the first time that gender mainstreaming has become official policy in the context of the UN's peace and security work, setting a new threshold of action for the Security Council, the UN system, and for all member states in the "new security environment."

On the ground, this resolution has translated into important procedural changes for UN country missions as well as a new focus on the individual security needs, particularly those of women, in conflict situations across the globe. A recent example is the UN's Global Open Day for Women and Peace Initiative, which it organized during the summer of 2010. This interagency project established official meetings between Special Representatives of the UN Secretary-General and other high-level officials and local women advocates in 20 post-conflict countries "to hear their concerns, and discuss how to increase women's participation in sustainable conflict resolution, peacemaking and peacebuilding" (http://www.unifem.org). Early reports indicate that many of these exchanges have been extremely powerful, especially for those heads of mission who have never actually heard from local women in any context.

One UN entity that has perhaps advanced the furthest in locating women in implementing SCR 1325 is the Department of UN Peacekeeping Operations (DPKO). DPKO has implemented significant organizational changes from the adoption of an internal action plan on 1325 to the establishment of a Gender Team at its UN headquarters to institutionalization of gender advisors or Gender Units in all peacekeeping missions established after 2000 (Tryggestad, 2009). With some select support from member-states, DPKO has also overseen the deployment of the first all-female unit of peacekeepers, which the UN first sent to Liberia in 2007. In 2011, the United Nations–African Union Mission in Darfur (UNAMID) began training the first all-female police contingent in Sudan. The establishment of these units is important as they seek to empower local women and further institutionalize gender-based violence as serious threats relevant to rebuilding security sectors in post-conflict societies. Gender training is also becoming a more standard procedure in peacekeeping missions. At minimum, these procedural shifts illustrate a move from an ad hoc consideration, at best, to a more systematic consideration of gender perspectives by the Council in peace missions.

Possibly one of the greatest achievements of SCR 1325 has been its ability to frame gender equality and women's rights as issues relevant to, if not central to, security provision. This has meant not only recognition of women's unique security needs during and after conflict, but acceptance of the notion that women's security is essential to the fundamental goal of the Security Council—the promotion and protection of international peace and security. This instrumental argument frames women's protection and participation as a resource to use to improve the overall outcome of the existing mission. This represents a significant expansion of what constitutes a security issue and how countries transitioning from armed conflict have the opportunity to redefine state security (Hudson 2009).

Sources:

Rehn, Elisabeth, and Ellen Johnson Sirleaf. 2002. *Women, War and Peace: The Independent Experts' Assessment on the Impact of Armed Conflict on Women and Women's Role in Peace-building.* New York: United Nations Development Fund for Women (UNIFEM).

United Nations Organization, 2012. UN Women, "Women, War and Peace."

Tryggestad, Torunn L., 2009. 'Trick or Treat? The UN and Implementation of Security Council Resolution 1325 on Women, Peace and Security,' *Global Governance,* Vol. 15, pp. 539–557.

Hudson, Natalie F. 2009. *Gender, Human Security, and the United Nations: Security Language as a Political Framework for Women.* New York/London: Routledge.

The rise to prominence of non–state actors (NSAs) underscores the state's diminished role relative to many contemporary security concerns. Since the end of the Cold War, we should not underestimate the degree to which such international actors as multinational corporations (MNCs), nongovernmental organizations (NGOs), transnational terrorist networks, paramilitaries, private military contractors (PMCs), policy think tanks, peace advocates, and even individuals have altered the long-standing rules of global politics. This "party-crashing" by non–state actors altered the status quo in the global system with direct ramifications for security thinking and action.

Consider, for instance, a number of recent cases where non–state actors played a significant role in world affairs. Such cases include the direct involvement of the NGO umbrella Coalition for an International Criminal Court in the negotiations shaping the Rome Statute and the ICC, the crucial role that remittances transmitted along diaspora networks play in funding terrorist cells and their activities, and the hugely significant role of one Spanish judge (Baltasar Garzon) in bringing former Chilean dictator Augusto Pinochet to justice. These and many other similar examples point to two crucial dimensions of structural change in the contemporary security environment: the rise to the fore of non–state actors as sources of both collective security threats and responses, and the potential that non–state actors in either capacity may foster and perpetuate a weakening of state capacity in the security realm. Although these developments do not mean that states are unimportant in contemporary global politics, they do illustrate that state sovereignty has at least eroded from what it was a few decades, or even just a few years, ago.

Intensifying Threats: The "Dark Side" of Interdependence   Characterizations of a new security environment are dependent not only on changing rules and new actors, but also on recognition of new or previously overlooked sources of insecurity. At an abstract level, we can understand these sources of insecurity as unintended outcomes produced by the **complex interdependence** that defines our current era of globalization.

The benefits of interdependence are many and often celebrated (Keohane & Nye, 2001; Friedman, 2007). Yet at the same time, the depth and expanse of networked interactions between and among societies and individuals is not without its hazards. Most notable among these is the increased sensitivity and vulnerability of an ever-greater number of actors, including states, to an increasingly wide range of security threats (Baldwin, 1980). To a very real extent, we can view globalization as the main impetus driving the emergence of a new security environment. Certainly, the political, social, economic, cultural, and intellectual processes of globalization, as well as the backlash against these processes, pose a very real security challenge. Put simply, just as we enjoy the benefits that a smaller globe brings in terms of communication and access to a diverse array of consumer goods and services, globalization has also produced violent protests and conflict rooted in frustrations about those transformations and the unequal benefits they yield.

Yet it is not just protest and violence by globalization's discontents that is important here. The increasing intensity and penetration of global interdependence has also created a degree of densely networked and weakly governed connections

Complex interdependence
A term referring to the broad and deep interdependence of issues and actors in the contemporary global political system, and the ways in which this condition structures and conditions the conduct of global politics.

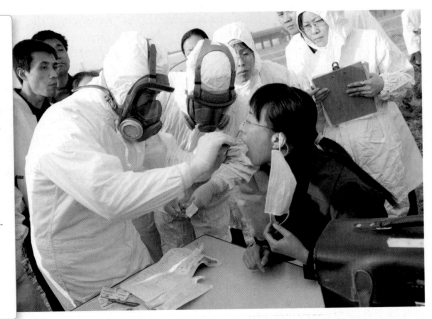

The dramatic response of public officials to threats of "Avian flu" (the H1N1 virus) symbolizes the rising impact of "nontraditional" security threats (such as the spread of disease) and the ways in which increasingly dense and expansive transnational linkages exacerbate these problems and their security implications. In this photo, public health professionals in China work to inoculate citizens from the virus in order to prevent the type of crippling epidemic that could undermine national, regional, and global security.

in commerce, transport, energy and natural resources, migration, and information technology. These changes have raised both the profile and stakes of these globalized activities, wiping away the dichotomy between security and all other issues that was commonplace in previous generations.

Whether in the rise of transnational terrorism, potential global epidemics such as HIV/AIDS or the Avian flu, the activities of multiple and competing organized crime networks, the proliferation of weapons of mass destruction as well as the easy exchange of conventional arms, or a variety of other developments, the new security environment provides an account of what we might consider the "dark side" of interdependence.

Contemporary Security Challenges

Although this new security environment has changed the way both individuals and state decision-makers perceive security, conflict and violence remain very real concerns for all involved actors. The following sections discuss contemporary security challenges ranging from more traditional military security concerns to ones that present newer threats. It is also helpful to remember that in the new security environment, the challenges the proliferation of various types of armaments pose is no longer something that we associate solely with states as was once the case. As we discuss the security challenges that weapons ranging from small arms to **weapons of mass destruction** (**WMD**) present, we fully recognize that states are not the only users or potential users of those tools of international interaction.

Weapons of mass destruction (WMD)
Often referring to nuclear weapons, but also including biological and chemical weapons. Weapons of mass destruction warfare refers to the application of force between countries using biological, chemical, and/or nuclear weapons.

The International Arms Trade The international arms trade is a booming industry. The estimated value of all arms transfer agreements worldwide in 2008 was $55.2 billion, with close to 60% of that value going to developing nations (SIPRI, 2009). For some, arms sales can help create balances of power that forestall conflict.

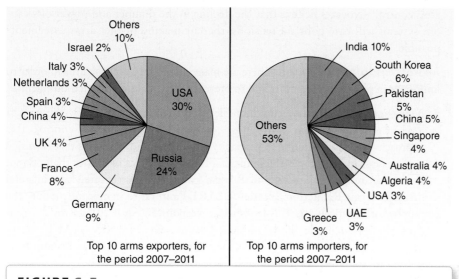

Top 10 arms exporters, for
the period 2007–2011

Top 10 arms importers, for
the period 2007–2011

FIGURE 6.5
The global arms trade

World arms sales during the years 2007–2011 for the 15 largest arms exporters alone totaled about $110 billion. A few countries dominated sales, as the pie chart on the left indicates. The pie chart on the right shows that imports were a bit more broadly distributed—although you will note that tense relationship dynamics (China/India, India/Pakistan, China/Taiwan, Turkey/Greece, and the Middle East as a whole) account for a good proportion of the demand for arms.

However, in other cases, the influx of arms, ranging from major systems such as combat aircraft and tanks to small arms and light weapons, only fuels regional and local violence by arming repressive states and insurgent groups. From either perspective, it is clear that the global sale of arms poses one of the greatest challenges of the 21st century to global, national, and human security.

A range of geopolitical factors (such as the maintenance of key strategic allies to economic factors, or the promotion of weapons deals that serve to subsidize the defense industrial bases of arms-exporting countries) drive the industry. As Figure 6.5 shows, the United States was the leader in the export of arms for the period 2007–2011, accounting for 30% of the arms trade (SIPRI, 2012). Moreover, the volume of U.S. arms exports during that period was 24% higher than the previous 5-year period (2002–2006)—making agreements valued at $37.8 billion, up dramatically from $25.4 billion in 2007. Russia (24%) and Germany (9%) rounded out the top three global arms exporting nations (SIPRI, 2012). These numbers largely speak to the trade in major conventional arms and weapons systems, which is the best known, most lucrative, and best monitored aspect of the global arms business.

Attempting Arms Control To enhance security, states and international organizations have long sought to monitor, and limit, the international exchange and production of weapons. **Arms control** involves limiting the numbers and types of weapons that countries possess. This approach aims at reducing military (especially offensive) capabilities and lessening the damage even if war begins. Additionally,

Arms control
A variety of approaches to the limitation of weapons. Arms control ranges from restricting the future growth in the number, types, or deployment of weapons; through the reduction of weapons; to the elimination of some types (or even all) weapons on a global or regional basis.

arms control advocates believe that the decline in the number and power of weapons systems will ease political tensions, thereby making further arms agreements possible.

Approaches to Arms Control   There are many methods to control arms in order to limit or even reduce their number and to prevent their spread. These methods include:

Strategic Arms Reduction Treaties (START I and II)
START I (1991) and START II (1993), provided for large cuts in the nuclear arms possessed by the United States and the Soviet Union (later the Russian Federation). START I was the first arms control treaty to reduce, rather than merely limit, the strategic offensive nuclear arsenals of the United States and the Soviet Union. START II established nuclear warhead and bomb ceilings of 3,500 for the United States and 2,997 for Russia by the year 2003 and also eliminated some types of weapons systems.

Intermediate-Range Nuclear Forces Treaty (INF)
A 1987 agreement between the United States and the Soviet Union signed by U.S. President Ronald Reagan and General Secretary Mikhail Gorbachev, the treaty eliminated nuclear and conventional ground-launched ballistic and cruise missiles with intermediate ranges defined between 500–5,500 km (300–3,400 miles).

Anti-Personnel Mine Ban Convention (aka the Ottawa Treaty)
A treaty drafted and signed in 1997 that aims at eliminating anti-personnel landmines around the world through specific terms requiring parties to cease production of anti-personnel mines, destroy existing stockpiles, and clear away all mined areas within their sovereign territory. Associated with the public diplomacy of Canadian diplomat Lloyd Axworthy and the late Princess Diana (U.K.), as of late 2011, there were 159 states-parties to the treaty, with two states (the Marshall Islands and Poland) signing but not ratifying the treaty and 35 states remaining nonsignatories.

- *Numerical restrictions:* Placing numerical limits above, at, or below the current level of existing weapons is the most common approach to arms control. This approach specifies the number or capacity of weapons and/or troops that each side may possess. In some cases the numerical limits may be at or higher than current levels. For example, the U.S. and Russian governments structured two bilateral **Strategic Arms Reduction Treaties (START I and II)** to significantly reduce the number of American and Russian nuclear weapons. In April 2010, Russian President Dmitry Medvedev and President Obama signed a "New START" treaty imposing new limits on ready-to-use, long-range nuclear weapons and committing both states to reduce the two biggest nuclear arsenals on the globe.

- *Categorical restrictions:* This approach to arms control involves limiting or eliminating certain types of weapons. The **Intermediate-Range Nuclear Forces Treaty (INF)** eliminated an entire class of weapons—intermediate-range nuclear missiles. The new **Anti-Personnel Mine Ban Convention (aka the Ottawa Treaty)** and the **Convention on Cluster Munitions** outlaw the use of weapons that often affect innocent civilians given their indiscriminate use and their ability to long outlast armed conflict.

- *Development, testing, and deployment restrictions:* This method of limiting arms involves a sort of military birth control, ensuring that weapons systems never begin their gestation period of development and testing or, if they do, they are never deployed. The advantage of this approach is that it stops a specific area of arms building before it starts. For instance, the countries that have ratified the nuclear **Treaty on the Non-Proliferation of Nuclear Weapons (NPT)** and that do not have such weapons agree not to develop them. Similarly, the **Comprehensive Test Ban Treaty (CTBT)** establishes restrictions on various forms of nuclear testing, with the overall goal of retarding the utility and effectiveness of nuclear weapons by limiting their research and development.

- *Geographic restriction:* An approach that prohibits the deployment of any weapons of war in certain geographic areas. The deployment of military weapons in Antarctica, the seabed, space, and elsewhere is, for example, banned. There can be geographic restrictions on specific types of weapons, such as the Treaty for the Prohibition of Nuclear Weapons in Latin America (1989).

- *Transfer restrictions:* This method of arms control prohibits or limits the flow of weapons and weapons technology across international borders. Under the NPT, for example, countries that have nuclear weapons or nuclear weapons technology pledge not to supply either to nonnuclear states.

- *Monitoring and Reporting:* In 2001, at the UN Conference on Curbing Illicit Trafficking of Small Arms and Light Weapons (SALW) in All Its Aspects, states committed to voluntarily instituting better controls to mark and trace weapons so that they could trace arms involved in conflict and human rights abuses to their source countries. From a human rights and humanitarian law perspective, this is critical for addressing civilian deaths as SALW account for an estimated 60–90% of the 100,000+ conflict deaths each year (Small Arms Survey, 2011) and tens of thousands of additional deaths outside of war zones. They are also the weapons of choice for many terrorists.

Barriers to Arms Control Limiting or reducing arms is an idea that most people favor. Yet arms control has proceeded slowly and sometimes not at all (Figure 6.6). The devil is in the details, as the old maxim goes, and it is important to review the continuing debate over arms control to understand its history and current status. None of the factors that we are about to discuss is the main culprit impeding arms control, nor is any one of them insurmountable. States are making important advances on a number of fronts, but together, these factors form a tenacious resistance to arms control.

A variety of security concerns make up a formidable barrier to arms control. Some analysts do not believe that countries can maintain adequate security if they disarm totally or substantially. *Worries about the possibility of future conflict* are probably the greatest security concern about arms control, a concern compounded by the

Convention on Cluster Munitions
This treaty, adopted by 107 states in Dublin, Ireland, on May 30, 2008, prohibits all use, stockpiling, production, and transfer of cluster munitions (a form of air-dropped or ground-launched explosive weapon that releases or ejects smaller munitions).

Treaty on the Non-Proliferation of Nuclear Weapons (NPT)
A multilateral treaty concluded in 1968, then renewed and made permanent in 1995. The parties to the treaty agree not to transfer nuclear weapons or in any way to "assist, encourage, or induce any nonnuclear state to manufacture or otherwise acquire nuclear weapons." Nonnuclear signatories of the NPT also agree not to build or accept nuclear weapons.

Comprehensive Test Ban Treaty (CTBT)
Bans all nuclear explosions in all environments for military or civilian purposes. The United Nations General Assembly adopted it on September 10, 1996, but it has not entered into force as of 2012.

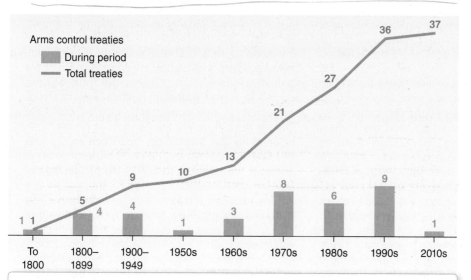

FIGURE 6.6

Arms control treaties

The development and use of increasingly devastating weapons has spurred greater efforts to limit them. This graph shows the number of treaties negotiated during various periods and the cumulative total of those treaties. The real acceleration of arms control began in the 1960s in an effort to restrain nuclear weapons. Of the 37 treaties covered here from 1675 to 2007, 26 (70%) were concluded between 1960 and 1999.

Note: Treaties limited to those that went into force and that dealt with specific weapons and verification rather than peace in general, material that could be used to make weapons, and other such matters.

Data source: Web sites of the Federation of American Scientists, the UN Department for Disarmament Affairs, and the U.S. Department of State, and various historical sources.

history matters

The Evolution of Arms Control

Despite the pervasiveness of armaments in the global system, attempts to limit and control their introduction, development, and proliferation have a long history. Arms control has evolved significantly, beginning with broad-based efforts, such as The Hague Conventions of 1898 and 1907, to restrict arms as a means to the end of eliminating war. These two comprehensive treaties encompassed regulations of the laws of war on land and sea, prohibitions against certain forms of weapons such as projectiles, gases, and explosives, provisions against the use of force to recover economic debts, and protections of neutral countries and parties during wartime. Along with the Kellogg–Briand Pact (formally designated the "General Treaty for the Renunciation of War," and signed by approximately two dozen countries in 1928), these agreements reflected the rise of liberal internationalism in the early part of the 20th century, and the efforts of such liberal internationalists to combat the fundamental insecurity that the problem of war through legal and institutional constraints posed.

As arms control efforts evolved during the 20th century, they became increasingly more limited and specialized in scope. This reflected the persistence of war, the resurgence of power politics, and the insecurity caused by the breadth and sophistication of available armaments. Governments designed most of these initiatives to impede the development, spread, and refinement of specific types and categories of weapons. Most prominent were the various attempts aimed at controlling so-called "NBC" (nuclear, biological, and chemical) weapons during the Cold War. The specter of arms races proved frightening enough to engender a variety of international arms control agreements involving the United States and the Soviet Union. Such agreements (some bilateral in scope, others multilateral) dealt with the testing, spread, and delivery of nuclear weapons (the Limited Test Ban Treaty in 1963; the Nuclear Non-Proliferation Treaty in 1968; the Anti-Ballistic Missile Treaty in 1972), the absolute and relative size of nuclear arsenals (the Strategic Arms Limitation Treaty in 1972, and its successor, SALT II, in 1979), and the elimination of a category of delivery vehicles for nuclear warheads (the Intermediate Nuclear Forces agreement of 1987).

Aside from nuclear weapons, some governments and NGOs made multilateral efforts to ban the production of biological weapons (the Biological Weapons Convention in 1972) and the production, stockpiling, and use of chemical weapons (the Chemical Weapons Convention, concluded in 1993).

Improved relations between the United States and the former USSR (supplanted in bilateral arms control negotiations by the Russian Federation) brought about the Strategic Arms Reduction Treaties (in 1991 and 1993) mandating significant reductions in the size of each state's nuclear arsenals. Some governments and NGOs also made efforts to extend the international ban on nuclear weapons testing (through the Comprehensive Test Ban Treaty of 1996) to include all underground, atmospheric, and outer space detonations. Yet the fragmentation of the security arena and the emergence of "new" security concerns had profound effects on both the focus and the effectiveness of international arms control efforts. NGOs and prominent advocates such as the late Princess Diana of the United Kingdom sought to shift the focus of arms control to human (rather than state-level) concerns, embodied in new agreements such as the 1999 Ottawa Treaty (officially the Convention on the Prohibition of the Use, Stockpiling, Production and Transfer of Anti-Personnel Mines and on their Destruction) as well as a UN-led effort to restrict the proliferation of light weapons.

The extensive spread and use of light arms in the many complex intrastate conflicts in the aftermath of the Cold War underscores the degree to which multilateral treaties concerning more prominent and sophisticated forms of weaponry are ill-suited to the emerging security challenges of this period. Arms control initiatives of that type persist, as is evident in the renewal of the START process and the signing of the "New START Treaty" between the United States and Russia in April 2010. At the same time, efforts to build up the capacity of international law and institutions to deal with the insecurity caused by contemporary armed conflict suggest that new developments in global security demand fresh approaches, which may place a reduced emphasis on negotiated, multilateral arms control treaties.

self-help nature of an anarchical global political system. For example, the Cold War and its accompanying huge arms buildup had no sooner begun to fade than fears about the threat of terrorists and **rogue states** with WMDs escalated in the aftermath of 9/11. This concern has, for instance, accelerated the U.S. effort to build a national missile defense system.

At least to some degree, nuclear proliferation is also a product of insecurity and the dynamic of the security dilemma. India's drive to acquire nuclear weapons was, in part, a reaction to the nuclear arms of China to the north. India's program to defend itself against China then raised anxieties in Pakistan, which had fought several wars with India. So, the Pakistanis began their program. "Today we have evened the score with India," Pakistan's prime minister exulted, after his country's first test.[6] Similarly, North Korea has repeatedly maintained that it needs nuclear weapons to act as a deterrent against foreign aggression, therefore "defending the sovereignty of the country and the nation and socialism and ensuring peace and security on the Korean peninsula and the region" (Korean Central News Agency, March 2009).

Doubts about the value of arms control are another security concern that restrains arms control. Those who are skeptical about arms control and its supposed benefits begin with the belief that humans arm themselves and fight because the world is dangerous. Given this view, skeptics believe that states should achieve political settlements before they negotiate arms reductions. Therefore, such analysts reject the idea that arms control agreements necessarily represent progress. In fact, it is even possible from this perspective to argue that more, not fewer, weapons may increase security in that they help to establish a rank hierarchy of power that makes stable interactions between states more likely.

In contrast, other analysts agree with Homer's observation in the Odyssey (ca. 700 BCE) that "the blade itself incites to violence." Theory B in Figure 6.7 represents this and demonstrates the belief that insecurity leads countries to have arms races, which lead to more insecurity and conflict in a hard-to-break cycle (Gibler, Rider, & Hutchison, 2005). From this perspective, the way for states to increase security is by reducing arms, not increasing them.

While the logic of arms races seems obvious, empirical research has not confirmed that arms races always occur. Similarly, it is not clear whether decreases in arms cause, or are caused by, periods of improved global cooperation. Instead, a host of domestic and systemic factors influence a country's level of armaments. What this means is that the most probable answer to the chicken-and-egg debate about which should come first, political agreements or arms control, lies in a combination of these theories. That is, arms, tension, and wars all promote one another, as Theory C in Figure 6.7 depicts.

Rogue states
Controversial term some international theorists apply to states that are (or are perceived to be) in noncompliance with the majority of prevailing rules, norms, and laws in the global system and therefore constitute a threat to order. This may mean, among other things, a state governed by authoritarian rule that severely restricts human rights, sponsors or condones terrorism, or seeks to obtain or promote the spread of weapons of mass destruction.

Reflecting the tragic circumstances facing many children, as well as adults, who are killed and maimed by old landmines every year, this sign—erected with the help of UNICEF—warns of a minefield in Sri Lanka.

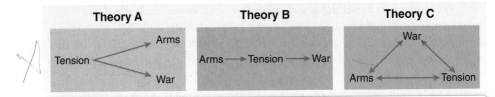

FIGURE 6.7

Arms, tension, and war

Theory A approximates the realist view, and Theory B fits the liberal view of the causal relationship between arms, tension, and use. Theory C suggests that there is a complex causal interrelationship between arms, tension, and war in which each of the three factors affects the other two.

Concerns about verification and cheating constitute a third barrier to arms control stemming from security concerns. The problem is simple: Countries suspect that others will cheat, a suspicion embodied in one of Ronald Reagan's favorite maxims when discussing arms control negotiations with the Soviet Union: "trust, but verify." This worry was a significant factor in the rejection of the CTBT by the U.S. Senate. A chief opponent characterized the treaty as "not effectively verifiable" and therefore "ineffectual because it would not stop other nations from testing or developing nuclear weapons. . . . The CTBT simply has no teeth."[7]

There have been great advances in verification procedures and technologies. Many arms control treaties provide for on-site inspections (OSI) by an agency such as the IAEA, but in some cases states can hide weapons and facilities from OSI. National technical means (NTM) of verification using satellites, seismic measuring devices, and other equipment have also advanced rapidly. These have been substantially offset, however, by other technologies that make NTM verification more difficult. For example, scientists have miniaturized nuclear warheads to the point where one could literally hide one in a good-sized closet. Dual-use chemicals make it difficult to monitor the Chemical Weapons Convention (CWC), and the minute amounts of biological warfare agents that could inflict massive casualties make it daunting to monitor the Biological Weapons Convention (BWC). Therefore, in the last analysis, virtually no amount of OSI and NTM can ensure absolute verification.

Because absolute verification is impossible, the real issue is which course is more dangerous: (1) coming to an agreement when there is, at least, some chance that the other side might be able to cheat, or (2) failing to agree and living in a world of unrestrained and increasing nuclear weapons growth? Sometimes, the answer may be number 2. Taking this view while testifying before the U.S. Senate about the Chemical Weapons Convention, former Secretary of State James A. Baker III counseled, "The [George H. W.] Bush administration never expected the treaty to be completely verifiable and had always expected there would be rogue states that would not participate." Nevertheless, Baker supported the treaty on the grounds that "the more countries we can get behind responsible behavior around the world . . . the better it is for us."[8]

In addition to international barriers, a number of significant national barriers exist as well. For example, not all leaders favor arms control, and even those who do often face strong opposition from powerful opponents of arms control who, noted previously, are skeptical of arms control in general or of a particular proposal. Additionally, opposition to arms control often stems from such domestic barriers as national pride and the interrelationship among military spending, the economy, and politics.

National pride is one domestic barrier to arms control. The adage in the Book of Proverbs that "pride goeth before destruction" is sometimes applicable to arms acquisitions. Whether we are dealing with conventional or nuclear arms, national pride is a primary drive behind their acquisition. For many countries, arms represent a tangible symbol of strength and sovereign equality. "EXPLOSION OF SELF-ESTEEM" read one newspaper headline in India after that country's nuclear tests in 1998.[9] "LONG LIVE NUCLEAR PAKISTAN" read a Pakistani newspaper headline soon thereafter. "Five nuclear blasts have instantly transformed an extremely demoralized nation into a self-respecting proud nation," the accompanying article explained.[10] Such emotions have also seemingly played a role in Iran's alleged nuclear weapons program. "I hope we get our atomic weapons," Shirzad Bozorgmehr, editor of *Iran News*, has commented. "If Israel has it, we should have it. If India and Pakistan do, we should, too," he explained.

Military spending, the economy, and politics interact to form another domestic barrier to arms control. Supplying the military is big business, and economic interest groups pressure their governments to build and to sell weapons and associated technology. Furthermore, cities that are near major military installations benefit from jobs provided on the bases and from the consumer spending of military personnel stationed on the bases. For this reason, defense-related corporations, defense plant workers, civilian employees of the military, and the cities and towns in which they reside and shop are supporters of military spending and foreign sales. Additionally, there are often bureaucratic elements, such as ministries of defense, in alliance with the defense industry and its workers. Finally, both interest groups and bureaucratic actors receive support from legislators who represent the districts and states that benefit from military spending. This alliance between interest groups, bureaucracies, and legislators forms an **"iron triangle"** at the heart of the military-industrial complex.

Iron triangle
A close and mutually beneficial arrangement between interest groups, the bureaucracy, and legislators within a given political system that forms the basis for the military-industrial complex.

Weapons of Mass Destruction   While the proliferation of WMDs represents another urgent security issue of the 21st century, the problem is distinct from conventional weapons and the arms trade in a number of critical ways. WMDs, which include biological, chemical, and nuclear weapons, are among the most lethal and destructive in the world. Further, the use of WMDs usually involves indiscriminate killing and long-term suffering affecting both civilians and combatants alike. The dropping of the atomic bomb over Hiroshima and Nagasaki in 1945 clearly illustrates this dramatic and devastating impact. In the pages that follow, we will deal briefly with biological and chemical weapons, and then turn to a more extensive examination of nuclear weapons and strategy. Although it is common to categorize these three weapons into the category of WMD, it is important to highlight nuclear weapons because unlike biological and chemical weapons, no preventative or protective measures exist to mitigate the effects of a nuclear attack. Thus, there is a taboo against their use in ways different from biological and chemical weapons.

Biological Weapons Biological warfare, which involves the use of pathogens such as viruses, bacteria, or other disease-causing biological agents or toxins as weapons, is not new. As early as the 6th century BCE, the Assyrians poisoned enemy wells with a parasitic fungus called rye ergot that caused gangrene and convulsions. More catastrophically, the Tartar army besieging Kaffa, a Genoese trading outpost in the Crimea in 1346, catapulted plague-infected corpses and heads over the walls to spread the disease among the defenders. Many of those who fled back to Italy carried the disease with them and, according to some historians, set off the Black Death that killed millions of Europeans. North America first experienced biological warfare in 1763 when, during an Indian uprising, the British commander in North America, Sir Jeffrey Amherst, wrote to subordinates at Fort Pitt, "Could it not be contrived to send the smallpox among those disaffected tribes of Indians?"[11] As it turns out, Sir Jeffrey's prompting was unnecessary. Soldiers at the fort had already given disease-infected blankets to members of the Shawnee and Delaware tribes.

The specter of biological warfare still looms large. Although the 1972 Biological Weapons Convention (BWC) bans the production, possession, and use of germ-based **biological weapons**, there are persistent rumors that some countries maintain bioweapons stocks or are seeking them. North Korea, Iran, Russia, and Syria are most often mentioned. Relatively recent evidence of bioweapons activity gives credence to such possibilities. For example, a top Russian official admitted in 1992 that the Soviet Union had been violating the BWC by conducting biological weapons research and, among other things, had amassed 20 tons of smallpox solution. The UN-led inspections of Iraq after the 1991 Persian Gulf War indicated that the country also had a germ warfare program that had, at minimum, produced 132,000 gallons of anthrax and botulism toxins. Anthrax has also become a security threat to the United States, particularly in 2001 when someone sent a small amount of anthrax spores through the U.S. Postal Service to government and media offices, killing several and significantly disrupting the mail service. Although the government ultimately blamed the U.S. anthrax attacks on a U.S. scientist with access to military bioweapons programs, there are ongoing fears about the potential use of this biological agent. The U.S. military, for example, requires that all its personnel receive the anthrax vaccine.

Although there has not been a large-scale biological attack to date, many scientists and policy makers continue to see a significant security risk with no regard for state borders or national boundaries. With ongoing advances in the field of biotechnology, both the know-how and the materials necessary to mount a biological attack are becoming more accessible, as are the tools and facilities essential for doing so. In this way, many fear that terrorists could also find it easier to produce and weaponize disease materials. Thus, bioterrorism has emerged as a

Biological weapons
Living organisms or replicating entities (viruses) that reproduce or replicate within their host victims. May be employed in various ways to gain a strategic or tactical advantage over an adversary, either by threats or by actual deployments.

potential security threat and an area of action for many policy makers. Despite these fears, many urge caution as terrorists have yet to employ a biological agent. According to Milton Leitenberg, a biological-weapons expert at the Center for International and Security Studies at the University of Maryland, "I don't think the threat is growing, but quite the opposite. . . . The idea that four guys in a cave are going to create bioweapons from scratch—that will be never, ever, ever" (Johnson, *Wall Street Journal*, 2010:1).

Chemical Weapons   Of the three components of WMDs, **chemical weapons** are the most prevalent because they are relatively easy and inexpensive to produce. They have earned the nickname of "the poor man's atomic bomb." As one CIA director told Congress, "Chemicals used to make nerve agents are also used to make plastics and [to] process foodstuff. Any modern pharmaceutical facility can produce biological warfare agents as easily as vaccines or antibiotics."[12] Troops widely used mustard gas during World War I, and it proved very lethal. Following the horrors of that war, the international community adopted the 1925 Geneva Protocol banning the use (not the production or possession) of chemical weapons. This treaty is still in effect today, and has been supplemented by the Chemical Weapons Convention (CWC), a multilateral treaty that entered into force in 1997. This treaty bans not only the use but also the production of chemical weapons, including in its provisions a timetable for their eventual destruction.

> **Chemical weapons**
> Devices that use chemical agents that inflict death or harm to human beings. They are classified as weapons of mass destruction.

Despite these international agreements, states recently have used chemical weapons, albeit rarely. Both Iran and Iraq used them during their grueling war (1980–1988), and Iraq used them internally to attack rebelling Kurdish and Shiite populations. Recordings of meetings later captured by U.S. forces chillingly verify the personal involvement of Saddam Hussein in the use of chemical weapons. In one meeting Saddam reminded other participants, "Chemical weapons are not used unless I personally give the orders." When Iraq's vice president asked if chemical weapons are effective, Saddam replied, "Yes, they're very effective if people don't wear masks." "You mean they will kill thousands?" the vice president wonders. "Yes, they will kill thousands," the president assures him.[13] And so they did, in numerous attacks directly administered by Saddam's first cousin Ali Hassan al-Majid (aka "Chemical Ali"). The most egregious of these attacks resulted in the deaths of approximately 5,000 people in a 1988 assault on the Kurdish city of Halabja, and untold numbers of Kurds and Shiites also perished or were ravaged by illness as a result of chemical attacks in response to various uprisings in the late 1980s and early 1990s.

UN inspections in Iraq after the Persian Gulf War (1991) also uncovered huge stores of chemical weapons, including over 105,000 gallons of mustard gas; 21,936 gallons of tabun, sarin, and other nerve gases; and over 453,000 gallons of other chemicals associated with weapons. Munitions contained some of this supply, such as 12,786 artillery shells filled with mustard gas and 18 warheads or bombs filled with nerve agents. There is no evidence that Iraq used any chemical weapons during the war, but there were traces of mustard gas and sarin on the battlefield. These may have been released inadvertently when the allied attacks destroyed Iraqi weapons depots, and some analysts suspect that exposure to these chemicals may be the cause of Gulf War syndrome, which has afflicted many veterans of the war.

Nuclear Weapons   As made horrifyingly clear during World War II, **nuclear weapons** are by far the world's most destructive weapons. Nuclear weapons include both *fission* weapons, like the atomic bomb, as well as *fusion* weapons, like the hydrogen bomb. The latter tend to be smaller and less expensive to produce. Of course, either category is potentially lethal to large numbers of people, making the proliferation of nuclear weapons states in recent years one of, if not the most serious sources of insecurity at the global, national and local level.

Roughly as old as nuclear weapons themselves are efforts to limit their spread, or to disarm those states that have acquired nuclear weapons capabilities. As is reflected in the two primary multilateral treaty instruments dedicated to nuclear arms control—the Nuclear Non-Proliferation Treaty (NPT) and the Comprehensive Test Ban Treaty (CTBT)—the twin strategies of **non-proliferation** and **disarmament** are the primary avenues by which the international community has sought to control nuclear weapons. During the Cold War, the parameters of nuclear bipolarity clearly dictated these approaches to controlling nuclear weapons. With respect to non-proliferation, the NPT restricted lawful possession of nuclear weapons to the initial five members of the so-called nuclear club (the U.S., USSR, U.K., France, and China), with all other signatories to the treaty agreeing to renounce nuclear weapons aspirations. In return for agreeing to this condition, these five states pledged to make meaningful progress toward nuclear disarmament—progress that the limits on testing and research stipulated by the Partial Test Ban Treaty (which entered into force in 1963) and later the CTBT (adopted in 1996, but yet to enter into force) further advanced. The limited pursuit of disarmament, as well as the perceived inequities in the NPT, both served to limit the effectiveness of multilateral efforts to control nuclear weapons during the Cold War, although the "Nuclear Club" made significant strides at the bilateral level, particularly between the United States and USSR.

Nuclear Weapons States and Their Arsenals   The world joined in a collective sigh of relief when the Cold War ended. Almost overnight, worries about the threat of nuclear war virtually disappeared from the media and from general political discussion. Unfortunately, the perception of significantly greater safety is illusory. It is true that the number of strategic nuclear weapons has declined. Nevertheless, many extremely powerful nuclear weapons remain in the arsenals of several states, and the interest in acquiring nuclear weapons by nonnuclear weapons states has seemingly intensified, as is reflected in the addition of India, Pakistan, and North Korea to the ranks of nuclear weapons states in recent years (Figure 6.8).

The United States and Russia. With enormous stockpiles inherited from the Cold War, the United States and Russia remain the nuclear Goliaths. In 2006, the U.S. deployed a strategic-range (5,550 kilometers/3,416.8 miles) arsenal that included 5,021 nuclear warheads and bombs and 951 **strategic-range delivery vehicles** (missiles and bombers). Russia's deployed strategic inventory was 3,500 weapons and 639 delivery

---

Nuclear weapon
An explosive device that derives its destructive force from nuclear reactions, either fission or a combination of fission and fusion.

Non-proliferation
Limitation of the production or spread of nuclear or chemical weapons.

Disarmament
The act of reducing, limiting, or abolishing a category of weapons.

Strategic-range delivery vehicles
Delivery vehicles for nuclear weapons, such as land- or submarine-based ballistic missiles and long-range heavy bombers, capable of attacking targets at distances greater than 5,500 kilometers. These delivery systems confer tremendous strategic advantage to states possessing them, and consequently have often been a great source of instability as well as a target of arms control efforts, such as between the United States and USSR/Russia.

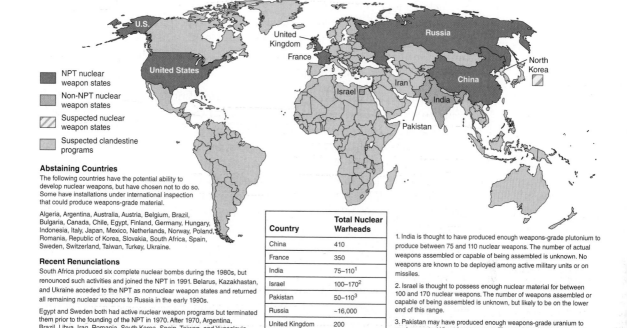

Abstaining Countries

The following countries have the potential ability to develop nuclear weapons, but have chosen not to do so. Some have installations under international inspection that could produce weapons-grade material.

Algeria, Argentina, Australia, Austria, Belgium, Brazil, Bulgaria, Canada, Chile, Egypt, Finland, Germany, Hungary, Indonesia, Italy, Japan, Mexico, Netherlands, Norway, Poland, Romania, Republic of Korea, Slovakia, South Africa, Spain, Sweden, Switzerland, Taiwan, Turkey, Ukraine.

Recent Renunciations

South Africa produced six complete nuclear bombs during the 1980s, but renounced such activities and joined the NPT in 1991. Belarus, Kazakhstan, and Ukraine acceded to the NPT as nonnuclear weapon states and returned all remaining nuclear weapons to Russia in the early 1990s.

Egypt and Sweden both had active nuclear weapon programs but terminated them prior to the founding of the NPT in 1970. After 1970, Argentina, Brazil, Libya, Iraq, Romania, South Korea, Spain, Taiwan, and Yugoslavia all had active programs researching nuclear weapons options. All of these programs were terminated by the early 1990s, except for Libya's, which was renounced in December 2003.

Legend:
- NPT nuclear weapon states
- Non-NPT nuclear weapon states
- Suspected nuclear weapon states
- Suspected clandestine programs

Country	Total Nuclear Warheads
China	410
France	350
India	75–110[1]
Israel	100–170[2]
Pakistan	50–110[3]
Russia	~16,000
United Kingdom	200
United States	~10,300
Total	**~27,600**

1. India is thought to have produced enough weapons-grade plutonium to produce between 75 and 110 nuclear weapons. The number of actual weapons assembled or capable of being assembled is unknown. No weapons are known to be deployed among active military units or on missiles.

2. Israel is thought to possess enough nuclear material for between 100 and 170 nuclear weapons. The number of weapons assembled or capable of being assembled is unknown, but likely to be on the lower end of this range.

3. Pakistan may have produced enough weapons-grade uranium to produce up to 110 nuclear weapons. The number of actual weapons assembled or capable of being assembled is unknown. Pakistan's nuclear weapons are reportedly stored in component form, with the fissile core separated from the nonnuclear explosives.

FIGURE 6.8

Nuclear weapons status 2005

As this figure depicts, the possession and spread of nuclear weapons remains a front-burner global security issue, due to the destructive power of the weapon, the size of existing arsenals, and the clandestine nature of some nuclear weapons programs.

Data Source: Carnegie Endowment for International Peace, Deadly Arsenals, http://www.carnegieendowment.org/files/DeadlyII.

---

vehicles. Additionally, the United States has about 500 deployed tactical (shorter-range, battlefield) nuclear weapons and Russia has some 2,330. Both countries also keep a substantial number of nuclear warheads and bombs in reserve. In 2010, Russia had a nuclear inventory of approximately 12,000 and the United States had 9,600—constituting a huge majority of the 22,600 nuclear weapons known to be stockpiled worldwide.

Washington and Moscow have both long relied on a triad of strategic weapons systems that includes (1) submarine-launched ballistic missiles (SLBMs) carried aboard ballistic missile nuclear submarines (SSBNs), (2) land-based intercontinental ballistic missiles (ICBMs), and (3) bombers. Most ICBMs are located in silos, although Russia has some that are railroad-mobile. ICBMs and SLBMs carry up to 10 warheads, with multiple warhead missiles having multiple independent reentry vehicle (MIRV) capability. This allows each warhead to attack a different target. The most powerful of these explosive devices is currently deployed on Russia's SS-18 ICBMs, each of which carries 10 MIRV warheads, each with the explosive power of 750 kilotons of TNT. The largest U.S. weapons are D-5 SLBMs that carry six 475-kiloton warheads.

Nuclear weapons designed for tactical use also come in a relatively miniaturized form. Among currently deployed tactical nuclear weapons, the explosive power of U.S. B-61 bombs can be as low as 0.3 kilotons (30 tons of TNT), a yield that is approximately nine times as powerful as the ammonium nitrate bomb that destroyed the Federal Building in Oklahoma City on April 19, 1995.

Other Nuclear Weapons States. China, France, Great Britain, India, and Pakistan all openly possess nuclear weapons, with North Korea claiming nuclear weapons status (a claim accepted by the **International Atomic Energy Agency**) and Israel possessing an undeclared nuclear weapons arsenal. All told, these states add another 1,300 or so nuclear devices to the volatile mix of over 13,000 deployed tactical and strategic nuclear devices. China, for example, has about 130 nuclear warheads and bombs, of which 40 are deployed on bombers, 12 on single warhead SLBMs, and 78 on single warhead missiles with ICBM or near-ICBM ranges. Additionally, several countries, most notably Iran, have or are suspected of having nuclear weapons development programs, and another 30 countries have the necessary technology base to build nuclear weapons (Figure 6.9).

Nuclear Deterrence and Strategy There are issues about a country's nuclear arsenal and doctrines that seldom enter the public debate, but that are crucial to an effective and stable arsenal. The two main issues are (1) how to minimize the chance of nuclear war and (2) how to maximize the chance of survival if a nuclear war does occur. It is not possible here to review all the factors that impinge on these issues, but we can illustrate the various concerns by examining deterrence and then two strategy issues, first-strike use and national missile defense.

The concept of deterrence remains at the center of the strategy of all the nuclear powers. Deterrence is persuading an enemy that attacking you will not be worth the cost. Deterrence relies on two factors. *Capability* is one. Effective deterrence requires that even if you are attacked, you must be able to preserve enough strength to retaliate powerfully. Of all current strategic weapons systems, SLBMs are least vulnerable to attack and, therefore, the most important element of deterrence. Fixed-silo ICBMs are the most vulnerable for destruction in an attack. *Credibility* is another factor of deterrence. An opponent must also believe that you can and will use your weapons if attacked. You might be thinking at this point, "Why would a country not respond to an attack?" In the sometimes perverse logic of nuclear war, as we shall see, there are times when doing so might not be an option. This leads some analysts to believe that relying exclusively on retaliation is not a credible deterrent stance and that, therefore, countries should be able and willing to initiate a nuclear war in an extreme circumstance.

Mutually assured destruction (MAD) advocates would base deterrence exclusively on having the ability and will to deliver a devastating counterstrike. They believe that one best achieves deterrence if each nuclear power's capabilities include (1) a sufficient number of weapons that are (2) capable of surviving a nuclear attack by an opponent and then (3) delivering a second-strike retaliatory attack that will destroy that opponent. In essence, this approach is *deterrence through punishment*. If each nuclear power has these three capabilities, then they achieve a mutual checkmate. The result, MAD theory holds, is that no power will start a nuclear war because doing so will lead to its own destruction (even if it destroys its enemy).

International Atomic Energy Agency (IAEA) The world's center of cooperation in the nuclear field. It was set up in 1957 as the world's "Atoms for Peace" organization within the United Nations family. The Agency works with its member-states and multiple partners worldwide to promote safe, secure, and peaceful nuclear technologies.

Mutually assured destruction (MAD) A situation in which each nuclear superpower has the capability of launching a devastating nuclear second strike even after an enemy has attacked it. The crux of the MAD doctrine is that possessing an overwhelming second-strike capacity prevents nuclear war due to the rational aversion of the other side to invite massive retaliation.

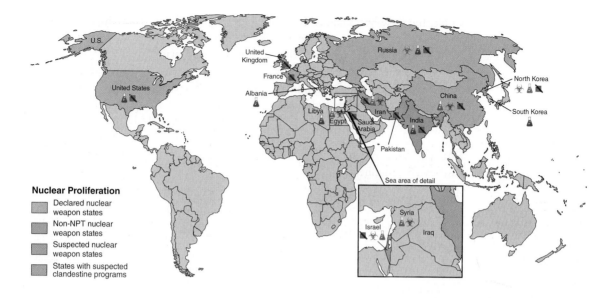

FIGURE 6.9

WMD proliferation status 2005

As this figure depicts, folding in the status of chemical and biological weapons programs and their spread magnifies the security threat posed by weapons of mass destruction.

Data Source: Carnegie Endowment for International Peace, Deadly Arsenals, http://www.carnegieendowment.org/files/DeadlyII.

Nuclear utilization theory (NUT) is an alternative approach to deterrence. Its advocates contend that the MAD strategy is a crazy gamble because it relies on rationality and clear-sightedness when, in reality, there are other scenarios (which we discussed earlier) that could lead to nuclear war. Therefore, NUT supporters prefer to base deterrence partly on *deterrence through damage denial* (or limitation). This requires the ability and willingness to destroy enemy weapons before the weapons explode on one's own territory and forces. The ways to do this are to prevent the launch of weapons by either destroying an enemy's command and communications structure or the weapons themselves before launching the weapons and/or destroying the weapons during flight.

Both U.S. and Russian nuclear doctrines have historically been a mixture of MAD and NUT strategies. The approaches of most of the lesser nuclear powers, such as

> **Nuclear utilization theory (NUT)**
> Pioneered by Herman Kahn, this theory asserts that it is possible for a limited nuclear exchange to occur and that nuclear weapons are simply one more rung on the ladder of escalation.

China, the U.K., and France, are almost purely oriented around the MAD doctrine. The U.S. posture under the George W. Bush administration took on a decidedly NUT orientation, in concert with the emphasis on preemption at the heart of the Bush Doctrine (Glaser & Fetter, 2006). The renewed interest in nuclear disarmament expressed by the Obama administration, and the March 2010 bilateral agreement between the United States and Russia ("Measures to Further Reduction and Limitation of Strategic Offensive Arms"), signal a shift back toward a MAD footing.

Energy and Natural Resources   In recent years, the term **energy security** has figured prominently in the policy discourse of major government officials. In a speech at Georgetown University in late March 2011, U.S. President Obama went as far as to say that U.S. national security depends on America's access to a secure and affordable energy supply (Obama, 2011). This is not surprising given that the United States, like many industrialized states, relies heavily on imported supplies of energy, linking energy policy to foreign policy in critical ways. From concerns about the availability of energy supplies outstripping rising world demand to the targeting of oil supplies by terrorists and insurgents, governments around the world have prioritized energy policy. Put simply, secure energy supply has direct implications for security at global, national, and individual levels. States must meet the demand for energy or economies will crumble.

> **Energy security**
> Term for an association between national security and the availability of natural resources for energy consumption. The uneven distribution of energy supplies among countries has led to significant vulnerabilities and insecurity.

While there is no all-encompassing definition of energy security, most analysts focus on sources of energy, including oil, natural gas, coal, nuclear power, hydropower, and wood, that are reliable and affordable both in terms of supply and delivery (Kalicki & Goldwyn, 2005). Continuing to have an adequate supply of oil, gas, and mineral resources is an increasing concern for the international community. With the accelerating development of such populous states as India and China, global demand and consumption are rising at alarming rates. Further, as political leaders and citizens learn more about climate change and its causes, we will likely see more restrictions on the use of fossil fuels. For many policy makers then, energy security has come to focus on diversifying supplies—both in terms of primary sources of fuel as well as investing in alternative forms of energy.

A sufficient and diverse supply only works, however, if states can ensure unhindered delivery of energy. Safe delivery is also a growing concern for policy makers, particularly as the energy supply system has become more globalized and states continue to overstretch and overburden fragile networks. As Michael Klare (2004) argues, these networks are often vulnerable to attack by terrorists, insurgents, pirates, and criminal bands trying to disrupt established governments or some international presence. The conduct of power politics can also hinder delivery. This is the case, for example, with the former Soviet republics and their reliance on Russia for oil and natural gas. On several recent occasions, Russia has threatened to or actually did cut off the flow of energy to Ukraine, Georgia, and the Baltic states. During the summer of 2010, Russia once again began cutting the natural gas supply to Belarus in a dispute over pricing, although many believe that the disputes have much more to do with punishing governments that are unfriendly to Moscow. This dispute has the potential to affect a number of European states given that Gazprom—the world's biggest producer and exporter of natural gas and Russia's most powerful company—exports energy to over 30 countries and provides approximately 25 percent of the European Union's gas supply.

These dual concerns of adequate supply and safe delivery are most evident in the case of petroleum—the world's single most important form of energy. While the United States and China continue to be the top consumers of the world's oil, there has been a shift in the center of gravity of top producers and exporters of oil from the Global North to the Global South. Top exporters include Saudi Arabia, Russia, United Arab Emirates, Iran, Venezuela, Nigeria, and Alergia—many of which are members of the powerful **Organization of the Petroleum Exporting Countries (OPEC)**. This IGO wields significant control over the production and pricing of the world's oil and affects military alliances and trade relationships around the globe, particularly as anxiety levels about future availability of adequate petroleum supplies continue to rise.

> **Organization of the Petroleum Exporting Countries (OPEC)** An intergovernmental organization of 12 oil-producing countries made up of Algeria, Angola, Ecuador, Iran, Iraq, Kuwait, Libya, Nigeria, Qatar, Saudi Arabia, United Arab Emirates, and Venezuela.

In addition, analysts estimate that almost half of the world's oil fields are nearing the end of their most productive years, while at the same time there has been a decline in new oil field discoveries. As output and new discovery peak, places such as the Gulf of Mexico tend to be some of the most difficult areas in which to drill in terms of new technology, growing environmental concerns, and many new unknown risks. Very clearly, the April 2010 BP oil spill in the Gulf of Mexico provided vivid illustration of these difficulties.

In general, the resource wars cited by Klare (2002) have direct and important ramifications for security, regardless of the security referent (global, state, or human) that one favors. The connection can be *direct*, with competition and pressure on the capacity of the natural environment to provide needed resources and/or absorb pollution making individuals, groups, and nations insecure. Such dynamics, which may lead to the reduction in arable land, depletion of freshwater supplies, or deforestation (to name just a few), make all those dependent on the natural environment for their livelihood and survival (which, of course, is all of us . . .) less secure.

The nexus between security and the environment can also be *indirect*, with resource competition and pressures on local ecosystems intensifying existing causes of insecurity (such as armed conflicts). The lucrative appeal of diamonds, for instance, significantly worsened conflicts in Sierra Leone and Liberia in the 1990s, attracting mercenary and paramilitary activity and providing a direct source of funds to the combatants, thereby sustaining the conflict. Whether one views the link between natural resources and the environment and security as direct or indirect, the key factor—as Homer-Dixon (1994) and others have pointed out—is scarcity, whether brought about by the depletion and degradation of the natural resource base, overconsumption related to population pressures or migration, or unequal concentration and access.

CRITICAL THINKING QUESTIONS

1. What is the basis for the traditional approach to security studies? On what key concepts and core assumptions does it rest?

2. What precipitated the move to "broaden" and "deepen" security studies, beginning in the 1980s? What are some of the leading examples of these efforts?

3. What are the three main reference points for security prevailing today? What security "threats" or problems do we most often associate with each?

4. What were the origins of the "new security environment"? What are its crucial defining features?

chapter **summary**

- Security remains central to the conduct and understanding of global politics. At the same time, it is increasingly a contested concept whose meaning is very much contingent on the frame of reference you employ to analyze it.

- The chosen frame of reference for security shapes the object of concern when thinking about security, and sometimes leads to radically different views on what constitutes a severe or significant security threat, as opposed to a more moderate or even low-level concern.

- One useful tool for thinking about these disparate views of security is Barry Buzan's (1991) five sectors approach. Whether one's security focus resides at the global, state, or individual level, Buzan contends that we can locate security concerns in one (or more) of five sectors:

  - *military security:* concerns produced by the reciprocal interaction of the armed offensive and defensive capabilities and/or perceptions of states and their leaders

  - *political security:* concerns produced in relation to the organization stability (or instability) of states, governing systems, and ideologies

  - *economic security:* concerns generated by limited or unequal access to economic resources (including financial capital and markets) needed to sustain an acceptable level of social welfare

  - *societal security:* concerns triggered by either excessive adherence *or* real/perceived threats to traditional patterns of language, culture, religious and national identity, or custom

  - *environmental security:* concerns prompted by threats to the local, regional, or global ecosystem and the natural resource base on which human life depends

- While states no longer equate military security with security *per se*, it retains a high degree of importance—both in its own right, and in its interactions with other types of security threats and challenges. In this way we can see where, for example, an environmental security concern (e.g., a sudden decline in arable land) might trigger a military security concern (e.g., the outbreak of armed conflict over land rights and access), or vice versa (where, for instance, an ongoing civil war might reduce the availability of or access to arable land).

- In the end, it is crucial not to overlook the continuing importance of the state and the logic of anarchy. The persistent absence of any effective central governing authority in the global system makes anarchy just as relevant for consideration in the new security environment as it was in the old. As an engine for continued insecurity in our world, the lack of such governing authority—and the violent contests it spawns both between and within states—remains the primary driver of armed conflict in global politics, as we will see in the next chapter.

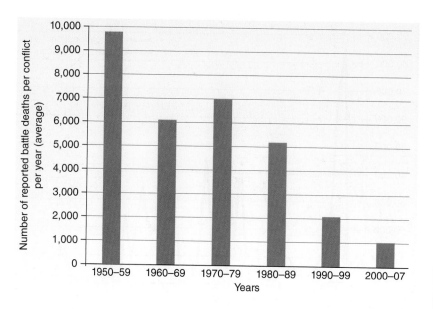

FIGURE 7.8
Average number of battle deaths per conflict per year, 1950–2007
There has been a clear, though far from consistent, decline in the deadliness of armed conflict since the end of the Korean War. In the 1950s, the average armed conflict killed nearly 10,000 people a year; by the new millennium, the average had fallen to just over 1,000.

Data Sources: Peace Research Institute Oslo; Uppsala Conflict Data Programme/Human Security Report Project.

Although they do not necessarily account for all deaths (especially civilian deaths) related to armed conflict, as Figure 7.8 shows, battle deaths are in steep decline, especially since the end of the Cold War (Lacina, Gledistch, & Russett, 2006; Mack, 2005). In part, we can explain this decline in the number of battle deaths by the broader shift in war and armed conflict away from major interstate wars to the more frequent but usually lower-intensity phenomenon of intrastate wars. Such conflicts are often protracted and devastating for the society in question. Yet from the standpoint of intensity, by virtue of the fact that they usually do not involve the mass mobilization of the entire society to the war effort or the unfettered employment of the technologically sophisticated military arsenal of one or more states as interstate wars do, the aggregate level of sustained violence is of a lower order (Figure 7.9).

Other Patterns and Trends

The preceding reveals a mixed picture of warfare as a phenomenon in decline, yet still vitally important. The fact that more than half of all armed conflicts occurring since the end of World War II remain active offers sufficient proof of the persistence of conflict in the contemporary era (Eriksson & Wallensteen, 2004). These aggregate patterns and trends aside, it is also the case that warfare has changed in qualitative terms over the centuries. Technological advances, the infusion of nationalism, the changing scope and costs of war, and innovations in strategy are each areas in which the very nature of war and how nations and/or states conduct it has changed.

Technology has rapidly escalated the ability to kill. There have been "advances" in the ability to manufacture weapons with an awesome capacity to kill and destroy, as well as in the ability to deliver those weapons at increasing distances and speed. Such changes are evident in technological innovations such as things we take for granted (gunpowder, the internal combustion engine), as well as those that occupy a prominent position in global political discourse (nuclear fission and fusion, intercontinental ballistic missiles). More recently, the infusion of cutting-edge scientific and

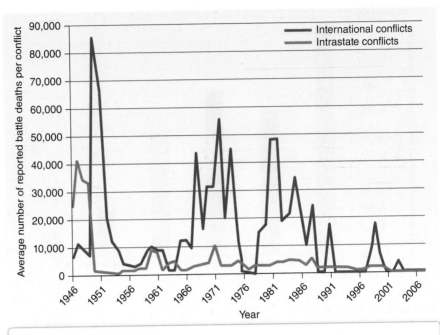

FIGURE 7.9

Reported battle deaths per state-based armed conflict: International conflicts versus intrastate conflicts, 1946–2008

With very few exceptions, international conflicts have been and remain far more deadly than intrastate conflicts.

Data Sources: Peace Research Institute Oslo; Uppsala Conflict Data Programme/Human Security Report Project.

technological advances in the areas of robotics and artificial intelligence into warfare has resulted in new classes and categories of weaponry (such as "unmanned aerial vehicles" [UAVs or "drones"]) featuring highly destructive capabilities, but involving little risk or even human involvement for those employing them.

Nationalism has also qualitatively changed warfare. Before the 19th century, the houses of nobles generally fought wars with limited armies. The American (1776) and French (1789) Revolutions, and the era of popular sovereignty and mass politics that followed, changed that. The revolutionary French state declared that military service was a patriotic duty and instituted the first comprehensive military draft in 1793. The idea of patriotic military service, coupled with the draft, allowed France's army to be the first to number more than a million persons. Subsequently, in the 19th and 20th centuries, nation-states mostly fought each other in interstate wars, with increases in intensity and in numbers involved as entire societies mobilized in service of the war effort (a phenomenon that we sometimes refer to as "total war").

The scope and cost of war have expanded as a result of technology and nationalism. Entire nations have become increasingly involved in wars. Before 1800, no more than 3 in 1,000 people of a country participated in a war. By World War I, the European powers called 1 of 7 people to arms. Technology increased the need to mobilize the population for industrial production and also increased the capacity for, and the rationality of, striking at civilians. Nationalism made war a movement of the masses, increasing their stake and also providing justification for attacking the enemy nation (Mann, 1992). One result is the blurred distinction between military and civilian targets. Modern technology has also reversed the connection between war effort and the nation (Coker, 2002). The high-tech forces the United States and its allies deployed against Iraq (1991, 2003) and Yugoslavia (1995, 1999) and the quick victories over the opposing regular military forces that ensued largely separated the war effort from the daily lives of Americans.

War as an endeavor has always been and remains costly, both in terms of blood and treasure. Preparations, waging war, and repairing the damage have always been expensive, but the increasing technological sophistication of war and of the military arsenals of many of the most militarized states has in some ways escalated these costs. This is true not only with respect to the staggering financial costs of waging and preparing for war—particularly when employing high-tech weaponry at great distances from the battlefield—but also in human terms, given the potentially high death and casualty tolls that we associate with modern warfare. While proponents of such innovations in weaponry argue that they are likely to correspond with greater precision and therefore reduced deaths and casualties for all parties concerned (including the state employing them), we cannot minimize their destructive capacity. Yet another way to look at the costs of waging or preparing for war is for us to consider global military spending (Figure 7.10).

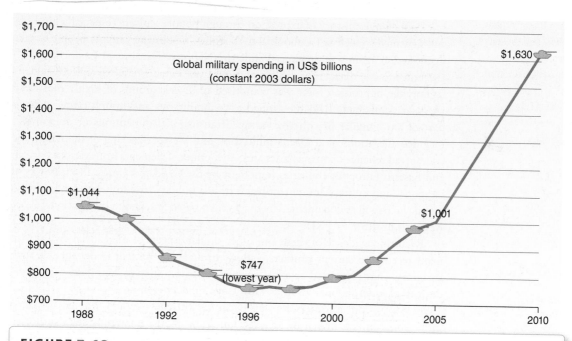

FIGURE 7.10

Global military spending

Global military spending peaked in the late 1980s, at the end of the Cold War, then declined into the mid-1990s, reaching a low point in 1996 and remaining fairly steady through the rest of the 1990s. Beginning in 2000, arms spending began to accelerate rapidly, increasing about 25% in constant 2003 dollars (adjusted for inflation) to over $1.6 trillion in 2010.

Data Source: Stockholm International Peace Research Institute (SIPRI), 2011.

Libyan rebel forces, coordinated by the National Transitional Council, proved adept in the field if sometimes fractured politically. These fractures persist and continue to provide obstacles for crafting a stable post-Gaddafi political order in Libya.

THE CHANGING CONTEXT OF WAR

The end of the Cold War has ushered in significant changes in the structure and context of the global system, with direct ramifications for the nature and conduct of war. The vast majority of wars today seem to conform with a "new pattern of conflict" defined by "challenges to existing state authority" rather than territory or other conventional national interests (Wallensteen & Axell, 1995:345). These challenges play out in many ways, with the defining thread the lack of centralized state control over the prosecution of war.

This dynamic was clearly evident in the Libyan civil war—including, but not limited to, the organic uprising of everyday Libyans against Gaddafi's regime that triggered the conflict, as well as both sides targeting civilians. Opposition to Gaddafi's rule had a longer history of expression through popular culture (especially hip hop) and new media (such as Facebook and YouTube), mobilizing younger people to take direct action against the regime. While the National Transitional Council (NTC) attempted to coordinate the rebellion and construct a shadow state to replace Gaddafi's regime, the opposition force was comprised of diverse groups of highly motivated irregular combatants who functioned as paramilitaries and militia rather than as part of any singular or cohesive "army." Transnational dimensions of the conflict included allegations of al Qaeda infiltration and Western backing of the rebels, the widespread reliance on mercenaries and other criminal elements from various African and Eastern European countries (especially by the Gaddafi regime), and transfers of weaponry and military equipment by air from a military base in Belarus to Gaddafi's regime in Tripoli as documented by the Sweden-based Stockholm International Peace Research Institute (SIPRI).

Recurring evidence of these and other similar aspects of the Libyan civil war in many recent and current conflicts—all occurring apart from, or in defiance of, state authority—has prompted scholars to question the utility of "standard theoretical devices of international politics" for explaining contemporary warfare (Holsti, 1996:25). With major interstate wars declining in frequency, and internal and often intractable conflicts driven by identity, unfolding amidst unraveling state authority, and fueled by scarcity rising to the fore, some view previous conceptions of warfare as insufficient (Henderson & Singer, 2002).

"Old" Wars: Origins and Logic

By the late 1990s a number of scholars of conflict and security studies responded to perceived changes in the structure and arrangements of global politics by introducing the conceptual device of **"new" wars**. Assertions of the changed nature and context of

"New" wars
Low-intensity but protracted armed conflicts often taking place within the boundaries of a state, between contending identity groups and irregular forces associated with them, and waged in such a way that distinctions between civil and military authority and combatants and noncombatants lack relevance.

contemporary warfare beg the question of what came before. In the view of proponents of the "new" wars thesis, "**old**" **wars** originated in a specific place and era (Western Europe from the 16th to 19th century) undergoing a complete social metamorphosis (Kaldor, 1999). This metamorphosis transformed war from a feudal endeavor to a thoroughly modern one. Whereas armed conflict was formerly a contest of honor and skill as well as a display of power, which vassals launched at the behest of monarchs and waged through the proxy of knights and mercenaries, the forces of modernity brought armed conflict under the complete and total control of the state.

The state's centrality in the global political system is intertwined with the evolution of modern warfare. This is borne out in the key developments in the evolution of "old" warfare, and the state's central position in those developments. Included among these are the formation of professional standing armies to wage war; the creation of public-sector finance and the establishment of permanent taxation systems to fund those armies and their military campaigns; the introduction of the convention of *raison d'etat* ("reason of state") as a central, even sufficient justification for said wars; and the promulgation of rules attempting to govern the conduct of war. These are all characteristics of "old" or "modern" warfare (evident in such widely chronicled conflicts as World War I) that we take for granted today, but which did not exist prior to the modern state's establishment and consolidation (Mann, 1992).

The historical relationship between the state and war has been so extensive (and mutually reinforcing) that "old" wars are essentially exercises in statecraft, along the lines of that which the famous 19th-century Prussian strategist Carl von Clausewitz described (see the "Thinking Theoretically" box). Masterful generals and diplomats from ancient to modern time have recognized the intimate connection between force and diplomacy that Clausewitz spoke to in *On War*. The great Chinese strategist Sun Tzu in *The Art of War* (about 500 BCE) counseled, "A government should not mobilize its army out of anger. . . . Act when it is beneficial; desist when it is not." Cleverly inverting Clausewitz's view, China's Premier Zhou Enlai in 1954 referred to diplomacy as "a continuation of war by other means."

"New" Wars: Origins and Logic

The archetype of the Clausewitzian "old" war held that wars were the product of rational calculation. Political leaders utilized the state's tools over which they presided to deploy overwhelming force against similarly organized opponents in a contest over competing national interest(s). Conversely, scholars have characterized contemporary conflicts as "wars of the third kind"—successors to the limited war of 18th- and 19th-century

> **"Old" wars**
> Derived from Clausewitzian thought and reflected in the wars of the 19th and early 20th centuries. "Old"wars refer to wars fought by and through the state and its organized, professional standing armies in pursuit of the national interest. Key distinctions typifying the "modern" state (disaggregated civil and military authority, distinctions between combatants and noncombatants, etc.) shaped the conduct of such wars.

> So-called "new" wars tend to originate in fundamental clashes between identity groups, fueled by transnational flows of money, weapons, combatants, and ideas. One of the first, and perhaps best, examples of a "new" war occurred in Bosnia-Herzegovina with the breakup of Yugoslavia in the early 1990s. This photo depicts the types of paramilitaries and irregular forces that were central actors in that, and other, "new" wars.

statecraft, and the total war of the 20th-century world wars (Rice, 1988). They have also referred to them as "internal conflicts" (Brown, 1996), "new" wars (Kaldor, 1999), "small wars" (Harding, 1994), and "protracted social conflicts" (Azar, 1990).

Regardless of the terminology that we use to describe them, this emerging view of contemporary conflict rests on three propositions: Such conflicts are increasingly likely to be carried out by actors other than states, for causes other than traditional national interests, and by means and tactics other than those associated with regular, professionalized standing armies. New wars are identity-fueled and chaotically disorganized conflicts that a range of official and irregular combatants wage and that **remittances**, organized crime, and transnational networks moving money, arms, and people sustain. Further, the key distinctions at the heart of modern society and central to "old" wars have been deeply eroded (Shaw, 1999). In "new" wars such as those in Bosnia-Herzegovina, Nagorny-Karabakh, Sierra Leone, Afghanistan, and Colombia (to name a few), armed conflict is advanced without much regard for separation between internal and external political and social realms, public and private goods and activities, civilian and military authority, or even between states of "war" and "peace" (Münkler, 2004).

Globalization as Catalyst Why are "new" wars happening now? "New" war theorists point to globalization as a phenomenon that has radically recast nearly all forms of social behavior, including war. While globalization is obviously not something that began in 1991, there is a decided emphasis on the intensity and extensity of the current wave of globalization and the acceleration of these dynamics as the catalyst for "new" wars.

Political scientists can naturally lump in armed conflict with the unfettered flow of goods, services, and capital, mass migration, and transboundary problems such as pollution and disease, as phenomena that have become "globalized." The forces of globalization have also unleashed a well-documented backlash against the processes of globalization and their perceived beneficiaries. Scholars have characterized this backlash around various divides such as **"jihad v. McWorld"** (Barber, 1996), a **"clash of civilizations"** (Huntington, 1996), or "globalization and its discontents" (Stiglitz, 2002). Regardless of one's perspective on the merits or pitfalls of globalization, it is important to recognize that globalization has both integrative and fragmentary effects—with the latter a significant factor underlying "new" wars.

The Crisis of the State "New" war theorists contend that globalization triggers two simultaneous and interrelated "crises." The first of these stems from states' increasing inability to control their internal and external relations. This diminished control leaves the state (and especially weak states) struggling to contend with the causes, dynamics, and implications of **transnationalism** and globalization in the realm of collective violence, as well as in the realms of commerce, health, migration, and the environment.

At the same time that an increasing number of states have proven unable to cope with the negative effects of the disruptive, polarizing, and seemingly haphazard processes of globalization, millions of individuals view these processes as threats. Furthermore, the spillover of globalization into the realm of collective violence poses a

Remittances
A transfer of money by an expatriate to persons in his or her home country.

"Jihad v. McWorld"
A thesis advanced by political theorist Benjamin Barber (1992, 1996) claiming that global politics is increasingly defined by the tensions between the homogenizing tendencies of globalization (the "McWorld" culture) and the fragmented backlash of tribalism (the "Jihad" culture).

"Clash of civilizations"
Samuel P. Huntington's thesis (1993, 1996) that the source of future conflict will be along "civilizational" (e.g., cultural) lines, with conflicts emerging at the "fault lines" or interfaces of the most contentious of the world's major civilizational units.

Transnationalism
Social, political, economic, and cultural activities and processes that transcend and permeate the borders and sovereign authority of states.

real, direct, and enhanced threat to the security of individuals. At the very juncture when state capacity is most pivotal—in the midst of the chaotic violence and lawlessness of "new" wars—the inefficacy, particularly of weak states, is apparent.

The Crisis of Identity

At the same time, some scholars believe that "new" wars produce a second "crisis" of identity, fueled by a **"particularistic identity politics"** driving "new" wars (Kaldor, 1999). In "old" and "new" wars alike, the manipulation of group identity by elites is important, as is the resonance of group identity within the populace. Taken together, these factors are crucial to the process of creating and sustaining a climate whereby the use of violence in relation to a real or perceived grievance is acceptable, if not desirable.

"New" wars are violent contests between inclusive and exclusive notions of social organization, which the social-psychological distinctions of "in-group" and "out-group" prompt. These occur around ethnic, religious, linguistic, or other cognitive signifiers (Druckman, 1994). These distinctions are often rooted in deep-seated historical and cultural grievances (whether real or imagined), grievances sustained through a mix of exaltation (of the in-group's honor, past, and traditions), demonization (of the out-group's motives and actions), and the manufacturing of a sense of perpetual threat (Stein, 2001). Such identities are usually historically derived and therefore have broader and more sustained appeal in the face of challenges to the nation-state, particularly given the degree of romanticized myth-making that we associate with them.

We should not overlook the extent to which the twin crises of the state and identity are mutually reinforcing, at least in the view of "new" war theorists. With the capacity of all states (and particularly weak states) exposed by globalization, the decline of personal fealty (pledge of allegiance of one person to the other) to the state further undermines state capacity and, by extension, national cohesion. In such a context, it is natural that individuals would look to other sources for both security and identity reinforcement. In this way, ethnic, religious, or other so-called **primordial identities** serve as appealing replacements for national identity. This transfer of political identity from nation-state to sub-state group lies at the heart of "new" wars.

Waging and Sustaining "New" Wars

In "new" wars, the basic calculus of warfare in terms of strategy and tactics is transformed. That is not to say that "new" wars lack a political dimension. We associate "new" wars with an effort by sub-state groups (with transnational support networks) to contest, hijack, or weaken the state's authority. However, in strategic terms the employment of violence in "new" wars veers drastically from the pursuit of traditional political or military objectives. Ultimately, "new" wars are those advanced and shaped by the desire to sow and reap the gains of fear and hatred on which a radical identity politics turn. Combatants engaged in "new" wars are singularly unified in the pursuit of political power and economic gain, and roundly dismissive of unifying ideologies, restraints on the use of force, or concerns with perceived political legitimacy. Rather than a tool to advance the national interest, in "new" wars violence is both the means to an end, and an end onto itself.

The chief point of departure for "new" wars is that the combatants' interests and the source of mobilization are one and the same; namely, the defense and advancement

"Particularistic identity politics"
A narrow, zero-sum conception of political identity that tends to generate fragmentation and intercommunal violence along national, ethnic, religious, or linguistic lines. Such identity politics are often employed by elites in such fragmented societies to consolidate power through zealous appeals to one identity group and derogation of the "other."

Primordial identities
A term that refers to the view advanced by some political and social theorists that a given identity may be deeply embedded or "hardwired" in a person's consciousness. Such identities override other possible sources of identity and other possible influences on an individual's perceptions of social and political phenomena—which can produce extreme intolerance and violence toward members of other identity groups.

Targeting civilians, systematic rape, and forced population displacement (as depicted in this photo)—along with war profiteering and mercenary activity—are all features of the long-running internal conflict within the Democratic Republic of the Congo. This conflict, which began with the fall of long-time dictator Mobutu Sese Seko in 1997, is sometimes referred to as "Africa's World War," involving a multiplicity of states and non–state actors and featuring horrific war crimes and crimes against humanity.

of one's own group relative to the much-demonized "other." This is often established and maintained through the selective and targeted use of violence to expel or eliminate any challengers, particularly those of the out-group(s), by political elites seeking to foster intercommunal violence in order to gain or consolidate political and economic power. In "new" wars, population displacement, massacres, widespread and systematic human rights violations, and organized criminal activity transform from ancillary outcomes to deliberate war strategies.

In "new" wars, a combination of paramilitaries, mercenaries, organized crime syndicates, and various other irregular forces substitute for standing, professionalized, hierarchically organized state armies. These irregular forces straddle and intentionally blur the distinction between combatants and noncombatants— as a result of both their own murky status as well as their favored targets. The object of "new" war violence is typically not the corresponding irregular forces of other competing groups, but civilians (Snow, 1996). As a result, nations repeatedly and egregiously violate rules governing the conduct of war embodied in various international treaties and conventions (such as the Geneva Conventions). In the process, core distinctions at the heart of "modern" society and "old" wars—such as between combatants and noncombatants—are stretched to the point of irrelevance. Such circumstances promote the adaptability and opportunism of shadowy and violent criminal networks, utilizing their structures to equal measure in the pursuit of war booty and the conduct of organized criminal activity on one hand, and the prosecution of intercommunal violence on the other (Berdal, 2003).

Arms production and trade has become globalized, as has organized crime, whether connected to brokering arms transfers or providing other goods and services convertible into revenue streams for sustaining and expanding armed conflicts. Those revenues, combined with remittances drawn from transnational communities of exiles and other supporters, are easy to launder and even easier to transfer within a deregulated global financial system. At the same time, the basis of "new" wars in clashing identities serves as a natural animus for recruiting, fundraising, and propagandizing along such networks, wherever émigré and refugee communities with strong kin loyalties flourish. Combatants are drawn from all quarters of the globe, and are relatively easy to recruit and move into and out of conflict zones using the channels of transnational (oftentimes **diaspora**) networks (Jung, 2003).

Diaspora
The movement, migration, or scattering of people away from an established homeland.

ASYMMETRICAL WARFARE: TERRORISM

When a quadrennial survey taken in 1999 asked Americans to name two or three top foreign policy concerns, only 12% mentioned terrorism. Four years later, with 9/11 on their minds, 75% of Americans identified terrorism as a critical threat, beyond any other foreign policy issue—a place of prominence it continues to enjoy (CCGA, 2010). While the shadow of terrorism may be greater than its actual presence, it remains an important translation of political violence. In large part, this importance stems from the fact that it is perhaps the most notable translation of **asymmetric warfare**—a term that refers to the organized and purposeful use of force by a weaker actor against a stronger one. This aspect of terrorism—that it is a tactic a weaker actor employs against a stronger one—applies to virtually every current or historical example of terrorism.

> **Asymmetric warfare**
> A strategy of conflict employed by a weaker actor in contending with a stronger one, in an attempt to "level the playing field." Terrorism is the most often cited example of asymmetric warfare, given the disparities in power and capabilities that often exist between states and non–state actors. Unconventional weapons, such as biological, chemical, or nuclear weapons, are also appealing instruments of asymmetric warfare.

The overall prominence of terrorism in general, and of one transnational terrorist group (al Qaeda) in particular, is exemplified even in the Libyan civil war. Gaddafi's repeated claims that the rebels were supported and infiltrated by al Qaeda turned typically bizarre (culminating in claims that al Qaeda was influencing the rebels to oppose his rule and turn to violence by slipping hallucinogens into the milk, coffee, and nondairy creamers ordinary Libyans used), but overall were designed to try to elicit international support by attempting to link the rebellion to a worldwide scourge. For their part, the NTC and other rebel forces took great pains to denounce al Qaeda and renounce Islamic fundamentalism publicly (although Islamic fundamentalist groups and parties were clearly part of the opposition). In August 2011, NATO's Supreme Allied Commander, James G. Stavridis, even went as far as to acknowledge "flickers" of al Qaeda activity among the rebels—in part on the basis of previous evidence in U.S. intelligence circles of significant Libyan presence within al Qaeda.

Definition and Scope

One of the main challenges of examining terrorism is that it defies efforts to define it. This is not just a semantic problem. It has affected initiatives to establish treaties and other international efforts to combat terrorism—all while the scope and impact of terrorism internationally has grown.

Seeking a Definition The UN and other national and international agencies have struggled for years to draft a comprehensive treaty on terrorism. They have concluded several treaties, including one in 2005 to thwart nuclear terrorism. However, a general agreement has failed in part because of disagreements over how even to define terrorism. These differences occur across states (the U.S. and U.K. definitions vary widely, for instance) and even between and among governmental agencies within states (various agencies of the U.S. government employ different definitions). On the global stage, many non-Western states stress that we should not consider armed struggles for national liberation against occupation or against discriminatory political regimes as terrorism.

While recognizing this lack of consensus, it is, however, important to establish how the word is used here. Terrorism is a form of political violence, carried out by individuals, nongovernmental organizations, or covert government agents or units,

that specifically targets civilians using clandestine methods. This definition stresses that terrorism focuses on harming some people in order to create fear in others by targeting civilians and facilities or systems (such as transportation) on which civilians rely (Kydd & Walter, 2006). The terrorists' objective is not just killing and wounding people and destroying physical material. Equally important targets are the emotions of those who see or read about the act of violence and become afraid or dispirited (Hoffman, 2006).

Although the tactics are similar, it is useful to distinguish between *domestic terrorism*, which includes attacks by local nationals within their country against a purely domestic target for domestic reasons; *international terrorism*, which involves terrorists attacking a foreign target, either within their own country or abroad; and *transnational terrorism*, which consists of transnational terrorist activities carried out by densely globally networked actors operating covertly across multiple national borders simultaneously. The attack on the Oklahoma City federal building in 1995 that killed 168 people and injured 800 more was an example of domestic terrorism. The kidnapping and murder of 11 Israeli athletes and one West German police officer by the Palestinian terrorist organization Black September at the 1972 Summer Olympics in Munich is an example of international terrorism, and al Qaeda's 9/11 attack on the World Trade Center in New York and the Pentagon in Arlington, Virginia, is an example of transnational terrorism.

This definition of terrorism clearly reflects the prevailing view in the global system that terrorism is a form of political violence that non–state actors rather than states employ. This perspective does not mean that all military actions states undertake are acceptable or permissible, nor does it mean that states cannot enmesh themselves in terrorist activities as supporters, sponsors, or beneficiaries. However, we can more accurately classify acts of violence that resemble terrorist activities—especially, but not only, the targeting of civilians—when states carry them out as war crimes under the principles of *jus in bello* (just conduct of war) and the various international conventions concerning war that follow from those principles. In light of this point, it seems clear that this definition places a premium on the intentional targeting of civilians as a distinguishing feature of terrorism—which by inference rejects the relativist claim many terrorist organizations and their sympathizers advance that the "ends" (political objectives) necessarily justify the "means" (targeting of civilians). An example of this logic was evident in an audiotape released on the Internet in 2005 by Abu Musab al-Zarqawi, the former leader of al Qaeda in Iraq (killed by a U.S. air strike in 2006), stressing that it was "acceptable to

Though definitional debates persist, terrorism tends to embody the spirit of former U.S. Supreme Court Justice Stewart Potter's comment regarding the definition of pornography: We know it when we see it. Without a doubt, the 9/11 attacks, by targeting civilians in a spectacular fashion designed to elicit major worldwide attention to a cause, meet any conceivable definition of what constitutes an act of terrorism.

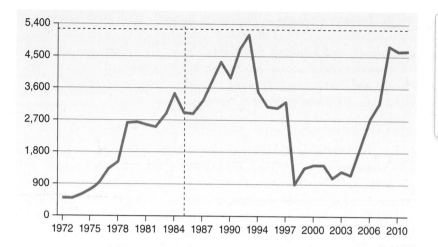

FIGURE 7.11
Frequency of terrorist
incidents per year,
1972–2010

Data Source: Global Terrorism
Database (GTD), University of
Maryland.

kill all infidels with all the kinds of arms that we have . . . even if armed infidels and
women and children are killed together."

Frequency and Extent   Incidents of terrorism are a regular occurrence, as evident in Figure 7.11. Also noteworthy is that while domestic terrorism as such is not
our focus here, domestic terrorism is more common and claims more lives than
international or transnational terrorism. Since 2004, domestic terrorist attacks have
far exceeded international attacks in number and lethality, largely because
of the sectarian violence in Iraq. For the most part, we can attribute this
difference to transnationalism, which makes the distinction between
"domestic" and "international" terrorism largely irrelevant. Geographically, as Figure 7.12 shows, terrorism has touched all the regions of the

FIGURE 7.12
Number of terrorist incidents by
region, 2000–2010

Data Source: Global Terrorism Database (GTD),
University of Maryland.

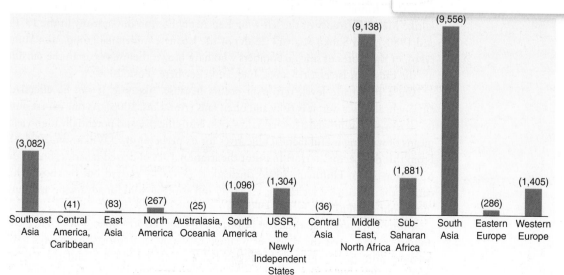

world, but between 2000 and 2010, terrorist incidents of all types have been most common in South Asia (34% of all incidents), the Middle East and North Africa (32% of all incidents), and Southeast Asia (11%). Conversely, Western Europe weathered 5% of all incidents, while North America was relatively insulated from terrorism. The spectacular and devastating 9/11 attack notwithstanding, only 0.9% of all terrorist incidents since 2000 have occurred in North America.

Causes of Terrorism

Although the September 11, 2001, attacks brought it to the front of the global agenda, terrorism has long existed. Understanding the causes of terrorism and its recent record are important parts of combating it (Laqueur, 2004; Sinclair, 2004).

Untangling the causes of terrorism is much like trying to understand why war occurs. At the *system level of analysis,* it is possible to argue that such political violence is in part a product of unequal global distribution of wealth (Ehrlich & Liu, 2005; Piazza, 2006). This inequality is hardly new, but globalization has brought the wealth gap into sharper focus. That reality points to another frequently articulated system level explanation for terrorism—the profound clash between Western liberalism and other views of politics, society, and economic activity. Globalization has proven dislocating and threatening not only in its impact but also for what it represents, inspiring a sociocultural backlash in many states and societies (Mousseau, 2003).

State- or societal-level analysis of terrorism often points to the emergence of terrorism in political systems when there are either few (or no) available nonviolent options for the expression of political views or when political violence is an attractive alternative that will call attention to the group and its agenda (Weinberg, 2001; Gurr, 1998). States' actions also clearly elicit terrorism, as we see with the foreign policy behavior of Israel and the United States in the Middle East, which provides constant fodder for jihadi terrorism, which al Qaeda and its affiliates perpetuate. On the *individual level of analysis,* one can seek to analyze the psychology and motivation of terrorists themselves. We can extend this inquiry to leaders such as Osama bin Laden, Ulrike Meinhof (leader of the left-wing Red Army Faction in Germany in the 1970s and 1980s), and Shoko Asahara (leader of the Japanese millennial group Aum Shinryko), or the scores of suicide bombers who have blown themselves up in the pursuit of "the cause" in Israel, Sri Lanka, Iraq, and elsewhere (Post, 2004).

On a pragmatic level, terrorism occurs because, like war, it can be effective, although, also like war, it is risky and often fails (Abrahms, 2006). As one expert puts it, "Terrorism has proved a low-cost, low-risk, cost-effective and potentially high-yield means of winning useful tactical objectives for its perpetrators" (Wilkinson, 2005:4). From this perspective, terrorism is not the irrational act of crazed fanatics (Bueno de Mesquita, 2005; Hoffman, 2006). Instead, it is usually carried out by those who consider it a necessary, legitimate, effective, and available tool for advancing and pursuing political aims (Crenshaw, 1988).

Moreover, prevailing social conditions are ripe for terrorist operations. First, technology has increased the power of weapons available to terrorists. Explosives have become more deadly, huge airliners can become piloted missiles, and there is an increasing danger of terrorists obtaining the material and means to launch a biological, chemical, or radiological attack. Second, increased urbanization has brought people together so that they are easier targets, especially when gathered in such high-profile places as skyscrapers and sports stadiums. With eerie premonition, a U.S. senator warned in 1999 that Americans were vulnerable to attack on targets that terrorists might select "for their symbolic value, like the World Trade Center in the heart of Manhattan."[1] Third, modern communications have also made terrorism more efficacious because the terrorist's goal is not to kill or injure, as such. Instead, the aim of terrorism is to gain attention for a cause or to create widespread anxiety that will, in turn, create pressure on governments to negotiate with terrorists and accede to their every demand. Without the media to transmit the news of their acts, terrorist attacks would affect only their immediate victims, which would not accomplish terrorists' goals (Nacos, 2007).

Sources of Terrorism

Two sources of political terrorism concern us here. One is state-sponsored terrorism. The second comprises transnational terrorist groups. As we shall see, they are closely linked.

State-Sponsored Terrorism   While we reflect the perspective of most scholars of terrorism that consider it a form of political violence non–state actors perpetrate, to argue that uniformed military personnel serving in the armed forces of a state are not proper terrorists does not mean that states themselves cannot engage in terrorism. For one, states can participate in **state-sponsored terrorism**, in which an established government's clandestine operatives or others who a country has specifically encouraged, funded, trained, equipped, and/or granted sanctuary carry out terrorist activities and operations.

From the U.S. perspective, the State Department has historically listed Cuba, Iran, Iraq, Libya, North Korea, Sudan, and Syria among state sponsors of terrorism. For their part, each of these countries has vehemently denied involvement in terrorism, and some of the U.S. allegations would fall outside the definition of terrorism that we use here. Not all would, though. For example, state terrorism would include Syria's involvement in the 2005 assassination of former Lebanese Prime Minister Rafiq Hariri, a strong opponent of Syria's long-time infiltration of Lebanon. Some have accused the United States of engaging in state terrorism. "We consider the United States and its current administration as a first-class sponsor of international terrorism, and it along with Israel form an axis of terrorism and evil in the world," a group of 126 Saudi scholars wrote in a joint statement.[2] Supporting examples include Washington's alleged complicity in political assassinations and other forms of state terrorism practiced internally by some countries in Latin America and elsewhere during the anticommunist fervor of the Cold War.

Transnational Terrorist Groups   The global changes that have given rise to a rapid increase in the number of international nongovernmental organizations have also expanded the number of transnational terrorist groups that are organized and

> **State-sponsored terrorism**
> Describes terrorism sponsored by nation-states. As with terrorism, the precise definition, and the identification of particular examples, are subjects of heated political dispute. In general, state-sponsored terrorism is associated with providing material support and/or sanctuary to terrorist or paramilitary organizations.

operate internationally and that commit **transnational terrorism**. One source, the U.S. State Department, identifies 40 such groups, including al Qaeda and its various regional and local affiliates, and there are dozens of other such organizations that the State Department has accused of terrorist activity or support. Transnational terrorist organizations are notable both for the global and transboundary reach, scope, and targeting of their activities and planning, as well as their ability to utilize the networked structure of global society to draw upon the needed materiel (weapons, money) and human (recruits) resources and promote their message (ideas and objectives) to sustain that global and transboundary scope and reach. In many ways they are among the most skillful manipulators of globalization, utilizing things like financial deregulation, relaxed border standards (especially within the EU), and the Internet and other information and communications technologies to sustain and expand their activities and support.

Al Qaeda is surely the most prominent terrorist organization today, and its origins and operations provide a glimpse into the emergence and evolution of transnational terrorism more generally. Al Qaeda (loosely translated from Arabic as "the Base") was founded by Osama bin Laden (the disaffected son of a wealthy Saudi family), along with Ayman al-Zawahiri (an Egyptian physician and then-head of the group Egyptian Islamic Jihad) in the late 1980s to encourage Arab support for and participation in a campaign of *jihad* against the Soviet occupiers in Afghanistan. Upon helping drive the Soviet forces from Afghanistan in 1989, al Qaeda's focus shifted to the United States. Bin Laden was particularly outraged by the presence of U.S. forces in Saudi Arabia near Mecca and Medina, two of the three holiest places (along with Jerusalem) of Islam, and by American support of what he saw as Israel's oppression of Palestinian Muslims. Reflecting this view (although not with any formal theological training or authority), bin Laden issued a 1998 *fatwa* (religious edict) entitled "Jihad Against Jews and Crusaders," which proclaimed that "to kill the Americans and their allies—civilians and military—is an individual duty for every Muslim who can do it in any country in which it is possible to do it."[3]

Subsequently, bin Laden and his followers fashioned and drew from the strength of a loose, horizontal network of cells distributed across the globe to mastermind a number of terrorist attacks, of which the most spectacular and devastating were the 9/11 attacks. The group and its affiliates have also been linked to other terrorist activities ranging from the 2005

> **Transnational terrorism**
> Terrorism carried out either across national borders or by groups that operate in more than one country.

> Some scholars of contemporary terrorism have argued that the major terrorist threat to the West stems from so-called third wave or "homegrown" terrorists, who are individuals born in countries like the U.S., U.K., or France that are inspired by, but not formally associated with, al Qaeda. A classic example of just such a terrorist is the Alabama-born Islamist militant Omar Hammami, 27, also known as Abu Mansur al-Amriki. Here, Hammami speaks during a news conference held by the militant group al-Shabab at a farm in southern Mogadishu's Afgoye district in Somalia.

rush-hour attack on the London bus and subway system, in which four bombs killed 56 commuters, to the violent insurgency against the Iraqi government during the U.S. occupation. While al Qaeda remains a prominent example of transnational terrorism and continues to pose a significant security threat to many states, bin Laden's death in a U.S. military attack on his compound in Abottabad, Pakistan, in May 2011, as well as the organization's marginal influence on recent transformative events in the Arab world, have led some to debate its present and future effectiveness (Byman, 2011). One prominent scholar has pointed to al Qaeda's greatest legacy as its role in ushering in a **"third wave" of terrorism** plaguing many Western states and carried out by individuals not only living in, but in some cases native-born citizens of, those states and inspired by if not formally associated with "al Qaeda central" (Sageman, 2008).

"Third wave" of terrorism
A thesis advanced by some scholars of terrorism (Sageman, 2008) that contends that the most recent wave of transnational terrorism is being advanced by "homegrown" Islamic radicals living in, and citizens of, Western countries and loosely inspired by al Qaeda.

TOOLS OF CONFLICT MANAGEMENT

Despite the troubling prevalence of armed conflict, global politics features many different approaches and avenues for limiting and restraining war. Even in the Libyan civil war, outside parties attempted forays into conflict management. Perhaps the most notable were efforts by the UN Security Council. A body with collective security responsibilities, it authorized its member-states to employ coercive diplomacy against Gaddafi's reactionary regime. This came primarily through sanctions freezing the Gaddafi government's assets and referring allegations of crimes against humanity to the International Criminal Court for investigation (UNSC Res 1970, February 26, 2011). Later the UNSC invoked the UN Charter's Chapter VII to authorize the creation of a "no-fly zone" over Libya and the use of "all necessary measures" to defend civilians (UNSC Res 1973, March 17, 2011). Additionally, the African Union proposed mediation of the dispute between Gaddafi's regime and the rebels— an overture that the National Transitional Council (NTC), which was coordinating the opposition, rejected. Although none of these efforts proved effective at forestalling the Libyan civil war, they represent a small range of the possibilities that third parties can and do introduce in the effort to avert or limit war. Here, we will look at some of the more common efforts to limit the outbreak of war and armed conflict or to reduce its damaging consequences—efforts that we lump under the broad heading of "conflict management."

In the field of international relations, we best understand conflict management as any effort to control or contain an ongoing conflict between politically motivated actors operating at the state or sub-state level, through third-party involvement (Burton & Dukes, 1990). Conflict management is centrally concerned with making an ongoing conflict less damaging to the parties directly engaged in it. Conflict management also often originates from a third party's concern with containing the conflict's damaging and destabilizing effects to other semi-involved or noninvolved parties ("horizontal escalation"), as well as containing the conflict's escalation of violent goals and their implementation ("vertical escalation"). Finally, conflict management operates from the premise that a conflict's escalation or intensification is not inevitable. Rather, the goal of conflict management is to deny "victory" to the aggressor(s), or perhaps more accurately, to deny the utility of aggression.

We utilize conflict management approaches when the prospects for conflict resolution seem far-off, but the dynamics of the conflict demand that a third party do something to contain it (Von Hippel & Clarke, 1999). In cases where the conflict's escalation or intensification seems likely, third parties can stem it in numerous ways. Two leading international conflict management scholars have grouped these approaches into four broad categories (Bercovitch & Regan, 2004). A mix of actor objectives and means employed define these approaches. They are:

- *threat-based* (including the use and/or threat of force and other tools to compel other parties);
- *deterrence-based* (including the use and/or threat of force, and various instruments of coercive diplomacy to deter other parties);
- *adjudicatory* (including legal, extralegal, and normative institutions and approaches to craft and reach legal settlements with other parties);
- *accommodationist* (including traditional and nontraditional diplomatic means to broker agreement with other parties).

Threat-based and deterrence-based approaches correspond most clearly with the threat and/or use of "hard" (coercive) power in the pursuit of interest. The main difference is the desired objective. Adjudicatory approaches rely heavily on the recognition of, and appeal to, a system of norms and rights and a legal architecture arrayed around them. Finally, approaches predicated on accommodation emphasize the utility of "soft" (persuasive) power as a means to pursue interests. Each of these approaches, whether in relation to conflict or its management, carries with it different ramifications and consequences, entails different costs, and demands different resources.

Collective Security

Active third-party efforts to limit inter- and intrastate conflicts and contain their negative effects are largely, although not exclusively, 20th-century phenomena. Even so, the underlying impetus behind conflict management is the pursuit of collective security, which has a longer track record worth investigating in order to gain purchase on the emergence of international conflict management.

Political scientists base collective security on three core ideas: first, that armed aggression is an unacceptable form of international political behavior; second, that we should construe an act of aggression directed against any one member in good standing in the international community as a breach of security and an act of aggression directed against all parties; and third, that the provision of security (including the prevention and reversal of acts of aggression) is the duty of all actors in the global political system. To this end, as Baylis (2001:264) points out:

> collective security involves a recognition by states that 1) they must renounce the use of military force to alter the status quo, and agree to settle their disputes peacefully; 2) they must broaden their conception of the national interest to take account of the interests of the international community as a whole; and 3) they must overcome the fear which dominates world politics and learn to trust one another.

history matters

International Conflict Management: Brief History of an Idea(l)?

The impetus to manage international conflict so as to provide stability and order is as old as conflict itself. Ancient China was home to experiments in cooperative leagues of independent states in the seventh and sixth centuries BCE, in which limiting warfare was a primary objective. Collective security and conflict management were also present in the Pan-Hellenist leagues of classical Greece. While amassing ever-increasing wealth and power was the chief objective, it is also clear that imperial Rome, as well as some of its chief subordinate units, undertook policing and enforcement action against disloyal subject nations and against external enemies in order to maintain *Pax Romana*. Later, Renaissance Italy's institutionalized alliances, like the League of Venice (1495) and the wider Holy League that Pope Pius V arranged (1571), provided mechanisms for harnessing armed violence for collective benefit (such as for defense against outside enemies) while otherwise limiting its use.

Another prominent attempt to create a collective security system was the Concert of Europe. Strictly speaking, the Concert of Europe (which included the United Kingdom, Austria, Prussia, and Russia) describes a period of peace between major European powers that prevailed from 1815 to 1854. However, the Concert of Europe's significance and legacy were much broader, as an informal system of conflict management that remained intact until the 1870–1871 Franco-Prussian war and the 1914 outbreak of World War I. Like the Roman Empire, the Concert architects' primary incentive was the preservation of order to enable the pursuit of self-interest. Nonetheless, members undertook ad hoc enforcement operations that contained potential conflicts and other destabilizing events and practices, including campaigns against slave traders and pirates, as well as missions to stabilize and pacify peripheral areas such as the Balkans, Lebanon, and Cyprus throughout the 19th and early 20th centuries.

With organized violence remaining a prominent and unrestricted tool of statecraft actors in the Concert, it was hardly a surprise when the entire system collapsed amid imperial rivalry and alliance obligations, culminating in World War I. The first attempt at a truly institutionalized approach to restraining international conflict came with the creation of the League of Nations in 1919. The massive devastation of World War I served as a chief pretext to its founding, but so too did recognition that the alliance structures canvassing Europe in the years leading up to the war were insufficient for limiting the outbreak, recurrence, or destructive results of conflict.

The League of Nations sought to remedy this situation by broadening its membership in order to commit to conflict management beyond Europe's borders. With the introduction of Wilson's Fourteen Points following The Hague conventions of 1899 and 1907, nations embraced the idea that an organization could manage conflict and limit its effects. Accordingly, these countries ascribed conflict management as the League of Nation's core function. This is evident in examining the League's Covenant, which went so far as to account for the possibility of using military force on the League's behalf to uphold the provisions of the Covenant (Article 16.2). Among these provisions were declarations that established peace and security as a concern to all League members (Article 11.1), and defining an act of war by any League member as an act of war against all (Article 16.1).

Early League efforts at conflict management and security provision were successful, if limited. Prominent illustrations include the peacekeeping/policing role it granted to troop deployments to the Saar valley, the "free city" of Danzig, and Upper Silesia. However, more significant challenges to the League's collective security and conflict management capabilities paved the way for the organization's undoing. Especially noteworthy were the League's ineffectual responses to Japan's invasion of Manchuria in 1931, and Italy's attack on Ethiopia in 1935—cases where the League's conflict management efforts were absent due to a lack of political will and available resources. Despite the emergence of successor organizations with conflict management and collective security mandates—including, most notably, the United Nations—these problems, evident not only in the League of Nations, but also in the various prior conflict management initiatives, continue to plague efforts to manage international conflict and limit its destructive impacts.

Conflict management and collective security share a common point of origin in seeking to promote and enforce norms governing the behavior and interactions among states and other actors on the world stage—in particular, the norm of armed conflict as an undesirable means for settling disputes.

The emphasis on the security of the international community is what distinguishes collective security systems from pure alliances. Alliances usually exist just as a means for each of their members to respond to an external threat, remaining self-regarding in both interest and action. On the other hand, other-regarding interests and actions, particularly regarding the obligation of all to join in a shared, collective response to aggression, define collective security systems. Examples of regional or global institutionalized collective security arrangements include the North Atlantic Treaty Organization, or NATO (1949) and, in part, the United Nations (1945), as well as various other organizations, including the Organization of American States, or OAS (1951), the Organization for African Unity (1963), now the African Union (2002), the Association of Southeast Asian Nations, or ASEAN (1967), and the Organization for Security and Cooperation in Europe, or OSCE (established as the Conference on Security and Cooperation in Europe, 1973).

Peacekeeping

Peacekeeping
The use of military means in a noncoercive posture by an international organization such as the United Nations to prevent a recurrence of military hostilities, usually by acting as a buffer between combatants in a suspended conflict. The international force is neutral between the combatants and must have been invited to be present by the combatants.

State-building
The process of creating both a government and the legal structures of a country and the political identification of the inhabitants of the country with the state and their sense of loyalty to it.

Peacekeeping is a frequently misused term in international relations. Some have used the term to refer to very dissimilar operations. These include the deployment of UN forces to the Sinai in 1956 (to defuse the Suez crisis) or to Cyprus following the Turkish invasion in 1974, extended and multifaceted UN operations in places such as Timor-Leste or Kosovo, mixed operations with stabilization and **state-building** as well as military components (such as NATO's ISAF deployment in Afghanistan), and nakedly self-interested military interventions (such as the U.S.-led *Operation Iraqi Freedom* in Iraq).

As Diehl (1994) points out, if we use peacekeeping to refer to any effort by third parties to terminate an armed conflict, the essence of peacekeeping becomes hopelessly obscured. Using the term in reference to operations where peace is not the first objective (or an objective at all) seems to contradict any basic notions of peace or efforts to "keep" it. In addition, while the fast-and-loose use of the term has significant implications for the study of peacekeeping, it is also important from a policy standpoint, as a poor grasp of the *concept* may contribute to misuse of the *practice* (Rieff, 1994).

Peacekeeping operations involve the introduction of armed military personnel into conflict zones, deploying armed military (as well as civilian police) personnel in a noncoercive posture. As Figure 7.13 indicates, the UN has carried out the bulk of peacekeeping operations today and in the past, although regional organizations and other arrangements can and have provided peacekeeping.

Peacekeeping operations differ dramatically from traditional military operations, which seek to deter or defeat opponents, seizing territory and other key strategic assets in the process. We can plausibly characterize a wide variety of activities as peacekeeping tasks, including but not limited to observation, fact-finding, monitoring ceasefires, and interposition (Bellamy, Williams, & Griffin, 2009). Peacekeeping forces typically carry out mandated responsibilities (specified in multilateral agreements, peace agreements, or resolutions passed by the UN or regional organizations) to monitor ceasefires, maintain buffer zones, and otherwise facilitate security. In more

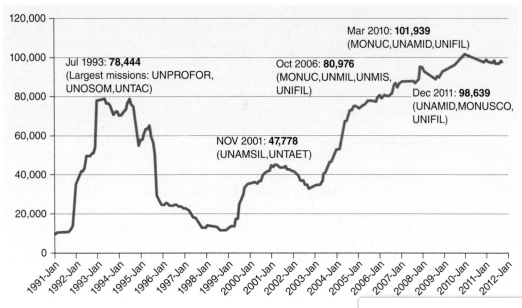

FIGURE 7.13

UN peacekeeping deployments since 1991—total forces and major operations

Data Source: UN Department of Peacekeeping Operations.

recent years, peacekeeping operations have expanded to include various tasks related to political administration, infrastructure rebuilding, and the promotion of civil society (sometimes called "wider" or **multidimensional peacekeeping**). Whatever form they take or place they occur, peacekeeping features three distinctive emphases: a limited reliance on coercive force, impartiality, and reliance on consent.

Limited Force   Peacekeeping deployments can be numerous in terms of personnel, but are always lightly armed. The typical peacekeeper possesses no more than a rifle or small arms, and the typical peacekeeping deployment is arrayed around the use of transport and logistics equipment (such as helicopters and armored personnel carriers) rather than those better suited for offensive action (such as tanks, fighter planes, and aircraft carriers). The lightly armed character of peacekeepers is an intentional reflection of what peacekeeping is and what it seeks to achieve. The extent to which peacekeepers are armed and equipped is consistent with their need to exercise their right to self-defense, and to possess a visible and credible deterrent capability, but does not go beyond that. Since peacekeeping forces are frequently involved in monitoring ceasefires, patrolling demilitarized zones, and other similar actions, this capability is crucial. Equally crucial is that peacekeeping forces are not armed to a level that they pose a threat to the parties to the conflict or to the population at-large.

Impartiality   The neutral nature of the character, activities, and composition of peacekeeping operations also distinguishes them from other forms of conflict management. Resolutions and statements sharply condemning the conflict in question and the behavior of one or more parties to it often precipitate the launching of peacekeeping deployments. However, for peacekeeping to be effective, we must direct it at containing the behavior of the parties rather than at their underlying intentions or grievances.

Multidimensional peacekeeping
A method of peacekeeping when soldiers, military officers, police, and civilian personnel from many countries monitor and observe peace processes that emerge in post-conflict situations and assist conflicting parties to implement the peace agreement they have signed. Such assistance comes in many forms, including promoting human security, confidence-building measures, power-sharing arrangements, electoral support, strengthening the rule of law, and economic and social development.

The requirement of impartiality has both strategic and political dimensions. Within any peacekeeping deployment, the peacekeepers' behavior must be impartial in order to avoid lending strategic or tactical advantage to any one party to the conflict. From a political standpoint, the practice of peacekeeping is wholly dependent on maintaining the view that peacekeepers (especially when provided the auspices of the UN or some other international organization) are neutral. Since the forces and funds committed to peacekeeping operations come from nation-states, impartiality is crucial. Therefore, as a condition for supporting the operation, the state must assure that its impartiality remains at the forefront.

Reliance on Consent   Another crucial aspect of peacekeeping operations is that they are contingent on securing permission from the government(s) of the host state or states where they will be deployed. This means that peacekeepers require the consent of warring parties before they can enter into a conflict. This is wholly unique to peacekeeping, and is emblematic of the central role state sovereignty occupies in peacekeeping. For both political and legal reasons, peacekeeping has been and remains fundamentally oriented around upholding state sovereignty and defending the principle of noninterference—making consent from the warring parties an essential condition of any peacekeeping operation.

The centrality of consent is closely related to other defining aspects of peacekeeping. Peacekeeping is a reactive activity that occurs after conflicts abate. It is also a military operation with highly limited rules of engagement using low levels of force. Given these factors, it stands to reason that securing consent from the warring parties is crucial to the success of peacekeeping operations. Further, by virtue of recognizing and reinforcing the authority of the warring parties, the peacekeeping deployment is established as a nonthreatening entity that does not seek to gain military or strategic advantage relative to any or all of the parties to the conflict.

Peace Enforcement

Peace enforcement
The use of military means in a semicoercive posture by an international organization such as the United Nations to introduce and enforce peace in an ongoing conflict setting. Peace enforcement operations relax some of the restrictions on peacekeeping, allowing for more expansive rules of engagement and for deployment without full consent of the warring parties.

Peace enforcement refers to a concerted initiative organized under international auspices to impose the conditions for peace, including the prevention of a resurgence of violent conflict (Johnston, 2001). As such, it is a very different form of peace operation, born of the recognition of the limitations of peacekeeping for the effective management of certain types and forms of conflict. Former UN Secretary-General Boutros Boutros-Ghali popularized the term "peace enforcement," as we conventionally understand it, in his 1992 policy proposal, "An Agenda for Peace." That document called for the creation of "peace enforcement" units consisting of military forces at the disposal of the UN, chiefly to monitor and enforce cease-fire agreements. Since that time, prominent peace enforcement operations have included the Australian-led International Force for East Timor (INTERFET) in 1999–2000, NATO's *Operation Allied Force* in Kosovo beginning in 1999, and the United Nations Organization Mission in the Democratic Republic of the Congo (MONUC), initiated in 1999.

Boutros-Ghali popularized the use of the term "peace enforcement" to distinguish it from peacekeeping. In the complex, dynamic, and intensely violent environments characterizing most contemporary intrastate conflicts, the interposition of impartial and lightly armed forces as a buffer between the warring parties is unlikely to provide a sufficient deterrent to the continuation or intensification of armed conflict. Conversely, peace enforcement operations seek to create or impose, by force, a cessation in hostilities so as to provide the conditions amenable to the crafting of a long-term peaceful settlement. This difference is not merely one of degree, but of kind, as the defining features of peace enforcement outlined below suggest.

Rules of Engagement The first and most distinguishing feature of peace enforcement is the **rules of engagement (ROE)**. Unlike peacekeeping operations, personnel engaged in peace enforcement operations generally possess the authority to use armed force not only in self-defense, but in other circumstances as well. Chief among these circumstances are the imperatives of defending noncombatants who are under attack or threat of attack or to engage on a military basis with armed combatants who are violating the terms of the cease-fire or other enforced or introduced peace arrangements. In this sense, a third party may use coercive force in a traditional (strategic) fashion, along the lines of what might occur in a conventional military operation.

Resource Requirements The provision and maintenance of public security, safety, and order is a paramount goal of peace enforcement operations. Accordingly, peace enforcement operations require extensive and sophisticated training and weaponry, far beyond that of traditional peacekeeping operations. The condition of noncompliance from warring parties that elicits peace enforcement in the first place also requires personnel engaged in such operations to possess advanced and customized military training, as well as a level of sophisticated armaments, support equipment, and infrastructure befitting a military operation in which a party is likely to encounter significant opposition.

Limited Consent and Impartiality Peace enforcement operations occur when an outside party needs to impose the conditions for peace. In some cases, the parties to the conflict may not desire termination of the hostilities at all. Peace operations in this sort of conflict environment almost always require the infusion of force by a third party, along with the introduction of quasi-offensive ROE previously discussed. Taken together, these factors contribute another key distinguishing feature of peace enforcement operations; namely, that—unlike traditional peacekeeping—they typically do not feature the parties' full consent, and may proceed without securing consent at all.

Despite this difference concerning consent, peace enforcement shares peacekeeping's operational emphasis on impartiality. A central tenet of peace enforcement operations is that the persistence of violence is the chief destabilizing force that peace enforcement must surmount in order to promote the necessary order and stability necessary to further the peace process. The main "enemy" of any peace enforcement operation, therefore, is the persistence of organized aggression, not any of the warring parties. By design, peace enforcement operations usually strive to maintain neutrality and implement their mandate in an even-handed fashion that sustains and enhances the conditions for peace, but does not target or assist any party to the conflict.

Legal Authority The militarily robust nature of peace enforcement represents an important qualitative difference between peace enforcement and most other forms of conflict management. A related difference is that peace enforcement operations

> **Rules of engagement (ROE)**
> Rules defining acceptable conduct by members of the armed forces engaged in a theater of conflict during operations or in the course of their duties. Typically the rules of engagement are clearly stipulated by political leaders and military commanders to military personnel, and are formulated to advance strategic goals while ensuring compliance with the laws of war.

require (and sometimes receive) a different form of legal authorization than do peace-keeping missions or other conflict management initiatives. We can best explain this difference in the sanctioning of peace enforcement operations with reference to the UN Charter. Although peace enforcement can be (and is) provided by non-UN sources, the distinction that we make in terms of legal sanction and within the UN Charter applies conceptually to non-UN operations as well.

We can best understand traditional or "wider" peacekeeping operations as extensions of Chapter VI of the UN Charter (subtitled "Pacific Settlement of Disputes"). Historically, Chapter VI actions also include mediation, negotiation, and a range of other diplomatic ventures emanating from the UN organization. On the other hand, peace enforcement operations more closely resemble the impulse of Chapter VII of the Charter (subtitled "Action with Respect to Threats to the Peace, Breaches of the Peace and Acts of Aggression")—the chapter NATO invoked to justify "all necessary means" for their third-party intervention in Libya's civil war in the spring and summer of 2011.

Clearly, peace enforcement poses a problem for a global political system based on the normative and legal construct of state sovereignty. Peace enforcement operations represent an instance when actors other than states (such as the UN and various RGOs) can employ coercive military force, while also suggesting that these actors can legitimately exercise the authority to determine why, when, and how an outside (third) party may employ military force. In this way, peace enforcement offends the sensibilities and challenges the logic of those who would point to the state as the central and most legitimate actor in the system—especially on occasions where a state employs it *without* UN authorization, as in NATO's *Operation Allied Force* in Kosovo in 1999. Peace enforcement also clashes with the norm of noninterference derived from and sustained by the concept of state sovereignty, and articulated in international law through the UN Charter—making peace enforcement not only difficult to implement on a practical level, but also controversial.

Mediation

Mediation

In global politics, a method of conflict management and resolution in which a third party seeks to generate a settlement that is acceptable to the original parties in an armed conflict or dispute.

Mediation is nearly ubiquitous in modern life, prominent in the legal profession, business world, and even interpersonal relationships. Mediation is also a key function of governments. In the view of social contract theorists such as Thomas Hobbes and John Locke, the mediation of disputes between citizens is one of the most important tasks of (representative) government—one that they can ideally employ before such conflicts escalate and turn violent. Not surprisingly, then, mediation is a principal component of conflict management in global politics.

As a form of international conflict management, mediation is most likely to occur when a conflict is protracted, the parties are at an impasse, neither party is prepared to absorb further costs or escalate the dispute, and both parties are ready to engage in dialogue and welcome mediation (Bercovitch, 1984). As two of the most prominent experts on international mediation (I. William Zartman and Saadia Touval) aptly summarize:

> Mediation is a form of third-party intervention in a conflict. It differs from other forms of third-party intervention in conflicts in that it is not based on the direct use of force and it is not aimed at helping one of the participants to win. Its purpose is to bring the conflict to a settlement that is acceptable to both

challenge your **assumptions**

Is the Expansion of International Law the Key to Limiting War?

Despite the continued absence of a world court or arbitrator with compulsory jurisdiction over states, the existence and use of international tribunals and standing courts to adjudicate international disputes has grown dramatically over the last century, especially since the end of the Cold War. As one longitudinal study found, 63% of the total international judicial activity (5,598 out of 8,895 cases) occurred after 1989. The 1990s witnessed the creation of more international courts than any other decade. All of this suggests the expansion of international legal authority, which in turn will limit the propensity of states and other actors to resort to armed violence to settle disputes by providing nonviolent mechanisms for conflict resolution.

As an approach to limiting war, international adjudication clearly does offer a number of distinct advantages. The rulings of courts and tribunals impose a detailed, fixed, and final decision that the parties to the conflict—if they have expressed their willingness to consent to the tribunal's authority—are obligated to accept. Submitting inter- or intrastate disputes to legal judgment by a standing international court with jurisdiction over matters related to war (such as the International Criminal Court) or to an ad hoc tribunal established to mete out justice in relation to a particular conflict (such as the Special Court for Sierra Leone, or the International Criminal Tribunal for the former Yugoslavia) also provides the parties with due process. Shifting the terms of the conflict or dispute from the ambiguity, polarization, and volatility that typically surrounds inter- and intrastate conflicts to one that is defined and governed by "due process" (established, consistent, and fair legal rules, principles, precedents, and procedures) reaffirms the idea of the rule of law, which is a key to restoring order in post-conflict societies.

At the same time, a legalist approach has its disadvantages. Arbitrators and judges are typically concerned only with resolving the immediate dispute, and proceedings unfold according to a particular set of rules and processes. As a result, while the rulings can in some cases establish precedents, the immediate and major impact of most rulings and judgments extends only to the parties in the dispute. Also, adjudication is an inherently adversarial process. Legal arguments can in some cases

lead courts or arbitrators to render "zero-sum" rulings. While these rulings may be binding, they also may lead to dissatisfaction in one or more parties to the conflict, potentially sowing the seeds for a renewal of hostilities.

Adjudication also clearly shifts a great deal of control to the court or arbitrator(s). While courts or arbitrators are pledged to principles of fairness and equity, the parties to the conflict could interpret this enhanced authority as threatening. Compounding this problem is the fact that both or all concerned parties may not accept a relevant international court's jurisdiction (such as the ICJ or ICC). Even in the event that the parties overcome these problems, international courts and tribunals are slow-moving, with significant delays between petition of the court and the case appearing on the docket—delays that may prompt a return to violence in heated and protracted international or intrastate conflicts.

What do you think? Is adjudication a tool we can effectively use to restrain contemporary armed conflict? Or is it, as some legal experts claim, the epitome of utopian idealism?

Sources:

Alter, Karen. 2003. "Do International Courts Enhance Compliance with International Law?" *Review of Asian and Pacific Studies* 25: 51–77.

Posner, Eric A. and John C. Yoo. 2004. "A Theory of International Adjudication," *John M. Olin Law & Economics Working Paper* No. 206 (2nd Series), University of Chicago School of Law (February 2004).

Romano, Cesare P.R. 1999. "The Proliferation of International Judicial Bodies: The Pieces of the Puzzle," 31 *New York University Journal of International Law and Politics* 709–751.

Sarat, Austin and Joel B. Grossman. 1975. "Courts and Conflict Resolution: Problems in the Mobilization of Adjudication," *American Political Science Review* 69(4): 1200–1217.

Simmons, Beth A. 1998. "Compliance with International Agreements," *Annual Review of Political Science* 1: 75–93.

Spangler, Brad. 2003. "Adjudication," in *Beyond Intractability,* Guy Burgess and Heidi Burgess (eds.). Boulder, CO: Conflict Research Consortium, University of Colorado.

sides and consistent with the third party's interests. . . . Mediation is best thought of as a mode of negotiation in which a third party helps the parties find a solution that they cannot find by themselves. (Zartman & Touval, 2007:437–438)

Third-party mediation of both interstate and intrastate conflicts has increased dramatically since the end of World War II. Consider, for instance, that in cases of international crisis alone (only one kind of international dispute), 84% (135 out of 161) of all offers and/or incidences of mediation since 1918 have occurred since 1945 (Brecher & Wilkenfeld, 2000). By another scholar's count, 255 of 310 inter- or intrastate conflicts occurring between 1945 and 1975 featured some form of official mediation (Princen, 1992). During the Cold War, mediation was provided by the superpowers (the United States in the Middle East after 1948; the USSR between India and Pakistan in the 1960s), regional or former colonial powers (Kenya in territorial disputes between Nigeria and Cameroon in the 1970s and 1980s; the United Kingdom in the Rhodesia–Zimbabwe dispute of the late 1970s), and the UN, along with a sampling of RGOs (the UN in the Falklands/Malvinas conflict of 1981–1982; the Arab League in the various Yemeni conflicts of the 1970s and 1980s; the Organization of African Unity in the various conflicts over the Ogaden region between Ethiopia and Somalia). Mediation was also frequently provided by so-called middle powers (Canada in the Suez crisis of 1956; Algeria in the U.S.–Iran hostage crisis of 1979–1981) as well as, in some instances, non–state actors (the Society of Friends in the Angolan civil war).

Given the complexity of many post–Cold War conflicts, as well as the level and intensity of violence, the range of actors prepared to intervene as mediators is remarkable. Inter- as well as intrastate conflict mediation since the end of the Cold War has come from sources both expected (e.g., the United States in Bosnia and the Middle East; the UN in the Red Sea Islands dispute between Yemen and Eritrea) and unexpected (e.g., Tanzania in the Great Lakes conflicts; Djibouti in the Ethiopia–Eritrea war). Newer sources of mediation, such as RGOs, NGOs, and private individuals have become especially prominent given changes not only in the nature of the conflicts themselves, but as a result of the proliferation and intrusion of such actors into the traditionally state-dominated arena of international security and law.

Scholars' efforts dedicated to conceptual clarification of mediation as a form of conflict management allow us to identify and isolate certain features that distinguish mediation from other conflict management forms.

Mediation Must Involve Third Parties   By definition, mediation involves one (or more) actors that are not privy to the original dispute in efforts to resolve that dispute. These actors bring their own interests and agendas into the dispute, which demand attention and typically alter any dispute's prevailing dynamic. The introduction of one or more third parties and their agendas can actually further complicate things. Yet at the same time, the infusion of mediators may bring new energies and ideas to a conflict management process that is stalemated, or to a conflict that seemingly defies management.

Consider the prominent example of the U.S. third-party mediation at the 1978 Camp David summit. The degree to which President Carter hitched his administration's entire foreign policy to a breakthrough between Egypt and Israel raised the stakes for the principals as well as the United States. Carter's effort refashioned resolution of the dispute around the objective of an Egypt–Israeli peace treaty, making successful mediation a matter of U.S. national interest (NIDR, 1992). The intense, hands-on effort that followed broadened, and in some ways further complicated, an already complex relationship between Egypt and Israel, while exposing U.S. policies in the Middle East, as well as perceptions that these policies (including the provision of military and economic aid) tilted heavily toward Israel, to the detriment of Egypt and the other Arab states. This perception continues to dog U.S. mediation of the Israeli–Palestinian dispute. At the same time, the higher stakes accompanying Carter's mediation were essential to compel the two adversaries toward a workable peace accord.

One of the most prominent examples of third-party mediation of an international dispute remains that of President Carter's efforts to broker a peace treaty between Egypt and Israel at the presidential retreat at Camp David (Maryland) in 1978. Despite a stalemate, the intense personal commitment of Carter to the process—along with generous doses of economic and military aid to both parties—ultimately produced a peace accord and diplomatic recognition of Israel by Egypt, the first Arab state to do so.

Mediation Is Nonviolent   The second defining feature of mediation is the absence of the mediator's application of violence or physical force. This is crucial to the very essence of mediation. As Bercovitch et al. (1991:8) define it, mediation is "a process of conflict management where disputants seek the assistance of, or accept an offer of help from, an individual, group, state, or organization to settle their conflict or resolve their differences *without resorting to physical force*" (emphasis added). Given the prevailing dynamic of international anarchy, which, depending on one's view of global politics, makes a resort to violence possible, likely, or wise, mediation must rely on something other than the direct use of force in order to distinguish itself from other, more coercive, forms of political behavior.

Mediators Are (Technically) Impartial   The third defining aspect of mediation is impartiality. Three features define impartiality in this context. The first is that the mediator's activities must be driven by a desire to secure an outcome that is acceptable to both sides of the dispute. Second, and on a related note, this outcome is not tantamount to granting "victory" to one side by tilting the formal outcome in its favor. Finally, as the term suggests, impartiality requires that the mediator possess a genuine and overriding interest in managing and even resolving the conflict—meaning that this interest must take precedence over any other (self-regarding) interest(s) attached to mediation, such as heightened prestige or securing strategic advantage.

Impartiality is important for more than its own sake. It is a central tenet of effective mediation. This is not because impartiality is or seems just or virtuous, but because it prompts and sustains the trust building that is central to effective mediation. Recall that one recurring theme in the definitions of mediation is the contribution of mediators to facilitating solutions to disputes that the parties themselves either can't or won't. Whatever disputes or differences are significant enough to precipitate a resort to armed violence are likely to be deep-seated and difficult to overcome. Yet to the extent that mediation offers at least a possibility of doing so, whether in Nicaragua, Nagorny-Karabakh, or Northern Ireland, it is because the outside party or parties are not bound by or beholden to the disputes or differences that prompted and sustained the conflict.

CRITICAL THINKING QUESTIONS

1. Why does a single, agreed-upon definition of "war" remain elusive? What are some of the central features defining war in your view?

2. What trends are evident in the incidence, type, and intensity of armed conflicts today? What accounts for these trends?

3. What is (are) the catalyst(s) and sustaining force(s) for "new" wars?

4. What explains the persistence and pervasiveness of global terrorism—what are its main causes and sources?

5. What are the major approaches to conflict management? What distinguishes them from one another? Which, in your view, is or could be the most effective—and why?

chapter summary

This chapter provides a broad overview of the intentional and systematic use of armed conflict for political ends. While varying definitions of war—or, for that matter, the lack of an accepted definition of terrorism—signify the complexities involved, what is relatively straightforward is that arguments for war's obsolescence ring hollow, as conflict remains a central feature of global politics. This is no doubt due to war's continuing appeal and ready availability. Violence persists as a means for states to pursue their interests, and—as we have seen here—*especially* as a tool for contending factions within a state (as in Libya) or as an instrument of asymmetric warfare that terrorist groups employ. Even with the NTC's consolidation of political authority after the military victory and their capture and killing of Gaddafi himself in October 2011, a low-level insurgency led by former Gaddafi loyalists continues as of the time of this writing, with divides between and among various tribal groups and their militias proving a significant obstacle to constructing a new and stable political order in Libya going forward.

Beyond the general conclusion that war remains far from obsolete, this chapter also demonstrates that:

- Armed conflict today is overwhelmingly more likely to take place within the bounds of a state (intrastate conflict)—with or without the involvement of "outside" (third-party) actors—than it is between two or more states (interstate conflict).

- Relatedly, most armed conflict today is likely to be of a lower intensity in terms of deaths and casualties, while persisting and proving difficult to resolve given the nature of intrastate conflict and the issues and actors involved.

- To some extent, the shift from interstate wars to intrastate armed conflicts is related to, and explained by, "particularistic identity politics"—a narrow but intense group identity that brings identity groups within states into direct and violent conflict with one another. This problem is especially acute in societies where the state is weak and lacks capacity, or where it is viewed to serve the interest of one identity group at the expense of the other(s).

- Globalization and transnational forces and processes have a direct impact on war and armed conflict, especially intrastate conflicts. The relative ease of movement of people, goods, money, and ideas can and does trigger and sustain armed conflicts—as the "new" wars thesis reflects.

- Globalization and transnational forces and processes also have a direct impact on terrorism, increasing its scope and profile and, relatedly, its appeal as a form of asymmetric warfare for non–state actors. As terrorism continues to evolve, it is likely to continue to exploit these forces and processes to plan and carry out operations and attract recruits.

- Multiple and different tools for managing armed conflict—including collective security institutions, peacekeeping and peace enforcement, and third-party mediation—exist, with varying track records of success. In general, their prospects for effective utilization likely depend on the application of the most appropriate "tool" for a particular conflict, as well as the need for greater material resources and support from the international community at-large, and more powerful states in particular.

key **terms**

aggression
asymmetric warfare
"clash of civilizations"
Concert of Europe
defensive realism
diaspora
diversionary theory of war
"end of history"
"jihad v. McWorld"
mediation
militarism

multidimensional peacekeeping
"new" wars
offensive realism
"old" wars
"particularistic identity politics"
peace enforcement
peacekeeping
preemption
primordial identities
relative deprivation
remittances

rules of engagement (ROE)
security dilemma
self-defense
state-building
statecraft
state-sponsored terrorism
"third wave" of terrorism
transnationalism
transnational terrorism

International Law and Transitional Justice

chapter 8

On April 26, 2012, a United Nations-backed court convicted former Liberian president Charles Taylor of war crimes and crimes against humanity committed during Sierra Leone's civil war. Shown here are victims watching the televised court decision and witnessing, for the first time, the international community convicting a former head of state. The litany of Taylor's gruesome crimes include overseeing massive rape campaigns, enslavement camps, and systematic torture, including amputations.

LEARNING OBJECTIVES

This chapter introduces and examines the sources of, prospects for, and debates concerning international legal authority in what remains in many ways a state-centric international system. Upon completion of the chapter, you will be able to:

- Recognize the fundamental ways in which international law differs from national (domestic) law

- Understand the philosophical roots, historical evolution, and major sources of international law and the international legal system

- Grasp some of the major international legal norms, customs, and practices, including diplomatic immunity, head of state immunity, *pacta sunt servanda*, *jus gentium*, and legal personhood

- Assess the major issues involving compliance with and enforcement of international law

- Be familiar with the functioning and authority of major international and regional courts and other methods of adjudication

- Identify and evaluate the underlying sources of and continuing debates concerning international humanitarian law (e.g., the "laws of war")

Since the end of the World War II, the global community has made great strides in the development and implementation of international law. Although international law and justice have long been aspirations of the global community, it wasn't until the 20th century that the world began to systematically pursue justice and accountability at international, regional, local, and most important, individual levels. Traditional approaches to international law and justice have long focused on the relationships between sovereign states on topics ranging from the laws of the sea to the laws of war. Modern developments, however, also include the legal relationships between and among international organizations, individuals, non–state actors and multinational corporations—all entities "capable of possessing the characteristics of international legal personality" (Epps, 2009:3). This chapter focuses on these more recent developments in international law and justice and the way in which this evolution impacts global actors and their pursuit of self-interest. While it would be naïve to ignore the reality that most actors in the system emphasize their own interests, it is important to recognize how these interests overlap and reinforce each other in ways that can reflect the interests of the broader global community in terms of the common good.

It is useful to begin considering how international law differs from domestic law. The difference between global and domestic systems is not so much the motives of the actors as the fact that domestic systems place greater restraints on the pursuit of self-interest than the international system (Joyner, 2005). *Legal systems* are one restraint on the power-based pursuit of self-interest in a domestic system. Hierarchical structures exist for making law (legislatures), for enforcing law (police and military), and for interpreting law (judiciaries). These bind individuals and groups to domestic legal systems. Ideas about *justice* also restrain the pursuit of power in domestic systems. What is just and what is legal are not always the same. Justice involves what is "right" here, not just what is legal. Whether the word is *just, moral, ethical,* or *fair,* there is a greater sense in domestic systems than there is in the international system that justice should prevail, that the ends do not always justify the means, and that those who violate the norms should suffer penalties. Surely, there is no domestic system in which everyone acts justly (Amstutz, 2005). Yet the sense of justice that citizens in stable domestic systems have does influence their behavior.

At the global level, such authoritative structures are largely absent. There is no international executive, legislature, or judiciary. **Compulsory jurisdiction** does not exist, and anarchy often enables chaos and violence. Furthermore, differences in culture and historical experiences lead people and nations to develop very different conceptions of what is right and just. Despite these significant obstacles, international law exists and increasingly functions in impactful ways across the globe. In April 2012, for example, the world witnessed an international court convicting a head of state for **war crimes** and **crimes against humanity** for the first time since the Nuremburg trials after World War II. An international tribunal, called the **Special Tribunal for Sierra Leone (STSL)**, found Charles G. Taylor, the former president of Liberia and once powerful warlord, guilty of arming, supporting, and guiding a brutal rebel movement that committed mass atrocities in Sierra Leone during its civil war in the 1990s. The rebel groups in Sierra Leone were notorious for gruesome tactics, including the systematic and widespread mutilation of thousands of civilians, to terrorize the country as they captured diamond mines to fund their insurgency. The prosecution proved to a panel of three judges, from Ireland, Samoa, and Uganda, that Mr. Taylor was guilty of "aiding and abetting" these crimes, including murder, rape,

a wide range of actions by the EU executive and legislative institutions, and it can also determine whether the laws and actions of member-countries violate EU law. The ECJ's caseload, which Figure 8.3 illustrates, is one mark of its substantial jurisdiction and growing importance.

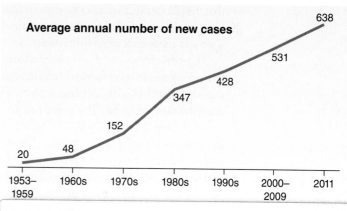

FIGURE 8.3

EU court of justice cases

One measure of the importance of the European Court of Justice is its work-load. It has increased steadily as indicated in this figure showing the average number of new cases filed annually with the ECJ. The court has jurisdiction over EU legislative and executive actions as well as over some laws passed by EU member-countries.

Data Source: Calculated using data from the 2006 and 2011. European Court Annual Reports.

Effectiveness of International Courts   There are some important limits on the impact of the ICJ and other international courts. The *jurisdictional limits* that we just discussed are one restraint. *Lack of enforcement* is a second impediment to the effectiveness of international courts. All courts rely heavily on the willingness of those within their jurisdiction to comply voluntarily or, when that fails, on a powerful executive branch to enforce court decrees. Effective domestic courts have these supports. By contrast, countries are often reluctant to follow the decisions of international courts, which, unlike the courts in most countries, are not backed up by an executive branch with powerful enforcement authority.

The International Court of Justice   The ICJ has only limited effectiveness. The UN Secretariat, which is the ICJ executive branch, does not have the authority or power to enforce ICJ rulings. This allows countries to sometimes ignore ICJ rulings. In *United States of America v. Mexico* (2003), for example, the ICJ upheld Mexico's claim that the United States was violating the Vienna Convention on Consular Relations (1963) by not ensuring that U.S. states allow arrested Mexican nationals to contact their country's diplomatic representatives. The ICJ directed the United States to do so and to provide relief to the prisoners who had been denied their treaty rights. The United States had ratified the convention in 1969, but the Bush administration responded to the ICJ ruling by announcing it was withdrawing U.S. consent to the treaty provision allowing the ICJ to decide cases under the treaty. Many legal experts doubted whether such presidential authority existed, but the Supreme Court inferentially upheld it by refusing to hear a case asking for enforcement on the ICJ decision.

Fortunately for global peace and justice, not all ICJ cases end this way. The ICJ sometimes does play a valuable role. Its rulings help define and advance international law. Furthermore, the court can contribute by giving countries a way, short of war, to settle a dispute once diplomacy has failed. The current ICJ case filed in 2004 by Bulgaria against Ukraine over their maritime border in the Black Sea provides a good example. More important than the details of the dispute is the fact that, unlike many disputes throughout history over land and maritime borders that have resulted in war, the existence of the ICJ provides Bulgaria and Ukraine with a way to come to a peaceful resolution.

ICJ advisory opinions also help resolve issues between IGOs and may even help establish general international law. In separate actions, the UN General Assembly and the World Health Organization each asked the ICJ to rule on the legality of using nuclear weapons. The court ruled in 1996 that "the threat or use of nuclear weapons would generally be contrary to the rules of international law applicable in armed conflict," except arguably "in an extreme circumstance of self-defense, in which the very survival of a state would be at stake." Among other impacts, the ICJ's ruling puts any leader considering the use of nuclear weapons except in extremis on notice that he or she could wind up the defendant in some future war crimes trial.

Regional Courts Like the ICJ, this group of courts has struggled to make an impact. The two European regional courts, the ECJ and ECHR, have been by far the most effective of the regional courts.

The ECJ is particularly notable for the number of cases it hears (638 in 2011) and its authority to make decisions and to have those rulings followed in areas that were once clearly within the sovereign realm of states. As Figure 8.4 shows, the rulings of the ECJ have tended to promote EU integration by finding for plaintiffs who argue that the policy of one or another member-country violates EU law. In one example, the court ruled in 2001 that Germany was discriminating against women by barring them from serving in combat positions in the military. Soon thereafter, Germany changed its policy and its armed forces began to train women for combat. An important pending decision relates to Microsoft Corporation's appeal of a decision by the EU Commission fining the software giant $613 million for monopolistic practices such as bundling Media Player and other programs with its Windows operating system. That ruling will have a major financial impact on Microsoft and, by extension, on both the U.S. stock market and possibly the way that software is sold all over the world.

Evaluating Judicial Effectiveness Given the limitations on the ICJ's effectiveness and that of most regional courts, it is tempting to write them off as having little more than symbolic value. Such a judgment would be in error. Whatever the outcome of a specific case, there is evidence that countries are gradually becoming more willing to utilize the ICJ, the ECJ, and other international courts and to accept their decisions. The map of the ICJ's justices and cases in Figure 8.2 shows that countries around the world have justices on the court

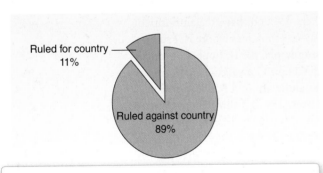

FIGURE 8.4
EU Court of Justice decisions
The European Union's Court of Justice has promoted EU integration by usually ruling in favor of the plaintiffs who bring a case against their home country claiming that one of its laws or policies clashes with EU law. In 2011, on complaints that an EU member-country had failed to meet its obligations under EU law, the court found for the plaintiff and against the country in 72 cases, dismissing the complaint in only 9 cases.

Data Source: 2011 European Court Annual reports.

and almost half are or have been a party to its cases. Now more than 60 countries, including Canada, India, and the United Kingdom, adhere to the optional clause giving the ICJ compulsory jurisdiction over their international legal disputes. In sum, it is true that the international judicial system is still primitive, but each of the over 160 opinions issued by the PCIJ and the ICJ since 1922 is one more than the zero instances of international adjudication in previous centuries.

APPLYING INTERNATIONAL LAW AND JUSTICE

Perhaps the major challenge in applying international law stems from the vast disparities in national legal systems and even legal cultures across the globe. Whereas most people around the world undoubtedly value justice and the rule of law, the social norms and cultural values that inform a given society's conception of justice or shape a given society's system of laws and preferences for how to enforce those laws can and do differ drastically. Laws are in many ways a reflection of dominant social norms concerning acceptable and unacceptable or deviant behavior. Therefore, one can see where creating and enforcing a unified body of international law to encompass nearly 200 nation-states and the societies and social preferences that they govern—not to mention untold additional numbers of sub-state and non-state actors—is difficult, to be sure. Among other challenges facing the effective translation of international law, we will discuss two here—the promotion of legal standards and justice amid differing cultural values and ideals, and the application and enforcement of international legal rights and responsibilities to states and individuals. Let us first step back and critically think about what it means to serve justice and who that justice really serves, issues explored in the "Thinking Theoretically" box that follows.

The daunting nature of these obstacles for crafting and advancing a robust system of international law has resulted in the emergence of highly politicized debates concerning the nature and scope of international law and jurisprudence, particularly surrounding accusations from some in the non-Western world that contemporary international law bears too much of the West's imprint. The ongoing "story" of Charles Taylor unfolding throughout this chapter is clearly applicable in this regard. Whereas few around the world would defend the brutal methods that the Liberian strongman employed in his rise to power, or in fomenting civil war in neighboring Sierra Leone, significant debates have emerged and persist concerning the nature of the charges that prosecutors brought against him and even the legal authority of the Special Court for Sierra Leone (SCSL). Taylor's conviction by the SCSL for war crimes including murder, enslavement, and the promotion of widespread and systematic rape is in many ways a landmark for international justice, both in advancing the continuing challenge to the notion of **head-of-state immunity** and in the successful exercise of jurisprudence by a "hybrid" (national/international) court. At the same time, in claiming that the court served largely a political function, critics have pointed to the fact that Western powers such as the U.S. and U.K. (along with Canada and the Netherlands) exclusively funded the SCSL, as well as the court's role in ensuring Taylor's ouster and isolation from power (Cheng, 2012).

Head-of-state immunity The notion, derived from a strict interpretation of state sovereignty, that a person's conduct as head of state or high-ranking political official renders that person "above the law" and not culpable for any criminal activity carried out in the dispatch of his or her responsibilities.

thinking theoretically

When Is Justice *Really* Served?

Despite the relative newness of international courts, political theorists have had much to say on their responsibilities, legitimacy, and jurisdiction. Some theorists argue that their role should be merely to assuage transboundary conflicts and wrongs that are brought to them by arresting and punishing criminals and expunging the evildoers from public life. Others see the courts serving a much wider, sociological purpose of holding perpetrators accountable for crimes in the eyes of their victims and their communities. This public recognition and punishment not only serves criminal justice goals, but promotes reconciliation, a human rights culture, and respect for the rule of law. Recent cases dealing with some of the world's worst criminals, such as Saddam Hussein, Osama bin Laden, and Muammar el-Qaddafi, outside of international courts, raise fundamental questions about the capacity of such judicial bodies to deal with contemporary armed conflict and violence.

For example, Saddam Hussein, captured by U.S. military forces in 2003, faced his charges in the specially created Iraqi High Criminal Court and Iraqi Special Tribunal. The court gave the illusion of domestic jurisdiction while actually being presided over by the United States. The court prosecuted Hussein for war crimes, crimes against humanity, and genocide,

amongst others—crimes recognized as under the jurisdiction of the ICC. What, then, are the implications of not trying this case in the ICC? The court ultimately convicted Hussein, sentenced him to death, and executed him for his crimes. Had the ICC tried the case, the death penalty would not have been an option. Some argue that Hussein's death is the only true justice that could have emerged, and thus it was necessary that he was tried in this court. Following this precedent, it would seem that ICC trials should come secondary to the desires of individual nations (in this case the United States). This undermines the ICC's jurisdiction and subsequent hope for this institution to be a powerful actor in bringing global justice.

Hussein's case, at least, went through some form of judicial process. Bin Laden and Qaddafi were both killed extrajudicially—bin Laden by U.S. military forces and Qaddafi by Libyan rebel forces. The global community breathed a collective sigh at both of their deaths, and at bin Laden's death President Barack Obama declared, "Justice has been done." There is no doubt that they were among the worst of the worst, killing innocent victims in the pursuit of personal power, but should a national military or rebel forces have determined their crimes, their punishment, and taken their lives? It is important to remember that simply

Law and Justice in a Multicultural World

As the international legal system evolves to better recognize and respect the rights and preferences of a diverse range and number of peoples, the challenge to reconcile differing conceptions of "justice" and differing translations of that concept into law are magnified. Most of international law and many of the prevailing ideas about justice that influence world politics are based on the concepts and practices of the West. This reality is a reflection of a disproportionately Euro-centric influence in constructing and advancing international law in conjunction with the Westphalian state system, and obviously not a reflection of the innate superiority or intrinsic appeal of Western conceptions of justice and law or definitions of legal rights. The Western orientation that prevails in international law has come under increasing scrutiny and criticism by scholars and practitioners, particularly from the Global South, as the international system has evolved to include greater attempts at global governance and as non-Western states and societies have amassed greater power and influence over global politics.

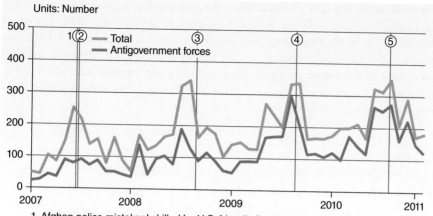

Units: Number

1. Afghan police mistakenly killed by U.S. friendly fire
2. U.S. air strike kills Afghan children
3. Afghanistan: 76 civilians die in air strike, ministry claims
4. Afghanistan election: on the eve of the poll
5. Afghan police and children die in shoot-out

FIGURE 8.6

Afghan civilian deaths, monthly breakdown

Civilian casualties are a central concern in the realm of *jus in bello*. While these numbers have historically been difficult to track, a number of nongovernmental and intergovernmental organizations have remained committed to telling this part of the story, particularly in the wars in Afghanistan and Iraq. Recent estimates by Human Rights Watch point to small but substantial increases in civilian deaths in these war-torn regions. In Afghanistan in 2011, for example, the UN mission documented 2,332 civilian deaths and 3,649 injuries for a total 5,981 civilian casualties, an increase of almost 10% in deaths and injuries compared to 2010. While antigovernment forces are responsible for a majority of these deaths, NATO and government forces account for close to 20% of this total number.

Data Source: The Guardian, 10 March 2011.

could see—the care that goes into it, the humanity that goes into it."[8] As Figure 8.6 illustrates, civilian deaths in Afghanistan have also been significant for a number of years and overall have increased from 2009 through 2011. These staggering numbers are more than simply "collateral damage." They represent individual people who died and countless families destroyed—all complicating our understanding of when military intervention is justified and when the costs of the means may outweigh the potential benefits of the end.

Applying International Law and Justice to Individuals

As previously noted, particularly in the case study of Charles Taylor, international law has begun to deal with the actions of individuals, particularly in holding people in positions of power accountable for their roles in committing and ordering mass atrocity. At least three key institutional benchmarks have marked the development, beginning with the post–World War II tribunals and then reigniting international focus with the ad hoc tribunals of the 1990s and finally culminating with the establishment of the ICC.

Post–World War II Tribunals   The first modern instances of individuals charged with crimes under international law came in the aftermath of the horrors of World War II. In the Nuremberg and Tokyo war crimes trials, German and Japanese military and civilian leaders were tried for waging aggressive war, for war crimes, and for crimes against humanity. Twelve Germans and seven Japanese were sentenced to death. Many Germans and Japanese also went to prison. These tribunals established three important precedents:

- Leaders can be criminally responsible for war crimes that they ordered.
- Leaders are responsible for war crimes committed by their subordinates unless such leaders tried to prevent the crimes or punish perpetrators.
- Obeying orders is not a valid defense for having committed atrocities.

The power behind these precedents, however, has always been compromised given that the tribunals clearly reflected a narrow pursuit of justice. Nuremberg and Tokyo were cases of victor's justice and punishment for the vanquished and therefore lacked lasting legitimacy.

Ad Hoc War Crimes Tribunals   After an absence of nearly 50 years, international tribunals reemerged in the 1990s. The atrocities that occurred in Bosnia and in Rwanda during this time were a driving force in this process. In both places, people on all sides were abused, injured, and killed. In Bosnia, it was the Muslims who were the principal victims and the Serbs who inflicted the majority of mass atrocities, including death and degradation between 1990 and 1995. In Rwanda the Hutus were the murderous aggressors in 1994, and the Tutsis the victims of genocide in a ghastly slaughter that the 2004 film *Hotel Rwanda* and the 2005 HBO special *Sometimes in April* revisited. The violence was horrific, widespread, and systematically employed. In Bosnia, for example, Serbian forces executed more than 8,000 Bosnian Muslim men and boys in a matter of days in Srebrenica in 1995. In Rwanda, close to 800,000 Tutsis and any Hutu sympathizers were killed in about three months' time.

Beyond the mass murders, in both conflicts, rape emerged as a strategic weapon of war. Rape is a weapon against women, men, and communities overall. Rape is a heinous and violent crime against women, but in this context, the aggressors also targeted such acts at the men in the communities, particularly fathers, husbands, brothers, and sons. In this context, rape constitutes an attack on their honor and central identity as men. Further, the long-term impacts of rape range from death of women to serious health consequences. Many communities shun women who have been raped, particularly those who become pregnant as a result. Forced impregnation also emerged in these conflicts as a means of genocide or ethnic cleansing.

The atrocities in Bosnia and Rwanda shocked the conscience of the world, particularly as the media brought images from these regions to our newspapers and televisions. This jarring reality led the UN Security Council to establish an International Criminal Tribunal for the Former Yugoslavia (ICTY) in 1993, and another for Rwanda (ICTR) in 1994. The tribunal for the Balkans sits in The Hague, the Netherlands. The Rwanda tribunal is located in Arusha, Tanzania. In 1999, the authority of the Balkans tribunal expanded to include war crimes in Kosovo.

The Hague tribunal has indicted over 160 individuals as war criminals, and as of 2009, had completed proceedings for over 100 of those indicted. Of those whose trials were completed by mid-2005, 90% have been convicted, have received sentences of up to 40 years in prison, and have been transferred to other countries in Europe to serve their time (Kerr, 2004). The most important of the trials was that of Slobodan Milosevic, because of his prominence and stature as the former president of Yugoslavia. However, he died in 2006 of heart failure before his trial was complete. The tribunal expects to complete all its initial trials by 2014 and the appeals process by 2016.[9] Still, as the photo on this page illustrates, a number of leading commanders from the Serbian military forces have been convicted of war crimes and crimes against humanity.

In 2009, the International Criminal Tribunal for the former Yugoslavia handed down its first decisions in what is known as the "Kosovo Six" Trial. The court acquited one man and convicted the other five for war crimes and crimes against humanity. These five senior political, military, and police officers were some of the highest ranking Serbs during the 1999 war in Kosovo when over 700,000 ethnic Albanians were expelled across borders into Albania and many more were killed, robbed, raped, and tortured.

The Rwanda tribunal has made headway more slowly than its counterpart in The Hague, but it became the first international tribunal since the Tokyo War Crimes trials after World War II to punish a head of government when, in 1998, former Rwandan Prime Minister Jean Kambanda pleaded guilty to genocide and was sentenced to life in prison. Through early 2012, the tribunal has completed the trials of 69 individuals, all but 10 of whom were convicted. Hutu civilian and military leaders have comprised most, but not all, of the convicted and accused. For instance, a Belgian-born Italian citizen, Georges Henry Joseph Ruggiu, who was a radio journalist in Rwanda, was sentenced to 12 years in prison for inciting genocide. Among the many other chilling calls to mayhem he broadcast in 1994: "You [Tutsi] cockroaches must know you are made of flesh. . . . We will kill you."[10] The ICTR set another critical precedent when it found Jean-Paul Akayesu guilty of acts of genocide, including rape, as a strategy against Tutsi women.

Following a somewhat different pattern, a joint UN–Sierra Leone tribunal was established in 2002. It sits in Freetown, the capital of Liberia, and is guarded by UN peacekeepers. This court's mission is to deal with war crimes that occurred during the civil war in Sierra Leone (1996–2002). There, three rebel groups killed and mutilated many thousands of noncombatants in an attempt to terrorize the population. Some of the tragedy that befell the country was captured in the 2006 film, *Blood Diamond,* with Leonardo DiCaprio. As of early 2012, 21 individuals had been indicted, and 20 have been captured or had their case closed due to death. This, of course, includes the trial, conviction, and pending sentencing of Charles Taylor. Taylor's trial was so explosive that it had to be moved to The Hague where a special session of the court tried him.

Yet another joint tribunal, this time linking the UN and Cambodia, has recently begun the proceeding for a handful individuals. It is intended to prosecute members of Cambodia's former Khmer Rouge regime for the deaths of approximately 1.7 million people (about 25% of the population) during its reign of terror (1975–1979). It is uncertain, however, whether the tribunal will ever get under way, much less achieve any success amid the complexities of Cambodian politics. Among other issues, Cambodian Prime Minister Hun Sen was once a low-ranking Khmer Rouge official. Notably, we can easily apply these critiques, to some extent, to all the tribunals that we have mentioned insofar as they only prosecute a select few and many perpetrators go unpunished in these countries. More problematic is the fact that many war criminals were part of the peace processes and were able to negotiate positions of power in the newly emerging government. These challenges raise serious questions about the ability of such ad hoc courts to justly punish perpetrators, combat cultures of impunity, and restore the rule of law in ways that are timely and victim-focused.

The International Criminal Court In 1998, in light of the many limitations of the ad hoc tribunals since the end of the Cold War and in the context of a long-standing movement within the UN to create a permanent international criminal court, member-states convened a global conference in Rome to create such a court. During the conference, most countries favored establishing a court with broad and independent jurisdiction. A smaller number of countries, including the United States, wanted a much weaker ICC. The crux of U.S. opposition to a strong ICC was the fear that U.S. leaders and military personnel might become targets of politically motivated prosecutions. "The reality is that the United States is a global military power and presence. . . . We have to be careful that it does not open up opportunities for endless frivolous complaints to be lodged against the United States as a global military power," explained the U.S. delegate to the talks.[11] The U.S. stand drew strong criticism. For one, an Italian diplomat expressed disbelief "that a major democracy . . . would want to have an image of insisting that its soldiers be given license never to be investigated."[12]

While some of the U.S. reservations were met, such as preventing the Court from having universal jurisdiction even over nonparty states, over 80% of the 148 countries attending ultimately voted to create a relatively strong court. Only seven states rejected the statute in Rome; notably the United States, Israel, India, and China were among them. The statute entered into force on April 12, 2002, and currently 120 states (Figure 8.7) have ratified the treaty. The ICC has jurisdiction over four crimes and can only prosecute crimes committed since the treaty was ratified in April 2002. The crimes include genocide (according to the Genocide Convention of 1948), crimes against humanity, war crimes (according to the Geneva Conventions), and crimes of aggression (addressed for the first time at the 10-year review conference in June 2010). According to the statute, crimes against humanity refer to widespread and systematic crimes, including murder, enslavement, forcible transfer, torture, rape, enforced prostitution, and enforced disappearance committed during times of civil strife and even peace. In this way, the court focuses on crimes that represent a policy or a plan rather than just random acts of violence.

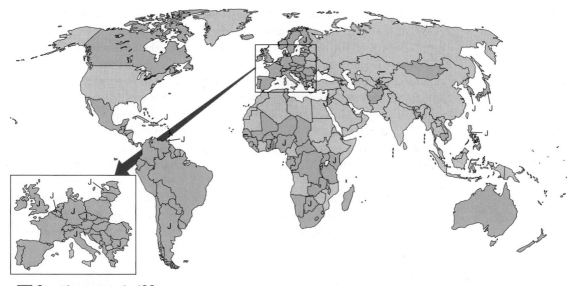

Countries party to the ICC

J Countries with current ICC Judges

FIGURE 8.7

Countries that are party to the ICC treaty

More than half the world's countries, including most of Europe and Latin America, have now signed and ratified the International Criminal Court treaty. The widely dispersed home countries of the court's judges is also evident in this map. Gambia's Fatou Bensouda was recently elected to serve as the chief prosecutor of the ICC. This former Gambian justice minister is only the second to hold this position, following Luis Moreno-Ocampo of Argentina, who held the job for the court's first nine years of existence.

The ICC does not have universal jurisdiction. Three "trigger mechanisms" exist for bringing a case under the jurisdiction of the court. The initiation of an ICC investigation can be triggered by a state that is party to the statute, by the Security Council (SC), or by the prosecutor, as long as the crime occurred on territory of a state that is party to the statute, or on a vessel or aircraft that is registered to that state, or if the perpetrator is a national of a state that is party to the statute. The only other time that the ICC can act in a nonparty situation is if that nonparty state consents or if the SC refers it to the court, as in the recent SC referral of the current president of North Sudan, President al-Bashir. If the SC refers a situation to the court, then and only then does the court have universal jurisdiction. ICC jurisdiction is also limited by the principle of complementarity codified in the statute. Thus, the ICC can consider a case if, and only if, the domestic judicial system is "unwilling or unable to genuinely" investigate or prosecute the alleged crime. Such a situation would most likely occur because of a lack of national infrastructure or a collapse of the state's domestic judicial system. Of course, unwillingness to investigate or prosecute is not as easy to identify.

The countries party to the ICC treaty met in 2003 and elected the court's 18 judges and its other top officials, including its chief prosecutor. The court began to operate the following year. Several African countries soon filed complaints with the ICC in 2005 alleging atrocities by various forces in the long and gruesome fighting in the central African area that encompasses parts of the Democratic Republic of the Congo, Uganda, Sudan, and the Central African Republic, and the ICC prosecutor has launched investigations and issued indictments in these areas. There are numerous trials under way, and in early 2012, the court concluded its first trial, finding Thomas Lubanga Dyilo guilty of the war crime of conscripting and enlisting children and using them to participate actively in violence and hostilities in the Democratic Republic of the Congo. He faces a maximum sentence of life imprisonment. Currently, the ICC is opening initial investigations in Libya, Kenya, and Côte d'Ivoire.

Somewhat innovatively, the ICC has focused some of its resources on the victims. The court established the Trust Fund for Victims, which develops activities and programs with the victims themselves as partners with the goal of helping them rebuild their families and communities and regain their place as contributing members of society. The Trust Fund for Victims administers both reparations, including restitution and compensation, and rehabilitation for the benefit of the victims.

There is little doubt that the creation of the ICC represents an important step in the advance of international law. However, French President Jacques Chirac was guilty of overstatement when he proclaimed, "Starting now, all those who might be inclined to engage in the madness of genocide or crimes against humanity will know that nothing will be able to prevent justice."[13] One issue is that the ICC treaty has not been ratified by a number of the world's major powers, including such notable countries as the United States, China, Russia, and India.

U.S. opposition remains adamant. President Clinton signed the treaty for technical reasons, but declined to submit it to the Senate for ratification unless it made revisions. Strengthening the U.S. stand, Congress passed the American Servicemembers' Protection Act (2002) barring U.S. cooperation with the ICC and authorizing the president to use force to free any American held by the ICC. President Bush agreed, and in 2002 the State Department informed the UN that the United States did not intend to ratify the ICC Treaty and did not believe there were any U.S. legal obligations arising from the earlier U.S. signing of the treaty. Bush also threatened to veto all UN peacekeeping operations unless the Security Council exempted U.S. troops from possible prosecution by the ICC. This issue has been resolved for now by a series of one-year exemptions the Security Council gave to U.S. peacekeepers. The Bush administration had also negotiated bilateral "Article 98 agreements" (for a clause in the ICC treaty) with 100 countries agreeing that neither country would surrender the other's citizens to the ICC for prosecution. Sometimes these agreements have been possible because another government agreed with Washington about the ICC; at other times U.S. threats of foreign aid cutoffs or other pressures have promoted agreement. What most Americans think about the ICC is unclear. As Figure 8.8 indicates, American views on the court depend on the question, in part because most Americans know little or nothing about the ICC.

Given its hegemonic role in the international system, the U.S. position on the court is sure to be important—perhaps critical to its success (Johansen,

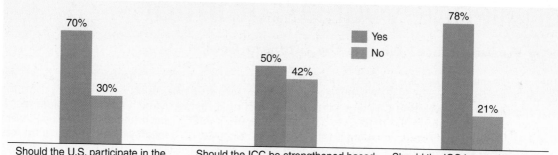

FIGURE 8.8

U.S. opinions of the ICC

If you ask Americans a general question about having the International Criminal Court try war criminals, as the left question does, you elicit a high level of support for the ICC. However, the support wanes slightly if you ask Americans if the ICC should be strengthened on the idea that the international community needs robust global judicial organizations. Still, the U.S. has not signed let alone ratified the Rome Statute. Further, while the last question reflect strong U.S. support for using the ICC to combat international terrorism, we have to wonder how supportive Americans would be if those terrorists were U.S. citizens.

Data Source: Chicago Council on Global Affairs 2010 National Survey of American Public Opinion.

2006; Ralph, 2005). Given U.S. focus on the economy, terrorism, and the Middle East, little change from the status quo is likely. However, some observers are optimistic about the U.S. stance in the long run. For one, the ICC's chief judge, Philippe Kirsch of Canada, predicts, "In the end, this court is going to become universal. It will not happen overnight. I think it may take a few decades to reach universality, but I believe it is only a question of time."[14] Perhaps Judge Kirsch is correct and American attitudes will eventually change. Even the Bush administration relented just a bit when in 2005 it abstained rather than vetoed the Security Council resolution that referred the situation in Darfur to the ICC for investigation and possible prosecution. The Obama administration followed by showing support through its backing of the SC resolution that referred Sudanese President al-Bashir to the ICC.

In addition to the ICC's complex relationship with major powers like the United States and China, the emerging caseload and initial trials raise important questions about the pursuit of justice and the many ways that justice is incomplete and imperfect. The fact that many people in Sierra Leone and Liberia were not even aware of Charles Taylor's conviction begs the question, "Justice for whom?"[15] The "Challenge Your Assumptions" box that follows takes this critical question one step further, "Justice for what end?" and encourages us to really consider the cost and benefit of pursuing justice across the globe.

The Pragmatic Application of Law and Justice

As this chapter demonstrates, the pursuit of law and justice is complicated, and at times can compete with and even contradict other international goals related to reconciliation, peace, security, and order. Within and across cultures, people differ

challenge your assumptions

Why Pursue Justice? What Is the Ultimate Goal?

The idea that states can and should deal with perpetrators of violent crimes committed during armed conflict or repressive rule is relatively new. Only since the end of the Cold War has the international community pursued the prosecution of perpetrators of mass atrocities. From Rwanda to the former Yugoslavia to the Democratic Republic of the Congo, the world is holding political and military leaders responsible for war crimes, crimes against humanity, and genocide, and transitional justice has become a growth industry for scholars and policy makers alike.

This increasing focus on transitional justice, however, raises important questions about the goals of justice in areas emerging from conflict. From prosecuting criminals to deterring future atrocities to bringing psychological closure to victims to facilitating reconciliation among war-torn communities to building human rights-based political institutions, transitional justice institutions can serve a wide range of interests and goals. What is more is that these interests do not always go hand-in-hand. At times, they can even be contradictory.

The International Criminal Court (ICC) is attempting to resolve these conflicting views of justice by defining the "interests of justice" with three elements: enforcing justice on behalf of the international community, ending impunity for the most serious criminals, and emphasizing the interests of the victims. However, many questions of interpretation and implementation remain. For example, are each of these elements equal? Is it okay to sacrifice one of the elements in the pursuit of another?

The issuance of an arrest warrant for Omar al-Bashir, the sitting President of Sudan, brings to light this tension as the indictment initially incited more violence and local unrest as the international community pursued "justice" for the war crimes and the crimes against humanity that Bashir and the government-supported Janjaweed committed in Darfur. Since 2002, two rebel groups have been at war with the Sudanese government through the Janjaweed counterinsurgency movement, with fighting primarily occurring within Darfur. One third of the population in Darfur is displaced; tens of thousands have been killed as a result of the fighting. As a result of his actions and despite the urgings of the Citizens Organizations of Sudan, the International Criminal Court issued a warrant for the arrest of Sudanese President Omar al-Bashir in March of 2009. The ICC claimed that al-Bashir's crimes were too heinous to go unpunished and that his arrest was in the interest of justice.

On March 5, 2009—the day after the ICC issued the warrant—al-Bashir expelled 13 humanitarian aid agencies from Sudan and ordered all other aid organizations to leave within the year. The effect was immediate. About 60% of the population was without access to any kind of medical or humanitarian aid. Al-Bashir claimed that they were passing erroneous information on his activities to the ICC, but the rest of the world saw it for was it was. He was punishing the people of Sudan for the actions of the international community. These same people who were now without aid were those who had already been displaced or affected by the military conflict—they were the "victims" whose interests were to be a priority in the pursuit of justice.

How could this situation have been handled differently? Should it have been? President al-Bashir was responsible for the murder, rape, torture, and forced displacement of hundreds of thousands of his own people. The international community demanded attention and action for the genocide in Darfur, and the ICC indictment and arrest warrant was just that. The justice the international community sought only brought with it greater abuses and suffering, but is this an inherent fault of the ICC or the way in which it handled al-Bashir's case? Is the pursuit of justice worth the risk of violent backlash? How do we need to balance or prioritize this tension between justice and peace moving forward?

Sources:

Jones, S. 2010. In the Pursuit of Justice: a Comment on the Arrest Warrant for President Al Bashir of Sudan. *Eyes on the ICC*, [Online]. 6.1, 13–42.

Selective Justice. *New African*, [Online]. 484, 10–15.

Wakabi, W. 2009. Aid Expulsions Leave Huge Gap in Darfur's Health Services. *The Lancet*, [Online]. 373.9669, 1068–1069.

on what counts as just and moral. The line between victim and perpetrators is not always clear. Of course, resources are always limited. However, we raise these critiques not as a source of immobility and defeat, but rather to challenge you to consider several critical questions regarding the prudence of applying standards of law, justice, and morality.

Can ends justify means? One conundrum is whether we can justify an act that by itself is evil if it is done for a good cause. Some believe that ends never justify means. The German philosopher Immanuel Kant took a position of **moral absolutism** in his *Groundwork on the Metaphysics of Morals* (1785) and argued that ends never justify means. He therefore urged us to "do what is right though the world should perish."

Others disagree and argue that, faced with complex choices, lofty goals do sometimes justify acts that most people consider morally abhorrent in the abstract. Terrorism is a case in point. For example, the Middle East terrorist group Hamas justifies suicide bombings against Israeli civilians on the grounds that the "heroic martyrdom operations . . . represent the sole weapon" available to the Palestinian people. The statement goes on to argue that "denying the Palestinian people the right of self-defense and describing this as terrorism, which should have been linked with the occupation [of Palestinian lands by Israel], violates all laws and norms which granted the people the right of self-defense" and that "considering the Palestinian resistance as a terrorist act and an outlaw legitimizes occupation because it delegitimizes its resistance."[16] This complex and protracted conflict raises critical questions about who is really violating international law, which violations are more problematic than others, and how do we approach situations where all sides are committing various war crimes, crimes against humanity, or fundamental human rights abuses?

In practice, the primitive international legal system can make the strict application of strong moral principles, adherence to international law, and other such altruistic acts unwise and even dangerous. Clearly, most of us do not take such an absolute position, nor do we practice **amorality**. Many people adhere to **moral relativism**. They believe that we must place actions in context. Consider the example of child soldiers. Insurgency groups often forcibly recruit or abduct children to serve in their armed forces. These children often witness their families and villages perish at the hands of these violent groups. These groups then become the only "family" they know, giving them food, drugs, and most important, a sense of belonging. Undoubtedly, children begin as child soldiers, but they often turn into violent perpetrators that torture, rape, and kill civilians in the war, sometimes becoming official adults during the course of the armed conflict. International efforts to address these children must take into account this complex scenario, where children are both victims and perpetrators, considering children's agency as such efforts address the psychological, social, and practical needs of reintegrating these children back into society, especially when it comes to the different experiences and needs of girl and boy soldiers (MacKenzie, 2009).

Should we judge others by our own standards? The issue about whether to judge others rests on two controversies. The first, which we have already addressed, is whether one should apply standards of international law and justice given the

Moral absolutism
A philosophical viewpoint that contends that the ends alone cannot and should not justify the means, or that morality should be the absolute guide for human decisions and actions.

Amorality
The philosophical viewpoint that morality cannot and/or should not be a guide for human actions and decisions.

Moral relativism
A philosophical viewpoint that contends that ascertaining the morality of human actions or decisions requires careful appreciation of the context in which said actions or decisions take place, and the moral and ethical standards that entail within that particular context.

divergent values of a multicultural world. Some claim that doing so is cultural imperialism. Others believe that at least some universal standards exist.

A second objection to any country or even the UN imposing sanctions or taking other action against a country for committing supposedly illegal, unjust, or immoral acts is that it violates the sovereignty of the target country. Americans overwhelmingly supported sanctions and even war against Iraq for its invasion of Kuwait in 1990. Most Americans would have been outraged over the violation of U.S. sovereignty, however, had the UN imposed sanctions on the United States for what many, perhaps most, people around the world considered the illegal U.S. invasion of Iraq in 2003. A third concern stems from what one might call "selective interventions." The United States has intervened in Haiti and Iraq at least partly in the name of democracy, yet in 1990, it sent its forces to defend Saudi Arabia and liberate Kuwait, both of which are ruled by distinctly undemocratic monarchies. Strong U.S. sanctions exist against communist Cuba, but U.S. trade with communist China is booming. Such selective interventions lead to a fourth concern: the suspicion that the invocation of international law and justice is often a smokescreen to cover old-fashioned imperialist intentions (Welsh, 2004; Orford, 2003).

Is it pragmatic to apply standards of legality and justice? Another objection to trying to apply moral principles is based on self-interest. Realists maintain that national interest sometimes precludes the application of otherwise laudable moral principles. They further contend that trying to uphold abstract standards of justice casts a leader as a perpetual Don Quixote, a pseudo knight-errant whose wish "To dream the impossible dream; to fight the unbeatable foe; . . . [and] to right the unrightable wrong," while appealing romantically, is delusional and perhaps dangerous.[17] From this perspective, states only abide by international law when it is in their national interest to do so, but they are skeptical about long-term gains of giving up any sovereign control in the global interest of law and order. Thus, international law applies to different states differently, depending on the state's position in the system. Standards of law and justice apply differently to the United States or China than to, say, a smaller, less powerful state in Latin America, Southeast Asia, or Africa.

This theoretical perspective, however, fails to account for all the middle-power states that contribute significantly to the development and implementation of international law and justice. Scholar Alison Brysk (2009) refers to these states as "global good Samaritans"—those who courageously stand up for what is right, pursuing global norms committed to justice, human dignity, and the rule of law. They might even recall the remonstration of President John F. Kennedy, who, evoking Dante Alighieri's *The Divine Comedy* (1321), commented, "Dante once said that the hottest places in hell are reserved for those who in a period of moral crisis maintain their neutrality."[18] More pragmatically, advocates of applying principles of law and justice contend that greater justice is necessary for world survival. This argument deals, for example, with resource distribution. It contends that it is unjust to support a system in which a large part of the world remains both impoverished and without self-development possibilities. The inevitable result, according to this view, will be a world crisis that will destroy order as countries fight for every declining resource.

One way out of the dilemma about when and to what degree law, justice, and other principles should apply to foreign policy may be to begin with the observation that it is not necessary to choose between moral absolutism and amorality. Instead, there is a middle ground of moral relativism that relies on **moral pragmatism** as a guiding principle. The serenity prayer, for example, is one that asks for the courage to change the wrongs one can, the patience to accept the wrongs that one cannot change, and the wisdom to know the difference. From this perspective, a decision-maker must ask, first, whether any tangible good is likely to result from a course of action and, second, whether the good will outweigh negative collateral consequences. By the first standard, taking high-flown principled stands when it is impossible or unlikely that you will affect the situation is quixotic. By the second standard, applying standards of justice when the overall consequences will be vastly more negative also fails the test of prudence. However, not taking action when change is possible and when the good will outweigh the bad fails the test of just behavior.

Moral pragmatism
The idea that there is a middle ground between amorality and moral absolutism that acts as a guide to human actions, particularly in regard to international law.

THE FUTURE OF INTERNATIONAL LAW AND JUSTICE

The often anarchic and inequitable world makes it easy to dismiss idealistic talk of conducting international relations according to standards of international law and justice. This view, however, was probably never valid and certainly is not true now. An irreversible trend in world affairs is the rapid growth of transnational interaction among states and people. As these interactions have grown, so has the need for regularized behavior and for rules to prescribe that behavior. For very pragmatic reasons, then, many people have come to believe, as one analyst notes, that "most issues of transnational concern are best addressed through legal frameworks that render the behavior of global actors more predictable and induce compliance from potential or actual violators" (Ratner, 1998:78). The growth of these rules in functional international interactions has been on the leading edge of the development of international law. Advances in political and military areas have been slower, but here too there has been progress. Thus, as with the United Nations, the pessimist may decry the glass as less than half full; whereas, in reality, it is encouraging that there is more and more water in the previously almost empty glass.

All the signs point to increasing respect for international law and a greater emphasis on adhering to at least rudimentary standards of justice. Violations of international standards are now more likely to draw criticism from the world community. It is probable, therefore, that international law will continue to develop and to expand its areas of application. So too will moral discourse have an increasing impact on the actions of international actors. There will certainly be areas where growth is painfully slow. A particular barrier is the change in the U.S. attitude from being a champion of international law and legal institutions after World War II to being more skeptical, and always exceptional, today (Murphy, 2004). There will also be those who violate the principles of law and justice and who sometimes get away with their unlawful and unjust acts. However, just as surely, there will be progress.

CRITICAL THINKING QUESTIONS

1. What do you think are the major obstacles to the effective implementation and enforcement of international law? Are these obstacles unique to global politics—and if so, how and why?

2. In the view of some international legal scholars, international law has progressed the furthest on matters of so-called functional politics. Do you agree with this assessment? What examples from this chapter do (or do not) support this claim?

3. How and in what ways has international law impacted state sovereignty and related concepts such as head-of-state immunity and crimes against humanity in recent years? What examples in this chapter stand out in this regard?

4. Is a robust system of international law possible, given the extensive political, social, and cultural diversity that defines our world? What are the arguments for and against such a system?

chapter **summary**

- We can best understand international law as primitive in comparison to domestic law, particularly when taking into account the relatively limited capacity for enforcement and adjudication. At the same time, the international legal system has evolved rapidly and expanded significantly in recent decades, with important implications for the conduct of global politics.

- Competing legal philosophies (such as natural and positive law), as well as differing legal norms and systems and cultural values, all pose fundamental challenges to the development and implementation of a coherent body of international law.

- International law is derived from multiple sources, including norms and principles, customs, and treaties. The emergence and evolution of international law over the past century has triggered the push to the codification of law in treaties and conventions, which are closer to "hard" law and thus have greater potential for enforceability.

- Adjudication in general, and the creation and use of standing international and regional courts and tribunals, have been leading factors in the growth and development of international law since the end of the Cold War.

- The push for an expanded concept of legal personhood in international law—to include individuals as well as other non–state actors—represents a shift in legal practice with the potential to dramatically expand the scope of legal rights and responsibilities subsumed within the international legal system.

The United States and most of Europe have also parted ways on a range of political issues. There was broad resentment of President George W. Bush's unilateralist approach to foreign policy and many of his specific policies. Europeans were distressed by his refusal to support the Kyoto Protocol on the environment, by his rejection of the International Criminal Court, by his abrogation of the Anti-Ballistic Missile Treaty, and, perhaps most of all, by his military action against Iraq. These political strains have intensified the U.S.-European rivalry and entwined it with European concerns about U.S. hegemony. Most European leaders believe that increasing the size and unity of the European Union is one way to maintain their region's global power and, especially, to counterbalance the United States. Barack Obama's election to the presidency signalled a change in the relationship. For instance, Britain's *Daily Telegraph* called Obama's 2008 victory a "watershed" and a "remarkable triumph of hope over adversity." One German commentator wrote that "The election of Barack Obama was an act of self-liberation for America." Responses from other European countries have also been mostly favorable, seeing President Obama as more open to collaboration transnationally than his predecessor. And clearly, collaboration on European debt issues in 2012 suggested that Mr. Obama indeed understood the shared transatlantic economic fate.[10]

This political context, then, provides the background for our examination of the major global economic institutions. Even though tensions exist within the North, these institutions remain the foundation of Northern economic health and the preservation of those economies' dominant place within the global system.

Trade Cooperation and Development: The WTO

We begin our examination with the institution that arguably has the greatest daily impact on global commerce: the World Trade Organization (WTO). As we discussed

Although the economic cost of war is often secondary to the military result, war and conflict produce significant negative impacts on national and global economies. Those impacts are felt for many years after a conflict ends, as the rebuilding develops post-conflict.

challenge your assumptions

How Should the U.S. Handle the Chinese Economic Challenge?

China and the United States may be on an economic collision course. The path to conflict begins with the U.S. trade deficit with China, as Figure 9.3 shows. It has been steadily mounting and reached $295 billion in 2011. U.S. officials put part of the blame for the deficit on China's halfhearted effort to deal with the illegal production of everything from music, movies, and software to machinery. The U.S. entertainment and software industries alone estimated that they lost $2.6 billion to such piracy. U.S. officials also claimed that Beijing is maintaining an artificially high yuan-to-dollar exchange value when the dollar has weakened against most currencies. Repeated demands by U.S. officials that China mend its ways have been backed by Congress, which has recurrently threatened to enact stringent U.S. tariffs on Chinese goods unless Beijing gives way. A third U.S. allegation is that China provides economic subsidies to many industries that give them an unfair advantage.

Recent history is not one of swift or hardline U.S. action. In 2007 the Bush administration ramped up the pressure on Beijing. In March, the United States imposed increased tariffs on glossy paper and intimated that other Chinese goods might also face increased barriers. In April, Washington filed two complaints with the World Trade Organization (WTO), one alleging that China was failing to enforce antipiracy rules and the other protesting against policies restricting access to U.S. products and services in China. Supporters of this action said that they represented a limited but important step to demonstrate U.S. resolve to challenge China. The tariff move was the first time in 20 years that a U.S. president had ordered a tariff hike against Chinese goods. Critics offered two opposite opinions. Some

argued that China was already making concessions, and applying more pressure would be counterproductive. From the opposite perspective, others charge that the Bush administration was making mini-moves designed more to diffuse efforts in Congress to enact strong moves against China than to persuade it to reform.

At the November 2011 Asia-Pacific Cooperation (APEC) summit, President Obama renewed pressure on China to liberalize its economic practices. He pressed the Chinese to make sure that Chinese economic policies did not disadvantage trading partners. He specifically mentioned the need to allow the Chinese currency to reach its real value and pushed for stricter Chinese protections of intellectual property. As he put it, "Enough is enough. . . . These practices aren't secret: I think everybody understands that they've been going on for quite some time. We're going to continue to be firm."[11]

What Do You Think?

Imagine you are a U.S. senator deciding on whether to vote on three competing measures.

- One is a resolution urging the White House to follow quiet diplomacy and persuade China to continue its economic reforms.
- The second resolution supports the continuation of limited sanctions.
- The third is a bill to impose a 25% tariff on all U.S. imports from China until the president certifies that China is fulfilling its obligations.

Which would you choose and why? What are the advantages and disadvantages of each policy?

Doha Round
The ninth and latest round of trade negotiations to reduce barriers to global commerce.

in "History Matters," the WTO grew out of the series of international agreements under the auspices of the General Agreement on Tariffs and Trade (GATT). The organization's initial membership of 23 countries has expanded to 153 members, and most of the nonmember countries are seeking to join. In keeping with the GATT's original mission, the reduction of trade barriers, the WTO has sponsored a series of trade negotiations, called *rounds*, which have greatly enhanced the free flow of trade and capital. Although the founders established the WTO as a general trade organization, its latest series of negotiations, the **Doha Round**, heavily

in 2010) were the African Development Bank ($4.1 billion), the Asian Development Bank ($13 billion), the Inter-American Development Bank ($15 billion), and the European Bank for Reconstruction and Development ($30 billion), which focuses on projects in the LDCs in Eastern Europe and in Russia and the former Soviet republics. There are other regional banks, but they are not as well funded, as exemplified by the Caribbean Development Bank, which, despite its region's pressing needs, only had the assets to make $299 million in loans in 2010. In addition to the development banks, numerous IGOs are dedicated to promoting economic cooperation and development among groups of countries based on their geographical region (such as the 12-member Black Sea Economic Cooperation Zone), culture, or some other link (for example, the 21-member Arab Monetary Fund).

An even more common type of international effort involves one or another Free Trade Agreement (FTA). These are treaties among two or more countries to reduce or eliminate tariffs and other trade barriers and to otherwise promote freer economic exchange. Before discussing FTAs in depth, it is important to note that different IGOs, governments, and studies designate them with different names and accompanying acronyms. Here we will use **regional trade agreement (RTA)** to designate an FTA among three or more countries within a region, and **bilateral trade agreement (BTA)** for an FTA between two countries or between an RTA and any other nonmember country. There is no precise count of FTAs, but the WTO estimates that there are about 30 RTAs and perhaps another 270 BTAs. We will begin with and emphasize multilateral regional economic cooperation, but we will also take up bilateral activity at the end of the section.

RTAs range from the tiny Melanesian Spearhead Group (Fiji, Papua New Guinea, Solomon Islands, and Vanuatu) to the huge European Union. Only a few countries are not members of an RTA, and numerous countries are in two or more. Some are little more than shell organizations that keep their goals barely alive, yet each represents the conviction of its members that, compared to standing alone, they can achieve greater economic prosperity by working together through economic cooperation or even economic integration. RTAs are particularly important to the development plans of the South. One indication is that about 75% of them have memberships that are exclusively made up of or include LDCs, and several others mix EDCs and LDCs as members. This pattern is evident in the following discussion of the major RTAs.

Regional trade agreement (RTA)
A broad term the World Trade Organization uses to define bilateral and cross-regional agreements as well as multilateral regional ones.

Bilateral trade agreement (BTA)
A free trade agreement between two countries or between a regional trade agreement and any other nonmember country.

The Western Hemisphere

Proposals for regional economic cooperation date back to a U.S. effort in 1889 to create a hemispherical free trade zone that would reduce trade barriers among the hemisphere's countries and adopt common external tariff and nontariff barriers. The notion of RTAs in the Western Hemisphere then lay dormant for almost a century until globalization began to convert the idea into reality. In this context, you may want to review the discussion of the European Union from chapter 5, as the EU is certainly the largest and most successful regional consortium in the world and began by focusing on trade and gradually expanded into almost every sphere of European sociopolitical life.

The North American Free Trade Agreement The largest RTA in the Western Hemisphere, measured in trade volume, is the **North American Free Trade Agreement (NAFTA)** among Canada, Mexico, and the United States. The 2,000-page agreement, which took effect in 1994, established schedules for reducing tariff and nontariff barriers to trade by 2004 in all but a few hundred of some 20,000 product categories and by 2009 for all products. NAFTA also reduced or eliminated many restrictions on foreign investments and other financial transactions and facilitated transportation by allowing trucking largely unimpeded access across borders. There is a standing commission with representatives from all three countries to deal with disputes that arise under the NAFTA agreement.

NAFTA has had an important impact on the three trading partners. Intra-NAFTA trade is a key component of the exports of all three partners, as the data on merchandise trade in Figure 9.6 reflects. Mexico and Canada are especially dependent on intra-NAFTA trade, with each sending between 80% and 90% of their exports to the United States and to one another. The United States is least dependent, albeit still heavily so, with NAFTA trade accounting for 26% of U.S. exports.

A vigorous debate continues in each of the three countries about the pros and cons of NAFTA. Canada is the least affected because it has relatively little interchange with

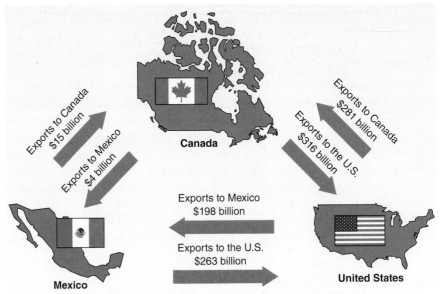

Exports to Canada
$15 billion

Exports to Mexico
$4 billion

Canada

Exports to Canada
$281 billion

Exports to the U.S.
$316 billion

Exports to Mexico
$198 billion

Exports to the U.S.
$263 billion

Mexico

United States

Total Intra-NAFTA trade for 2011: $1.12 trillion

FIGURE 9.6

Intra-NAFTA trade

The North American Free Trade Agreement has accounted for a rapid rise in trade among Canada, Mexico, and the United States since the treaty went into effect in 1994. There are plans for a Western Hemisphere free trade zone, the Free Trade Area of the Americas, although there are many political and economic roadblocks to completing such a zone in the short term.

Date Source: http://www.census.gov/foreign-trade/balance/c1220.html

Mexico and because preexisting U.S.–Canada trade was already quite high. For Americans, there certainly have been losses. Many American businesses have relocated their facilities to Mexico, establishing *maquiladoras*, manufacturing plants just south of the border, to produce goods for export to the United States. According to a U.S. Department of Labor study, U.S. job losses from this shift of production and from Mexican imports totaled 507,000 between late 1993 and late 2002. Yet economists point out that those jobs would have probably gone to other LDCs anyway if

Although NAFTA and other trade agreements should in theory facilitate free trade, they also tend to increase the volume of trade among member countries. That means longer waits at borders and in some ways produces perverse impacts on free trade (at least for the short term).

they had not shifted to Mexico. Furthermore, American consumers benefited from lower prices for goods imported from Mexico. Such gains often are less noticed, however, than are losses. As one economist explains, "The gains are so thinly spread across the country that people don't thank NAFTA when they buy a mango or inexpensive auto parts."[37] NAFTA has had the greatest effect on Mexico, in large part because both the size and strength of its economy are so much less than those of the United States and Canada. Some aspects have been clearly positive. NAFTA has diversified Mexico's economic base by increasing the percentage of its exports that are manufactured goods. The country's *maquiladora* program, dating back long before NAFTA, was set up to promote industrialization by giving special tax and other advantages to industries in a zone near the U.S. border. However, after NAFTA went into effect, the *maquiladora* zone boomed, doubling its production and tripling its workers by 2000. Then fortunes turned down in the zone, in part because of competition from China for the U.S. market. More recent data, however, shows a new upswing. Moreover, Mexico's GDP growth rate nearly tripled in the decade after NAFTA, compared to the decade before it. Mexico's 2005 per capita GNP of $7,310 was 25% higher than that of Chile, the next wealthiest country in Central and South America. Reflecting on such data, Mexican President Vicente Fox contended, "NAFTA gave us a big push. It gave us jobs. It gave us knowledge, experience, technological transfer."[38]

It is also true for Mexicans, as well as for Americans and Canadians, that NAFTA has had some very negative effects on some, such as displaced workers. Some segments of Mexico's economy have been particularly hard hit, such as corn farmers in central and southern Mexico who have suffered greatly from the incoming tidal wave of subsidized U.S. corn, increasing about 1,400% between 1993 and 2004. Many Mexicans also worry about the loss of their culture amid the influx of Pizza Huts, KFC outlets, and other elements of American culture.

The Free Trade Area of the Americas   At the same time that NAFTA came into effect in 1994, efforts were under way to create a much broader hemispheric RTA, tentatively named the Free Trade Area of the Americas (FTAA), which would include all or most of the countries in North, Central, and South America, and in the Caribbean. To that end, the heads of every country in the Western Hemisphere except Cuba, which was barred at U.S. insistence, met in 1994 at the Summit of the Americas in Miami, Florida, and agreed to create a free trade zone in the hemisphere by 2005. Soon, the optimistic predictions of the summit meeting gave way to difficult and slow negotiations. Subsequent summits in Santiago, Chile (1999), Quebec City, Canada (2001), Monterrey, Mexico (2004), and Mardel Plata, Argentina (2005) failed to reach any breakthroughs, and 2005, the original target date for an FTAA agreement, passed into history without one.

The disagreements that have ensnared the FTAA negotiations are very similar to the North–South issues that have beset the WTO's Doha Round, which we discussed earlier. As much as the hemisphere's LDCs are anxious to improve their access to U.S. markets, they are equally nervous about dropping their protections and drowning in a tidal wave of American imports and services, and about having American investors snap up local businesses and other property. The growing anti-American tone of Venezuela's Hugo Chávez and funds flowing into the country's treasury from surging oil prices increased the opposition to the FTAA even more. In fact, Chávez is trying to expand an existing limited trade agreement among Venezuela, Bolivia, Cuba, and Nicaragua into a much larger Bolivarian Alternative of the Americas encompassing much of Latin America and the Caribbean. "The idea here is to promote cooperation between countries of the South—seeking out complementary exchanges in terms of trade and technological transfer—rather than, as has traditionally been the case, further extending North–South dependencies," a Venezuelan official explained.[39]

There is also resistance to the FTAA in the United States, especially among some interest groups. Unions fear that American jobs will wind up in the hands of underpaid Central and South Americans. Agricultural organizations are determined to protect their subsidies. Other groups fear that an FTAA will eventually increase labor migration, as the EU has done among its member-countries, leading to a greater inflow of Latin Americans into the United States than already exists. For now, then, the FTAA's fate remains cloudy at best.

Mercosur   Whatever the FTAA's future, a number of countries have undertaken or continued efforts to establish or expand their own trade treaties. The **Southern Common Market (Mercosur)** is of particular note. Argentina, Brazil, Paraguay, and Uruguay established Mercosur in 1995. Venezuela has joined since then as a full member, and Bolivia, Chile, Colombia, Ecuador, and Peru have become associate members. Including just its five full and five associate members, Mercosur is a market of 372 million people with a combined GDP of over $2.3 trillion, as Figure 9.7 shows.

A number of issues, including Argentina's economic crisis and some countries' concerns about the powerful role that Brazil plays in Mercosur, have slowed the negotiations to expand and strengthen it, but other factors exist that are pushing for its enlargement and invigoration. One is the desire to provide a counterweight to the United States in the hemisphere. "We have to unite," Brazil's President Lula da Silva told an audience. "We need to create a South American nation. The more policies we have in common, the better we will be able to succeed in big negotiations, above

Southern Common Market (Mercosur)
A regional organization that emphasizes trade relations, established in 1995 among Argentina, Brazil, Paraguay, and Uruguay, with Bolivia, Chile, Peru, and Venezuela as associate members.

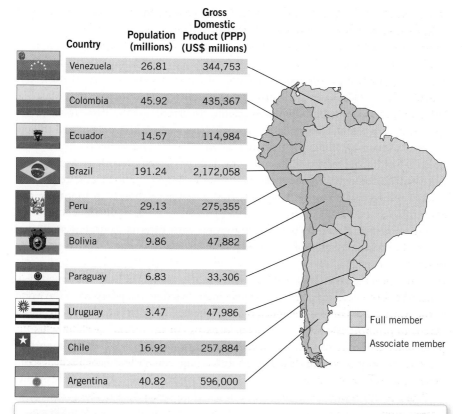

Country	Population (millions)	Gross Domestic Product (PPP) (US$ millions)
Venezuela	26.81	344,753
Colombia	45.92	435,367
Ecuador	14.57	114,984
Brazil	191.24	2,172,058
Peru	29.13	275,355
Bolivia	9.86	47,882
Paraguay	6.83	33,306
Uruguay	3.47	47,986
Chile	16.92	257,884
Argentina	40.82	596,000

Full member

Associate member

FIGURE 9.7

Mercosur

Mercosur is an important RTA. A key issue fo the Western Hemisphere is whether it, NAFTA, and other RTAs will merge into a single FTAA or remain divided, overlapping, and to a degree competitive.

Data Sources: http://en.wikipedia.org/wiki/List_of_South_American_countries_by_GDP_(PPP); http://en.wikipedia.org/wiki/South_America

all in trying to break down WTO's protectionist barriers and prevent the FTAA becoming an instrument that suffocates our chances of growth."[40]

Taking a step in that direction, the South American leaders agreed at summits in 2004, and again in 2007, to seek to merge Mercosur and the Andean Community (Bolivia, Colombia, Ecuador, Peru) into a Union of South American Nations that would eventually emulate the EU with its own currency, a continental parliament, and a common passport. Mercosur itself also continues to develop, and all the countries of the Andean Community of Nations are now either full or associate members. Additionally, Mercosur may reach north, and there are at least informal membership discussions with Mexico. Mercosur also established a parliament that convened for the first time in 2007. Their respective home governments appointed its first members, but, like the EU, beginning in 2010, Mercosur elected its parliament by direct popular vote. The RTA has also expanded its scope by negotiating a number of BTAs with individual countries, including one with India in 2007.

Asia and the Pacific

In Asia, the first RTA was the Association of Southeast Asian Nations (ASEAN) established in 1967. It now includes Brunei, Cambodia, Indonesia, Laos, Malaysia, Myanmar (Burma), the Philippines, Singapore, Thailand, and Vietnam. The ASEAN countries have a combined population of over 568 million, a GNP of about $1.1 trillion, and total exports of about $1.4 trillion. Like the EU and some other RTAs, ASEAN is also expanding its responsibilities to include development, health, and other matters. The disaster management program that it developed in 2002 facilitated a coordinated response when a 2004 tsunami devastated coastal areas in Indonesia and other member-countries. ASEAN is working to forge greater political cooperation among its members and to bargain as a group with external countries and other trade organizations. Some observers view the RTA as a counterbalance to China in the region.

Asia-Pacific Economic Cooperation (APEC)
A regional trade organization founded in 1989 that now includes 21 countries.

More recently, **Asia-Pacific Economic Cooperation (APEC)** was founded in 1989. Its website declares that it is the "only intergovernmental grouping in the world operating on the basis of non-binding commitments . . . [with] no treaty obligations required of its participants . . . decisions made by consensus, and commitments . . . undertaken on a voluntary basis." Despite its amorphous nature, APEC is important because among its 21 members are most of the countries of the greater Pacific Ocean region, including China, Japan, Russia, and the United States. Additionally, APEC members account for 41% of the world population, about 50% of the global GDP, and over 40% of world trade. There is a small APEC secretariat based in Singapore, but it is symbolic of APEC's still-tentative status that it has not added a word such as "organization" or "community" to the end of its name.

Somewhat like the G-8, APEC facilitates numerous routine economic consultations among members. Its focus, however, is the annual APEC summit meeting, which serves as a forum for discussions among the United States, Japan, China, and other leading members. Although APEC does not claim to be moving toward RTA status, there have been agreements in principle, for example, to achieve "free and open trade and investment" in the Asia-Pacific region. Japan and the United States are to remove all their barriers by the year 2010, with the rest of the APEC members achieving a zero-barrier level by 2020. It remains unclear whether this will occur, given such factors as China's huge trade surplus with the United States and Japan's uncertain economy. Beyond this, few specific agreements have resulted from these summits, but they are part of a process of dialogue that helps keep lines of communication open. Among other Asia/Pacific RTAs are the 14 island-states of the South Pacific Regional Trade and Economic Cooperation Agreement, and the South Asian Preferential Trade Agreement among India and six other countries.

Other Regions

The impulse for regional ties has not been confined to the Americas and the Asia-Pacific region. In Europe, the 27-member European Union is by far the most extensive regional effort. Other European or partly European RTAs are the four-member

European Free Trade Association and the Commonwealth of Independent States, which includes the former Soviet republics. Given the expanded coverage of the EU in chapter 5, further commentary here is unnecessary other than to point out that with a population about 50% larger than the U.S. population and with a collective GNP that rivals that of the United States, the EU is a powerful economic force. To some degree, competing with it is one factor that has driven the creation of other RTAs, including NAFTA. Among the most important RTAs in Africa are the 19-member Common Market for Eastern and Southern Africa, northern Africa's 24-member Community of Sahel Saharan States, the 15-member Economic Community of West African States, the 11-member Economic Community of Central African States, and the 15-member South African Development Community. Another range of RTAs are based in the Middle East. These include the Gulf Cooperation Council and its six oil-wealthy members. All these share a common purpose of increasing the members' economic strength. Yet because most RTAs are made up of countries with weak economies, their goal is something akin to trying to build a solid structure on quicksand.

Bilateral Trade Agreements

Countries have long concluded bilateral trade agreements with one another, but, as with RTAs, recent years have seen a rapid expansion of BTAs between countries and between RTAs and individual countries. The WTO estimates that at least 270 and probably many more RTAs are currently in effect. The United States, for example, has concluded BTAs with 21 individual countries including Australia, Chile, Israel, Morocco, and South Korea, and with one RTA, the five-member Southern African Customs Union (Botswana, Lesotho, Namibia, South Africa, and Swaziland). Among the U.S. BTAs is the confusingly named Central American Free Trade Association—Dominican Republic (CAFTA-DR). In addition to the United States and the Dominican Republic, it includes Costa Rica, El Salvador, Guatemala, Honduras, and Nicaragua. Despite its RTA-like name, CAFTA-DR is a series of similar bilateral trade agreements between the United States and the other countries, and those countries with each other. It is important to inquire into the impact of RTAs and BTAs before concluding our discussion. They have the advantages of opening trade, investment, and other forms of economic interchange among countries. That is good insofar as it generally improves the economic circumstances of most people in all the countries party to any FTA. Such agreements also can potentially create commonalities and ease tensions among nations and lead to greater regional cooperation on many fronts. The current EU serves as an example of what can evolve from a very limited RTA.

Yet there are also downsides to RTAs and BTAs. One is that their proliferation has created a patchwork of agreements that undermine global trade liberalization (Haftel, 2004). This may harm, rather than advance, the South's economic development. According to the WTO's director-general, RTAs are an unsatisfactory substitute for global trade liberalization because "they are by their very nature discriminatory. None has really succeeded in opening markets in sensitive areas like agriculture. They add to the complexities of doing business by creating a multiplicity of rules. And the poorest countries tend to get left out in the cold."[41]

CRITICAL THINKING QUESTIONS

1. Which theoretical perspective best characterizes how you think the global political economy really works?

2. What are the primary goals for creating, maintaining, and expanding the dominant global economic institutions? Have they been successful in achieving those goals? Why or why not?

3. Does global economic interaction yield increased welfare for all or only for a select few? Explain your thinking.

4. Will regional economic integration lead to political integration? Give some examples to support your answer and think back to the chapter on international organization, as well.

chapter summary

- Economics and politics are closely intertwined aspects of global politics. This interrelationship has become even more important in recent history. Economics has become more important internationally because of dramatically increased trade levels, ever-tightening economic interdependence between countries, and the growing impact of global economics on domestic economics. The study of global political economy examines the interaction between politics and economics.

- There are many technical aspects to explaining and understanding the international political economy, and it is important to understand such concepts as gross domestic product, gross national product, and current and real dollars, among other concepts mentioned early in this chapter.

- We can divide the approaches to understanding global political economy roughly into three groups: economic nationalism, internationalism, and critical radicalism.

- The core of the economic nationalist doctrine is the realist idea that the state should harness and use national economic strength to further national interest. Therefore, the state should shape the country's economy and its foreign economic policy to enhance state power.

- Internationalists tend to be liberals (or neoliberals) who believe that global economic relations should and can be harmonious because prosperity is available to all and we can most likely achieve and preserve it through cooperation. The main thrust of internationalism is to separate politics from economics in order to create prosperity by freeing economic interchange from political restrictions.

- Critical radicals hold that world politics is based on the division of the world into wealthy and poor; dominant and dependent. Put directly, the EDCs keep the LDCs weak and poor in order to exploit them. Critical radicals tend to focus on how the global system is structured to maintain the relationships of dominance and dependence. They also believe that only a radical restructuring of the global system will produce betterment for the LDCs.

Cuba, in 2000). The leaders adopted the "Doha Program of Action," which reiterated a number of earlier declarations and pledged its signatories to "continue strengthening the unity and solidarity among countries of the South, as an indispensable element in the defense of our right to development and for the creation of a more just and equitable international order."[5] The follow-up of the 2005 meeting, the 2008 summit in Geneva, Switzerland, unfortunately ended without agreement on agricultural tariffs, even if the Doha principles remained theoretically in place. That document asserted the need for policy change in these areas:

- *Trade reforms*, such as lowering EDC barriers to agricultural imports, which will expand and stabilize markets for LDC exports.

- *Monetary reforms* that will create greater stability in the exchange rates of LDC currencies and will also moderate the sometimes sudden and significant ebb and flow of FDI and FPI into and out of the LDCs.

- *Institutional reforms* that will increase the South's influence over policies of the International Monetary Fund, the World Bank, and other such international financial agencies. Currently, as chapter 9 details, wealthy countries dominate decision-making in these institutions.

- *Economic modernization* of LDCs with significant assistance by EDCs through such methods as relaxing patent rights to permit easier technology transfers to LDCs.

- *Greater labor migration* for LDC workers seeking employment in more prosperous EDCs.

- *Elimination of economic coercion*, including the use of sanctions, which the South tends to see as a tool by which EDCs punish and control LDCs.

- *Economic aid* to the South by the North that steadily increases to meet the UN's target of 0.7% of each EDC's GNP, which it spends on promoting the development of LDCs. The current aid level is a bit over 0.2%.

- *Debt relief* granted by EDCs, the World Bank, and the IMF, based on reducing the money owed to them by many LDCs and eliminating the debt for the poorest LLDCs. Currently, LDCs owe about $2.4 trillion and have annual debt service payments over $400 billion.

The North's Response to the South's Reform Agenda   To say that the North has ignored the South's plight would be inaccurate. It would also be misleading to assert that the North has gone very far to meet the South's demands. One reason for the North's limited response is the view of many that the main barriers to the South's development are internal issues, including political instability, inefficient market controls, and corruption. Taking that view, in 2002, President George W. Bush told one international development conference that LDCs had not done enough to reform themselves and that, "The lesson of our time is clear: When nations close their markets and opportunity is hoarded by a privileged few, no amount—no amount—of development aid is ever enough." Instead of more aid, the president continued, the LDCs needed to accept "a higher, more difficult, more promising call . . . to encourage sources that produce wealth: economic freedom, political liberty, the rule of law and human rights."[6]

history matters

UNCTAD: A Voice for the Global Poor?

World War II was a turning point for many structures and relationships in the global system. First, it shifted from a multipolar global system, where Britain, France, Germany, Italy, Japan, the Soviet Union, and the United States balanced each others' power, to a bipolar system, where the United States and the Soviet Union engaged in a Cold War for nearly 50 years. The decline of the traditional European world powers and their global colonial empires was another critical trend that produced a tremendous influx of poor, corrupt, and often violent countries. We usually refer to this underclass of countries as the *less developed countries* (LDCs). As **decolonization** progressed after World War II, these newly independent countries recurrently sought global roles commensurate with their status as sovereign states and UN members.

One of the primary forums for gaining a voice in global affairs is the UN Conference on Trade and Development (UNCTAD). As described on its website, UNCTAD:

promotes the development-friendly integration of developing countries into the world economy. UNCTAD has progressively evolved into an authoritative knowledge-based institution whose work aims to help shape current policy debates and thinking on development, with a particular focus on ensuring that domestic policies and international action are mutually supportive in bringing about sustainable development.

Established in 1964, UNCTAD's early success centered on providing a voice for the growing number of developing countries in the UN context. Calling themselves the Group of 77, these newly independent countries brought trade and development issues to the fore of global debates, even if the EDCs were less than receptive to their efforts. Today, numbering 131 countries, the Group of 77 remains a primary forum for pursuing development issues and seeks to do so with the power of numbers. Even though it is difficult to point to many tangible UNCTAD successes in global development policy, the forum has given voice to issues that otherwise would have received little attention. Some landmark UNCTAD achievements include:

- Adoption of the **Generalized System of Preferences (GSP)** in 1968 under GATT. The GSP provided for improved access for LDCs to EDC markets.

- UN General Assembly Passage of the **New International Economic Order (NIEO)** in 1974. The NIEO called for changes to the global terms of trade, greater development assistance flowing from the EDCs to the LDCs, and a restructuring of global

Decolonization
The undoing of colonialism; this mostly focused on dismantling the European colonial empires built in the 19th century.

Generalized System of Preferences (GSP)
A program designed to promote economic growth in the developing world by providing preferential entry for products from designated beneficiary countries and territories.

New International Economic Order (NIEO)
A term that refers to the goals and demands of the South for basic reforms in the global economic system.

President Obama has been somewhat more receptive to development demands, but his 2012 budget request focused a significant portion of development assistance on strategic interests. For instance, although he requested $9.8 billion for the Global Health Initiative, he also requested significant funds for Iraq, Afghanistan, and Pakistan. Such priorities give credence to the argument of Economic Nationalists that economic policy is, and should be, focused on promoting national goals for the Northern donors.[7]

Domestic resistance within the EDCs has also limited Northern responses to the LDCs. Many of the changes that the LDCs want are very unpopular in the EDCs. Greater labor migration is an example. One survey of the United States, Canada, Japan, and four Western European EDCs found that an average of 71% of their people opposed increased immigration.[8] Foreign aid also faces stiff opposition in most EDCs. A recent poll of Americans found 64% thinking that U.S. foreign aid was too high and only 9% thinking it was too low. Another 24% thought the aid level was about right, and 2% were unsure.[9] The result of this attitude in the

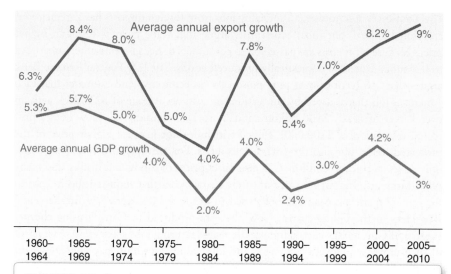

FIGURE 10.5

World trade and GDP

World trade measured in exports, which generate GDP, has grown faster in each period between 1960 and 2010 than did the collective GDPs of the world's countries. This means that exports have played an important role in driving overall economic growth. Globalization supporters point to such data to show that freer trade is having an overall positive impact on world economic circumstances.

Data Source: IMF. imf.org

growth helps drive economic expansion, as Figure 10.5 shows. More specifically, for example, the U.S. government calculates that because of trade liberalization since the founding of GATT in 1947, the income of the average American household is $9,000 higher than it otherwise would have been.[13]

A corollary of this argument, according to internationalists, is that development of the South will increase EDC prosperity. Although assisting the LDCs will require a substantial short-term cost to the North in aid, debt reductions, and other assistance, many analysts argue that in the long run this investment would create a world in which many more of the 1.3 billion Chinese, 1.1 billion Indians, and the other 3 billion people living in LDCs could buy products labeled "Made in America," visit the United States as tourists, and otherwise benefit the U.S. economy, not to mention those of other EDCs.

Benefits of Specialization   Another advantage of globalization, according to internationalists, is based on the long-standing theory that all countries will benefit if each sells what it can produce most efficiently. Among those who have propounded this idea are English economists David Ricardo, in *On the Principles of Political Economy and Taxation* (1817), and John Stuart Mill in *Principles of Political Economy* (1848). Ricardo developed the theory of "comparative advantage," which held that everyone would benefit if each country produced and exported its most cost-efficient products. Based on this view, Mill argued that trade's "advantage consists in a more efficient employment of the productive forces of the world."

The Cost of Protectionism   Protecting jobs from foreign imports has a tremendous emotional appeal, but most economists argue that trade barriers result in higher prices because tariff costs are passed on to consumers or because consumers are forced to buy more expensive domestically produced goods. The U.S. Federal Reserve Bank argues that "protectionism is pure poison for an economy" and estimates that each American job that is saved by protectionism costs an average of $231,289, with an overall cost of nearly $100 billion annually to U.S. consumers.[14] How does a protected job cost over $200,000? The cost includes not just the higher price of the protected items, but also downstream products. For example, protecting sugar not only raises its price to consumers, it also raises prices of candy, soft drinks, and many other products. The higher price of candy also exposes that industry and its jobs to foreign competition. Manufacturers used to produce LifeSavers, Jaw Breakers, and Red Hots in the Chicago area. Now, they are produced in Canada using cheaper sugar, and Chicago has lost half its candy manufacturing jobs since 1970. As a result of such moves, employees lose wages and jobs, companies must pay unemployment compensation, and the rippling costs can add up.

Promotion of Competition   Internationalists also argue that free economic interchange promotes beneficial competition. Without foreign competition, the argument goes, domestic manufacturers have a captive market, which can have a variety of ill effects, such as price fixing and lack of innovation. For example, during the 1980s and 1990s, American automakers did not begin to offer U.S. consumers well-built, inexpensive, fuel-efficient small cars until pressure from foreign competition forced them to reshape their product and modernize their production techniques.

Providing Development Capital   Internationalists maintain that free economic interchange increases investment capital flow to the LDCs. The IMF calculates that between 1997 and 2005 alone, a net $1.3 trillion (investments minus withdrawals) in foreign direct investment (FDI) flowed into LDCs to bolster their economic development, and FDI also benefits EDCs. It is also the case that MNC-directed investments provide EDCs with a wide variety of economic benefits. Jobs are one benefit. Foreign-owned MNCs employ 6.3 million people in the United States, pay them $350 billion a year, and contribute tens of billions of dollars in U.S. federal, state, and local taxes.

Noneconomic Advantages   Arguably, there are also several noneconomic advantages to internationalism. These include advancing world cooperation, decreasing violence, and promoting democracy.

Global Cooperation   A political argument internationalists make is that free economic interchange promotes world cooperation. The logic is that if countries can trade together in peace, their interactions will bring greater contact and understanding. Cooperation will then become the rule rather than the exception, and this will lead to political interaction and cooperation. The move toward the political integration of Europe, which began with economic cooperation, is the most frequently cited example.

Decreased Violence   Another political argument for free economic interchange is that it decreases violence by promoting interdependence, which makes fighting more difficult and more unlikely (McDonald, 2004; Pevehouse, 2004). In the words of one

is to make "all workers, communities and countries competitors for these corporations' favor.'" This competition, he worries, has set off "a 'race to the bottom' in which wages and social and environmental conditions tend to fall to the level of the most desperate" (Brecher, 1993:685). Critics of globalization also charge that, among other evils, the race to the bottom will mean gutting desirable social programs. Europe has built an extensive social welfare support system through government programs and mandates on industries (such as health insurance for workers, paid vacations, and other benefits). Such programs and benefits are costly, however, and European economies struggle to meet them while also keeping the price of their products low enough to be competitive in world markets or even at home compared to imported goods and services. Similarly, critics worry that countries attempting to maintain high standards of environmental protection or institute new safeguards will see companies move their production facilities and jobs elsewhere.

A Critical Radical Postscript

To return to the point with which we began this portion of the chapter, the clash between internationalism and economic nationalism is likely fundamental to understanding the political economic trajectory of the coming decades (Helleiner & Pickel, 2005). The rapid globalization process that began after World War II has brought the world much closer to a truly global economy than seemed possible not long ago. The EDCs have generally prospered, and even most of the LDCs have improved their health, education, and many other social conditions.

However, these two dominant perspectives have yet to captivate the thinking of many policy makers and citizens, especially in the developing world. To them, an alternative future based on global restructuring, economic redistribution, and the establishment of equity and human rights as guiding principles in North–South relations is the only path to a global future of long-term peace, stability, and prosperity. Such a future could build on the constructs put forth in the New International Economic Order and later in the Millennium Development Goals, but would require a substantial change in policy attitudes from Northern political elites who buy into one of the two more dominant perspectives just discussed.

So, if we were to think about a future more in line with a critical radical view, we might start with some of the following fundamental principles:

- **Fair trade** This approach to global exchange would refocus attention away from profit as the first goal of commerce. Promoting worker rights and acceptable living standards would be the starting place for a more people-centric form of prosperity.

- **Human rights** As we will discuss in the next chapter, LDCs have long argued for greater emphasis on economic rights relative to the civil and political rights that have historically taken center stage for the North.

- **Social justice** The legacy of colonialism persists in the South and will not disappear anytime soon. However, will the global community accept a policy program that begins from the assumption that some degree of global wealth redistribution is essential to global peace and security?

The interesting dilemma, then, from both policy and scholarly perspectives, is whether the collective (and some would argue, moral) power the South possesses in pursuit of greater economic equity can overcome the wealth and structurally entrenched interests of the Global North. For now, it is more likely that the internationalists or the economic nationalists will have more to say about the shape of the global economic future. However, the economic crisis of the early 21st century has given many a chance to reconsider those older models.

CRITICAL THINKING QUESTIONS

1. What signs of economic progress can developing world countries identify?

2. What are the primary roadblocks to development for countries in the South?

3. How effective are current global economic institutions in promoting development?

4. To what extent do you view global political economy as a product of global politics?

5. Which of the three theoretical perspectives best describes the current state of the global political economy?

6. Which of the three theoretical perspectives might best provide a framework or roadmap forward for coping with global political economic development?

chapter summary

- As we discussed in the previous chapter, the world is generally divided into two economic spheres: a wealthy North and a much less wealthy South. There are some overlaps between the two spheres, but in general the vast majority of the people and countries of the South are much less wealthy and less industrialized than the people and countries of the North. The South also has a history of direct and indirect colonial (neocolonial) control by countries of the North.

- A wealth gap persists between North and South. By some measures, economic and social conditions in the South have improved in recent decades. However, those improvements mask the reality of ongoing poverty and desperate living conditions in many locations in the Global South.

- Again, taken in tandem with our discussion in the previous chapter, it is clear that there is economic competition across a number of different classes of countries: North–North competition, North–South competition, and South–South competition.

- Numerous IGOs and international programs focus on economic cooperation, and many give the development of the South some priority. The largest general IGO, the UN, maintains a number of efforts aimed at general economic development, with an emphasis on the less developed countries (LDCs).

the entire shift on their feet. According to the investigations, "some say they stand so long that their legs swell until they can hardly walk" (Duhigg & Barboza, A1:2012). Further, human rights activists point to the dangerous and seriously risky working conditions in these factories, from toxic cleaning chemicals for iPhone screens, to several recent explosions that have killed and injured numerous employees.

Foxconn currently employs 1.2 million and is responsible for assembling approximately 40% of the smartphones, computers, and other electronics sold worldwide. Thus, Foxconn's decisions to keep labor costs down and production up sets standards with which other manufacturers must compete. Foxconn supplies Apple, Hewlett-Packard, and Dell, among other **multinational corporations,** with the cheapest possible devices just about as quickly as these electronic firms conceive them. In this way, consumer demand for affordable and high volume products is a major factor for this human rights issue. Consumers play a significant role in the supply process, and we cannot be uninformed about the origins of our cell phones and tablets and what it took to get those products to us quickly and at the lowest price possible.

We will return to this case study throughout the chapter as it highlights the many actors involved in human rights abuses and more important our shared responsibility to promote and protect basic rights of individuals. From individual consumers to major corporations to parts manufacturers to states and intergovernmental organizations, we all bear responsibility as global citizens in promoting the common good.

These protestors from SACOM—Students and Scholars Against Corporate Misbehavior—are demonstrating outside a Foxconn meeting demanding that this major Chinese employer provide better working conditions for its employees. Foxconn, one of Apple's major suppliers, has recently received global attention for reports of unsafe and abusive labor practices.

THE NATURE OF HUMAN RIGHTS

Consider the following events that have defined the 21st century: democratic movements challenging and overthrowing authoritarian governments in the context of the Arab Spring; prisoner abuse of suspected terrorists at Guatanamo Bay in the context of the War on Terror; multinational corporations moving manufacturing jobs to low-wage countries with lax labor laws; rural villages and urban poor in developing countries dying from preventable diseases because of the lack of clean water and access to basic medicine; men and women organizing to establish the right to marry and found a family regardless of sexual orientation; and

Human rights
Inalienable fundamental rights to which a person is inherently entitled simply because he or she is a human being. Conceived as universal and egalitarian, these rights may exist as natural rights or as legal rights, in both national and international law.

Universal Declaration of Human Rights
Adopted by the UN General Assembly in 1948, it is the most fundamental internationally proclaimed statement of human rights in existence.

Multinational corporations (MNCs)
Private enterprises that have production subsidiaries or branches in more than one country.

Enlightenment
A cultural movement of intellectuals in 18th-century Europe and America whose purpose was to reform society and advance knowledge. It promoted science and intellectual interchange and opposed superstition, intolerance, and abuses in church and state.

Natural law
A system of law that is purportedly determined by nature, and thus universal.

First generation rights
Based on the principles of individualism and noninterference, these are "negative" rights based on the Anglo-American principles of liberty. Developed under a strong mistrust of government, they have evolved into "civil" or "political" rights.

Proscriptive rights
Obligations on a society and its government to try to provide a certain qualitative standard of life that, at a minimum, meets basic needs.

Second generation rights
Based on the principles of social justice and public obligation; they tend to be "positive" rights, based on continental European conceptions of liberty as equality. The notion has evolved into what we now call "social" or "economic" rights.

increased trafficking of women, girls, and boys across national borders where they are forced into prostitution, domestic servitude, agricultural work, and other forms of forced labor. What all of these distinct events have in common is that it is difficult to talk about them and more important to act on them without invoking the modern-day language of human rights. This language is not inconsequential because "to assert a human right is to make a fundamentally political claim: that one is entitled to equal moral respect and to the social status, support, and protection necessary to achieve that respect" (Goodhart, 2009:4). Human rights have become a part of mainstream politics, and even those who don't consider themselves politically inclined are familiar with and use the human rights framework for analysis and activism.

The Emergence of Rights Language

Political theorists have long been thinking and writing about the rights of man. Prior to the 20th century, this language emerged gradually, most notably with the development of the European **Enlightenment**. Prior to the Enlightment, philosophers advocated rights they derived from **natural law** as inherent duties that people had to one another and to God. The dominant religious institution of the day, Christianity, divinely sanctioned this moral order. With the Enlightenment, however, these natural rights that emerged from the laws of nature increasingly focused on the secular origins of individual freedoms and liberties rather than a divine moral order.

Political philosopher John Locke articulated this reasoning by focusing on the fundamental freedoms (natural rights) that individuals have by simply being human. From this perspective, these rights of individuals predate national and international law, and no state can usurp them. Individuals should not be "deprived of life, liberty, or property without due process of law." We often refer to this first group of human rights as **first generation rights**.[2] These rights focus on civil liberties and political freedoms and for many serve as the core to a rights system based on equality and nondiscrimination. Some international relations scholars have classified these rights as **proscriptive rights**, those policies and actions that governments cannot do to groups. Discrimination based on race, ethnicity, gender, or sexual orientation is a good example of a breach of such rights. The obligation to respect many of these proscriptive rights extends to private individuals, organizations, and corporations, and protections include freedom of speech, religion, and association as well as rights to a fair trial and rights to vote. We can also refer to these rights as negative rights, as they focus rights providers on refraining from intervening or interfering.

Human rights, however, also include those positive rights that require rights providers to act to ensure that all people are not deprived of and have equal access to basic needs and goods. **Second-generation rights** are largely centered on economic and social rights, such as economic subsistence, education, nutrition, sanitation, work, housing, and health care. For some international relations scholars, these **prescriptive rights** include the essentials that a society and its government are arguably prescribed (obligated) to try to provide in order to assure certain qualitative standards of life for everyone in the community.

International scholars and policy makers are increasingly debating the degree to which we should use proscriptive and prescriptive rights as a standard to judge state

thinking **theoretically**

Justifying the Origins of Human Rights

Human rights as a societal norm is a modern innovation, but the moral and philosophical justifications date back centuries before the UDHR's establishment in 1948. Political philosophers like Jeremy Bentham, Thomas Hobbes, and John Locke laid the normative framework for the debates over the rights of mankind that ensued. How one justifies the existence of human rights determines what he or she defines as "rights" and how one best achieves and protects those rights. Two justifications framing the opposite ends of the spectrum are natural law and legal positivism—one maintaining that human rights are inherent protections that all people can claim, and one asserting that human rights exist only when there are legal guarantees to them.

Perhaps the most widely accepted justification for human rights is embedded in the notion of natural law, particularly as John Locke's liberal ideal conceptualizes them. Proponents of natural rights claim that natural law is the only way to establish the universality of rights. All people are entitled to certain rights, and no government, culture, or civilization is morally allowed to usurp those rights. In his *Second Treatise of Government*, Locke argued that even in a state of nature (where there is no government or societal norms to govern behavior) all men are free and equal to pursue their own interests. They are limited, however, to only those actions that do not impose on the freedom of others. Thus, Locke's argument states that just by being human, all people have a natural right to their lives, property, and liberty that predate national and international law. Liberalism, grounded in equality and freedom, espouses a belief in these same natural rights. From this perspective, human rights are moral demands that translate into laws that organizations protect.

Other theorists start with the laws in explaining human rights and why they are what they are. Such theorists, known as legal positivists, might accept that humans possess inherent rights like those listed above; however, the establishment of legal documents and the creation of an international human rights regime have superceded the task of justifying human rights. The UDHR, written more than 60 years ago, created the framework for today's human rights. While natural law theorists argue that rights existed before the UDHR and

subsequent conventions, legal positivists would argue that the nations neither acknowledged nor enforced them. It was as if they did not exist. From this perspective then, legal scholars and institutions, not philosophers, should undertake the task of defining human rights, for it was only after the signing of the human rights conventions that there was any global consensus on the legitimacy of these rights. This approach to rights essentially holds that universal human rights exist because they are codified in international law with near global recognition. Critics of legal positivism argue that narrowing the construction of rights to legal manifestations alone fails to account for the way that rights claims most often emerge—when they are violated and/or denied. Such critics argue that the existence of rights most often predates the treaties that articulate them.

From these two examples, one can see how distinct theoretical perspectives derive unique understandings of the origins of human rights and how we should define and respect human rights worldwide. The difficulty, however, lies in identifying "new" or "emerging" rights. These rights are those which nations or organizations have never codified into legal documents or debated in moral arguments because we either assumed that such rights already existed or we find that such rights had only recently been denied. People do not recognize many rights as rights until individuals or groups are denied or deprived of these rights. Human rights scholar Jack Donnelly (1989) refers to this as the "possession paradox." Much like oxygen, people are unaware of certain rights that they possess until they are denied. Once denied, however, it is obvious that it is essential and necessary to live a life of dignity as set forth in the UDHR. Some of the new, "emerging" rights include environmental human rights (clean water, air, and soil) and technology-related human rights (access to information). The difficulty herein lies with providing philosophical and legal support for these rights, so that we may guarantee them for future generations.

Source:
Donnelly, Jack. 1989. *Universal Human Rights in Theory and Practice*. Ithaca, NY: Cornell University Press.

Prescriptive rights
The essentials a society and its government are arguably obligated to try to provide in order to assure that certain qualitative standards of life exist for everyone in the community.

Third generation rights
Remaining largely unofficial, this broad spectrum of rights includes group and collective rights, rights to self-determination, rights to economic and social development, rights to a healthy environment, rights to natural resources, rights to communicate, rights to participation in cultural heritage, and rights to intergenerational equity and sustainability.

policy and practice. For example, the United States, which emphasizes proscriptive rights, regularly criticizes China for a wide range of rights abuses. A U.S. State Department annual review of global human rights characterized China as an "authoritarian state" whose "human rights record throughout the year remained poor" on such matters as freedom of speech and religion.[3] China countered by accusing the United States of violating prescriptive human rights. "Human rights protection provided by the U.S. Constitution is very limited," a Chinese government report asserted. It noted, for instance, that in the United States there is no right to "food, clothing, shelter, education, work, rest, and reasonable payment."[4]

One source of differing views about proscriptive and prescriptive rights is linked to a society's conceptions of individual success or failure: Is it based on each person's effort or on outside forces such as that person's place in society? Most Americans and Canadians believe that individuals are responsible for their personal success and other conditions, but throughout much of the rest of the world a majority disagrees. According to a 2011 Pew Research Study, the Global Attitudes Project, nearly 60% of Americans believe it is more important for everyone to be free to pursue their life's goals without interference from the state, while just 35% say it is more important for the state to play an active role in society so as to guarantee that nobody is in need. In contrast, at least 6 in 10 in Spain, France (64%), and Germany (62%), and in Britain 55% say the state should ensure that nobody is in need; about 4 in 10 or fewer consider being free from state interference a higher priority.[5] In short, they believe that outside forces, not personal actions, are the most important factor in determining an individual's success or failure in life. The differences in these views on the appropriate role of the state in "promoting" individual human rights have substantial implications on state policy and programming at local, national, and even international levels.

Not everyone, however, is comfortable with these distinctions between categories of rights. For example, political philosopher Henry Shue (1980) has criticized the negative and positive categories of rights as an artificial and even problematic division because it often leads to the prioritization of one set of rights over the other. Shue maintains that it is irrelevant whether torture tactics or food deprivation lead to an individual's death. Both are sources of fundamental human rights violations and therefore equally important and indivisible. In other words, people cannot live a life of dignity without both security and subsistence and those rights are intrinsically intertwined. Rights providers are obligated to avoid depriving people of necessary rights, to protect people from deprivation of those rights, and to aid people when they are deprived.

This holistic approach to human rights brings us to **third generation rights**, or those rights focused on the communal aspects of being human. These rights, which we can label group or solidarity rights, extend rights conceptualizations to consider those rights we best realize and protect in collectives. This stands in contrast to the individual nature and realization of the first and second generation rights. Group rights demand that we implement them jointly, based upon the agreement and will of the collective. Such rights include the right to a clean environment, the right to development, the right to natural resources, and the right to self-determination. Because the rights-holders and duty-holders in this category of rights are not easily identifiable, these rights are some of the most controversial and least institutionalized.

Whatever the focus, though, one scholar suggests that the most fruitful way to think about human rights is to begin with the idea that "ultimately they are supposed to serve basic human needs." These basic human needs, which generate corresponding rights, include, among others (Galtung, 1994:3, 72):

- "Survival needs—to avoid violence": The right of individuals and groups to be free from violence.

- "Well-being needs—to avoid misery": The right to adequate nutrition and water; to movement, sleep, sex, and other biological wants; to protection from diseases and from adverse climatological and environmental impacts.

- "Identity needs—to avoid alienation": The right to establish and maintain emotional bonds with others; to preserve cultural heritage and association; to contribute through work and other activity; and to receive information about and maintain contact with nature, global humanity, and other aspects of the biosphere.

- "Freedom needs—to avoid repression": The right to receive and express opinions, to assemble with others, to have a say in common policy; and to choose in such wide-ranging matters as jobs, spouses, where to live, and lifestyle.

As you read this chapter, consider how you think about and categorize rights. How do you make sense of human rights? Do you tend to prioritize certain rights over others? Does the international community need to ensure certain rights, such as basic education and nutrition, in order to enjoy other rights, such as the right to vote, or vice versa? Do you agree with Shue and find the fundamental human rights to be indivisible and if so, which rights constitute the fundamental ones?

The Modern Human Rights Movement

The horrific human rights violations that defined World War II, particularly the mass torture and killing of an estimated 70 million Chinese and Tibetans under Mao, over 20 million by Stalin in the USSR, and approximately 6 million Jews in Germany, catalyzed the modern human rights movement. The Holocaust united the international community in groundbreaking ways in an effort to prevent genocide from ever occurring again. This powerful event, in addition to other global crises such as the disappearances in Latin America in the 1970s or the oppressive Apartheid regime in South Africa, proved to be critical motivators in mobilizing individuals and raising a global consciousness about systematic abuses of human rights by the state. The power of people in the movement, from elite actors like South Africa's Nelson Mandela to ordinary people like the Madres of the Plaza del Mayo, an association of Argentinean mothers whose children were "disappeared" by the military dictatorship between 1976 and 1983, continue to drive the movement and shape the development of organizations. As **nongovernmental organizations (NGOs)** became increasingly influential in naming and shaming major human rights violations and sharing information and utilizing technology in innovative ways, these non–state actors also emerged as critical components of the developing movement.

Nongovernmental organizations (NGOs) International (transnational) organizations with private memberships.

UN Charter Signed on June 26, 1945, the Charter serves as the foundational treaty of the United Nations. All members are bound by its articles.

Nelson Rolihlahla Mandela, born in 1918 in South Africa, served as the first ever democratically elected President of South Africa from 1994 to 1999. Before his election, he was a leader in the anti-apartheid movement and cofounder of the armed wing of the African National Congress (ANC). During the country's long struggle against the repressive white minority, Mandela went to prison for 27 years for his role in the anti-apartheid movement. Since he left office, Mandela has been a global leader in promoting reconciliation, combatting poverty, and eliminating inequality throughout Africa.

State actors also contributed in positive ways to the momentum of the human rights movement, particularly in the codification of international human rights norms and laws. For example, the **United Nations Charter** first gave formal and authoritative expression to the concept of human rights and defined the UN's central role in driving the movement. It is impossible to fully grasp the human rights movement without an appreciation of its close relation to and reliance upon international organizations at global and regional levels. IGOs, in collaboration with NGOs, individuals, religious groups, professional organizations, and foundations have been critical to the movement's success.

Human Rights in International Law

It was in the context of the United Nations that international human rights law began to take shape and set standards for conduct for states. The founding and most far reaching legal document outlining the fundamental human rights is the Universal Declaration of Human Rights (UDHR), which the UN General Assembly overwhelmingly adopted on December 10, 1948. Drafted as a "common standard of achievement for all peoples and nations," the Declaration spells out basic economic, social, cultural, civil, and political rights for all to enjoy. In this way, the UDHR promotes a universal approach to human rights by declaring in Article 1, "All human beings are born free and equal in dignity and rights," and by further proclaiming in Article 2, "Everyone is entitled to all the rights and freedoms set forth in this Declaration, without distinction of any kind." Overall, the UDHR consists of a preamble and 30 principles (listed in abbreviated form in Figure 11.1) that have come to reflect the cornerstone of international human rights law. This comprehensive document has become the bar for normative standard setting in this field.

Notably, however, this document is a declaration and does not directly bind states legally in the way an international treaty, convention, or covenant does. Still, its overwhelming passage, its perceived legal authority, and its ongoing influence today in practice makes it a reasonable part of global norms. It is now the most translated document in the world, existing in nearly 360 languages (http://www.un-ngls.org/spip.php?article614). For legal scholars, this is a clear example of **customary law**.

Customary law
In international law, this refers to the Law of Nations or the legal norms that have developed through the customary exchanges between states over time, whether based on diplomacy or aggression.

1. All human beings are born free and equal in dignity and rights.
2. Everyone is entitled to all the rights and freedoms without distinction of any kind, such as race, color, sex, language, religion, political or other opinion, national or social origin, property, birth, or other status.
3. Everyone has the right to life, liberty, and security of person.
4. No one shall be held in slavery or servitude.
5. No one shall be subjected to torture or to cruel, inhuman, or degrading treatment or punishment.
6. Everyone is equal before the law and entitled to equal protection of the law.
7. No one shall be subjected to arbitrary arrest, detention, or exile.
8. Everyone is entitled in full equality to a fair and public hearing by an independent and impartial tribunal.
9. Everyone charged with a penal offense has the right to be presumed innocent until proved guilty.
10. No one shall be subjected to arbitrary interference with his privacy, family, home, or correspondence, nor to attacks upon his honor and reputation.
11. Everyone has the right to freedom of movement and residence within the borders of each state, the right to leave any country, including his own, and to return to his country.
12. Everyone has the right to seek and to enjoy in other countries asylum from persecution.
13. Men and women of full age, without any limitation due to race, nationality, or religion, have the right to marry and to found a family. They are entitled to equal rights as to consent to marriage, during marriage, and at its dissolution.
14. Everyone has the right to own property alone as well as in association with others.
15. Everyone has the right to freedom of thought, conscience, and religion and to express their beliefs in public and in private.
16. Everyone has the right to freedom of opinion and expression to seek, receive, and impart information and ideas through any media.
17. Everyone has the right to freedom of peaceful assembly and association. No one may be compelled to belong to an association.
18. Everyone has the right to take part in their country's government directly or through freely chosen representatives.
19. Everyone has the right to equal access to public services in his country.
20. The will of the people shall be the basis of the authority of government expressed in periodic elections which shall be by universal and equal suffrage and shall be held by secret vote or by equivalent free voting procedures.
21. Everyone has the right to work, to choose their work, to reasonable work conditions, and to protection against unemployment.
22. Everyone has the right to equal pay for equal work.
23. Everyone has the right to form and to join trade unions.
24. Everyone has the right to an adequate standard of living, including food, clothing, housing, medical care, and other necessary social services regardless of age, health, or any other circumstance beyond their control.
25. Mothers and children are entitled to special assistance and to equal help, regardless of marital or any other circumstance.
26. Everyone has the right to education. It shall be compulsory and free, at least at the elementary level. Parents have a prior right to choose the kind of education given to their children.
27. Everyone has the right freely to participate in the cultural life of the community, to enjoy the arts and to share in scientific advancement and its benefits.
28. Everyone has the right to the protection of the moral and material interests resulting from any scientific, literary or artistic production of which he is the author.
29. Everyone must uphold these rights, except as determined by law to be necessary to meet the just requirements of morality, public order, and the general welfare in a democratic society.
30. Nothing in this Declaration may be interpreted as implying for any State, group, or person any right to engage in any activity or to perform any act aimed at the destruction of any of the rights and freedoms set forth herein.

FIGURE 11.1

Basic principles of human rights as codified in the UDHR (Abbreviated Version)

The UDHR is one of the most comprehensive, yet simple, international human rights agreements to date. The figure above is a shortened version of the rights articulated in the UDHR. However, as this chapter highlights, the devil is in the details, and how these principled aspirations translate into law, policy, and most important, practice is anything but simple and straightforward.

International Covenant on Civil and Political Rights (ICCPR)
A multilateral treaty the United Nations General Assembly adopted on December 16, 1966, and in force from March 23, 1976. It commits its parties to respect the civil and political rights of individuals, including the rights to life, freedom of religion, freedom of speech, freedom of assembly, electoral rights, and rights to due process and a fair trial.

International Covenant on Economic, Social, and Cultural Rights (ICESCR)
A multilateral treaty the United Nations General Assembly adopted on December 16, 1966, and in force from January 3, 1976. It commits its parties to work toward the granting of economic, social, and cultural rights to individuals, including labor rights, the right to health, the right to education, and the right to an adequate standard of living.

International Bill of Human Rights
An informal name given to one General Assembly resolution and two international treaties, including the Universal Declaration of Human Rights (adopted in 1948), the International Covenant on Civil and Political Rights (1966) with its two Optional Protocols, and the International Covenant on Economic, Social, and Cultural Rights (1966).

Following the UDHR, states took steps to further enunciate these basic rights in the context of two multilateral treaties: the **International Covenant on Civil and Political Rights (ICCPR, 1966)** and the **International Covenant on Economic, Social, and Cultural Rights (ICESCR, 1966)**. Together, these three agreements constitute the **International Bill of Human Rights**. More than 80% of countries have ratified each pact, which means that national governments commit to undertake and to put into place domestic legislation and other policy measures compatible with and supportive of the treaty obligations and duties. There are, however, some major exceptions. For example, China has not become a party of the ICCPR, and the United States has not ratified the ICESCR. Further, many states have ratified these treaties but have laws, policies, and customs in place that directly violate the standards set forth in the two covenants. For a list of states that are party to the covenants, go to the Office of High Commissioner for Human Rights website at http://www.ohchr.org/EN/Pages/WelcomePage.aspx.

In addition to these two basic treaties and the Universal Declaration, numerous other UN-sponsored treaties address the rights of specific groups, including women, children, ethnic, racial, and religious groups, indigenous peoples, migrants, and peoples with disabilities. There are also several multilateral treaties that address specific types of abuse. One, the Convention against Torture and Other Cruel, Inhuman or Degrading Treatment or Punishment (1984) has drawn considerable recent attention because of confirmed and alleged abuses of prisoners by U.S. personnel in Iraq, Afghanistan, and elsewhere. The treaty, to which the United States became a party in 1994, defines torture as "any act by which severe pain or suffering, whether physical or mental, is intentionally inflicted on a person for such purposes as obtaining . . . information [or a confession]." Additionally, the treaty specifies, "No exceptional circumstances whatsoever, whether a state of war or a threat of war, internal political instability or any other public emergency, may be invoked as a justification of torture." U.S. military tribunals have punished some low-ranking military personnel who committed indisputable abuses, and it is now clear that some tactics the Bush Administration and the U.S. Department of Defense authorized for use during questioning of suspected terrorists violate international treaty obligations. As Figure 11.2 illustrates, however, it is not just the United States that seems to be engaging in more torture. Globally, the respect for the right not to be tortured was in decline well before 9/11.

In addition to UN-sponsored treaties, a number of regional conventions and judicial arms of IGOs supplement the global community's effort to protect and promote human rights. The best developed of these are in the European Union (EU) and include two human rights covenants and the European Court of Human Rights. Domestic courts also increasingly apply human rights law (Jayawickrama, 2003). Additionally, many NGOs, such as Amnesty International and Human Rights Watch, are concerned with a broad range of human rights and work toward their protection and enforcement. These groups work independently and in cooperation with the UN, regional organizations, and state actors to further human rights. They add to the swell of information about and criticisms of abuses and help promote the adoption of international norms that support human rights.

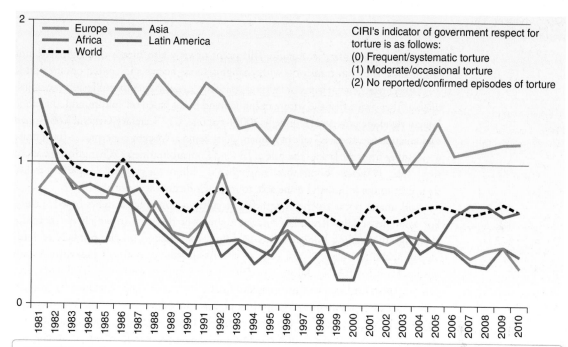

FIGURE 11.2

Average respect for right to be protected against torture, 1981–2010

The downward trend depicted here shows an overall decline in states' respect for international laws against torture. In other words, the use of torture by government is actually increasing and not just since 9/11. While this trend certainly varies by region, we see the most concerning decline in Africa, according to the CIRI data.

Data Source: http://humanrightsdata.blogspot.com.

Critiques of Human Rights Theory and Practice

Society has built the modern human rights movement upon the logic of universality. Given the natural law backdrop of the Enlightenment, this idea that all humans possess the same, immutable rights is not surprising. This perspective begins with the idea that rights originate from outside a society. For some, the source is the very nature of human existence. They contend that people inherently possess such rights as the right to life, which nobody has the right to legitimately abridge. Another external source, theology, leads many to believe that a deity grants rights and therefore humans may not transgress them. Whatever the specific source, those who contend that rights originate outside a society and transcend it are universalists. **Universalism**, in the realm of human rights, suggests that humanity comes before culture and traditions. In other words, people are human first and members of cultures second.

There are, however, a number of important challenges to the assumed universalism by human rights politics and practice. One argument, **cultural relativism**, rejects the idea that people and their rights can (or should) separate from or precede the societies in which they live. Cultural relativists argue that human rights are normative values appropriate to the cultures out of which they emerge, and they criticize the mainstream international human rights movement for lacking respect for different cultural, religious, and philosophical traditions. Relativists therefore assert that in a world of diverse cultures, no single standard of human rights exists or is likely to exist short of the world

Universalism
A belief that human rights are derived from sources external to society, such as from a theological, ideological, or natural rights basis.

Cultural relativism
The principle that an individual human's beliefs and activities are understood by others in terms of that individual's own culture.

becoming homogenized culturally. This point of view also means that rights are not immutable. They can transform with changing social norms and contemporary values.

Others reject such claims of cultural relativism as poor attempts to justify the unjustifiable. They argue that the nature of humankind is not based on culture, and, therefore, human rights are universal (Donnelly, 2003). For one, UN Secretary-General Kofi Annan told an audience, there is "talk of human rights being a Western concept, . . . [but] don't we all suffer from the lack of the rule of law and from arbitrariness? What is foreign about that? What is Western about that? And when we talk of the right [of people] . . . to live their lives to the fullest and to be able to live their dreams, it is universal."[6]

Still, many point to the way different cultures construct a rights-based society. For example, scholar Rhonda Callaway points out the ways in which Asian values challenge the leading human rights paradigm that focuses on the primacy of individual rights. She argues, "the crux of the Asian values argument lies with certain unique features of Asian culture, specifically the emphasis on family, hard work, frugality, respect for law and authority, and finally, deference (and reverence) to authority," which can and often do trump the rights of individuals (2007:112). Further, this cultural difference leads to a greater emphasis on economic and social rights over political rights as the needs of the community take precedence. Many Asian cultures perceive the Western focus on individuals as problematic and even a detriment to the order of civil society. Take, for example, the case of Singapore, which does not extend all the **Miranda rights** and other legal protections given to suspects in the United States. Singapore also imposes punishment that Americans might think is "cruel and unusual," including the extremely painful beating of a convict's bared buttocks with a rattan cane for about 30 crimes ranging from attempted murder to vandalism. To defend their position, Singapore officials point to the fact that people there are threatened by a vastly lower crime rate than in most major U.S. cities. "We believe that the legal system must give maximum protection to the majority of our people. We make no apology for clearly tilting our laws and policy in favor of the majority."[7]

This connection between "the West" and human rights leads us to a second critique of the modern human rights movement; that is, the argument that human rights are nothing more than an imperialistic modern-day tool. From this perspective, human rights are a political maneuver that Western nations have used to promote their interests and to bolster Western power throughout the globe. For example, arguments from this camp point to the fact that the major organizations committed to human rights advocacy, from IGOs like the UN to NGOs like Human Rights Watch, are largely constructed, funded, and run by Western powers. Further, critics focus on the selectivity of human rights advocacy and how that advocacy often masks ulterior and far less altruistic motives. The "Challenge Your Assumptions" box develops one of these important critiques.

Another important critique focused on the power embedded in human rights discourse and practice comes from feminist scholars and activists who point to the ways in which the concept has been narrow and biased and manipulated for particular interests. Historically, the "rights of man" and even the rights originally codified in the U.S. Constitution denied rights to women, among many others. While the modern human rights movement has recognized gender equality rights, in the International Bill of Rights and women's rights specifically in the Convention on the Elimination of All Forms of Discrimination Against Women (CEDAW, 1979), we still have a long way to go.

Miranda rights
A U.S. criminal procedural rule that requires law enforcement to warn criminal suspects in police custody (or in a custodial interrogation), before they are interrogated, of their Fifth Amendment right against compelled self-incrimination.

challenge your assumptions

Are Human Rights a Form of Modern-Day Imperialism?

Discussions of imperialism often imply historical narratives about European dominance and expansion through violent colonial conquest. Many assume that it is a problem of the past, whereby powerful states would claim land as their colonies, ruling with an iron fist for nationalistic and economic gains. Imperialism as a modern phenomenon is not part of mainstream political discourse. Anthropologist Dr. Laura Agustín, however, argues that imperialist values run rampant in modern society, particularly in the context of the global human rights movement. Consider human rights "activists" today who often combine celebrity status with their charity. For example, Hollywood went through a phase where the best accessory was a child from an underdeveloped country and now everyone wants a pair of TOMS shoes, a for-profit company that matches every pair of purchased shoes with new shoes for a child in need. Critics like Agustín argue that the promotion of human rights has become an industry in the United States, a tool to force American culture and ideology onto other countries and peoples in the name of human rights—another imperialist venture.

The human rights movement has spent much of its existence treading the line between promoting human rights values and promoting Western, capitalist, and democratic values. Cultural relativists argue that the Universal Declaration of Human Rights (UDHR) cannot and should not be universal, because some of its ideas stand in contradiction to how some communities organize themselves, and their commitment to communal existence rather than individual rights. Asian cultures, for example, often grant primacy to collective rights of groups over individuals, where land pressures demand that the community's welfare trump individual needs. For others, universalism is a direct affront to religious beliefs unique to different groups. To simply force them to change that practice would not only be insensitive to the years of tradition and practice that stand behind their beliefs, but a violation of the right to religious freedom. Currently, the United States is dealing with this issue in the context of the right to health care, particularly women's health. The right of women to plan their families and control their reproductive health (as codified in the Committee on the Elimination of Discrimination Against Women [CEDAW]), and therefore, their right to access affordable contraception is posing serious challenges to the Obama administration as Catholic Church leaders strongly oppose this "right" as it is currently constructed in the federal health care mandate. They view this as a direct affront to the Church's moral teachings. Because morality often drives the human rights movement, universality can lead to a form of imperialism. Agustín uses *New York Times* reporter Nicholas Kristof as an example of this Western, imperial approach. Kristof has investigated and written many reports on human trafficking in foreign countries, looking at prostitution and brothels as the enemy of freedom. He has participated in police raids on brothels and has even purchased a slave to give her freedom. In the media's eyes (and his 1,000,000+ Twitter followers) Kristof is a hero. They believe that by closing these brothels or buying these slaves, he is improving lives, giving young girls a "second chance."

The reality, however, is that the "rescued victims" often "choose" to return to oppressive situations. They are poor, uneducated, and most important, unloved, with no social safety nets, thus often finding freedom worse than enslavement. They are ideal prey for traffickers. When a brothel closes, desperation ensues, and they are willing to search for any job. Traffickers exploit this, and through fraud, force, or coercion lure them into sex trafficking. Kristof's stories revolve around the thrilling tale of their rescue where good triumphs evil. There is no reader interest in their reintegration to society and this is where the real work begins. This latter story is not nearly as exciting, requiring a much longer term attention span and much greater investment from the human rights movement and society more broadly.

Kristof's dedicated readers and other human rights activists might argue that, at least, he is doing something and trying to prevent human rights violations. Agustín purports that this rhetoric is again reminiscent of colonial days where any signs of development served to quell the doubters. If Kristof saves one woman from sex trafficking, but creates an environment in which 25 more will be trafficked, do we count that as a victory? If he saves one, but does nothing about the increasing demand for cheap labor, whether in the sex industry or in agribusiness, is this really working toward the common good? This situation is nebulous and requires that you consider both the intended and unintended consequences of the human rights movement.

Source:
http://www.lauraagustin.com/

For example, feminists are very critical of the emphasis on law and top-down approaches to human rights protection. This legalist bias focuses attention on rights violated in the public sphere by state actors, which completely ignores the majority of human rights abuses that women in the world suffer. Human rights violations for many women occur in "private" contexts of family and community and are generally perpetrated by non-state actors, such as spouses and family members (Bunch & Reilly, 1994). As seen in Figure 11.3, just because a state signs a treaty to protect and promote women's rights does not mean those rights are actually put into policy and practice at the local level in small communities, rural villages, and private households.

While these select critiques do not necessarily lead us to an outright rejection of human rights, they do remind us of the power of language as it translates in law and as we apply it in policy. The critiques highlight the need for our vigilance and unwavering curiosity about what assumptions we are making when we use the human rights framework. Who counts as human? Which rights are most essential? Do rights priorities vary across time and space? Keep these concerns in mind as we now move to the next section and explore in greater detail the human rights issues that surround some of the world's most oppressed and vulnerable groups.

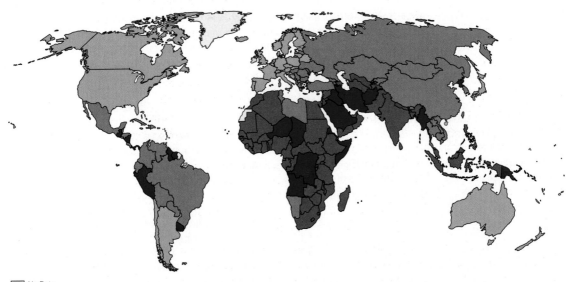

☐ No Data
☐ The laws are consonant with CEDAW and are well enforced by the government; such enforcement is a high priority of the government
▨ The laws are consonant with CEDAW; these are mostly enforced, and the government appears to be fairly proactive in challenging cultural norms that harm women
▨ The laws are consonant with CEDAW; there is spotty enforcement; the government may or may not signal its interest in challenging cultural norms harmful to women
▨ Laws are for the most part consonant with CEDAW, with little effective enforcement; improving the situation of women appears to be a low priority for the government
■ There is vitually no enforcement of laws consonant with CEDAW, or such laws do not even exist

FIGURE 11.3

Discrepant government behavior concerning women 2010

This map illustrates the extent to which national laws coincide with rights and protections outlined in the international treaty on women, CEDAW. Importantly, this data goes beyond just assessing whether the laws exist, but accounts for actual implementation and enforcement of the laws. Thus, it gives a better sense of women's legal rights and the rule of law that women experience on a daily basis.

Data Source: Womanstats Project.

CURRENT ISSUES IN HUMAN RIGHTS

Since the emergence of the modern state in 1648, the state's right to sovereign control over what happens within its borders has often made human rights concerns obsolete. The rights of people have, up until recently, been strictly a matter of domestic control, and therefore, any form of foreign intervention in the internal affairs of a sovereign state would constitute a significant violation of state sovereignty, and in some cases, international law. Many states, such as China and Russia, remain vocal supporters of the primacy of state sovereignty as a global organizing system. For instance, both states vetoed a UN Security Council Resolution in February 2012, which essentially rejected the Arab League's call for Syrian President Bashar al-Assad to step down and stop the massive killing of civilians. In addition, China has rejected any interference from the West or elsewhere on its domestic rights policies, from its treatment of political dissidents, to its censorship of information technology, to its lack of protection for its workers. According to national labor laws, for example, Chinese workers (many of which are migrants) do not have the right to organize or the right to a livable wage. For Chinese officials, these are matters best left to the state. However, as the case study demonstrates, this issue already involves a range of non–state actors inside and outside of China's borders, from the media to MNCs to human rights advocacy organizations. It is difficult to imagine how some genuinely can regard such an issue as purely a domestic matter.

This attitude is changing, and increasingly governments are experiencing international pressure to respect the basic rights of their citizens. It is in this context that IGOs, NGOs, and even individuals, as we described earlier, have helped to set human rights standards and global expectations that are chipping away at legal boundaries of state sovereignty, particularly since the end of the Cold War. Challenging the sovereign authority of the state is not just happening in the context of war and national security interests, but increasingly, the international community is intervening in the name of human rights. One more recent example has been the emergence of the 2005 UN **Responsibility to Protect (R2P)** initiative that sets forth a set of principles, based on the idea that sovereignty is not a privilege, but a responsibility, a duty. This norm provides a framework for action obligating states to intervene in cases where massive human rights abuses are occurring. This call to action provides the justification for using tools that already exist, including mediation, early warning mechanisms, economic sanctioning, and **Chapter VII** powers from the UN Charter to prevent and stop mass atrocities. It was this framework for action that drove the international community to act in the case of Libya in 2011, with a NATO-led humanitarian intervention to aid the Libyan people in bringing down long ruling autocrat, Muammar Gaddafi.

From Russia to China to Libya and Syria, these cases highlight how human rights continue to be a defining feature of the 21st century, in complicated and uneven ways. Human rights challenges are enormous, in terms of the plethora of issues at stake, as well as the varied strategies of activism and the ethical choices behind those centers of activity. Technology has played a significant factor in this ideational development. There is a much more extensive and graphic detailing of human rights through television and the Internet. Hearing and reading about human rights abuses do not have

Responsibility to Protect (R2P)
A global United Nations initiative doctrine, endorsed by the UN in 2005, which is based on the idea that sovereignty is not a privilege, but that sovereignty confers responsibilities on states and their leaders—first and foremost, to ensure the well-being of their citizens.

Chapter VII
Part of the Charter of the United Nations that deals with action with respect to threats to peace, breaches of the peace, and acts of aggression.

The KONY 2012 campaign by *Invisible Children* has emerged as one of the leading human rights issues of this year. The symbol of the campaign is an upside-down triangle, illustrating how the masses—ordinary people like you and me—can affect change throughout the world. It is an effort to make "the many" more powerful, through the use of social media, to influence the actions of those few at the top in decision-making roles. The symbol raises important questions about power: who has it, who doesn't, and how it can best be utilized.

Convention on the Rights of the Child (CRC) (1989)
A human rights treaty setting out the civil, political, economic, social, health, and cultural rights of children.

anywhere near the emotional impact of seeing images of violence, torture, and other abuses in vivid color on the television screens and computer monitors in the intimate surroundings of our homes. Such images are harder to ignore than reporting in other media and have added to slowly changing attitudes about abuses. The impact of technology, and social media in particular, on the human rights movement is abundantly clear in the *Invisible Children* campaign to find, arrest, and try Joseph Kony, the leader of the Lord's Resistance Army operating in Northern Uganda, the Central African Republic, the Democratic Republic of the Congo, and South Sudan, for war crimes and crimes against humanity. *Invisible Children*, a U.S.-based NGO, has started the campaign, "Kony 2012," with a 30-minute video that went viral, receiving over 40 million views within the first few days. The video has received some criticism, but nonetheless, has received media attention from all major international and U.S.-based news sources. Although the awareness-raising effort is incredible, time will tell whether or not the campaign can bring Kony to justice. Still, the following sections discuss how real changes have started to take hold. Human rights groups have made progress, and some human rights rhetoric has translated into realities on the ground.

Human Rights Problems

Despite the development of international human rights norms and laws, human rights violations continue to occur in every country in the world, often in horrific and systematic ways. For example, the **Convention on the Rights of the Child (1989)** is one of the most widely ratified international treaties. Somalia, South Sudan, and the United States are the only three states not to have ratified the treaty. Still, the world's children suffer tremendously. The UN's Special Representative for Children and Armed Conflict estimates that there are at least 250,000 child soldiers worldwide, which is likely an underestimation given the difficulty in collecting accurate data from war-torn regions. Child soldiers are often forced to kill their own parents, make their abductors their new families, serve as sex slaves for other soldiers, and become addicted to drugs and/or alcohol. However, children do not have to live in war zones to experience serious human rights abuses. According to UNICEF, one out of four children in developing countries is underweight, and undernutrition contributes to nearly five million child deaths each year in developing countries. From physical security to food security, even children have no protection or fulfillment of their basic rights.

Another vulnerable group of people today are those who have been forcibly displaced. **Refugees**, asylum-seekers, **internally displaced persons** and economic migrants suffer the full range of human rights abuses as they are forced to leave their homes, livelihoods, and communities. Rights abuses occur during and after the migration, while many spend years in exile. While no continent is immune from mass displacement, most of the world refugees are located in the poorest developing countries. As of 2011, the **UN High Commissioner for Refugees (UNHCR)** monitors nearly 34 million people around the world who have been uprooted for a variety of reasons, including approximately 15 million refugees, mostly in Africa and the Middle East. According to the 1951 Convention Relating to the Status of Refugees, states are required to protect the basic rights of those granted refugee status as well as the right of resettlement and legal protection from deportation, or forcible return to their country of origin. The fundamental principle here is that people should never be forced into harm's way. Unfortunately, this definition of refugee only covers about one-third of the world's displaced, and therefore, the legal status only protects a certain percentage of this population. Further, the human rights challenges for these groups have only intensified in the wake of globalization and the "war on terror" as states are increasingly concerned about terrorism, illegal migration, organized crime, and even jobs. We can no longer assume that immigrants are innocent victims. Liberal societies that previously welcomed such people with open arms must now heed caution. In many cases, nations automatically perceive some of these "victims" as threatening, or even criminal.

From women to indigenous populations to suspected terrorists, we do not lack groups that are experiencing serious violations of human rights. Even though we have many international laws and organizations in place working to protect the rights of people across the globe, it is easy for us to become disillusioned by the widespread abuse, violence, exploitation, and negligence that many people encounter on a daily basis. Thus, it is critical to understand the reasons for implementing human rights law. There have been instances of notable achievements and success stories, particularly since the adoption of the UDHR. What is more is that people continue to advocate and fight for change.

Barriers to Progress on Human Rights

Unfortunately, because a state signs and ratifies a treaty does not mean that it always complies

Refugee
A person who is outside his or her country of origin or habitual residence because he or she has suffered persecution on account of race, religion, nationality, political opinion, or because he or she is a member of a persecuted "social group."

Internally displaced persons (IDP)
Someone who is forced to flee his or her home, but who remains within his or her country's borders.

UN High Commissioner for Refugees (UNHCR)
Established December 14, 1950, by the UN General Assembly, the UNHCR is mandated to lead and coordinate action to protect refugees and resolve refugee problems worldwide. Its primary purpose is to safeguard the rights and well-being of refugees.

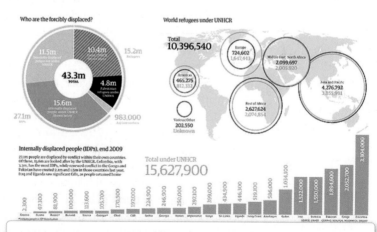

According to the annual *Global Trends* report by the UN High Commissioner for Refugees (UNHCR), the world is now experiencing the highest numbers of displaced people since the end of the Cold War. There are now approximately 27.1 million internally displaced people and 15.6 million refugees. Conflicts in places like Afghanistan, Iraq, the Democratic Republic of the Congo, and Sudan drive a large percentage of these forcibly displaced. Top receiving countries of refugees include Pakistan, Jordan, and Iran.

Data Source: UNHCR Statistics. Illustrated by Paul Scruton for the Guardian.

with it. Iraq ratified both the ICCPR and the ICESCR in 1971, yet throughout its 33 years, Saddam Hussein's regime egregiously abused many, even most, of the rights set forth in both covenants. The impact of such treaties, the efforts of IGOs and NGOs, and the general progress of human rights, as we have noted, have been mixed. Enforcement is often lacking, and in some ways, human rights laws challenge the international community to rethink what it means to hold states accountable to their normative and legal commitments.

One of the most significant challenges to turning legal rhetoric into reality on the ground is the power of state sovereignty. Countries ardently guard it and reject outside criticism of their internal practices. When in 2007 a reporter asked a Chinese Foreign Ministry spokesperson about a resolution in Germany's Bundestag criticizing China's labor camps for political dissidents, he replied testily, "The question you mentioned involves China's internal affairs. We are opposed to irresponsible remarks on China's internal affairs by other countries including the German parliament."[8] Although the sovereignty argument as a defense has weakened, it still remains powerful. Smaller countries and those of the South are particularly sensitive to what they see as a pattern of powerful countries in the North criticizing weaker countries in the South while refusing to accept criticism themselves and generally being unwilling to criticize one another. Especially alarming for countries of the South is the assertion that such human rights violations give other countries the right to intervene, a course of action that they never contemplate with regard to a powerful state. Thus, for many in the South, the human rights campaign seems tinged with neocolonialism and perhaps even racism. This division clearly emerges when we look at some of the world's best and worst in terms of human rights practices, as seen in Figure 11.4.

A second and closely related problem is the claim that cultural standards are different, and, therefore, what is a human rights violation in one country is culturally acceptable in another (De Bary, 2004). This is part of the argument that we discussed earlier about the source of law and whether cultural relativism is an acceptable standard. Like the matter of sovereignty, the issue of law based in cultural standards is particularly sensitive for the South because the Universal Declaration of Human Rights and, to a lesser degree, the ICCPR, the ICESCR, and some of the other major human rights treaties were written at a time when the West dominated the UN much more than it does today. See the "History Matters" box on the drafting of the UDHR for a better understanding of who contributed to this important document.

A third problem is political selectivity, which disposes all countries to shock when opponents transgress human rights and ignore abuses by themselves, by their allies, and by countries that they hope to influence. The United States regularly proclaims its commitment to the global spread of democracy, yet continues to support the governments of Saudi Arabia and several other unabashedly authoritarian regimes. Making matters worse, the self-proclaimed U.S. role of championing democracy and human rights was badly undercut by disclosures including secret prisons abroad under CIA auspices in which authorities questioned prisoners using tactics that are illegal in the United States. This is **rendition**, or the turning over of prisoners for questioning by other governments that operate without the limits on prisoner treatment that bind American officials. There has been documented evidence of abuses inflicted on prisoners in Iraq's Abu Ghraib prison and elsewhere and on Muslim detainees at Guantánamo

Rendition
In law, a surrender or handing over of persons or property, particularly from one jurisdiction to another.

Top 13 Countries		Bottom 10 Countries	
Denmark	30	Burma	2
Iceland	30	Eritrea	2
Austria	29	Iran	2
New Zealand	29	China	3
Norway	29	Korea, Democratic People's Republic of	3
Australia	28	Yemen	3
Belgium	28	Zimbabwe	3
Finland	28	Saudi Arabia	4
Liechtenstein	28	Congo, Democratic Republic of	5
Luxembourg	28	Nigeria	5
Netherlands	28		
San Marino	28		
Sweden	28		

FIGURE 11.4

Best and worst human rights records by state, 2010

The CIRI Human Rights Data Project scores states' human rights practices based upon 14 indicators, ranging from physical integrity rights to civil liberties to worker's rights to the rights of women. The best score a country can receive is 30, while the worst score would be 0. The world average was 18 and the U.S. scored 26 (tied for 5th place).

Data Source: CIRI Human Rights Data Project (www.humanrightsdata.org).

Bay. When the U.S. State Department issued its 2005 report on human rights and criticized numerous other countries, many of them retorted that, in essence, Americans should address their own abuses before pointing a finger at anyone else. The Russian Foreign Ministry charged that the report once again showed a "double standard" and that, "Characteristically off-screen is the ambiguous record of the United States itself." Venezuela's vice president portrayed the United States as "not qualified from any point of view" to lecture others on human rights, and a Mexican official said that Washington criticizing other countries' human rights records was like "the donkey talking about long ears"—the Spanish-language equivalent of "the pot calling the kettle black."[9]

A fourth problem is that concern with human rights remains a fairly low priority for most countries. In the abstract, most people support advancing human rights, but in more applied situations it becomes clear that support is shallow. For example, a recent survey that asked people in the United States and India about important foreign policy goals for their country found that promoting human rights ranked 11th of 14 possible goals among Americans and 11th of 11 possible goals among Indians.[10] We can also say, however, that while still not at the forefront of concern of most people, the importance that nations have given to human rights has increased in recent years and that increased sensitivity is strengthening international pressure on those abusing the rights of others.

These challenges highlight the fundamental nature of the human rights regime— states are the primary enforcers for international human rights. While the international

history matters

Who Actually Wrote the Universal Declaration of Human Rights?

Immediately following World War II, the world looked very different than we know it today. Many nations that we now know did not exist, others were still under direct colonial rule, and many were slowly recovering from debilitating war losses. The emergence of the United Nations (UN) meant further concentration and institutionalization of power in the hands of Western states, particularly the Allies. Given that the Universal Declaration of Human Rights (UDHR) emerged in the context of the UN, it is no wonder that many critics of the UDHR maintain that it is a biased document that conceptualizes rights from a Western, white, male, and European perspective. This critique is not entirely historically accurate. In fact, a relatively diverse set of international actors who encouraged an inclusive process and a document more universal in scope drafted the UDHR.

A Panamanian representative in the General Assembly's first session initially proposed creating a human rights document, thus putting human rights on the official UN agenda.[11] This demonstrates a willingness by part of the global South to recognize a universal system of rights. Even more telling is participation of representatives from diverse nations on the Commission on Human Rights Drafting Committee. China's

Peng-Chun Chang was the Commission's Vice-Chair. He incorporated elements of Confucian philosophy to both explain the foundation of human rights and resolve conflict between Committee members. His greatest contribution to the document's universalism was his resolute refusal to allow mentions of God or the nature of spirituality in the UDHR. The Committee's Rapporteur, Charles Habib Malik, was of Lebanese descent. There were also Drafting Committee members from Chile and the USSR.[12] There also were many other opportunities for global representatives to provide input on the drafting process, including writing the actual proposals and then conducting reviews in the context of the third committee, which read and debated every line of the declaration. When the UN brought the UDHR to a vote, almost every represented nation at the time had the opportunity to voice concerns. Thus, the argument that the UDHR was a primarily Western, Judeo-Christian document is simply wrong.

A more relevant argument is that the UDHR was a document written by and for educated elites, with little input or recognition of common people—those most likely to make human rights appeals. Mr. Malik, for example, attended Harvard before he founded the

community, especially IGOs, NGOs, and individuals, play a number of important roles in terms of raising awareness, agenda-setting, naming and shaming, and lobbying states, they do not possess coercive powers as do states. From economic sanctions to peacekeeping interventions, states can enforce human rights standards in other states and even among non–state actors. Increasingly, non–state actors, from MNCs, private contracting firms, and insurgent movements, are proving to pose substantial threats to the protection and promotion of rights during times of war and times of peace.

Thus, while it would be wrong for us to overestimate the advance of human rights, we would equally err not to recognize that we have achieved progress in the advancement of human rights by declarations of principle, by numerous treaties, and by the work of the UN, Amnesty International, and other IGOs and NGOs. The frequency and horror of the abuses that they highlight are increasingly penetrating the international consciousness and disconcerting the global conscience. This awareness has a positive effect on the world stage.

Human Rights Progress

It would be naïve to argue that the world has even begun to come close to resolving its numerous human rights issues. It would be equally wrong to deny that we

philosophy department at Beirut's American University. Eleanor Roosevelt, the Committee Chairperson, led a privileged life as First Lady of the United States. Their backgrounds made them good candidates to draft the declaration, but it also placed them in a very different, privileged mindset. They could easily understand the philosophical and theoretical reasoning for the enumerated rights, but they were not entirely aware of the range of rights issues that people face in local communities and the problems that they might encounter in implementing the declaration at that level. This is true as different communities have claimed group rights and protections as collectives, such as the indigenous, the disabled, or women. Article 5, for example, forbids torture and inhumane treatment or punishment. These terms are so broad that most people could not define the exact meaning. Does that include domestic violence, for example? What about the practice of female circumcision in some African nations? Proponents of female circumcision might argue that Article 27 guarantees the right to participate in the community's culture—wherein the process is part of a girl's transition to womanhood. In this way, the UDHR did not even begin to grapple with local level cultural complexities and challenges.

Implementing the UDHR at the ground level has stirred many debates on the indivisibility of rights and whether the human rights regimes grant certain rights, such as civil and political, over other rights, like economic and social rights. The issue at hand is not whether the world should accept these "Western" rights, but how the rights that educated, mostly male elites created translate into action for everyday life for ordinary people. Still, it is important to understand the UDHR's drafting process and the ways in which it was both radical and limited and the many voices that were involved in the creation of one of the most important global documents of the 20th century.

Sources:

Department of Public Information. 2012. *The Universal Declaration of Human Rights: An Historical Record of the Drafting Process* [Homepage of Dag Hammarskjold Library], [Online]. Available: http://www.un.org/Depts/dhl/udhr/.

Glendon, M. "A World Made New" in *International Human Rights in Context*, edited by Steiner, H., Alston, P., & Goodman, R. U.K.: Oxford University Press. 139–142.

National Coordinating Committee for UDHR50 1998. August 27, 1998-last update. *Questions and Answers About the UDHR* [Homepage of Franklin and Eleanor Roosevelt Institute], [Online]. Available: http://www.udhr.org/history/question.htm#_Toc397930435.

have made a start and that one aspect of globalization is the increased concern for and application of human rights principles (Cardenas, 2004; Tomuschat, 2004). The way to evaluate the worth of the efforts we are about to discuss is to judge their goals and to see them as the beginnings of a process that only a few decades ago did not exist at all. Whatever country you live in, the protection of human rights has evolved over an extended period and is still far from complete. The global community has now embarked on an effort similar to most countries' efforts (Hawkins, 2004). It will take time, however, and it will be controversial (Monshipouri et al., 2003).

The UN is at the center of the international human rights effort. It has sponsored numerous human rights treaties that, along with human rights in general, the **Office of the United Nations High Commissioner on Human Rights (OHCHR)** monitors. From 1946 through early 2006, the UN Commission on Human Rights (UNCHR) was also a leading UN organization on human rights. It consisted of 53 member-countries the United Nations Economic and Social Council (ECOSOC) elected for 3-year terms. During its annual meetings it was often the site of clashes over human rights. However, it was plagued by numerous problems. One was a penchant for regularly condemning Israel for violating the rights of Arabs

Office of the United Nations High Commissioner on Human Rights (OHCHR)
Established by a General Assembly Resolution in 1993 and mandated to promote and protect the enjoyment and full realization, by all people, of all rights established in the UN Charter and in international human rights laws and treaties.

Navi Pillay serves as the UN High Commissioner for Human Rights, coordinating human rights activities throughout the UN system and supervising the work of the Human Rights Council in Geneva, Switzerland. Her previous experience as a lawyer from South Africa, as judge for the International Criminal Court, and as President of the International Criminal Tribunal in Rwanda guides her work as the world's leading advocate for human rights for all.

UN Human Rights Council (UNHRC)
An intergovernmental body within the United Nations system responsible for strengthening the promotion and protection of human rights around the globe and for addressing situations of human rights violations and make recommendations on them.

while just as regularly ignoring the human rights violations of many other countries. Adding to the dismay in many quarters about the commission, ECOSOC regularly named countries with poor human rights records as members. Making matters even worse, in 2003 the commission elected authoritarian Libya, which has a deplorable human rights record, to its chairmanship. Then in 2004, ECOSOC elected Sudan to the Commission virtually at the same time that the Security Council was calling on Khartoum to cease its genocidal policies in Darfur.

Responding to such absurdities, the UN General Assembly in 2006 replaced the UNCHR with a new organization, the **UN Human Rights Council (UNHRC)**. It is a 47-member body that the General Assembly elects, and its members are supposed to uphold the highest human rights standards. Nevertheless, the United States was one of the few countries that voted against creating the UNHRC, arguing that there was little to keep it from repeating the flaws of the UNCHR. Time will tell, but the initial election of members was not especially auspicious. The scores of the 47 members, using Freedom House's 2006 rating of countries' civil liberties records, from 1 (best) to 7 (awful), averaged a not-too-bad 2.6. However, 43% of the members fell into the dubious 4 and below categories, including Cuba with a bottom-dwelling score of 7. In another discouraging turn, the council soon followed the defunct UNCHR's practice of paying inordinate attention to alleged human rights abuses by Israel. This issue of objective balance soon led the UN Secretary-General to write an open letter in which he said that to advance human rights, "We must realize the promise of the Human Rights Council, which so far has clearly not justified all the hopes that so many of us placed in it." He went on to say that he was "worried by its disproportionate focus on violations by Israel," and he urged, "Instead, the Council's agenda should be broadened to reflect the actual abuses that occur in every part of the world."[13]

Concerns with the council led Washington to decline to seek a council seat in 2006, 2007, and 2008. A State Department official explained, "We believe that the [council] has thus far not proved itself to be a credible body in the mission that it has been charged with. There has been a nearly singular focus on issues related to Israel, for example, to the exclusion of examining issues of real concern to the international system, whether that's in Cuba or Burma or in North Korea. . . . We hope that over time, this body will expand its focus and become a more credible institution representative of the important mission with which it is charged."[14]

While the establishment of the Human Rights Council was a significant achievement, at some level it presumes a willingness of states to comply and to be transparent. There is, of course, the new **Universal Periodic Review (UPR)** in which all states have to defend their human rights record to the global community on a regular basis. This mechanism assumes, however, that states will submit their reports to the Universal Periodic Review, that the reports will be honest reflections of reality on the ground, and that the input from the Council and High Commissioner will be strong and influential in state policy going forward. As human rights scholar David Forsythe finds, "the change from the Commission to the Council [has] amounted to a repackaging of old wine in a new bottle, although some [still] hold out hope for progress over time" (2012:96). On this latter point, it is worth noting how proactive the Council has been in 2011 and 2012 in sending independent investigators into Syria, documenting and condemning human rights abuses occurring on all sides, and pushing the international community, particularly the Security Council, to intervene. The international body is playing a critical role in raising awareness about the gross and systematic human rights violations currently happening in Syria and is attempting to set the international security agenda accordingly.

Universal Periodic Review (UPR)
A unique process that involves a review of the human rights records of all 192 UN member-states once every 4 years.

HUMAN RIGHTS ADVOCACY

Returning to the case of human rights abuses of Chinese workers, note that within several weeks after the *New York Times* broke the story about working conditions in China in factories responsible for assembling some of our favorite Apple products, the firms involved took action. Foxconn announced that it would sharply raise salaries and reduce overtime. Apple responded by asking an independent group, the Fair Labor Association, to conduct audits of several of its factories in China, starting with Foxconn. Apple is the first technology company to be admitted to the Fair Labor Association, and the company has promised to implement association audits in facilities that assemble more than 90% of Apple products.

While we do not know how these audits may or may not change abusive labor practices or conditions, particularly once the media frenzy has dissipated, the case highlights the complex nature of human rights advocacy. It shows the power of the media and of information in bringing these issues to the attention of the global community. The case also demonstrates the interconnected nature of human rights violations and human rights protections. From consumers to activists to the business community to government officials, we are all a part of the story of workers' rights in China and elsewhere. An essential part of this narrative depends upon how institutions measure and govern human rights—and the violations of those rights.

Measuring and Monitoring Human Rights

Increasingly, human rights scholars and practitioners are recognizing the critical need, as well as the challenges, to systematically measure and report on global human rights standards. Measurement is not only important for advocates attempting to make their case to state actors, but also for human rights research aimed at improving accountability mechanisms for such standards. We measure human rights to *describe and document* situations and events, and we use the raw information to serve a number of important functions. Human rights scholar Todd Landman (2004, 2007) argues that measurement enables us to *classify* different rights violations and abusers, to *monitor* the degree to which states promote and protect human rights, to *recognize patterns* of the causes and consequences of human rights violations, and lastly, to *advocate* for necessary rights improvements at local, national, and global levels. Human rights measures can focus on events, like the disappearances in Latin America; on standards, such as the democratic principles coded in the Freedom House scales; on surveys, which focus on individual perceptions of protected or abused rights; and on socioeconomic statistics, such as the **Human Development Index (HDI)** or measures of gross domestic product (GDP).

Human Development Index (HDI)
A composite statistic used to rank countries by level of human development.

While policy makers are usually looking for these kinds of "hard" data sources, there are a number of significant challenges in collecting both the necessary qualitative and quantitative information to make such concrete assessments. To begin, when we start measuring human rights, we are assuming that everyone agrees on what exactly constitutes the fulfillment of a particular right. What makes a good measurement a reflective indicator? Take, for example, the concept of women's rights. When trying to gauge the development of women's rights in Afghanistan or Iraq, for example, we often look at whether or not women are voting in the democratic elections. While the right to vote is certainly important, just because a woman has the right to vote does not mean she feels safe enough to actually travel to the election polls or that she is literate enough to read the ballot. When it comes to women's right to work, many point to the increasing number of women in the workforce worldwide, but does access to jobs necessarily translate into empowerment and dignity for women? This measure of women's rights does not, for example, take into account women's wages compared to men, even in the United States where women make approximately $0.80 for every dollar a man earns in a similar position. While this number varies in different job sectors, this average across the industries leads to significant income differences over one's lifetime. Measuring women's rights by looking at the increasing percentages of women in the workforce also assumes that women's working conditions are healthy and that at the end of the week they actually have control over how they spend their earned income.

These examples illustrate the difficulty in measuring human rights. Often, information is easily biased and highly incomplete. Even government reports frequently are suspect in terms of reliability. Reports are often intentionally vague or information is simply missing. Further, some organizations simply underreport certain human rights violations, making them very difficult to figure out. For example, estimates on the number of people who are "victims" of human trafficking vary from approximately 3 million (International Labor Organization estimates) to 27 million (U.S. State Department estimates). This gap is dramatic and has serious implications for who counts as a trafficking "victim," how they are treated, and policies designed at prevention and prosecution. There are many obstacles to measuring human rights—both in terms of problems and progress. However, these obstacles are not insurmountable and we must overcome them. The international community needs more comprehensive—as well as disaggregated—data that it can cross-check from a variety of sources in order for the human rights

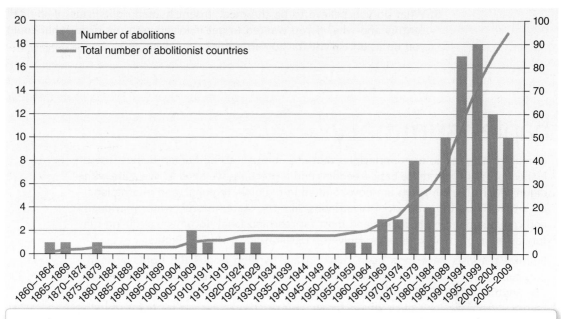

FIGURE 11.5

Global trends in laws prohibiting the death penalty

According to Amnesty International, the death penalty is legal in only about one quarter of the world's countries. In the last 25 years, 67 governments have abolished the death penalty, 5 have abolished it for ordinary crimes, and an additional 35 have abolished the death penalty in practice, if not by law per se. For some, this trend reflects an emerging abolitionist norm toward the death penalty. However, this norm is by no means universal, with states like the U.S. actually seeing overall increases in the number of people executed.

Data Source: Amnesty International.

CRITICAL THINKING QUESTIONS

1. Review the basic human rights principles codified in the UDHR (see Figure 11.1) and consider the various ways that your state might interpret these rights and translate them into policy. Then select one principle and compare and contrast at least two different interpretations for this right (e.g., right to life, right to marry, right to be free from torture). Why are these different interpretations significant, and what does this say about actual implementation of these basic moral principles in real world political systems?

2. There are a number of critiques of the universalism assumed in the human rights regime. Choose one critique and explain it. Do you agree or disagree with this critique? Why?

3. What do you see as the most significant barrier to human rights promotion and protection in the world today and why? Then discuss at least one possible way to realistically address this barrier.

4. Why is measuring and monitoring important for human rights advocacy?

5. What do you believe to be the most urgent human rights issue of the 21st century and why? If you wanted to get involved with this issue, what could you do as an activist for human rights?

chapter **summary**

- Human rights are the moral principles that are universal to all human beings. These inalienable rights are those basic freedoms and protections we need to live a life with dignity. Many human rights are now codified in national, regional, and international laws that shape the way social institutions, like the state, interact with individuals and communities. The founding and most far reaching legal document outlining the fundamental human rights is the Universal Declaration of Human Rights.

- Political theorists have long been thinking and writing about the rights of man, particularly those derived from natural law, as inherent duties that people had to one another and to God. With the Enlightenment, however, these natural rights that emerged from the laws of nature increasingly focused on the secular origins of individual freedoms and liberties rather than a divine moral order.

- First-generation rights focus on civil and political rights and for many serve as the core of a rights system based on equality and nondiscrimination. Some classify these rights as proscriptive rights, those policies and actions that governments cannot do to groups.

- Second-generation rights are largely centered on economic and social rights, such as economic subsistence, education, nutrition, sanitation, work, housing, and health care. These prescriptive rights include the essentials that a society and its government are arguably obligated to try to provide in order to assure certain qualitative standards of life for everyone in the community.

- Third-generation rights, or those focused on the communal aspects of being human, refer to solidarity rights unique to certain groups in a particular context. These group rights can be wide-ranging, from self-determination rights to the right to development to the right to a healthy environment.

- The modern human rights movement has been catalyzed by a combination of powerful events, like the Holocaust, the growth and influence of IGOs and NGOs, the leadership of key individuals and grassroots movements, the expansion of international human rights law, and the developments in information technology connecting these various actors across the globe.

- Criticisms of the universal approach embedded within the human rights movement include arguments concerned with cultural relativism, modern forms of imperialism, and feminist activism.

- While the human rights movement has many notable achievements, barriers to progress still exist. Gaps in treaty interpretation and failures in law enforcement as well as political selectivity highlight the fundamental (and often problematic) nature of the human rights regime—states are the primary enforcers for international human rights.

then the world is approaching, or may have even reached, a crisis of carrying capacity—the potential of no longer being able to sustain its population in an adequate manner or being able to absorb its waste. To put this as an equation that illustrates what can happen when we push the boundaries of carrying capacity:

Exploding population	×	Spiraling per capita resource consumption	×	Mounting waste and pollutant discharges	=	Biosphere catastrophe

If the neotraditionalists are correct in their equation, then a primary goal should be to ensure that we do not reach or, for safety's sake, even approach full carrying capacity. That will not be easy, however, because another fundamental goal of humans has been and remains to increase their economic well-being and to reap the other benefits, such as better health, that come with prosperity. The world's economically developed countries (EDCs) have largely achieved that goal. The world's less developed countries (LDCs) are intent on also doing so. Industrialization and science are key elements of development, yet they are two-edged swords in their relationship to the environment and the quality of human life. On the positive side, industrialization has vastly expanded global wealth, especially for the EDCs. Science has created synthetic substances that enhance our lives. Medicine has dramatically increased our chances of surviving infancy and has extended adult longevity. Yet, on the negative side, industry consumes natural resources and discharges pollutants into the air, ground, and water. Synthetic substances enter the food chain as carcinogens, refuse to degrade, and have other baleful effects. Similarly, decreased infant mortality rates and increased longevity have been major factors promoting the world's rapid population growth.

Given that all these factors are part of modernization and unlikely to reverse, the dilemma is how to achieve sustainable development, the process of protecting the biosphere while simultaneously advancing human socioeconomic development. Can

This favela in Rio drives home the pressures that unrestrained urbanization has on many regional ecosystems. Such crowding creates extreme pressure for adequate waste disposal and the delivery of many other public needs, especially in LDCs.

history matters

Sustainable Development

We can identify international environmental agreements as far back as the 1300s, but most international measures to preserve ecosystems did not emerge until the late 20th century.[6] The Earth's bounty of resources is not infinite and internal state regulation is not enough. States have worked to establish agreements that regulate the behavior of various actors with the goal of preserving ecosystems and even reversing damage.

The most comprehensive of these efforts has focused on the pursuit of sustainable development, as the two UN-sponsored Earth Summits in 1992 and 2002 indicated. The legacies of both summits illustrate the tension between environmental protection and economic growth and the way state sovereignty can limit progress. The "Thinking Theoretically" feature discussed efforts to solve global environmental problems that are fundamentally transboundary in nature. Realities of the territorial state system that still define contemporary international relations often constrain solutions to these problems.

Earth Summit I

The 1992 **UN Conference on Environment and Development (UNCED)** in Rio symbolized the growing concern with the environment and sustainable development. Popularly dubbed Earth Summit I, mostly the heads of state represented the 178 countries in attendance. About 15,000 NGO representatives attended a nearby conference. The official conference produced Agenda 21 (a 112-topic, nonbinding blueprint for sustainable development in the 21st century) and two treaties (the Convention on Biological Diversity and the United Nations Framework Convention on Climate Change).

Earth Summit I also featured the politics of environmental protection. The LDCs argued that the burden of sustainable development should fall substantially on the EDCs because they were responsible for most of the pollution and depletion of resources. LDCs contended that they should be exempt because the EDCs had already developed. Some in the LDCs suspect that EDC efforts to restrict their development may be part of a neocolonial effort to keep the LDCs weak and dependent. LDCs maintained that they were too poor to develop their resources in a sustainable way, and, therefore, EDCs should significantly increase aid to help LDCs. Most of the EDCs disagreed with these LDC positions.

"We do not have an open pocketbook," President George H. W. Bush observed.[7] Similarly, the South avoided restrictions on such activities as deforestation. "Forests are clearly a sovereign resource. . . . We cannot allow forests to be taken up in global forums," Malaysia's chief negotiator asserted.[8] It would be an overstatement to call the conference a failure because important global initiatives normally gestate for an extended period, and the two treaties, Agenda 21, and the attention that the conference generated globally helped firmly plant the environment on the world political agenda.

UN Conference on Environment and Development (UNCED) Often called Earth Summit I or the Rio Conference, this gathering in 1992 was the first to bring together most of the world's countries to address the range of issues associated with sustainable development.

the biosphere survive if we bring the 5.4 billion people who live in the LDCs up to the standard of living—with all its cars, air conditioners, throwaway plastic containers, and other biosphere-attacking amenities—enjoyed by the 1 billion people in the EDCs? How? The "History Matters" feature illustrates these tensions between the North and South well, and focuses on the Earth Summits.

Central to what you should ponder as you read the rest of this chapter is if and how we can meet the legitimate, but resource-consuming and waste-creating modernization goals of LDCs without severely damaging the environment. For example, think about what consumption would be like if India, with its 1.1 billion people, were as economically developed as the United States and had the same

Earth Summit II

A decade later, delegates from almost all of the world's countries and representatives from some 8,000 NGOs gathered in Johannesburg, at Earth Summit II, the **World Summit on Sustainable Development (WSSD)**, to address what the UN Secretary-General called the "gap between the goals and promises set out in Rio and the daily reality [of their accomplishment]."[9] The political disputes, however, that had bedeviled Earth Summit I also afflicted the WSSD, creating what an Indonesian diplomat portrayed as "a battle, a conflict of interest between developed and developing countries."[10] The United States and some other EDCs were unwilling to provide LDCs with substantially increased aid or to accept environmental restrictions. The EDCs opposed the creation of international agencies to monitor and enforce mandatory standards. One U.S. official insisted that the only path to progress was for "both developing and developed nations" to agree to mutual restrictions.[11] Yet the Secretary-General asserted, "The richest countries must lead the way . . . and they contribute disproportionately to global environmental problems."[12]

The EDCs announced some new funding commitments, and the conference adopted important new, albeit voluntary, targets for reducing pollution and resource depletion. Providing a perspective, the UN Secretary-General advised, "I think we have to be careful not to expect conferences like this to produce miracles." Instead, he suggested, "What happens is the energy that we create here, the commitments that have been made, and what we do on the ground as individuals, as civil society, as community groups, and as governments and private sector."[13]

Earth Summit III

The preparations for the Rio+20 Summit in June 2012 centered on seven critical themes in sustainable development.[14] They are:

- Jobs—focusing attention on the impact of the global economic crisis;
- Energy—a central variable in the environment–development relationship;
- Cities—focusing on the unique environmental challenges of urbanization in the developing world;
- Food—centering on rethinking how food is grown, shared, and consumed;
- Water—access to fresh water and waste water treatment is critical to personal and environmental health;
- Oceans—care of our oceans has an array of impacts on health, weather, food, air, and beyond;
- Disasters—coping with disasters is a recurrent challenge for humankind and is a special challenge in the developing world.

The Summit concluded by issuing "The Future We Want" stating that the parties "renew our commitment to sustainable development and to ensuring the promotion of an economically, socially and environmentally sustainable future for our planet and for present and future generations." http://daccess-dds-ny.un.org/doc/UNDOC/LTD/N12/436/88/PDF/N1243688.pdf?OpenElement.

resource use and waste patterns. There are now 6.6 million cars in India. There would be 535 million if automobiles were as commonplace there as in the United States. One impact would be astronomically increased pressure on petroleum supplies. The additional cars and other accoutrements of a developed economy would put India on the road to consuming as much petroleum per capita as Americans. Since the United States uses about 30 times more petroleum per capita than does India, annual oil consumption in India would skyrocket from 36 billion gallons to 1.1 trillion gallons. In addition to the drain on the world's oil supply, this would increase pollution enormously. For one, carbon dioxide (CO_2) emissions would rise ominously. Americans discharge about 20 times more CO_2 per capita than do Indians, but India already

World Summit on Sustainable Development (WSSD) Often called Earth Summit II, this conference was held in Johannesburg in 2002. It was attended by almost all countries and by some 8,000 NGOs.

These Chinese textile workers exemplify the high level of industrial activity taking place in rapidly developing economies like China. LDCs often argue that they shouldn't be held to high environmental standards when the current EDCs weren't held to them during their periods of industrialization.

emits about 1.7 billion metric tons of CO_2 annually. That figure would rise to about 34 billion metric tons, escalating the threat to the environment. It is not necessary to continue this example to make the point that if Indians, as they have a right to do, achieve the same level of prosperity as Americans and also have the same resource consumption and waste pattern as prevails today in the United States, that would be very bad for the ecological future of the planet.

Furthermore, if you were to bring the rest of the LDCs up to the U.S. level of resource use and emissions discharge, then you would hyper-accelerate the depletion of natural resources and the creation of pollution. At current rates of increase, LDC emissions of CO_2 will surpass those of EDCs in about 10 years, and if LDCs discharged CO_2 at the same per capita rate as the EDCs, then current world emissions would be over double the already-too-high level. Clearly, this is not acceptable. Less clear is what to do. Other than doing nothing, the options fall into two broad categories: restricting development and paying the price for environmentally sustainable development.

Option 1: Restrict/Roll Back Development   Preserving the environment by consuming less is one possibility. Those who advocate stringent programs believe that even if they seem unpalatable to many people now, eventually we will be better off if we make the sacrifices necessary to restrain development and preserve the environment.

Objections to such solutions leap to mind. Are we, for instance, to suppress LDC development? If people in India do not acquire more cars, if Chinese are kept in the fields instead of in factories, and if Africans continue to swelter in the summer's heat without air conditioners, then we can partly avoid accelerated resource use and pollution discharges. As we saw in chapter 10, however, the LDCs are asserting their right to industrialize and to acquire the conveniences of life, such as cars and air conditioning, on an equal basis with the EDCs. As such, the LDCs reject any suggestion that they restrain their development. No one can "try to tell the people of Beijing that they can't buy a car or an air-conditioner" because they pollute, cautions one Chinese energy official. "It is just as hot in Beijing as it is in Washington."[15]

Another solution would be for the people of the North to use dramatically fewer resources and to take the necessary steps to reduce pollution by drastically curtailing some of the luxuries that they currently enjoy. This could include forfeiting SUVs and other large passenger vehicles, commuting by public transportation instead of by car, or keeping the heat down in winter and using air conditioners only sparingly in the summer. Polls show that most people favor the theory of conservation and environmental protection. Yet practice indicates that, so far, most people are also unwilling to suffer a major reduction in their conveniences or standards of living. Efforts to get more Americans to use mass transit, for example, have had very little success. There are other possibilities that would apply greater pressure on the public to conserve. The government could levy a steep gas-guzzler tax on any private passenger vehicle that gets, say, less than 25 miles per gallon (mpg). How would you react to such a tax of $1,000 at the time of sale for each mpg under 25 mpg that the vehicle got? That would raise the price of a 17-mpg SUV an extra $8,000. Yet, another approach would be to dramatically raise gasoline taxes, an option that we present to you later in this chapter in "Challenge Your Assumptions" on p. 472.

Option 2: Pay for Environmentally Sustainable Development

Another possibility is to pay the price to create and distribute technologies that will allow the LDCs to maximize the balance between economic development and environmental protection. Without modern technology and the money to pay for it, China, for example, poses a serious environmental threat. China now stands second behind the United States in terms of national CO_2 emissions. China's increased industrialization is one factor, but a second important factor is that China generates most of its commercial power by burning coal. The problem is that coal produces 45% more CO_2 per unit of energy generated than gasoline, 41% more than heating oil, and 97% more than natural gas. China annually consumes over 2 billion tons of coal, about 38% of the world total. This, combined with the country's economic development, is a major reason why China's CO_2 emissions rose 57% between 1990 and 2004, while the rest of the world's emissions increased 19%. Even on a per capita basis, China's emissions surged more than four times the global per capita increase.

There are choices, but each has trade-offs. One choice is to install pollution control equipment, such as stack scrubbers, to clean the emissions from burning coal. That would aid the environment, but it would be hugely expensive. For example, a recent proposal to retrofit a huge coal-fired generating plant in Bulgaria with stack scrubbers and other equipment, which would clean up its sulfur dioxide emissions by 95%, came with an estimated price tag of $650 million. Bulgaria had EU backing for the project, and China and other LDCs would need similar support to meet the costs of reducing the discharge of pollutants. Another choice China could make is to consume more oil to decrease the use of coal. Oil imports are vastly expensive, however, and act as a drag on the country's socioeconomic development. Increased oil consumption at the level China would need would also rapidly accelerate the depletion of the world's finite petroleum reserves. Moreover, the new oil fields that firms are finding often lie offshore, and drilling endangers the oceans.

Another choice is using hydroelectricity to provide relatively nonpolluting energy. This requires dam construction that floods the surrounding countryside, displaces its residents, and spoils the pristine beauty of the river valley downstream. China, for example, is trying to ease its energy crunch and simultaneously develop clean hydroelectric power by building the massive $25 billion Three Gorges Dam and hydroelectric project on the Yangtze River. The project, which rivals the Great Wall of China in scope, will vastly increase the availability of clean power to rural provinces by generating 18,200 megawatts of electricity without burning highly polluting coal.

These before and after photos show the impact of building the Three Gorges Dam in China. The left photo shows some of the agricultural land lost to the dam, which was built to provide more electricity generation to fuel China's rapid economic rise.

The dam will also help stem floods that have often caused catastrophic damage and death downstream. To accomplish these benefits, however, the dam will create a 370-mile-long reservoir, inundating over 200 cities, towns, and villages, and forcing 1.3 million people from their homes. The rising water will submerge numerous archeological sites and what many consider one of the most scenic natural areas in the world. Moreover, a collapse of the dam from structural failure, earthquake or other natural disaster, or military attack could cause a flood of unimaginable proportions. Critics also charge that the reservoir covers some 1,500 factories, hospitals, dumps, and other sites containing human and industrial waste, and the water will become contaminated as pollutants seep into it. The Three Gorges project is an almost perfect illustration of the difficulty of sustainable development.

Although the project will ease some environmental problems (in this case, coal burning), it will also have an adverse impact on people and create or worsen other environmental problems. Even if you can cut such Gordian knots, you will encounter other problems: the short-term costs of environmental protection in terms of taxes to pay for government programs; the high costs of products that companies manufacture in an environmentally acceptable way and that are themselves environmentally safe; and the expense of waste disposal in an ecologically responsible manner.

Moreover, since the LDCs are determined to develop economically, yet must struggle to pay the costs of environmentally sound progress, the North will have to extend significant aid to the South to help it develop in a relatively safe way. We need money to create nonpolluting energy resources, to install pollution control devices in factories, and to provide many other technologies. The costs will be huge, with some estimates exceeding $120 billion a year. We need billions more each year to help the LDCs stem their—and the world's—spiraling population.

Is the North willing to pay this price? Polls show that people in many countries are concerned about global climate change, ozone layer destruction, deforestation, wildlife destruction, and acid rain. Cross-national polls also regularly find that a majority of respondents say that their governments should do more to protect their country's environment and also to be involved in the global environmental effort. Yet, surveys additionally find that a majority of citizens think that their tax burdens are already too heavy and are reluctant to support large expenditures on environmental programs. In an indication about how Americans might respond to the question posed in the earlier "Challenge Your Assumptions" box, a 2007 survey recorded 58% of Americans rejecting and only 38% approving (with 4% unsure) the idea of increased gasoline taxes as a way to cut consumption and ease global climate change.[16] Given Americans' historic antipathy to foreign aid, it is hard to imagine much support for higher taxes to pay other countries to protect the environment.

GLOBAL CARRYING CAPACITY: POPULATION PROBLEMS AND PROGRESS

On Tuesday, October 12, 1999, the world population passed the 6 billion mark. That is a stunning number. Humans in their modern form date back about 40,000 years, and their number did not reach 1 billion until 1804. It took only another 195 years, to 1999, to get to the 6 billion mark. The jump from 5 billion to 6 billion had only taken 12 years. The world is awash in humanity, with China alone having more people than had been on Earth in 1804. The upward spiral has begun to slow, but only slightly. Current UN projections, as Figure 12.1 depicts, show the world population continuing to grow to 9 billion by midcentury. Given a reasonably finite amount of resources and ability to absorb waste, this growing population presents a challenge to Earth's carrying capacity. That will be an especially acute problem in some regions because their populations will continue to grow at a relatively rapid rate. Sub-Saharan

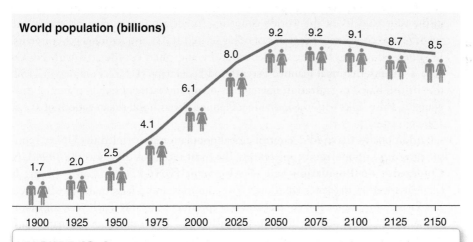

FIGURE 12.1

World population growth

The UN expects the world population to peak at 9.2 billion by midcentury, to stabilize briefly at that level, and then to gradually decline. Adding another 2.7 billion more people between 2005 and 2050 will strain Earth's resources, especially given the increased use of resources and the generation of waste due to economic development.

Data Source: UN Population Division.

Africa will be the most troubled. Statisticians project its population to grow annually by 2.43% between 2005 and 2115, while they project the world population to grow at an annual rate of just 1.14%. The percentages may seem small, but they mean that sub-Saharan Africa will have about 9 million more people a year than it would have at the 1.14% rate.

The acceleration of population growth beginning about 1950 occurred for several reasons. High fertility rates is one. Between 1950 and 1970, the average woman had five children, with an average between six and seven children per family in the LDCs. That overall rate has fallen, but the world population continues to grow too fast. Fewer deaths is a second and increasingly important factor. Better health means that more infants survive to grow up and that adults live longer. In 1950, 20 of every 1,000 people worldwide died each year; now only 9 of every 1,000 do. A third factor causing population growth is the population base multiplier effect. This is a problem of mathematics. During the next decade, some 3 billion women will enter their child-bearing years. At the current fertility rate, these women will have 7.5 billion children, who in turn will have yet more children. Thus, the population will continue to grow until the world fertility rate falls to 2.1, the approximate replacement rate at which each set of parents has two surviving children.

Global Recognition of the Population Problem

The United Nations has led the effort to control global population growth. Among the UN divisions and associated agencies involved, the United Nations Population Fund (UNFPA) is the largest. It began operations in 1969, and focuses on promoting family planning services and improving reproductive health in LDCs. During its history, UNFPA has provided over $6 billion to support population programs in the vast majority of the world's countries. In addition to its own programs, the agency helps coordinate programs of other related IGOs and national governments. UNFPA's efforts are further supplemented by and often coordinated with NGOs such as the International Planned Parenthood Federation (IPPF). Founded in 1952, this British-based organization operates its own international family planning programs and also links with the individual Planned Parenthood organizations of about 150 countries.

Additionally, the need to control global population growth led the UN to sponsor three world population conferences. The most recent of these was the 1994 **UN Conference on Population and Development (UNCPD)** in Cairo, Egypt. It brought together delegates from over 170 countries and a large number of NGOs and focused on population control and on reproductive health. Each year, for example, about 529,000 women (99% of whom live in LDCs) die from pregnancy and childbirth complications. Abortion was the most controversial issue at the conference. Abortion is widely available in about 60% of countries, fairly restricted in another 15%, and very restricted or unavailable in the remaining 25%. According to the **World Health Organization (WHO)**, induced abortions (those that occur for other than natural causes) end about 22% of pregnancies. Abortions performed in unsafe conditions, either in countries where it is illegal or severely restricted, or in countries with an inadequate health care system, are a major threat to women's health. WHO estimates that about 68,000 women a year die from unsafe abortions. In some

UN Conference on Population and Development (UNCPD)
A UN-sponsored conference that met in Cairo, Egypt, in September 1994. The conference called for a program of action to include international, national, and local programs to foster family planning.

World Health Organization (WHO)
A UN-affiliated organization created in 1946 to address world health issues.

countries that both restrict abortions and are exceptionally poor, an estimated more than half of maternal mortality is the result of illegal abortion.

Controversy at the conference centered on how far it should go toward supporting abortion as a health measure or even as a population control approach. Predominantly Muslim countries were particularly opposed to the conference's support of abortion, with the Sudanese government charging that this would result in "the spread of immoral and irreligious ideas."[17] The Roman Catholic Church was also critical, with the Pope warning the conference not to "ignore the rights of the unborn."[18] Among those with a supportive view was Norway's Prime Minister Gro Harlem Brundtland who charged, "Morality becomes hypocrisy if it means accepting mothers' suffering or dying in connection with unwanted pregnancies and illegal abortions and unwanted children."[19]

The result of this conflict was a compromise, with the language in the conference report promoting safe abortion qualified by the phrase, "in circumstances in which abortion is legal," and the caveat, "In no case should abortion be promoted as a method of family planning." The 1994 Cairo conference unanimously approved a "Program of Action" calling for spending $5.7 billion annually by the year 2000 on international programs to foster family planning. Funding never reached that goal, but the heightened awareness of the population problem and the closely associated issue of women's reproductive health and the delegates' and others' post-conference activity did help to increase funding from $1.3 billion in 1993 to $2.2 billion in 2000. Most important, maternal mortality has declined by about one-third since the conference.

Fertility rate
The average number of children born to a woman over her lifetime in a given society.

Approaches to Reducing the Birthrate

There are two basic approaches to reducing the birthrate. Social approaches provide information about birth control and encouragement to practice it by making birth control devices and pills, sterilization, and, in some cases, abortion programs available. The combined efforts of national governments, UNFPA and other IGOs, and NGOs have had an impact. During the early 1960s, the contraceptive prevalence rate (the percentage of couples practicing contraception) in the LDCs was only 9%. Now it is 60%. This contraceptive prevalence rate falls off drastically in the least developed countries (LLDCs), where it is only 40%.

Economic approaches to population growth also work. There is a clear relationship between poverty and the number of children a woman bears. The **fertility rate**, the average number of children a woman

These South African women are passing out condoms in a mining community. They turn out each week to promote safe sex in their community. In many countries of the world, the effectiveness of birth control and safe sex programs is constrained by cultural attitudes.

will have, is 1.7 in high-income countries, 2.1 in middle-income countries, and 3.7 in low-income countries. How does one explain the link between population and wealth? One view is that overpopulation causes poverty. This view reasons that with too many people, especially in already poor countries, there are too few resources, jobs, and other forms of wealth to go around. Perhaps, but that is only part of the problem, because it is also true that poverty causes overpopulation. The low-income countries tend to have the most labor-intensive economies, those in which children are economically valuable because they help their parents with farming or, when they are somewhat older, provide cheap labor in mining and manufacturing processes. As a result, cultural attitudes in many countries have come to reflect economic utility. Having a large family is also an asset in terms of social standing in many societies with limited economic opportunities.

Furthermore, women in low-income countries have fewer opportunities to limit the number of children they bear. Artificial birth control methods and counseling services are less readily available in these countries. Also, women in LDCs are less educated than are women in EDCs. It is therefore harder to convey birth control information, especially written information, to women in LDCs. Additionally, they have fewer opportunities than do women in EDCs to gain paid employment and to develop status roles beyond that of motherhood. The lack of educational and economic opportunities is related to both the use of contraception and the fertility rate.

The evidence that poverty causes population increases has spurred efforts to advance the economic and educational opportunities available to women as an integral part of population control. This realization was one of the factors that led the UN to designate 1975 as International Women's Year and to kick off the Decade for Women. That year the UN also convened the first World Conference on Women (WCW). In 1976, the establishment of the UN Development Fund for Women (UNIFEM, after its French name) followed these initiatives. The Fund works through 10 regional offices to improve the living standards of women in LDCs by providing technical and financial support to advance the entry of women into business, scientific and technical careers, and other key areas. UNIFEM also strives to incorporate women into the international and national planning and administration of development programs and to ensure that issues of particular concern to women such as food, security, human rights, and reproductive health are kept on the global agenda. The UN also established the International Research and Training Institute for the Advancement of Women with the task of carrying out research, training, and information activities related to women and the development process. Headquartered in the Dominican Republic, the institute conducts research on the barriers that impede the progress of women in social, economic, and political development.

The Impact of International Population Control Efforts

The effort to reduce global population growth is a success story. Part of the credit goes to the work of IGOs, NGOs, and national governments. Improved economic conditions in many LDCs and the slowly improving economic and educational status of women in many countries have also played a role. As a result, the average global fertility rate has declined dramatically, as Figure 12.2 illustrates. The goal is 2.1, which is about the stable replacement rate. The UN expects the global population to reach that standard by midcentury. After that the UN expects the fertility rate to drop below the replacement rate, which will for a time, at least, decrease the world population late in this century. As recently as 1994, the population was expanding at 94 million a year, and the UN was estimating that it would reach 11.6 billion by 2150. Now the UN projects the population to peak at more than 2 billion people short of that. That is stellar news, but it merits two cautions. One is that population is hard to predict. A UN worst-case scenario projects the population at 14 billion at the end of this century and peaking at 36 billion in 2300. Also, despite the slowdown, the substantial population increase that is looming will challenge Earth's carrying capacity.

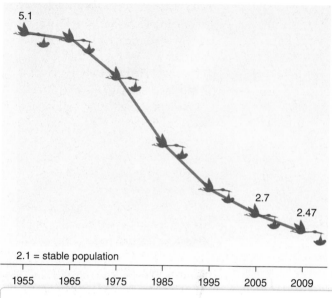

FIGURE 12.2
World fertility rates
The number of children the average woman bears has dropped by over 50% since the 1950s. This welcome change is the result of numerous factors, including the work of international agencies to improve educational and economic opportunities for females and to provide information and other forms of assistance to women who wish to practice planned parenthood.

Data Sources: UN Population Division, *World Population to 2003* (UN: New York, 2004).; World Bank.

ASSESSING NATURAL RESOURCE PRESSURES

Recent decades have witnessed increased warnings that we are using our resources too quickly. Most studies of the rates at which we are depleting energy, mineral, forest, land, wildlife, fishery, and water resources have expressed a level of concern ranging from caution to serious alarm.

Petroleum, Natural Gas, and Minerals

The supply of oil, gas, and mineral resources is one area of concern. At the forefront of this concern are the cost and supply of energy resources. World energy needs are skyrocketing. Global energy production increased 80% between 1960 and 2005. Burning fossil fuels (coal, oil, and gas) generates 75% of the output. Following in declining order are burning wood, crop residue, and other forms of biomass; then, nuclear energy. Such environmentally friendly sources as hydroelectric, solar, geothermal, and wind power produce only 3% of energy. At one time the world had an estimated 2.3 trillion barrels of oil beneath its surface. Current known reserves are a bit more than half of that. At the rate that we are consuming oil—34 billion barrels

Pictures such as this one from the BP Deepwater Horizon oil rig have become synonomous with environmental disaster. This event in the Gulf of Mexico reignited the debate about the risks of off-shore drilling and energy generation more generally.

in 2007—simple math would suggest that the world's oil wells will go dry in 2046. Natural gas supplies are a bit better, but at current reserves and use we will deplete them in 2072. However, projections are tricky because demand changes, because energy companies sometimes discover new oil and gas sources, and because technological advances, such as new techniques in deep sea drilling, tap previously unusable deposits. For example, known reserves of petroleum actually increased from 1.01 trillion barrels in 1996 to 1.32 trillion barrels in 2007. Nevertheless, petroleum and natural gas reserves are a concern because the supply is indisputably exhaustible and because new finds are smaller and less attractive to utilize. They are often deeper, under the ocean, and in environmentally sensitive land areas. These realities and the dramatic rise in oil prices in 2007–2008 prompted increased demand for hybrid vehicles and further research and development of alternative fuels and renewable energy sources. The Obama administration has made alternative fuels a high priority in its policy agenda, but it may well confront continuing resistance from some business sectors.

The story for natural gas is nearly the same. New discoveries, enhanced extraction methods, and other factors may have an impact on the timing, but the bottom line is that the supply is finite and at some point, perhaps within the lifetime of those born today, human beings will exhaust it. Coal will last almost 500 years at current consumption rates, but it is a major pollutant if not controlled by expensive technology. The development of hydroelectric power is attractive in some ways, but it is expensive to develop, and damming rivers creates environmental and social problems. Nuclear power is another alternative, and some countries rely heavily on it. For example, nuclear power generates 80% of France's electricity. However, only 30 countries generate nuclear power, and on average it amounts to only about 20% of their total commercial energy production. Additionally, there are high costs and obvious hazards to nuclear power. Some people advocate developing wind, solar, geothermal, and other such sources of power. So far, though, cost, production capacity, and other factors have limited the application of these energy sources and will continue to do so unless there are major technological breakthroughs.

Another factor in the supply and demand for energy is usage patterns. With 10% of the world population, the EDCs consumed 50% of the energy. However, in terms of increasing use, LDC energy consumption increased 105% between 1975 and 2005, while the increase in energy consumption by EDCs was lower at 76%. This pattern indicates that while the North may bear much of the responsibility to date for the resources that we use to create the energy and the waste products that we discharge, no solution is possible unless the South is a full participant. In addition to oil and natural gas, we are rapidly depleting many other minerals. Based on world reserves and world use, some minerals that are in particularly short supply (and estimates of the year that Earth's supply will be exhausted given known reserves) include copper (2056), lead (2041), mercury (2077), tin (2053), and zinc (2042). Certainly, discoveries of new sources or the decline of consumption based on conservation or the use of substitutes could extend those dates. However, it is also possible that the time interval to depletion could shorten if, for instance, extraction rates accelerate as LDCs develop.

The resource puzzle, as mentioned, is how to simultaneously (1) maintain the industrialized countries' economies and standards of living, (2) promote economic development in the South, which will consume increased energy and minerals, and (3) manage the problems of resource depletion and environmental damage involved in energy and mineral production and use. If, for instance, the South were to develop to the same economic level as the North, if the LDCs' energy-use patterns were the same as the North's currently are, and if the same energy resource patterns that now exist persisted, then petroleum reserves would almost certainly soon be dry. Natural gas and many other minerals probably also would quickly follow oil into the museum of geological history.

Forests and Land

For many who will read this book, the trees that surround them and the very land on which they stand will hardly seem like valuable natural resources and will certainly not seem endangered. That is not the case. There are serious concerns about the depletion of the world's forests and the degradation of its land.

Forest Depletion   The depletion of forests and their resources concerns many analysts. Data compiled by the UN Food and Agriculture Organization (FAO) and other sources indicate that the increase in world population and, to a lesser degree, economic development, have been destroying the world's forests. Some 1 billion people depend on wood as an energy source, and they have depleted many forests for fuel to cook food and heat homes. They are also clearing forests to make room for farms and grazing lands. Forests and woodland still cover about 30% of Earth's land area. Once, however, they occupied 48% of the land area, and tree cover has been declining by about 1% every 10 years. Logging is a major factor, but hydroelectric projects are drowning forests and strip-mining for minerals is razing the trees. Acid rain and other environmental attacks increase the toll on forestation. The result is that in recent years we have lost annually an average 35,000 square miles of forest, an area about the size of Portugal.

Forest loss is greatest in the LLDCs, whose forests are disappearing at the rate of 1% every 2 years. Tropical forests, which account for over 80% of all forest losses, are in particular peril. Fifty years ago, tropical forest covered 12% of Earth's land surface; now just 6% is covered. The Amazon River basin's tropical forest in Brazil and the surrounding countries is an especially critical issue. This ecosystem is by far the largest of its kind in the world, covering 2.7 million square miles, about the size of the 48 contiguous U.S. states. The expanding populations and economic needs of the region's countries have exerted great pressure on the forest. For example, the Amazon basin has recently been losing 9,000 square miles, an area about the size of Massachusetts, of forest every year.

LDCs recognize the problem, but economic need drives them to continue to clear forests for farming, building material, roads and other facilities, and many other domestic uses. Wood and wood products, such as paper, pulp, and resins are also valuable exports, annually bringing in about $100 billion in needed earnings to the LDCs. It is easy to blame the LDCs for allowing their forests to be overcut, but many in those countries ask what alternative they have. "Anyone who comes in and tells us not to cut the forest has to give us another way to live," says an official of Suriname. "And so far, they haven't done that." Instead, what occurs, charges the country's president, is "eco-colonialism" by international environmental organizations trying to prevent Suriname from using its resources.[20]

Deforestation has numerous negative consequences. One is global climate change, which we discuss in a later section. Another consequence of forest depletion is that wood in many areas has become so scarce and so expensive that poor urban dwellers have to spend up to a third of their meager incomes to heat their homes and cook. Poor people in rural areas have to devote the entire time of a family member to gather wood for home use. The devastation of the forests is also driving many forms of life into extinction. A typical 4-square-mile section of the Amazon basin rain forest contains some 750 species of trees, 125 species of mammals, 400 species of birds, 160 species of reptiles and amphibians, and perhaps 300,000 species of insects. The loss of biodiversity has an obvious aesthetic impact, and there are also pragmatic implications. Some 25% of modern pharmaceutical products are "green medicines" that contain ingredients originally found in plants. Extracts from Madagascar's rosy periwinkle, for example, are an ingredient in drugs to treat children's leukemia and Hodgkin's disease. Taxol is a drug derived from the Pacific yew for use in cancer chemotherapy, and a soil fungus is the source of the anticholesterol drug Mevacor. Many plants also contain natural pesticides that could provide the basis for the development of ecologically safe commercial pesticides to replace the environmental horrors, such as DDT, of the past.

Fortunately, the story of the world's forests is not all bleak. Recent research indicates that overall forest depletion may have stopped. One study found that about half of the countries with the largest forests are having positive forest growth. "This is the first time we have documented that many countries have turned the corner, that gradually forests are coming back," commented a scholar involved in the study. The head of the Food and Agriculture Organization's forest division cautioned that while he was glad about the study's "positive indications of an important change," he also felt that the lack of good data on forests in many parts of the world meant it would be wise not to be overly optimistic.[21]

> Borneo forests have become terraced agricultural land in this photo. As countries work to feed their populations and seek export revenue, the pressure to deforest large areas rises.

Land Degradation Not only are the forests beleaguered, so is the land. Deforestation is one of the many causes of soil erosion and other forms of damage to the land. Tropical forests rest on thin topsoil. This land is especially unsuited for agriculture, and it becomes exhausted quickly once the forest is cut down and crops are planted or grazing takes place. With no trees to hold soil in place, runoff occurs, and silt clogs rivers and bedevils hydroelectric projects. Unchecked runoff can also significantly increase the chances of river floods, resulting in loss of life and economic damage, and deadly mudslides down barren slopes with no trees to hold the dirt in place.

According to the United Nations Environment Programme (UNEP), 3.5 million square miles (about the size of China or the United States) of land are moderately degraded, 1.4 million square miles (about equal to Argentina) are strongly degraded, and 347,000 square miles (about the same as Egypt) are extremely degraded and beyond repair. At its worst, desertification occurs. More of the world's surface is becoming desertlike because of water scarcity, timber cutting, overgrazing, and overplanting. The desertification of land is increasing at an estimated rate of 30,600 square miles a year, turning an area the size of Austria into barren desert. Moreover, that rate of degradation could worsen, based on UNEP's estimate that 8 billion acres are in jeopardy.

Forest and Land Protection   Because almost all of the world's land lies within the boundaries of a sovereign state, international programs have been few. Desertification is one area in which there has been global action. Almost all countries are party to the Convention on Desertification (1994), which set up a structure to monitor the problem and to assist countries in devising remedial programs to reclaim barren land. There have also been some advances at the regional level. Most European countries abide by a 1979 treaty to reduce acid rain, and addressing that issue was the main goal of the Canada–U.S. Air Quality Agreement (1991). More recently, and addressing another problem, leaders of seven central African countries agreed in 2005 to a treaty to protect their region's rain forest, which is second in size to the one in the Amazon basin.

There is also progress at the national level in the preservation of forest and land resources, as well as on other resource and environmental concerns. Membership in environmental groups has grown dramatically. In several European countries and in the European Union, green parties have become viable political forces. For example, they have 42 of the seats (5%) in the European Parliament, and Germany's Green Party has 51 seats (8%) in the Bundestag. The growing interest in flora and fauna is also increasing the ecotourism trade, which some sources estimate makes up as much as a third of the nearly $500 billion annual tourism industry. For this reason, many countries are beginning to realize that they can derive more economic benefit from tourists than from loggers wielding chain saws.

Wildlife

World wildlife is amazingly diverse. These life forms (and the approximate number of known species for each) include mammals (4,300), reptiles (6,800), birds (9,700), fish (28,000), mollusks (80,000), insects (11,000,000), and arachnids (44,000).

Global Pressure on Wildlife   The march of humankind has driven almost all the other creatures into retreat and, in some cases, into extinction. Deforestation, land clearing for settlement and farming, water diversion and depletion, and pollution are but a few of modernization's by-products that destroy wildlife habitat.

There are pragmatic, as well as aesthetic, costs. The venom of the Brazilian pit viper is a vital component of the blood-pressure drug, Capoten, and vampire bat saliva is the basis of an anti-blood-clotting drug, now in clinical trials, to prevent heart attacks and stroke.

While some species are the unintended victims of development, others are threatened because they have economic value. The estimated $10 billion annual illegal trade in feathers, pelts, ivory, and other wildlife products is leading to the capture and sale or slaughter of numerous species, including many that are endangered. Poachers are killing tigers because their bodies are so valuable. A pelt fetches up to $15,000. Powdered tiger humerus bone, said to cure typhoid fever and other ailments, sells for $1,450 a pound, and men in some parts of the world pay $1,200 for a tiger's penis in the hope that eating it will improve their virility. Other endangered animals wind up on someone's dinner plate. Rising prosperity in China has increased the number of *ye wei* (wild taste) restaurants, where for $100 or so you can indulge in a buffet of elephant, tiger, and other exotic fare (Marshall, 2006). Much of the slaughter occurs in LDCs, but the EDCs are not guiltless. For example, poachers illegally kill more than 40,000 bears each year in the United States in part to harvest their gall bladders. These supposedly relieve a range of ailments (including hemorrhoids) and sell for up to $3,000 when smuggled abroad.

Note that on the issue of wildlife, like many other matters in this chapter, there are optimists who believe that the problem is grossly overstated. According to one analyst, "a fair reading of the available data suggests a rate of extinction not even one–one-thousandth as great as the one the doomsayers scare us with." He cautioned against ignoring "possible dangers to species," but stressed, "We should strive for a clear and unbiased view of species' assets so as to make sound judgments about how much time and money to spend on guarding them."[22] Other analysts have agreed with that assessment (Lomborg, 2001).

Protecting Wildlife   Although the world's list of endangered species is still growing, these threatened species are also now gaining some relief through the Convention on the International Trade in Endangered Species (CITES, 1975) and the 167 countries that are party to it. CITES added elephants to the list of endangered species in 1989, and the legal ivory trade has dropped from 473 tons in 1985 to zero. Poachers are still killing about 500 elephants a year for their ivory, but that is far better than the annual toll of 70,000 elephants during the last decade before they were protected under CITES. Wild cats, reptiles, and other types of wildlife have also found greater refuge, and the international sale of their skins has declined drastically. The global trade in live primates, birds, and reptiles has seen similar decreases. Individual countries have also acted to suppress poaching and punish those engaged in the illegal sales of wildlife. In 2003, for example, Chinese officials impounded 1,276 illegal pelts from 32 tigers, 579 leopards, and 665 otters that had been smuggled into the country. It was the largest seizure in China's history and a particularly helpful sign from a region that is the destination of a great deal of the illegal trade in wildlife, especially in parts used in traditional medicine. Note that penalties are especially stringent for such activity in China, which has executed at least 28 wildlife smugglers since 1990.

Freshwater

"Water, water everywhere, nor any drop to drink," cries out an adrift seaman in Samuel Taylor Coleridge's *Rime of the Ancient Mariner* (1798). We cannot quite say that of the world's freshwater, but there is less of it than you might think. Yes, 71% of Earth's surface is covered by water, but 97% of it is salt water and another 2% is frozen in the polar ice caps. This leaves only 1% readily available for drinking, watering livestock, and irrigating crops. Moreover, pollution is depleting or tainting some of the freshwater supply that exists. Freshwater use, after tripling between 1940 and 1975, has slowed its growth rate to about 2% to 3% a year. Much of this is due to population stabilization and conservation measures in the EDCs. Still, because the world population is growing and rainfall is a constant, the world needs an additional 7.1 trillion gallons each year just to grow the necessary extra grain to feed the expanding population.

Complicating matters even more, many countries, especially LDCs, have low per capita supplies of water, as you can see on the map in Figure 12.3. The world per capita availability is 8,549 cubic meters (1 m³ = 264.2 gallons), but it is unevenly distributed. Indeed, about 20% of countries have an annual availability of less than 1,000 cubic meters of water per person. Given the fact that Americans annually use 1,682 cubic meters of water per capita, the inadequacy of less than 1,000 cubic meters is readily apparent.

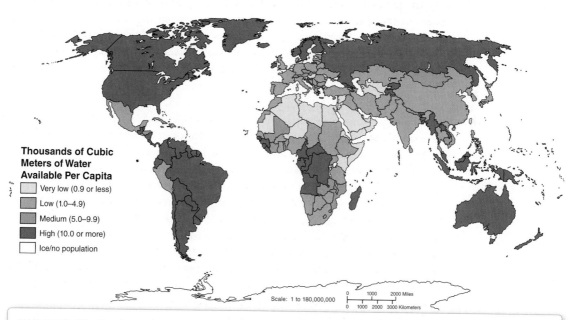

Thousands of Cubic Meters of Water Available Per Capita
- Very low (0.9 or less)
- Low (1.0–4.9)
- Medium (5.0–9.9)
- High (10.0 or more)
- Ice/no population

Scale: 1 to 180,000,000

FIGURE 12.3

Per capita water availability

A report by the United Nations Commission on Sustainable Development warns that 1.2 billion people live in countries facing "medium-high to high water stress."

Data Source: World Resources Institute, 2006.

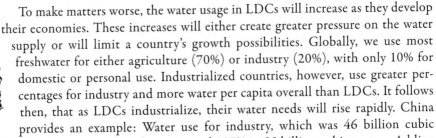

To make matters worse, the water usage in LDCs will increase as they develop their economies. These increases will either create greater pressure on the water supply or will limit a country's growth possibilities. Globally, we use most freshwater for either agriculture (70%) or industry (20%), with only 10% for domestic or personal use. Industrialized countries, however, use greater percentages for industry and more water per capita overall than LDCs. It follows then, that as LDCs industrialize, their water needs will rise rapidly. China provides an example: Water use for industry, which was 46 billion cubic meters in 1980, has increased 107% to 95 billion cubic meters. Adding to the problem in many countries, fertilizer leaching, industrial pollution, human and animal wastes, and other discharges are contaminating a great deal of drinking water.

Compounding demands on the water supply even further, global population growth means that the water supply worldwide will decline by one-third by 2050, leaving 7 billion people in 60 countries facing a water shortage. "Of all the social and natural crises we humans face, the water crisis is the one that lies at the heart of our survival and that of our planet Earth," the director-general of the United Nations Educational, Scientific, and Cultural Organization (UNESCO) has commented.[23]

If this projection proves accurate, it could lead to competition for water and to international tensions. There are, for example, 36 countries with a water *dependency ratio* above 50; that is, they get more than 50% of their freshwater from rivers that originate outside their borders. The security of these countries would be threatened if upstream countries diverted that water for their own purposes or threatened to limit it as a political sanction. For example, Israel, which has 2.041 cubic meters of water per capita, also has a dependency ratio of 55, with a majority of its water sources originating in the surrounding, often hostile, Arab states. Such possibilities have led some analysts to suggest that in the not-too-distant future the access to water supplies could send thirsty countries over the brink of war.

Such concerns are not new. Two Sumerian city-states negotiated the first known water treaty 4,500 years ago to end their dispute over water in the Tigris River. Just since 1820, according to the UN, more than 400 treaties have been concluded relating to water as a limited and consumable resource. Nevertheless, old disputes reemerge and new ones break out. Such disputes recently moved the head of UNEP to contend that there is an "urgent need" for IGOs to "act as the water equivalent of marriage counselors, amicably resolving differences between countries . . . [that] may be straying apart."[24]

The Seas and Fisheries

The saltwater oceans and seas cover about two-thirds of Earth's surface. The water may not be useful for drinking or irrigation, but the seas are immensely valuable resources. This section covers the fish and the other foods that the seas provide. We will discuss marine pollution later in this chapter under environmental concerns.

Pressures on the Seas and Fisheries Human food requirements put increasing pressure on the ocean's fish, mollusks, and crustaceans. The importance of marine life as a source of food plus the demands of a growing world population increased the marine (saltwater) catch from 17 million tons in 1950, to 62 million tons in 1980, to 84 million tons recently. Salt water accounts for 63% of the world's fisheries production, with aquaculture providing 30%, and freshwater wild fisheries supplying the remaining 7%. Given an estimate by the Food and Agriculture Organization (FAO) that the sustainable annual yield of Earth's oceans is no more than 96 million tons, it is clear that a critical point is approaching rapidly. One recent study concluded that 29% of species that provide seafood had either been fished so heavily or so damaged by pollution or loss of habitat, such as reef destruction, that they had been reduced to 10% of peak levels. Most other species were also depleted to a greater or lesser degree. "I don't have a crystal ball and I don't know what the future will bring, but this is a clear trend," one researcher commented. "There is an end [to the marine fisheries] in sight, and it is within our lifetimes."[25] Given that the world's fisheries supply 15% of the animal protein humans consume, the danger to the fisheries poses a health threat to countries that rely on fish for vital protein supplies. Asia and Africa are especially imperiled, where fish contribute 20% or more to the often inadequate animal protein in the diet of the regions' inhabitants (Williams, 2005).

These shrimping boats are charging into the sea off China at the end of a 2-month long no-fishing season. Overfishing is a significant issue across the world's oceans and has even become a flashpoint for armed conflict in some instances.

Protecting Fisheries One major step at the global level came in 1994 when the UN's Convention on the Law of the Sea went into effect. Agreed to by 148 countries, but excluding the United States, the treaty gives countries full sovereignty over the seas within 12 miles of their shores and control over fishing rights and oil and gas exploration rights within 200 miles of their shores. That should improve conservation in these coastal zones. Additionally, the UN has established an International Seabed Authority, headquartered in Jamaica. It will help regulate seabed mining in international waters and will receive royalties from those mining operations to help finance ocean-protection programs.

There are also national and international efforts in other areas. A huge decline in demersal fish (such as cod, flounder, and haddock) in the northwest Atlantic prompted Canada and the United States to severely limit catches in rich fishing grounds such as the Grand Banks and the Georges Bank off their North Atlantic coasts. On an even broader scale, 99 countries, including all the major fishing countries, agreed in 1995 to an international treaty that will regulate the catch of all the species of fish (such as cod, pollock, tuna, and swordfish) that migrate between national and international waters. The treaty was part of the rapidly growing number of international pacts to regulate the marine catch that have made fishing, as one diplomat put it, "no longer a free-for-all situation."[26]

Despite its relatively minor economic impact, there is no issue of marine regulation that sparks more emotion than the control of whaling. At the center of the controversy is the International Whaling Commission (IWC), which was established in 1946. With whale populations plummeting and some species nearing extinction, the IWC banned commercial whaling in 1986. That did not end whaling, however. Norway, although an IWC member, objects to the ban and under a loophole in the IWC treaty takes about 1,000 whales a year. Japan takes another 700 whales under the pretext of scientific study, which is permitted under IWC rules, and Iceland takes 60 for science. A number of other countries or indigenous peoples add to the annual whale harvest, which totals about 1,900. Whalers take about 80% of whales each year, which are minke whales, but they also harpoon more than a half dozen other types, including sperm and humpback whales.

The controversy over whaling has occasioned strong clashes at each year's IWC meeting. Japan leads the move to abolish the moratorium, saying that the number of many species of whales makes the ban no longer necessary. However, Japan was more willing to compromise on these issues at the 2007 meeting. Critics accuse Japan of using its foreign aid to win votes on the IWC and point, for example, to the decision of landlocked Laos to join the IWC in 2007, soon after the Laotian prime minister visited Tokyo and reconfirmed its aid package to his country. However, Great Britain and other countries that oppose Japan have also been active in encouraging other landlocked, but anti-whaling countries like Slovakia to join the IWC. Those who advocate whaling claim that the minke population, which is between 300,000 and 1 million, will support limited commercial whaling. They also argue that whaling can provide an important source of food and income. As an official from Dominica put it, "This is a creature like all others that people depend upon for food, and therefore because of its abundance we think that we can take a limited amount and make some money out of it."[27] The whaling issue has also become enmeshed with issues of national pride. "There is a consensus in Japan that as part of the natural right for a sovereign nation it is perfectly right to continue whaling," explained a Japanese Ministry of Foreign Affairs official.[28] Advocates for the moratorium argue that we know too little about whale numbers and reproduction to allow commercial whaling. As for whaling for supposedly scientific study, a U.S. government statement typifies the anti-whaling view: "The United States believes that lethal research on whales is not necessary, and that the needed scientific data can be obtained by well-established nonlethal means."[29]

ASSESSING ENVIRONMENTAL QUALITY

In the carrying capacity equation we discussed near the beginning of this chapter, the growing world population and its increasing consumption of resources are only part of the problem. The third part of that equation is the increasing waste and pollution from the excretions of over 7 billion people and the untold billions of domestic animals that they keep for food or companionship and from the discharges of polluting gases, chemicals, and other types of waste into the water, air, and ground by industry, governments, and individuals.

The state of the biosphere is related to many of the economic and resource issues that we have been examining. Like the concerns over those issues, global awareness and activity are relatively recent and are still in their early stages. We have already discussed several concerns that have an environmental impact, such as desertification, deforestation, and biodiversity loss. The next sections look at threats to the quality of the ground on which we walk, the water that we drink, the air that we breathe, and to the dangers that global climate change and ozone layer depletion pose.

Ground Quality

It seems almost comical to observe that there are serious concerns about the dirt getting dirty. Ground quality is no joke, however. Industrial waste and other discharges have polluted large tracts of land, some of the largest construction projects engineered by mankind are garbage dumps (euphemistically called landfills), and destructive farming techniques have depleted the soil of its nutrients in many areas.

International Ground Quality Issues Land pollution is a significant problem, but the territorial dominance of states usually leaves this issue outside the realm of global action. Exporting solid waste for disposal does, however, have a global impact. With their disposal sites brimming and frequently dangerous, EDCs annually ship millions of tons of hazardous wastes to LDCs. Financial considerations have persuaded some LDCs to accept these toxic deliveries. Along with sending old tires, batteries, and other refuse to LDCs, the EDCs also practice *e-dumping,* shipping millions of discarded computers and other electronic devices overseas for disposal. Some 63 million computers become obsolete in the United States each year, and many of those end up overseas, supposedly for recycling. According to one report, "The Digital Dump: Exporting Reuse and Abuse to Africa," Nigeria alone receives 400,000 such computers each month.[30] What occurs, though, is that people sometimes extract small amounts of valuable minerals, such as gold, platinum, silver, copper, and palladium from some motherboards, and the rest of the unit is dumped, where it adds to ground and water pollution. In the view of one NGO report, "The export of e-waste remains a dirty little secret of the high-tech revolution."[31]

Although some shipping and receiving countries widely condemn and outlaw this practice—in essence, using LDCs as disposal sites—the UN reports that "the volume of transboundary movements of toxic wastes has not diminished." Even more alarmingly, the report warns, "The wastes are sent to poor countries lacking the infrastructure for appropriate treatment. They are usually dumped in overpopulated areas in poor regions or near towns, posing great risks to the environment and to the life and health of the poorest populations and those least able to protect themselves."[32] A closely associated international aspect of ground pollution is that it is often caused by waste disposal by **multinational corporations (MNCs)**, which may set up operations in LDCs because they have fewer environmental regulations.

Multinational corporations (MNCs) Private enterprises that have production subsidiaries or branches in more than one country.

International Efforts to Protect Ground Quality There has been progress on international dumping. The 1992 Convention on the Control of Transboundary Movements of Hazardous Wastes and Their Disposal (the Basel Convention), which 105 countries originally signed in Switzerland, limits such activity.

It has since been ratified by 172 countries, with the United States among the missing. There have also been several regional agreements, including the Bamako Convention (1998), which includes almost all African states and bans the transboundary trade in hazardous wastes on their continent, and the Waigani Convention (2001), which takes the same measures for its parties in the South Pacific. The limits in the Basel Convention were stiffened further in reaction to the continued export of hazardous wastes under the guise of declaring that the materials were meant for recycling or as foreign aid in the form of recoverable materials. At one time Great Britain alone annually exported up to 105,000 tons of such toxic foreign aid to LDCs, a practice that one British opposition leader called the "immoral . . . dumping of our environmental problems in someone else's backyard."[33] Now all such shipments for recycling and recovery purposes are banned.

Water Quality

There are two water environments: the marine (saltwater) environment and the freshwater environment. The quality of both is important.

International Water Quality Issues

Marine pollution has multiple sources. Spillage from shipping, ocean waste dumping, offshore mining, and oil and gas drilling combine for a significant part of the pollutants that pour into the oceans, seas, and other international waterways. Petroleum is a particular danger. Spills from tankers, pipelines, and other parts of the transportation system during the 1990s dumped an annual average of 110,000 tons of oil into the water, and discharges from offshore drilling accounted for another 20,000 tons. The flow of oil from seepage and dumpsites on land or oil discharge into inland waters making their way to the ocean are yet other large man-made sources, annually adding about 41,000 tons of oil to the marine environment. Some spills are spectacular, such as the August 2003 grounding on Pakistan's coast of the Greek oil tanker Tasman Spirit, which spilled 28,000 tons (7.5 million gallons), but less noticed are the many smaller spills that add to the damage.

Other major carriers of marine pollution are rivers, which serve as sewers transporting human, industrial, and agricultural waste and pollutants into the seas. The runoff from fertilizers is a major pollutant, and their annual global use at about 153 million metric tons is nearly quadruple what it was in 1960. The exploding world population, which creates ever-more intestinal waste, adds further to pollution. Many coastal cities are not served by sewage treatment facilities. Sewage is the major polluter of the Mediterranean and Caribbean seas and the ocean regions off East Africa and Southeast Asia. Industrial waste is also common. Because they often have neither modern equipment nor standards, discharges are especially common and dangerous in LDCs. During 2006, for example, China's State Environmental Protection Administration (SEPA) recorded 161 "serious" spills and many more minor ones off the coast of China, leading SEPA's deputy director to characterize 2006 as "the grimmest year for China's environmental situation."[34]

Of these pollutants, the influx of excess nitrogen into the marine system is especially damaging. Human activities, such as using fertilizers and burning fossil fuels, add about 210 million metric tons to the 140 million metric tons of nitrogen that natural processes generate. Excess nitrogen stimulates *eutrophication,* the rapid growth of algae and other aquatic plants. When these plants die in their natural cycle, the decay process strips the water of its dissolved oxygen, thereby making it increasingly uninhabitable for aquatic plants, fish, and other marine life. To make matters worse, some algae blooms are toxic and take a heavy toll on fish, birds, and marine mammals. The Baltic, Black, Caribbean, and Mediterranean seas, and other partly enclosed seas, have been heavily afflicted with eutrophication, and even ocean areas such as the northeast and northwest coasts of the United States have seen a significant increase in the number of algae blooms in the past quarter century. Inasmuch as 99% of all commercial fishing takes place within 200 miles of continental coasts, such pollution is especially damaging to fishing grounds.

Freshwater pollution of lakes and rivers is an international as well as a domestic issue. The discharge of pollutants into lakes and rivers that form international boundaries (the Great Lakes, the Rio Grande) or that flow between countries (the Rhine River) is a source of discord. Additionally, millions of tons of organic material and other pollutants that we dump into the inland rivers around the world eventually find their way to the ocean. Acid rain and other contaminants that drift across borders also cause freshwater pollution.

International Efforts to Protect Water Quality   Marine pollution control has been on the global agenda for some time, and we have made progress. One of the first multilateral efforts was the International Maritime Organization, founded in 1958, in part to promote the control of pollution from ships. Increased flows of oil and spills led to the International Convention for the Prevention of Pollution from Ships (1973). More recently, 43 countries, including the world's largest industrial countries, agreed to a global ban effective in 1995 on dumping industrial wastes in the oceans. The countries also agreed not to dispose of nuclear waste in the oceans. These efforts have made a dramatic difference for marine oil spills. During the 1970s, the average year saw 314,000 tons of oil spew into the oceans and seas. That spillage was down to 29,000 tons a year during 2000–2004. National governments are also taking valuable enforcement steps, with, for instance, the U.S. Justice Department fining 10 cruise lines a total of $48.5 million between 1993 and 2002, which hopefully went to clean-up efforts.

On another front, 152 countries (excluding Russia and the United States) have ratified the Stockholm Convention on Persistent Organic Pollutants (2001), a treaty that bans 12—the dirty dozen—pollutants, such as various insecticides, PCBs, and dioxins, that scientists have linked to birth defects and other genetic abnormalities. These pollutants contaminate water either directly, through seepage from the land, or from rainfall, and eventually enter the food chain. Some also cause other forms of destruction. DDT

Waste disposal, whether in water rich areas or not, is a challenging problem for any society. But in country's where the effectiveness of many public services have not kept pace with economic development, scenes like this one from China's Hainan province are far too common.

(**d**ichlorodiphenyl**t**richloroethane), for example, has attacked eagle and other populations by significantly reducing the chances that eggs will hatch.

Air Quality

Air is the most fundamental necessity of the biosphere. It sustains life, but it can also contain pollutants that can befoul lungs as well as the land and water. Moreover, the world's air currents ignore national boundaries, making air quality a major global concern.

International Air Quality Issues   The quality of the air that we breathe has deteriorated dramatically since the beginning of the industrial revolution. Now, air pollution from sulfur dioxide (SO_2), nitrogen dioxide (NO_2), and particulate matter (PM, such as dust and soot) causes about 2 million deaths a year, according to WHO. The majority of those are in Asia, where most of the major cities exceed WHO guidelines for suspended particles. For example, Beijing's SO_2 concentration is 4.5 times higher than the WHO's health standard, the city's NO_2 level is 3 times higher, and its suspended particulate matter is 5 times higher.

Using SO_2 as an illustration, we can dig a bit deeper in air quality issues. Sulfur is common in raw materials such as petroleum, coal, and many metal ores. SO_2 is emitted when we burn such materials for fuel or during such industrial processes as petroleum refining, cement manufacturing, and metal processing. SO_2 has numerous deleterious effects. It can cause or aggravate respiratory problems, especially in the very young and the elderly. The sulfurous gas in the atmosphere forms an acid when combined with water, and the resulting acid rain contaminates water resources and attacks forests. The damage from acid rain has followed. The United States, Canada, and Europe were the first to suffer. Especially in the northern part of the United States and in Canada, there has been extensive damage to trees, and many lakes have become so acidified that it has killed most of the fish. Europe has also suffered extensive damage. About a quarter of the continent's trees have sustained moderate to severe defoliation. The annual value of the lost lumber harvest to Europe alone is an estimated $23 billion. The ecotourism industry in once-verdant forests around the world is also in danger, imperiling jobs. The death of trees and their stabilizing root systems increases soil erosion, resulting in the silting up of lakes and rivers. The list of negative consequences could go on, but that is not necessary to make the point that acid rain is environmentally and economically devastating.

Protecting Air Quality   On the positive side, annual EDC emissions of air pollutants have declined dramatically. Since 1940, for instance, U.S. emissions have dropped 51% for SO_2, 30% for NO_2, and 80% for particulate matter. Unfortunately, spiraling levels of air pollution in the LDCs is more than offsetting the improvement in the EDCs. This is particularly true in Asia. There, analysts expect rapid industrialization, combined with the financial inability to spend the necessary tens of billions of dollars to control SO_2 emissions, to more than triple annual SO_2 emissions, from 34 million tons in 1990 to about 115 million tons in 2020. Even now, according to the World Bank, China has 16 of the 20 most polluted cities globally. Among the ill effects, China's Ministry of Science and Technology estimates that air pollution annually kills 50,000 newborn babies.

There have been several international efforts to address air quality. Some regional agreements, such as the 1985 Helsinki Protocol for reducing SO_2 emissions in Europe, have been followed by improved air quality (Ringquist & Kostadinova, 2005). Various international agencies, such as UNEP and WHO, work to warn against the danger of air pollution and help countries reduce it. Some funding is also available. For example, about 6% of the loans that the World Bank made in 2004 were for environmental improvement programs. Increasingly, a wide range of IGOs and NGOs are becoming involved in pushing an environmental agenda. The publicity surrounding the award of the 2007 Nobel Peace Prize to Al Gore and other participants on the Intergovernmental Panel on Climate Change (IPCC) is a case in point.

In the end, though, countries will have to be at the forefront of the effort to improve air quality. The costs are significant. In 2007, China's government pledged to spend $180 billion over 5 years on environmental protection. With 90% of the country's SO_2 emissions, 70% of its NO_2 emissions, and a significant part of its PM discharges produced by burning coal, China plans to devote about 10% of its environmental funds to such efforts as flue gas desulfurization. China predicts that it can meet WHO SO_2 standards by 2020, but that is a significant technological and budgetary challenge.

The Ozone Layer

Atmospheric ozone (O_3) absorbs ultraviolet (UV) rays from the sun. About 90% of all O_3 is within the ozone layer, which surrounds Earth 10 to 30 miles above the planet. Without it, human life could not exist.

Ozone Layer Depletion   There is little doubt that the ozone layer has thinned or that the consequences are perilous. Emissions of chlorofluorocarbons (CFCs), a chemical group prevalent in refrigerators, air conditioners, products such as Styrofoam, many spray can propellants, fire extinguishers, and industrial solvents, are attacking the ozone layer. The chemical effect of the CFCs is to deplete the ozone by turning it into atmospheric oxygen (O_2), which does not block ultraviolet rays. This ozone layer thinning increases the penetration through the atmosphere of ultraviolet-B (UV-B) rays, which cause cancers and other mutations in life-forms below. Chapter 1 noted the impact of this on Americans. Australia and New Zealand have measured temporary increases of as much as 20% in UV-B radiation, and light-skinned Australians have the world's highest skin cancer rate. Another possible deleterious effect of increased UV-B bombardment came to light during a study of the water surrounding Antarctica. Over the area, a hole 3.86 million square miles in size—about the size of Europe and with as much as a 70% depletion of atmospheric O_3—occurs annually. There scientists found evidence of a 6 to 12% decline in plankton organisms during the period of the annual ozone hole. Such losses at the bottom of the food chain could restrict the nutrition and health of fish and eventually of humans farther up the food chain. Ozone levels over the rest of the world have declined less than over the South Pole, but they are still down about 10% since the 1950s.

Protecting the Ozone Layer   Among its other accomplishments, the UNEP sponsored a 1987 conference in Montreal to discuss protection of the ozone layer. There, 46 countries agreed to reduce their CFC production and consumption by

Global climate change
The significant and lasting change in weather patterns over periods ranging from decades to millions of years. Both anthropogenic (human induced) and natural causes have been identified by climate scientists.

Greenhouse gases (GHGs)
Carbon dioxide, methane, chlorofluorocarbons, and other gases that create a blanket effect by trapping heat and preventing the nightly cooling of Earth.

Greenhouse effect
The accumulation of carbon dioxide and other gases in Earth's atmosphere that causes rising global temperatures.

50% before the end of the century. Country participants negotiated subsequent amendments to the Montreal Convention at quadrennial conferences, the last of which took place in Montreal in 2007, to commemorate the 20th anniversary of the convention. At that meeting, signatories agreed to accelerate phasing out CFCs, as there is belief that CFC reduction also plays a role in combating climate change.

As a result of the original 1987 agreement, there is relatively good news on ozone depletion. The annual buildup of CFC concentrations reversed itself from 5% in the 1980s, to a slight decline beginning in 1994, only 7 years after the Montreal Convention. Somewhat modifying this good news is the fact that the CFC buildup had increased so rapidly in the years before 1987, that it will take many decades before the damage substantially reverses. Moreover, even that is far from certain. The most important caveat has to do with the economic advancement of the LDCs. The substitutes for CFCs in refrigerants and other products are expensive, and the cost estimates of phasing out CFCs worldwide range up to $40 billion. Therefore LDCs will be hard-pressed to industrialize and provide their citizens with a better standard of living while simultaneously abandoning the production and use of CFCs. For example, refrigerators, which not long ago were rare in China, are becoming increasingly commonplace. China has pledged to end CFC production by 2010, but it still has 27 CFC plants operating, and ending production with outside help now would be better than ending it (hopefully) alone later.

Global Climate Change

Over the past two decades, **global climate change** has become the leading global environmental concern and point of controversy. Global climate change's place at center stage was symbolized in 2007 by former Vice President Al Gore Jr., as he stepped up to claim his Oscar award for the documentary *An Inconvenient Truth*. Gore told the Hollywood audience and several hundred million television viewers that addressing global climate change was not just a political issue, but a moral issue. "We have everything we need to get started," he urged, "with the possible exception of the will to act." As if to second the call to action, singer Melissa Etheridge also received an Oscar for the movie's theme song, "I Need to Wake Up." There can be little doubt that Earth is warming, but what Gore and many others believe is that its cause is the accumulation in the upper atmosphere of carbon dioxide (CO_2) and other **greenhouse gases (GHGs)**, especially methane and chlorofluorocarbons, generated mostly by human activity. These gases create a blanket effect, trapping heat and preventing the nightly cooling of Earth. Reduced cooling means warmer days, which produces the **greenhouse effect**. This is similar to the way that an agricultural greenhouse builds up heat by permitting incoming solar radiation to come in, but hinders the outward flow of heat.

Climate change is not just about rising temperatures, but also focuses our attention on the increased incidence of severe weather. This May 2011, post-tornado scene from Joplin, Missouri, is only one instance of severe weather from a very active tornado season that year.

climate change of the next half century would come to between $5 trillion and $8 trillion. We can put this into context by taking that year's global GNP ($31.5 trillion), projecting it out over 50 years ($1.56 quadrillion), and calculating that $8 trillion would come to 0.5% of that total. Compounding the puzzle even more, the longer-term the economic projections are, the less reliable they inevitably become. Regarding such projections, one economist commented, "Going past 2050, the cleverness really has to kick in."[43]

The Costs of Halting or Substantially Slowing Global Climate Change   Projections of what it will cost economically and in terms of lifestyle to address global climate change also range widely, with neotraditionalists saying that the cost will be high and the modernists prone to predicting lower costs. It would take volumes to cover the different cost estimates, and resolving them is impossible because they rest on vastly different assumptions, just as do the estimates of the economic impact of climate change. What is safe to say is that there will be significant costs that will have an impact on people's wallets or their lifestyles or both. Consider, for example, one existing proposal for a U.S. tax on CO_2 emissions of $14 a ton to promote conservation and to raise money to combat global climate change.[44] That translates to an added tax of about 12 cents a gallon on gasoline. Given that Americans drive 9,800 miles a year per capita (not per driver) and the U.S. government estimates that the average private vehicle gets 17.1 mpg, that comes to an added annual tax of $69 per person, or $276 for a family of four. The cost of electricity from coal- and oil-fuel plants would also increase, and people would pay more for a wide range of goods because of the added cost of producing and delivering them. Surely, such costs might be lower than the expense of dealing with the damage from climate change. The bottom line, as one economist puts it, is "There's no easy way around the fact that if global warming is a serious risk, there will be serious costs" from its damage, the costs to address it, or both.[45] There is also wisdom in the observation, "It's important for the people arguing for action to make the case that it's worth it, rather than the promise that it will be free."[46]

The International Response to Global Climate Change   The early movement toward addressing global climate change came at the World Climate Conference (WCC, 1990), at which most EDCs other than the United States made nonbinding pledges to stabilize or reduce greenhouse gas emissions, and Earth Summit I's Global Warming Convention (1992, more formally the United Nations Framework Convention on Climate Change, UNFCCC), whereby virtually all countries, including the United States, agreed to ease pressure on the climate and to work toward a global solution through annual meetings to discuss policy.

The Kyoto Protocol   During the 1997 round of these discussions in Kyoto, Japan, delegates drafted a supplement to the treaty called the **Kyoto Protocol**. This agreement came after intense negotiations, often divided along familiar North–South lines. The South wanted the EDCs to cut GHG emissions by 12% to 15% by 2012, and to provide the LDCs with massive new aid to cut pollution. Most EDCs found neither of these proposals acceptable. The EDCs wanted the LDCs to commit to upper limits on future emissions, but the LDCs rejected this idea,

Kyoto Protocol
A supplement to the Global Warming Convention (1992) that requires the economically developed countries to reduce greenhouse gas emissions by about 7% below their 1990 levels by 2012 and encourages, but does not require, less developed countries to reduce emissions.

arguing, "Very many of us are struggling to attain a decent standard of living for our people. And yet we are constantly told that we must share in the effort to reduce emissions so that industrialized countries can continue to enjoy the benefits of their wasteful lifestyle."[47] The compromise was to require the EDCs to reduce GHG emissions by about 7% below their 1990 levels by 2012, and to urge, but not require, LDCs to do what they can to restrain GHG emissions. The protocol specified that it would go into effect when ratified by at least 55 countries representing at least 55% of the world's emissions of GHG at that point. Some participants met those standards in 2005, and by mid-2007, 173 countries had ratified the treaty (Fisher, 2004).

Of the handful of countries that have not ratified the treaty, the United States is the most prominent. Although Vice President Gore was the chief U.S. negotiator in Kyoto and signed the protocol on behalf of the United States, President Clinton did not send it to the Republican-controlled Congress for ratification because he knew it faced certain death there. Among other indications, the Republican leader in the Senate condemned the Kyoto Protocol as a "flawed treaty" that would cripple the U.S. economy.[48] The election of President Bush in 2000 ended any immediate chance of U.S. adherence to the treaty. One reason he cited for his opposition is the lack of requirements for LDCs. "It is ineffective, inadequate, and unfair to America," he told reporters, "because it exempts 80% of the world, including major population centers such as China and India, from compliance."[49] Bush also argued that complying with "the Kyoto treaty would severely damage the United States' economy." Placing himself squarely in the camp of environmental optimists, he argued, "We can grow our economy and, at the same time, through technologies, improve our environment."[50]

Recent Developments   More recently, the debate over what to do about global climate change has heated up anew. The change has been driven by the increasingly certain IPCC declarations that global climate change is man-made, amid increasingly dramatic warnings about the impact of global climate change; by the campaign of Al Gore and such other events as the Live Earth concerts held around the world in July 2007, featuring entertainers including Bon Jovi, Madonna, and Snoop Dogg; and by the 2007 Democratic recapture of Congress and the end of Bush's presidency in 2009.

Among other initiatives, in 2007, Great Britain introduced global climate change for the first time as a topic in the UN Security Council, arguing that it presented a threat to world security. British Foreign Secretary Margaret Beckett contended, "Our responsibility in this Council is to maintain international peace and security, including the prevention of conflict. An unstable climate will exacerbate some of the core drivers of conflict, such as migratory pressures and competition for resources."[51] However, the ongoing North–South divide stymied the British effort, with China's representative rejecting the initiative on the grounds that "the developing countries believe that the Security Council has neither the professional competence in handling climate change, nor is it the right decision-making place for extensive participation leading up to widely acceptable proposals."[52] The European countries and Canada also pushed hard for a strong statement of the G-8 leaders (see chapter 9) at their 2007 meeting in Germany, but the United States insisted on moderating the language.

In part, all such efforts were skirmishes leading up to the 2007 round of WCC talks held in Bali, Indonesia, and its agenda for extending the Kyoto Protocol beyond 2013 (the year that it expires) and expanding its limitations on GHG emissions. After much discord, primarily centering on differences between the United States and European approaches to the issues at hand, the WCC produced a roadmap for future negotiations as the primary Bali outcome. Unfortunately, it was also clear that the many participants were negotiating from the assumption that the next U.S. administration would be more cooperative on climate change than Bush 2. Nonetheless, regardless of the U.S. approach, it remains clear that developing world countries will bear the brunt of negative climate change impacts in the near term. In addition, how the world copes with the "industrializing threats" that China and India pose is likely the gravest threat to real progress on climate change, even if the Obama administration is more inclined to engage in this debate. And who knows what the 2012 United States' presidential election will bring in terms of the American perspective on coping with climate change.

Arguably, the Durban conference held in late 2012 made some progress on GHG mitigation, but critics of the agreement contend that what was decided is too little, too late and little more than a pledge to try to continue talking about the threats posed by climate change. If nothing else, Durban was a success in keeping the UNFCCC process on track for the future when many saw the process as dead or at least dying. It also signified a recommitment by the EU and some other industrialized countries to the Kyoto Protocol beyond its 2013 expiration. However, we might consider Durban "a failure in terms of the expectations of certain countries, like the small island states . . . who wanted a much stronger agreement."[53] Such states face the most direct and imminent climate impacts in the coming years. In the end, it is not illogical to assume that the need to adapt to significant climate impacts (like rising sea levels, temperature impacts, and changing growing seasons) may prompt more fruitful action in future rounds of negotiations. As one climate activist recently said, the need for climate "adaptation may be the back-door" to progress on climate mitigation.[54]

CRITICAL THINKING QUESTIONS

1. Is the concept of sustainable development applied fairly to all countries around the world?

2. Are multilateral organizations and conferences effective ways to pursue environmental quality? Why or why not?

3. How urgent is the need for action to preserve or remediate environmental quality around the globe?

4. Which environmental issues are the most pressing for the global community to engage? Explain your answer.

5. What are the major roadblocks to global environmental cooperation historically and in the years ahead?

chapter summary

- This chapter focuses on global ecological concerns and cooperation. Self-interest—some people would say the demands of survival—compels us to attend to issues concerning the world's expanding population, the depletion of natural resources, the increase of chemical discharges into the environment, and the impact of these trends on the global biosphere.

- A key concept and goal is sustainable development. The key questions are how to ensure that LDCs develop industrially, how to maintain the standard of living in the EDCs, and how to also simultaneously protect the environment. Given the justifiable determination of the LDCs to develop economically, the potential for accelerated resource depletion and pollution production is very high.

- There is a wide range of views about how great the threats to the biosphere are and what we can and should do to address them.

- Population is a significant problem facing the world, with the global population surpassing the 7 billion mark.

- At the center of any concept about sustainable development, and sustainability more generally, are decisions about how to balance population growth with our use of resources.

- Increasing population and industrialization have rapidly accelerated the use of a wide range of natural resources. It is possible, using known resources and current use rates, to project that petroleum, natural gas, and a variety of minerals will be totally depleted within the present century. The world's forests, its supply of freshwater, and its wildlife are also under population and industrialization pressure. There are many international governmental and nongovernmental organizations and efforts, symbolized by the 1992 Earth Summit and its following summits, to address these problems.

- Population growth and industrialization are also responsible for mounting ground pollution, water pollution, air pollution, global climate change, and ozone layer depletion due to atmospheric pollution. Work in other areas, such as reducing CO_2 emissions, has only just begun and is difficult because of the high costs.

- The efforts at international cooperation discussed in this chapter return us to fundamental questions about pursuing agreement and action at the global level. As we discussed in chapter 4 on globalization, those on the local level increasingly are feeling and coping with many global issues. Many environmental problems illustrate the global-local linkage clearly.

- It is easy to view the vast extent of the problems facing the globe, to measure the limited effort we are making to resolve them, and to dismiss the entire subject of international cooperation as superficial. It is true that we are not doing nearly enough. However, it is also true that only a very few decades ago nobody was doing anything. From that limited historical vantage point, the progress we have made over the past 50 years is encouraging, though in a muted way. The primary question is whether we will continue to expand our efforts and whether we will do enough soon enough to forestall truly catastrophic environmental problems.

key terms

adaptation
anthropogenic
biosphere
carrying capacity
ecosystem
fertility rate
global climate change
Green Revolution

greenhouse effect
greenhouse gases (GHGs)
Kyoto Protocol
mitigation
modernists
multinational corporations
(MNCs)
neotraditionalists

sustainable development
UN Conference on Environment
and Development (UNCED)
UN Conference on Population and
Development (UNCPD)
World Health Organization (WHO)
World Summit on Sustainable
Development (WSSD)

glossary

Adaptation The process or outcome of a process that leads to a reduction in harm or risk of harm or to realization of benefits associated with climate variability and climate change. [12]

Adjudication Referral of an ongoing dispute to an impartial third-party tribunal (either a board of arbitrators or a standing court) for the rendering of a binding legal decision. [8]

Aggression In its broadest sense, aggression is behavior, or a disposition, that is forceful, hostile, or attacking. It may occur either in retaliation or without provocation. In global politics, aggression is reflected in the tensions between states that produce arms races, militarized interstate disputes, and war. While there is no universally accepted definition of aggression in international law, an unprovoked military attack by one state on another is a commonly understood act of aggression. [7]

Alliance A formal political association between two or more parties, made in order to advance common goals and to secure common interests. [6]

Amorality The philosophical viewpoint that morality cannot and/or should not be a guide for human actions and decisions. [8]

Anarchical global system The traditional structure of world politics in which there is no central authority to set and enforce rules and resolve disputes. [1]

Anarchy A fundamental concept in the study of global politics derived from the insights of Thomas Hobbes regarding the "state of nature," which contends that global politics is best understood as a self-help struggle for survival between and among states and other actors given the lack of any effective overarching central governing authority in the system. [1, 2, 6]

Anthropogenic Caused or produced by humans. [12]

Anti-Personnel Mine Ban Convention (aka. the Ottawa Treaty) A treaty drafted and signed in 1997 that aims at eliminating anti-personnel landmines around the world through specific terms requiring parties to cease production of anti-personnel mines, destroy existing stockpiles, and clear away all mined areas within their sovereign territory. Associated with the public diplomacy of Canadian diplomat Lloyd Axworthy and the late Princess Diana (U.K.), as of late 2011, there were 159 states-parties to the treaty, with two states (the Marshall Islands and Poland) signing but not ratifying the treaty and 35 states remaining nonsignatories. [6]

Arms control A variety of approaches to the limitation of weapons. Arms control ranges from restricting the future growth in the number, types, or deployment of weapons; through the reduction of weapons; to the elimination of some types (or even all) weapons on a global or regional basis. [6]

Arrearages The state of being behind in the discharge of obligations, often an unpaid or overdue debt. [5]

Asia-Pacific Economic Cooperation (APEC) A regional trade organization founded in 1989 that now includes 21 countries. [9]

Asymmetric warfare A strategy of conflict employed by a weaker actor in contending with a stronger one, in an attempt to "level the playing field." Terrorism is the most often cited example of asymmetric warfare, given the disparities in power and capabilities that often exist between states and non–state actors. Unconventional weapons, such as biological, chemical, or nuclear weapons, are also instruments of asymmetric warfare. [7]

Autarky/autarkic state A completely or nearly completely inwardly directed society with little or no connections to the outside world. [2]

Authoritarian A government that centralizes and exercises power and administers society with little or no input from or participation by the governed. [2]

Authoritarianism A type of restrictive governmental system in which people are under the rule of an individual, such as a dictator or king, or a group, such as a party or military junta. [3]

Balance of power A concept that describes the degree of equilibrium (balance) or disequilibrium (imbalance) of power in the global or regional system. [2, 6]

Balancing Refers to the act of states responding to the threat of an emergent (international) power or coalition of powers by banding together to balance against that emergent state or states. Balancing behavior typically requires a coordination of effort and objectives among numerous countries in order to effectively forestall or limit the perceived instability associated with an unchecked rising power—with the chief objective stability, order, and *stasis* in the system. One of the most prominent historical examples of a balancing arrangement was the Concert of Europe, which prevailed through much of the 19th century. [6]

Bandwagoning Refers to the act of a weaker sovereign state or states joining a stronger (international) power or coalition as a subordinate partner with the expectation of deriving gains by riding on the "coattails" of that rising power. Quincy Wright coined the term in *A Study of War* in 1942, but it was popularized by Kenneth Waltz in his 1979 work *Theory of International Politics* and further refined by Steven Walt in his 1987 book *The Origins of Alliances*. [6]

Behavioralism A mid-twentieth century turn toward promoting the study of social and political phenomena using the scientific method—including, but not limited to, hypothesis testing and empirical analysis. [2]

Bilateral trade agreement (BTA) A free trade agreement between two countries or between a regional trade agreement and any other non-member country. [9]

Biological weapons Living organisms or replicating entities (viruses) that reproduce or replicate within their host victims. May be employed in various ways to gain a strategic or tactical advantage over an adversary, either by threats or by actual deployments. [6]

Biosphere Earth's ecological system (ecosystem) that supports life—its land, water, air, and upper atmosphere—and the living organisms, including humans, that inhabit it. [12]

Bipolarity/bipolar system A type of international system with two roughly equal actors or coalitions of actors that divide the international system into two "poles" or power centers. [2, 6]

Bloc Grouping of materially interdependent and (often) ideologically aligned states. [2]

Bounded rationality A concept developed by the Nobel Prize winning economist Herbert Simon that suggests the rational choices of individuals are in fact bound or limited by the reality that time pressures, imperfect information, and bias influence those choices. [2]

Bretton Woods System of monetary management that established the rules for commercial and financial relations among the world's major industrial states in the mid-twentieth century. The Bretton Woods system was the first example of a fully negotiated monetary order intended to govern monetary relations among independent nation-states. [9]

Bureaucracy The bulk of the state's administrative structure that continues even when political leaders change. [2, 5]

Capabilities In global politics, the power and influence available to an actor as a function of its tangible power assets. [2]

Capitalism An economic system based on the private ownership of the means of production and distribution of goods, competition, and profit incentives. [9]

Carrying capacity The number of people that an environment, such as Earth, can feed, provide water for, and otherwise sustain. [12]

Cartel An international agreement among producers of a commodity that attempts to control the production and pricing of that commodity. [10]

Chapter VII Part of the Charter of the United Nations that deals with action with respect to threats to peace, breaches of the peace, and acts of aggression. [11]

Chemical weapons Devices that use chemical agents that inflict death or harm to human beings. They are classified as weapons of mass destruction. [6]

"Clash of civilizations" Samuel P. Huntington's thesis (1993, 1996) that the source of future conflict will be along "civilizational" (e.g., cultural) lines, with conflicts emerging at the "fault lines" or interfaces of the most contentious of the world's major civilizational units. [6, 7]

Classical liberalism A subdivision of liberal thought that is optimistic about human nature and believes that people can achieve more collectively than individually, that people understand this, and, therefore, given the opportunity people will seek to work together in their common, long-term interests. [1]

Classical realism A subdivision of realist thought that believes the root cause of conflict is the aggressive nature of humans. [1]

Codify To write down a law in formal language. [8]

Cognitive consistency The psychological tendency of individuals to hold fast to their prevailing view of how the world works, and to discount ideas and information that may contradict that view. [2]

Cognitive dissonance A discordant psychological state in which an individual encounters and attempts to process information that contradicts his or her prevailing understanding of a subject. [2]

Cold War The confrontation that emerged following World War II between the bipolar superpowers, the Soviet Union and the United States. Although no direct conflict took place between these countries, it was an era of great tensions and global division. [2]

Collective security Stemming from the belief that peace and stability are global public goods, collective security holds that an act of aggression against one state constitutes an act of aggression against all members in good standing of the international community, and therefore is deserving of a collective response. A fundamental premise underpinning the peace and security strategies and operations of the UN, numerous other international organizations, and many states. [6]

Commodity agreements International agreements to stabilize commodity prices in the interest of producers and consumers. They can include mechanisms to influence market prices by adjusting export quotas and production when market prices reach certain trigger price levels. [10]

Communism An ideology that originated in the works of Friedrich Engels and Karl Marx; it is essentially an economic theory. As such, it is the idea that an oppressed proletariat class of workers would eventually organize and revolt against those who owned the means of production, the bourgeoisie; a political system of government applied in China, and elsewhere, wherein the state owns the means of production as a system to expedite Engels and Marx's economic theory. [3]

Competent authority In the just war tradition, the premise that the "right" to wage war can only be extended from a legitimate source of authority with the moral and legal standing to issue such an order. The classical translation of "competent authority" in just war theory was clerical officials, whereas the modern translation associates such authority with the sovereign state and, in some cases, international organizations. [8]

Complex interdependence A term most associated with the liberal theorists Robert Keohane and Joseph Nye (see *Power and Interdependence*, 1977), complex interdependence refers to the broad and deep interdependence of issues and actors in the contemporary global political system, and the ways in which this condition structures and conditions the conduct of global politics. Many scholars point to complex interdependence, as a byproduct of globalization, as evidence of both the existence and future prospects of cooperation in global politics—particularly emphasizing the extent of international institutions that have emerged in attempts to "govern" the multiple and complex interactions associated with it. [1, 2, 5, 6]

Complex peacekeeping International, multidimensional operations comprising of a mix of military, police, and civilian components working together to lay the foundations of a sustainable peace; tasks include traditional monitoring and ceasefire enforcement as well as the monitoring of democratic elections, disarmament programs, and human rights documentation. [5]

Comprehensive Test Ban Treaty (CTBT) Bans all nuclear explosions in all environments for military or civilian purposes. The United Nations

General Assembly adopted it on September 10, 1996, but it has not entered into force as of 2012. [6]

Compulsory jurisdiction In international law, the premise that states or other parties are or would be compelled to submit in full to the legal authority of a standing international court. Jurists view compulsory jurisdiction as key to the successful functioning of a court and legal system. In international legal practice, compulsory jurisdiction remains something of an ideal, as most courts—such as the International Court of Justice—feature a system of jurisdiction in which states consent to the court's jurisdiction on a negotiated, ad hoc basis. [8]

Concert of Europe The balance of power that existed in Europe from the end of the Napoleonic Wars (1815) to the outbreak of World War I (1914). Its founding powers included Austria, Prussia, the Russian Empire, and the United Kingdom, the "Quadruple Alliance" responsible for the downfall of the First French Empire. The chief function of the Concert of Europe was maintaining stability and averting major wars between and among the great powers of the continent, while also policing skirmishes and disputes along its periphery. [2, 7]

Conditionality The policy of the International Monetary Fund, the World Bank, and some other international financial agencies to attach conditions to their loans and grants. These conditions may require recipient countries to devalue their currencies, to lift controls on prices, to cut their budgets, and to reduce barriers to trade and capital flows. Such conditions are often politically unpopular, may cause at least short-term economic pain, and are construed by critics as interference in recipient countries' sovereignty. [9]

Containment A cornerstone of U.S. foreign policy during the Cold War, devised by George Kennan, that sought to prevent the spread of communism through a mix of coercive

diplomacy, strong alliances, and military strength. [6]

Convention on Cluster Munitions This treaty, adopted by 107 states in Dublin, Ireland, on May 30, 2008, prohibits all use, stockpiling, production, and transfer of cluster munitions (a form of air-dropped or ground-launched explosive weapon that releases or ejects smaller submunitions). [6]

Convention on the Rights of the Child (CRC) (1989) A human rights treaty setting out the civil, political, economic, social, health, and cultural rights of children. The Convention generally defines a child as any human being under the age of 18. [11]

Credibility In global politics, the power and influence available to an actor as a function of its reputation and ability and willingness to follow through on its commitments and threats. [2]

Crimes against humanity As defined by the Rome Statute (establishing the International Criminal Court) in 1998, actions that "constitute an assault on human dignity or grave humiliation or degradation of one or more human beings." Crimes against humanity—which can include murder, extermination, torture, rape, and other inhumane acts—are not isolated events, but rather official government policy or a systematic practice tolerated or condoned by a government or *de facto* political authority. [8]

Critical radicalism Theory that views economic structure as a primary factor shaping political relationships and the power they engender. Critical radicals contend that the world is divided between have and have-not countries and that the *haves* (the EDCs) work to keep the *have-nots* (the LDCs) weak and poor in order to exploit them. To change this structural situation, critical radicals generally favor a restructuring of the economic system to end the uneven distribution of wealth and power. [9]

Cultural relativism The principle that an individual human's beliefs and activities are understood by others in terms of that individual's own culture. [11]

Current dollars The value of the dollar in the year for which it is reported. Sometimes called *inflated dollars*. Any currency can be expressed in current value. [9]

Customary law In international law, this refers to the Law of Nations or the legal norms that have developed through the customary exchanges between states over time, whether based on diplomacy or aggression. [11]

Debt crisis When a national government cannot pay the debt it owes and seeks, as a result, some form of assistance. [10]

Decolonization The undoing of colonialism, the unequal relation of polities in which one people or nation establishes and maintains dependent territory over another. [10]

Defensive realism An explanation of war and armed conflict in international relations rooted in the realist appreciation of states, power, and anarchy. Defensive realists contend that war is a by-product of the anarchical nature of the international system; states and their leaders typically do not choose war, but the mutual and sometimes incompatible quest for security by states inherently produces armed conflict. [7]

Democracy A system of government that at minimum extends to citizens a range of political rights and a range of civil liberties that are important to free government. [3]

Democratic A type of government established on the premise that input and consent from the governed are necessary to the exercise of power and administration of society—and that the governed have an obligation to participate fully as citizens in the political system. [2]

Democratic internationalism The theoretical perspective that the basic political and moral concerns of people will conflict with imperial domination and violence, and thus, people can, through political activity from below, place a (democratic) check on abuses of power and inclinations to go to war. [4]

Dependency theory The belief that the industrialized North has created a neo-colonial relationship with the South in which the less developed countries are dependent on and disadvantaged by their economic relations with the capitalist industrial countries. [9]

Deterrence Persuading an opponent not to carry out an undesirable action by combining both sufficient capabilities and credible threats so as to forestall that action. [6]

Development capital Equity funding for the expansion of established and profitable firms, which is generally less risky and more rewarding than funding new ventures. [9]

Diaspora The movement, migration, or scattering of people away from an established homeland. [7]

Diplomatic immunity The notion, long embedded in international norms and practice, that holds that official diplomatic emissaries of a sovereign state are to be largely immune from prosecution under the laws and procedures of the foreign country to which they are dispatched. Formalized in the Vienna Convention on Diplomatic Relations (1961), diplomatic immunity has a much longer history in customary law as a reciprocal practice designed to facilitate the work and ensure the safe passage of foreign diplomats by removing the potential for legal and political persecution. [8]

Diplomatic recognition The formal recognition of one state's sovereignty by another, extended through the establishment of an embassy and/or consular relations and subsequent diplomatic interactions. Diplomatic recognition is a key defining condition of state sovereignty, suggesting the relational and subjective aspect of sovereignty. [3]

Disarmament The act of reducing, limiting, or abolishing a category of weapons. [6]

Discrimination In the just war tradition, the premise that the conduct of war must be directed solely toward enemy combatants, and not toward noncombatants, who should be immune from attack, injury, or reprisal. [8]

Diversionary theory of war Identifies a war a country's leader instigates in order to distract its population from their own domestic strife. [7]

Doha Round The ninth and latest round of GATT negotiations to reduce barriers to international free economics interchange. The round is named after the 2001 WTO ministerial meeting in Doha, Qatar, where agreement to try to negotiate a new round of reductions in barriers by 2005 was reached. [9]

Due process The legal principle that the state must respect in full the rights of the individual within the legal system, allowing judges to define matters of fundamental fairness and justice. [8]

Dumping Any type of predatory pricing, especially in the context of international trade. It occurs when manufacturers export a product to another country at a price either below the price charged in its home market, or in quantities normal market competition cannot explain. [10]

Economic nationalism The realpolitik theory that the state should use its economic strength to further national interests. By extension, economic nationalists advocate using state power to build a state's economic strength. To accomplish their ends, economic nationalists rely on a number of political-economic strategies that often result in the exploitation of weaker countries. [9]

Economically developed countries (EDCs) Countries with high levels of economic development. Indicators include low birth, death, and infant mortality rates; less than 10% of the workforce in agriculture; and high levels of nutrition, secondary schooling, literacy, electricity consumption per head, and among the highest levels of GDP per capita globally. [9]

Ecosystem A biological system consisting of all the living organisms in a particular area and the nonliving components with which the organisms interact, such as air, minerals, soil, water, and sunlight. [12]

"End of history" In the study of global politics, the "End of History" refers to Francis Fukuyama's thesis (1989, 1992) that the end of the Cold War marked the complete and total triumph of liberalism and therefore the end of "history" (defined by the 19th-century German philosopher Friedrich Hegel as the dialectical struggles produced by the existence of contending ideologies). [6, 7]

Energy security Term for an association between national security and the availability of natural resources for energy consumption. The uneven distribution of energy supplies among countries has led to significant vulnerabilities. [6]

The Enlightenment A cultural movement of intellectuals in 18th-century Europe and America whose purpose was to reform society and advance knowledge. It promoted science and intellectual interchange and opposed superstition, intolerance, and abuses in church and state. [3, 11]

Ethnonational group/ethnonationalism A strain of nationalism that is marked by the desire of an ethnic community to have absolute authority over its own political, economic, and social affairs. Therefore, it denotes the pursuit of statehood on the part of an ethnic nation. Ethnonationalist movements signify the perception among members of a particular ethnic group that the group's interests are not being served under prevailing political arrangements. [3]

Euro (€) The official currency of the Euro zone, used by 17 of the 27 member-states of the EU. [5]

European Coal and Steel Community (ECSC) A six-nation international organization that served to unify Western Europe during the Cold War and created the foundation for the modern-day developments of the European Union. The ECSC was the first organization based on the principles of supranationalism. [5]

European Commission A 27-member commission with shared executive power that serves as the bureaucratic organ of the European Union. [5]

European Communities (EC) Established in 1967, the EC was a single unit whose plural name (Communities) reflects the fact that it united the European Coal and Steel Community, the European Economic Community, and the European Atomic Energy Community under one organizational structure. The EC evolved into the European Union beginning in 1993. [5]

European Council An EU institution, formally recognized in the Treaty of Lisbon in 2009, comprising the heads of state or government of the EU member-states, along with the President of the European Commission and the President of the Council of the European Union. [5]

European Court of Human Rights (ECHR) A supranational court located in Strasbourg, France, originally established by the European Convention on Human Rights in 1959 to adjudicate complaints concerning the violation of the human rights stipulated in that agreement from individuals or other states against the 47 states that are parties to the Convention. The ECHR's authority has been formally recognized by the Council of Europe, but it is not formally an institution of the European Union (though all member-states of the EU are members of the Council of Europe and parties to the European Convention on Human Rights). [8]

European Court of Justice (ECJ) A supranational court that serves as the "high court" in the European Union (astride the Court of First Instance and Court of Auditors) and is responsible for the enforcement of European Union "community law" and ensuring its application across and within all 27 current EU member-states. Based in Luxembourg, the ECJ was first established by the Treaty of Paris (creating the European Coal and Steel Community, the earliest forerunner to the EU) in 1952. It is comprised of one judge per member-state, though typically hears cases in panels of 3, 5, or 13 justices. Individuals, private firms, and various other non–state actors as well as member-states are parties to the ECJ. [5, 8]

European Parliament (EP) The 626-member legislative branch of the European Union. Representation is determined by population of member-countries and is based on 5-year terms. [5]

European Union (EU) The European regional organization established in 1993 when the Maastricht Treaty went into effect. The EU encompasses the still legally existing European Communities (EC). When the EC was formed in 1967, it in turn encompassed three still legally existing regional organizations formed in the 1950s: the European Coal and Steel Community (ECSC), the European Economic Community (EEC), and the European Atomic Energy Community (EURATOM). [4, 5]

Exceptionalism The belief of some that their nation or identity group is better than others. [3]

Exchange rates The values of two currencies relative to each other—for example, how many yen equal a dollar or how many yuan equal a euro. [9]

Failed/failing state(s) Countries in which political and economic upheaval are compounded by the fact that all or most of the citizens give their primary political loyalty to an ethnic group, a religious group, or some other source of political identity rather than the state itself. Such states are so fragmented that no one political group can govern effectively, undermining the capacity of the state and the security and well-being of those residing in the affected society. [3, 6]

Fascism An ideology that advocates extreme nationalism, with a heightened sense of national belonging or ethnic identity. [3]

Fertility rate The average number of children who would be born to a woman over her lifetime if she were to experience the exact current age-specific fertility rates through her lifetime, and were she to survive from birth through the end of her reproductive life. [12]

First generation rights Based on the principles of individualism and non-interference, these are "negative" rights based on the Anglo-American principles of liberty. Developed under a strong mistrust of government, they have evolved into "civil" or "political" rights. [11]

Fiscal year (FY) A budget year, which may or may not be the same as the calendar year. The U.S. fiscal year runs from October 1 through September 30 and is referred to by its ending date. Thus, FY2007 ran from October 1, 2006, through September 30, 2007. [1]

Flexible response A defense strategy John F. Kennedy implemented in 1961 to address his administration's skepticism of Dwight Eisenhower's "New Look" and its policy of massive retaliation. Flexible response calls for mutual deterrence at strategic, tactical, and conventional levels, giving the United States the capability to respond to aggression across the spectrum of warfare, not limited only to nuclear arms. [6]

Foreign direct investment (FDI) Buying stock, real estate, and other assets in another country with the aim of gaining a controlling interest in foreign economic enterprises. Different from portfolio investment, which involves investment solely to gain capital appreciation through market fluctuations. [9]

Former Soviet republics (FSRs) These are 15 independent states that seceded from the Union of Soviet Socialist Republics in its dissolution in December 1991. They include Armenia, Azerbaijan, Belarus, Estonia, Georgia, Kazakhstan, Kyrgyzstan, Latvia, Lithuania, Moldova, Russia, Tajikistan, Turkmenistan, Ukraine, and Uzbekistan. [10]

Frustration-aggression theory A psychologically based theory that frustrated societies sometimes become collectively aggressive. [2]

Functional relations Sometimes referred to as "low politics," a term that designates more routine and less politically fraught activities in global politics such as trade, diplomatic interactions, and communications. International law and global governance has expanded further in functional relations due to the relative willingness of states to concede more sovereignty relative to these areas of activity. [8]

Functionalism A theoretical perspective that explains cooperation between governance structures by focusing on the basic needs of people and states to interact on specific issue areas, such as communications, trade, travel, health, or environmental protection activity. [5]

Fundamental attribution error (correspondence bias) The tendency to overrate or overemphasize personality and disposition when explaining the observed behavior of others, while underrating or underemphasizing situational or contextual factors. Also known as *correspondence bias,* this concept suggests that the exact opposite tendency is the case when seeking to comprehend one's own behavior—personality and disposition are deemphasized, and context and situational factors taken into account. [2]

Fundamentalist/traditionalist Someone who holds very conservative religiously based political values and typically wishes to incorporate those beliefs into legal and political systems. [4]

Fungible A term common to the study of economics referring to the degree of convertibility of currency or other economic assets into a desired good or service. [2]

G-20 A standing forum for economic summitry amongst sectoral policy officials (finance, environment, etc.) and heads-of-state from the world's largest and fastest growing economies. Chiefly designed to promote high-level exchanges regarding major economic and political issues, with the goal of brokering consensus. The G-20's origins lie in the G-8, a similar forum whose members included the U.S., Canada, U.K., France, Japan, Germany, Italy, and Russia. In recent years, the G-8 expanded, beginning with coordination with the 'Outreach 5' (Brazil, China, India, Mexico, South Africa) in 2005. As of September 2009, the G-8 was officially supplanted by the G-20 (established in 1999), which includes all of the aforementioned countries and Argentina, Australia, Indonesia, Saudi Arabia, South Korea, Turkey, and the EU. [1]

Gay, Lesbian, Bisexual, and Transgender (GLBT) In use since the 1990s, the term is intended to emphasize diversity of sexuality and gender identity and is sometimes used to refer to anyone who is nonheterosexual instead of exclusively to people who are homosexual, bisexual, or transgender. [11]

Gender opinion gap The difference between males and females along any one of a number of dimensions, including foreign policy preferences. [2]

General Agreement on Tariffs and Trade (GATT) A series of multilateral trade negotiations that reduced tariffs after World War II and continued into the early 1990s. Became the WTO in 1993. [4, 9]

Generalized System of Preferences (GSP) A program designed to promote economic growth in the developing world by providing preferential duty-free entry for up to 4,800 products from 129 designated beneficiary countries and territories. GSP was instituted on January 1, 1976, by the Trade Act of 1974. [10]

Genocide The deliberate and systematic destruction of, or effort to destroy, in whole or in part, an ethnic, racial, religious, or national group. [6]

Global capital The overall volume of financial resources and transactions in the global economy. [1]

Global civil society The vast and voluntary assemblage of groups operating across borders and separate from governments with the aim of influencing the world. Constitutes ideas, institutions, organizations, and individuals located and operating between the family, the state, and the market. [4]

Global climate change The significant and lasting change in the distribution of weather patterns over periods ranging from decades to millions of years. Both anthropogenic (human induced) and natural causes have been identified by climate scientists. [12]

Global North Refers to the 57 countries with high human development that have a Human Development Index (HDI) about .8 as reported in the United Nations Development Program Report 2005. Most, but not all of these countries (with the exception of Australia and New Zealand) are located in the Northern Hemisphere. [9]

Global politics Used to describe the substantive focus of this book. Signifies that many interactions in today's world no longer fit with the term "international," which implies that states remain the sole purveyors of global political activity. [1]

Global security The efforts a community of nations takes to protect against threats that are transnational in nature. The responses to these threats are usually multilateral, often involving regional and/or international organizations. [6]

Global South Countries, most of which are in the Southern Hemisphere, that

have medium development (88 countries with an HDI less than .8 and greater than .5) and low human development (32 countries with an HDI less than .5). Some 20 countries do not provide information necessary to develop their HDI, thus the Global South is made up of some 133 countries out of a total of 197. Most of them are in South and Central America, Asia, and Africa. [9]

Globalization A multifaceted concept that represents the increasing integration of economics, communications, and culture across national boundaries. [1, 4, 6, 10]

Green Revolution Refers to a series of research, development, and technology transfer initiatives occurring between the 1940s and the late 1970s, that increased agriculture production around the world, beginning most markedly in the late 1960s. [12]

Greenhouse effect The process by which the accumulation of carbon dioxide and other gases in Earth's upper atmosphere arguably causes an increase in temperature by creating a thermal blanket effect; this prevents some of the cooling that occurs at night as Earth radiates heat. [12]

Greenhouse gases (GHGs) Carbon dioxide, methane, chlorofluorocarbons, and other gases that create a blanket effect by trapping heat and preventing the nightly cooling of Earth. [12]

Gross domestic product (GDP) A measure of income within a country that excludes foreign earnings. [4, 9]

Gross national product (GNP) A measure of the sum of all goods and services produced by a country's nationals, whether they are in the country or abroad. [9]

Group of Eight (G-8) The seven economically largest free market countries: Canada, France, Germany, Great Britain, Italy, Japan, and the United States, plus Russia (a member on politic issues since 1998). [9]

Group of 77 (G-77) The group of 77 countries of the South that cosponsored

the Joint Declaration of Developing Countries in 1963 calling for greater equity in North–South trade. This group has now come to include about133 members and represents the interests of the less developed countries of the South. [10]

The Hague system Name given to the peace conferences held in the Netherlands in 1899 and 1907 where the global community issued the first formal statements of the laws of war and war crimes. [5]

Hard power The use or threatened use of material power assets by an actor to compel one or more other actors to undertake a desired action, or not undertake an undesirable one. Hard power relies on coercion. [2]

Head-of-state immunity The notion, derived from a strict interpretation of state sovereignty, that a person's conduct as head of state or high ranking political official renders that person "above the law" and not culpable for any criminal activity carried out in the dispatch of his or her responsibilities. This principle has come under increasing scrutiny and legal challenges in recent years, as embodied in legal proceedings undertaken against former heads-of-state such as Augusto Pinochet, Slobodan Milosevic, Omar al-Bashir, and Charles Taylor. [8]

Hegemony A systemic arrangement whereby one predominantly powerful actor possesses both the disproportionate material capabilities and the will to introduce, follow, and enforce a given set of rules to lend order and structure to that system. Hegemony also requires "buy-in" from at least some of the other actors concerned who stand to benefit from the rules the hegemon introduces and enforces. [2]

Heuristic devices A range of psychological strategies that allow individuals to simplify complex decisions. Such devices include evaluating people and events in terms of how well they coincide with your own belief system

("I am anticommunist; therefore all communists are dangerous"), stereotypes ("all Muslims are fanatics"), or analogies ("appeasing Hitler was wrong; therefore all compromise with aggressors is wrong"). [2]

High-value, low-probability problems The nature of most problems or threats, in which the likelihood of a given individual being impacted are very low, but the consequences if it occurs are very serious. [1]

Holy Roman Empire (HRE)/Holy Roman Emperor The domination and unification of a political territory in Western and Central Europe that lasted from its inception with Charlemagne in 800 to the renunciation of the imperial title by Francis II in 1806. [3]

Human development An approach to the study of international development that emphasizes the functioning and capabilities of individuals as an appropriate means for assessing the economic, social, and political development of a society. Common points of emphasis and measurement include equity, sustainability, and empowerment. [2]

Human Development Index (HDI) A composite statistic used to rank countries by level of human development. [11]

Human rights Inalienable fundamental rights to which a person is inherently entitled simply because he or she is a human being. Conceived as universal and egalitarian, these rights may exist as natural rights or as legal rights, in both national and international law. [11]

Human security An emerging paradigm for understanding global vulnerabilities, proponents of which challenge the traditional notion of national security by arguing that the proper referent for security should be the individual rather than the state. Human security holds that a people-centered view of security is necessary for national, regional, and global stability. [6]

Human trafficking The illegal trade of human beings for the purposes of reproductive slavery, commercial sexual exploitation, forced labor, or a modern-day form of slavery. [11]

Identity politics A situation in which most if not all political issues and debates are filtered through and revolve around competing and conflicting group identities. Particularly common in states or societies in which there are multiple identity groups with unresolved historical grievances [3]

Ideological/theological school of law A set of related ideas in secular or religious thought, usually founded on identifiable thinkers and their works, that provides a coherent legal framework. [8]

Idiosyncratic analysis An individual-level analysis approach to decision-making that assumes that individuals make foreign policy decisions and that different individuals are likely to make different decisions based on unique personal characteristics such as personality, health, personal biography, and so forth. [2]

Imperialism A term synonymous with colonialism, recalling the empire building of the European powers in the 19th century. The empires were built by conquering and subjugating Southern countries. [9]

Individual-level analysis An analytical approach that emphasizes the role of individuals as either distinct personalities or biological/psychological beings. [2]

Industrial capitalism An economic system based on private ownership of the means of production, where markets rely on increasing production, expanding markets, and the unrestricted movement of capital and labor across borders. [4]

Intergovernmental organizations (IGOs) International/transnational bodies that are composed of member-countries. [1]

Intermediate-Range Nuclear Forces Treaty (INF) A 1987 agreement between the United States and the Soviet Union signed by U.S. President Ronald Reagan and General Secretary Mikhail Gorbachev, the treaty eliminated nuclear and conventional ground-launched ballistic and cruise missiles with intermediate ranges defined between 500 and 5,500 km (300–3,400 miles). [6]

Intermestic The merger of *inter*national and do*mestic* concerns and decisions. [1]

Internally displaced persons (IDPs) Someone who is forced to flee his or her home, but who remains within his or her country's borders. At the end of 2006, there were an estimated 24.5 million IDPs in some 52 countries. [11]

International Atomic Energy Agency (IAEA) A critical organization in the nuclear non-proliferation regime, especially in its role in conducting international inspections of national nuclear facilities. It was set up in 1957 as the world's "Atoms for Peace" organization within the United Nations family. The agency works with its member-states and multiple partners worldwide to promote safe, secure, and peaceful nuclear technologies according to the NPT. [5, 6]

International Bill of Human Rights An informal name given to one General Assembly resolution and two international treaties established by the United Nations. It consists of the Universal Declaration of Human Rights (adopted in 1948), the International Covenant on Civil and Political Rights (1966) with its two Optional Protocols, and the International Covenant on Economic, Social, and Cultural Rights (1966). [11]

International Conference on Financing for Development (ICFD) A UN-sponsored conference on development programs for the South that met in Monterrey, Mexico, during March 2002. Fifty heads of state or government, as well as over 200 government cabinet ministers, leaders from NGOs, and leaders from the major IGOs attended the conference. [10]

International Court of Justice (ICJ) Also known as the *World Court,* the ICJ is a standing international court established after World War II and serves as the primary judicial organ of the United Nations. The ICJ is headquartered in The Hague (the Netherlands) and consists of 15 judges serving rotating 9-year terms. Its main function is to settle international legal disputes submitted to it by states, and to provide advisory opinions on legal matters submitted by international organizations and agencies and the UN General Assembly. [8]

International Covenant on Civil and Political Rights (ICCPR) A multilateral treaty the United Nations General Assembly adopted on December 16, 1966, and in force from March 23, 1976. It commits its parties to respect the civil and political rights of individuals, including the rights to life, freedom of religion, freedom of speech, freedom of assembly, electoral rights, and rights to due process and a fair trial. As of March 2012, the Covenant had 74 signatories and 167 parties. [11]

International Covenant on Economic, Social, and Cultural Rights (ICESCR) A multilateral treaty the United National General Assembly adopted on December 16, 1966, and in force from January 3, 1976. It commits its parties to work toward the granting of economic, social, and cultural rights to individuals, including labor rights, the right to health, the right to education, and the right to an adequate standard of living. As of June 2012, the Covenant had 70 signatories and 160 parties. [11]

International Criminal Court (ICC) The first permanent global tribunal established to try individuals for war crimes, genocide, crimes against humanity, and crimes of aggression. [8]

International financial institutions (IFIs) Global financial institutions established or chartered by multiple states. Their owners or shareholders are generally national governments, although other international institutions and organizations occasionally function as shareholders also. Many of the most prominent IFIs are multilateral development banks, such as the World Bank. [1]

International institutions Broadly comprise various formal and informal entities where, in many cases, international public authority is vested in an institution that qualifies as an international organization with an international legal personality. [5]

International law The body of principles, customs, and rules regulating interactions among and between states, international organizations, individuals, and in more limited cases, multinational organizations. These binding legal obligations can serve multiple purposes, from establishing expectations and order to protecting the status quo to legitimizing the use of force or humanitarian intervention. [5, 8]

International Labor Organization (ILO) An international organization responsible for drawing up and overseeing international labor standards. It is the only "tripartite" United Nations agency that brings together government representatives, employers, and workers to jointly shape policies and programs. [11]

International Monetary Fund (IMF) The world's primary organization devoted to maintaining monetary stability by helping countries to fund balance-of-payment deficits. Established in 1947, it now has 185 members. [4, 9]

International organizations Organizations with an international membership, scope, and presence. There are essentially two types of international organizations—intergovernmental organizations (IGOs), which are global or regional in membership and scope and whose members are states,

and nongovernmental organizations (NGOs), whose members are non–state actors of various types from the nonprofit or for-profit sector [1].

International relations (IR) Used in this book to describe the academic study of global politics. Thus, when discussing theoretical approaches, for example, we use the term "international relations theory," as that is the commonly used term in our field. [1]

Internationalism Also called *liberal internationalism,* this theoretical approach holds that entities should and can conduct international economic relations cooperatively. Internationalists believe that the international economy is a non-zero-sum game in which prosperity is available to all. They favor freeing trade from political restrictions to spread prosperity and other forms of economic interchange. [9]

Iron triangle A close and mutually beneficial arrangement between interest groups, the bureaucracy, and legislators within a given political system that forms the basis for the military-industrial complex. [6]

Irredentism A minority population's demand to unify with its homeland (typically an adjoining state), or when the state in question claims the area in which that minority lives. [3]

"Jihad v. McWorld" A thesis advanced by political theorist Benjamin Barber (1992, 1996) claiming that global politics is increasingly defined by the tensions between the homogenizing tendencies of globalization (the "McWorld" culture) and the fragmented backlash of tribalism (the "Jihad" culture). [7]

Jus ad bellum Loosely translated from the Latin as "just right to wage war," the primary decision-law of just war theory that is intended to provide the minimal moral and legal criteria necessary to justify a resort to war. Steeped in centuries of Western political thought and jurisprudence, *jus ad bellum* and just war theory more generally have profoundly shaped international law with respect to war and legal dilemmas pertaining to it. [8]

Jus in bello Loosely translated from the Latin as "justice in war," the component of just war theory that is intended to provide the minimal moral and legal criteria necessary to govern proper conduct in war. Steeped in centuries of Western political thought and jurisprudence, *jus in bello* and just war theory more generally have had an extensive impact on the promulgation and attemped enforcement of the "laws of war," as embodied in international conventions such as the Geneva Conventions. [8]

Jus post bellum Loosely translated from the Latin as "justice after war," the third and least developed component of just war theory that is intended to provide the minimal moral and legal criteria necessary to define and assess just outcomes after war. [8]

Just cause A prominent criterion of the *jus ad bellum* decision-law of just war theory that holds that the reason for going to war must reflect or equate with some plausible translation of justice—such as the need to protect innocent lives from imminent danger or to correct a grave public evil—and cannot be solely or primarily based in retribution. [8]

Kyoto Protocol A supplement to the Global Warming Convention (1992) that requires the economically developed countries to reduce greenhouse gas emissions by about 7% below their 1990 levels by 2012 and encourages, but does not require, less developed countries to reduce emissions. [12]

Last resort The basic (and highly restrictive) underlying premise of just war theory and in particular *jus ad bellum* that holds that military force can and should only be employed after all other peaceful alternatives have been exhausted. [8]

League of Nations The first attempt to establish an international organization with global reach in terms of membership and issue areas. It existed between the end of World War I and the beginning of World War II and was the immediate predecessor of the United Nations. [5, 11]

Least developed countries (LLDCs) Those countries in the poorest of economic circumstances. In this book, this includes those countries with a per capita GNP of less than $400 in 1985 dollars. [10]

Legal personhood Any party possessing both rights and responsibilities under the law, within a given legal system. Legal personhood in international law has traditionally been restricted to states, but has been expanded in recent decades (in conjunction with different courts and tribunals) to encompass individuals, corporations, and other non–state actors. [8]

Less developed countries (LDCs) Countries, located mainly in Africa, Asia, and Latin America, with economies that rely heavily on the production of agriculture and raw materials and whose per capita GDP and standard of living are substantially below Western standards. [5, 9]

Levels of analysis A social scientific approach to the study of global politics that analyzes phenomena from different perspectives (system, state, individual). [2]

Liberalism/liberal The view that people and the countries that represent them are capable of finding mutual interests and cooperating to achieve them, by forming ties between countries and also by working together for the common good through global organizations and according to international law. See *Classic liberalism* and *Neoliberalism*. [1]

Limited membership council A representative organizational body of the UN that grants special status to members who have a greater stake, responsibility, or capacity in a particular area of concern. The UN Security Council is an example. [5]

Lisbon Treaty Signed on December 13, 2007, and entering into force in December 2009, this international agreement amends the two treaties (Maastricht Treaty and the Treaty Establishing the European Community) that form the constitutional basis of the EU. [5]

Maastricht Treaty The most significant agreement in the recent history of the European Union (EU). The EU's 12 member-countries signed this treaty in February 1992, and it entered into force in November 1993. It outlines steps toward further political-economic integration. [5]

Majority voting A system used to determine how votes should count. The theory of majoritarianism springs from the concept of sovereign equality and the democratic notion that the will of the majority should prevail. This system has two main components: (1) each member casts one equal vote, and (2) the issue is carried by either a simple majority (half plus one vote) or, in some cases, an extraordinary majority (commonly two-thirds). [5]

Manufactured goods Items that required substantial processing or assembly to become usable. Distinct from primary products, such as agricultural and forestry products, that need little or no processing. [9]

Maquiladora A Mexican name for manufacturing operations in a free trade zone, where factories import material and equipment on a duty-free and tariff-free basis for assembly, processing, or manufacturing and then re-export the assembled, processed, and/or manufactured products, sometimes back to the raw materials' country of origin. [10]

Maritime borders Customary legal divisions of the world's oceans into maritime areas encompassing maritime limits and zones, delineating international waters, and granting exclusive national rights concerning passage, navigation, and dominion over mineral and biological resources. Efforts to codify maritime boundaries were a primary impetus for the United Nations Convention on the Law of the Sea, which entered into force in 1994 and currently has 163 parties. [8]

Marxist theory The philosophy of Karl Marx that the economic (material) order determines political and social relationships. Thus, history, the current situation, and the future are determined by the economic struggle, termed *dialectical materialism*. [9]

Mediation In global politics, a method of conflict management and resolution in which a third party seeks to generate a settlement that is acceptable to the original parties in an armed conflict or dispute. [7]

Merchandise trade The import and export of tangible manufactured goods and raw materials. [9]

Microstates Countries with small populations that cannot survive economically without outside aid or that are inherently so militarily weak that they are inviting targets for foreign intervention. [3]

Militarism The belief or desire of a government or people that a country should maintain a strong military capability and be prepared to use it aggressively to defend or promote national interests. [7]

Military-industrial complex A term first coined by former U.S. President Dwight Eisenhower (in his farewell address) that refers to political and economic relationships between legislators, national armed forces, and the defense industrial base that supports them. These relationships include political contributions, political approval for defense spending, lobbying to support bureaucracies, and beneficial legislations and oversight of the industry. [6]

Military necessity A criterion of just war theory (*jus in bello*) that holds that, at all times in the conduct of war, only the minimum necessary amount of force sufficient to satisfy

the overriding goal of advancing the military defeat of one's adversary should be employed. To satisfy the criterion, attacks should be directed only at military targets to serve military objectives, so as to contribute to a strategic advantage while limiting excessive death and destruction. [8]

Millennium Development Goals (MDGs) In 2000, 189 nations made and committed to eight global goals aimed at poverty reduction, education, public health, and human rights. This pledge encompasses eight specific goals to achieve by 2015. [5, 10]

Millennium Summit A meeting among many world leaders at the UN headquarters in New York City in 2000 to discuss the role of the UN at the turn of the 21st century. World leaders ratified the United Nations Millennium Declaration. [10]

Miranda rights A U.S. criminal procedural rule that requires law enforcement to warn criminal suspects in police custody (or in a custodial interrogation), before they are interrogated, of their Fifth Amendment right against compelled self-incrimination. [11]

Mitigation Action to reduce greenhouse gas emissions (GHGs) to slow or stop global warming. [12]

Modernists Those who believe in humankind's mastery of the environment, and possess great faith in technology to solve existing and future environmental problems. Modernists contend that ecosystem carrying capacity can be extended through technological advances. Dominant view in industrialized world for the last several hundred years. Modernists are sometimes referred to as *exclusionists*, as they view mankind as separate from the environment. [12]

Monarchism A political system that is organized, governed, and defined by the idea of the divine right of kings, or the notion that because a person is born into royalty, he or she is ordained to rule. [3]

Monetary relations The entire scope of international money issues, such as exchange rates, interest rates, loan policies, balance of payments, and regulating institutions (for example, the International Monetary Fund). [9]

Montreal Protocol A 1989 international treaty designed to protect the ozone layer by phasing out the production of numerous substances that scientists have proved are responsible for ozone depletion. [5]

Moral absolutism A philosophical viewpoint that contends that the ends alone cannot and should not justify the means, or that morality should be the absolute guide for human decisions and actions. [8]

Moral pragmatism The idea that there is a middle ground between amorality and moral absolutism that acts as a guide to human actions, particularly in regard to international law. [8]

Moral relativism A philosophical viewpoint that contends that ascertaining the morality of human actions or decisions requires careful appreciation of the context in which said actions or decisions take place, and the moral and ethical standards that entail within that particular context. [8]

Multidimensional peacekeeping A method of peacekeeping when soldiers, military officers, police, and civilian personnel from many countries monitor and observe peace processes that emerge in post-conflict situations and assist conflicting parties to implement the peace agreement they have signed. Such assistance comes in many forms, including promoting human security, confidence-building measures, power-sharing arrangements, electoral support, strengthening the rule of law, and economic and social development. [7]

Multinational corporations (MNCs) Private enterprises that have production subsidiaries or branches in more than one country. [1, 4, 9, 12]

Multinational states Countries in which there are two or more sizeable and recognized nationalities. [3]

Multipolar sytem A world political system in which power is primarily held by four or more international actors. [2]

Multistate nation A nation that has substantial numbers of its members living in more than one state. [3]

Munich analogy A belief among post–World War II leaders, particularly Americans, that aggression must always be met firmly and that appeasement will only encourage an aggressor. Named for the concessions made to Adolf Hitler by Great Britain and France at Munich during the 1938 Czechoslovakian crisis. [2]

Mutually assured destruction (MAD) A situation in which each nuclear superpower has the capability of launching a devastating nuclear second strike even after an enemy has attacked it. The crux of the MAD doctrine is that possessing an overwhelming second-strike capacity prevents nuclear war due to the rational aversion of the other side to invite massive retaliation. [6]

Nation A group of culturally and historically affiliated people who feel a communal bond and who feel they should govern themselves to at least some degree. [3]

Nation-state A politically organized territory that recognizes no higher law, and whose population politically identifies with that entity. *See* State. [3]

National security The requirement to maintain the survival of the state through the use of economic diplomacy, power projection, and political power. Originally (and still largely) focused on amassing military strength to forestall the threat of military invasion by powerful adversaries, national security is now construed to encompass a broad range of factors impinging on a nation's nonmilitary or economic security, material interests, and values. [6]

Nationalism The belief that the nation is the ultimate basis of political loyalty and that one's nation is entitled to self-government. *See* Nation-state. [3, 4]

Nativism A political attitude demanding favored status for certain established inhabitants of a nation-state relative to the claims of newer immigrants. Nativism usually translates into opposition to immigration and multiculturalism, as well as policies that restrict the political or legal status of specific ethnic or cultural groups on the basis of perceived or alleged difference or incompatibility with "established" national traits, customs, and practices. [3]

Natural law/naturalist school of law A system of law that is purportedly determined by nature, and thus universal. Classically, natural law refers to the use of reason to analyze human nature—both social and personal—and deduce binding rules of moral behavior. Proponents of natural law believe that the common features and traits of humanity—such as the rational faculties of the individual—necessitate and justify a common legal standard and set of rights and obligations that entail to all human beings. [8, 11]

Neocolonialism The notion that EDCs continue to control and exploit LDCs through indirect means, such as economic dominance and co-opting the local elite. [9, 10]

Neofunctionalism A theoretical perspective that explains cooperation between governance structures by focusing on the basic needs of people and states to interact on specific issue areas, such as communications, trade, travel, health, or environmental protection activity. Different from functionalism, these practical needs are defined by elites rather than grassroots, from the top down rather than the bottom up. [5]

Neoliberal institutionalism (NLI) Embraces and builds on the liberal school of thought that states are rational-unitary actors and that they can cooperate through international regimes and institutions; focus is on long-term benefits instead of short-term goals. [1, 5]

Neoliberalism/neoliberal The view that conflict and other ills that result from the anarchical global system can be eased by building global and regional organizations and processes that will allow people, groups, countries, and other global actors to cooperate for their mutual benefit. [1]

Neorealism/neorealist The view that the self-interested struggle for power among countries is caused by the anarchical nature of the global system, which leaves each state solely responsible for its safety and welfare and forces each state to pursue its interests in competition with other states. [1]

Neotraditionalists Believe in ecological limits and the need to reduce ecological stress. Emphasize conservation and the search for environmental solutions that reduce humanity's impact on ecosystems. Ecosystem carrying capacity is finite. Neotraditionalists are sometimes referred to as *inclusionists*, as they view humankind as part of nature. [12]

New International Economic Order (NIEO) A term that refers to the goals and demands of the South for basic reforms in the global economic system. [10]

New security environment A catch-all term referring to the emergence of a multiplicity of "new" (or perhaps, newly recognized) threats to the security of states, individuals, and the global system in the contemporary (post–Cold War) world. Such threats transcend the traditional understanding of security threats and are often associated with weak or failing governments and poverty, inequality, and underdevelopment. [6]

"New" wars Low-intensity but protracted armed conflicts often taking place within the boundaries of a state, between contending identity groups and irregular forces associated with them, and waged in such a way that distinctions between civil and military authority and combatants and noncombatants lack relevance. "New" wars are a function of globalization, in that they are often prompted by failing state authority and sustained by myriad transnational connections including the relatively easy movement of money, weapons, and combatants. [7]

New World Order Refers to any period of history featuring a dramatic change in dominant norms and values and the associated balance of power. [6]

Newly industrializing countries (NICs) Less developed countries whose economies and whose trade now include significant amounts of manufactured products. As a result, these countries have a per capita GDP significantly higher than the average per capita GDP for less developed countries. [10]

Noncompulsory jurisdiction A loose form of legal jurisdiction in which the authority of a court or other adjudicatory body is contingent on the consent of parties to which the body of law applies. In international law, much jurisdiction has been and remains noncompulsory, particularly relative to states. [8]

Nongovernmental organizations (NGOs) International (transnational) organizations with private memberships. [1, 4, 11]

Non-proliferation Limitation of the production or spread of nuclear or chemical weapons. [6]

Non–state actors (NSAs) Entities participating or acting in the sphere of global politics; organizations with sufficient power to influence and cause change in politics that are not belonging to or existing as a state structure or established institution of a state. [6]

Nontariff barriers (NTBs) A nonmonetary restriction on trade, such as quotas, technical specifications, or unnecessarily lengthy quarantine and inspection procedures. [10]

Non-zero-sum game A contest in which gains by one or more players can be achieved without being offset by losses for any other player or players. See *Zero-sum game*. [1]

Norms Unwritten rules, principles, or standards of behavior that create social expectations about how states and individuals ought to behave and interact in the global community. [2, 4, 5]

North American Free Trade Agreement (NAFTA) An economic agreement among Canada, Mexico, and the United States that went into effect on January 1, 1994. [9]

Nuclear utilization theory (NUT) Pioneered by Herman Kahn, this theory asserts that it is possible for a limited nuclear exchange to occur and that nuclear weapons are simply one more rung on the ladder of escalation. [6]

Nuclear weapon An explosive device that derives its destructive force from nuclear reactions, either fission or a combination of fission and fusion. [6]

Offensive realism An explanation of war and armed conflict in international relations rooted in the realist appreciation of states, power, and anarchy. Offensive realists contend that war is a result of the inherently aggressive tendencies of states and their leaders, who capitalize on the condition of anarchy and purposefully choose war as a tool of advancing their interests and amassing greater power. [7]

Office of the United Nations High Commissioner on Human Rights (OHCHR) Established by a General Assembly Resolution in 1993 and mandated to promote and protect the enjoyment and full realization, by all people, of all rights established in the UN Charter and in international human rights laws and treaties. Mandate includes preventing human rights abuses, securing respect for all human rights, and promoting international cooperation to protect human rights. [11]

Official development assistance (ODA) Often referred to as foreign aid, ODA refers to concessional financial flows from the EDCS to the LDCs. It can take the form of grants or loans with interest rates below normal market rates (thus, it is considered concessional and not commercially driven). [10]

"Old" wars Derived from Clausewitzian thought and reflected in the wars of the 19th and early 20th centuries. "Old" wars refer to wars fought by and through the state and its organized, professional standing armies in pursuit of the national interest. Key distinctions typifying the "modern" state (disaggregated civil and military authority, distinctions between combatants and noncombatants, etc.) shaped the conduct of war. In such wars, entire societies were mobilized for the war effort, producing all-encompassing wars between multiple states marked by massive casualties and destruction. [7]

Operational code A perceptual phenomenon that describes how an individual acts and responds when faced with specific types of situations, based on her or his understanding of the nature and efficacy of politics combined with her or his fundamental worldview and values. [2]

Optimistic bias The psychological tendency of individuals—particularly those in positions of power—to overrate their own potential for success, and underrate their own potential for failure. [2]

Organization for Economic Cooperation and Development (OECD) An organization that has existed since 1948 (and since 1960 under its present name) to facilitate the exchange of information and otherwise to promote cooperation among the economically developed countries. In recent years, the OECD has started accepting a few newly industrializing and former communist countries in transition as members. [9]

Organization of the Petroleum Exporting Countries (OPEC) An intergovernmental organization of 12 oil-producing countries made up of Algeria, Angola, Ecuador, Iran, Iraq, Kuwait, Libya, Nigeria, Qatar, Saudi Arabia, United Arab Emirates, and Venezuela. [6]

Overstretch A concept developed by the historian Paul Kennedy (1987), among others, that suggests a recurring historical tendency of powerful actors to overextend themselves by taking on superfluous but costly foreign policy commitments that erode their power by depleting their financial resources and invoking domestic discord and upheaval. [2]

P5 Refers to the five permanent members of the UN Security Council who have the power to veto resolutions. These include China, France, Russia, the United Kingdom, and the United States. [5]

Pacta sunt servanda Loosely translated from Latin as "treaties are to be served/carried out," an important international norm that treaty agreements between states, and the provisions and obligations contained therein, should be considered to have binding legal force. [8]

"Particularistic identity politics" Often the catalyst of "new" wars, a narrow, zero-sum conception of political identity that tends to generate and further fragment intercommunal violence along national, ethnic, religious, or linguistic lines. Such identity politics are often employed by elites in fragmented societies to consolidate power through zealous appeals to one identity group and derogation of the "other." [7]

Peace enforcement The use of military means in a semicoercive posture by an international organization such as the United Nations to introduce and enforce peace in an ongoing conflict setting. Peace enforcement operations relax some of the restrictions on peacekeeping, allowing for more expansive rules of engagement and for deployment without full consent of the warring parties. [7]

Peacekeeping The use of military means in a noncoercive posture by an international organization such as the United Nations to prevent a recurrence of military hostilities, usually by acting as a buffer between combatants in a suspended conflict. The international force is neutral between the combatants and must have been invited to be present by the combatants. [7]

Plenary body A session that is fully attended by all qualified members. [5]

Polarity The number of predominantly powerful actors in the global system at any given point in time. [2]

Political asylum An international legal right to entry and sanctuary within a sovereign state afforded by Article 14 of the Universal Declaration of Human Rights (UDHR) to individuals forced to leave a country or political system in which they are experiencing persecution on grounds of race, nationality, religion, political opinions, membership, and/or participation in any social group or activities. [8]

Political communities As defined by the political scientist Karl W. Deutsch (1957), social groups with a process of political communication, some machinery for establishing and enforcing collective agreements, and some popular habits of compliance with those agreements. [3]

Political culture A concept that refers to a society's general, long-held, and fundamental practices and attitudes. These are based on a country's historical experience and on the values (norms) of its citizens. These attitudes are often an important part of the internal setting in which national leaders make foreign policy. [2]

Popular sovereignty A political doctrine that holds that sovereign political authority resides with the citizens of a state. According to this doctrine, the citizenry grant a certain amount of authority to the state, its government, and, especially, its specific political leaders (such as monarchs, presidents, and prime ministers), but do not surrender ultimate sovereignty. [3]

Population aging A scenario in which a large and increasing proportion of a given society is approaching or at an age in which active participation in public and private life is unlikely. [2]

Positivist school of law Those who believe that varying social and cultural contexts necessitate and justify a variable legal standard and set of rights and obligations that are determined by individual states and societies in ways that are consistent with the norms and values of the people living in those states and societies. [8]

Predatory states States governed by corrupt and repressive regimes that "prey" on the population and assets of the state and society they govern for the purpose of personal enrichment, and to the detriment of the collective well-being. [6]

Preemption Sometimes referred to as "anticipatory war," a strategy of warfare predicated on the legitimacy and desirability of using military force against a security threat prior to that threat fully materializing in the form of an attack against one's own state or interests. This differs by degree from preventative war, in which military force is employed to eliminate *potential* threats. [7]

Prescriptive rights The essentials that a society and its government are arguably obligated to try to provide in order to assure that certain qualitative standards of life exist for everyone in the community. [11]

Primary products Agricultural products and raw materials, such as minerals. [9]

Primordial identities A term that refers to the view advanced by some political and social theorists that a given identity may be deeply embedded or "hardwired" in a person's consciousness. Such identities override other possible sources of identity and other possible influences on an individual's perceptions of social and political phenomena—which can produce extreme intolerance and violence toward members of other identity groups. [7]

Proportionality (of ends desired) In the just war tradition, the *jus ad bellum* criterion that holds that a "just" war is one in which the expected benefits of waging a war must be viewed in proportion to the expected evils/negative consequences and outcomes—with the former exceeding the latter. [8]

Proportionality (of means) In the just war tradition, the *jus in bello* criterion that holds that a "just" war is one in which the conduct of the war is governed by consideration of incidental injury and harm to noncombatants, with the benefits of such an act considered in relation (proportion) to such harm, and weighed accordingly. [8]

Proscriptive rights Obligations on a society and its government to try to provide a certain qualitative standard of life that, at a minimum, meets basic needs and perhaps does not differ radically from the quality of life enjoyed by others in the society. These rights are usually expressed in such terms as "the government shall . . . ." [11]

Protectionism Using tariffs or nontariff barriers, such as quotas or subsidies, to protect a domestic economic sector from competition from imported goods or services. [10]

Protestant Reformation The religious movement initiated by Martin Luther in Germany in 1517 that rejected the Catholic Church as the necessary intermediary between people and God. [3]

Public goods In economics, goods that are nonrivalrous and nonexcludable. Nonrivalry means that consumption of the good by one individual does not reduce availability of the good for consumption by others; nonexcludability means that no one can be excluded effectively from using the good. [5]

Purchasing power parity (PPP) A measure of the relative purchasing power of different currencies. It is measured by the price of the same goods in different countries, translated by the exchange rate of that country's currency against a base currency, usually the U.S. dollar. [9]

Rally effect The tendency during a crisis of political and other leaders, legislators, and the public to give strong support to a chief executive and the policy that leader has adopted in response to the crisis. [2]

Rational actors An assumption derived largely from microeconomics that contends that individuals in society are prone to make informed, systematic, and self-interested /self-serving choices and decisions based on a careful accumulation and weighting of all relevant information. [2]

Real dollars Dollars that have been adjusted for inflation. [9]

Realism/realist The view that world politics is driven by competitive self-interest, and, therefore, that the central dynamic of the global system is a struggle for power among countries as each tries to preserve or, preferably, improve its military security and economic welfare in competition with other states. See *Classical realism* and *Neorealism*. [1, 5]

Reasonable hope for success: *a priori* Also referred to as *probability of success,* the *jus ad bellum* criterion that holds that war cannot and should not be waged for a fruitless or ill-defined cause, or where disproportionate means must be employed in order to achieve a measure of success. A clear definition and articulation of "success" should be identified by the potential belligerent in advance of the decision to actually use force. [8]

Refugee A person who is outside his or her country of origin or habitual residence because he or she has suffered persecution on account of race, religion, nationality, political opinion, or because he or she is a member of a persecuted "social group." [11]

Regime theory Derived from liberal tradition, regime theory argues that international institutions or regimes affect the behavior of states or other international actors on a specific issue, such as nuclear weapons or human rights, by promoting and upholding norms and rules governing behavior. It assumes that cooperation is possible in the anarchic system of states, as regimes are by definition instances of international cooperation. [5]

Regime type The type of government prevailing in a given society. [2]

Regional trade agreement (RTA) A broad term the World Trade Organization uses to define bilateral and cross-regional agreements as well as multilateral regional ones. [9]

Relative deprivation The experience of recognizing one's own absolute deprivation in relation to affluence and material abundance enjoyed by others. Relative deprivation is enhanced in scenarios in which information about disparities in wealth and standards of living becomes more widely available to those who are relatively worse off. [7]

Remittances A transfer of money by an expatriate to persons in his or her home country. [7]

Rendition In law, a surrender or handing over of persons or property, particularly from one jurisdiction to another. [11]

Responsibility to Protect (R2P) A global United Nations initiative doctrine, endorsed by the UN in 2005, which is based on the idea that sovereignty is not a privilege, but that sovereignty confers responsibilities on states and their leaders—first and foremost, to ensure the well-being of their citizens. [6, 11]

Right intention The *jus ad bellum* criterion, following from the existence of a "just cause," that speaks to the motivation for war on the part of the potential belligerent. Primarily assessed as whether the actor's aim or objective in going to war is consistent with the just cause that actor has identified and articulated. An expressed desire to harm or punish the enemy is not considered a "right intention." [8]

Rogue state(s) Controversial term some international theorists apply to states that are (or are perceived to be) in noncompliance with the majority of prevailing rules, norms, and laws in the global system and therefore constitute a threat to order. This may mean, among other things, a state governed by authoritarian rule that severely restricts human rights, sponsors or condones terrorism, or seeks to obtain or promote the spread of weapons of mass destruction. [2, 6]

Rules of engagement (ROE) Rules defining acceptable conduct by members of the armed forces engaged in a theater of conflict during operations or in the course of their duties. Typically the rules of engagement are clearly stipulated by political leaders and military commanders to military personnel, and are formulated to advance strategic goals while ensuring compliance with the laws of war. [7]

Salience/salient In public opinion research, the issues or questions that are more meaningful and significant (or "matter" more) to a greater proportion of people. [2]

Sanctions Economic, diplomatic, or military actions put in place to punish a state in an attempt to coercively force states to comply with legal obligations. [5]

Secessionism Motivated by a quest for political self-determination, a minority population's desire to break away from an existing state and form a new sovereign state. [3]

Second generation rights Based on the principles of social justice and public obligation; they tend to be "positive" rights, based on continental European conceptions of liberty as equality. The notion has evolved into what we now call "social" or "economic" rights. [11]

Secretariat The administrative organ of the United Nations, headed by the Secretary-General. [5]

Secretary-General (SG) The Secretary-General is the head of the Secretariat of the United Nations and serves as the UN spokesperson. Many other IGOs also use the term secretary-general to designate their organizational leader. [5]

Securitization Assumes a sectoral approach to security in which multiple realms of security concerns (military, political, social, economic, environmental, etc.) are introduced as a means of defining, analyzing, and responding to differing security threats. [6]

Security In global politics, a condition associated with individual nation-states, the global system, and/or individual human beings in which the subject is insulated from harm or the threat of harm and its well-being is ensured. [6]

Security dilemma Given anarchy, the tendency of states and other actors to undertake actions to enhance their own security in a "self-help" system tends to threaten other states or actors who are uncertain of the original state's intentions. This is a dilemma in that the original action, intended to make the state or actor more secure, has the opposite effect. Security dilemmas are a frequent cause of arms races and wars, and reveal the extent to which misperceptions and the lack of information about states' actions and intentions are destabilizing factors in global politics. [6, 7]

Self-defense A countermeasure that involves defending oneself, one's property, or the well-being of another from harm. The use of the right of self-defense as a legal justification for the use of force in times of danger is available in many jurisdictions, but the interpretation varies widely. [7]

Self-determination The concept that a people should have the opportunity to control or follow their own political destiny through self-government. [3, 5]

Services trade Trade based on the purchase (import) from the sale (export) to another country of intangibles such as architectural fees; insurance premiums; royalties on movies, books, patents, and other intellectual properties; shipping services; advertising fees; and educational programs. [9]

Smoot–Hawley Tariff Act Senator Reed Smoot and Representative Willis C. Hawley signed this act into law on June 17, 1930. The act raised U.S. tariffs on over 20,000 imported goods to record levels. [9]

Social contract A concept associated with liberal political philosophers such as Locke, Kant, and Thomas Paine that refers to an implicit understanding agreed to by those who merged into a society and created a government. The social contract details the proper functions of and prohibitions on government as well as the obligations of citizens. [3]

Social media Internet-based programs that allow for the creation and exchange of user-generated content and interactive dialogue between individuals and groups using Web-based and mobile-based technologies. [4]

Soft power The use or prospective use of material or ideational power assets by an actor to induce another actor or actors to undertake a desired action, or not undertake an undesirable one. Soft power relies on persuasion. [2]

Southern Common Market (Mercosur) A regional organization that emphasizes trade relations, established in 1995 among Argentina, Brazil, Paraguay, and Uruguay, with Bolivia, Chile, Peru, and Venezuela as associate members. [9]

Sovereignty The most essential defining characteristic of a state. The term strongly implies political independence from any higher authority and also suggests at least theoretical equality. [1]

Special drawing rights (SDRs) Reserves held by the International Monetary Fund that the central banks of member-countries can draw on to help manage the values of their currencies. SDR value is based on a *market basket* of currencies, and SDRs are acceptable in transactions between central banks. [9]

Special Tribunal for Sierra Leone A judicial body established by the government of Sierra Leone and the United Nations with the authority to prosecute persons bearing responsibility for violations of international humanitarian law and/or Sierra Leonean law during the civil war in Sierra Leone, beginning in 1996. Notable as a "hybrid" (national/international) court, as well as for issuing the first conviction of an African head of state (former Liberian President Charles Taylor) for war crimes committed while a sitting head-of-state. [8]

State A political actor that has sovereignty and a number of characteristics, including territory, population, organization, and recognition. [1]

State-building The process of creating both a government and other legal structures of a country and fostering the political identification of the inhabitants of the country with the state and their sense of loyalty to it. [3, 7]

State-level analysis An analytical approach that emphasizes the actions of states and the internal (domestic) causes of their foreign policies. [2]

State of nature A theoretical time in human history when people lived independently or in family groups and there were no societies of nonrelated individuals or governments. [3]

State sovereignty A central tenet of global politics first established in the Treaty of Westphalia, that holds that the administrative unit of the state (presuming it satisfies the basic criteria of a sovereign state) has the sole right to govern its territory and people, free from outside interference. [2, 3]

State-sponsored terrorism Describes terrorism sponsored by nation-states. As with terrorism, the precise definition, and the identification of particular examples, are subjects of heated political dispute. In general, state-sponsored terrorism is associated with providing material support and/or sanctuary to terrorist or paramilitary organizations. [7]

Statecraft The use of military, economic, diplomatic, and ideational tools by statepersons in the pursuit of clearly defined foreign policy objectives and national interests. [2, 7]

Stateless nation A nation that does not have political expression through a sovereign state. [3]

Strategic Arms Reduction Treaties (START I and II) START I (1991) and START II (1993) provided for large cuts in the nuclear arms possessed by the United States and the Soviet Union (later the Russian Federation). START I was the first arms-control treaty to reduce, rather than merely limit, the strategic offensive nuclear arsenals of the United States and the Soviet Union. START II established nuclear warhead and bombing ceilings of 3,500 for the United States and 2,997 for Russia by the year 2003 and also eliminated some types of weapon systems. [6]

Strategic-range delivery vehicles Delivery vehicles for nuclear weapons, such as land- or submarine-based ballistic missiles and long-range heavy bombers, capable of attacking targets at distances greater than 5,500 kilometers. These delivery systems confer tremendous strategic advantage to states possessing them, and consequently have often been a great source of instability as well as a target of arms control efforts, such as between the U.S. and USSR/Russia. [6]

Subsidies Assistance paid to a business or economic sector. Most subsidies are made by the government to producers or distributed as subventions in an industry to prevent the decline of that industry or an increase in the prices of its products or simply to encourage it to hire more labor. [10]

Supranational organization An organization that is founded and operates, at least in part, on the idea that international organizations can or should have authority higher than individual states and that those states should be subordinate to the supranational organization. [5]

Sustainable development The ability to continue to improve the quality of life of those in the industrialized countries and, particularly, those in the less developed countries while simultaneously protecting Earth's biosphere. [12]

Sweatshops A negatively connoted term for any working environment that is unacceptably difficult or dangerous. Employees often work long hours for very low pay, regardless of laws mandating overtime pay or a minimum wage. [11]

System-level analysis An analytical approach that emphasizes the importance of the impact of global conditions (economics, technology, power relationships, and so forth) on the actions of states and other actors. [2]

Tariff A tax, usually based on a percentage of value, that importers must pay on items purchased abroad; also known as an import tax or import duty. [10]

Theocracy A political system that is organized, governed, and defined by spiritual leaders and their religious beliefs. [3]

Theory An interconnected set of ideas and concepts that seeks to explain why things happen and how events and trends relate to one another. Theories allow us to explain and even predict the occurrence of various phenomena. [1]

Third generation rights Initially proposed in 1979 by the Czech jurist Karel Vasak at the International Institute of Human Rights in Strasbourg, these are rights that go beyond civil and social. Remaining largely unofficial, this broad spectrum of rights includes group and collective rights, rights to self-determination, rights to economic and social development, rights to a healthy environment, rights to natural resources, rights to communicate, rights to participation in cultural heritage, and rights to intergenerational equity and sustainability. [11]

"Third wave" of terrorism A thesis advanced by some scholars of terrorism (Sageman, 2008) that contends that the most recent wave of transnational terrorism is being advanced by "homegrown" Islamic radicals living in, and citizens of, Western countries and loosely inspired by al Qaeda. [7]

Thirty and Eighty Years' Wars Two partly concurrent periods of declared and undeclared warfare during the 16th and 17th centuries throughout Europe, involving the Holy Roman Empire and various opponents of its centralizing imperial rule. These wars, and their resolution through the terms of the Peace of Westphalia in 1648, helped transform medieval Europe into the "modern," state-based system. [3]

Totalitarianism A political system in which the ruling regime recognizes no limit to its authority and seeks to regulate and control every and all aspects of public and private life. [3]

Trade barriers Government-induced restrictions on international free trade that can take the form of tariffs, import quotas, licensing, subsidies, embargos, and currency devaluations. [4]

Transaction costs Impediments to commercial or other cooperative ventures stemming from a lack of trust between and among involved parties rooted in concerns about the enforceability of agreements. [2]

Transitional justice A wide range of judicial and nonjudicial processes and mechanisms associated with a society's attempts to redress the legacies of massive human rights abuses and work toward accountability, justice, and reconciliation. [8]

Transnational advocacy networks (TANs) IGOs, NGOs, and national organizations that are based on shared values or common interests and exchange information and services. [4]

Transnational crime Organized illegal activity that occurs across borders and challenges the jurisdiction of national governments with the goal of obtaining financial or other material benefit. Such offenses can include terrorist activity, money laundering, drug trafficking, human trafficking, organ trafficking, and the sale of small arms and light weapons, many of which are interconnected and interdependent. [4]

Transnational terrorism Terrorism carried out either across national borders or by groups that operate in more than one country. [7]

Transnationalism Social, political, economic, and cultural activities and processes that transcend and permeate the borders and authority of states. [2, 4, 7]

Treaty of Amsterdam Treaty that made substantial changes to the Maastricht Treaty by emphasizing citizenship and the rights of individuals; striving for more democracy through increased powers for the European Parliament; a Community area of freedom, security, and justice; the beginnings of a common foreign and security policy; and the reform of the institutions in the run-up to enlargement. [5]

Treaty of Nice This treaty amended the Maastricht Treaty and Treaty of Rome by reforming the institutional structure of the European Union to withstand eastward expansion. [5]

Treaty of Westphalia The treaty that ended the Thirty Years' War (1618–1648). The treaty signals the birth of the modern state system and the end of the theoretical subordination of the monarchies of Europe, especially those that had adopted Protestantism, to the authority of the Roman Catholic Church and the Holy Roman Empire. While the date of 1648 marked an important change, the state as a sovereign entity had begun to emerge earlier and continues to evolve. [2, 6]

Treaty on the Non-Proliferation of Nuclear Weapons (NPT) A multilateral treaty concluded in 1968, then renewed and made permanent in 1995. The parties to the treaty agree not to transfer nuclear weapons or in any way to "assist, encourage, or induce any non-nuclear state to manufacture or otherwise acquire nuclear weapons." Nonnuclear signatories of the NPT also agree not to build or accept nuclear weapons. [6]

UN Charter Signed on June 26, 1945, the Charter serves as the foundational treaty of the United Nations. All members are bound by its articles. The Charter also states that obligations to the United Nations prevail over all other treaty obligations. [5, 11]

UN Conference on Environment and Development (UNCED) Often called Earth Summit I or the Rio Conference, this gathering in 1992 was the first to bring together most of the world's countries, a majority of which were represented by their head of state or government, to address the range of issues associated with sustainable development. [12]

UN Conference on Trade and Development (UNCTAD) A UN organization established in 1964 and currently consisting of all UN members plus the Holy See, Switzerland, and Tonga that holds quadrennial meetings aimed at promoting international trade and economic development. [10]

UN Conference on Population and Development (UNCPD) A UN-sponsored conference that met in Cairo, Egypt, in September 1994 and was attended by delegates from more than 170 countries. The conference called for a program of action to include spending $17 billion annually by the year 2000 on international, national, and local programs to foster family planning and to improve the access of women in such areas as education. [12]

UN Development Programme (UNDP) An agency of the UN established in 1965 to provide technical assistance to stimulate economic and social development in the economically less developed countries. The UNDP has 48 members selected on a rotating basis from the world's regions. [10]

UN General Assembly (UNGA) The main representative body of the United Nations, composed of all 192 member-states where each state has one vote. [5]

UN Human Rights Council (UNHRC) An intergovernmental body within the United Nations system responsible for strengthening the promotion and protection of human rights around the globe and for addressing situations of human rights violations and making recommendations on them. Meeting in Geneva, Switzerland, the Council is made up of 47 United Nation member-states that the UN General Assembly elects. [11]

UN Security Council (UNSC) The main organ of the United Nations charged with the maintenance and promotion of international peace and security. The Security Council has 15 members, including 5 permanent members. [5]

UN Trusteeship Council Suspending operation on November 1, 1994, with the independence of Palau, the major goals were to promote the advancement of the inhabitants of Trust Territories and their progressive development toward self-government or independence. [5]

Unanimity voting A system used to determine how votes should count. In this system, in order for a vote to be valid, all members must agree to

the proposed measure. Abstention from a vote may or may not block an agreement. [5]

Unipolar system A type of international system that describes a single country with complete global hegemony or preponderant power. [2]

United Nations High Commissioner for Refugees (UNHCR) Established December 14, 1950, by the UN General Assembly, the UNHCR is mandated to lead and coordinate action to protect refugees and resolve refugee problems worldwide. Its primary purpose is to safeguard the rights and well-being of refugees. [11]

Universal Declaration of Human Rights Adopted by the UN General Assembly in 1948, it is the most fundamental internationally proclaimed statement of human rights in existence. [5, 11]

Universal Periodic Review (UPR) A unique process that involves a review of the human rights records of all 192 UN member-states once every four years. [11]

Universalism A belief that human rights are derived from sources external to society, such as from a theological, ideological, or natural rights basis. [11]

Uruguay Round The eighth round of GATT negotiations to reduce tariffs and nontariff barriers (NTBs) to trade. The eighth round was convened in Punta del Este, Uruguay, in 1986 and its resulting agreements were signed in Marrakesh, Morocco, in April 1994. [9]

Vienna Convention on the Law of Treaties An international treaty that entered into force in 1980 codifying the norm of *pacta sunt servanda* ("agreements must be kept") and establishing the legal force of international treaties between states. The VCLT defines a treaty as "an international agreement concluded between states in written form and governed by international law," and affirms that

every state possesses the capacity and right to conclude treaties. [8]

War crimes Violations of the laws of war (e.g., international humanitarian law) including the murder or mistreatment of prisoners of war; wanton destruction of cities, towns, villages, or other civilian areas; the murder or mistreatment of civilians; and the forced deportation of civilian residents of an occupied territory to internment camps. The definition of war crimes has developed over the centuries as part of customary international law, with the codification of war crimes and enforcement and punishment provisions beginning in the mid-nineteenth century with the first of the four Geneva Conventions, and continuing in The Hague Conventions of 1899 and 1907. The Rome Statute (1998) rendered war crimes one of the "core crimes" falling under the jurisdiction of the International Criminal Court. [8]

Weapons of mass destruction (WMD) Often referring to nuclear weapons, but also including biological and chemical weapons. Weapons of mass destruction warfare refers to the application of force between countries using biological, chemical, and/or nuclear weapons. [6]

Weighted voting A voting formula that counts votes depending on what criterion is deemed to be the most significant, such as population or wealth. [5]

World Bank Group Four associated agencies that grant loans to LDCs for economic development and other financial needs. Two of the agencies, the International Bank for Reconstruction and Development (IBRD) and the International Development Association (IDA), are collectively referred to as the World Bank. The two other agencies are the International Finance Corporation (IFC) and the Multilateral Investment Guarantee Agency (MIGA). [9]

World Health Organization (WHO)
A UN-affiliated organization created in 1946 to address world health issues. [12]

World Summit on Sustainable Development (WSSD) Often called Earth Summit II, this conference was held in Johannesburg in 2002. It was attended by almost all countries and by some 8,000 NGOs, and it established a series of calls for action and timetables for ameliorating various problems. [12]

World systems theory The view that the world is something of an economic society brought about by the spread of capitalism and characterized by a hierarchy of countries and regions based on a gap in economic circumstance, by a division of labor between capital-intensive activities in wealthy countries and labor-intensive activities in poor countries, and by the domination of lower tier countries and regions by upper tier ones. [9]

World Trade Organization (WTO)
The organization, founded in 1995, that implements and enforces the General Agreement on Tariffs and Trade (GATT) and mediates trade-related disputes between and among states-parties to the GATT. [4, 9]

Xenophobia Fear of foreigners or other "out-groups." [3]

Zero-sum game A contest in which gains by one player can only be achieved by equal losses for other players. See *Non-zero-sum game.* [1]

Zionism The belief that the Jewish people constitute a unified and exceptional nation and are therefore entitled to an independent homeland within the lands of historical Israel. [3]

endnotes

CHAPTER 1

1. *New York Times,* January 21, 2005.

2. http://www.cbsnews.com/stories/ 2010/08/02/earlyshow/main6735984. shtml?tagmncol;lst;1

3. Pew Research Center report, July 30, 2006.

4. *Washington Post,* February 3, 2005.

5. National Geographic Society, "National Geographic—Roper 2002 Global Geographic Literacy Survey," November 2002.

6. CNS News, October 26, 2004.

7. http://www.bea.gov/newsreleases/ international/intinv/intinvnewsrelease.htm

8. Former Assistant Secretary of Defense Lawrence J. Korb, quoted in the *New York Times,* January 22, 1996.

9. CNS News, October 26, 2004.

CHAPTER 2

1. Henry A. Kissinger, *Diplomacy* (1994), quoted in *Newsweek,* April 11, 1994.

2. *Washington Post,* February 12, 2002.

3. *Washington Post,* January 10, 2007.

4. *Washington Post,* February 12, 2002.

5. *Washington Post,* October 30, 2002.

6. *New York Times*, September 21, 2001.

7. Quote from Frank Newport, editor-in-chief, The Gallup Poll. Available online at: http://www.gallup.com/poll/summits/ islam.asp.

8. Pew Research Center, "Views of a Changing World: War with Iraq Further Divides Global Publics," June 3, 2003.

9. *New York Times,* October 12, 2001.

10. Pew Research Center, "Views of a Changing World: War with Iraq Further Divides Global Publics," June 3, 2003.

11. Bush made his remarks during an interview with Linda Douglas of KNBC, Jim Lampley of KCBS, and Paul Moyer of KABC in Los Angeles, CA, on June 15, 1991. See the Public Papers of the Presidents of the United States, U.S. Government Printing Office (GPO).

12. Richard Brookhiser, "The Mind of George W. Bush," *Atlantic Monthly,* April 2003, pp. 55–69.

13. Transcript of joint press conference, October 21, 2001. Available at the American Presidency Project, University of California, Santa Barbara. http://www.presidency.ucsb.edu/

14. *Investor's Business Daily/Christian Science Monitor* poll, 2002. Data provided by The Roper Center for Public Opinion Research, University of Connecticut.

15. "Scientific Balance of Power," *Nature,* 439 (February 9, 2006), pp.646–647.

CHAPTER 3

1. *New York Times*, October 6, 1995.

2. *Ibid.*

3. *New York Times*, June 8, 1994.

4. Chicago Council on Global Affairs, *Global Views 2004: American Public Opinion and Foreign Policy.*

5. Chicago Council on Global Affairs/ German Marshall Fund. Methodology survey, June 2002. Data provided by The Roper Center for Public Opinion Research, University of Connecticut.

6. From "Patrie" in *Dictionaire Philos-ophique,* 1764.

7. Comment by anthropologist Eugene Hammel in the *New York Times,* August 2, 1994.

8. *New York Times,* April 10, 1994.

9. Statement in "Report of the Secretary-General on the Work of the Organiza-tion," quoted in the *Hartford Courant*, September 9, 1999.

10. *Time,* March 12, 1990.

11. Address to Congress by President Woodrow Wilson, February 11, 1918.

12. Political scientist Rupert Emerson of Harvard University, quoted in Wiebe (2001), p.2.

13. *Washington Post,* September 23, 1996.

14. *Washington Post,* 2010.

15. *Business Insider,* 2011.

16. *New York Times,* February 26, 1992.

17. From Woodrow Wilson's *The State: Ele-ments of Historical and Practical Politics* (1911); available at the Woodrow Wilson International Center for Scholars website (http://www.wilsoncenter.org).

18. Maurice Glele-Ahanhanzo, Special Rapporteur of the UN Commission on Human Rights. InterPress Service World News, September 20, 1998.

19. *Le Monde,* May 8, 1998.

20. National Public Radio transcript, November 21, 2006.

21. *New York Times,* January 28, 1998.

22. John English, quoted in the *Sydney (Australia) Morning Herald*, November 26, 2006.

23. Masoud Barzani, Kurdistan Democratic Party, quoted in the *New York Times,* February 18, 2005.

24. *Voice of America* online, November 30, 2006.

25. Martha Brill Olcott, Carnegie Endow-ment for International Peace, *Kansas City Star,* November 26, 2001.

26. Quote from Consortiumnews.com, February 7, 2000.

27. *Washington Post*, March 14, 2005.

CHAPTER 4

1. http://www.theatlantic.com/magazine/ archive/1992/03/jihad-vs-mcworld/3882/

2. http://www.petrostrategies.org/Learning_ Center/oil_transportation.htm# Shipping%20Costs

3. "Gartner Says Worldwide Mobile Connections Will Reach 5.6 Billion in 2011 as Mobile Data Services Revenue Totals $314.7 Billion" (PDF). *Gartner.* 2010-07-09. http://www.gartner.com/ it/page.jsp?id=1759714

4. *Washington Post,* January 29, 2000.

5. *Washington Post,* November 19, 2000. President Clinton's remark was during a

speech at the Vietnam National University, Hanoi, Vietnam, November 17, 2000.

6. http://epp.eurostat.ec.europa.eu/ statistics_explained/index.php/ Foreign_language_learning_statistics

7. *Washington Post,* January 29, 2000.

8. MPAA Theatrical Market Statistics 2010. http://www.mpaa.org/ Resources/93bbeb16-0e4d-4b7e-b085-3f41c459f9ac.pdf

9. *Time,* November 18, 1993.

10. State of the Union message transcript, *Washington Post,* January 28, 2000.

11. *Washington Post,* December 23, 2006.

12. http://csonet.org/

13. Randall L. Tobias, Director of U.S. Foreign Assistance and USAID Administrator Address before the U.S. Conference of Catholic Bishops, Washington DC, December 13, 2006.

14. The former diplomat was Jonathon Clarke, president of the American Journalism Foundation, quoted in the *Washington Diplomat,* June 2001.

15. All data on attitudes toward European and national political identification in this section are drawn from the *Eurobarometer* 59, Spring 2003.

16. Richard M. Nixon, *Beyond Peace* (New York: Random House, 1994), excerpted from *Time,* May 2, 1994.

17. The Pew Research Center for People and the Press, "Views of a Changing World," June 2003.

18. The Reverend J. Bryan Hehir of Harvard University, quoted in the *New York Times,* August 24, 1994.

19. http://www.biographyonline.net/ spiritual/pope-john-paul.html

20. The Pew Research Center for People and the Press, "What the World thinks in 2002."

21. Gallup Poll Web site. http://www. gallup.com/poll/releases/pr020308.asp

22. USA-CNN-Gallup poll, reported in the *Arizona Republic,* March 5, 2002.

23. Literacy: UN Daily News 2010, *Literacy Has Empowering Effect on Women, UN Officials Say,* UN News Centre, New York.

24. Management positions: Grant Thornton International 2009, *Women Still Hold Less than a Quarter of Senior Management Positions in Privately Held Businesses*, Grant Thornton International, London.

25. Employment: United Nations 2011, *Millennium Development Goals Report 2011*, United Nations, New York.

26. Violence against women: UNiTE to End Violence Against Women 2009, *Violence Against Women,* UN Department of Public Information, New York.

27. UNDP, 1995, p. 1.

28. *New York Times*, September 16, 1995.

29. www.ipu.org

30. *New York Times,* April 10, 1995.

31. *New York Times,* April 10, 1995.

CHAPTER 5

1. "The History of the European Union and European Citizenship," on the website www.historiasglo20.org.

2. Yearbook of International Organizations 2005/2006, Vol 5(3).

3. Non-Aligned Movement. 2009. XV Summit of the Non-Aligned Movement. Sharm El Sheikh. http://www.namegypt. org/en/AboutName/MembersObservers AndGuests/Pages/default.aspx. The Group of 77. 2011. The Group of 77-Members. The Group of 77, Geneva. http://www.g77.org/doc/members.html

4. BBC News, February 11, 2003.

5. Valery Fyodorov, director of the Center for Political Trends in Moscow, quoted in the *Christian Science Monitor,* February 11, 2003.

6. Churchill made the widely quoted statement on June 26, 1954, while visiting the United States.

7. Address to the General Assembly, July 16, 1997, UN Document SG/ SM/6284/Rev.2.

8. World Federalist Movement. www.wfm.org/

9. President Frederick J.T. Chiluba of Zambia, quoted in the *New York Times*, October 23, 1995.

10. Permanent Mission of Germany to the United Nations at http://www.new-york-un.diplo.de/Vertretung/newyorkvn/ en/Startseite.html.

11. UN press release GA/9692, December 20, 1999.

12. International Monetary Fund. January 09, 2012. IMF Members' Quotas and Voting Power. Washington, D.C. http://www.imf.org/external/np/sec/ memdir/members.aspx

13. *New York Times*, March 6, 1995.

14. BBC online, October 16, 2006.

15. Address to the Council on Foreign Relations, New York, January 19, 1999, UN document SG/SM/6865.

16. Focal Point for Women. September 2010. The Status of Women in the United Nations System and in the Secretariat. UN Women, New York. http://www.un.org/womenwatch/ osagi/pdf/As-of-31-December-2009.pdf

17. *Asia Times*, January 10, 2007.

18. United Nations, Secretary-General, "Renewing the United Nations: A Programme for Reform," Report to the General Assembly, Document A/51/950, July 14, 1997.

19. General Assembly. September 8, 2010. Composition of the Secretariat: Staff Demographics. United Nations, New York. http://daccess-dds-ny.un.org/ doc/UNDOC/GEN/N10/510/57/ PDF/N1051057.pdf?OpenElement

20. *Washington Post,* April 29, 2006.

21. U.S. General Accountability Office, "The United Nations Reforms Progressing, but Comprehensive Assessment Needed to Measure Impact," Report GAO-04-399, February 2004.

22. Department of Public Information. December 24, 2011. Fifth Committee, Concluding Session, Recommends $5.15 Billion Budget for 2012-2013, Including Financing for 29 Special Political Missions. United Nations, New York. http://www.un.org/News/ Press/docs/2011/gaab4021.doc.htm .

23. United Nations. 2011. Is the United Nations a Good Value for the Money? United Nations, New York. http://www. un.org/geninfo/ir/index.asp?id=150

24. *New York Times,* September 12, 1995.

25. United Nations Peacekeeping. November 30, 2011. Peacekeeping Fact Sheet. United Nations, New York.

http://www.un.org/en/peacekeeping/resources/statistics/factsheet.shtml

26. Address to "Empower America," Washington, D.C., October 16, 1998, UN Document SG/SM/6404.

27. General Assembly. July 26, 2010. United Nations Development Programme Financial Reports and Audited Financial Statements for the Biennium Ended 31 December 2009. United Nations, New York. Available at http://www.beta.undp.org/content/dam/undp/documents/about/transparencydocs/UNBOA audit report A65_5_add_1 for biennium 2008 to 2009.pdf. Operations Support Group. February 28, 2011. Income and Expenditures. UNDP, New York. http://www.beta.undp.org/content/undp/en/home/operations/transparency/income_expenditures.html

28. UNHCR. 2012. UNHCR—What We Do. UN Refugee Agency, New York. http://www.unhcr.org/pages/49c3646cbf.html

29. *Time,* October 30, 1995.

30. Press conference, December 16, 2006, UN press release.

31. Address at Princeton University, November 24, 1997, UN Document SG/SM/6404.

32. *New York Times,* July 17, 1997.

33. UNICEF. February 2011. The State of the World's Children 2011. UNICEF, New York. http://www.unicef.org/sowc2011/pdfs/SOWC-2011-Main-Report_EN_02092011.pdf

34. BBC World Service Poll, March 2005.

35. *Washington Post,* April 12, 2005.

36. *New York Times,* January 8, 1997.

37. *New York Times,* September 18, 1994.

38. Communication Department of the European Commission. 2011. EU Administration. EU, Brussels. http://europa.eu/about-eu/facts-figures/administration/index_en.htm

39. European Commission. December 19, 2011. The EU Budget 2011 in Figures. EU, Brussels. http://ec.europa.eu/budget/figures/2011/2011_en.cfm

40. *Daily Mail,* February 2, 2007.

41. European Parliament. 2012. European Parliament News. EU, Brussels.

http://www.europarl.europa.eu/news/en/headlines/

42. European Parliament. July 17, 2009. Percentage of Men/Women Members of the European Parliament. EU, Brussels. http://www.europarl.europa.eu/sides/getDoc.do?language=en&type=IMPRESS&reference=20090629BRI57511&secondRef=ITEM-003-en

43. BBC, March 29, 2005.

44. Court of Justice of the European Union. 2012. CURIA - General Presentation. EU, Luxembourg. http://curia.europa.eu/jcms/jcms/Jo2_6999/

CHAPTER 6

1. *Labor,* September 6, 1947.

2. To a lesser extent, the end of the Cold War brought into focus concerns about excesses in defense spending as an impetus for rethinking security and the appropriate allocation of economic and societal resources. See Tickner (1995) and Booth (1995) on this.

3. For an influential discussion of the changing character of war in the post–Cold War era, see Mary Kaldor, *New and Old Wars: Organized Violence in a Global Era* (Cambridge, UK: Polity Press, 1999). For a critique of Kaldor's argument, see Mats Berdal, "How 'New' Are 'New Wars'? Reflections on Global Economic Change and War in the Early 21ˢᵗ Century," *Global Governance* 9 (October–December 2003): 477–502.

4. A special issue of *Security Dialogue,* 2004 *35*(3), illustrates the controversial aspects of this concept theoretically, analytically, and practically speaking.

5. Schwartz, Peter, and Doug Randall. 2003. *An Abrupt Climate Change Scenario and its Implications for United States National Security.* (New York: Environmental Defense).

6. *New York Times,* May 29, 1998.

7. Statement of Senator Richard G. Lugar (R-IN), October 7, 1999.

8. *New York Times,* September 13, 1996.

9. *The Hindu,* May 13, 1998.

10. *The Pakistan Observer,* May 31, 1998.

11. Quoted in BBC, February 17, 2011.

12. John M. Deutch quoted in the *New York Times,* February 25, 1996.

13. *New York Times,* January 9, 2007.

CHAPTER 7

1. Senator Pat Roberts (R-Kansas), quoted in the *Washington Post National Weekly Edition,* October 1–7, 2001.

2. *Washington Post,* April 24, 2002.

3. Statement of the *World Islamic Front,* "Jihad against Jews and Crusaders," February 23, 1998. Available online on the website of the Federation of American Scientists. http://www.fas.org/irp/world/para/docs/980223-fatwa.htm

CHAPTER 8

1. *Washington Post,* October 23, 2006.

2. Address at Ditchley Park, United Kingdom, June 26, 1998. Quoted in UN Document SG/SM/6313.

3. All quotes from President George W. Bush in this section taken from his Address to the Nation, March 17, 2003.

4. CNN.com, February 24, 2003.

5. *New York Times,* March 11, 2003.

6. Quoted at http://www.why-war.com/news/2002/10/12/iraqwarn.html.

7. Phyllis Bennis of the Institute for Policy Studies, quoted in Margot Patterson, "Beyond Baghdad: Iraq Seen as First Step to Extend U.S. Hegemony," *National Catholic Reporter,* December 12, 2002.

8. Radio Free Europe release, April 9, 2003.

9. International Criminal Tribunal for the Former Yugoslavia 2012, *About the ICTY* [Homepage of UN ICTY], [Online]. http://www.icty.org/sections/AbouttheICTY

10. CNN.com. June 1, 2000.

11. *New York Times,* August 13, 1997.

12. *New York Times,* June 15, 1998.

13. *Washington Post,* April 12, 2002.

14. Interview of April 29, 2002, in Judicial Diplomacy on the Web. http://www.diplomaticjudiciaire.com/UK/ICCUK7.htm

15. http://www.aljazeera.com/news/africa/2012/04/201242693846498785.html

16. Statement of the Islamic Resistance Movement, Hamas-Palestine, issued December 17, 2001, in reaction to the speech of President Arafat. http://www.jmcc.org/new/01/dec/hamasstate.htm

17. "The Impossible Dream (The Quest)" was composed by Mitch Leigh, with lyrics written by Joe Darion, for the 1965 musical *Man of La Mancha,* based on the novel *The Adventures of Don Quixote* by Cervantes.

18. Kennedy's Remark on June 24, 1963, can be found in the *Public Paper of the President of the United States: John F. Kennedy, 1963.*

CHAPTER 9

1. Jessica Yellin (2011). "Obama faces tall order at G-20."

2. Michael Moynihan, "Is the 'Free Market' Tea Party Anti-Free Trade?" http://reason.com/blog/2010/09/30/is-the-free-market-tea-party-a, 9/30/2010

3. Lori Wallach, "After Incurring Largest Democratic House Opposition Vote in His Presidency, Obama Backs Trade Deals That Government Studies Say Will Increase Trade Deficit," *Public Citizen,* http://www.citizen.org/pressroom/pressroomredirect.cfm?ID=3438, 10/21/2011.

4. *Labor,* September 6, 1947.

5. *Global Views 2004: American Public Opinion and Foreign Policy,* Chicago Council on Foreign Relations.

6. Interpress Service World News, November 29, 2001.

7. *Hartford Courant,* May 19, 2005.

8. As quoted in Robert A. Pastor. *Congress and the Politics of U.S. Foreign Economic Policy, 1929-1976,* Berkeley: University of California Press, p. 86.

9. Chicago Council on Foreign Relations, *Global Views 2008: American Public Opinion and Foreign Policy.*

10. Cnn.com Wire Staff. (2011) "Obama touts cooperation with Asia, calls out China." http://www.cnn.com/2011/11/14/politics/obama-apec-summit/index.html?hpt=ias_c1

11. Reinhardt, Andy, "Europe Reacts to Obama's Victory," *BusinessWeek,* November 5, 2008, on the Web at http://www.businessweek.com/globalbiz/content/nov2008/gb2008115_581184.htm?chan=globalbiz_europe+index+page_top+stories.

12. *Washington Post,* September 15, 2003.

13. *Guardian Unlimited,* September 5, 2003.

14. BBC, April 24, 2007.

15. Reuters, April 30, 2007.

16. Speech to the U.S. Chamber of Commerce, Washington, D.C., April 23, 2007.

17. Tom Miles and Juliane von Reppert-Bismarck, (2011) "Fifty economists ask Obama to 'step up' on trade," Rueters.com, September 2. http://www.reuters.com/article/2011/09/02/us-trade-doha-idUSTRE7814SO20110902

18. See http://www.imf.org/external/np/pp/eng/2010/070710.pdf, p. 6.

19. Inter Press Service News Agency, April 17, 2002.

20. Walden Bello, from "Justice, Equity and Peace Are the Thrust of Our Movement," acceptance speech at the Right Livelihood Award ceremonies, Swedish Parliament, Stockholm (December 8, 2003).

21. President Eduardo Duhalde of Argentina (2002–2003), quoted in the *Washington Post,* January 15, 2002.

22. Jeffrey D. Sachs, "IMF 'Cure' Is Adding to Crisis in Argentina," op-ed piece in the *Irish Times,* May 4, 2002.

23. Artemio Lopez, chief economist for Equis Research, quoted in the *Washington Post,* May 3, 2002.

24. President Nestor Kirchner, quoted by BBC News, May 26, 2003.

25. *Washington Post,* April 30, 2002.

26. BBC News, September 11, 2003.

27. Johan Norberg, "Three Cheers for Global Capitalism," *American Enterprise Online* (June 2004).

28. BBC, March 21, 2005.

29. *Wall Street Journal,* May 1, 2007.

30. *International Herald Tribune,* June 11, 2007.

31. Comments in a speech, January 22, 1999, on the Web at www.oneworld.net/guides/imf_wb/front.shtml.

32. BBC.com, June 9, 2007.

33. Professor John Kirton of the University of Toronto G-8 Information Centre, quoted by the BBC, July 12, 2005.

34. Nicholas Bayne, "Impressions of the Evian Summit, 1–3 June 2003," 2003 Evian Summit: Analytical Studies, G-8 Information Centre, University of Toronto, http://www.g7.

35. *Rolling Stone,* July 11, 2005.

36. Reuters, July 13, 2005.

37. Gary Hufbauer of the Institute for International Economics, quoted in the *Virginian-Pilot,* January 14, 2004.

38. *BusinessWeek,* December 22, 2003.

39. *Miami Herald,* April 28, 2007.

40. *Miami Herald,* September 13, 2003.

41. *New Zealand Herald,* January 14, 2004.

CHAPTER 10

1. "World Bank Projects Global Slowdown, with Developing Countries Impacted," Press Release No: 2012/236/DEC, worldbank.org.

2. Note that these statistics use World Bank definitions and not UN ones.

3. *Hartford Courant,* March 12, 1995.

4. The Accra Declaration, at http://www.unctad.org/en/docs/tdl413_en.pdf.

5. G-77 at www.g77.org/southsummit2/en/intro.html.

6. President Bush's comments were made to the International Conference on Financing for Development in Monterrey, Mexico, as quoted in the *Hartford Courant,* March 23, 2002.

7. Reinhardt, Andy, "Europe Reacts to Obama's Victory," *BusinessWeek,* November 5, 2008, on the Web at http://www.businessweek.com/globalbiz/content/nov2008/gb2008115_581184.htm?chan=globalbiz_europe+index+page_top+stories.

8. Pew Research Center, "Views of a Changing World," 2003.

9. Gallup Poll, February 2004; data provided by Roper Center for Public Opinion Research, University of Connecticut.

10. BBC online, March 25, 2007.

11. Charles Duhigg and David Barboza, "In China, Human Costs Are Built Into an iPad," *New York Times.* http://www.nytimes.com/2012/01/26/business/ieconomy-apples-ipad-and-the-human-costs-for-workers-in-china.html?_r=1&ref=general&src=me&pagewanted=all

12. Productivity Commission, Government of Australia, "Measures of Restrictions on Trade in Services Database," *Canberra,* March 8, 2005.

13. John K. Veroneau, "Introduction," *eJournal USA,* an Electronic Journal of the U.S. Department of State, January 2007.

14. U.S. Federal Reserve Bank of Dallas, "2002 Annual Report, The Fruits of Free Trade," W. Michael Cox and Richard Alm.

15. BBC, March 22, 2002.

16. Associated Press, February 5, 2002.

17. *New York Times,* November 2, 1996.

18. Representative Joseph Gaydos in the *Congressional Record,* April 13, 1988.

19. Frank J. Gaffney Jr., "China's Charge," *National Review,* June 28, 2005.

20. Quoted in Charles R. Smith, "Rand Report Warns of Conflict with China," June 20, 2001, on the NewsMax website at http://www.newsmax.com/.

21. White House press release, May 20, 2002.

22. "Obama eases restrictions to Cuba." http://www.guardian.co.uk/world/2009/apr/13/barack-obama-cuba-policy-change

CHAPTER 11

1. http://www.ilo.org/global/about-the-ilo/lang--en/index.htm

2. The idea of the generation of rights was coined by Karel Vasak in the 1970s to reflect the rallying cry of the French Revolution—liberty, equality, and fraternity.

3. U.S. State Department, Bureau of Democracy, Human Rights, and Labor, Country Reports on Human Rights Practices, 2002, released March 31, 2003.

4. *New York Times,* March 5, 1997.

5. Pew Research Center, Global Attitudes Project, 2011. http://www.pewglobal.org/files/2011/11/Pew-Global-Attitudes-Values-Report-FINAL-November-17-2011-10AM-EST.pdf

6. Address at the University of Tehran on Human Rights Day, December 10, 1997, UN Document SG/SM/6419.

7. *New York Times,* May 5, 1994.

8. China, Ministry of Foreign Affairs, Foreign Ministry spokesperson Jiang Yu's regular press conference, May 8, 2007.

9. http://www.udhr.org/history/question.htm#_Toc397930435

10. http://www.un.org/Depts/dhl/udhr/

11. *Washington Post,* March 4, 2005.

12. Chicago Council on Global Affairs, *The United States and the Rise of China and India: Results of a 2006 Multination Survey of Public Opinion* (Chicago: Chicago Council on Global Affairs, 2006).

13. Secretary-General Kofi Annan, "Address to Mark International Human Rights Day," New York City, December 8, 2006, text in a UN press release, December 8, 2006.

14. U.S. State Department, Daily Press Briefing, Sean McCormack, spokesman, March 6, 2007.

15. McCarthy, M. 2011. "Feds probe $4.5 billion college licensing industry," *USA Today,* 01 December. http://content.usatoday.com/communities/gameon/post/2011/12/feds-launch-probe-of-45-billion-collegiate-licensing-industry-img-college-licensin-company-clc-us-department-of-justice/1#.T0z2W_GPV2B

16. Dreier, P. 2001. "The Campus Anti-Sweatshop Movement," *The American Prospect,* 19 December. http://prospect.org/article/campus-anti-sweatshop-movement

17. Office on Drugs and Crime 2012, *What is Human Trafficking,* United Nations Office on Drugs and Crime. http://www.unodc.org/unodc/en/human-trafficking/what-is-human-trafficking.html

18. See, for example, http://www.guestworkeralliance.org/category/justice-at-hersheys-2/.

CHAPTER 12

1. *New York Times,* May 20, 1997.

2. http://www.riob.org/IMG/pdf/Dominique_Fougeirol_RIOB_Debrecen_Mekong.pdf

3. http://live.unece.org/env/lrtap/welcome.html

4. Dennis Pirages (1989) uses the terms "exclusionists" and "inclusionists" instead of "modernists" and "neotraditionalists," respectively.

5. Christopher Flavin, et al., State of the World 2003 (World-Watch Institute: Washington, D.C. 2005), p. 5

6. See Prof. Ron Mitchell's International Environmental Agreements Project at http://iea.uoregon.edu/page.php?file=home.htm&query=static for an extensive database of international environmental agreements starting at 1300.

7. *Hartford Courant,* June 8, 1992.

8. *Hartford Courant,* June 6, 1992.

9. September 2, 2003, on the WSSD site at http://www.un.org/events/wssd/.

10. Reuters, June 7, 2002.

11. Undersecretary of State for Global Affairs Paula Dobriansky, on the website of the U.S. Embassy in Indonesia at http://www.usembassyjakarta.org.

12. September 2, 2003, on the WSSD site at http://www.un.org/events/wssd.

13. September 4, 2003, on the WSSD site at http://www.un.org/events/wssd.

14. http://www.uncsd2012.org/rio20/index.php?menu=123#jobs

15. *New York Times,* November 29, 1995.

16. CBS News/*New York Times* poll, April, 2007; data provided by The Roper Center for Public Opinion Research, University of Connecticut.

17. *New York Times,* August 31, 1994.

18. *L'Observatore Romano,* n.d.

19. *New York Times,* September 6, 1994.

20. *New York Times,* September 4, 1995.

21. Quotes are from the *New York Times,* November 14, 2006, reporting on an article by Pekka Kauppi, Jesse Ausubel, and others in the Proceedings of the National Academy of Sciences.

22. Julian Simon, "Environmentalists May Cause the Truth to Become Extinct," an op-ed piece in the *Hartford Courant,* June 15, 1992.

23. *Washington Post,* March 5, 2003.

24. *Arizona Republic,* March 23, 2003.

25. Boris Worm of Dalhousie University in Nova Scotia, Canada, quoted in the *New York Times,* November 3, 2006.

26. Satya Nandan of Fiji, chairman of the conference that in 1995 concluded the Agreement for the Implementation of the Law of the Sea Convention Relating to the Conservation and Management of Straddling Fish Stocks and Highly Migratory Fish Stocks; quoted in the *Hartford Courant,* August 4, 1995.

27. BBC, June 22, 2005.

28. BBC, June 15, 2006.

29. U.S. Department of State press release, August 7, 2003.

30. Report by the NGO, Basel Action Group, quoted in the *New York Times,* October 24, 2005.

31. Quote is from the *Asia Times,* August 8, 2003. The NGOs that issued the report were the Basel Action Network and the Silicon Valley Toxics Coalition.

32. UN Human Rights Commission, UN Document E/CN.4/ 1998/10, "Adverse Effects of the Illicit Movement and Dumping of Toxic and Dangerous Products and Wastes on the Enjoyment of Human Rights," January 20, 1998.

33. *Manchester Guardian Weekly,* March 20, 1994.

34. *Guardian Unlimited,* January 6, 2007.

35. James Schlesinger, an op-ed piece in the *Hartford Courant,* January 27, 2004.

36. IPCC, Working Group III Report, "Mitigation of Climate Change," May 4, 2007, and Working Group I Report, "The Physical Science Basis," February 2, 2007.

37. *New York Times,* September 6, 2000.

38. Claudia Tebaldi, a scientist at the National Center for Atmospheric Research quoted in the *Washington Post,* October 21, 2006.

39. CNN.com, May 31, 2003.

40. *New York Times,* February 29, 2000.

41. *New York Times,* August 19, 2000.

42. Nicholas Stern, head of the U.K. Government Economic Service, quoted in the *Washington Post,* October 31, 2006.

43. John M. Reilly, an economist at the M.I.T. Joint Program on the Science and Policy of Global Change, quoted in the *New York Times,* December 12, 2006.

44. The proposal was made by Harvard economist Richard Cooper.

45. W. David Montgomery, economist at Charles River Associates, quoted in the *New York Times,* December 12, 2006.

46. Yale environmental law and policy professor Dan Esty quoted in the *Washington Post,* October 31, 2006, A18.

47. Mark Mwandosya of Tanzania, head of the LDC caucus in Kyoto quoted in the *New York Times,* November 20, 1997.

48. *New York Times,* December 12, 1997.

49. *New York Times,* December 13, 1997. Bush's remark was made while still a presidential hopeful.

50. *Washington Post,* June 5, 2002.

51. *New York Times,* April 7, 2007.

52. *New York Times,* April 7, 2007.

53. "Durban climate change: the agreement explained." http://www.telegraph.co.uk/earth/environment/climatechange/8949099/Durban-climatechange-the-agreement-explained.html

54. Off-the-record interview with Mark A. Boyer, February 2011.

references

Abbott, Kenneth W., and Duncan Snidal. 1998. "Why States Act through Formal International Organizations." *Journal of Conflict Organization*, 42/1:3–32.

Abrahms, Max. 2006. "Why Terrorism Does Not Work." *International Security*, 31/2:42–78.

Agah, Yonov Frederick. 2012. "WTO Dispute Settlement Body Developments in 2010: An Analysis." *Trade, Law and Development*, 4/1:241–250.

Alter, Karen. 2003. "Do International Courts Enhance Compliance with International Law?" *Review of Asian and Pacific Studies*, 25:51–77.

Amstutz, Mark R. 2005. *International Ethics: Concepts, Theories, and Cases in Global Politics*. Lanham, MD: Rowman & Littlefield.

Anderson, Benedict. 1991. *Imagined Communities: Reflections on the Origin and Spread of Nationalism*. New York/London: Verso.

Andrade, Lydia M. 2003. "Presidential Diversionary Attempts: A Peaceful Perspective." *Congress & the Presidency*, 30:55–79.

Anheiner, Helmut, Marlies Glasius, and Mary Kaldor. 2004. *Global Civil Society*. Cambridge, UK: Polity Press.

Arend, Anthony Clark. 2003. "A Methodology for Determining an International Legal Rule." In *International Law: Classic and Contemporary Readings*, 2nd ed., ed. Charlotte Ku and Paul F. Diehl. Boulder, CO: Lynne Reinner.

Axtmann, Roland. 2004. "The State of the State: The Model of the Modern State and Its Contemporary Transformation." *International Political Science Review*, 25/3:259–279.

Axworthy, Lloyd. 2001. "Human Security and Global Governance: Putting People First." *Global Governance*, 7:19–23.

Azar, Edward E. 1990. *The Management of Protracted Social Conflict: Theory and Cases*. Aldershot: Dartmouth.

Bajpai, Kanti. 2000. "Human Security: Concept and Measurement," Kroc Institute Occasional Paper #19: OP1 (August 2000). South Bend, IN: Kroc Institute, University of Notre Dame.

Baldwin, David A. 1979. "Power Analysis and World Politics: New Trends versus Old Tendencies." *World Politics*, 31/2:161–194.

Baldwin, David A. 1980. "Interdependence and Power: A Conceptual Analysis," *International Organization*, 34/4:471–506.

Baldwin, David A. 1997. "The Concept of Security," *Review of International Studies*, 23/1:5–26.

Baradat, Leon P. 2003. *Political Ideologies*, 8th ed. Englewood Cliffs, NJ: Prentice-Hall.

Barash, D. 2011. "Why We Needed Bin Laden Dead," *Chronicle of Higher Education*, 57/37:B14–B15.

Barber, Benjamin R. 1992. "Jihad vs. McWorld," *The Atlantic Monthly*, May 1992.

Barber, Benjamin R. 1996. *Jihad vs. McWorld: How Globalism and Tribalism Are Reshaping the World*. New York: Ballantine Books.

Barber, James D. 1985. *Presidential Character*, 3rd ed. Englewood Cliffs, NJ: Prentice-Hall.

Barnett, Michael, and Martha Finnemore. 2004. *Rules for the World: International Organizations in Global Politics*. Ithaca: Cornell University Press.

Bassam, T. 2010, "The Politicization of Islam into Islamism in the Context of Global Religious Fundamentalism." *Journal of the Middle East & Africa*, 1/2:153–170.

Bassiouni, C. 2007. "Ceding the High Ground: The Iraqi High Criminal Court Statute and the Trial of Saddam Hussein." *Case Western Reserve Journal of International Law*, 39/1:21–97.

Baylis, John. 2001. "International and Global Security in the Post–Cold War Era." In *The Globalization of World Politics*, 2nd ed., ed. J. Baylis and S. Smith. Oxford: Oxford University Press.

BBC News. 2010. "What is Wikileaks?" December 7, 2010. Available online at: http://www.bbc.co.uk/news/technology-10757263. Last accessed March 14, 2012.

BBC News. 2010. "Q&A: Mexico's Drug-Related Violence." Available online at: http://www.bbc.co.uk/news/world-latin-america-10681249. Last accessed December 12, 2010.

Bellamy, Alex J. 2006. *Just Wars: From Cicero to Iraq*. London: Polity.

Bellamy, Alex J., and Paul D. Williams. 2011. "The New Politics of Protection? Côte d'Ivoire, Libya, and the Responsibility to Protect." *International Affairs*, 87/4:825–850.

Bellamy, Alex J., Paul Williams, and Stewart Griffin. 2010. *Understanding Peacekeeping*, 2nd ed. Cambridge: Polity.

Bennett, Scott, and Allan C. Stam. 2004. *The Behavioral Origins of War*. Ann Arbor: University of Michigan Press.

Bercovitch, Jacob. 1984. *Social Conflicts and Third Parties: Strategies of Conflict Resolution*. Boulder, CO: Westview Press.

Bercovitch, Jacob, J. Theodore Anagnoson, and Donnette L. Wille. 1991. "Some Conceptual Issues and Empirical Trends in the Study of Successful Mediation in International Relations." *Journal of Peace Research*, 28/1:7–17.

Bercovitch, Jacob, and Patrick Regan. 2004. "Mediation and International Conflict Management: A Review and Analysis." In *Multiple Paths to Knowledge in International Relations*, ed. Zeev Maoz, Alex Mintz, T. Clifton Morgan, Glenn Palmer, and Richard J. Stoll. Lanham, MD: Lexington.

Berdal, Mats. 2003. "How 'New' Are 'New Wars'? Global Economic Change and the Study of Civil War." *Global Governance*, 9/4:477–502.

Betsill, Michele M., and Harriet Bulkeley. 2004. "Transnational Networks and

Global Environmental Governance: The Cities for Climate Protection Program." *International Studies Quarterly,* 48/2:471–487.

Bhagwati, Jagdish. 2004. *In Defense of Globalization.* Oxford, UK: Oxford University Press.

Bilder, Richard B. 2007. "Adjudication: International Arbitral Tribunals and Courts." In *Peacemaking in International Conflict: Methods and Techniques* (revised edition), ed. I. William Zartman. Washington, DC: U.S. Institute of Peace Press.

Bobrow, Davis B. 1996. "Complex Insecurity: Implications of a Sobering Metaphor: 1996 Presidential Address." *International Studies Quarterly,* 40/4:435–450.

Boehmer, C. 2006. Neoliberal Institutionalism. University of Texas El Paso, El Paso, TX. Available at http://utminers.utep.edu/crboehmer/Neo-Liberal%20Institutionalism.pdf

Bohas, Henri-Alexandre. 2003. "A New Middle Age: A Post-Westphalian Approach to the European Union." Paper presented at "Challenge and Prospects for the European Union in a Globalizing World." Research Conference of the European Union Center of California, Claremont, CA.

Booth, Ken. 1991. *New Thinking about Strategy and International Security.* London: HarperCollins.

Booth, Ken. 2005. *Critical Security Studies and World Politics.* Boulder, CO: Lynne Rienner.

Booth, Ken, and Nicholas Wheeler. 2008. *The Security Dilemma: Fear, Cooperation, and Trust in World Politics.* Basingstoke: Palgrave Macmillan.

Boulding, Kenneth E. 1956. "General Systems Theory—The Skeleton of Science." *Management Science,* 2/3:197–208.

Boyer, Mark A., and Michael J. Butler. 2005. "Public Goods Liberalism: The Problems of Collective Action." In *Making Sense of International Relations Theory,* ed. Jennifer Sterling-Folker. Boulder, CO: Lynne Rienner.

Brecher, Jeremy. 1993. "Global Village or Global Pillage." *Nation,* December 6.

Brecher, Michael, and Jonathan Wilkenfeld. 2000. *A Study of Crisis.* Ann Arbor: University of Michigan Press.

Breuning, Marijke. 2003. "The Role of Analogies and Abstract Reasoning in Decision-Making: Evidence from the Debate over Truman's Proposal for Development Assistance." *International Studies Quarterly,* 47:229–245.

Brewer, Paul R., Kimberly Gross, Sean Aday, and Lars Willnat. 2004. "International Trust and Public Opinion about World Affairs." *American Journal of Political Science,* 48/1:93–116.

Brown, Michael, ed. 1996. *The International Dimensions of Internal Conflict.* Cambridge, MA: MIT Press.

Brown, Oli, Anne Hammill, and Robert McLeman. 2007. "Climate Change as the 'New' Security Threat: Implications for Africa." *International Affairs,* 83/6:1141–1154.

Brown, Seyom. 1998. "World Interests and the Changing Dimensions of Security." In *World Security: Challenges for a New Century,* 3rd ed., ed. Michael T. Klare and Yogesh Chandrani. New York: St. Marin's Press.

Brysk, Alison. 2009. *Global Good Samaritans: Human Rights as Foreign Policy.* Oxford: Oxford University Press.

Bueno de Mesquita, Bruce. 2002. "Domestic Politics and International Relations." *International Studies Quarterly,* 46:1–10.

Bueno de Mesquita, Ethan. 2005. "The Quality of Terror." *American Journal of Political Science,* 49/3:515–531.

Bull, Hedley. 1977. *The Anarchical Society: A Study of Order in World Politics.* London: Macmillan.

Bunch, Charlotte, and Niamh Reilly. 1994. *Demanding Accountability: The Global Campaign and Vienna Tribunal for Women's Human Rights.* Rutgers University, Center for Women's Global Leadership.

Burton, John, and Frank Dukes. 1990. *Conflict: Practices in Management, Settlement, and Resolution.* New York: St. Martin's Press.

Butler, Michael J. 2012. "Ten Years After: (Re) Assessing Neo-Trusteeship and UN Statebuilding in Timor-Leste." *International Studies Perspectives,* 13/1:85-104.

Butler, Michael J. 2012. *Selling a "Just" War: Framing, Legitimacy, and U.S. Military Intervention.* New York/Basingstoke: Palgrave Macmillan.

Buzan, Barry. 1991. *People, States, and Fear: The National Security Problem in International Relations,* 2nd ed. Boulder, CO: Lynne Rienner.

Byman, Daniel. 2011. "Terrorism after the Revolutions: How Secular Uprisings Could Help (or Hurt) Jihadists." *Foreign Affairs,* 90/3:48-54.

Callaway, Rhonda. 2007. "The Rhetoric of Asian Values." In *Exploring International Human Rights: Essential Reading,* ed. Rhonda Callaway and Julie Harrelson-Stephens. Boulder, CO: Lynne Rienner.

Caplow, Theodore, and Louis Hicks. 2002. *Systems of War and Peace.* Lanham, MD: University Press of America.

Caporaso, James A. 2005. "The Possibilities of a European Identity." *Brown Journal of World Affairs,* 12/1:65–75.

Caprioli, Mary. 2000. "The Myth of Women's Pacifism." In *Taking Sides: Clashing Views on Controversial Issues in World Politics,* 9th ed., ed. John T. Rourke. Guilford, CT: McGraw-Hill/Dushkin.

Caprioli, Mary. 2004. "Feminist IR Theory and Quantitative Methodology: A Critical Analysis." *International Studies Review,* 6/2:253–269.

Caprioli, Mary, and Peter F. Trumbore. 2005. "Rhetoric versus Reality: Rogue States in Interstate Conflict." *Journal of Conflict Resolution,* 49/4:770–791.

Cárdenas, Emilio J., and María Fernanda Cañas. 2002. "The Limits of Self-Determination." In *The Self-Determination of Peoples: Community, Nation, and State in an Interdependent World,* ed. Wolfgang F. Danspeckgruber. Boulder, CO: Lynne Rienner.

Cardenas, Sonia, 2004. "Norm Collision: Explaining the Effects of International Human Rights Pressure on State Behavior." *International Studies Review,* 6/2:213–242.

Caron, D. 2006. "Towards a Political Theory of International Courts and Tribunals." *Berkeley Journal of International Law,* 24/2:401–422.

Carter, Ralph G. 2003. "Leadership at Risk: The Perils of Unilateralism." *PS: Political Science & Politics,* 36/1: 17–22.

C.A.S.E. Collective, 2006. "Critical Approaches to Security in Europe: A Networked Manifesto." *Security Dialogue*, 37/4:443–487.

Chan, Steve. 2004. "Influence of International Organizations on Great-Power War Involvement: A Preliminary Analysis." *International Politics*, 41:27–143.

Cederman, Lars-Erik, Andreas Wimmer, and Brian Min. 2010. "Why Do Ethnic Groups Rebel? New Data and Analysis." *World Politics*, 62/1:87–119.

Chayes, Abram, and Antonia Handler Chayes. 1995. *The New Sovereignty: Compliance with International Regulatory Agreements*. Cambridge, MA: Harvard University Press.

Checkel, Jeffrey T. 1999. "Social Construction and Integration." *Journal of European Public Policy*, 6/4:545–560.

Cheng, Christine. 2012. "Charles Taylor Trial Highlights ICC Concerns." *Al Jazeera*, April 27, 2012. Available online at: http://www.aljazeera.com/indepth/opinion/2012/04/20124268513851323.html. Last accessed July 17, 2012.

Chernoff, Fred. 2004. "The Study of Democratic Peace and Progress in International Relations." *International Studies Review*, 6/1:49–65.

Chicago Council on Global Affairs. 2004. *Global Views 2004: American Public Opinion and Foreign Policy*. Chicago Council on Global Affairs.

Chicago Council on Global Affairs. 2006. *Global Views 2006: The United States and the Rise of China and India*. Chicago Council on Global Affairs.

Chicago Council on Global Affairs (CCGA). 2010. *Global Views 2010—Constrained Internationalism: Adapting to New Realities*. Available at: http://www.thechicagocouncil.org/UserFiles/File/POS_Topline%20Reports/POS%202010/Global%20Views%202010.pdf. Last accessed November 12, 2010.

Chittick, William O., and Lee Ann Pingel. 2002. *American Foreign Policy: History, Substance and Process*. New York: Seven Bridges Press.

Claude, Inis L., Jr. 1964. *Swords into Plowshares: The Problems and Progress of International Organizations*, 3rd ed. New York: Random.

Clausewitz, Carl von. 1976. *On War*, edited and translated by M. Howard and P. Paret. Princeton, NJ: Princeton University Press.

Cline, William. 2004. *Trade Policy and Global Poverty*. Washington, DC: Institute for International Economics.

Coate, Roger, and Jacques Fomerand. 2004. "The United Nations and International Norms: A Sunset Institution?" Paper presented at the annual meeting of the International Studies Association, Montreal, Canada.

Coates, Neal. 2005. "The United Nations Convention on the Law of the Sea, the United States, and International Relations." Paper presented at the annual meeting of the International Studies Association, Honolulu, HI.

Cohn, Carol. 1987. "Sex and Death in the Rational World of Defense Intellectuals." *Signs*, 12/4:687–718.

Coker, Christopher. 1992. "Post-modernity and the End of the Cold War: Has War Been Disinvented?" *Review of International Studies*, 18:189–198.

Coleman, Isobel. 2010. *Paradise Beneath Her Feet: How Women Are Transforming the Middle East*. New York: Random House, Council on Foreign Relations.

Conversi, Daniele. 2002. *Ethnonationalism in the Contemporary World: Walker Connor and the Study of Nationalism*. London: Routledge.

Conversi, Daniele, ed. 2004. *Ethnonationalism in the Contemporary World*. Oxford, UK: Routledge.

Conway, David. 2004. *In Defense of the Realm: The Place of Nations in Classical Liberalism*. Aldershot, UK: Ashgate.

Cooper, Andrew. 2008. *Celebrity Diplomacy*. Boulder, CO: Paradigm Publishers.

Cotton, James. 2007. "Timor-Leste and the Discourse of State Failure." *Australian Journal of International Affairs*, 61/4:455–470.

Cowles, Maria Green, and Desmond Dinan. 2004. *Development in the European Union*. Houndsmills, UK: Palgrave Macmillan.

Cozette, Murielle. 2004. "Realistic Realism? American Political Realism, Clausewitz and Raymond Aron on the Problem of Means and Ends in International Politics." *Journal of Strategic Studies*, 23/3:428–453.

Cramer, Jane Kellett. 2006. "'Just Cause' or Just Politics?" *Armed Forces & Society*, 32/2:178–201.

Crenshaw, Martha. 1988. "Theories of Terrorism: Instrumental and Organizational Approaches." In *Inside Terrorist Organizations*, ed. David Rapoport. New York: Columbia University Press.

Cunningham, Karla J. 2003. "Cross-Regional Trends in Female Terrorism." *Studies in Conflict & Terrorism*, 26/3:171–195.

Daalder, Ivo H., and James M. Lindsay. 2003. *America Unbound: The Bush Revolution in Foreign Policy*. Washington, DC: Brookings Institution Press.

Dag Hammarskjold Library. January 9, 2012. Dag Hammarskjold: The UN Years. United Nations, New York. Available at http://www.un.org/depts/dhl/dag/index.html

Danspeckgruber, Wolfgang. 2002. *The Self-Determination of Peoples: Community, Nation, and State in an Interdependent World*. Boulder, CO: Lynne Rienner.

Day, Gerald W. 1981. "The Impact of the Third Crusade upon Trade with the Levant." *The International History Review*, 3/2:159–168.

De Bary, William Theodore. 2004. *Nobility and Civility: Asian Ideals of Leadership and the Common Good*. Cambridge: Harvard University Press.

de Hoop Scheffer, Jaap. 2005. "Keynote Address by NATO Secretary-General." Victoria University Institute of Policy Studies and New Zealand Institute of International Affairs, Wellington, New Zealand. 31 March 2005. Available online at: http://www.nato.int/docu/speech/2005/s050331a.htm. Last accessed March 11, 2011.

Delahunty, Robert J., and John Yoo. 2005. "Against Foreign Law." *Harvard Journal of Law & Public Policy*, 29/1:291–329.

de Nevers, Renée. 2006. "The Geneva Conventions and New Wars." *Political Science Quarterly*, 121/3:369–396.

de Nevers, Renée. 2006. "Modernizing the Geneva Conventions." *The Washington Quarterly*, 29/2:99–113.

Dessler, Andrew E., and Edward A. Parson. 2006. *The Science and Politics of Global Climate Change: A Guide to the Debate.* Cambridge: Cambridge University Press.

Deutsch, Karl W., et al. 1957. *Political Community and the North Atlantic Area: International Organization in the Light of Historical Experience.* Princeton, NJ: Princeton University Press.

Diehl, Paul F. 1994. *International Peacekeeping.* Baltimore, MD: Johns Hopkins University Press.

DiIulio, John J. 2003. "Inside the Bush Presidency: Reflections of an Academic Interloper." Paper presented at the conference on The Bush Presidency: An Early Assessment, Woodrow Wilson School, Princeton University, Princeton, NJ.

Dinan, Desmond. 2004. *Europe Recast: A History of European Union.* Boulder, CO: Lynne Rienner.

Donnelly, Jack. 1989. *International Human Rights.* Boulder, CO: Westview.

Donnelly, Jack. 1999. "The Social Construction of International Human Rights." In *Human Rights in Global Politics,* ed. Tim Dunne and Nicholas Weaver. Cambridge, UK: Cambridge University Press.

Donnelly, Jack. 2003. *Universal Human Rights in Theory and Practice.* Ithaca, NY: Cornell University Press.

Doyle, Michael W. 1983. "Kant, Liberal Legacies, and Foreign Affairs." *Philosophy and Public Affairs,* 12/3:205–235.

Drainville, André C. 2004. *Contesting Globalization: Space and Place in the World Economy.* Oxford, UK: Routledge.

Druckman, Daniel. 1994. "Nationalism, Patriotism and Group Loyalty: A Social Psychological Perspective." *Mershon International Studies Review,* supplement to *International Studies Quarterly,* 38:43–68.

Duhigg, Charles, and David Barboza. 2012. "In China, Human Costs Are Built into an iPad." *New York Times.* Available at http://www.nytimes.com/2012/01/26/business/ieconomy-apples-ipad-and-the-human-costs-for-workers-in-china.html?_r=1&pagewanted=all

Dyson, Stephen Benedict. 2006. "Personality and Foreign Policy: Tony Blair's Iraq Decisions." *Foreign Policy Analysis,* 2/3:289–306.

Dyson, Stephen Benedict, and Thomas Preston. 2006. "Individual Characteristics of Political Leaders and the Use of Analogy in Foreign Policy Decision Making." *Political Psychology,* 27/2:265–288.

Eatwell, Roger. 2006. "Explaining Fascism and Ethnic Cleansing: The Three Dimensions of Charisma and the Four Dark Sides of Nationalism." *Political Studies Review,* 4/3:263–278.

Eckhardt, William. 1991. "War-Related Deaths since 3000 B.C." *Bulletin of Peace Proposals,* 22:437–443.

Edwards, Martin S. 2006. "Public Opinion Regarding Economic and Cultural Globalization: Evidence from a Cross-National Survey." *Review of International Political Economy,* 13/4:587–608.

Ehrlich, Paul R., and Jianguo Liu. 2002. "Some Roots of Terrorism." *Population and Environment,* 24/2:183–192.

Eichengreen, Barry. 2008. *Globalizing Capital: A History of the International Monetary System,* 2nd ed. Princeton University Press.

el-Battahani, Atta. 2006. "A Complex Web: Politics and Conflict in Sudan." In *Peace by Piece: Addressing Sudan's Conflicts. Accord: An International Review of Peace Initiatives,* 18. London: Conciliation Resources.

Elms, Deborah Kay. 2004. "Intellectual Property Rights, Drug Access, and the Doha Round," GUISD/Pew Case Studies Center, case no. 271. Washington, DC: Georgetown University Institute for the Study of Diplomacy.

Enders, Walter, and Todd Sandler. 2006. "Distribution of Transnational Terrorism among Countries by Income Class and Geography after 9/11." *International Studies Quarterly,* 50/2:367–394.

Enloe, Cynthia. 1990. *Bananas, Beaches, and Bases: Making Feminist Sense of International Politics.* Berkeley: University of California Press.

Epps, Valerie. 2009. *International Law,* 4th ed. Durham, NC: Carolina Academic Press.

Epstein, Joshua. 2003. *War and Gender: How Gender Shapes the War System and Vice Versa.* Cambridge: Cambridge University Press.

Eriksson, Mikael, and Peter Wallensteen. 2004. "Armed Conflict, 1989–2003." *Journal of Peace Research,* 41:625–636.

Erskine, Toni. 2003. *Can Institutions Have Responsibilities? Collective Moral Agency and International Relations.* New York/Basingstoke: Palgrave Macmillan.

Etheredge, Lloyd S. 2001. "Will the Bush Administration Unravel?" *The Government Learning Project.* Online.

Etzioni, Amitai. 2004. "A Self-Restrained Approach to Nation-Building by Foreign Powers." *International Affairs,* 80/1:1–17.

Farer, Tom J. 2003. "The Prospect for International Law and Order in the Wake of Iraq." *American Journal of International Law,* 97/3:621–628.

Ferguson, Niall. 2004. "A World without Power." *Foreign Policy,* 143 (July/August):32–40.

Ferguson, Yale H. 2005. "Institutions with Authority, Autonomy, and Power." *International Studies Review,* 7/2:331–333.

Finnenmore, Martha. 2004. *The Purpose of Intervention: Changing Beliefs about the Use of Force.* Ithaca, NY: Cornell University Press.

Fisher, Dana R. 2004. *National Governance and the Global Climate Change Regime.* Lanham, MD: Rowman & Littlefield.

Fleming, Matthew H., John Roman, and Graham Farrell. 2005. "The Shadow Economy." *Journal of International Affairs* (July): Columbia University of International Public Affairs.

Foot, Rosemary, S. Neil MacFarlane, and Michael Mastanudo, eds. 2003. *U.S. Hegemony and International Organizations.* New York: Oxford University Press.

Forsythe, David P. 2006. "United States Policy toward Enemy Detainees in the 'War on Terrorism.'" *Human Rights Quarterly,* 28/2:465–491.

Forsythe, David, P. 2012. *Human Rights in International Relations,* 3rd ed. New York: Cambridge.

Foster, Dennis, M., and Glenn Palmer. 2006. "Presidents, Public Opinion, and Diversionary Behavior: The Role of Partisan Support Reconsidered." *Foreign Policy Analysis,* 2/3:269–290.

Fox, Jonathan. 2004. "The Rise of Religious Nationalism and Conflict: Ethnic Conflict and Revolutionary Wars, 1945–2001." *Journal of Peace Research,* 41:715–731.

Fox, Jonathan, and Shmeul Sandler. 2004. *Bringing Religion into International Relations.* New York: Palgrave Macmillan.

Freedom House. 2007. *Freedom in the World: The Annual Survey of Political Rights & Civil Liberties, 2005–2006.* New Brunswick, NJ: Transaction.

Freedom House. 2012. *Freedom in the World—2012.* Available online at: http://www.freedomhouse.org/report/freedom-world/freedom-world-2012. Last accessed May 14, 2012.

Friedman, Thomas. 2005. *The World Is Flat: A Brief History of the Twenty-First Century.* New York: Farrar, Straus & Giroux.

Fukuyama, Francis. 1989. "The End of History?" *The National Interest* (Summer 1989).

Fukuyama, Francis. 1992. *The End of History and the Last Man.* New York: Simon & Schuster.

Fukuyama, Francis. 2004. *State-Building: Governance and World Order in the 21st Century.* Ithaca, NY: Cornell University Press.

Gallie, Walter Bryce. 1956. "Essentially Contested Concepts." *Proceedings of the Aristotelian Society,* 56:167–198.

Galtung, Johan. 1994. *Human Rights in Another Key.* Cambridge, UK: Polity Press.

Gartzke, Erik, and Quan Li. 2003. "War, Peace, and the Invisible Hand: Positive Political Externalities of Economic Globalization." *International Studies Quarterly,* 47/4:561–586.

Geisler, Michael, ed. 2005. *National Symbols, Fractured Identities.* Hanover, NH: University Press of New England.

Geller, Daniel S., and John A. Vasquez. 2004. "The Construction and Cumulation of Knowledge in International Relations: Introduction." *International Studies Review,* 6/4:1–12.

Gellner, Ernest. 1983. *Nations and Nationalism.* Ithaca, NY: Cornell University Press.

George, Alexander L. 1969. "The 'Operational Code': A Neglected Approach to the Study of Political Leaders and Decision-Making." *International Studies Quarterly,* 13/2:190–222.

Ghosn, Faten, Glenn Palmer, and Stuart Bremer. 2004. "The MID3 Data Set, 1993–2001: Procedures, Coding Rules, and Description." *Conflict Management and Peace Science,* 21:133–154

Gibler, Douglas M., Toby J. Rider, and Marc L. Hutchison. 2005. "Taking Arms against a Sea of Troubles: Conventional Arms Races during Periods of Rivalry." *Journal of Peace Research,* 42:131–147.

Gijsberts, Mérove, Louk Hagendoorn, and Peer Scheepers. 2004. *Nationalism and Exclusion of Immigrants: Cross-National Comparisons.* Aldershot, UK: Ashcroft.

Gilbert, Daniel T., and Malone, Patrick S. 1995. "The Correspondence Bias." *Psychological Bulletin,* 117: 21–38.

Gilbert, Mark F. 2003. *Surpassing Realism: The Politics of European Integration since 1945.* Lanham, MD: Rowman & Littlefield.

Gitlin, Todd. 2003. "America's Age of Empire." *Mother Jones* (January/February): online.

Glahn, Gerhard von, and James Larry Taulbee. 2007. *Law Among Nations: An Introduction to Public International Law,* 9th ed. New York: Pearson.

Glaser, Charles L., and Steve Fetter. 2006. "Counterforce Revisited: Assessing the Nuclear Posture Review's New Missions." *International Security,* 30/2:84–126.

Goldsmith, Jack L., and Stephen D. Krasner. 2003. "The Limits of Idealism." *Daedalus,* 132:47–63.

Goldsmith, Jack L., and Eric A. Posner. 2005. *The Limits of International Law.* New York: Oxford University Press.

Goldstone, P. R. 2007. "Pax Mercatoria: Does Economic Interdependence Bring Peace?" *Audit of the Conventional Wisdom,* MIT Center for International Studies, 7/12 (August):1–4.

Goodhart, Michael. 2009. *Human Rights: Politics and Practice.* Oxford: Oxford University Press.

Gray, Christine, and Benedict Kingsbury. 1993. "Developments in Dispute Settlement." In *The British Year Book of International Law 1992,* Vol 63. New York: Oxford University Press.

Gray, Colin S. 1994. "Force, Order, and Justice: The Ethics of Realism in Statecraft." *Global Affairs,* 14:1–17.

Greenhill, Brian. 2010. "The Company You Keep: International Socialization and the Diffusion of Human Rights Norms." *International Studies Quarterly,* 54/1:127–146.

Gruenberg, Leon. 1996. "The IPE of Multinational Corporations." In *Introduction to International Political Economy,* ed. David N. Balaam and Michael Veseth. Upper Saddle River, NJ: Prentice-Hall.

Gurr, Ted Robert. 1998. "Terrorism in Democracies: Its Social and Political Bases." In *Origins of Terrorism: Psychologies, Ideologies, Theologies, States of Mind,* ed. Walter Reich. Baltimore, MD: Johns Hopkins University Press.

Haftel, Yoram Z. 2004. "From the Outside Looking In: The Effect of Trading Blocs on Trade Disputes in the GATT/WTO." *International Studies Quarterly,* 48/1:121–149.

Haftel, Yoram Z., and Alexander Thompson. 2006. "The Independence of International Organizations: Concept and Applications." *Journal of Conflict Resolution,* 50/2:253–275.

Hamill, James. 1998. "From Realism to Complex Interdependence? South Africa, Southern Africa, and the Question of Security." *International Relations,* 14/3:1–30.

Handelman, Don. 2004. *Nationalism and the Israeli State: Bureaucratic Logic in Public Events.* London: Berg Publishing.

Harbom, Lotta, and Peter Wallensteen. 2010. "Armed Conflicts, 1946–2009." *Journal of Peace Research,* 47/4:501–509.

Harding, Jeremy. 1994. *Small Wars, Small Mercies: Journeys in Africa's Disputed Nations.* London: Penguin.

Hawkins, Darren. 2004. "Explaining Costly International Institutions: Persuasion and Enforceable Human Rights Norms." *International Studies Quarterly,* 48/4:779–806.

Heasley, James E., III. 2003. *Organization Global Governance: International Regimes and the Process of Collective Hegemony.* Lanham, MD: Lexington Books.

Heater, Derek. 2004. *Citizenship: The Civic Ideal in World History, Politics, and Education*. Houndsmills, UK: Palgrave Macmillan.

Hechter, Michael. 2000. *Containing Nationalism*. Oxford, UK: Oxford University Press.

Held, David, and Anthony G. McGrew. 2000. *The Global Transformations Reader: An Introduction to the Globalization Debate*. London: Polity.

Heldt, Birger. 1999. "Domestic Politics, Absolute Deprivation, and the Use of Armed Force in Interstate Territorial Disputes, 1950–1990." *Journal of Conflict Resolution*, 43/4:451–478.

Helleiner, Eric, and Andreas Pickel, eds. 2005. *Economic Nationalism in a Globalizing World*. Ithaca, NY: Cornell University Press.

Henderson, Errol, and J. David Singer. 2002. "New Wars and Rumors of New Wars." *International Interactions*, 28/2:165–190.

Henderson, Errol A. 2004. "Mistaken Identity: Testing the Clash of Civilizations Thesis in Light of Democratic Peace Claims." *British Journal of Political Science*, 34/3:539–554.

Herrmann, Richard K., and Jonathan W. Keller. 2004. "Beliefs, Values, and Strategic Choice: U.S. Leaders' Decisions to Engage, Contain, and Use Force in an Era of Globalization." *Journal of Politics*, 66/2:557–580.

Herz, John H. 1950. "Idealist Internationalism and the Security Dilemma." *World Politics*, 2:157–180.

Hewitt, J. Joseph, Jonathan Wilkenfeld, and Ted Robert Gurr. 2010. *Peace and Conflict 2010*. Boulder, CO: Paradigm.

Hobsbawm, Eric J. 1990. *Nations and Nationalism since 1780: Programme, Myth, Reality*. Cambridge: Cambridge University Press.

Hobson, John M. 2005. "The Enduring Place of Hierarchy in World Politics: Tracing the Social Logics of Hierarchy and Political Change." *European Journal of International Relations*, 11/1:63–98.

Hoffman, Bruce. 2006. *Inside Terrorism* (rev. and expanded ed.). New York: Columbia University Press.

Hoffmann, Stanley. 2003. "World Governance: Beyond Utopia." *Daedalus*, 132:27–35.

Holsti, K. J. 2004. *Taming the Sovereigns: Institutional Change in International Politics*. New York: Cambridge University Press.

Holsti, Kalevi. 1996. *The State, War, and the State of War*. Cambridge: Cambridge University Press.

Holsti, Ole R. 2004. *Public Opinion and American Foreign Policy*. Ann Arbor: University of Michigan Press.

Homer-Dixon, Thomas F. 1994. "Environmental Scarcities and Violent Conflict: Evidence from Cases." *International Security*, 19(1):5–40.

Horne, John. 2002. "Civilian Populations and Wartime Violence: Toward an Historical Analysis." *International Social Science Journal*, 26:426–435.

Horowitz, Michael, Rose McDermott, and Allan C. Stam. 2005. "Leader Age, Regime Type, and Violent International Relations." *Journal of Conflict Resolution*, 49/45:661–685.

Hossay, Patrick. 2002. *Contentions of Nationhood: Nationalist Movements, Political Conflict and Social Change in Flanders, Scotland, and French Canada*. Lanham, MD: Lexington Books.

Hudson, Valerie M. 2005. "Foreign Policy Analysis: Actor- Specific Theory and the Ground of International Relations." *Foreign Policy Analysis*, 1/1:1–11.

Hudson, Natalie F. 2009. *Gender, Human Security, and the United Nations: Security Language as a Political Framework for Women*. New York/London: Routledge.

Hughes, Barry 1985. *World Futures: A Critical Analysis of Alternatives*. Baltimore: Johns Hopkins University Press.

Human Security Centre. 2010. "Human Security Brief 2009/10." Human Security Centre, Simon Fraser University. Available at: http://www.hsrgroup.org/human-security-reports/20092010/overview.aspx

Huntington, Samuel P. 1993. "The Clash of Civilizations." *Foreign Affairs*, 72/3:56–73.

Huntington, Samuel P. 1996. *The Clash of Civilizations and the Remaking of World Order*. New York: Simon & Schuster.

Ignazi, Piero, and Mark Kesselman. 2004. "Extreme Right Parties in Western Europe." *Political Science Quarterly*, 119/2:369–371.

International Trade Union Confederation 2008. *The Global Gender Pay Gap*, ITUC, Brussels.

Jackson, Robert, and Georg Sørensen. 2003. *Introduction to International Relations: Theories and Approaches*, 2nd ed. Oxford, UK: Oxford University Press.

James, Patrick. 2002. *International Relations and Scientific Progress: Structural Realism Reconsidered*. Columbus: Ohio State University Press.

Jaquette, Jane S. 1997. "Women in Power: From Tokenism to Critical Mass." *Foreign Policy*, 108:23–97.

Jayawickrama, Nihal. 2003. *The Judicial Application of Human Rights Law: National, Regional and International Jurisprudence*. Cambridge, UK: Cambridge University Press.

Jervis, Robert. 1976. *Perception and Misperception in International Politics*. Princeton, NJ: Princeton University Press.

Jervis, Robert. 1978. "Cooperation under the Security Dilemma." *World Politics*, 30:167–214.

Johansen, Robert C. 2006. "The Impact of U.S. Policy toward the International Criminal Court on the Prevention of Genocide, War Crimes, and Crimes against Humanity." *Human Rights Quarterly*, 28/2:301–331.

Johnson, Dominic D. P. 2004. *Overconfidence and War: The Havoc and Glory of Positive Illusions*. Cambridge, MA: Harvard University Press.

Johnson, James T. 1999. *Morality and Contemporary Warfare*. New Haven: Yale University Press.

Johnson, Keith. 2010. "Gains in Bioscience Cause Terror Fears." *Wall Street Journal*, August 11, 2010. Available online at: http://online.wsj.com/article/SB10001424052748703722804575369394068436132.html. Last accessed February 12, 2012.

Johnston, Douglas, ed. 2003. *Faith-Based Diplomacy: Trumping Realpolitik*. New York: Oxford University Press.

Johnston, Nicola. 2001. "Peace Support Operations." From *Inclusive Security, Sustainable Peace: A Toolkit for Advocacy and Action*. Denver, CO: Hunt Alternatives Fund.

Jok, J. M. 2011. "Diversity, Unity, and Nation Building in South Sudan." USIP Special Report no. 287. Washington, DC: United States Institute of Peace.

Jones, S, 2010. "In the Pursuit of Justice: A Comment on the Arrest Warrant for President Al Bashir of Sudan." *Eyes on the ICC* [Online]. 6/1:13–42.

Joyner, Christopher C. 2000. "The Reality and Relevance of International Law in the Twenty-First Century." In *The Global Agenda: Issues and Perspectives*, ed. Charles W. Kegley Jr. and Eugene R. Wittkopf. Boston: McGraw-Hill.

Joyner, Christopher C. 2005. *International Law in the 21st Century: Rules for Global Governance*. Lanham, MD: Rowman & Littlefield.

Jung, Dietrich, ed. 2003. *Shadow Globalization, Ethnic Conflicts, and New Wars*. London: Routledge.

Jung, Hwa Yol. 2002. *Comparative Political Culture in the Age of Globalization*. Lanham, MD: Lexington Books.

Jutta, Joachim. 2003. "Framing Issues and Seizing Opportunities: The UN, NGOs, and Women's Rights." *International Studies Quarterly*, 47:247–274.

Kahneman, Daniel, and Jonathan Renshon. 2007. "Why Hawks Win." *Foreign Policy*, 158:34–38.

Kaldor, Mary. 1999. *New and Old Wars: Organized Violence in a Global Era*. Stanford: Stanford University Press.

Kalicki, Jan H., and David L. Goldwyn. 2005. *Energy and Security: Toward a New Foreign Policy Strategy*. Washington, DC: Woodrow Wilson Center Press.

Kaplan, Robert D. 1994. "The Coming Anarchy." *Atlantic Monthly*, 273/2:44–76.

Karns, Margaret P., and Karen A. Mingst. 2009. *International Organizations: The Politics and Processes of Global Governance*, 2nd ed. New York: Lynne Rienner.

Karns, Margaret P., and Karen A. Mingst. 2012. *International Organizations: The Politics and Processes of Global Governance*, 2nd ed. Boulder, CO: Lynne Rienner.

Keck, Margaret, and Kathryn Sikkink. 1998. *Activists Beyond Borders: Advocacy Networks in International Politics*. Ithaca, NY: Cornell University Press.

Kellett, Peter. 2006. *Conflict Dialogue: Working with Layers of Meaning for Productive Relationships*. Thousand Oaks, CA: Sage.

Keohane, Robert O. 1998. "International Institutions: Can Interdependence Work?" *Foreign Policy*, 110:82–96.

Keohane, Robert O., and Joseph S. Nye Jr. 2001. *Power and Interdependence: World Politics in Transition*, 3rd ed. New York: Addison-Wesley.

Kerr, Rachel. 2004. *The International Criminal Tribunal for the Former Yugoslavia*. Oxford, UK: Oxford University Press.

Keshk, Omar M. G., Brian M. Pollins, and Rafael Reuveny. 2004. "Trade Still Follows the Flag: The Primacy of Politics in a Simultaneous Model of Interdependence and Armed Conflict." *Journal of Politics*, 66/4:1155–1182.

Kindleberger, Charles P. 1973. *International Economics*. Homewood, IL: R.D. Irwin, Inc.

Kindleberger, Charles. 1986. *The World in Depression, 1929-1939*. Berkeley: University of California Press.

Kindleberger, Charles. 2006. *A Financial History of Western Europe*. London: Routledge;

King, Gary, and Christopher J. L. Murray. 2001. "Rethinking Human Security." *Political Science Quarterly*, 116/4:585–610.

Kirkpatrick, David D. 2011. "Egypt Erupts in Jubilation as Mubarak Steps Down." *New York Times*, February 11, 2011; A1.

Kinsella, David, and Bruce Russett. 2002. "Conflict Emergence and Escalation in Interactive International Dyads." *Journal of Politics*, 64:1045–1069.

Kissinger, Henry A. 1979. *The White House Years*. Boston: Little, Brown.

Kissinger, Henry A. 1994. *Diplomacy*. New York: Simon & Schuster.

Klabbers, Jan. 2006. "The Right to Be Taken Seriously: Self-Determination in International Law." *Human Rights Quarterly*, 28/1:186–206.

Klare, Michael T. 2002. *Resource Wars: The New Landscape of Global Conflict*. New York: Henry Holt.

Klare, Michael T. 2004. "Bush-Cheney Energy Strategy: Procuring the Rest of the World's Oil." *Foreign Policy in Focus* (January 2004).

Koh, Harold Hongju. 1997. "Why Do Nations Obey International Law?" *Yale Law Journal*, 106/2599.

Kolstø, Pål. 2006. "National Symbols as Signs of Unity and Division." *Ethnic and Racial Studies*, 29/4:67–701.

Krause, Keith, and Michael C. Williams, eds. 1997. *Critical Security Studies*. Minneapolis: University of Minnesota Press.

Krause, Keith, and Michael Williams. 1996. "Broadening the Agenda of Security Studies: Politics and Methods." *Mershon International Studies Review*, 40/2:229–254.

Krasner, Stephen D. 1983. *International Regimes*. Ithaca, NY: Cornell University Press.

Kristof, Nicholas D., and Sheryl WuDunn. 2009. *Half the Sky: Turning Oppression into Opportunity for Women Worldwide*. New York: Knopf.

Kuziemko, Ilyana, and Eric Werker. 2006. "How Much Is a Seat on the Security Council Worth? Foreign Aid and Bribery at the United Nations." *Journal of Political Economy*, 114/5:905–930.

Kydd, Andrew H., and Barbara F. Walter. 2006. "The Strategies of Terrorism." *International Security*, 31/1:49–79.

Lacina, Bethany, Nils Petter Gleditsch, and Bruce Russett. 2006. "The Declining Risk of Death in Battle." *International Studies Quarterly*, 5/30:673–680.

Lal, Deepak. 2004. *In Praise of Empires: Globalization and Order*. New York: Palgrave Macmillan.

Landman, Todd. 2004. "Measuring Human Rights: Principle, Practice and Policy." *Human Rights Quarterly*, 26 (November): 906-931.

Landman, Todd. 2006. *Studying Human Rights*. New York: Routledge.

Lang, Anthony F., ed. 2003. *Just Intervention*. Washington, DC: Georgetown University Press.

Langlois, Catherine C., and Jean-Pierre P. Langlois. 2006. "When Fully Informed States Make Good the Threat of War: Rational Escalation and the Failure of Bargaining." *British Journal of Political Science*, 36/4:645–669.

Laqueur, Walter. 2004. *No End to War: Terrorism in the Twenty-First Century*. New York: Continuum International.

Larémont, Ricardo Réne. 2005. *Borders, Nationalism, and the African State*. Boulder, CO: Lynne Rienner.

Lasswell, Harold D. 1936. *Politics: Who Gets What, When, How*. New York, London: Whittlesey House, McGraw-Hill Book Co.

Laursen, Steffen Terp. 2011. "Mesopotamian Ceramics from the Burial Mounds of Bahrain, c.2250–1750 BC." *Arabian Archaeology and Epigraphy*, 22/1:32–47.

Layne, Christopher. 2006. "Impotent Power? Re-examining the Nature of America's Hegemonic Power." *National Interest*, 85:41–47.

Layne, Christopher. 2006a. "The Coming of the United States' Unipolar Moment." *International Security*, 31/2:7–41.

Leitner, Kara, and Simon Lester. 2006. "WTO Dispute Settlement from 1995 to 2005: A Statistical Analysis." *Journal of International Economic Law*, 9/1:219–231.

Lemkin, Rafael. 1944. *Axis Rule in Occupied Europe*. Washington, DC: Carnegie Endowment for International Peace.

Leonard, Eric K. 2007. "Establishing an International Criminal Court: The Emergence of a New Global Authority?" GUISD/Pew Case Studies Center, case no. 258. Washington, DC: Georgetown University Institute for the Study of Diplomacy.

Levy, Jack S. 1988. "Domestic Politics and War." *Journal of Interdisciplinary History*, 18/3:653–673.

Li, Quan, and Rafael Reuveny. 2003. "Economic Globalization and Democracy: An Empirical Analysis." *British Journal of Political Science*, 33:29–54.

Li, Quan, and Drew Schaub. 2004. "Economic Globalization and Transnational Terrorism: A Pooled Time-Series Analysis." *Journal of Conflict Resolution*, 48/2:230–258.

Lobell, Steven E. 2004. "Historical Lessons to Extend America's Great Power Tenure." *World Affairs* (Spring). Online.

Lomborg, Bjørn, 2001. *The Skeptical Environmentalist: Measuring the Real State of the World*. New York: Cambridge University Press.

Lomborg, Bjørn. 2003. "Debating the Skeptical Environmentalist." In *Taking Sides: Clashing Views on Controversial Issues in World Politics*, 11th ed., ed. John T. Rourke. Guilford, CT: McGraw-Hill/Dushkin.

Longman, Phillip. 2004. "The Global Baby Bust." *Foreign Affairs*, 83/3:64–79.

Lopez, George. 2004. "Containing Iraq: Sanctions Worked." *Foreign Affairs*, 83/4:90–103.

Mack, Andrew. 2005. *Human Security Report 2005*. New York: Oxford University Press.

Mackenzie, Megan. 2009. "Securitization and Desecuritization: Female Soldiers and the Reconstruction of Women in Post-Conflict Sierra Leone." *Security Studies*, 18/2:241–261.

Maley, Willy. 2003. *Nation, State, and Empire in English Renaissance Literature: Shakespeare to Milton*. London: Palgrave.

Mallory, Ian A. 1990. "Conduct Unbecoming: The Collapse of the International Tin Agreement." *American University International Law Review*, 5/3:835–892.

Mann, Michael. 1993. *The Sources of Social Power: Volume 2, The Rise of Classes and Nation States 1760–1914*. Cambridge: Cambridge University Press.

Mann, Michael E. 2012. *The Hockey Stick and the Climate Wars: Dispatches from the Front Lines*. New York: Columbia University Press.

Mansfield, Edward D., and Jack Snyder. 1995. "Democratization and the Danger of War." *International Security*, 20/1:5–38.

Marshall, Andrew. 2006. "Making a Killing." *Bulletin of the Atomic Scientists*, 62/2:36–42.

Marshall, Monty G., and Ted Robert Gurr. 2005. *Peace and Conflict, 2005: A Global Survey of Armed Conflicts, Self-Determination Movements, and Democracy*. College Park, MD: Center for International Development and Conflict Management, University of Maryland.

Martin, Andrew, and George Ross, eds. 2004. *Euros and Europeans: Monetary Integration and the European Model of Society*. Cambridge, UK: Cambridge University Press.

Marx, Anthony W. 2003. *Faith in Nation: Exclusionary Origins of Nationalism*. New York: Oxford University Press.

Mastanduno, Michael. 1998. "Economics and Security in Statecraft and Scholarship." *International Organization*, 52/4:825–854.

Mathiason, John. 2007. *Invisible Governance: International Secretariats in Global Politics*. Bloomfield, CT: Kumarian.

Mathews, Jessica Tuchman. 1989. "Redefining Security." *Foreign Affairs*, 68/2:162–177.

McIntosh, David D. 1998. "The Muscular Mediator: Richard Holbrooke and the Dayton Peace Conference," Working Paper 98-1, Harvard Program on Negotiation.

Maurer, Andreas. 2003. "The Legislative Powers and Impact of the European Parliament." *Journal of Common Market Studies*, 41:227–248.

Mayda, Anna Maria, and Dani Rodrik. 2005. "Why Are Some People (and Countries) More Protectionist than Others?" *European Economic Review*, 49/6:1393–1430.

McDonald, Patrick J. 2004. "Peace through Trade or Free Trade?" *Journal of Conflict Resolution*, 48/4:547–572.

McDonald, Patrick J. 2007. "The Purse Strings of Peace." *American Journal of Political Science*, 51/3:569–582.

McDowall, David. 2004. *A Modern History of the Kurds*. New York: I.B. Tauris.

Mearsheimer, John J. 1990. "Back to the Future: Instability in Europe after the Cold War." *International Security*, 15/1:5–56.

Mearsheimer, John J. 2001. *The Tragedy of Great Power Politics*. New York: W. W. Norton.

Mearsheimer, John J., and Stephen Walt. 2003. "An Unnecessary War." *Foreign Policy*, 134:50–59.

Meernik, James, and Michael Ault. 2005. "The Diverted President: The Domestic Agenda and Foreign Policy." Paper presented at the annual convention of the International Studies Association, Honolulu, HI.

Melander, Erik. 2005. "Political Gender Equality and State Human Rights Abuse." *Journal of Peace Research,* 42:149–166.

Meunier, Sophie. 2000. "What Single Voice? European Institutions and EU–US Trade Negotiations." *International Organization,* 54/2:103–135.

Migdal, Joel S. 2004. "State-Building and the Non-Nation-State." *Journal of International Affairs,* 58/1:17–47.

Minorities at Risk Project. 2005. College Park, MD: Center for International Development and Conflict Management. Available at http://www.cidcm.umd.edu/mar/

Mistry, Dinshaw. 2004. "Military Technology, National Power, and Regional Security: The Strategic Significance of India's Nuclear, Missile, Space, and Missile Defense Forces." In *South Asia's Nuclear Security Dilemma,* ed. Lowell Dittmer. New York: M.E. Sharpe.

Mitchell, Ronald. 2012. *International Environmental Agreements Database Project.* Available at: http://iea.uoregon.edu/page.php?file=home.htm&query=static

Mitchell, Sara McLaughlin, and Brandon C. Prins. 2004. "Rivalry and Diversionary Uses of Force." *Journal of Conflict Resolution,* 48/6:937–961.

Mitrany, David. 1946. *A Working Peace System.* London: Royal Institute of International Affairs.

Mittelman, James. 1997. "The Dynamics of Globalization." In *Globalization: Critical Reflections,* ed. James H. Mittelman. Boulder, CO: Lynne Rienner.

Monshipouri, Mahmood. 2004. "The Road to Globalization Runs through Women's Struggle: Iran and the Impact of the Nobel Peace Prize." *World Affairs,* 167/1:3–14.

Monshipouri, Mahmood, Neil Englehart, Andrew J. Nathan, and Kavita Philip, eds. 2003. *Constructing Human Rights in the Age of Globalization.* Armonk, NY: M. E. Sharpe.

Moore, Rebecca R. 2001. "China's Fledgling Civil Society." *World Policy Journal,* 18/1:56–66.

Moore, Will H., and David J. Lanoue. 2003. "Domestic Politics and U.S. Foreign Policy: A Study of Cold War Conflict Behavior." *Journal of Politics,* 65:376–397.

Morefield, Jeanne. 2004. *Covenants without Swords: Idealist Liberalism and the Spirit of Empire.* Princeton, NJ: Princeton University Press.

Morgenthau, Hans J. 1945. "The Evil of Politics and the Ethics of Evil." *Ethics,* 56/1:1–18.

Morgenthau, Hans J. 1948. *Politics among Nations: The Struggle for Power and Peace.* New York: Alfred A. Knopf.

Morgenthau, Hans J. 1973, 1986. *Politics among Nations.* New York: Knopf. Morgenthau's text was first published in 1948 and periodically thereafter. Two sources are used herein. One is the fifth edition, published in 1973. The second is an edited abstract drawn from pp. 3–4, 10–12, 14, 27–29, and 31–35 of the third edition, published in 1960. The abstract appears in Vasquez 1986:37–41. Pages cited for Morgenthau 1986 refer to Vasquez's, not Morgenthau's, book.

Mousseau, Michael. 2003. "Market Civilization and Its Clash with Terror." *International Security,* 27/3:5–29.

Mueller, John. 1989. *Retreat from Doomsday: The Obsolescence of Major War.* New York: Basic Books.

Mueller, John. 2004. *The Remnants of War.* Ithaca, NY: Cornell University Press.

Muldoon, James P., Jr. 2003. *The Architecture of Global Governance.* Boulder, CO: Westview.

Murphy, John. 2004. *The United States and the Rule of Law in International Affairs.* New York: Cambridge University Press.

Münkler, Herfried. 2004. *The New Wars.* London: Polity.

Nabulsi, Karma. 2004. "The Peace Process and the Palestinians: A Road Map to Mars." *International Affairs,* 80/2:221–231.

Nacos, Brigitte L. 2007. *Mass-mediated Terrorism: The Central Role of the Media in Terrorism and Counterterrorism,* 2nd ed. Lanham, MD: Rowman & Littlefield.

Namkung, Gon. 1998. "Japanese Images of the United States and Other Nations: A Comparative Study of Public Opinion and Foreign Policy." Doctoral dissertation. Storrs, CT: University of Connecticut.

Nasr, Vali. 2011. "If the Arab Spring Turns Ugly." *New York Times.* August 28, 2011; SR4.

National Institute for Dispute Resolution (NIDR). 1992. *A Conversation on Peacemaking with Jimmy Carter.* Washington, DC: National Institute for Dispute Resolution. Fifth National Conference on Peacemaking and Conflict Resolution in Charlotte, NC, 7 June 1991. PBS.com. http://www.pbs.org/wgbh/amex/carter/peopleevents/e_peace.html

National Geographic Society. 2006. *2006 National Geographic-Roper Survey of Geographic Literacy.* http://www.nationalgeographic.com/roper2006/

Navaretti, Giorgio Barba, and Anthony J. Venables. 2004. *Multinational Firms in the World Economy.* Princeton: Princeton University Press.

Norris, Pippa, and Ronald Inglehart. 2004. *Sacred and Secular: Religion and Politics Worldwide.* New York: Cambridge University Press.

Nussbaum, Bederman. 2001. *International Law in Antiquity.* Cambridge, MA: Cambridge University Press.

Nye, Joseph S., Jr. 2000. *Understanding International Conflicts,* 3rd ed. New York: Longman.

Nye, Joseph S., Jr. 2002. "Globalism versus Globalization." *Globalist,* April 15. Online.

Nye, Joseph S., Jr. 2004. *Soft Power: The Means to Success in World Politics.* New York: Public Affairs.

Nye, Joseph S., Jr. 2004a. "The Decline of America's Soft Power." *Foreign Affairs,* 83/3:16–21.

Obama, Barack H. 2011. "Remarks by the President on America's Energy Security." Office of the Press Secretary, The White House. Available online at: http://www.whitehouse.gov/the-press-office/2011/03/30/remarks-president-americas-energy-security. Last accessed September 8, 2011.

O'Leary, Brendan. 1997. "On the Nature of Nationalism: An Appraisal of Ernest Gellner's Writings on Nationalism." *British Journal of Political Science,* 27:191–222.

Oneal, John R., and Bruce M. Russett. 1997. "The Classical Liberals Were Right: Democracy, Interdependence, and Conflict, 1950–1985." *International Studies Quarterly,* 41:267–294.

Opello, Walter C., Jr., and Stephen J. Rosow. 2004. *The Nation-State and Global Order: A Historical Introduction to Contemporary Politics.* Boulder, CO: Lynne Rienner.

Orford, Anne. 2003. *Reading Humanitarian Intervention: Human Rights and the Use of Force in International Law.* Cambridge: Cambridge University Press.

Organski, A.F.K., and Jacek Kugler. 1980. *The War Ledger.* Chicago: University of Chicago Press.

O'Rourke, Kevin H., and Jeffrey G. Williamson. 2002. "After Columbus: Explaining Europe's Overseas Trade Boom 1500–1800." *The Journal of Economic History,* 62/2:417–456.

Paquette, Laura. 2003. *Analyzing National and International Policy: Theory, Method, and Case Studies.* Lanham, MD: Lexington Books.

Paris, Roland. 2001. "Human Security: Paradigm Shift or Hot Air?" *International Security,* 26/2:87–102.

Park, Susan. 2005. "How Transnational Environmental Advocacy Networks Socialize International Financial Institutions: A Case Study of the International Finance Corporation." *Global Environmental Politics,* 5/4:95–119.

Pastor, Robert A. 1980. *Congress and the Politics of U.S. Foreign Economic Policy, 1929-1976.* Berkeley: University of California Press.

Pateman, Carole. 1988. *The Sexual Contract.* Stanford, CA: Standford University Press.

Peterson, V. Spike, and Anne Sisson Runyan. 2010. *Global Gender Issues in the New Millennium,* 3rd ed. Boulder, CO: Westview Press.

Pevehouse, Jon C. 2004. "Interdependence Theory and the Measurement of International Conflict." *Journal of Politics,* 66/1:247–272.

Pew Research Center for the People and the Press. 2002. Pew Global Attitudes Project 44-Nation Major Survey. Washington, DC: Pew Research Center for the People and the Press.

Pew Research Center for the People and the Press. 2003. *Views of a Changing World, 2003.* Washington, DC: Pew Research Center for the People and the Press.

Pew Research Center. 2006. "American Attitudes Hold Steady in Face of Foreign Crises." http://pewresearch.org/pubs/241/voters-focus-on-domestic-issues-despite-crises-abroad

Pew Research Center. 2007. "World Publics Welcome Global Trade—But Not Immigration," Pew Global Attitudes Project, October 4, 2007. Available online at: http://www.pewglobal.org/2007/10/04/chapter-2-views-of-immigration. Last accessed April 11, 2012.

Piazza, James A. 2006. "Rooted in Poverty? Terrorism, Poor Economic Development, and Social Cleavages." *Terrorism and Political Violence,* 18/1:159–177.

Pickering, Jeffrey, and Emizet F. Kisangani. 2005. "Democracy and Diversionary Military Intervention: Reassessing Regime Type and the Diversionary Hypothesis." *International Studies Quarterly,* 49/1:23–46.

Pilch, Frances. 2005. "Developing Human Rights Standards in United Nations Peacekeeping Operations." Paper presented at the annual meeting of the International Studies Association, Honolulu, HI.

Pirages, Dennis. 1989. *Global Technopolitics.* Dallas: Wadsworth.

Poole, Peter A., and Michael Baun. 2004. "Europe Unites: The EU's Eastern Enlargement." *Political Science Quarterly,* 119/2:368–369.

Posner, Eric A., and John C. Yoo. 2004. "A Theory of International Adjudication." *John M. Olin Law & Economics Working Paper* No. 206 (2nd Series), University of Chicago School of Law (February 2004).

Post, Jerrold M. 2004. *Leaders and Their Followers in a Dangerous World: The Psychology of Political Behavior.* Ithaca, NY: Cornell University Press.

Powell, Robert. 2006. "War as a Commitment Problem." *International Organization,* 60/1:169–203.

Princen, Thomas. 1992. *Intermediaries in International Conflict.* Princeton, NJ: Princeton University Press.

Program on International Policy Attitudes (PIPA). 2008. "Iraqi Public Opinion on the Presence of US Troops." Testimony of Dr. Steven Kull, Director, Program on International Policy Attitudes, University of Maryland before House Committee on Foreign Affairs, Subcommittee on International Organizations, Human Rights, and Oversight (July 23, 2008). Available online at: http://www.worldpublicopinion.org/pipa/articles/home_page/517.php. Last accessed May 10, 2012.

Pye, Lucian W., and Sidney Verba. 1965. *Political Culture and Political Development.* Princeton, NJ: Princeton University Press.

Ralph, Jason. 2005. "International Society, the International Criminal Court, and American Foreign Policy." *Review of International Studies,* 31/1:27–44.

Ratner, Steven R. 1998. "International Law: The Trials of Global Norms." *Foreign Policy,* 110:65–81.

Rehn, Elisabeth, and Ellen Johnson Sirleaf. 2002. *Women, War and Peace: The Independent Experts' Assessment on the Impact of Armed Conflict on Women and Women's Role in Peace-building.* New York: United Nations Development Fund for Women (UNIFEM).

Reilly, Niamh. 2009. *Women's Human Rights: Seeking Gender Justice in a Globalizing Age.* Cambridge, UK: Polity.

Reimann, Kim D. 2006. "A View from the Top: International Politics, Norms and the Worldwide Growth of NGOs." *International Studies Quarterly,* 50/1:45–68.

Renan, Ernest. 1995. "Qu'est-ce Qu'une Nation?" In *Nationalism,* ed. John Hutchinson and Anthony D. Smith. New York: Oxford University Press.

Renshon, Stanley A. 1995. "Character, Judgment, and Political Leadership: Promise, Problems, and Prospects of the Clinton Presidency." In *The Clinton Presidency: Campaigning, Governing, and the Psychology of Leadership,* ed. Stanley Renshon. Boulder, CO: Westview.

Renshon, Stanley A., and Deborah Welch Larson, eds. 2002. *Good Judgment in Foreign Policy: Theory and Application.* Lanham, MD: Rowman & Littlefield.

Rice, Edward E. 1988. *Wars of the Third Kind: Conflict in Underdeveloped Countries.* Berkeley: University of California Press.

Richardson, Lewis. 1960. *Statistics of Deadly Quarrels.* Pittsburgh, PA: Boxwood Press.

Rieff, David. 1994. "The Illusions of Peacekeeping." *World Policy Journal,* 11/3:1–18.

Ringquist, Evan J., and Tatiana Kostadinova. 2005. "Assessing the Effectiveness of International Environmental Agreements: The Case of the 1985 Helsinki Protocol." *American Journal of Political Science,* 49/1:86–114.

Robertson, G. 2011. "Why It Is Absurd to Claim That Justice Has Been Done." *The Independent.* Accessed April 2012 at http://www.independent.co.uk/opinion/commentators/geoffrey-robertson-why-its-absurd-to-claim-that-justice-has-been-done-2278041.html

Rodin, David. 2005. *War and Self-Defense.* New York: Oxford University Press.

Rodrigues, Maria Guadalupe Moog. 2004. *Global Environmentalism and Local Politics: Transnational Advocacy Networks in Brazil, Ecuador, and India.* Albany: State University of New York Press.

Romano, Cesare P. R. 1999. "The Proliferation of International Judicial Bodies: The Pieces of the Puzzle." *New York University Journal of International Law and Politics,* 31:709–751.

Rosato, Sebastian. 2003. "The Flawed Logic of Democratic Peace Theory." *American Political Science Review,* 97/4:585–602.

Rosen, Stephen Peter. 2004. *War and Human Nature.* Princeton: Princeton University Press.

Rosenau, James N. 2004. "Understanding World Affairs: The Potential of Collaboration." *Globalizations,* 1/2:326–339.

Rosenau, James N. 1994. "New Dimensions of Security: The Interaction of Globalizing and Localizing Dynamics." *Security Dialogue,* 25/3:255–281.

Ross, Lee. 1977. "The Intuitive Psychologist and His Shortcomings: Distortions in the Attribution Process." In L. Berkowitz, *Advances in Experimental Social Psychology,* 10. New York: Academic Press.

Rothschild, Emma. 1995. "What Is Security?" *Daedalus: Journal of the American Academy of Arts and Sciences,* 124/3:53–90.

Sageman, Marc. 2008. *Leaderless Jihad: Terror Networks in the Twenty-First Century.* Philadelphia: University of Pennsylvania Press.

Samuels, Richard J. 2006. "Japan's Goldilocks Strategy." *The Washington Quarterly,* 29/4:111–127.

Sarat, Austin, and Joel B. Grossman. 1975. "Courts and Conflict Resolution: Problems in the Mobilization of Adjudication." *American Political Science Review,* 69/4:1200–1217.

Schafer, Mark, and Stephen G. Walker. 2006. "Democratic Leaders and the Democratic Peace: The Operational Codes of Tony Blair and Bill Clinton." *International Studies Quarterly,* 50/3:561–583.

Schiff, Benjamin N. 2008. *Building the International Criminal Court.* New York: Cambridge University Press.

Schmidt, Brian C. 2004. "Realism as Tragedy." *Review of International Studies,* 30:427–441.

Schmitter, Philippe C. 2005. "Ernst B. Haas and the Legacy of Neofunctionalism." *Journal of European Public Policy,* 12/2:255–272.

Schmitz, Hans Peter. 2004. "Domestic and Transnational Perspectives on Democratization." *International Studies Review,* 6/3:403–421.

Schultze, Charles L. 2004. *Offshoring, Import Competition, and the Jobless Recovery.* Policy Brief 136. Washington, DC: Brookings Institution.

Schweller, Randall L. 2004. "Unanswered Threats: A Neoclassical Realist Theory of Underbalancing." *International Security,* 29/2:159–201.

Scully, Roger, and David M. Farrell. 2003. "MEPs as Representatives: Individual and Institutional Roles." *Journal of Common Market Studies,* 41:269–288.

"Selective Justice." 2009. *New African* [Online]. 484(May):10–15.

Senese, Paul D. 2005. "Territory, Contiguity, and International Conflict: Assessing a New Joint Explanation." *American Journal of Political Science,* 49/4:769–791.

Shah, Timothy Samuel, and Monica Duffy Toft. 2006. "Why God Is Winning." *Foreign Policy,* 155:38–43.

Shambaugh, George E. 2004. "The Power of Money: Global Capital and Policy Choices in Developing Countries." *American Journal of Political Science,* 48/2:281–311.

Sharp, Jeremy M. 2011. "Egypt in Transition," Congressional Research Service Report 7-5700 (August 23, 2011). Available online at: www.crs.gov. Last accessed September 10, 2011.

Shaw, Martin, 1999. "War and Globality: The Role and Character of War in the Global Transition." In *The New Agenda for Peace Research,* ed. Ho Won Jeong. Aldershot: Ashgate.

Sheehan, Michael. 2005. *International Security: An Analytical Survey.* Boulder, CO: Lynne Rienner.

Sheehan, Michael. 2008. "The Changing Character of War." In *The Globalization of World Politics: An Introduction to International Relations,* 4th ed., ed. John Baylis, Steve Smith, and Patricia Owens. New York: Oxford University Press.

Shue, Henry. 1980. *Basic Human Rights: Subsistence, Affluence and U.S. Foreign Policy.* New Jersey: Princeton University Press.

Silverman, Adam L. 2002. "Just War, Jihad, and Terrorism: A Comparison of Western and Islamic Norms for the Use of Political Violence." *Journal of Church and State,* 44:73–92.

Simmons, Beth A. 1998. "Compliance with International Agreements." *Annual Review of Political Science,* 1:75–93.

Simmons, Beth A., and Daniel J. Hopkins. 2005. "The Constraining Power of International Treaties: Theory and Methods." *American Political Science Review,* 99/4:623–631.

Simmons, Mark, and Peter Dixon. 2006. "Introduction." In *Peace by Piece: Addressing Sudan's Conflicts. Accord: An International Review of Peace Initiatives,* 18. London: Conciliation Resources.

Simon, Herbert. 1957. "A Behavioral Model of Rational Choice." In *Models of Man, Social and Rational: Mathematical Essays on Rational Human Behavior in a Social Setting*. New York: Wiley.

Sinclair, Andrew. 2004. *An Anatomy of Terror: A History of Terrorism*. New York: Palgrave Macmillan.

Singer, J. David. 1961. "The Level-of-Analysis Problem in International Relations." *World Politics*, 14/1:77–92.

Singer, J. David, and Melvin Small. 1972. *The Wages of War 1816-1965: A Statistical Handbook*. New York: Wiley.

Stockholm International Peace Research Institute (SIPRI). Annual Editions. SIPRI Yearbook. Oxford, UK: Oxford University Press.

Sjoberg, Laura, and Caron E. Gentry. 2007. *Mothers, Monsters, Whores: Women's Violence in Global Politics*. London: Zed Books.

Slaughter, Anne-Marie. 2003. "The Global Community of Courts." *Harvard International Law Journal*, 44:217–219.

Smith, Anthony D. 1994. "Gastronomy or Geology? The Role of Nationalism in the Reconstruction of Nations." *Nations and Nationalism*, 1/1:3–23.

Smith, Anthony D. 2004. *Chosen Peoples: Sacred Sources of National Identity*. Oxford, UK: Oxford University Press.

Smith, Gordon W., and George R. Schink. 1976. "The International Tin Agreement: A Reassessment." *Economic Journal*, 86:715–728.

Smith, Tom W., and Seokho Kim. 2006. "National Pride in Comparative Perspective, 1995/96 and 2003/04." *International Journal of Public Opinion Research*, 18/1: 128–136.

Snow, Donald M. 1996. *Uncivil Wars: International Security and the New Internal Conflicts*. Boulder, CO: Lynne Rienner Publishers.

Snyder, Robert S. 2005. "Bridging the Realist/Constructivist Divide: The Case of the Counterrevolution in Soviet Foreign Policy at the End of the Cold War." *Foreign Policy Analysis*, 1/1:55–71.

Solomon, Robert. 1982. *The International Monetary System, 1945–1981*. New York: Harper and Row.

Sommer, Michael. 2007. "Network of Commerce and Knowledge in the Iron Age: The Case of the Phoenicians." *Mediterranean Historical Review*, 22/1:97–111.

Spangler, Brad. 2003. "Adjudication." In *Beyond Intractability*, ed. Guy Burgess and Heidi Burgess. Boulder, CO: Conflict Research Consortium, University of Colorado. Available online at: http://www.beyondintractability.org/essay/adjudication/. Last accessed July 17, 2008.

Speer, James P., II. 1968. "Hans Morgenthau and the World State." *World Politics*, 20/1:207–227.

Stansfield, Gareth. 2005. "The Transition to Democracy in Iraq: Historical Legacies, Resurgent Identities, and Reactionary Tendencies." In *The Iraq War and Democratic Politics*, ed. Alex Danchev and John Macmillan. London/New York: Routledge.

Stein, Janice Gross. 2001. "Image, Identity, and the Resolution of Violent Conflict." In *Turbulent Peace: The Challenges of Managing International Conflict*, ed. C. A. Crocker, F. O. Hampson, and P. Aall. Washington, DC: United States Institute of Peace Press.

Stein, Janice Gross. 2002. "Psychological Explanations of International Conflict." In *Handbook of International Relations*, ed. Walter Carlsnaes, Thomas Risse, and Beth A. Simmons. London: SAGE.

Sterling-Folker, Jennifer. 1997. "Realist Environment, Liberal Process, and Domestic-Level Variables." *International Studies Quarterly*, 41:1–26.

Sterling-Folker, Jennifer. 2002. *Theories of International Cooperation and the Primacy of Anarchy: Explaining U.S. International Monetary Policy-Making after Bretton Woods*. Albany: State University of New York Press.

Stiglitz, Joseph E. 2002. *Globalization and Its Discontents*. New York: W. W. Norton.

Stipp, David. 2004. "Climate Collapse: The Pentagon's Weather Nightmare." *Fortune Magazine*, January 26, 2004.

Stockholm International Peace Research Institute (SIPRI). 2012. *SIPRI Fact Sheet, March 2012: Trends in International Arms Transfers, 2011*. Available at: http://books.sipri.org/files/FS/SIPRIFS1203.pdf. Last accessed April 17, 2012.

Stockholm International Peace Research Institute (SIPRI). 2009. *SIPRI Arms Transfer Database*. Available at: http://www.sipri.org/databases/armstransfers. Last accessed December 20, 2011.

Tabb, William K. 2004. *Economic Governance in the Age of Globalization*. New York: Columbia University Press.

Telhami, Shibley, and Michael Barnett, eds. 2002. *Identity and Foreign Policy in the Middle East*. Ithaca, NY: Cornell University Press.

Thomas, Nicholas, and William T. Tow. 2002. "The Utility of Human Security: Sovereignty and Humanitarian Intervention." *Security Dialogue*, 33/2:177–192.

Thompson, Alexander. 2006. "Coercion through IOs: The Security Council and the Logic of Information Transmission." *International Organization*, 60/1:1–34.

Tickner, J. Ann. 1992. *Gender in International Relations: Feminist Perspectives on Achieving Global Security*. New York: Columbia University Press.

Tickner, J. Ann. 2001. *Gendering World Politics: Issues and Approaches in the Post–Cold War Era*. New York: Columbia University Press.

Tir, Jiroslav, and Michael Jasinski. 2008. "Domestic-Level Diversionary Theory of War: Targeting Ethnic Minorities." *Journal of Conflict Resolution*, 52/5:641–664.

Tomuschat, Christian. 2004. *Human Rights: Between Idealism and Realism*. Oxford, UK: Oxford University Press.

Trumbore, Peter F. 2003. "Victims or Aggressors? Ethno-Political Rebellion and Use of Force in Militarized Interstate Disputes." *International Studies Quarterly*, 47:183–201.

Tryggestad, Torunn L. 2009. "Trick or Treat? The UN and Implementation of Security Council Resolution 1325 on Women, Peace and Security." *Global Governance*, 15:539–557.

Tusicisny, Andrej. 2004. "Civilizational Conflicts: More Frequent, Longer, and Bloodier?" *Journal of Peace Research*, 41/2:485–498.

Ullman, Richard. 1983. "Redefining Security." *International Security*, 8/1:129–153.

United Nations. 2012 *Millennium Development Goals.* Available online at http://www.un.org/millenniumgoals/

United Nations Commission on Human Security. 2003. *Human Security Now: Protecting and Empowering People.* New York: United Nations Publications.

United Nations Educational, Scientific and Cultural Organization (UNESCO). 2001. "What Agenda for Human Security in the Twenty-First Century?" UNESCO Division of Human Rights, Democracy, Peace and Tolerance, Social and Human Sciences Sector. Paris.

UN, Department of Economic and Social Affairs, Population Division. 2004. Online: http://www.undp.org/

United Nations Children's Fund (UNICEF). Annual editions. *State of the World's Children.* New York: Oxford University Press.

United Nations Development Programme (UNDP). Annual editions. *Human Development Report.* New York: Oxford University Press.

United Nations Development Program (UNDP). 1994. *Human Development Report 1994: New Dimensions of Human Security.* Available online at: http://hdr.undp.org/en/reports/global/hdr1994/. Last accessed November 11, 2011.

Uppsala Conflict Data Program (UCDP). 2012. UCDP/PRIO Armed Conflict Dataset; http://www.pcr.uu.se/research/ucdp/datasets/ucdp_prio_armed_conflict_dataset/. Uppsala University Department of Peace and Conflict Research. Last accessed March 30, 2012.

United Nations Intellectual History Project. Available online at http://www.unhistory.org/

Urquhart B. 2011. Learning from Hammarskjold. *New York Times.* Available at http://www.nytimes.com/2011/09/17/opinion/learning-from-hammarskjold.html?_r=1

U.S. Bureau of the Census. Annual editions. *Statistical Abstract of the United States.* Washington, DC.

U.S. Central Intelligence Agency (CIA). Annual editions. *World Fact Book.* Washington, DC: GPO.

U.S. Department of State. 2010. *2010 International Narcotics Control Strategy Report.* Bureau of International Narcotics and Law Enforcement Affairs. Available online at: http://www.state.gov/j/inl/rls/nrcrpt/2010/index.htm. Last accessed December 10, 2010.

U.S. Department of State. 2009. *2009 International Narcotics Control Strategy Report.* Bureau of International Narcotics and Law Enforcement Affairs. Available online at: http://www.state.gov/j/inl/rls/nrcrpt/2009/index.htm. Last accessed December 10, 2010.

van Creveld, Martin. 1991. *The Transformation of War.* New York: Free Press.

Vasquez, John A. 1995. "Why Do Neighbors Fight? Proximity, Interaction, or Territoriality." *Journal of Peace Research,* 32/3:277–293.

Vasquez, John. 1986. *Classics of International Relations.* Englewood Cliffs: Prentice Hall.

Voeten, Erik. 2004. "Resisting the Lonely Superpower: Responses of States in the UN to U.S. Dominance." *Journal of Politics,* 66:729–754.

Volgy, Thomas J., and Alison Bailin. 2002. *International Politics and State Strength.* Boulder, CO: Lynne Rienner.

Von Hippel, Karin, and Michael Clarke. 1999. "Something Must be Done." *The World Today,* 55/3:4–7.

von Stein, Jana. 2005. "Do Treaties Constrain or Screen? Selection Bias and Treaty Compliance." *American Political Science Review,* 99/3:611–622.

Wæver, Ole. 1995. "Securitization and De-securitization." In *On Security,* ed. Ronnie Lipshultz. New York: Columbia University Press.

Wakabi, W. 2009. "Aid Expulsions Leave Huge Gap in Darfur's Health Services." *The Lancet* [Online], 373/9669:1068–1069.

Walker, Stephen G., Mark Schafer, and Michael D. Young. 1998. "Systematic Procedures for Operational Code Analysis: Measuring and Modeling Jimmy Carter's Operational Code." *International Studies Quarterly,* 42/1:175–189.

Wallensteen, Peter, and Karin Axell. 1994. "Conflict Resolution and the End of the Cold War, 1989–93." *Journal of Peace Research,* 31/3:333–349.

Walt, Stephen M. 1985. "Alliance Formation and the Balance of World Power." *International Security,* 9/4:3–43.

Walt, Stephen M. 1987. *The Origins of Alliances.* Ithaca, NY: Cornell University Press.

Waltz, Kenneth N. 1959. *Man, the State, and War.* New York: Columbia University Press.

Waltz, Kenneth N. 1979. *Theory of International Politics.* Reading: Addison-Wesley.

Walzer, Michael. 2006. *Just and Unjust Wars: A Moral Argument with Historical Illustrations,* 4th ed. New York: Basic Books.

Waterbury, John. 1993. *Exposed to Innumerable Delusions: Public Enterprise and State Power in Egypt, India, Mexico, and Turkey.* Cambridge: Cambridge University Press.

Waugh, Daniel C. 2010. "'The Silk Roads in History." *Expedition,* 52/5:9–22.

Weber, Cynthia. 1999. *Faking It: U.S. Hegemony in a "Post-Phallic" Era.* Minneapolis: University of Minnesota Press.

Weber, Max. 1918. "Politics as a Vocation." In *Max Weber: Essays in Sociology,* translated and edited by H. H. Gerth and C. Wright Mills. 1946. New York: Oxford University Press.

Weinberg, Leonard. 1991. "Turning to Terror: The Conditions under Which Political Parties Turn to Terrorist Activities." *Comparative Politics,* 23/4:423–438.

Weiss, Thomas G., Tatiana Carayannis, and Richard Jolly. 2009. "The 'third' UN." *Global Governance: A Review of Multilateralism and International Organizations,* 15/1:123–142.

Welsh, Jennifer M., ed. 2004. *Humanitarian Intervention and International Relations.* Oxford, UK: Oxford University Press.

Wendt, Alexander. 2004. "The State as Person in International Theory." *Review of International Studies,* 30:289–316.

Whitworth, Sandra. 2004. *Men, Militarism, and UN Peacekeeping.* Boulder: Lynne Rienner.

Wiebe, Robert H. 2001. *Who We Are: A History of Popular Nationalism.* Princeton, NJ: Princeton University Press.

Wilkinson, David. 2004. "Analytical and Empirical Issues in the Study of Power–Polarity Configuration Sequences." Paper presented at a Conference of a Working Group on Analyzing Complex Macrosystems as Dynamic Networks, Santa Fe Institute, Santa Fe.

Wilkinson, Paul. 2005. *Terrorism versus Democracy: The Liberal State Response,* 2nd ed. London: Routledge.

Williams, Meryl J. 2005. "Are High Seas and International Marine Fisheries the Ultimate Sustainable Management Challenge?" *Journal of International Affairs,* 59/1:221–235.

Williams, Michael C. 2004. "Why Ideas Matter in International Relations: Hans Morgenthau, Classical Realism, and the Moral Construction of Power Politics." *International Organization,* 58/4:633–665.

Williams, Michael C. 2005. *The Realist Tradition and the Limits of International Relations.* New York: Cambridge University Press.

Williams, Paul D., ed. 2008. *Security Studies: An Introduction.* New York/ London: Routledge.

Williams, Rob M., Jr. 2003. *The Wars Within: People and States in Conflict.* Ithaca, NY: Cornell University Press.

Willig, Michael R., and Samuel M. Scheiner. 2011. "The State of Theory in Ecology." In *The Theory of Ecology,* ed. Samuel M. Scheiner and Michael R. Willig. Chicago: University of Chicago Press.

Wimmer, Andreas. 2002. *Nationalist Exclusion and Ethnic Conflict.* Cambridge, UK: Cambridge University Press.

Wohlforth, William C. 1999. "The Stability of a Unipolar World." *International Security,* 24/1:5–41.

Woodwell, Douglas. 2004. "Unwelcome Neighbors: Shared Ethnicity and International Conflict during the Cold War." *International Studies Quarterly,* 48/1:197–216.

World Bank. 2009. *World DataBank.* Available online at: http://databank. worldbank.org/data/home.aspx. Last accessed March 14, 2012.

World Bank. 2011. *World Development Indicators 2011.* Washington, DC: World Bank Publications.

World Bank. Annual editions. *World Development Report.* New York: Oxford University Press.

Wyn Jones, Richard. 1996. "Travel without Maps: Thinking about Security after the Cold War." In *Security Issues in the Post-Cold War World,* ed. M. Jane Davis. Cheltenham: Edward Elgar.

Wyn Jones, Richard. 2001. *Critical Theory and World Politics.* Boulder, CO: Lynne Rienner.

Yanik, Lerna K. 2006. "Major Powers, Global Arms Transfers, and Human Rights Violations." *Human Rights Quarterly,* 28/2:357–388.

Yarger, Harry R. 2010. *Short of General War: Perspectives on the Use of Military Power in the 21st Century.* U.S. Army War College: Strategic Studies Institute, Carlisle, PA.

Yom, S. L. 2002. *The United States and Islam: Fundamentalism and the Future.* Homepage of American Diplomacy Publishers. Available online at: http:// www.unc.edu/depts/diplomat/ archives_roll/2002_07-09/yom_usislam/ yom_usislam.html [2011]

Zakaria, Fareed. 1993. "Is Realism Finished?" *National Interest,* 32:21–32.

Zartman, I. William, and Saadia Touval. 2007. "International Mediation." In *Leashing the Dogs of War: Conflict Management in a Divided World,* ed. C. Crocker, F. Hampson, and P. Aall. Washington, DC: United States Institute of Peace Press.

Zartman, I. William. 2008. "Introduction: Toward the Resolution of International Conflicts." In *Peacemaking in International Conflict: Methods & Techniques,* rev. ed., ed. I. William Zartman. Washington, DC: U.S. Institute of Peace Press.

Zunes, Stephen. 2005. "The Influence of the Christian Right in U.S. Middle East Policy." *Middle East Policy,* 12/2:73–78.

credits

CHAPTER 1

Photo Credits Opener: © ArisMessinis/ AFP/Getty Images; p. 4: © Carolyn Kaster/ AP/Corbis; p. 6: © J Redden/UNHCR via Getty Images; p. 11: © Jon Feingersh/Blend Images LLC RF; p. 13: © Jim Watson/AFP/ Getty Images; p. 15: © Mike Sargent/AFP/ Getty Images; p. 17: © J. Scott Applewhite/ AP/Corbis; p. 22: © David Paul Morris/ Bloomberg via Getty Images; p. 28: © Ted Aljibe/AFP/Getty Images; p. 29: © David Buffington/Getty Images RF.**Text Credits** Figure1.1, p. 24: From *International Politics on the World Stage,* Brief 8/e by Rourke/Boyer, Figure 1.1, p. 8.Reprinted by permission of The McGraw-Hill Companies. Figure 1.2, p. 25: From *International Politics on the World Stage,* Brief 8/e by Rourke/Boyer, Figure 1.2, p. 9. Reprinted by permission of The McGraw-Hill Companies.

CHAPTER 2

Photo Credits Opener: © Getty Images; p. 35: © Lionel Bonaventure/AFP/Getty Images; p. 41: © AFP/Getty Images; p. 45: © Erik de Castro/Pool/epa/Corbis; p. 49: © Yaw Bibini/X02115/Reuters/Corbis; p. 50: © Design Pics/Alan Marsh RF; p. 51: © KCNA via Korean News Service/AFP/ Getty Images; p. 53: © Alexander Zemli- anichenko/AP/Corbis; p. 55: © Camera Press/ JitendraArya/Redux; p. 57: © P. Ughetto/ PhotoAlto RF.**Text Credits** Figure 2.1, p 27: From *International Politics on the World Stage,* 12/e by Rourke/Boyer, Figure 8.1, p. 237. Reprinted by permission of The McGraw-Hill Companies. Figure 2.2, p 38: Transatlantic Trends: Key Findings 2011 from http://www.gmfus.org/publications_/ T/TT2011_final_web.pdf. Used by permis- sion. Figure 2.3, p 46: Source: Rasmussen Reports; http://www.rasmussenreports. com/public_content/business/econ_survey_ questions/september_2009/toplines_ afghanistan_spetmber_23_24_2009. Figure 2.4, p 47: "Most Say Relations between Muslims and Westerners are Poor" from http://pewresearch.org/pubs/2066/muslims- westerners-christians-jews-islamic-extremism- september-11. Used by permission of Pew

Research Center's Global Attitudes Project. Figure 2.5, p 48: From *International Politics on the World Stage,* 12/e by Rourke/Boyer, Figure 3.2, p. 70. Reprinted by permission of The McGraw-Hill Companies. Figure 2.6, p 58: From *International Politics on the World Stage,* 12/e by Rourke/Boyer, Figure 8.8, p. 254. Reprinted by permission of The McGraw-Hill Companies. Figure 2.7, p 60: http://s.wsj.net/ public/resources/images/PT-AK368C_ OILch_NS_20081128164841.gif. Figure 2.8, p 64: From *International Politics on the World Stage,* 12/e by Rourke/Boyer, Figure 8.3, p 244. Reprinted by permission of The McGraw-Hill Companies. Figure 2.9, p 69: From *Interna- tional Politics on the World Stage,* 12/e by Rourke/Boyer, Figure 3.6, p 92. Reprinted by permission of The McGraw-Hill Companies. Figure 2.10, p 70: Source: Global Attitudes Center; The American-Western European Values Gap, (Survey Report). http://www. pewglobal.org/2011/11/17/the-american- westerneuropean-values-gap/?src_prc-headline. Figure 2.11, p 72: From *International Politics on the World Stage,* 12/e by Rourke/Boyer, Figure 3.7, p 94. Reprinted by permission of The McGraw-Hill Companies.

CHAPTER 3

Photo Credits Opener: © Roberto Schmidt/ AFP/Getty Images; p. 81: © RamziHaidar/ AFP/Getty Images; p. 82: © moodboard/ Getty Images RF; p. 83: © Raveendran/ AFP/Getty Images; p. 86: © Bettmann/ Corbis; p. 100: © Glow Images RF; p. 101: © Getty Images; p. 105: © AP Photo/Paul White; p. 112: © L'Osservatore Romano Vatican-Pool/Getty Images; p. 115: © AP Photo/Greg Baker; p. 116: © akg-images/ The Image Works; p. 117: © AFP/Getty Images; p. 118: © AP Photo/File; p. 127: © Maxim Marmur/AFP/Getty Images.**Text Credits** Figure 3.2, p 88: Perry Marvin, Myra Chase, James R. Jacob, Margaret C. Jacob, and Theodore H. Von Laue. Western Civilization: Ideas, Politics and Society, Fourth Edition. Copyright 1992 by Houghton Mifflin Company.Adapted with permission. Figure 3.3, p 93: From *International Politics on the World Stage,* 12/e by Rourke/Boyer,

Figure 4.2, p 118. Reprinted by permission of The McGraw-Hill Companies. Figure 3.4, p 95: *Source:* Pew Global Attitudes Project, 2007, http://www.pewglobal.org/ 2007/10/04/chapter-4-values-and-american- exceptionalism. Figure 3.5, p 97: *Source:* Pew Global Attitudes Project, 2007, http:// www.pewglobal.org/2007/10/04/chapter-2- views-of-immigration. Figure 3.6, p 98: From *International Politics on the World Stage,* 12/e by Rourke/Boyer, p 121. Re- printed by permission of The McGraw-Hill Companies. Figure 3.7, p 102: From *Inter- national Politics on the World Stage,* 12/e by Rourke/Boyer, p 127. Reprinted by permission of The McGraw-Hill Companies. Figure 3.9, p 109: Foreign Policy/Fund for Peace Failed States Index Map, 2011 http://www.fundfor- peace.org/global/?q=fsi. Used by permission. Figure 3.10, p 111: From *International Politics on the World Stage,* 12/e by Rourke/Boyer, p 175. Reprinted by permission of The McGraw-Hill Companies. Figure 3.11, p 113: *Source:* Pew Global Attitudes Center Novem- ber 17, 2011, http://www.pewglobal.org/ 2011/11/17/the-american-westerneuropean- values-gap/?src_prc-headline. Figure 3.12, p 114: From *International Politics on the World Stage,* 12/e by Rourke/Boyer, p 177. Reprinted by permission of The McGraw-Hill Companies. Figure 3.13, p 119: From *Inter- national Politics on the World Stage,* 12/e by Rourke/Boyer, p 110. Reprinted by permission of The McGraw-Hill Companies. Figure 3.14, p 121: From *International Politics on the World Stage,* 12/e by Rourke/Boyer, p 112. Reprinted by permission of The McGraw-Hill Companies. Figure 3.15, p 123: *Source:* The Middle East Political Research Center. http://www.meprc.com/?p_15. September 27th 2010. Figure 3.16, p 125: Map courtesy of Perry-Castañeda Library, University of Texas Libraries Collection. Available online at:http://www.lib.utexas.edu/maps/middle_ east_and_asia/afghanistan_ethnicities_map_ 4Dec2009.jpg.

CHAPTER 4

Photo Credits Opener: © Karen Bleier/ AFP/Getty Images; p. 137: © Jake Lyell/

Alamy; p. 144: © AP Photo/Barry Sweet; p. 148: © Stan Honda/AFP/Getty Images; p. 151 (left): © STF/AFP/Getty Images; p. 151 (right): © AP Photo/Eduardo Di Baia; p. 155: © Ingram Publishing RF; p. 160: © Carlos Cazalis/Corbis; p. 162: © Jean-Christophe Bott/epa/Corbis; p. 166: © Joe Raedle/Getty Images.**Text Credits** Figure 4.1, p 133: Source: http://www.economist.com/blogs/dailychart/2011/07/big-mac-index. Figure 4.2, p 138: Source: http://data.worldbank.org /indicator/IT.NET.USER/countries /1W?display=graph. Figure 4.3, p 141: Obesity Growth Rate in OECD Countries Available at http://expathealth.org/expat-trends/are-the-british-too-fat/. Used by permission. Figure 4.4, p 158: From *International Politics on the World Stage,* 12/e by Rourke/Boyer, p 122. Reprinted by permission of The McGraw-Hill Companies. Table 4.1, p 145: Source: Source: http://money.cnn.com/magazines/fortune/global500/2011/performers/companies/profi ts/.

CHAPTER 5

Photo Credits Opener: © ThonyBelizaire/AFP/Getty Images; p. 176: NASA; p. 180: © Monika Graff/Getty Images; p. 182: © Photodisc/Getty Images RF; p. 191: © Mustafa Ozer/AFP/Getty Images; p. 196: © C. Zachariasen/PhotoAltoRF; p. 202: © STRINGER/AFP/Getty Images; p. 208: © AristidisVafeiadakis/ZUMA Press/Newscom.**Text Credits** Figure 5.1, p 181: From *International Politics on the World Stage,* 12/e by Rourke/Boyer, Figure 7.1, p 175. Reprinted by permission of The McGraw-Hill Companies. Figure 5.2, p 184: From *International Politics on the World Stage,* 12/e by Rourke/Boyer, Figure 7.2, p 177. Reprinted by permission of The McGraw-Hill Companies. Figure 5.5, p 204: From *International Politics on the World Stage,* 12/e by Rourke/Boyer, Figure 7.5, p 196. Reprinted by permission of The McGraw-Hill Companies

CHAPTER 6

Photo Credits Opener: © Pedro Ugarte/AFP/Getty Images; p. 215: © Reuters/Reuters TV; p. 220: © Reuters/Aladin Abdel Naby; p. 223: © HO/Reuters/Corbis; p. 224: © KhaledDesouki/AFP/Getty Images; p. 231: © Design Pics/Darren Greenwood RF; p. 232: © AP Photo /Xinhua, Qian Zhen; p. 237: © Liba Taylor/Corbis.**Text Credits** Figure 6.1, p 216: From *International Politics on the World Stage,* 12/e by Rourke/Boyer, Figure 10.2, p 314. Reprinted by permission of The McGraw-Hill Companies. Figure 6.5, p 233: From *International Politics on the World Stage,* 12/e by Rourke/Boyer, Figure 10.6, p 324. Reprinted by permission of The McGraw-Hill Companies. Figure 6.6, p 235: From *International Politics on the World Stage,* 12/e by Rourke/Boyer, Figure 11.1, p 346. Reprinted by permission of The McGraw-Hill Companies. Figure 6.7, p 238: From *International Politics on the World Stage,* 12/e by Rourke/Boyer, Figure 11.4, p 357. Reprinted by permission of The McGraw-Hill Companies. Figure 6.8, p 243: Source: Carnegie Endowment for International Peace, www.ProliferationNews.org, *Deadly Arsenals* http://www.carnegieendowment.org/files/DeadlyII.ProlifMap12x10.FINAL[1].pdf. Figure 6.9, p 245: Source: Carnegie Endowment for International Peace, www.ProliferationNews.org, *Deadly Arsenals* http://www.carnegieendowment.org/files/DeadlyII.ProlifMap12×10.FINAL[1].pdf.

CHAPTER 7

Photo Credits Opener: © Marco Longari/AFP/Getty Images; p. 256: © Khaled-Desouki/AFP/Getty Images; p. 259: © Keystone/Getty Images; p. 260: © Ingram Publishing/AlamyRF; p. 268: © Mahmud Turkia/AFP/Getty Images; p. 269: © Craig Johnston/AFP/Getty Images; p. 272: © Junior D. Kannah/AFP/GettyImages; p. 274: © Carmen Taylor/WireImage; p. 278: © Farah AbdiWarsameh/ /AP/Corbis; p. 289: © Karl Schumacher/AFP/Getty Images.**Text Credits** Figure 7.2, p 257: From *International Politics on the World Stage,* 12/e by Rourke/Boyer, Figure 10.1, p 307. Reprinted by permission of The McGraw-Hill Companies. Figure 7.3, p 263: Source: UCDP Conflict Encyclopedia, www.ucdp.uu.se. Figure 7.10, p 269: From *International Politics on the World Stage,* 12/e by Rourke/Boyer, Figure 10.2, p 314. Reprinted by permission of The McGraw-Hill Companies. Figure 7.11, p 277: Frequency of Terrorist Incidents per year, 1972-2010 Global Terrorism Database (GTD), University of Maryland. Used by permission of National Consortium for the Study of Terrorism and Responses to Terrorism. Figure 7.12, p 277: Frequency of Terrorist Incidents by Region, 2000–2010 Global Terrorism Database (GTD), University of Maryland. Used by permission of National Consortium for the Study of Terrorism and Responses to Terrorism.

CHAPTER 8

Photo Credits Opener: © IssoufSanogo/AFP/GettyImages; p. 297: © Bettmann/Corbis; p. 305: © Ingram Publishing/AlamyRF; p. 306: © AP Photo/Dimitri-Messinis; p. 314: © AP Photo/Manish Swarup; p. 319: © Heinz Ruckermann/UPI/Newscom; p. 323: © AFP/Getty Images; p. 326: © JGI/Blend Images RF; p. 331: © Ingram Publishing/Superstock RF.**Text Credits** Figure 8.1, p 304: From *International Politics on the World Stage,* 12/e by Rourke/Boyer, Figure 9.1, p 283. Reprinted by permission of The McGraw-Hill Companies. Figure 8.2, p 307: From *International Politics on the World Stage,* 12/e by Rourke/Boyer. Reprinted by permission of The McGraw-Hill Companies. Figure 8.3, p 309: From *International Politics on the World Stage,* 12/e by Rourke/Boyer, Figure 9.3 p 287. Reprinted by permission of The McGraw-Hill Companies. Figure 8.4, p 310: From *International Politics on the World Stage,* 12/e by Rourke/Boyer, Figure 9.4, p 288. Reprinted by permission of The McGraw-Hill Companies. Figure 8.15, p 316: Is War Sometimes Necessary for Justice? From http://www.gmfus.org/publications_/TT/TT2011_final_web.pdf. Used by permission. Figure 8.6, p 321: The Guardian, 10 March 2011 – http://www.guardian.co.uk/news/datablog/2010/aug/10/afghanistan-civilian-casualties-statistics. Figure 8.7, p 325: From *International Politics on the World Stage,* 12/e by Rourke/Boyer, p 298. Reprinted by permission of The McGraw-Hill Companies. Figure 8.8, p 327: From *International Politics on the World Stage,* 12/e by Rourke/Boyer, Figure 9.7, p 299. Reprinted by permission of The McGraw-Hill Companies.

CHAPTER 9

Photo Credits Opener: © Monika Graff/The Image Works; p. 342: © Getty Images RF; p. 343: © Eduardo Garcia/Getty Images; p. 345: © Imaginechina via AP Images; p. 351: © Marwan Ibrahim/AFP/Getty Images; p. 357: © Spencer Platt/Getty Images; p. 361: The McGraw-Hill Companies inc./Ken Cavanagh Photographer; p. 364: © Mikhail Klimentyev/AFP/GettyImages; p. 367: © Joe Raedle/Newsmakers/Getty Images.**Text Credits** Figure 9.1, p 345: From *International Politics on the World Stage,* 12/e by Rourke/Boyer, Figure 12.3, p 383. Reprinted by permission of The McGraw-Hill Companies. Figure 9.2, p 347: From *International*

Politics on the World Stage, 12/e by Rourke/ Boyer, Figure 12.4, p 384. Reprinted by permission of The McGraw-Hill Companies. Figure 9.3, p 353: From *International Politics on the World Stage,* 12/e by Rourke/Boyer, Figure 12.10, p 398. Reprinted by permission of The McGraw-Hill Companies. Figure 9.4, p 354: From *International Politics on the World Stage,* 12/e by Rourke/Boyer, Figure 13.8, p 422. Reprinted by permission of The McGraw-Hill Companies. Figure 9.5, p 358: From *International Politics on the World Stage,* 12/e by Rourke/Boyer, Figure 13.9, p 426. Reprinted by permission of The McGraw-Hill Companies. Figure 9.6, p 366: From *International Politics on the World Stage,* 12/e by Rourke/Boyer, Figure 13.11, 437. Reprinted by permission of The McGraw-Hill Companies. Figure 9.7, p 369: From *International Politics on the World Stage,* 12/e by Rourke/ Boyer, Figure 13.12, p 437. Reprinted by permission of The McGraw-Hill Companies.

CHAPTER 10

Photo Credits Opener: © Olivier Hoslet/ epa/Corbis; p. 377: © Jeremy Nicholl/Alamy; p. 379: © Craig Lapp/NFB/Getty Images; p. 383: © MajidSaeedi/Getty Images; p. 391: © Alejandro Pagni/AFP/Getty Images; p. 393: © SeongJoon Cho/Bloomberg via Getty Images; p. 395: © Hassan Ammar/AFP/Getty Images; p. 396: © Design Pics/Keith LevitRF; p. 401: © Jonathan S. Landay/MCT/MCT via Getty Images; p. 405: © Brand X Pictures/ Punchstock RF.**Text Credits** Figure 10.1, p 378: From *International Politics on the World Stage,* 12/e by Rourke/Boyer, Figure 12.5, p 387. Reprinted by permission of The

McGraw-Hill Companies. Figure 10.2, p 382: From *International Politics on the World Stage,* 12/e by Rourke/Boyer, Figure 12.7, p 391. Reprinted by permission of The McGraw-Hill Companies. Figure 10.3, p 390: From *International Politics on the World Stage,* 12/e by Rourke/Boyer, Figure 12.9, p 396. Reprinted by permission of The McGraw-Hill Companies. Figure 10.4, p 394: From *International Politics on the World Stage,* 12/e by Rourke/Boyer, Figure 2.11, 402. Reprinted by permission of The McGraw-Hill Companies. Figure 10.5, p 399: From *International Politics on the World Stage,* 12/e by Rourke/ Boyer, Figure 13.13, p 442. Reprinted by permission of The McGraw-Hill Companies.

CHAPTER 11

Photo Credits Opener: © Anyka/AlamyRF; p. 411: © Mike Clarke/AFP/Getty Images; p. 416: © Media24/Gallo Images/Getty Images; p. 424: © Rex Features via AP Images; p. 425: © Guardian News & Media Ltd 2010; p. 430: © AFP/Getty Images; p. 433: © Salah Malkawi/Getty Images; p. 434: The McGraw-Hill Companies inc./Ken Karp, Photographer; p. 436: Courtesy of Dayton Human Trafficking Accords, University of Dayton. **Text Credits** Figure 11.2, p 419: Cingranelli, David L. and David L. Richards, 2012. The Cingranelli-Richards (CIRI) Human Rights Data Project.Version 2011.12.09, www. humanrightsdata.org, http://www.human-rightsdata.org. Used by permission. Figure 11.3, p 422: Map of Discrepant Government Behavior Concerning Women Data available at http:/womanstats.org/data/images/ map5.1discrepant_behavior_compressed.

jpg. Used by permission. Figure 11.4, p 426: Cingranelli, David L. and David L. Richards, 2010./ "The Cingranelli and Richards (CIRI) Human Rights Data Project" Human Rights Quarterly 32.2: 401-424. Used by permission. Figure 11.5, p 437: Global Trends in Laws Prohibiting the Death Penalty Availableathttp: //www.e-ir.info/2011/07/30/failure-to-comply-global-human-rights-norms-and-the-retention-of-capital-punishment/. Used by permission of the author, Thomas Thornley.

CHAPTER 12

Photo Credits Opener: © Flip Nicklin/ Minden Pictures; p. 445: © Chris Jackson/ Getty Images; p. 448: © STR/AFP/Getty Images; p. 450 (left): © Fritz Hoffmann/In Pictures/Corbis; p. 450 (right): © Du Huaju/ Xinhua Press/Corbis; p. 453: © Brent Stirton/ Getty Images; p. 456: U.S. Coast Guard photo; p. 458: © Mattias Klum/National Geographic/Getty Images; p. 462: © JGI/ Blend Images RF; p. 463: © Long Fu/Color China Photo/AP Images; p. 467: © STR/ AFP/Getty Images; p. 470: © Aaron Roeth Photography RF.**Text Credits** Figure 12.2, p 455: From *International Politics on the World Stage,* 12/e by Rourke/Boyer, Figure 15.5, p 502. Reprinted by permission of The McGraw-Hill Companies. Figure 12.3, p 461: From *International Politics on the World Stage,* 12/e by Rourke/Boyer, p 509. Reprinted by permission of The McGraw-Hill Companies. Figure 12.4, p 471: From *International Politics on the World Stage,* 8/e by John T. Rourke, Figure 12.2, p 376. Reprinted by permission of The McGraw-Hill Companies.